MOON

H A N D B O O K S

GUADALAJARA

BRUCE WHIPPERMAN

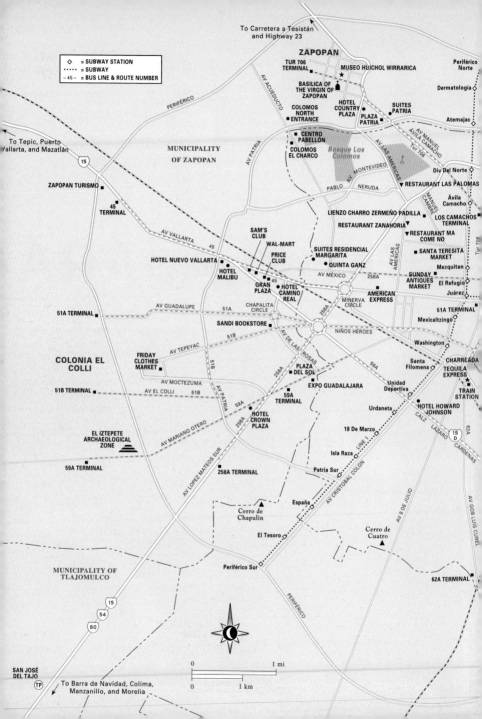

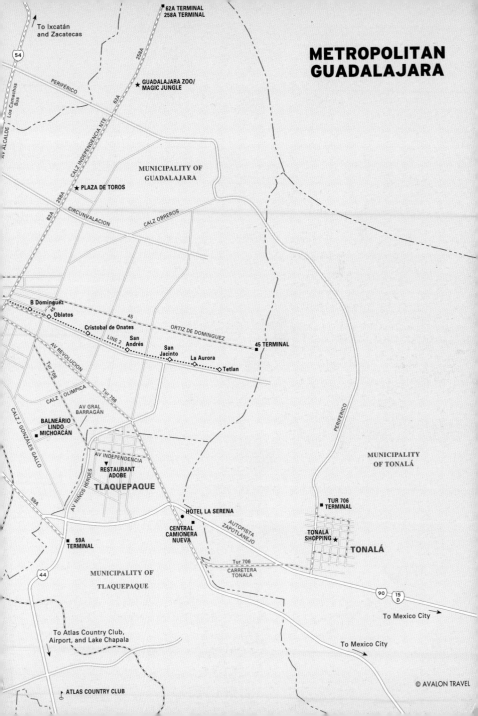

METROPOLITAN GUADALAJARA

To Ixcatán
and Zacatecas

54

PERIFÉRICO

62A TERMINAL
258A TERMINAL

★ GUADALAJARA ZOO/
MAGIC JUNGLE

MUNICIPALITY OF
GUADALAJARA

★ PLAZA DE TOROS

CIRCUNVALACION   CALZ OBREROS

B Dominguez
Oblatos
Cristobal de Onates   45   ORTIZ DE DOMINGUEZ
                    Line 2   San Andrés   45 TERMINAL
AV REVOLUCION   San
                    Jacinto   San
                              La Aurora
                              Tetlan

CALZ OLIMPICA   Tur 706
AV GRAL
BARRAGÁN

BALNEÁRIO
LINDO
MICHOACÁN

AV INDEPENDENCIA

RESTAURANT
ADOBE

TLAQUEPAQUE

HOTEL LA SERENA

CENTRAL
CAMIONERA
NUEVA

AUTOPISTA
ZAPOTLANEJO

59A
TERMINAL

44

MUNICIPALITY OF
TLAQUEPAQUE

Tur 706
CARRETERA
TONALA

MUNICIPALITY
OF TONALÁ

TUR 706
TERMINAL

TONALÁ
SHOPPING   ★   TONALÁ

90 15
    D

To Mexico City

To Atlas Country Club,
Airport, and Lake Chapala

To Mexico City

★ ATLAS COUNTRY CLUB

© AVALON TRAVEL

AV ALCALDE | Los Camachos
Bus

258A

62A

258A

62A

45

Tur 706

CALZ J GONZALES GALLO

AV NIÑOS HEROES

59A

PERIFÉRICO

DISCOVER
GUADALAJARA

Renowned the world over as the "most Mexican of cities," Guadalajara brims with delights, from the unmistakable aroma of hot corn tortillas to the soft strumming of a guitar in the night to the dazzling whirl of folkloric dancers' skirts and the insistent rap of their heels. Your dreams of old Mexico can come true in Guadalajara. It's a big but welcoming town, with sunny, temperate weather and broad, sweeping plazas made for strolling and decorated by fountains and venerable monuments. The city bursts with things to do, including dozens of fascinating museums and galleries, dance and music performances, and a cornucopia of delicious food, from savory Mexican home-style *comidas* to international gourmet cuisine.

With a metropolitan-zone population of more than four million, Guadalajara is Mexico's second-largest city and a major manufacturing and business center. It spreads across 100 square miles within a

Whimsical ironwork decorates a Tlaquepaque gate.

mile-high, mountain-rimmed valley, about 1,000 highway miles due south of El Paso, Texas, or about three hours by air from the major air gateways of Los Angeles and Houston. Manifold motivations propel its millions of visitors, who are so numerous that Guadalajara ranks second only to Mexico City as the country's most-visited destination. Many come to bask in Guadalajara's year-round spring-like weather, so lovely that the best time to visit is anytime. Students of all ages come to study the Spanish language, Mexican history, art, and culture, and to stay in the homes of Guadalajara families.

Others come to Guadalajara seeking a quiet retirement. Currently numbering in the tens of thousands, many expatriates have cashed out on their U.S. or Canadian homes and settled year-round in Guadalajara or along the shores of Lake Chapala. They can enjoy much more

Cuadras (rectangular pictures) depict deities of the indigenous pantheon.

luxurious houses than they had back home – often for a third the price – and still have enough left over to live on the interest.

A legion of both Mexican and foreign travelers, some of them professional buyers, come for Guadalajara's celebrated handicrafts. The selection is so lovely and reasonably priced that Guadalajara and its neighboring villages of Tlaquepaque and Tonalá have, collectively, become the de facto handicrafts capital of Mexico. The lanes of Tlaquepaque and Tonalá are lined with both quaint shops and factory stores, offering dozens of diverse products: papier-mâché so fine that it resembles bright sculpture, supple leather accessories and fine boots, glistening stoneware ceramics, gilded heirloom baroque reproductions, and delicately blown glassware, to name a few.

Many tens of thousands of businesspeople also come to buy and sell – not handicrafts, but electronics. Guadalajara is the burgeoning "Silicon Valley of the South," a label that has progressed far past a slogan. A list of the city's giant electronics plants – Sony, Hewlett-Packard, NEC, Motorola, Intel – reads like a who's who of the computer revolution.

Banners decorate Tlaquepaque's Avenida Independencia during the National Ceramics Fair.

Easily accessible, Guadalajara makes a convenient jumping-off point for other Mexican destinations, including Mexico City (one hour by air; six hours by road) and Puerto Vallarta (less than an hour by air; four hours by road). In the environs of Guadalajara itself, scenic road trips branch out in all directions. In less than an hour's travel south is Mexico's grandest lake, cloud-tipped Chapala. In the rustic lakeshore villages of Chapala and Ajijic (Ah-HEE-heek), you can stroll cobbled, bouganvillea-decorated streets, select from a trove of handicrafts and local arts, and sample the delicious offerings of many excellent restaurants. Venture just an hour farther from the city, and your horizon widens to include the monumental Guachimontones archaeological park, with its grand reconstructed conical pyramid, and the relaxing Hacienda El Carmen – fine for an overnight or two exploring the countryside by horseback, relaxing by the pool or the whirlpool tub, and being pampered in the spa. Alternatively, you can visit the pine-tufted rustic mountain villages of Mazamitla or Tapalpa. Along your path, be sure to sample some of the celebrated local treats, such as savory pit-barbecued lamb,

Teatro Degollado and Plaza Liberación

hot tamales stuffed with garden-grown green chard, smooth country cheeses, melt-in-your-mouth milk-caramel candy, homemade fresh-fruit jams and jellies and mountain wildflower honey.

Why does it seem that everyone who visits the region returns home with a fondness for Guadalajara? More than any of the city's many charms, it has to do with the people – mostly working and middle-class Mexican folks, often on family outings with kids along, all hankering for a bit of food and fun. Most first-time visitors catch on to this mood right away, and cannot resist joining in. The good feelings begin on their first stroll around town, and continue as long as they stay.

Sergio Bustamante's famous monkey sculptures at the Guadalajara Zoo

Contents

The Lay of the Land 14

Planning Your Trip 17

Explore Guadalajara 18
The Best of Guadalajara 18
The Heart of the City 19
Five Days for Serious Shoppers 20
Treasures of Old Mexico 21
A Week on the Road 22
A Breath of Fresh Air 24

Downtown 26
Sights 32
Entertainment and Events 44
Shopping 49
Accommodations 51
Food 55
Information and Services 58
Getting There and Around 60

West and North 68
Minerva-Chapultepec 70
Plaza del Sol-Chapalita 91
Zapopan 108

Tlaquepaque and Tonalá 118
Tlaquepaque 121
Tonalá 140

Lake Chapala 155
The Chapala Riviera 161

Guadalajara Getaways 184
San Juan de los Lagos 187
Mazamitla 193
Tapalpa 202
Chimulco and Bosque de Primavera 212
Guachimontones and Hacienda El Carmen 215
Tequila 220
Magdalena 227

Background 231
The Land 231
Flora and Fauna 233
History 238
Economy and Government 256
The People 261
Arts and Culture 264

Essentials 279
Getting There 279
Getting Around 289
Visas and Officialdom 293
Conduct and Customs 298
Accommodations 300
Shopping 302
Tips for Travelers 304
Tours, Guides, and Courses 309
Health and Safety 311
Information and Services 316

Resources... 319

Glossary 319
Spanish Phrasebook 322
Suggested Reading 328
Internet Resources 334

Index... 336

MAP CONTENTS

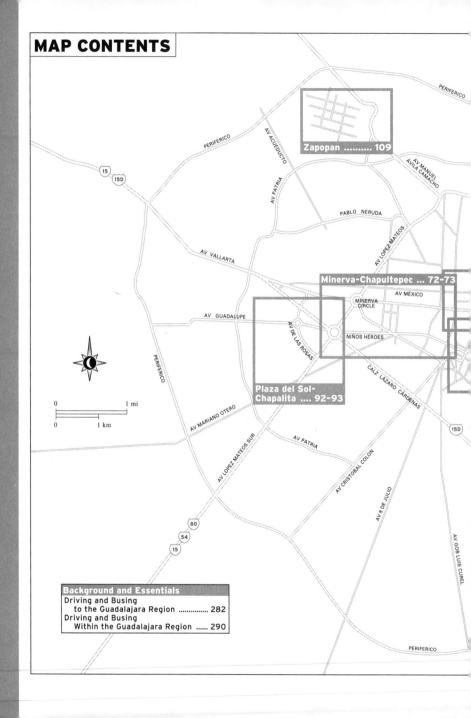

Zapopan 109

Minerva-Chapultepec ... 72-73

Plaza del Sol-
Chapalita 92-93

Background and Essentials
Driving and Busing
  to the Guadalajara Region 282
Driving and Busing
  Within the Guadalajara Region 290

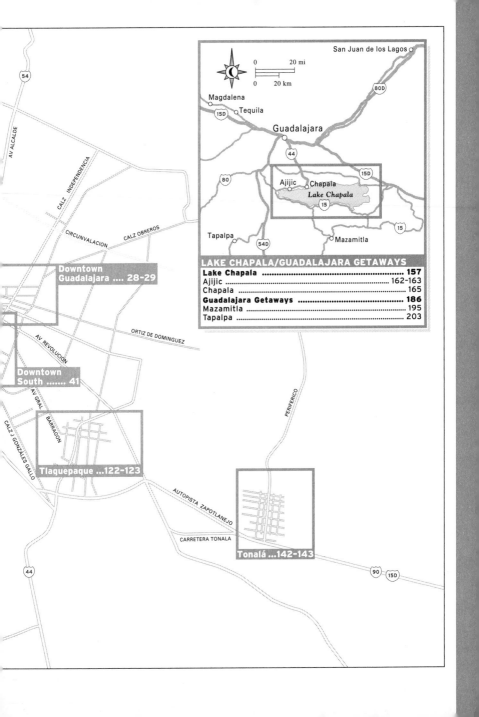

San Juan de los Lagos

0   20 mi

0   20 km

Magdalena

15D   Tequila

Guadalajara

44

80D

80

Ajijic   Chapala
Lake Chapala

15D

15

Tapalpa

54D

Mazamitla

15

LAKE CHAPALA/GUADALAJARA GETAWAYS

Lake Chapala **157**
Ajijic 162-163
Chapala 165
Guadalajara Getaways **186**
Mazamitla 195
Tapalpa 203

Downtown
Guadalajara 28-29

Downtown
South 41

Tlaquepaque ...122-123

Tonalá ...142-143

AV ALCALDE

CALZ INDEPENDENCIA

54

CIRCUNVALACION   CALZ OBREROS

ORTIZ DE DOMINGUEZ

AV REVOLUCION

AV GRAL

BARRAGON

CALZ J GONZÁLES GALLO

PERIFERICO

AUTOPISTA ZAPOTLANEJO

CARRETERA TONALA

44

90   15D

The Lay of the Land

DOWNTOWN

The heart of the *municipio* (township) of Guadalajara (pop. 1.8 million) is a bustling but pleasantly spacious, low-rise downtown. Buses empty squads of passengers curbside, subway trains scuttle underground, shoppers peruse department store displays, businesspeople relax for coffee-shop lunches, pigeons scurry and flutter, and families stroll broad, fountain-decorated plazas.

Highlights are the towering cathedral and the classic-facade Teatro Degollado. Nearby, via shop- and restaurant-lined pedestrian walkways, spreads the visionary-scale Plaza Tapatía, graced by its own monuments, including the Hospicio Cabañas, Latin America's largest colonial building and site of the José Clemente Orozco Art Museum, with a treasury of the art of the renowned muralist. Shoppers will enjoy the Magno Centro Joyero gold jewelry market and the adjacent Mercado Libertad, with a trove of appealing handicrafts.

WEST AND NORTH

The Minerva-Chapultepec, just a five-minute ride west of the city center, is a fashionable neighborhood of stately, tree-shaded homes, designer galleries, upscale malls, and fine restaurants. Highlights are the renowned Orozco murals in the Rectoría de la Universidad de Guadalajara, the towering neo-Gothic Templo Expiatorio, and the monumental Los Arcos, with its panoramic views.

To the southwest lies the Plaza del Sol-Chapalita district, home of a bustling mall and world-class exposition center. To the northwest, the leafy Chapalita neighborhood is a comfortable mix of Mexican businesses, upper-middle-class families, and North American retirees.

Zapopan (pop. 1.2 million), bordering Minerva-Chapultepec to the northwest, is home to the beloved Virgin of Zapopan. From the Virgin's basilica, Zapopan spreads across a wealthy domain of well-to-do neighborhoods, manufacturing parks, shopping malls, and restaurants. Beyond its urban edge, Zapopan's countryside encompasses a hinterland of rich farms, graceful old haciendas, lush pine-oak forests, and the semitropical canyon Barranca del Río Grande de Santiago.

TLAQUEPAQUE AND TONALÁ

Tlaquepaque (pop. 460,000), southeast of the Guadalajara city center, still retains the picturesque character of a colonial-era potter's village, while its handicrafts tradition has blossomed. Dozens of shops offer a galaxy of local ceramics, glassware, leather, pewter, decorator furnishings, and more. Visitors also flock to El Parián for good food and folkloric music and dance.

Tonalá (pop. 315,000), about five miles farther east, perches at Guadalajara's sleepy country edge. Its pre-Columbian handicrafts tradition continues in hundreds of workshops that offer leather, furniture, papier-mâché, brass, and blown glass. Primary Tonalá sights include its factory stores and the statue of the legendary Queen Cihalpilli.

LAKE CHAPALA

Lake Chapala and its diadem of shoreline villages—Chapala, San Antonio, Ajijic, and San Juan Cosala—a half hour south of Guadalajara's metropolitan zone, make up the celebrated Chapala Riviera. Its colony of North American and well-to-do Mexican residents supports a bounty of amenities: comfortable lodgings and good restaurants, handicrafts and fine arts, music and dramatic performances, and plenty of swimming, tennis, golf, walking, and hiking opportunities.

Boats at Chapala town pier line up, ready to ferry parties to historic Mezcala Island, stopping on the return for lunch at Alacranes Island. Kayaking is possible from almost anywhere along the lakeshore.

GETAWAYS

Several nearby getaways, varying from one to three hours by road from the city center, are rich in the enjoyments of old Mexico.

San Juan de los Lagos is home to the adored **Catedral Basílica,** the Virgin's precious **El Pocito** shrine.

For cool, pine-scented mountain air and rustic-chic cabin lodgings, choose **Mazamitla** or **Tapalpa.** The forest is prettier in Mazamitla, while Tapalpa's main excursions, **Las Piedrotas** giant rock monoliths and **El Salto del Nogal** waterfall, are more interesting. Of Guadalajara's country bathing springs, the first choice goes to **Chimulco** warm springs resort and RV park. **Bosque de Primavera** wilderness reserve offers a more rustic, off-trail adventure.

Farther west of Guadalajara, explore the **Guachimontones** archaeological zone and its monumental conical pyramid. Afterward, swim and picnic at the crystal spring **Balneario El Rincón,** or linger for an overnight at the graceful colonial-era **Hacienda El Carmen.** Continue west past the blue agave fields to the famed town of **Tequila** and its **Cuervo liquor distillery.** Afterward, relax at lovely canyon-view **Balneario La Toma.** Continue west a dozen miles to the opal center of **Magdalena.**

Planning Your Trip

WHEN TO GO

Although any time is a good time to visit Guadalajara, for some people, certain seasons may be more ideal than others. For example, if you want to join Guadalajara festivities, arrive during the May Fiesta Cultural de Mayo or during the Fiesta de Octubre, which peaks around the October 12 festival of the Virgin of Zapopan.

For others, weather may be a major consideration. Guadalajara visitors enjoy a generally mild-to-warm, two-season climate (a mostly dry winter–spring and a rainier summer), similar to (but a bit wetter than) some areas of Southern California. Days are warmest during the late spring, typically peaking around 90°F (32°C) by mid-afternoon. Winter days are cooler, with very comfortable highs around 70°F (21°C). During July, August, and September it rains, mostly moderately, with summer daytime highs at an ideal 80–82°F (27–28°C). Winter (December, January, and February) lows average a cool, but not cold, 40–45°F (5–7°C).

You can avoid most midday heat by visiting during late summer, fall, or winter. If you enjoy balmy evenings, visit during spring, summer, or fall. The best time to visit may be during the balmy, dry months of October and November, when you can largely avoid the rain of summer, the hot days of spring, and the cool nights of winter.

GETTING THERE

Most foreign visitors travel to Guadalajara via flights from one of many North American gateway airports, including Atlanta, Boston, Chicago, Dallas, Houston, Las Vegas, Los Angeles, Miami, New York, Phoenix, San Francisco, and Tucson.

For budget travelers, battalions of daily buses leave the border towns of Nogales, Arizona; Calexico and San Diego, California; and El Paso, Laredo, and McAllen, Texas.

Driving your car or RV to Guadalajara may be a viable option, especially for those who are planning a long trip or intend to do lots of camping in outlying areas. From the western United States, it's best to go via Nogales, Arizona; from the central or eastern United States, go via El Paso or Reynosa, Texas. Allow at least two days at the wheel from El Paso or a day and a half from Reynosa.

WHAT TO TAKE

"Men wear pants, ladies be beautiful" was once the dress code of one of western Mexico's classiest hotels. Most men vacationing in Guadalajara can get by without a jacket; women are fine with simple skirts or pants and blouses. Business travelers should bring along a light suit for more formal business functions.

What you pack depends on how mobile you want to be. If you're staying at a self-contained resort, you can take the two suitcases and one carry-on allowed by airlines. If you're going to be moving around a lot, condense everything down to one bag with wheels that doubles as a soft backpack. Pack prudently and tightly, choosing items that will do double or triple duty (such as a Swiss army knife).

Loose-fitting, hand-washable, easy-to-dry clothes make for trouble-free Guadalajara traveling. Synthetic or cotton-synthetic-blend shirts, blouses, pants, socks, and underwear will fit the bill for most every occasion. For breezy or winter nights, add a medium-weight jacket, a light sweater, and/or a stuffable windbreaker.

In all cases, leave expensive clothes and jewelry at home. Stow items that you cannot lose in your hotel safe or carry them with you in a sturdy zipped purse or a waist pouch on your front side.

Pack light enough to take an extra suitcase for bringing your goodies home (or ship them home).

Explore Guadalajara

THE BEST OF GUADALAJARA

This itinerary takes you throughout the *municipio* (township) of Guadalajara. It covers the top attractions downtown and in the surrounding suburban areas of Minerva-Chapultepec, Zapopan, Tlaquepaque, and Tonalá. Plazas, monuments, museums, shopping—there's a little bit of something for everyone. No car is needed for this itinerary; you can see all the highlights on foot or by taxi.

Days 1-2

Spend your first two days **downtown** hitting the highlights of the city. On your first day, stroll around the Plaza Liberación and Plaza Tapatía and visit the cathedral and monuments. On your second day, visit the south side of downtown, beginning at the Templo de San Francisco de Asis. Then spend the afternoon visiting the Museo de Arqueología, Museo de Paleontología, and Parque Agua Azul.

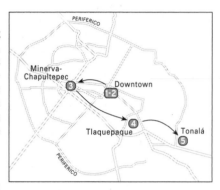

Day 3

Taxi west to the **Minerva-Chapultepec** district to view the Orozco murals and the adjacent Museo de Arte, at the University of Guadalajara, and the neo-Gothic Templo Expiatorio. Continue west by taxi for the airy view atop the Los Arcos monument. Stop for a short visit at the Casa Museo José Clemente Orozco. Spend the afternoon in **Zapopan,** visiting the basilica of the Virgin of Zapopan and the adjacent Museo Huichol Wirrarica. Enjoy dinner at the Grecian Restaurant Agios Agellos.

Day 4

Transfer by car or taxi to your **Tlaquepaque** hotel (Quinta Don José or Casa del Retoño). Stroll the Avenida Independencia pedestrian mall and peruse the many inviting handicrafts stores. Continue your shopping meander past the Tlaquepaque plaza, the adjacent colonial-era Santuario de Nuestra Señora de la Soledad, the parish church Parroquia San Pedro (don't miss the miniature Bible-story pageant). Take a break for lunch at either Casa Fuerte or El Adobe on Avenida Independencia. Finish your walk, visiting some of the Tlaquepaque factory shops and stores on Avenida Juárez. Enjoy dinner and the mariachi and folkloric dance show at El Parián (Wed., Sat., and Sun. at 3:30 and 9 P.M.; only strolling mariachis at other times).

Day 5

Taxi east a half hour to **Tonalá.** After a look at the remarkable bronze sculpture of Queen Cihualpilli in the town plaza, visit some shops along Madero-Hidalgo, the main shopping street. Be sure to include the Bazar de Sermel papier-mâché shop and the Galería Bernabe. Break for lunch at either El Boquinete or Los Geranios, then head north along Hidalgo to factory shops Los Caporales, Ken Edwards, and Artesanías Erandi. If you have more time, taxi to either Vidrios del Sol or Vidrios Jimón, on the south side of town. Return to Tlaquepaque for supper, at either Restaurant Sandwiches and Friends or Cenaduria La Única.

THE HEART OF THE CITY

In downtown Guadalajara, monuments, museums, arts, and entertainments abound. Covering the highlights of the city-center, this two-day itinerary is designed for folks on a tight schedule. If you have more time to spend in the region, consider combining this itinerary with excursions farther afield.

Day 1

Start your sightseeing at the cathedral (half hour), then continue north to the adjacent Plaza de los Hombres Ilustres and the neighboring Museo Regional (total one hour). Continue behind the cathedral to the broad Plaza Independencia, the Teatro Degollado, and, behind the Teatro, the monumental brass frieze Frisa de los Fundadores (half hour). Continue east to the expansive Plaza Tapatía and the adjacent Magno Centro Joyero (Great Jewelry Center) and the giant Mercado Libertad behind it, especially good for handicrafts shopping (90 minutes).

Stop for lunch at one of the *fondas* (permanent food stalls) at the mercado (upstairs), or one of the restaurants on the Plaza de Mariachis, on the market's south side. Spend most of the rest of your day admiring the grand murals and other works of José Clemente Orozco in the historic Hospicio Cabañas (Instituto Cultural Cabañas), Latin America's largest colonial building (90 minutes).

Afterward, before dinner, walk or taxi back to Plaza de Hombres Illustres by the cathedral and catch a *calandria* (horse-drawn carriage) ride around town. For dinner, head north of the cathedral a few blocks to (or have your calandria driver drop you at) the relaxing Restaurant San Miguel.

If you have time after dinner, take in a performance at either the Teatro Degollado or the Teatro Diana, or enjoy both dinner and mariachi entertainment at Restaurant Casa Bariachi, in the Minerva Chapultepec district west of downtown.

Day 2

On your second day, explore the sights south of the cathedral. Start by visiting the arresting 1937 Orozco mural in the Palacio de Gobierno, on the east side of Plaza de Armas, just south of the cathedral (half hour). Walk or taxi about six blocks south to the tree-shaded Plaza San Francisco and visit a pair of beloved, colonial-era churches, the Templo de San Francisco de Asis and the Capilla de Aranzazú (one hour). Meander south through the picturesque Nueve Esquinas district to the neighborhood square, Plaza Nueve Esquinas, and enjoy lunch at the restaurant Birrias Nueve Esquinas on the plaza (two hours).

After lunch, taxi south several blocks to the Museo de Arqueología (half hour) and continue across the street to Parque Agua Azul (90 minutes). For your afternoon finale, either do some serious handicrafts browsing at the Casa de Artesanías Agua Azul, north of the *parque*, or taxi to the far east side of Parque Agua Azul to the excellent Museo de Paleontología (one hour).

For evening food and entertainment, taxi to Restaurant Casa Bariachi if you didn't make it there yesterday, or drop in at one of the city-center restaurants, such as Sandy's, La Chata, or Sanborn's. Afterward, walk over to the Hotel Fénix for the live music in the lobby.

FIVE DAYS FOR SERIOUS SHOPPERS

Mexico is so stuffed with lovely, reasonably priced handicrafts (or *artesanías,* pronounced "ar-tay-sah-NEE-ahs") that many crafts devotees, if given the option, might choose Mexico over heaven. The livelihood of a sizable number of Guadalajaran families depends upon the sale of homespun items—clothing, utensils, furniture, forest herbs, religious offerings, adornments, toys, musical instruments—that either they or their neighbors make. Many crafts traditions reach back thousands of years to the beginnings of Mexican civilization. The work of generations of artisans has, in many instances, resulted in finery so prized that whole villages devote themselves to the manufacture of a single class of goods.

Shopping is a prime Guadalajara occupation. Many hundreds of factory shops in the *municipios* of Tlaquepaque and Tonalá produce a large percentage of Mexico's handicrafts and art, both fine and decorative. The range of available goods is enormous, notably stoneware figurines and place settings, sculpture, pewter, papier-mâché, rustic wood furniture and leather-covered *equipal* furniture, glassware, lampshades, and antique—especially baroque—reproductions.

Day 1

Serious shoppers should probably plan to stay at least two nights in **Tlaquepaque**. From the airport, check in to your Tlaquepaque hotel (Quinta Don José or Villas del Ensueño). Then spend the first day exploring the shops on **Avenida Independencia** (such as Antigua de Mexico, Bustamante, La Casa Canela, and Agustín Parra). Enjoy lunch or dinner at either Restaurant El Patio or Restaurant El Adobe.

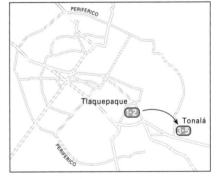

Day 2

After breakfast, visit the shops on **Avenida Juárez** (Jiménez Piel, Téte Ante Diseno, Fábricas Mona, Vitrales Albarrán, and Donaji). After lunch, visit some of Tlaquepaque's **factory shops** (Vidrios Soplados, El Cirio, Ann Kary, and Cerámicas Guadalajara) and see the artisans at work. If you have time, take a look inside the **Museo Regional de la Cerámica de Tlaquepaque**. In the mid-afternoon or evening, enjoy the mariachis and folkloric dance shows at El Parián entertainment center (Wed., Sat., and Sun. at 3:30 and 9 P.M.; strolling mariachis at other times).

Day 3

Take a taxi from Tlaquepaque to **Tonalá**. Check into your Tonalá hotel (Las Palomas or Mi Hotelito Bed and Breakfast), then spend the rest of the day visiting the shops (Carrusel, El Santuario, El Bazar de Sermel, Galería Bernabe) along the main shopping street, **Madero-Hidalgo**. Stop for lunch at Rinconada del Sol, Geranios, or El Boquinete. In the afternoon, take a break from shopping to see some of Tonalá's sights: The statue of **Queen Cihualpilli** on the central plaza, **Museo Regional Tonallán**, and **Museo National de la Cerámica** are all worth a stop.

Day 4

Spend the day on **factory tours**. Blown glass, high-fired stoneware, woodcrafts, and fine ironwork are all here, from several excellent sources: Caporales, Ken Edwards, Artesanías Erandi, Herrería Artística Covarrubias,

Vidrios del Sol, and more. The prices couldn't be better than right here at the source. After lunch, do a test run to see if you can fit all your new items in your suitcases. Not enough room? Find a shipping agent before the end of the business day and make arrangements to have your goods packed up securely and shipped home.

Day 5

Have some time before your flight leaves? If there's room left in your suitcase, stop enroute to the airport for last-minute bargains or those special items you just can't leave without, such as Tonala ceramic animals, an irresistible papier-mâché parrot, or brilliant opal jewelry.

TREASURES OF OLD MEXICO

FINE ART AND HANDICRAFTS

Guadalajara overflows with fine art and handicrafts. Dozens of galleries, both public and private, offer a treasury of paintings, murals, sculpture, ceramics, and photography. Primary among all of them are the José Clemente Orozco Art Museum in the Instituto Cultural Cabañas (Hospicio Cabañas), downtown; the Museo de Arte at the University of Guadalajara; the Museo Huichol Wirrarica in Zapopan; and the Museo Regional de Cerámica in Tlaquepaque. Additionally, scores of gallery and factory stores in Tlaquepaque and Tonalá offer a collective mountain of irresistible art, both fine and decorative, and handicrafts, sometimes so polished that they resemble fine art. Many other worthy private galleries, especially in the Minerva-Chapultepec district, offer similarly rich, mostly fine art and sculpture collections.

MUSIC AND DANCE

An abundance of national and international performances light up the stages year-round at the Teatro Degollado opera house and the Teatro Diana, both downtown. The University of Guadalajara Ballet Folklórico and the Jalisco Philharmonic Orchestra are the highlights of the theaters' varied offerings of operas, musicals, and plays.

Guadalajara's cultural ferment peaks during the Fiesta Cultural de Mayo (May Cultural Festival), an annual monthlong celebration of art, music, theater, and much more. Be sure to get the program, customarily in the May edition of the monthly *Infomart* booklet of the Cultura Guadalajara office (Pino Suárez 254, corner of Reforma downtown, tel. 33/3613-8021 and 33/3613-2218, culturaguadalajara@hotmail.com). Alternatively, you can access cultural events via the cultural schedule of the Guadalajara municipal government (Ayuntamiento de Guadalajara) at www.guadalajara.gob.mx/guiacultural.

HISTORY AND ARCHAEOLOGY

History and archaeology enthusiasts should include visits to the excellent downtown Museo Regional de Guadalajara, Museo de la Ciudad (Museum of the City), Museo de Arqueología, and Museo de Paleontología in their itineraries.

The same goes for both of Guadalajara's monumental archaeological sites, El Iztepete, at the metropolitan zone's southwest edge, and the Guachimontones conical pyramids, an hour's drive west of downtown.

El Iztepete, first explored in 1954, is believed to have been an important ceremonial and trading center for obsidian (volcanic glass) around A.D. 1–1000. Besides the main reconstructed 20-foot-high platform, other visible remains include a number of rubble-strewn, unreconstructed mounds, one of them a ball court, scattered around a quarter-square-mile zone.

Guachimontones, on the other hand, was first explored only recently, in 1998. The major reconstruction is a strikingly unusual conical stepped pyramid about 60 feet high, built around the beginning of the Christian era and abandoned four hundred years later. A number of similar but unreconstructed pyramids occupy the approximately 100-acre hillside site.

A WEEK ON THE ROAD

The Guadalajara region offers much more than just the city of Guadalajara itself. Escape the hustle and bustle of the metropolitan area on this weeklong road trip. This tour will take you into quiet countryside and forests, waterfalls and hot-springs resorts, and small towns along the Lake Chapala shoreline. For even more relaxation, slow down the pace by adding a couple extra days at any stop along the way. A car makes this itinerary easier, but it can also be done by combining bus trips and taxi rides.

Day 1

Depart Guadalajara for Lake Chapala by car, taxi, or bus. Check in to your hotel (La Nueva Posada, Los Artistas, Swan Inn) in **Ajijic,** then spend the afternoon strolling Ajijic's shady plaza or the garden of the Neill James Library, or go shopping at Ajijic's cluster of inviting handicrafts shops (Mi Mexico and Galería di Paola). After lunch (at Los Telares or David's), walk downhill to Lake Chapala's shore by the Ajijic pier. Families with children might substitute a couple hours at the Tobolandia water park. For dinner and live musical entertainment, try La Bodega, Melanie's, or La Rusa at the Hotel La Nueva Posada.

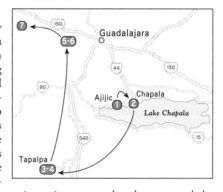

Day 2

Have breakfast at your hotel, then drive, taxi, or bus east to **Chapala town.** In your walk around town, be sure to include the Chapala town plaza and adjacent market; the pier downhill on the lakefront; the restored train station, now cultural center; and the Braniff mansion, now Restaurant Cazadores, for lunch. Afterward, return to the Chapala pier and hire a boat to Isla de los Alacranes and Isla de Mezcala. Return to Ajijic for dinner (Pedro's or Johanna's) and a good night's rest.

Day 3

After an early breakfast, drive or bus two-and-a-half hours west, then south, to **Tapalpa.** Lunch overlooking the *jardín* at Restaurant Paulino's. Stroll around the town, sampling the local homemade sweets (peach jam, bonbons, guava-nut cookies, milk-caramel candy, guava eggnog) at Dulcería del Centro and admiring the fetching homespun handicrafts (woodcrafts, wool weavings, pottery) at Artesanías La Hacienda.

From town, drive or taxi past the old paper mill and trout farm, continuing west to explore **Las Piedrotas** (The Big Rocks). If prepared, camp overnight; if not, return to Tapalpa for an evening stroll around the Tapalpa plaza and dinner at Los Girasoles before retiring to your hotel (Hostal Casa del Manzano, Hotel Casa de Maty, or Hotel Posada las Margaritas).

Day 4

After breakfast, head south on foot or by taxi or car via Atacco to the canyon of the Río Nogal and the waterfall **El Salto del Nogal.** Bring your bathing suit and a picnic or buy lunch at the canyon-rim *palapa* restaurant. Hike downhill to the pool at the bottom of the waterfall. If prepared, camp overnight; otherwise, return to your Tapalpa hotel.

Days 5-6

Head to the **Bosque de Primavera** and **Río Caliente** area. Check in at the Río Caliente Spa and spend some quality time soaking in the natural pools, enjoying spa treatments, and sallying out on a guided stroll through the surrounding forest.

Alternatively, off-the-beaten-track adventurers might want to enjoy the outdoor opportunities available in the Bosque de Primavera surrounding the Río Caliente Spa. In the luscious pine-oak forest, you can spread out with plenty of room (best on nonholiday weekdays) for tent or RV camping in the established campground. (The facilities are sparse, however, so bring everything you'll need.) You can enjoy plenty of pine-shadowed hiking trails, soaking pools at nearby local-style *balnearios* (bathing resorts), and unique wilderness camping opportunities right on the bank of the steaming Río Caliente.

Day 7

From Hotel Río Caliente Spa or the Bosque de Primavera, travel west an hour by car and spend a day (or more, if your schedule permits) exploring the monumental **Guachimontones** archaeological zone, including a swim in the cool, crystal-clear spring of **Balneario El Rincón.** Those who prefer luxury can have it at the old-world-style **Hacienda El Carmen.** At the other extreme, RVers and campers can set up at nearby Balneario El Rincón natural spring park, which kids love. Alternatively, you could stay at the modest Hotel Las Fuentes, which has a pool, and simply visit Guachimontones and Balneario El Rincón during the day.

A BREATH OF FRESH AIR

Your Guadalajara outdoor experience can begin right in town, with hiking, jogging, and wildlife-viewing opportunities at the big **Bosque Los Colomos** park, on the northwest side of town. Outside the city, you'll find many other ways to experience the great outdoors.

HIKING

Hiking opportunities are common in the Guadalajara region, notably in and around **Mazamitla, Tapalpa,** and the **Bosque de Primavera.** The wildflowers and wildlife commonly viewable in these temperate mountain zones are similar to those of the rural western United States. Foxes, wildcats, badgers, coyotes, and mountain lions are not uncommon, nor are birds such as hawks, vultures, doves, and owls. Unless you're highly experienced or fortunate, you'll see more animals and learn more about plants if you hire a guide. In Mazamitla, guides can be hired at the horse rental station. In Tapalpa, ask for a guide at the Tapalpa tourist information office or the Eko-Park booth at the town entrance. A guided wildlife-viewing hike is included with a stay at Hotel Río Caliente Spa in the Bosque de Primavera.

KAYAKING

Kayaking is best on **Lake Chapala.** Good launch spots dot the lake's northwest side around Chapala, Ajijic, and San Juan Cosala. Prepared kayakers could spend a whole week enjoying an idyllic Lake Chapala paddling and shore camping adventure. Serious paddlers should bring their own kayak and gear; little, if any, equipment is locally available.

BALNEARIOS

Except for Balneario Lindo Michoacán, downtown, most of the Guadalajara region's *balnearios* (bathing springs) are in scenic country spots, from half an hour to an hour's drive from the city center, all easily accessible by car, bus, or taxi. These spots are very popular and are likely to be more relaxing and tranquil on weekdays and crowded and noisy on Sundays and holidays.

The most accessible *balnearios* are the cool, crystalline springs at **Los Camachos,** along Highway 54 north of town.

Near Lake Chapala, **Tobolandia** water to-boggan park is 45 minutes south on the Chapala–Ajijic highway. At the east end of San Juan Cosala, droves of families enjoy **Motel Balneario San Juan Cosala,** a complex of natural warm-spring swimming pools and sports facilities.

One hour southwest of the city, at Villa Corona village, natural warm spring **Chimulco** offers lavish, shaded facilities. Nearby **Agua Caliente** offers about the same.

At La Venta, in the Bosque de Primavera forest reserve, three country *balnearios* offer relaxation in the naturally warm waters of the Río Caliente. The best developed is the **Balneario Cañon de las Flores.** Farther along the dirt access road, **Balneario Las Tinajitas** and another farther on (even more rustic) are more tranquil. Find them about 45 minutes west of the city, off Highway 15, about seven miles (11 km) west of the *periférico* (peripheral boulevard).

A couple miles west of Tequila, a pair of *balnearios* offers relaxing water diversions at the tropical edge of the Barranca (canyon of the Río Santiago), about an hour and 15 minutes west of the city. Guests at the very popular **Balneario La Toma** enjoy two big shaded pools, one of which is fed from a cliffside cave, perched on the airy canyon rim. The nearby **Balneario Paraíso** offers a small shaded swimming and wading pool, a bit of space for camping, and all the mangoes you can eat, in season.

TENT AND RV CAMPING

Although camping in lower elevation tropical zones requires no sleeping bag, mountain and winter camping in most of the Guadalajara region does. A compact tent that you and your partner can share is a must to protect against bugs, as is mosquito repellent. A first-aid kit is absolutely essential.

A sprinkling of private campgrounds and RV parks are available for fee use, mostly at locations in the *Guadalajara Getaways* chapter. Moving clockwise around the *Guadalajara Getaways* map, starting at Tapalapa, is **Eko Park Tapalpa** (with a big menu of outdoor adventures, including tenting), **Chimulco** RV park, **Agua Caliente** RV park and camping (next to Chimulco), **San José El Tajo** RV park and tenting, and **Balneario El Rincón** RV and tenting (by Guachimontones).

Additionally, some informal camping areas (with little or no facilities—bring everything you'll need) exist on communally owned forest lands. One of the most accessible and pristine is the **Bosque de Primavera,** on the south side of Highway 15 at La Venta, about 15 minutes by car or bus west of the *periférico.* You have a choice of tenting beneath the pines or beside the bathtub-warm Río Caliente.

Other areas ripe for informal camping are sprinkled around **Tapalpa.** One of the most popular is the scenic **Las Piedrotas** meadowlands preserve, a few miles outside of town. A fence limits access to foot traffic, so be prepared to carry your gear for about a quarter mile. Furthermore, if the water level is high enough (late summer–early fall), camping, fishing, kayaking, and boating opportunities are available at the **Presa del Nogal,** a reservoir and dam about four miles (seven km) south of Tapalpa town. Informal camping is also common at **El Salto del Nogal** waterfall.

DOWNTOWN

People flock to downtown Guadalajara (metropolitan area pop. 4 million, elev. 5,214 ft./1,589 m.) to shop, delighting in big selections at correspondingly small prices.

But that's only part of the fascination. Although Guadalajarans like to think of themselves as different (calling themselves, uniquely, "Tapatíos"), their city is renowned as the "most Mexican" of cities. Downtown visitors—a few foreign, but mostly ordinary Mexican folks—flock to the historic city center, especially on Sundays and holidays, to bask in Guadalajara's springlike sunshine, savor its music, relax beside its cooling fountains, and admire its grand monuments.

For foreign visitors, strolling downtown Guadalajara means relaxing and enjoying the local scene: *artesanos* making and selling handicrafts, *mariachis* strumming and singing, *cocineros* cooking up tacos, and everyone else, usually families with kids, taking it all in.

Among your downtown diversions, be sure to take advantage of some of the bargains that Guadalajara offers. For the best selection, make your first shopping stop at the grand Mercado Libertad, which displays everything from multicolored mounds of delectable fruits and vegetables to a small mountain of handicrafts (stone, wood, papier mâché, and glass) to leather (shoes, belts, purses, jackets), and loads more.

PLANNING YOUR TIME

You could easily spend a week exploring the museums, monuments, galleries, murals, and markets of downtown Guadalajara, but the

© BRUCE WHIPPERMAN

HIGHLIGHTS

Catedral de Guadalajara: The cathedral is a central spot from which start your downtown sightseeing. It contains the casket of the Virgin of Innocence, who was martyred in Rome during the third century A.D. and whose remains were brought to Guadalajara in 1788 (page 32).

Teatro Degollado: Feast your eyes on the theater's epic facade, depicting the allegory of Apollo and the nine muses. At the box office, get tickets for the Sunday folkloric ballet of the University of Guadalajara, or other world-class theatrical, dance, and musical performances (page 34).

Mercado Libertad: Stroll the market's manifold lanes of bright fruit and vegetables, fragrant flowers, pungent herbs and spices, and handicrafts. Enjoy a savory home-cooked lunch at one of the second-floor *fondas* (food stalls) (page 35).

Hospicio Cabañas: Latin America's largest colonial building houses a grand collection of the work of José Clemente Orozco, notably the stirring mural *Man of Fire*, which decorates the interior cupola of the monumental dome (page 36).

Palacio de Gobierno: This building is famous as the Jalisco state governor's office and for an arrestingly graphic Orozco mural that depicts Father Miguel Hidalgo, like an avenging angel, battling the demons of oligarchy and ignorance (page 40).

Parque San Francisco: Admire the facade of the Templo de San Francisco de Asis and the golden *retablos* (altarpieces) inside the Capilla de Nuestra Señora de Aranzazú (page 40).

Nueve Esquinas: "Nine Corners" is a picturesque village-within-a-city neighborhood. At Plaza Nueve Esquinas, enjoy a delicious lunch or dinner of regional specialties (page 42).

Parque Agua Azul: The south-of-downtown park features a botanical garden, a butterfly house, concerts, and plenty of shade and green grass. While you're here, visit the park's excellent paleontology museum (page 42).

Rodeos and Bullfights: Spend an exciting Sunday afternoon at a rodeo-like *charreada*. Watch dashing *charros* bust broncos, rope mustangs, and perform daredevil bull riding, and brightly costumed *charras* (cowgirls) execute a daring *escaramuza charra* (around-the-ring sidesaddle dash) (page 46).

The Tequila Express: Join Guadalajara's popular all-day party, which includes an hourlong scenic ride on the Tequila train, a tequila museum and distillery tour, a sumptuous Mexican buffet, and a brilliant folkloric dance and mariachi music extravaganza (page 48).

LOOK FOR **(** TO FIND RECOMMENDED SIGHTS, ACTIVITIES, DINING, AND LODGING.

TUR

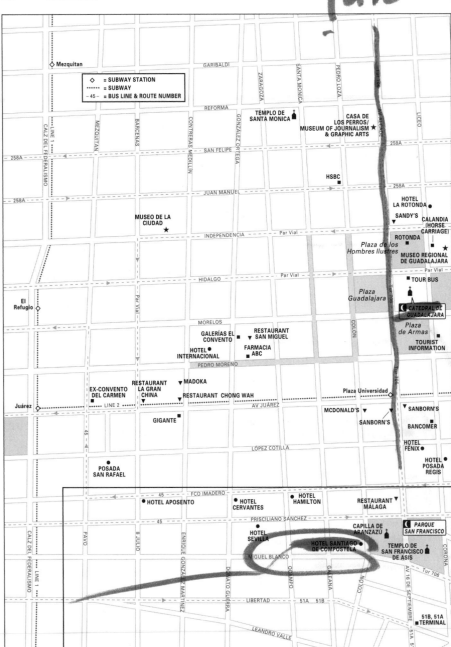

706

DOWNTOWN GUADALAJARA

Parque Morelos

To **RODEOS AND BULLFIGHTS**

SAN DIEGO

FEDERACIÓN

INDUSTRIA

REPÚBLICA

HIDALGO

OROZCO MURALS (INSTITUTO CULTURAL CABAÑAS)

HOSPICIO CABAÑAS

POST OFFICE

HOTEL DE MENDOZA

CONGRESO DEL ESTADO

PALACIO DE JUSTICIA

TEMPLO DE SANTA MARÍA DE GRACIAS

Plaza de la Liberación

FRISA DE LOS FUNDADORES

TEATRO DEGOLLADO

Plaza de los Fundadores

MORELOS MALL

TOURIST INFORMATION

LA RINCONADA

IMOLACIÓN DE QUETZALCOATL

TOURIST INFORMATION

Plaza Tapatía

CENTRO JOYERO

HOTEL FRANCÉS

PALACIO DE GOBIERNO

HOTEL ROMA

San Juan de Dios

Pedestrian Overpass

RODRIGUEZ

MERCADO LIBERTAD

LINE 2

AV JAVIER MINA

BANAMEX

HOLIDAY INN HOTEL & SUITES

Plaza de Los Mariachis

MONEY CHANGERS

AV ALVARO OBREGÓN

HOTEL UNIVERSO

TELECOMUNICACIONES

NIGHTCLUB

NIGHTCLUB

HOTEL LATINO

GIGANTES

SEE "DOWNTOWN SOUTH" MAP

HOTEL SAN FRANCISCO PLAZA

GÓMEZ FARIAS

HOTEL PLAZA DON QUIJOTE

AV REVOLUCIÓN

MEDRANO

ALDAMA

Tur 706

To Tlaquepaque, Tonalá, Hwy 90, and Hwy 80

0   100 yds

0   100 m

© AVALON TRAVEL

downtown area is compact enough that you can visit most of the highlights in two fairly leisurely days and still have time left over for shopping. (Hint: If you can, try to avoid sightseeing on Mondays, when most museums are closed, and Sundays, when some sights have shorter hours of operation.)

If you have only one or two days to spend downtown, it's best to stay at one of the comfortable hotels, such the **de Mendoza**, the **Francés,** or **La Rotonda,** all within a block or two of the city-center cathedral. If you have only one day, spend it hitting the highlights, especially the **Catedral de Guadalajara,** the **Hospicio Cabañas,** and the **Mercado Libertad.** Enjoy lunch at **La Rinconada** or **Sandy's** and dinner at **San Miguel.** For evening diversion, stroll over to the **Plaza de Mariachis** or, if you call ahead for a ticket, take in a performance at the **Teatro Degollago** or the **Teatro Diana.**

A good place to spend your second Guadalajara day is **Tlaquepaque,** strolling the trove of fine handicrafts shops along Avenidas Independencia and Juárez, and savoring lunch at **El Adobe.** Later, linger over dinner at **El Parián** entertainment center, enjoying the mariachi and folkloric dance show.

Alternatively, you might spend your second day perusing the museums around downtown Guadalajara, especially the **Museo de la Ciudad,** north of the cathedral, returning south for a view of the arresting Orozco mural at the **Palacio de Gobierno.** Continue on foot to south-side **Parque San Francisco** for a look at the precious **Templo de San Francisco de Asís** and the beloved **Capilla de Aranzazù.** Stroll a few blocks farther south, through the picturesque **Nueve Esquinas** historic district, for late lunch or early dinner at **Birrias Nueve Esquinas.**

With another day or two you could spend a couple of nights in a comfortable Tlaquepaque bed and breakfast, such as the **Quinta Don José** or the **Casa del Rotono.** On a second Tlaquepaque day, handicrafts enthusiasts would enjoy an excursion to **Tonalá** for a walking tour of some of the renowned **factory shops.** Top

your visit off with late lunch or early dinner at **Rincón del Sol** or **Los Geranios** before returning to Tlaquepaque.

With two more days, you could enjoy some out-of-town overnights. A good choice would be picturesque **Ajijic,** on the mountain-rimmed **Lake Chapala** shoreline. Topchoice bed-and-breakfast lodgings would be the **Hotel La Nueva Posada** in Ajijic or the **Quinta Quetzalcoatl** in Chapala. Spend your time exploring Ajijic's attractive collection of **handicrafts shops,** strolling the airy **Ajijic lakeshore,** and taking a breezy boat excursion from the **Chapala pier** for lunch at mid-lake Isla de los Alacranes or historic Isla Mezcala. Enjoy your evenings dining and dancing at some of Ajijic's better restaurants, such as **La Rusa,** at the Hotel La Nueva Posada, and **La Bodega.**

Other fruitful excursion possibilities would be a two-day Western excursion, with a couple of nights at the restful **Rancho Río Caliente,** including day trips to **Tequila** distillery town and the ancient, monumental **Guachimontones** pyramids. Alternatively, you might spend your second night at the rustic, inviting **Hacienda El Carmen** near Guachimontones, continuing on to Tequila the next day.

HISTORY
Before Columbus

The broad Atemajac Valley, where the Guadalajara metropolis now spreads, has nurtured humans for hundreds of generations. Discovered remains date back at least 10,000 years. The Río Lerma-Santiago—Mexico's longest river, which meanders westerly across five states, from central Mexico to the Pacific—has nourished Atemajac Valley cornfields for at least three millennia.

Ample food led to prosperity. Leisure classes developed, and by A.D. 300 high cultures were occupying western Mexico. In the present-day states of Jalisco, Nayarit, and Colima, they left grand pyramids and ceremonial plazas and sophisticated animal- and human-motif pottery in myriad bottle-shaped underground tombs.

(Intriguingly, similar tombs are also found in Colombia and Ecuador.)

The Guadalajara region's early residents' major monumental constructions remain: 2,000-year-old **Iztepete,** at Guadalajara's southwest edge, and the fascinating **Guachimontones,** grand circular pyramids, west of Guadalajara and north of Tequila.

During the next thousand years after Iztepete, waves of migrants swept across the Valley of Atemajac: Toltecs from the northeast, and the Aztecs much later from the west. As Toltec power declined during the 13th century, the Tarascan civilization took root in Michoacán to the southeast and filled the power vacuum left by the Toltecs. On the eve of the Spanish conquest, semiautonomous local chiefdoms, tributaries of the Tarascan emperor, shared the Atemajac Valley.

Conquest and Colonization

The fall of the Aztecs in 1521 and the Tarascans a few years later made the Atemajac Valley a plum ripe for the picking. In the late 1520s, while Cortés was absent in Spain, the opportunistic Nuño de Guzmán vaulted himself to power in Mexico City on the backs of the native peoples and at the expense of Cortés's friends and relatives. Suspecting correctly that his glory days in Mexico City were numbered, Guzmán cleared out just before Christmas 1529, at the head of a small army of adventurers seeking new conquests in western Mexico. They raped, ravaged, and burned their way west for a half dozen years, inciting dozens of previously peaceful tribes to rebellion.

Hostile Mexican attacks repeatedly foiled Guzmán's attempts to establish his western Mexico capital, which he wanted to name after his Spanish hometown, Guadalajara (from the Arabic *wad al hadjarah,* "river of stones"). Ironically, it wasn't until 1542, the year of Guzmán's death in Spain, six years after his arrest by royal authorities, that the present Guadalajara was founded. At the downtown Plaza de los Fundadores, a panoramic bronze frieze shows cofounders Doña Beatriz de Hernández and governor Cristóbal de Oñate christening

the soon-to-become-capital of the "Kingdom of Nueva Galicia."

The city grew; its now-venerable public buildings rose at the edges of sweeping plazas, from which expeditions set out to explore far-flung lands. In 1563, Miguel López de Legazpi and Father Andrés de Urdaneta sailed west to conquer the Philippines; the year 1602 saw Sebastián Vizcaíno sail for the Californias and the Pacific Northwest. In 1687 Father Eusebio Kino left for 27 years of mission-building in Sonora and what would become Arizona and New Mexico; finally, during the 1760s, Father Junípero Serra and Captain Gaspar de Portola began their arduous trek to discover San Francisco Bay and founded a string of California missions.

During Spain's Mexican twilight, Guadalajara was virtually an imperial city, the capital of **Nueva Galicia,** a western domain that encompassed the present-day states of Jalisco, Nayarit, Colima, Aguascalientes, and parts of Zacatecas, San Luis Potosí, Sinaloa, and Durango, a realm comparable in size to Old Spain itself.

Independence

The cry, "Death to the *gachupines,* viva México" by insurgent priest Miguel Hidalgo ignited rebellion on September 16, 1810. Buoyed by a series of quick victories, Hidalgo advanced on Mexico City in command of a huge ragtag army. But, facing the punishing fusillades of a small but disciplined Spanish force, Hidalgo lost his nerve and decided to occupy Guadalajara instead. Loyalist general Felix Calleja pursued and routed Hidalgo's forces at Calderón Bridge, a few miles north of Zapotlanejo, about 20 miles east of Guadalajara. Although Hidalgo and Ignacio Allende escaped, they were captured in the north a few months later. It wasn't for another dozen bloody years that others—Agustín de Iturbide, Vicente Guerrero, José María Morelos—from other parts of Mexico realized Hidalgo's dream of independence.

Guadalajara, its domain reduced by the republican federal government to the new state of Jalisco, settled down to the production of corn, cattle, and tequila. The railroad came, branched north to the United States and south to the Pacific, and, by 1900, Guadalajara's place as a commercial hub and Mexico's second city was secure.

Modern Guadalajara

After the bloodbath of the 1910–1917 revolution, Guadalajara's growth far outpaced the country in general. From a population of around 100,000 in 1900, the Guadalajara metropolitan zone ballooned to more than three million by 2000. People were drawn from the countryside by jobs in a thousand new factories, making everything from textiles and shoes to silicon chips and soda pop.

Handicraft manufacture, always important in Guadalajara, zoomed during the 1960s when waves of jet-riding tourists came, saw, and bought mountains of blown glass, leather, pottery, and metal finery.

During the 1980s, Guadalajara put on a new face while at the same time preserving the best part of its old downtown. An urban-renewal plan of visionary proportions created Plaza Tapatía—acres of shops, restaurants, and offices beside fountain-studded malls—incorporating Guadalajara's venerable theaters, churches, museums, and government buildings into a single grand open space.

Sights

Getting Oriented

Although the Guadalajara metropolis sprawls across 100 square miles, the treasured one-square-mile heart of the city is easily explored on foot. The cathedral at the corner of north–south Avenida 16 de Septiembre and Avenida Morelos marks the center of town. A few blocks south, another important artery, east–west Avenida Juárez, runs above the metro subway line through the main business district, while a few blocks east, Calzada Independencia runs beneath Plaza Tapatía and past the main market to the Museo de Arqueología and the green, grassy Parque Agua Azul a mile south.

THE CATHEDRAL AND CENTRAL PLAZAS

The twin steeples of the cathedral serve as an excellent starting point to explore the city-center plazas and monuments.

◖ Catedral de Guadalajara

The downtown cathedral, dedicated to the Virgin of the Assumption when it was begun in 1561, was finished about 30 years later. A potpourri of styles—Moorish, Gothic, Renaissance, and Classic—make up its spires, arches, and facades. Although an earthquake demolished its

steeples in 1818, they were rebuilt and resurfaced with cheery canary yellow tiles in 1854.

Inside, side altars and white facades climax at the principal altar, built over a tomb containing the remains of several former clergy, including the mummified heart of renowned Bishop Cabañas. One of the main attractions is the **Virgin of Innocence,** in the nave, left side, to the left of the entrance. The glass-enclosed figure contains the bones of a 12-year-old girl who was martyred in the third century and forgotten, only to be rediscovered in the Vatican catacombs in 1786 and shipped to Guadalajara in 1788. The legend claims she died protecting her virginity; it is equally likely that she was martyred for refusing to recant her Christian faith.

Somewhere in the nave (maybe near the main altar) you'll find either a copy of or the authentic **Virgen de Zapopan.** Between the beginning of June and October 12, the tiny, adored figure will be the authentic "La Generala," as she's affectionately known; on October 12, a tumultuous crowd of worshippers escorts her back to cathedral in Zapopan, where she remains until brought back to Guadalajara the next June.

Outside, broad plazas surround the cathedral: the **Plaza Guadalajara** (formerly Plaza Laureles), in front (west) of the cathedral,

© BRUCE WHIPPERMAN

The Catedral de Guadalajara incorporates a range of architectural styles.

then, moving counterclockwise, the **Plaza de Armas** to the south, **Plaza Liberación** to the east (behind), and the **Plaza de los Hombres Ilustres** to the north of the cathedral.

Plaza de los Hombres Ilustres

Across Avenida Morelos, the block-square Plaza de los Hombres Ilustres is bordered by 16 sculptures of Jalisco's eminent citizens. Their remains lie beneath the stone rotunda in the center; their bronze statues line the sidewalk. Right at the corner you'll find the figure of revered Jalisco governor Ignacio Vallarta; a few steps farther north stands the statue of José Clemente Orozco, legally blind when he executed his great works of art. Continue around the plaza, and you will be rewarded with a view of a recent addition to the Hombres Ilustres statues: the celebrated humanist and educator Irene Robledo Garcia.

Museo Regional de Guadalajara

Adjacent to and east of the Plaza de los Hombres Ilustres, the colonial building behind the lineup of horse-drawn *calandrias* housed the Seminario de San José for six generations following its construction in 1696. During the 1800s it served variously as a barracks and a public lecture hall, and, since 1918, it has housed the Museo Regional (60 Liceo, tel. 33/3614-9957 or 3614-2227, open Tues.–Sat. 9 A.M.–5:30 P.M., Sun. 9 A.M.–5 P.M.).

Tiers of rooms surrounding a tree-shaded interior patio illustrate local history. Exhibits begin with a hulking mastodon skeleton and a small garden of petrified trees and continue through a collection of whimsical animal and human figurines recovered from the bottle-shaped tombs of Jalisco, Nayarit, and Colima. Upstairs, find galleries of Jalisco history and colonial religious art, life-size displays of contemporary but traditional fishing methods at nearby Lake Chapala, and the costumes and culture of regional Cora, Huichol, Tepehuan, and México peoples.

Plaza Liberación

Back outside, head east two blocks down Avenida Hidalgo, paralleling the expansive Plaza Liberación behind the cathedral. On your left you will pass the baroque facades of the *congreso del estado* (state legislature) and the *palacio de justicia* (state supreme court) buildings.

Step inside the latter (open Mon.–Fri. 9 A.M.–7 P.M., Sat. 9 A.M.–1 P.M.) for a look at the mural above the staircase, off the patio to the right. Finished in 1965 by Guillermo Chavez Vega (see his signature in the top right corner), the mural dramatically interprets 19th-century Mexican and Jalisco history. The mural, although obviously Orozco-influenced, is not as arrestingly graphic as those of the master. A bilingual explanation, atop the staircase, identifies the main actors. In the center, Gómez Farías, Father of the Reform, Benito Juárez ("Respect for the rights of all is peace"), and Melchor Ocampo, author of the Laws of Reform, stride down the path of Mexico's nationhood. On the left, arch-villain López de Santa Anna holds the chains of slavery. On the right, white-bearded Jalisco governor Ignacio Vallarta lionizes Miguel Hidalgo: "The Reform Revolution would not have occurred without the push that Hidalgo initiated at Dolores."

© BRUCE WHIPPERMAN

The Catedral de Guadalajara's domed and steepled silhouette towers above the western edge of the Plaza Liberación.

Teatro Degollado

Outside, at the eastern end of the plaza, rises the timeless silhouette of the Teatro Degollado. The theater's classic, columned facade climaxes in an epic marble frieze, depicting the allegory of Apollo and the nine muses. The Degollado's resplendent grand salon is said to rival the gilded refinement of Milan's renowned La Scala. Overhead, its ceiling glows with Gerardo Suárez's panorama of canto IV of Dante's *Divine Comedy*, complete with its immortal cast—Julius Caesar, Homer, Virgil, Saladin—and the robed and wreathed author himself in the middle. Named for millionaire Governor Degollado, who financed its construction, the theater opened with appropriate fanfare on September 13, 1866, with a production of *Lucia de Lammermoor*, starring Angela Peralta, the renowned "Mexican Nightingale." An ever-changing menu of artists still grace the Degollado's stage, including an excellent local folkloric ballet troupe every Sunday morning. For information and tickets, visit or call the Degollado box office

(tel. 33/3614-4773, open daily 10 A.M.–1 P.M. and 4–7 P.M.).

Templo de Santa María de Gracia

Just to the north of (on the left as you face) the Teatro Degollado stands the austere silhouette of the Templo de Santa María de Gracia, Guadalajara's original (1549–1618) cathedral. The present building was begun in 1661 and completed about a century later.

Frisa de los Fundadores

Walk behind the Degollado, where a modern bronze frieze, the Frisa de los Fundadores (Frieze of the Founders) decorates its back side. Appropriately, a mere two blocks from the spot where the city was founded, the 68-foot sculpture shows Guadalajara's cofounders facing each other on opposite sides of a big tree. Governor Cristóbal de Oñate strikes the tree with his sword, while Doña Beatriz de Hernández holds a fighting cock, symbolizing her gritty determination (and that of dozens of fellow settlers) that Guadalajara's location should remain put.

EAST OF THE CATHEDRAL
Plaza Tapatía

The 17 acres of the Plaza Tapatía complex extend for several blocks across subplazas, fountains, and malls. Initially wide in the foreground of Plaza de los Fundadores, the Tapatía narrows between a double row of shops and offices, then widens into a broad esplanade and continues beside a long pool/fountain that leads to the monumental, domed Hospicio Cabañas a third of a mile away. Along the Tapatía's lateral flanks, a pair of long malls—continuations of Avenidas Hidalgo and Morelos—parallel the central Paseo Degollado mall for two blocks.

The eastern end of the Morelos mall climaxes with the striking bronze *escudo* (coat of arms) of Guadalajara. Embodying the essence of the original 16th-century coat of arms authorized by Emperor Charles V, the *escudo* shows a pair of lions protecting a pine tree (with leaves, rather than needles). The lions represent the warrior's determination and discipline, and the solitary pine symbolizes noble ideals.

Continue east, to where the Plaza Tapatía widens, giving berth for the sculpture-fountain *Imolación de Quetzalcoatl,* designed and executed by Víctor Manuel Contreras in 1982. Four bronze serpent-birds, representing knowledge and the spirit of humankind, stretch toward heaven at the ends of a giant cross. In the center, a towering bronze spiral represents the unquenchable flame of Quetzalcoatl, transforming all that it touches. Locals call the sculpture the "big corkscrew," however. Nearby, find the city **tourist information booth** (open daily approximately 9 A.M.–5 P.M.).

Adjacent, on the south flank of the plaza, rises a big former department store, now the **Magno Centro Joyero** retail jewelry complex. A fleet of shops display glittering, mostly gold necklaces, amulets, bracelets, and much, much more. Most shops are open daily 9 A.M. until around 6 or 7 P.M. (For more details, see the *Shopping* section.)

◀ Mercado Libertad

At this point, Avenida Independencia runs directly beneath Plaza Tapatía, past the adjacent

© BRUCE WHIPPERMAN

Flocks of pigeons are right at home in downtown Plaza Tapatía.

Campesinos enjoy a break beneath the shady willow trees that grace the rear patio of the Mercado Libertad.

sprawling Mercado Libertad, built in 1958 on the site of the traditional Guadalajara *tianguis* (open-air market), known since pre-Columbian times. Follow the elevated pedestrian walkway south to explore the Libertad's produce, meat, fish, herbs, food, and handicrafts stalls. (For more Mercado Libertad details, see the *Shopping* section.)

Plaza de los Mariachis

On Independencia, just south of the market, musicians at the Plaza de los Mariachis continue the second century of a tradition born when mariachi (cowboy troubadour) groups first appeared during the 1860s in Guadalajara. The musical hubbub climaxes Saturday nights and Sunday afternoons as musicians gather, singing while they wait to be hired for serenades and parties. (Note: A shootout at the Plaza de los Mariachis temporarily scared the mariachis and visitors away during 2006, although at this writing, many of the mariachis have returned. Nevertheless, the city government is considering changing the location of the Plaza de los Mariachis. Ask your hotel clerk for an update.) Alternatively, you can enjoy the mariachi shows at El Parián entertainment center in Tlaquepaque. See the *Tlaquepaque and Tonalá* chapter for details.

Hospicio Cabañas

Behind the long pool/fountain at the east end of Plaza Tapatía stands the domed neoclassic Hospicio Cabañas, the largest and one of the most remarkable colonial buildings in the Americas, designed and financed by Bishop Juan Ruiz de Cabañas; construction was completed in 1810. The purpose of the "Guadalajara House of Charity and Mercy," as the good bishop originally named it, a home for the sick, helpless, and homeless, was fulfilled for 170 years. Although it successfully served as an orphanage during the 1970s, time had taken its toll on the Hospicio Cabañas. The city and state governments built a new orphanage in the suburbs, restored the old building, and changed its purpose. It now houses the **Instituto Cultural Cabañas** (Cabañas 8, tel. 33/3818-2800, ext, 31016, open Tues.–Sat. 10:15 A.M.–5:45 P.M., Sun. 10:15 A.M.–3 P.M.),

JOSÉ CLEMENTE OROZCO

Born into middle-class comfort in Zapotlán, Jalisco, in 1883, Orozco was taken to Mexico City with his family when they resettled in 1888. Soon after José began studying architecture and art in 1908, he was strongly influenced by the work of noted political cartoonist José Guadalupe Posada. One of Orozco's biographers wrote that on his way to college classes, he would stop at Posada's workshop, where the master worked in view of everyone. Orozco later wrote, "This was the first stimulus that awoke my imagination and impulse to put those first figures down on paper."

And he did. After his formal education, Orozco started drawing bordello scenes and political cartoons, which he exhibited in 1916. Around the same time, Orozco, influenced by the apocalyptic early 19th-century work of Goya, completed and exhibited his famous drawing portfolio, *Mexico in Revolution*. This marked the beginning of his lifelong vocation of jolting the world awake to the suffering and futility of war.

Orozco's first public murals, completed in 1923, were judged too severe and were later altered or destroyed. Seeking more fertile ground, he moved to the United States in 1927 and completed a trio of important murals at Pomona College, the New School for Social Research, and Dartmouth College. Riding a crest of accomplishment, Orozco returned to Mexico in late 1934.

Now, with nothing to stop him, Orozco was free to create: "I favored black and the province forbidden by the Impressionists. Instead of red and yellow sunsets I painted pestilential shadows . . . and instead of nude Indians, drunk women and men."

As he matured, Orozco's work became

© BRUCE WHIPPERMAN

grander and even more starkly arresting. Between 1934 and 1940 he completed his Guadalajara masterpieces *Man of Fire* and *Hidalgo and the Liberation*, at the Hospicio Cabañas and the Palacio de Gobierno downtown, respectively, and *The People and Their Leaders*, at the University of Guadalajara rectory, west of downtown.

In the aftermath of his great Guadalajara triumphs, Orozco and his wife, Margarita Valladares, bought part of a farm, on Guadalajara's west-side suburb, in 1946. The Orozcos rebuilt the original house in 1948, including a large studio where José planned to create "works totally different than I've done until now." Unfortunately, time caught up with him. José Clemente Orozco passed away a year later, on September 7, 1949, at the age of 66.

BUILDING CHURCHES

Although European architects designed most of Mexico's colonial-era churches, embellishing them with old-world Gothic, Renaissance, baroque, and Moorish decorations, native artists added their own geometric, floral, and animal motifs. The result was a blend that manifested in intriguing variations all over Mexico.

Sometimes the native influence led to poor ("provincial") versions of European designs; other times (notably, the Templo de Nuestra Señora de Aranzazú and the Templo de Santa Monica in downtown Guadalajara) artists merged brilliant native decorations with the best of European-style vaults, arches, and columns.

THE LAYOUT

Mexican church design followed the Egypto-Greco-Roman tradition of its European models. Basically, architects designed their churches beginning with the main space of the **nave,** in the shape of a box, lined with high lateral windows. Depending on their origin and function, builders constructed three basic types of churches – the monk's **monastery or convent** (convento), the bishop's **cathedral** (catedral), and the priest's parish church (templo, parroquia).

With only masonry to work with, and often faced with the constant threat of earthquake, colonial-era builders raised massively thick walls, supported on the exterior with ponderous buttresses. Key elements were naves, with or without **transepts** (cruceros), cross spaces separating the nave from the altar, making the church plan resemble a Christian cross. They placed the **choir** (coro) above and just inside the entrance arch.

At the opposite, usually east, or sunrise, end of the church, builders sometimes extended the nave beyond the transept to include a **presbytery** (presbiterio), which was often lined with seats where church officials presided. Past that the building ended at the **apse** (ábside), the space behind the altar, frequently in semicircular or half-octagonal form. Within the apse rises the gilded **retable** (retablo) adorned with sacred images, attended by choirs of angels and cherubs.

Larger churches usually incorporated side altars, presided over by images of locally popular saints, nearly always including the Virgin of Guadalupe.

THE FACADE

Outside, in front, rises the facade (fachada), sometimes in a uniform style, but just as often a mixture of Renaissance, Gothic, and baroque, with some Moorish (mujedar) worked into the mix. A proliferation of columns nearly always

a center for the arts. Public programs include classes, films, and instrumental, chorale, and dance concerts.

Seemingly endless ranks of corridors pass a host of sculpture-decorated patios. Practice rooms resound with the clatter of dancing feet and the halting strains of apprentice violins, horns, and pianos. Exhibition halls and studios of the **José Clemente Orozco Art Museum** occupy a large fraction of the rooms, while the great muralist's brooding work spreads across a corresponding fraction of the walls. Words such as dark, fiery, nihilistic, even apocalyptic, would not be too strong to describe the pan-

oramas that Orozco executed (1938–1939) in the soaring chapel beneath the central dome. On one wall, an Aztec goddess wears a necklace of human hearts; on another, armored automaton-soldiers menace Indian captives; while in the cupola overhead, Orozco's *Man of Fire*, wreathed in flame, appears to soar into a hellishly red-hot sky.

NORTH OF THE CATHEDRAL

Return to the cathedral-front street (which continues, changing from 16 de Septiembre to Alcalde north of the cathedral) and walk north three-and-a-half blocks.

decorates Guadalajara church facades, from the classic Etruscan, Doric, Ionic, and Corinthian *(Toscano, Dórico, Jónico, Corintio)* pillars to spiraled Solomonic *(Salomónico)* barber's poles and bizarre *estipites. Estipite* columns, a baroque feature of plateresque facades (so-named for their resemblance to elaborate silverware designs), usually begin with a classical capital (base) but rise, curiously, like an inverted obelisk, widening to a pair or trio of elaborately carved prismatic blocks and narrowing quickly again to an identical capital at the top.

CONVENTS

The monastery- (or convent-) style churches, besides all of the above, included living and working quarters for members of the order, typically built around a columned patio called the **cloister** *(claustro).* A corridor through an arched porch *(portería)* adjacent to the nave usually led to the cloister, from which monks and nuns could quickly reach the dining hall, or **refectory** *(refectorio),* and their private rooms, or cells *(celdas).*

The missionary fathers designed their churches with an eye to handling the masses of natives whom they hoped to convert. For them, padres included an **atrium** *(atrio),* a large exterior courtyard in front of the facade. For the partly initiated natives, they often built an open chapel *(capilla abierta)* on one side of the atrium. Conversions also occurred at smaller open chapels *(pozas),* built at the corners of the atrium.

© BRUCE WHIPPERMAN

The Templo de San Francisco de Asis is noted for its monumental Solomonic spiral-columned facade.

Museum of Journalism and Graphic Arts

The neoclassic facade of the Museum of Journalism and Graphic Arts (open Tues.–Sat. 10 A.M.–6 P.M., Sun. 10:30 A.M.–3 P.M., tel. 33/3613-9285 or 33/3613-9286), popularly known as the **Casa de los Perros** (House of the Dogs), rises on the west side of Alcalde, between San Felipe and Reforma.

The museum maintains a schedule of temporary photography and other graphic arts exhibitions, film screenings, and a library. The permanent exhibits on the bottom floor display a copy of the front page of the original *El Despertador Americano,* an original linotype (automatic typesetting) machine, and a 1950s-vintage television studio mockup.

The present building occupies the site of Guadalajara's first printing press, founded at the same time as Guadalajara's first university, in 1792. Later, in December 1810, under the orders of rebel priest Miguel Hidalgo, Mexico's first insurgent newspaper, *El Despertador Americano,* was edited and printed by Francisco Severo Maldonado.

The building's popular name originates from the dog shelter maintained by an animal-lover who operated a tailor shop on the site during the mid-1800s. Although subsequent fighting destroyed the building during the 1858–1861 War of the Reform, new owners—tequila distiller Jesús Flores and his socially prominent wife, Ana González Rubio—replaced it with the present structure in 1896. In recognition of tradition, they topped the new building's French-style facade with a pair of cast-iron pointer terriers, prominently visible from the street.

Templo de Santa Monica

Walk two blocks west to the beloved old Templo de Santa Monica, built by Guadalajara's Jesuits between 1720 and 1733 (subsequently destroyed and rebuilt), on the block of Santa Monica between Reforma and San Felipe. Admire the resplendent original rococo *portada* (door portal), in midblock, flanked by two pairs of gloriously carved Solomonic columns, clad with stone vines, leaves, and grapes, spiraling upward toward heaven. Walk a half block north, to the corner of Flores, where, above the southwest street corner, a kindly St. Christopher carries the child Jesus on his giant shoulder.

Museo de la Ciudad

At the Museo de la Ciudad (Museum of the City) (open Tues.–Sat. 10 A.M.–5:30 P.M., Sun. 10 A.M.–2:30 P.M., tel. 33/3658-3706, 33/3658-2531, or 33/3658-2665), you'll find an excellent exposition of photos, drawings, paintings, papers, and artifacts depicting 500 years of Guadalajara history, from the conquest to the present. Don't miss the display showing the widening of Avenida Juárez during the 1950s, when engineers and workers, seemingly miraculously, moved the entire city telephone building 50 feet without a single service interruption. The Museum of the City is two blocks south and five blocks west of the Templo de Santa Monica on Independencia, north side, between Medellin and Barcenas.

SOUTH OF THE CATHEDRAL

A number of must-see Guadalajara sights sprinkle the mile-long district that begins just south of the cathedral.

Palacio de Gobierno

Just a block east and a half block south of the cathedral front, let the Palacio de Gobierno (open daily 9:30 A.M.–8:30 P.M.), on Armas's east side, be the first stop of your south-side walking tour. At the **city tourism information booth** *(módulo de información)* (open Mon.– Fri. 9 A.M.–3 P.M. and 4–7 P.M., Sat. and Sun. 10 A.M.–12:30 P.M.), just inside the entrance, ask for a copy of the superb all-color *Points of Interest* bilingual foldout map and guide. (Moreover, the sidewalk out front of the Palacio de Gobierno is a good spot to meet a local guide, Mr. Xiao Lin (tel. 33/3607-6786, donation only), who explains the murals inside.

The Palacio de Gobierno's main attraction is the epic 1937 **Orozco mural** in the stairwell, right side of the inner patio. Father Miguel Hidalgo, with torch in hand, like an avenging angel, leads Mexico's struggle against the evil stooges of Communism, Capitalism, Fascism, and Catholicism. Don't miss the villains, such as General Porfirio Díaz and the idiotic Benito Mussolini (middle right panel), or the heroes, such as mustachioed Emiliano Zapata (in campesino white cotton).

Parque San Francisco

Walk four blocks south along 16 de Septiembre to the busy corner of Prisciliano Sánchez. A beloved pair of old churches, the Capilla de Nuestra Señora de Aranzazú, ahead of you on the right side of 16 de Septiembre, and the dignified Templo de San Francisco de Asis on the left side, occupy the tree-shaded Parque San Francisco. The **Templo de San Francisco de Asis,** built through the initiative of Franciscan padres between 1668 and 1692, stands on the site of an earlier (1552) Franciscan church and convent. Its exterior climaxes in its facade of Solomonic columns spiraling upward like giant barber poles. The airy, towering nave shines with a glittering baroque *retablo* above and behind the altar.

Capilla de Nuestra Señora de Aranzazú

West, across 16 de Septiembre, the Capilla de Nuestra Señora de Aranzazú, built between

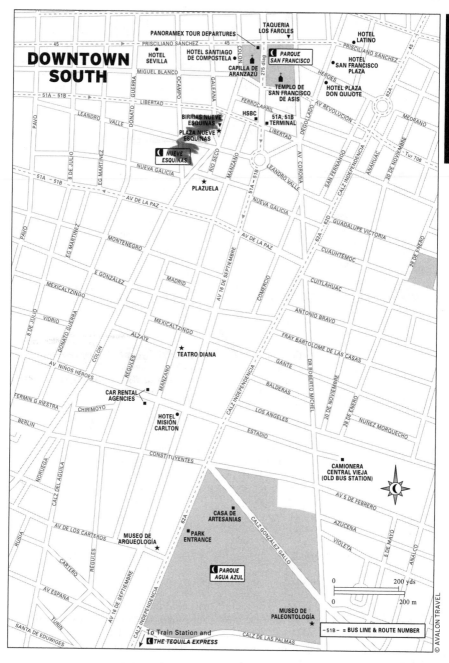

DOWNTOWN

DOWNTOWN SOUTH

PANORAMEX TOUR DEPARTURES
TAQUERIA LOS FAROLES
HOTEL LATINO
HOTEL SEVILLA
HOTEL SANTIAGO DE COMPOSTELA
PARQUE SAN FRANCISCO
HOTEL SAN FRANCISCO PLAZA
CAPILLA DE ARANZAZÚ
TEMPLO DE SAN FRANCISCO DE ASIS
HOTEL PLAZA DON QUIJOTE
BIRRIAS NUEVE ESQUINAS
HSBC
PLAZA NUEVE ESQUINAS
51A, 51B TERMINAL
NUEVE ESQUINAS
PLAZUELA
NUEVA GALICIA
GUADALUPE VICTORIA
CUAUHTÉMOC
CUITLAHUAC
ANTONIO BRAVO
FRAY BARTOLOME DE LAS CASAS
TEATRO DIANA
GANTE
BALDERAS
CAR RENTAL AGENCIES
LOS ANGELES
HOTEL MISIÓN CARLTON
ESTADIO
NUÑEZ MORQUECHO
CONSTITUYENTES
CAMIONERA CENTRAL VIEJA (OLD BUS STATION)
AV 5 DE FEBRERO
AZUCENA
CASA DE ARTESANIAS
VIOLETA
MUSEO DE ARQUEOLOGÍA
PARK ENTRANCE
PARQUE AGUA AZUL

0   200 yds
0   200 m

MUSEO DE PALEONTOLOGÍA

To Train Station and
THE TEQUILA EXPRESS

-51B- = BUS LINE & ROUTE NUMBER

© AVALON TRAVEL

The Capilla de Nuestra Señora de Aranzazú is famous for its grand golden *retablos* (altar pieces) inside.

1749 and 1752, complements the exterior majesty of San Francisco de Asis with its austerely simple facade. This changes inside, however, where you can pay your respects to the beloved Virgen de Aranzazú, who presides above the altar, beneath a divine, towering golden *retablo.* Beneath nearly as fine a *retablo,* on the western (right) side wall, you can pay your respects to the Lord of the Afflicted; on the opposite (east) wall, you can do the same with a duplicate of the celebrated Virgen de Zapopan. Before leaving the nave, pass a duplicate of the equally beloved Virgen de Talpa, near the door, and on the way, be sure not to miss the little glass case with a swarm of children's toys nearly covering the **Santo Niño de Atocha** (Holy Child of Atocha).

The tale of the Virgen de Aranzazú deserves retelling. Once upon a time in the remote Basque country of northern Spain, a shepherd stumbled upon an image of the Virgin and Child, caught in a thorn thicket. The amazed shepherd exclaimed to the image:

"¡Aranzazú!" ("You are in the thorns!"). After hearing the shepherd's story, the Basque country people adopted his Virgin as their own and subsequently carried the tradition to the New World. In Guadalajara, Franciscan padre Francisco Iñigo Vallejo, with the patronage of rich Basque *hacendados,* got the chapel built in her honor.

Nueve Esquinas

Continue south along Colón, the street that borders the west side of the Aranzazú church. Within a block you'll enter the colorful working-class *Nueve Esquinas* ("Nine Corners") district. Spruced-up 19th-century townhouse facades and hole-in-the-wall local workshops—printers, machine shops, electrical repair—decorate the narrow lanes.

After three short blocks you come to the neighborhood-center, **Plaza Nueve Esquinas,** bordered by a squad of *birria* **restaurants** *(birrerias),* so-named for the savory, traditional Guadalajaran pit-roasted meat (goat, pork, or beef) that they all serve. Make sure you have an appetite when you arrive, because a serving of *birria* here is an opportunity you won't want to miss. Of the several popular restaurants, the best seems to be **Birrias Nueve Esquinas** on Colón, at the plaza front.

Parque Agua Azul

To explore the worthwhile sights farther south, keep walking south, or hail a taxi (no more than $1.50) to carry you the 10 blocks (one mile, 1.6 km) to Parque Agua Azul (corner of Independencia and González Gallo, tel. 33/3619-0328 or 33/3619-0340, open Tues.–Sun. 10 A.M.–6 P.M., entrance fee approximately $1).

You can enjoy a whole day in the park, taking in a concert, strolling through a butterfly or bird house, snoozing on the lawn, and more. It's a green, shaded place where you can walk, roll, sleep, or lie on the grass. When weary of that, head for the bird park, admire the banana-beaked toucans and squawking macaws, and continue into the aviary, where free-flying birds flutter overhead. Nearby, duck into the *mariposario* and enjoy the flickering rainbow hues of *mariposas* (butterflies). Continue to the orchids in a towering hothouse, festooned with growing blossoms and misted continuously by a rainbow of spray from the center. Before other temptations draw you away, stop for a while at the open-air band or symphony concert in the amphitheater.

Museo de Paleontología de Guadalajara

Be sure to save an hour from your Parque Agua Azul stroll to visit the excellent, up-to-date Museo de Paleontología de Guadalajara (520 Michel, corner of González Gallo, 33/3619-7043, 33/3619-5560, or 33/3619-6576, paleontolo01@hotmail.com, open Tues.–Sat. 10 A.M.–6 P.M., Sun. 11 A.M.–4 P.M.), about a half mile east of the Agua Azul entrance, just outside the far eastern corner of Parque Agua Azul. Through a series of innovative permanent exhibits, the visitor explores the methods, tools, and content of paleontology. The grand finale is a transparent walkway over a life-sized model of one of Guadalajara's prime paleontological sites—a lake bed, rich in remains of Ice Age animals (saber-toothed tiger, giant sloth, mammoth), which visitors view and identify beneath their very feet. For more information, including a listing of the museum's classes, activities, and temporary exhibitions, visit www.guadalajara.gob.mx/dependencias/museopaleontologia/index.html. (Hint: If this handle is too error prone for you, simply go to the Google search page and enter Museo Paleontología de Guadalajara.)

Museo de Arqueología

Just across Calzada Indepedencia from Parque Agua Azul, the Archaeological Museum of Western Mexico (Nucleo Agua Azul 889, tel. 33/3619-0104, open Mon.–Sat. 10 A.M.–2 P.M. and 5–7 P.M., Sun. 10 A.M.–2 P.M.), between busy Avenida 16 de Septiembre and Calzada Independencia, displays an interesting collection of pre-Columbian artifacts from Jalisco, Colima, and Nayarit. The exhibits climax in the delightfully lifelike Colima figurines. Old men snooze, women gossip, children romp, while parrots squawk, dogs frolic, and armadillos scurry—all bringing, to the visitor's mind's eye, a long-dead civilization back to vibrant life. Also, notice the explanation of the uniquely intriguing "bottle tombs" *(tumbas de tiro)*, of a style found nowhere else but Colombia and Ecuador, as well as the exhibit (if they have one by the time you arrive—ask if they have a brochure *(folleto)* or other written material, of the Iztepete archaeological site at the southwest edge of town. (See the *West and North* chapter.)

Entertainment and Events

STROLLING THE PLAZAS

Afternoons any day, and Sunday in particular, are good for people-watching around Guadalajara's many downtown plazas. Favorite strolling grounds are the broad fountain and Plaza Guadalajara in front of the cathedral, the even broader Plaza Liberación behind the cathedral, and, especially in the evening, the pedestrian mall streets, such as Colón, Galeana, Morelos, and Moreno, which meander south and west from cathedral-front Plaza Guadalajara.

If you time it right, you can enjoy the concert that the Jalisco State Band has provided since 1898, in the **Plaza de Armas, just south** of the cathedral (Thurs. 6:30 P.M., Sun. 6 P.M.; mariachis Wed. 6:30 P.M.).

If you miss these, climb into a *calandria* (horse-drawn carriage) for a ride around downtown; carriages are available on Liceo between the rotunda and the history museum, just north of the cathedral, for about $15 an hour.

© BRUCE WHIPPERMAN

The Jalisco State Band performs weekly in the Plaza de Armas central kiosk.

Plaza de los Mariachis

In your wanderings, be sure to include the Plaza de los Mariachis, on the south side of Plaza Tapatía, at street level, adjacent to the big Mercado Libertad.

The best time to visit Plaza de los Mariachis is during the late afternoon or early evening, when you can take a sidewalk table, have a drink or snack, and enjoy the mariachis' sometimes soulful, sometimes bright, but always enjoyable offerings. (If you decide to hire mariachis to play some of your favorite Mexican tunes, establish the price, which should run about $1 per musician per song, beforehand.)

MUSIC AND DANCE
Performances

The **Teatro Degollado** hosts world-class opera, symphony, and ballet events. While you're in the Plaza Liberación, drop by the theater box office *(taquilla)* (tel. 33/3613-1115 or 3614-4773, open daily 10 A.M.–8 P.M.) and ask for a *lista de eventos*. You can also call (or ask your hotel desk clerk to call) the box office for reservations, tickets and information.

For a very typical Mexican treat, attend one of the regular Sunday 10 A.M. **University of Guadalajara folkloric ballet performances.** They're immensely popular; get tickets in advance.

Since the new south-side **Teatro Diana** (Av. 16 de Sept. 710, 33/3614-7940, info@teatrodiana.com, www.teatrodiana.com, box office open daily 11 A.M.–8 P.M.) opened its doors not long ago, it has filled the need for a second world-class performance hall in Guadalajara. The Diana's up-to-date, soft rising-tiered seating adds greatly to the visibility, audibility, and intimacy of the performances. And there are many performances, ranging from the Vienna Boys Choir and the Covent Garden Royal Ballet to the Mayumana Afro-Latin Dance troupe and the Iraida Noriega jazz trio. Find the Teatro Diana in the south-edge-of-downtown neighborhood, about a mile south of the cathedral.

MARIACHIS

Mariachis, those thoroughly Mexican troubadour bands, have spread from their birthplace in Jalisco throughout Mexico and into much of the United States. The name itself reveals their origin. "Mariachi" originated with the French *mariage*, or marriage. When French influence peaked during the 1864–1867 reign of Maximilian, Jaliscans transposed *mariage* to "mariachi," a label they began to identify with the five-piece folk bands that played for weddings.

The original ensembles, consisting of a pair of violins, *vihuela* (large eight-stringed guitar), *jarana* (small guitar), and harp, played exclusively traditional melodies. Song titles such as "Las Moscas" (The Flies), "El Venado" (The Stag), and "La Papaya" thinly disguised their universal themes, mostly concerning love.

Although such all-string folk bands still play in Jalisco, notably in Tecalitlán and other rural areas, they've largely been replaced by droves of trumpet-driven commercial mariachis. The man who sparked the shift was probably Emilio Azcárraga Vidaurreta, the director of radio station XEW, which began broadcasting in Mexico City in 1930. In those low-fidelity days, the subdued sound of the harp didn't broadcast well, so Azcárraga suggested the trumpet as a replacement. It was so successful the trumpet has become the signature sound of present-day mariachis.

Still, mariachis mostly do what they've always done – serenade sweethearts, play for weddings and parties, even accompany church masses. They seem to be forever strolling around town plazas on Saturday nights and Sunday afternoons,

looking for jobs. Their fees, which should be agreed upon before they start, often depend on union scale per song, per serenade, or per hour.

Sometimes mariachis serve as a kind of live jukebox that, for a coin, will play your old favorite. And even if it's a slightly tired but sentimental "Mañanitas" or "Cielito Lindo," you can't help but be moved by the singing violins, bright trumpets, and soothing guitars.

Traditional mariachis are making a comeback in Guadalajara.

© BRUCE WHIPPERMAN

You can also sample the offerings of the **Instituto Cultural Cabañas,** which sponsors many events, both experimental and traditional, including films, folkloric ballet performances, and art exhibitions. For more information, ask at the Hospicio Cabañas admission desk.

If you hanker for more (or different) musical entertainment, walk two blocks east of the cathedral to the **Hotel Frances** (Maestranza 35, tel. 33/3613-1190 or 33/3613-0936) to enjoy the mariachis, who play until around 11 P.M. on Fridays.

Nightclubs

A few clubs accommodate folks who want to unwind downtown. The lobby bar in the **Hotel Fénix** (Corona 160, tel. 33/3614-5714), just two blocks south of the cathedral, often offers evening music until about midnight. Call to confirm.

Devotees of discotheques might enjoy a visit to a pair of clubs (customarily crowded with 20- and 30-somethings most Friday and Saturday nights), on Maestranza, between Sánchez and Madero. The **Meridiana 60,** the more genteel of the two, is decorated inside with colored lights flashing on vine-draped walls and offers no cover and live salsa-rock music Wednesday–Saturday beginning at 10 P.M. (tel. 33/3613-8489, open 10 A.M.–2 A.M.).

A few doors south and across the street, **Bar-Discoteca Maskaras** (tel. 33/3614-8103, open daily 7 P.M.–3 A.M.) operates a downstairs bar and a no-cover upstairs discoteque. The door stays shut so neighbors can sleep and customers can hear each other talk downstairs.

FIESTAS

Although Guadalajarans always seem to be celebrating, the town really heats up during its three major annual festivals.

Starting the third week in June, the southeast neighborhood, formerly the separate village of Tlaquepaque, hosts the **National Ceramics Fair.** Besides celebrated stoneware, Tlaquepaque shops and stalls are stuffed with a riot of ceramics and folk crafts from all over Mexico, while cockfights, regional food, folk dances, fireworks, and mariachis fill the streets. See the *Tlaquepaque and Tonalá* chapter for details.

A few months later, the entire city, Mexican states, and foreign countries get into the **Fiesta de Octubre.** For a month, everyone contributes something, from ballet performances, plays, and soccer games to selling papier-mâché parrots and *elote* (corn on the cob) in the plazas.

Concurrently, Guadalajarans celebrate the traditional **Fiesta de la Virgen de Zapopan.** Church plazas are awash with merrymakers enjoying food, mariachis, dances (don't miss the Dance of the Conquest), and fireworks. The merrymaking peaks on October 12, when a huge crowd conducts the Virgin from the downtown cathedral to Zapopan. The merrymakers' number usually swells to a million faithful who escort the Virgin, accompanied by ranks of costumed saints, devils, Spanish conquistadors, and Aztec chiefs. (For a list of national fiestas, see the sidebar *Fiestas* in the *Background* chapter.)

◖ RODEOS AND BULLFIGHTS

Local associations of *charros* (gentleman cowboys) stage rodeo-like **charreadas** at Guadalajara *lienzos charro* (rodeo rings). The most reliable local *charreada* is at **Lienzo Charro de Jalisco,** where local *charros* stage colorful Sunday shows, beginning around noon, just beyond the southeast side of Parque Agua Azul (Calz. Dr. Michel 577, tel. 33/3619-0315). (See the *charreadas* sidebar for performance details.)

Late fall and winter are the main season for **corridas de toros,** or bullfights. The bulls charge and the crowds roar *"¡Olé!"* (oh-LAY) on Sunday afternoons at the Guadalajara Plaza de Toros (bullring), on Calzada Independencia about two miles north of the Mercado Libertad.

Watch for posters or ask at your hotel desk or the tourist information office (tel. 33/3688-1600) for *charreada* and *corrida de toros* details and dates.

CHARREADAS

Charrería, the sport of horsemanship, is a long-venerated Jalisco tradition. Boys and girls, coached by their parents, practice riding skills from the time they learn to mount a horse. Privileged young people become noble *charros* or *charras* or *coronelas* – gentleman cowboys and cowgirls – whose equestrian habits follow old aristocratic Spanish fashion, complete with broad sombrero, brocaded suit or dress, and silver spurs.

The years of long preparation culminate in the *charreada*, which entire communities anticipate with relish. Although superficially similar to an Arizona rodeo, a Jalisco *charreada* differs substantially. The festivities take place in a *lienzo charro*, literally, the passageway through which the bulls, horses, and other animals run from the corral to the ring. First comes the *cala de caballo*, a test of the horse and rider. The *charros* or *charras* must gallop full speed across the ring and make the horse stop on a dime. Next is the *piales de lienzo*, a roping exhibition during which an untamed horse must be halted and held by having its feet roped. Other bold performances include *jineteo de toro* (bull riding and throwing) and the super-hazardous *paso de la muerte*, in which a rider tries to jump upon an untamed bronco from his or her own galloping mount. *Charreadas* often end in a flourish with the *escaramuza charra*, a spectacular show of riding skill by *charras* in full, colorful dress.

© BRUCE WHIPPERMAN

If you ever happen upon a country *charreada*, be sure to stop and take in the action.

THE TEQUILA EXPRESS

Ride the very popular tourist train to the historic **Hacienda San José,** now preserved as both museum and liquor distillery of the Herradura tequila firm, in the town of Amatitán, a few miles east of the famed liquor town of Tequila. The tour amounts to an all-day party, and features nearly continuous food, drink, and music. The train stops at the ex-hacienda-distillery, where there is a viewing of the blue agave harvesting process, a distillery tour, a grand Mexican buffet, and a folkloric show, typically including folk dancing, mariachis, a roping exhibition, and handicrafts.

Tours depart from the rail station, about a mile south of downtown, mostly on Saturday and Sunday mornings, several times per month. It's best to buy your tickets at least six weeks in advance. Tariffs run around $70 per adult; kids 6–11, $48; children under six are free. Tickets are widely available: In the city center, get them at the Guadalajara Camara de Comercio (Chamber of Commerce) (Morelos 395, tel. 33/3614-3145, open Mon.–Sat. 9 A.M.–2:30 P.M. and 3:30–6 P.M.), on the Plaza Guadalajara, upstairs, corner of Colón, just a block west of the cathedral.

You may also buy Tequila Express tickets by credit card from **Ticketmaster** (tel. 33/3818-3800). It's best to have a local person, such as your hotel desk clerk, call for you.

For more information, visit www.tequilaexpress.com.mx, or call local toll-free tel. 01-800/503-9720.

You can also tour the Hacienda San José on your own Monday–Friday. For details, see the *Tequila* section in the *Getaways* chapter.

ENTERTAINMENT LISTINGS

For many more entertainment ideas, pick up the **events schedule** at the Instituto Cultural Cabañas, beyond the long pool/fountain at the east end of Plaza Tapatía, or the tourist information office in Plaza Tapatía, on Paseo Morelos, the mall extension of Avenida Morelos, behind the Teatro Degollado at Morelos 102.

Another good source of entertaining events is the weekly English-language *Guadalajara*

Reporter, always available at Sandi Bookstore (Tepeyac 718, Colonia Chapalita, tel. 33/3121-0863). If you still can't find a newsstand copy, contact the newspaper office (Duque de Rivas 254, Guadalajara 44130, tel. 33/3615-2177, www.guadalajarareporter.com), two blocks from the west-side Hotel Diana.

SPORTS AND RECREATION
Walking and Jogging

Walkers and joggers enjoy several spots around Guadalajara. Close in, the **Plaza Liberación** behind the cathedral provides a traffic-free (although concrete) jogging and walking space. Avoid the crowds with morning workouts. If you prefer grass underfoot, try **Parque Agua Azul** (open Tues.–Sat. 10 A.M.–6 P.M., entrance $1), on Calzada Independencia about a mile south of the Plaza Tapatía.

An even better jogging/walking space is the **Bosque Los Colomos** park (open daily 7 A.M.–7 P.M.)—hundreds of acres of greenery, laced with special jogging trails—four miles northwest from the city center, before Zapopan; take a taxi or bus #51C, which begins at the old bus terminal, near Parque Agua Azul, and continues north along Avenida 16 de Septiembre through downtown Guadalajara. By car, drive along Avenida Patria, northeast. Pass the Plaza Pabellón shopping center, on the right, at Avenida Aqueducto, and continue about another mile to the Colomos entrance gate, on the right, at 1805 Avenida Patria. For more information, call the park's *casa cultural* (tel. 33/3641-7633).

Tennis and Golf

Although central Guadalajara has few, if any, public tennis courts, the **Hotel Camino Real,** (Av. Vallarta 5005, tel. 33/3134-2424), on the west side, rents courts to the public. On the southern outskirts, on the airport-Chapala highway, about a mile south of the periferico, behind the big SCI electronics factory, the **Atlas Country Club** (tel. 33/3689-2620) rents tennis courts to non-members.

The hotels **Fiesta Americana** (Aurelio Aceves 225, Glorieta Minerva, tel. 33/3825-

3434), by the west-side Minerva Circle, and the **Crowne Plaza** (Av. López Mateos Sur 2500, tel. 33/3634-1034) both have courts for guests.

Swimming

Nearly all the luxury hotels have swimming pools. Nevertheless, three of the most convenient **downtown hotel pools** perch atop the moderately priced Hotels Roma, Santiago de Compostela, and Cervantes (see *Accommodations*). (However, the pools may not be heated, and thus comfortably usable only during the spring and summer; call ahead to check.)

If your hotel doesn't have a pool, go to the very popular **public pool and picnic ground** at Balneario Lindo Michoacán. Find it about two miles along González Gallo, southeast of Parque Agua Azul, at the corner Calzado J.

González Gallo (Río Barco 16) 9399, open daily 10 A.M.–5 about $6 adults, $3 kids).

Skating

Disco Roller roller rink (López Mateos Sur 4537, tel. 33/3631-5981, open daily 1:30–6 and 6:30–8:45 P.M.) also has a play area for little ones, plus video games and snacks. Find it on the corner across from the Office Depot.

The very pleasant **Iceland** ice-skating rink (Avenida Mexico 2582, just east of Avenida López Mateos Norte, tel. 33/3615-7876) is fun for all ages. Besides skating, admission gets you skate rental and free video games. Skating sessions are in two-hour time blocks beginning daily around 9:30 A.M. and continuing until 7 P.M. on weekdays and 9 P.M. on weekends.

Shopping

MERCADO LIBERTAD

The sprawling Mercado Libertad, at the east end of Plaza Tapatía, has several specialty areas distributed through two main sections. Most of the handicrafts are in the eastern, upper half. While some stalls carry guitars and sombreros, leather predominates—with jackets, belts, saddles, and the most *huaraches* (sandals) you'll ever see under one roof. Bargaining *es la costumbre* (is the custom). Competition, furthermore, gives buyers the advantage. If one seller refuses your reasonable offer, simply turning in the direction of another stall will often bring him to his senses. The upper floor also houses an acre of food stalls, many of them excellent.

The back courtyard leads past a lineup of bird-sellers and their caged charges to the Mercado Libertad's lower half, where produce, meat, and spice stalls fill the floor. (Photographers, note the photogenic view of the produce floor from the balcony above.) Downstairs, don't miss browsing intriguing spice and *yerba* (herb) stalls, which feature mounds of curious dried plants gathered from

the wild, often by village *curanderos* (traditional healers). Before you leave, be sure to look over the piñatas, which make colorful, unusual gifts.

MAGNO CENTRO JOYERO

For **jewelry** shopping, the Magno Centro Joyero complex, on the south edge of the Plaza Tapatía, is worth a visit. A battalion of shops, in a pair of airy, modern (ground and basement) stories, display mostly 10- and 14-carat gold necklaces, rings, amulets, bracelets, chains, and much more. The styles and prices reflect the modest incomes of most of the shoppers. Stones, while plentiful and sparkling, are usually glass or zircon imitations, although some authentic rubies *(rubis),* diamonds *(diamantes),* and emeralds *(esmeraldas),* are available in certain stores if you ask. Cultured pearls, however, are common and quite reasonably priced. Find most stores in the complex (tel. 33/3562-2011) open daily from about 9 A.M. until around 6 or 7 P.M. (For jewelry shopping details, see *Handicrafts* in the *Background* chapter.)

© BRUCE WHIPPERMAN

Tomatoes seem reddest and apples seem crispiest at the Mercado Libertad.

HANDICRAFTS

When shopping for handicrafts, it's always best to go to the source if possible. **Tlaquepaque** and **Tonalá** villages, southeast of the city center, are Guadalajara's most bountiful handicrafts sources. Access either of them with an easy taxi ride ($6) or air-conditioned bus TUR 706, or doable-with-difficulty bus #275 diagonal ride from Avenida 16 de Septiembre downtown. (See *Shopping* in the *Tlaquepaque and Tonalá* chapter.)

For Guadalajara's most bountiful handicrafts selection under one roof, go to the **Mercado Libertad** market, which sprawls at street level and below at the northeast east end of Plaza Tapatía. Most of the handicrafts are on the bottom, downstairs floor.

When you get hungry and weary of shopping, sample some of the many excellent hearty offerings from the acre of *fondas* (food stalls) in the market upstairs.

Of the sprinkling of downtown handicrafts shops, the most notable is the big government **Casa de Artesanías Agua Azul** (Calz. Gonzáles Gallo 20, open Mon.–Fri. 10 A.M.– 6 P.M., Sat. 10 A.M.–5 P.M., Sun. 10 A.M.– 3 P.M., tel./fax 33/3619-4664 or 33/3619-5179, iaj@prodigy.net.mx or promoiaj@prodigy.net. mx), by Parque Agua Azul, on the north-side corner of Independencia and González Gallo. You can choose from virtually everything— brilliant stoneware, handsome gold and silver jewelry, and endearing ceramic, brass, and papier-mâché animals—without actually going to Tonalá, Tlaquepaque, or Taxco.

Two other more centrally-located but much less extensive handicrafts sources in the Plaza Tapatía vicinity are at the **tourist information office** (Morelos 102) and the native vendors in the adjacent alley, called Rincón del Diablo.

If you happen to be near the city center, west of the cathedral, you might drop in at the **Galerías El Convento** complex, in a big restored mansion, on Donato Guerra at the corner of Morelos, four blocks west of the cathedral front, between Morelos and Pedro Moreno. Shops offer fine arts and handicrafts, from leather furniture and Tlaquepaque glass to baroque religious antiques and fine silver. Stop for a restful drink or meal at the excellent Restaurant San Miguel. (See *Food,* later in this chapter.)

DEPARTMENT STORES

For convenient, all-in-one shopping, including groceries, try **Gigante** (downtown on Juárez, corner of Martínez, tel. 33/3613-8638 or 33/3613-4006, open 24 hours daily). For even more under one air-conditioned roof, try the big **Gigante** at Plaza del Sol (Av. López Mateos Sur 2077, open daily 9 A.M.–9 P.M.).

For finer merchandise and bountiful fashion-conscious selections, try the popular mid-to-upscale **Fábricas de Francia** department store (at the downtown corner of Juárez and 16 de Septiembre, tel. 33/3678-5700, open Mon.– Sat. 11 A.M.–8:30 P.M., Sun. 11 A.M.–5 P.M.).

Accommodations

A wide range of recommendable hotels dot Guadalajara's downtown, within walking distance of museums, monuments, theaters, and shopping. A number of them have parking garages, a desirable option for auto travelers. Hotels farthest from the city-center cathedral plazas are generally the most economical.

AROUND THE CATHEDRAL

Several good hotels, mostly in the moderate price range, sprinkle the bustling blocks north and south of the cathedral.

Under $50

Right smack in the downtown action, the second-floor ◖ **Hotel Posada Regis** offers both economy and a bit of old-world charm (Corona 171, Guadalajara, Jalisco 44100, tel. 33/3614-8633 or tel./fax 33/3613-3026, posadaregis@usa.net, www.posadaregis.tripod.com, $26–45). Its clean and comfortable high-ceilinged rooms enclose a gracious Porfirian-era indoor lobby/atrium. Evening videos, friendly atmosphere, and a good breakfast/lunch café provide opportunities for relaxed exchanges with other travelers. The 19 rooms come with TV, phones, and fans, but no parking is included; credit cards are accepted.

A central location, comfortable (though a bit worn) rooms, and modest prices explain the popularity of the **Hotel Universo** (López Cotilla 161, Guadalajara, Jalisco 44100, tel./fax 33/3613-2815, fax 33/3613-4734, $42–50), on the corner of Cotilla and Degollado just three blocks south of the Teatro Degollado. Guests enjoy renovated, carpeted, and draped air-conditioned rooms with wood furniture and ceiling-to-floor tiled bathrooms. The 137 rooms and suites come with cable TV, phones, and parking; credit cards are accepted.

$50-100

The three-story, authentically baroque **Hotel Frances** (Maestranza 35, Guadalajara, Jalisco 44100, tel./fax 33/3613-1190 or 33/3613-0936, fax 33/3658-2831, reserva@hotelfrances.com,

www.hotelfrances.com, $65) rises among its fellow monuments on a quiet side street just a block south of the Teatro Degollado. The Frances, Guadalajara's first hotel, was built in 1610 and has been restored to its original splendor. The 40-odd rooms, all with bath, glow with polished wood, bright tile, and fancy frosted cut-glass windows. Downstairs, an elegant chandelier illuminates the dignified, plant-decorated interior patio and adjacent restaurant. However, to increase business, owners have installed live mariachi music downstairs on Fridays until around 11 P.M., which for some may not fit with the hotel's otherwise refined old-world ambience. Rates include parking, but fans only. Credit cards are accepted.

A choice north-side location, on a quiet side street a block north of the Cathedral, explains part of the success of the 33-room **Hotel La Rotonda** (Liceo 130, Guadalajara, Jalisco 44100, tel./fax 33/3614-1017, tel. 33/3658-0224, toll-free Mexico tel. 01-800/964-7800, larotonda@hoteleselectos.com, www.hoteleselectos.com, $55–65). Past the small reception of this former mansion, you enter a light courtyard, decorated by old-world stone arches, where guests linger over breakfast. Farther on, corridors lead past intimate rear patios. Most rooms open onto the upstairs courtyard-view balcony, bordered by potted plants and a gilded iron railing. Rooms vary in size, but all are floored with attractively rustic tiles and appointed with immaculate, up-to-date bathrooms and solid, polished hardwood furniture. Amenities include phones, cable TV, restaurant, bar, small events salon, fans, and parking; credit cards are accepted.

Guests at the **Quality Inn Centro Historico** (Av. Juárez 170, Guadalajara, Jalisco 44100, tel. 33/3614-8650, fax 33/3614-2629, toll-free U.S.-Canada tel. 877/424-6423, reservashtlroma@hotmail.com, www.choicehotels.com, $72), formerly the Hotel Roma, enjoy luxurious amenities—plush lobby, shiny restaurant/bar, rooftop rose garden, and (unheated) pool—usually available only at pricier hostelries. Rates may be discounted if you ask. All rooms come with TV, phones, a/c, parking, and limited wheelchair access; credit cards are accepted. Some rooms, although clean and comfortable, are small. Look before moving in.

The **Hotel Fénix** (Corona 160, Guadalajara, Jalisco 44100, tel. 33/3614-5714, fax 33/3613-4005, reservaciones@fenixguadalajara.com.mx, www.fenixguadalajara.com.mx, $80), just two blocks south of the cathedral, is a short walk to everything. The owners have managed to upgrade this rather basic small-lobby hotel into something more elaborate. The somewhat cramped result, while not unattractive, is often very busy. During the day, tour groups traipse in and out past the reception desk, while at night guests crowd the adjacent lobby bar for drinks and live combo music. Upstairs, the 172 air-conditioned rooms are spacious and comfortably furnished with American-standard motel amenities. Rooms come with TV, telephones, and parking, but no pool. You might try for a better deal in advance by booking a promotional package, such as an "executive package" of four nights for the price of three, including breakfast.

Over $100

The midsize colonial-facade **[C** **Hotel de Mendoza** (V. Carranza 16, Guadalajara, Jalisco 44100, tel. 33/3613-4646, fax 33/3613-7310, hotel@demendoza.com.mx, www.demendoza .com.mx, $100–130), only a couple of blocks north of the Teatro Degollado, is a longtime favorite of Guadalajara repeat visitors. Refined traditional embellishments—neo-Renaissance murals and wall portraits, rich dark paneling, glittering candelabras—grace the lobby, while upstairs, carpeted halls lead to spacious, comfortable rooms furnished with tasteful dark decor, including large baths, thick towels, and many other extras. The 100-odd rooms and suites feature cable TV, phones, a/c, a small pool, good refined restaurant, gym, jacuzzi, parking, and some wheelchair access. A third night (by reservation only) is sometimes free; credit cards are accepted.

The mid-sized **Holiday Inn Guadalajara Centro Historico** (211 Juárez, tel. 33/3613-1763, tel./fax 33/3560-1200, U.S.-Canada toll free tel. 888/465-4329, holidaycentro@prodigy. net.mx, www.holidayinn.com, $85–103) offers a host of close-in luxuries. Upstairs, the approximately 50 rooms are luxuriously appointed in soothing pastels, marble baths, plush carpets, and large beds. Rooms include cable TV, phones, a/c, parking, classy restaurant, gym, but no pool; credit cards are accepted.

WEST OF THE CATHEDRAL

A number of budget and moderately priced hotels dot the west-side blocks on or around Madero, within easy walking distance (up to eight blocks, 10 minutes) of the cathedral.

Under $50

The lackluster but very economical **Hotel Hamilton** (Madero 381, Guadalajara, Jalisco 44100, tel. 33/3614-6726, $12–19) offers a super-budget option. Although the 32 bare-bulb rooms with hot-water showers are plain and could use a good scrubbing, their steel doors, although drab, do enhance security. For maximum quiet and light, get a room in back, away from the street. Rooms come with fans and a hotel safe, but no parking.

A block south and a half block west, on Prisciliano Sánchez between Ocampo and Donato Guerra, the best-buy **[C** **Hotel Sevilla** (Prisciliano Sánchez 413, Guadalajara, Jalisco 44100, tel./fax 33/3614-9354 or 33/3614-9037, fax 33/3614-9172, $26–38) offers comfortable accommodations at modest prices. Its 80 plain but comfy rooms are furnished in dark brown wood with rugs to match. For more light and quiet, get an upper-story room away from the street. Amenities include a lobby with TV, private shower baths, parking, a hotel safe for storing valuables, and a restaurant open daily except Sunday. Rooms come with TV, fans, and telephones; parking is included.

The backpacker-friendly **Posada San Rafael** (López Cotilla 619, Guadalajara, Jalisco 44100, tel. 33/3614-9146, sanrafael@avantel.net or posadasanrafael@usa.net, www.sanrafael1.tripod.com), one block off Juárez near the corner of Calle 8 Julio, is about 10 blocks from the cathedral. Its simple but gaily decorated rooms with baths are spread around a light, colorfully restored central patio. Tightly managed by the friendly on-site owner, the prices are reasonable. Try for a room in the back, away from the noisy street. The 12 rooms come with fans.

$50-100

The gay-friendly **Hotel El Aposento** (The Lodging) (Fco. Madero 545, Guadalajara, Jalisco 44100, tel.33/3614-1612 or 33/3614-2609, elaposento3@yahoo.com, www.elaposento.com, $47–70) offers a bit of Porfirian charm at moderate prices. Several years ago, the enterprising owner of this bed-and-breakfast–style hostelry renovated this 19th-century-style hospital to a modern standard hotel. Now the 19 rooms surround an airy fountain-patio, where guests enjoy a full American-style breakfast, included with their lodging. The rooms, although air-conditioned, high ceilinged, and clean enough, are less than immaculate, with occasional rug spots and scratched paint. Many of the beds are spacious queen- and king-size; lamps are handy for reading, and cabinets and dressers are of polished wood. All rooms include attractively tiled baths with sink and shower, laundry, phones, parking, breakfast, and cable TV.

Closer in, only five blocks from the cathedral, where the pedestrian strolling mall begins on Moreno, stands the big, 110-room **Hotel Internacional** (Pedro Moreno 570, Guadalajara, Jalisco 44100, tel. 33/3613-0330, fax 33/3613-2866, hotelinternational_gdl@yahoo.com.mx, $60). Downstairs, a small lobby with comfortable chairs adjoins the reception area. In the tower upstairs, the 1960s-style rooms, most with city views, are clean and comfortable but varied. Look at more than one before moving in. Try for a discount below the asking price, which is high compared to the competition. (The hotel does, however, offer a 15 percent discount for a one-week rental.) Amenities include fans, some a/c, phones, TV, a café, and parking; credit cards are accepted.

Three blocks south, at the northeast corner of Prisciliano Sánchez and Donato Guerra, step up from the sidewalk and enter the cool, contemporary-classic interior of the **Hotel Cervantes** (442 Prisciliano Sánchez, tel./fax 33/3613-6686 or 33/3613-6846, reservaciones@hotelcervantes.com.mx, www.hotelcervantes.com.mx, $56–62). Everything, from the marble-and-brass lobby, the modern-chic restaurant and bar, unheated outdoor pool, and exercise room downstairs to the big beds, plush carpets, and shiny marble baths of the 100 rooms upstairs, seems perfect for the enjoyment of the predominantly business clientele. For such refinement, rates are surprisingly moderate. Rooms come with TV, phones, parking, and a/c; credit cards are accepted.

SOUTH OF THE CATHEDRAL

A number of good-value small and midsize hotels dot the south-side downtown neighborhood, close to the colorful Parque San Francisco and its pair of beloved old churches.

Under $50

The competent owners of the Hotel Universo also run a pair of good-buy hotels a block east of the Parque San Francisco. The **Hotel Latino** (Prisciliano Sánchez 74, Guadalajara, Jalisco 44100, tel. 33/3614-4484 or 33/3614-6214, $21–25) is one of Guadalajara's better cheap hotels. Although it's a plain, small-lobby hotel, the Latino's guests nevertheless enjoy a modicum of amenities. The 57 rooms in four stories (no elevator) are clean, carpeted, and thoughtfully furnished, albeit a bit worn around the edges. Baths are modern-standard, with shiny-tile showers and marble sinks. Rates are certainly right, and include a/c, cable TV, parking, and phone.

Just a block south, the authentically colonial **Hotel San Francisco Plaza** (Degollado 267, Guadalajara, Jalisco 44100, tel. 33/3613-8954, fax 33/3613-3257, $46–49) is replete with traditional charm. The reception area opens to an airy and tranquil inner patio, where big soft chairs invite you to relax amid a leafy garden of potted plants. In the evenings, the venerable arched stone corridors gleam with cut-crystal lanterns. Upstairs, the rooms are high ceilinged, with wooden handmade furniture, bedside reading lamps, and sentimental old-Mexico paintings on the walls. Each room has a phone, cable TV, fan, and a large, modern-standard bathroom with marble sink. Downstairs, guests enjoy an airy, reliable restaurant and an adjacent outside patio. Parking is included in the rate, and credit cards are accepted. (Hint: Choose a room on the hotel's south side, away from the bus noise and vibration on busy Prisciliano Sánchez.)

$50-100

If the Hotel San Francisco Plaza is full, you might try the much less charming but recommendable **Hotel Don Quijote Plaza** (Niños Héroes 91, Guadalajara, Jalisco 44100, tel. 33/3658-1299, fax 33/3614-2845, $47–71), a half block south of the Hotel San Francisco Plaza. The renovated 19th-century-vintage hotel, which advertises itself as gay friendly, has three tiers of 33 rooms that surround an inviting inner restaurant patio. The simply but comfortably furnished rooms include bath, telephone, TV, air-conditioning, and parking.

Over $100

If you can afford a bit more for refinements, go three blocks west to the (**Hotel Santiago de Compostela** (Colón 272, Guadalajara, Jalisco 44100, tel. 33/3613-8880, fax 33/3658-1925, toll-free Mexico tel. 01-800/365-5300, hotelsantiagocom@megared.net.mx, $77–87), a graceful, old-world-style hotel tucked on the west side of the lively Parque San Francisco. Past the small desk at the foyer, enter a light and elegant patio/bar/lobby, furnished with invitingly soft sofas. Upstairs, the five floors of 95 rooms, all opening onto the airy central atrium, are immaculate and comfortably appointed with carpets and furnishings invitingly decorated in earth tones. Four of the rooms have built-in spa tubs. Baths are deluxe, shiny, and spacious. A rooftop view pool-patio completes the attractive picture. Rates include phone, air-conditioning, cable TV, gym, business center, meeting rooms, and garage parking; credit cards are accepted.

About a mile farther south, at downtown's far southern edge, business travelers might consider the **Hotel Misión Carlton** (Av. Niños Héroes 125, Guadalajara, Jalisco 44100, tel. 33/3614-7272, fax 33/3613-5539, Mexico toll-free tel. 800/900-3800, reservaciones@misioncarlton.com, www.hotelesmision.com.mx, $85), formerly the Hilton. During the 1970s, investors wagered a pile of cash, based on a planned new southend financial center that never really panned out. The result was the present hotel, with a load of deluxe business facilities, including a convention center accommodating 4,000 people, a business and negotiating center, two restaurants, two bars, and 191 deluxe view rooms. Rates run about half those of comparable hotels around the west-side Guadalajara Expo convention center. If the Misión Carlton has a drawback, it's the small pool-patio, noisy (but sheltered by a wall) from traffic on the adjacent busy Avenida Niños Héroes.

BUS STATION AND AIRPORT HOTELS

Two hotels on the southeast edge of town offer interesting bus- and air-travel-related options, respectively. For bus travelers, the big long-distance Central Camionera bus station is at Guadalajara's far southeast edge, at least 20 minutes by taxi (figure $8) from the center. Bus travelers might find it convenient to stay at the sprawling, two-pool, moderately priced, relatively new **Hotel La Serena Terminal** (Carretera Zapotlanejo 1500, Guadalajara, Jalisco 45625, tel. 33/3600-0910, fax 33/3600-1974, reservas@aranzazu.com.mx, www.aranzazu.com.mx, $38). It's adjacent to the big bus terminal and has a restaurant. Bus and truck noise, however, may be a problem. Ask for a quiet *(tranquilo)* room. The 600 tidy and comfortable rooms all come with bath. Rooms vary; look at more than one before moving in.

For air travelers, the luxuriously spacious and airy **Aeropuerto Hotel Casagrande** (Calle Interior, Aeropuerto Internacional Miguel Hidalgo s/n, Guadalajara, Jalisco 45640, tel. 33/3678-9000, fax 33/3678-9002, Mexico toll-free tel. 01-800/366-4200, ventas@casagrande.com.mx or reserva@casagrande.com.mx, www.casagrande.com.mx, $115) is just outside the airport terminal exit door. Rate includes a deluxe double room with TV, phone, big bed, a/c, and a pool, restaurant, and bar downstairs. Promotional rates are sometimes available.

Food

Downtown Guadalajara is not overloaded with restaurants, and some of them even close early. (For much more variety and fine dining prospects, see *Food* in the *Tlaquepaque and Tonalá* chapter.)

AROUND THE CATHEDRAL
Coffee Shops and Light Fare

For breakfast, lunch, or supper, you can always rely on **Sanborns** (corner of Juárez and 16 de Septiembre, tel. 33/3613-6283, open Sun.–Fri. 6 A.M.–1 A.M., Fri. and Sat. open 24 hours), which retains the 1950s ambience of a Denny's in the middle of downtown. Entrées are mid-range, from breakfasts at around $5 to salads and sandwiches $3–6 and dinner plates $5–12.

For a local, more economical variation, head directly upstairs to **Restaurant Esquina** (open daily 7 A.M.–11 P.M.), on the same corner, or to the original **Sanborns** (tel. 33/3613-6267, 33/3613-6264, open daily 7:30 A.M.–11 P.M.), across the street. Besides a tranquil, refined North American–style coffee shop, it has a big gift shop upstairs and a bookstore, offering English-language paperbacks and magazines, downstairs.

Local coffee and conversation hangout **Madoka** (on Medillin between Juárez and Moreno, open daily 8 A.M.–11 P.M.), a few blocks west, is as much a cultural experience as it is an eatery. Loyal devotees enjoy many coffees ($1–2), plus a broad menu, from omelets and hamburgers to *carne asada* ($3–6).

For a light breakfast or a break during a hard afternoon of sightseeing, you have at least two options. Stop in at **Croissants Alfredo** bakery (tel. 33/3613-2694, open daily 7:30 A.M.–9 P.M.), on the north side of Plaza Liberación in front of and east of the Teatro Degollado. Their luscious goodies ($1–3)—flaky croissants, crisp cookies, tasty tarts, and good coffee—can keep you going for hours.

If you need a real break from Mexican cuisine, go to **McDonald's** (Juárez and Colón, one short block west of Sanborns, tel. 33/3613-

7307, open daily 8 A.M.–10 P.M.) for breakfast. An Egg McMuffin with ham, hash browns, and coffee runs about $4 until noon daily.

At the no-nonsense but worthy **Restaurant Málaga** (16 de Septiembre 210, tel. 33/3614-3815, open daily 7 A.M.–10 P.M.), the hardworking owner really does come from Málaga, Spain, and the food shows it: an eclectic list of hearty breakfasts ($3–7), which include hand-squeezed orange juice and good coffee. Additionally, they offer many salads and sandwiches ($3–7), desserts, and savory espresso. Credit cards are accepted.

The Restaurant Málaga's prices seem to have risen lately. You can get similar fare and good service a few blocks north, at the **Café Madrid** (on Juárez between Corona and 16 de Septiembre, tel. 33/3614-9504, open daily 7:30 A.M.–10 P.M.).

Mexican

The masterfully restored Porfirian **La Rinconada** Mexican-style restaurant (Morelos 86, tel. 33/3613-9914, open Mon.–Sat. noon–10 P.M.) is on the Morelos strolling mall, behind the Teatro Degollado. The mostly tourist and middle-class local customers enjoy La Rinconada for its good tacos, *tortas,* and enchiladas ($2–4), plus meat, fish, and fowl entrées ($4–8). Entertainment arrives in the form of the troubadours who wander in from the Plaza de los Mariachis nearby. By 4 P.M. many afternoons, two or three groups are filling the place with their melodies.

Nearby, a pair of clean places for good local food stand out. Try **La Chata** (Corona 126, between Cotilla and Juárez, next to Bancomer, tel. 33/3617-2853, open daily 1 P.M.–1 A.M.). Although plenty good for lunch ($4–8), *cena* (supper) ($4–10) is when the cadre of female cooks come into their own. Here you can have it all: tacos, *chiles rellenos,* tostadas, enchiladas, *pozole, moles,* and a dozen other delights you've probably never heard of, all cooked the way *mamacita* used to do it. Recent renovations and acceptance of credit cards have attracted a gentrified clientele and have consequently led to higher prices.

If La Chata's upscale jump has put it beyond your budget, go instead to **La Playita** (a half block north, on Juárez near Corona, tel. 33/3614-5747, open daily 9 A.M.–12:30 A.M.), with a similarly Mexican, but more economical, menu ($3–6).

NORTH AND WEST OF THE CATHEDRAL
Coffee Shops and Light Fare

For a bit of class, take a plaza-view table at **Sandy's** (Alcalde at Independencia, tel. 33/3345-4636, open Mon.–Fri. 7 A.M.–10:30 P.M., Sat. and Sun. 7 A.M.–midnight), a block north of the cathedral, at the mezzanine level. Snappy management, service with a flourish, and weekend evening live music make the typical, but tasty, coffee shop menu of soups, salads, sandwiches ($3–6), meat, pasta, and Mexican plates ($4–10) seem like an occasion.

If you're in the mood for a restful lunch or dinner, head west a few blocks to the airy interior patio of ◖ **Restaurant San Miguel** (east side of Donato Guerra, between Morelos and Pedro Moreno, tel. 33/3613-0809, open Tues.–Sat. 8:30 A.M.–midnight, Sun.–Mon. 8:30 A.M.–9 P.M.). Enjoy salad, soup, a sandwich ($4–6), or a full meal ($6–12) while you take in the tranquil, traditional ambience. Around you rise the venerable arches and walls of Guadalajara's oldest convent for women, founded by the sisters of Santa Teresa de Jesús in 1694. The old institution's topsy-turvy history mirrors that of Mexico itself. After its founding, it became the home for the Virgin of Zapopan until her present sanctuary was built decades later. In the 1860s, the nuns were expelled by the liberal forces during the War of the Reforms. They were allowed to return by President Díaz in 1895, only to be pushed out by revolutionary general Venustiano Carranza in 1914. The sisters bounced back, returning after the revolution subsided in 1919, but were again expelled by President Calles during the *cristero* rebellion in 1925. Liberal but conciliatory President Lázaro Cárdenas allowed their return in 1939. Finally, the mostly aged sis-

La Rinconada provides a pleasant spot for lunch.

ters vacated their old home, this time voluntarily and for the last time, in 1977.

Chinese

Continue a few blocks west along Juárez to **Restaurant La Gran China**, between Martinez and 8 Julio (Juárez 590, tel. 33/3613-1447, open daily noon–9 P.M.), where the Cantonese owner/chef puts out an authentic and tasty array of dishes. Despite the reality of La Gran China's crisp bok choy, succulent spareribs, and smooth savory noodles ($5–8), they nevertheless seem a small miracle here, half a world away from Hong Kong.

For a variation, try Gran China's plainer, more economical but equally authentic neighboring **Restaurant Chong Wah** (Juárez 558, tel. 33/3613-9950; open 11 A.M.–10 P.M.), half a block east at the corner of E. G. Martinez.

SOUTH OF THE CATHEDRAL

For local-style food, dining prospects are good around the Parque San Francisco, about five blocks south of the cathedral.

Mexican

The prime south-side spot is the **Plaza Nueve Esquinas,** on Colón just two blocks south of Parque San Francisco. Guadalajara families flock here afternoons and early evenings to feast on traditional Jalisco *birria,* served up by a half dozen surrounding restaurants. The best is **❖ Birrias Nueve Esquinas** (tel. 33/3613-6260, open daily 9 A.M.–7 P.M.). Specialties include *birria de chivo tatemada a fuego lento* (*birria* of goat roasted over a low fire, $8) and *barbacoa de borrego en pencos de maguey* (barbecued lamb in maguey leaf, $8). Alternatively, they offer plenty of more familiar goodies, such as lamb and home-style chicken soup, cheeseburgers with french fries, guacamole *con totopos* (with chips), salad, tacos, and quesadillas ($4–8).

At Corona 250, on the corner of Prisciliano Sánchez,on the north side of Parque San Francisco, stands the local favorite, street-front **Taquería Las Faroles.** Mexican traditional food lovers can have it all: six kinds of tacos, plus quesadillas, *gringas, torta ahogada* (Mexican dipped sandwich), and much more ($2–6).

Donuts

For melt-in-your-mouth donuts and good coffee, try **Dunkin' Donuts** (open daily 8 A.M.– 9 P.M.), across Corona from the Hotel Fénix.

EAST OF THE CATHEDRAL

For budget meals, local folks flock to the acres of **fondas** (permanent food stalls) on the second floor of the **Mercado Libertad** at the east end of Plaza Tapatía. Hearty home-style fare, including Guadalajara's specialty, *birria*—pork, goat, or lamb in savory, spiced tomato-chicken broth— is at its safest and best here. It's hard to go wrong if you make sure your choices are hot and steaming ($2–5). Market stalls, furthermore, depend on repeat customers and are generally very careful that their offerings are wholesome. Be sure to douse fresh vegetables with plenty of lime *(limón)* juice, however. Most of the *fondas* are open daily about 7 A.M.–6 P.M.

© BRUCE WHIPPERMAN

Contrary to popular perception, street stall food, as long as it's hot and made on the spot, remains a wholesome eating option.

Information and Services

TOURIST INFORMATION

The main state of Jalisco tourist information office is near the Plaza Tapatía on Paseo Morelos, the mall extension of Avenida Morelos, behind the Teatro Degollado (Morelos 102, tel. 33/3668-1600 or 33/3668-1601, fax 33/3668-1686, hgonzale@jalisco.gob.mx, www.visita.jalisco.gob.mx, open Mon.–Fri. 9 A.M.–8 P.M., Sat.–Sun. 10 A.M.–2 P.M.).

A second state of Jalisco tourist information source is the booth in the foyer of the Palacio de Gobierno, on Corona, a block southeast from the cathedral front (open Mon.–Fri. 9:30 A.M.–2:30 P.M. and 5–7 P.M., Sat.–Sun. 10 A.M.–12:30 P.M.). (Although the worthwhile www.visita.jalisco.gob.mx website is in Spanish, if you find it via the Google search engine you can click on "translate this page").

City of Guadalajara tourism (tel. 33/3616-9150 or 33/3818-3600, ext. 3165, ofvc@gdlmidestine.com, www.guadalajaramidestino.com) maintains at least two **tourist information booths** (*módulos de información*). Find one downtown, in the the Plaza Tapatía, approximately where the plaza broadens out, in the booth by the tall, corkscrew-shaped Imolación de Quetzalcoatl fountain.

City tourism's main office is in the Los Arcos arch, near the Minerva Circle, on Avenida Vallarta, about two miles west of downtown (tel. 33/3615-1182, open Mon.–Sat. 9 A.M.–6 P.M., Sun. 9 A.M.–4 P.M.). The tourist information booth is at street level, the administrative offices upstairs. Ask for a copy of city tourism's superb all-color *Points of Interest* bilingual foldout map and guide.

MONEY EXCHANGE

Change more types of money (Canadian, French, German, Italian, Japanese, Swiss, and U.S.) for the best rates at the downtown streetfront **Banamex** office and ATM (Juárez 237, corner of Corona, tel. 33/1226-3252, open Mon.–Fri. 9 A.M.–4 P.M.).

If Banamex is closed or its lines are too long, take your business around the corner to **BBV-Bancomer** (on Corona between Cotilla and Juárez, open Mon.–Fri. 9 A.M.–4 P.M.).

For longer business hours, including Saturdays, go to **HSBC,** with a pair of downtown branches (Libertad 410, open Mon.–Fri. 8 A.M.–7 P.M., Sat. 8 A.M.–3 P.M., tel. 33/3658-0869, 33/3658-1125), the other is across the street from the cathedral front (at the northwest corner of Alcalde and Juan Molina, tel. 33/3613-2501, 33/3614-7515, open the same hours).

After bank hours, go to one of the dozens of *casas de cambio* (money changers), a block east of Banamex, on Cotilla between Maestranza and Corona.

Guadalajara's only **American Express** branch is on the west side of town, about three miles west of the city center at Plaza Los Arcos (Av. Vallarta 2440, tel. 33/3818-2323, fax 33/3616-7665, open Mon.–Fri. 9 A.M.–6 P.M., Sat. 9 A.M.–1 P.M.). American Express provides both travel agency and member financial services, including personal-check and travelerscheck cashing.

CONSULATES

Several countries maintain Guadalajara consular offices. The **U.S. consulate** (Progreso 175, tel. 33/3268-2100 and 33/3268-2200) is between Cotillo and Libertad about a mile and a half west of the city center. Service hours for American citizens are Monday–Friday 8 A.M.–11 P.M.

The **Canadian consulate** (Aurelio Aceves 225, local 31, open Mon.–Fri. 8:30 A.M.–2 P.M. and 3–5 P.M., tel. 33/3615-6215, fax 3615-8665) is in the Hotel Fiesta Americana near the intersection of Avenidas López Mateos and Vallarta, about three miles west of the city center. For emergencies after business hours, call the Canadian consulate in Mexico City at tollfree tel. 800/706-2900.

Contact the **British consulate** (tel. 33/3343-9505); the **German consulate** (Madero 215, tel. 33/3613-9623); the **French consulate** (López

Mateos 484, tel. 33/3616-5516, Mon.–Fri. 9:30 A.M.–2 P.M.); the **Italian consulate** (López Mateos 790, corner E. Parra, tel. 33/3616-1700 or 33/3616-8688, fax 33/3616-2092, open Tues.–Fri. 11 A.M.–2 P.M.); and the **Spanish consulate** (tel. 33/3640-0450, 33/3630-0822, open Mon.–Fri. 8:30 A.M.–1 P.M.).

Consular agents from a number of other countries customarily hold Guadalajara office hours and may be reachable through the **Consular Association of Guadalajara** (tel. 33/3616-0629).

If all else fails, consult the local Yellow Pages under *"Embajadas, Legaciones y Consulados."*

MEDICAL SERVICES

If you need a doctor or hospital, ask your hotel desk or, in an emergency, go to the **Hospital Americas** (Av. Americas 932, Guadalajara 44620, tel. 33/3817-3141 or 33/3817-3004), with many specialists on call. The hospital accepts the coverage of many American HMOs; all staff is U.S.–trained and all hospitalization is in private rooms, with TV, phone, and private bathroom.

Alternatively, go to the highly recommended **Hospital del Carmen** (tel. 33/3813-0042, emergencies tel. 33/3813-1224).

For routine medications, one of the most widely accessible pharmacies is the Guadalajara chain, **Farmacia ABC,** with many branches. You'll find one downtown (518 P. Moreno between M. Ocampo and D. Guerra, tel. 33/3614-2950, open daily 7:30 A.M.–10 P.M.).

Equally good is the **Farmacia Guadalajara** also with many branches, such as at Plaza del Sol (tel. 33/3121-6515), and **24-hour delivery service** (tel. 33/3818-1818).

POLICE AND FIRE

For downtown police and fire emergencies, dial the emergency numbers 060 or 080.

POST AND COMMUNICATIONS
Mail

The downtown **Guadalajara post office** is two blocks north of the Teatro Degollado, just past the Hotel Mendoza (at Independencia and V. Carranza, tel. 33/3614-2482, open Mon.–Fri. 8 A.M.–7 P.M., Sat. 9 A.M.–1 P.M.).

Telephone Services and Internet Access

Telecom (tel. 33/3613-8584, open Mon.–Fri. 8 A.M.–6 P.M., Sat. 9 A.M.–noon) offers public telephone and fax downtown, at Degollado and Madero, below the city *juzgado* (jail).

Connect with the Internet downtown at handy **Ciber@z** Internet store (tel. 33/3658-1162, open daily 8 A.M.–midnight), on Plaza de Los Fundadores, behind the Teatro Degollado.

Publications

Among the best Guadalajara sources of English-language magazines is **Sanborns** (corner of Juárez and 16 de Septiembre, open daily 7:30 A.M.–11 P.M., tel. 33/3613-6267 or 33/3613-6264), the gift, book, and coffee shop chain, downtown. Others are at **Plaza Vallarta** (Av. Vallarta 1600, tel. 33/3615-5894, open 7 A.M.–1 A.M.) and **Plaza del Sol** (2718 López Mateos Sur, tel. 33/3647-2510 or 33/3647-2514, open daily 7 A.M.–1 A.M.).

You can usually get an English-language newspaper, such as *USA Today* or the *Miami Herald* Mexico edition, at one of the newsstands edging the Plaza Guadalajara (formerly Plaza Laureles), across from the cathedral.

While you're downtown, if you see a copy of the informative local weekly the *Guadalajara Colony Reporter,* buy it. Its pages will be stuffed with valuable items for visitors, including local events calendars, restaurant and performance reviews, meaty feature articles on local customs and excursions, and entertainment, restaurant, hotel, and rental listings. (If you can't find one, contact the *Reporter* office (tel. 33/3615-2177, fax 33/3615-2177, reporter@megared.net.mx, www.guadalajarareporter.com) to find out where you can get a copy.)

Additionally, suburban southwest-side **Librería Sandi** (Tepeyac 718, Colonia Chapalita, Guadalajara, tel. 33/3121-0863, open Mon.–Fri. 9:30 A.M.–7 P.M. and Sat. 9:30 A.M.–2 P.M.) always has the *Reporter,* plus the best selection of English-language books in the Guadalajara region.

Language and Cultural Courses

The University of Guadalajara's very professional **Centro de Estudios Para Extranjeros** (Study Center for Foreigners) (Tomás V. Gómez 125, P.O. Box 1-2130, Guadalajara, Jalisco 44100, tel. 33/3616-4399, fax 33/3616-4013, cepe@corp.udg.mx, www.cepe.udg.mx) conducts an ongoing program of cultural studies for visitors. Besides formal language, history, and art instruction, students may also opt for live-in arrangements with local families. Write or visit them at their **west-side center,** three blocks north of the Los Arcos monumen-tal arch, on Tomas V. Gómez, between Avenidas Mexico and Justo Sierra; telephone first for a *cita* (appointment).

PHOTOGRAPHY

The several branches of the **Laboratorios Julio** chain offer quick photofinishing and a big stock of both digital and film photo supplies, including professional 120 transparency and negative rolls. There's a big downtown branch (Colón 125 between Juárez and Cotilla, tel. 33/3614-2850, open Mon.–Sat. 10 A.M.–8 P.M., Sun. 11 A.M.–7 P.M.) and a west-side store (Av. Americas 425, corner of Manuel Acuña, tel. 33/3344-5470, open Mon.–Fri. 9 A.M.–7:30 P.M. and Sat. 9 A.M.–2:30 P.M.), among others.

Getting There and Around

GETTING THERE

A squadron of air carriers, both Mexican and U.S., connect the **Guadalajara Airport** (officially the Miguel Hidalgo International Airport, code-designated GDL) with many U.S. and Mexican destinations.

Mexican Carriers

Mexicana Airlines (U.S. toll-free tel. 800/531-7921, Mexico toll-free tel. 01-800/502-2000, or in Guadalajara reservations tel. 33/3837-7000, arrivals and departures tel. 33/3688-5775, www.mexicana.com) flights connect with U.S. destinations Chicago, Las Vegas, Los Angeles, Oakland, Portland, Sacramento, San Francisco, and San Jose, and Mexican destinations Los Cabos, Mexicali, Mexico City, Puerto Vallarta, and Tijuana. Furthermore, Mexicana's low-price subsidiary airline **Klik** connects with Cancùn and Mérida.

Aeroméxico and partner line **Aerolitoral** (U.S. toll-free tel. 800/237-6639, Mexico toll-free tel. 800/021-4000, www.aeromexico.com) flights connect with U.S. destinations Las Vegas, Los Angeles, Ontario, and Phoenix, and Mexican destinations Acapulco, Chihuahua, Culiacán, Hermosillo, Juárez, Mexico City, Monterrey, Puerto Vallarta, Tijuana, and Torreón.

Aerocalifornia (U.S. toll-free tel. 800/237-6625, Guadalajara reservations tel. 33/3615-4393, flight information tel. 33/3688-5514) connects with U.S. destinations Los Angeles and Tucson and Mexican destinations Culiacán, Durango, Hermosillo, La Paz, Los Cabos, Los Mochis, Mazatlán, Mérida, Mexico City, Monterrey, Puebla, Tijuana, and Torreón.

Aviacsa Airlines (Mexico toll-free reservations tel. 01-800/006-2200, Guadalajara flight information 33/3688-6033 or 33/3123-1751) connects with Mexican destinations Mexicali, Mexico City, Monterrey, and Tijuana.

Azteca Airlines (Mexico toll-free reservations tel. 01-800/229-8322, Guadalajara flight information 33/3630-4616) connects with the U.S. destination Ontario (Southern California), and Mexican destinations Cancun, Mexico City, and Tijuana.

Avolar Airlines (Mexico toll-free tel. 01-800/212-8652, Guadalajara arrivals and departures tel. 33/3688-8064) connects with Mexican destinations Cuernavaca, Culiacan, La Paz, Los Mochis, and Tijuana.

Volaris Airlines (Mexico toll-free tel. 01-800/122-8000, Guadalajara arrivals and departures 33/3688-8029) connects with Mexican destinations Monterrey, Tijuana, and Toluca.

U.S. Carriers

American Airlines (U.S. toll-free tel. 800/433-7300, Mexico toll-free tel. 01-800/904-6000, www.aa.com) connects Guadalajara daily with Dallas; **Delta Air Lines** (U.S. toll-free tel. 800/221-1212, Mexico toll-free tel. 01-800/123-4710, www.delta.com) connects daily with Atlanta and Los Angeles; **Continental Airlines** (U.S. toll-free tel. 800/231-0856, Mexico toll-free tel. 01-800/900-5000, www.continental.com) connects daily with Houston; **U.S. Airways** (formerly America West, U.S. toll-free tel. 800/235-9292 or 800/292-2274, Mexico toll-free tel. 001-800/235-9292 or 001-800/292-2274, www.usairways.com) connects with Phoenix; **Alaska Airlines** (U.S. toll-free tel. 800/426-0333, Mexico toll-free tel. 001-800/426-0333, www.alaskaair.com) connects with Los Angeles; **America Trans Air** (ATA) (U.S. toll-free tel. 800/435-9282, Mexico toll-free tel. 001-800/435-9282, Guadalajara arrivals and departures tel. 33/3688-5929, 33/3688-6531) connects with Chicago.

For information and reservations for all of the above, you may also contact a travel agent, such as American Express (tel. 33/3818-2323 or 33/3818-2325).

Airport Arrival and Departure

Airport arrival is simplified by money exchange counters and a Hong Kong Shanghai Banking Corporation (HSBC) bank (tel. 33/3688-5689, open Mon.–Fri. 8 A.M.–7 P.M., Sat. 8 A.M.–3 P.M., 24-hour ATM), to the right as you exit the terminal door.

Right next to the HSBC bank, find a friendly travel agent, **Agencia del Lago** (open Mon.–Sat. 9 A.M.–7 P.M., tel. 33/3688-5100 or 33/3688-5105), which makes hotel reservations, air reservations, car rentals, and other travel services.

Many **car-rental agencies** maintain arrival hall booths: **Avis** (tel. 33/3688-5656 or 33/3688-5784); **Alamo** (tel. 33/3613-5551 or 33/3613-5560, alamogdl@prodigy.net.mx); **Aries** (tel. 33/3688-5400 or 33/3688-5272, fax 33/3688-4007); **Arrasa** (tel. 33/3615-0522); **Budget** (tel. 33/3613-0027 or 33/3613-0286, fax 33/3613-0943 or 33/3688-5531); **Dollar** (33/3688-5956 or 33/3688-5958, dollar@megared.net.mx); **Hertz** (tel. 33/3688-5633 or 33/3688-6080, fax 33/3688-6070); **National** (tel. 33/3614-7175 or 33/3614-7994, fax 33/3688-5645); and **Optima** (tel. 33/3688-5532 or 33/3812-0437).

Ground transportation is likewise well organized for shuttling arrivers the 12 miles (19 km) along Chapala Highway 44 into town. *Colectivo* van seats go for $2 per person downtown at the terminal exit curbside. Private taxi *taxi especiales* tickets ($18 for 1–4 people downtown, $25 to Lake Chapala) are sold at booths *(taquillas)* at both departure and arrival ends of the terminal.

Travelers on a tight budget can save money by riding the red and white Autotransportes Guadalajara-Chapala bus (designed for local people, but usable by everyone), which stops in front of the terminal (on the right side, after you exit, in front of Aeropuerto Hotel Casa Grande) and continues either downtown to the old bus station (Camionera Central Vieja) or to nearby Zapote village, where, on the highway, you can catch another, similar bus, bound for Lake Chapala.

Many simple and economical card-operated public telephones are also available; buy telephone cards ($3, $5, or $10) at the snack bar by the far right-hand terminal exit. You'll also find a newsstand (lobby floor), bookstore (upstairs), and many crafts and gift shops convenient for last-minute business and purchases.

Airport departure is equally simple, as long as you save enough for your international departure tax of $19 ($12 federal tax, $7 local), unless it's already included in your ticket.

If you have time before your departure, spend it comfortably at one of the two good Wings restaurants, one downstairs and one upstairs.

Don't lose your tourist card. If you do, be prepared with a copy or some evidence (such as a ticket stub to verify your Mexico arrival date) to present to airport Migración (arrive at the terminal early) to avoid a fine and red tape.

By Car or RV

Four major routes connect the Guadalajara region to the rest of Mexico. To or from **Tepic-Compostela-Puerto Vallarta,** federal Highway 15 winds about 141 miles (227 km) over the Sierra Madre Occidental crest. Highway 15D, the *cuota* (toll) expressway, although expensive ($30 for a car, RVs much more), greatly increases safety, decreases wear and tear, and cuts the Guadalajara–Tepic driving time from five to two-and-a-half hours. The *libre* (free) route, by contrast, has two oft-congested lanes that twist steeply up and down the high pass and bump through towns. For safety, allow around five hours via the *libre* route to and from Tepic.

To and from **Puerto Vallarta,** bypass Tepic via the toll *corta* (cutoff) that connects Highways 15 and 15D (at Chapalilla) with Highway 200 (at Compostela). Figure on four hours total if you use the entire toll expressway (about $35), six-and-a-half hours if you don't.

To and from **Barra de Navidad** in the southwest, traffic winds smoothly (but sometimes slowly) along two-lane Highway 80 for the 190 miles (306 km) to and from Guadalajara. Allow around five hours downhill (southbound), five and a half uphill (northbound).

An easier road connection to and from Barra de Navidad runs through Manzanillo and Colima along *autopistas* (superhighways) 200, 110, and 54D. Easy grades allow a leisurely 55 mph (90 kph) most of the way for this 192-mile (311-km) trip. Allow about four hours to or from Manzanillo; add another hour for the additional smooth 38 miles (61 km) of Highway 200 to or from Barra de Navidad (follow the Manzanillo town toll bypass).

To or from Lake Chapala in the south, the four level, straight lanes of Highway 44 whisk traffic safely the 33 miles (53 km) to or from Guadalajara in about 45 minutes.

By Long-Distance Bus: Old Terminal

Guadalajara has two bus terminals, one new, one old. The new terminal in the southeast suburb offers mostly first- and luxury-class long-distance direct connections to outlying Jalisco destinations and most other parts of Mexico.

The old terminal, **Camionera Central Vieja,** occupies about two square city blocks on the southeast edge of downtown, two blocks east of Calzada Independencia and a block north of Parque Agua Azul. From here, second-class buses head out for hundreds of Guadalajara region towns, villages, and crossroads, mostly west, south, and east of the city.

At the old terminal, the buses occupy a large interior lot sandwiched between ticketing halls: *sala A* on the north side (Calle Los Angeles) and *sala B* on the south side (Calle 5 de Febrero).

Sala B, which services **west and southwest destinations,** handles most of the traffic. It has a modicum of services, including lots of phone booths operable with economical Ladatel phone cards, luggage lockers (east end), and food counters. The following are listed from east to west:

Transportes Ceocuitatlán (say-oh-kwee-that-LAHN) (tel. 33/3619-3989 or 33/3619-8891) serves west and northwest destinations, including the *periférico* (end of Av. Vallarta) west, La Venta and the Bosque de Primavera, Amatitán, Tala, Tequila, and Magdalena.

Transportes Tlajomulco (no phone) connects with the southern outskirts destinations of San Miguel Cuyutlán, Tlajomulco, Cuescomititlán, Las Cuatas, and along Chapala Highway 44 south past the airport.

"Azul" (blue) **Autobuses Guadalajara-Talpa-Mascota** (tel. 33/3619-7079 or 33/3124-1902) connects, via Highway 70 and Ameca, with far southwestern Jalisco destinations of Talpa and Mascota.

Autobuses Sur (no phone) connects with southern destinations of charmingly picturesque Tapalpa mountain town, plus Atemajac de Brizuela, Amacueca, Santa Ana, and Ciudad Guzmán.

"Servicios Coordinados" **Flecha Amarilla** (tel. 33/3619-4533) connects with southwestern destinations of Ameca, Cocula, Villa Corona (*balnearios* Chimulco and Aguascalientes), Navajas, La Villita, and Cruz Vieja.

Transportes Guadalajara Bella Vista (tel. 33/3619-2619) connects with southwest destinations past the *periférico* (end of López Mateos), Acatlán, and Villa Corona (*balnearios* Chimulco and Aguascalientes).

Transportes Guadalajara-La Vega-Cocula (tel. 33/3650-3033) connects via Highway 15 with southwest destinations of Etzatlán, La Vega (reservoir fishing), and Cocula.

Transportes Tenamaxtlenses (tel. 33/3619-0853) connects via Highway 80 and Villa Corona with far southwest destinations of Soyatlán, Tenamaxtlán, Atengo, Juanacatlán, and Tecolotlán.

Autocamiones del Pacífico (tel. 33/3619-9654) connects via Highway 80 with the far southwest villages of El Limón, Tolimán, La Villa, Los Guajes, Chiquilistán, and Tuxcacuesco.

Omnibus de la Ribera (tel. 33/3650-0605) connects south via Avenida López Mateos with the Lake Chapala northwest shore towns of Zapotitán, Las Cuatas, Buena Vista, Jocotepec, and warm-spring resort San Juan Cosala.

Sala A, on the opposite, north side of the bus lot, services **southern to eastern destinations.** Moving from the building's east to west end:

Autotransportes Guadalajara-Chapala (tel. 33/3619-5675), the major Lake Chapala line, connects with north-shore destinations of Chapala, Ajijic, and Jocotepec. Luxury- and first-class tickets are available.

Transportes Ciénega (tel. 33/3619-3337) connects southeast with Rodeo, Atequiza, and Atotonilco.

"Servicios Coordinados" **Flecha Amarilla** (tel. 33/3619-4533) connects with southwestern destinations of Ameca and Tala.

ADO (Autobuses del Oriente) (tel. 33/3679-0453) connects with southern and eastern destinations of La Laja, La Punta, La Jauja, and Zapotlanejo.

By Long-Distance Bus: New Terminal

The long-distance Guadalajara **Camionera Central Nueva** (New Central Bus Terminal) is at least 20 minutes by taxi (about $8) from the city center. The huge modern complex sprawls past the southeast-sector intersection of the old Tonalá Highway (Carretera Antigua Tonalá) and the Zapotlanejo Autopista (Freeway) Highway 90. Tell your taxi driver which bus line you want or where you want to go, and you'll be dropped at one of the terminal's seven big *módulos* (buildings). For arrival and departure convenience, you might consider staying at the adjacent moderately priced **Hotel La Serena** (see *Accommodations*, earlier in this chapter).

Each of the seven *módulos* is self-contained, with restrooms, cafeteria or snack bar, stores offering snack foods (but few fruits or veggies), bottled drinks, common medicines and drugs, and handicrafts. Additionally, *módulos* 1, 3, and 7 have public long-distance telephone and fax service. *Módulos* 2 and 3 have kept luggage service, *módulo* 3 has hotel reservations agent Sendetur ($70 and up, Guadalajara, Mazatlán, Acapulco, Puerto Vallarta, and Mexico City).

Dozens of competing bus lines offer departures. The current king of the heap is **Estrella Blanca,** a giant bus operator that manages a host of subsidiaries, notably Elite, Turistar, Futura, Transportes del Norte, Transportes Norte de Sonora, and Transportes Chihuahuenses. Second-largest and trying harder is **Flecha Amarilla,** which offers "Servicios Coordinados" through several subsidiaries. Trying even harder are the biggest independents: Omnibus de Mexico, Enlaces Terrestres Nacionals ("National Ground Network"), Transportes Pacífico, and Autobuses del Occidente, all of which would very much like to be your bus company.

To northwest **Pacific Coast** destinations, go to *módulo* 3. Take Estrella Blanca first-class subsidiary **Elite** (tel. 33/3679-0485, toll-free 01-800/507-5500), via Tepic and Mazatlán, to the U.S. border at Nogales, Mexicali, or Tijuana. Alternatively, ride first-class Transportes

Pacífico (tel. 33/3600-0211) for the same northwest Pacific destinations as Elite. For southwest Pacific Coast destinations, go by **Transportes Pacífico** (tel. 33/3600-0211), in *módulo* 3 or *módulo* 4, for small southwest Nayarit coastal towns and villages such as Las Varas, La Peñita, and Rincón de Guayabitos, en route to Puerto Vallarta. Moreover, you can ride second-class **Transportes Norte de Sonora** west and northwest (tel. 33/3679-0463), *módulo* 4, to smaller northern Nayarit and Sinaloa towns, such as Tepic, San Blas, Santiago Ixcuintla-Mexcaltitán, Acaponeta-Novillero, and Escuinapa-Teacapan.

For far southern Pacific destinations of **Zihuatanejo, Acapulco,** and the **Oaxaca coast** you can go one of two ways: Direct to Acapulco by **Futura** (*módulo* 7) east to Toluca, then south, via Cuernavaca, all in one long day, bypassing Mexico City (one or two buses per day). Alternatively, go less directly via Elite (*módulo* 3) west to Tepic or Puerto Vallarta (or by a **Flecha Amarilla** affiliate, tel. 33/3600-0770, *módulo* 1, south to Tecomán), where you must transfer to a Zihuatanejo-Acapulco southbound Elite bus. This may necessitate an overnight in either Tepic, Puerto Vallarta, Barra de Navidad, Manzanillo, or Tecomán and at least two days traveling (along the scenic, untouristed Pacific route, however), depending upon connections. Finally, in Acapulco, connections will be available southeast to the Oaxaca coast.

If you're bound southeast directly to the city of **Oaxaca,** go conveniently by Futura (*módulo* 7) to Mexico City Norte (North) station, where you transfer, via ADO (Autobuses del Oriente) or Omnibus Cristóbal Colón, southeast direct to Oaxaca City.

Also at *módulo* 4, allied lines Autocamiones del Pacífico and Transportes Cihuatlán (tel. 33/3600-0076 second-class or tel. 33/3600-0598 first class), together offer service south along scenic mountain Highway 80 to the Pacific via Autlán to **Melaque, Barra de Navidad,** and **Manzanillo.**

For eastern to southern destinations in **Jalisco, Guanajuato, Aguascalientes,** **Michoacán,** and **Colima,** go to either *módulo* 1 or 2. In *módulo* 2, ride first-class **ETN** (tel. 33/3600-0501) east to Celaya, León, and Aguascalientes, or west and southwest to Uruapan, Morelia, Colima, Manzanillo, and Puerto Vallarta. In *módulo* 1, Flecha Amarilla subsidiary lines (tel. 33/3600-0398) offer service to a swarm of northeast destinations, including León, Guanajuato, and San Miguel de la Allende, and southeast and south to Uruapan, Morelia, Puerto Vallarta, Manzanillo, Barra de Navidad, and untouristed villages—El Super, Careyes, La Manzanilla, Tomatlán, and El Tuito—on the Jalisco coast. From *módulo* 2, **La Linea** and **La Linea Plus** (tel. 33/3600-0055) offer departures southeast to Michoacán destinations of Zamora, Zitácuaro, Quiroga, Pátzcuaro, Uruapan, and Morelia. Also in *módulo* 2, **Autotransportes Sur de Jalisco** second-class buses offer southern departures, via old Highway 54 or *autopista* 54D, via Sayula, Ciudad Guzmán, Colima, to Tecomán, thence southeast via the Michoacán coast to Lázaro Cárdenas, or northwest via Cuyutlán to Manzanillo.

Omnibus de Mexico (tel. 33/3600-0085 or 33/3600-0718) dominates *módulo* 6, offering broad service in all directions. To the north and northeast, buses connect to the U.S. border at Juárez via Zacatecas, Saltillo, Durango, Torreón, Fresnillo, and Chihuahua; to Monterrey via Saltillo; and northeast, via Tampico, to the U.S. border at Reynosa and Matamoros. Moreover, buses connect east, with Mexico City, and west, with Tepic.

Additionally, Omnibus de Mexico offers first-class connections south, with Ciudad Guzmán, Colima, and Manzanillo, and north with regional destinations of Nochistlán and Colotlán.

In *módulo* 7, Estrella Blanca subsidiary lines mostly offer connections north. For example, ride first-class Transportes Chihuahuenses (tel. 33/3679-0404) north via San Juan de los Lagos, Zacatecas, Durango, Torreón, Chihuahua, all the way to the border at Ciudad Juárez. You may also ride luxury-class Turistar (tel. 33/3679-0404) either along the same routes as Transportes Chihuahuenses or north-easterly via San Juan de los Lagos, Zacatecas, Saltillo, and Monterrey to Matamoros, at the U.S. border.

By Train
Passenger rail service to and from Guadalajara has been stopped by the privatization of Mexican Railways' Pacific route. Unless future government subsidies offset private losses, Pacific passenger trains will have gone the way of buggy whips and Stanley Steamers.

GETTING AROUND
The historical heart of Guadalajara is accessible by most folks on foot. If you don't feel like walking, hail a taxi. Short taxi trips within a mile of the city center shouldn't cost more than $2. For longer trips outside of the city center, you can opt for the **subway** or one of the oft-crowded city buses.

If you're going to be doing a lot of independent traveling by car or bus in Guadalajara, get a copy of the very reliable **Guia Roji Red Vial Ciudad de Guadalajara** city map. It's available at Sanborns gift shop/restaurant (see *Publications* earlier in this chapter).

By City Bus
Most city buses are an experience not for the faint of heart. They are plentiful but often packed with commuters. People are generally courteous despite the crowding. Nevertheless, keep your purse buttoned and your wallet secure in a deep front pocket or waist pack.

One important bus exception is the air-conditioned **TUR** bus line. Being air-conditioned, it is more expensive but much less crowded (figure about $1) than the ordinary buses. An especially handy TUR bus is TUR 706, which you can catch downtown along main north-south street 16 de Septiembre. The TUR 706 gives access to a huge, touristically important area of Guadalajara, running diagonally from Zapopan in the northwest, continuing southeast right past the city center cathedral, through Tlaquepaque, all the way to Tonalá and back.

City buses stop at regular marked bus *paradas* (pah-RAH-dahs), or stops. If you want the bus to stop, stand on the curb, face traffic, and hold your arm straight out, parallel to the ground.

For trips into the suburbs, a number of useful **city bus routes** diverge from the city center. Go conveniently to the **inner western suburb** (restaurants and upscale Centro Magno shopping center) via the quiet **Par Vial** electric bus, from the corner of Independencia and Alcalde, one block north of the cathedral. For the inner or **far western suburbs** (Gran Plaza shopping center) ride a westbound **bus #45** from the corner of 16 de Septiembre and Prisciliano Sánchez, bordering Plaza (or Parque) San Francisco, five blocks south of the cathedral.

For the **southwestern** suburbs (luxury hotels, Plaza del Sol shopping center, Guadalajara Expo convention center) ride either **westbound bus #258A** (corner of Alcalde and San Felipe, three blocks north of the cathedral) or

A leisurely way to get around downtown is to rent a *calandria* (horse-drawn carriage) just north of the cathedral.

SUBWAY, GUADALAJARA STYLE

Since the early 1990s, Guadalajarans have enjoyed a new underground train system, which they call simply the **Tren Ligero,** or "Light Train." It's nothing fancy, a kind of Motel 6 of subway lines – inexpensive, efficient, and reliable. A pair of intersecting lines, Linea 1 and Linea 2, carry passengers in approximately north-south and east-west directions, along a total of 15 miles (25 km) of track. The station most visitors see first is the Plaza Universidad (on Linea 2), accessible by staircases that descend near the city-center intersection of Juárez and Colón, by the Sanborn's coffee shop at the southwest corner.

If you want to take a ride, deposit the specified number of pesos in the machines, which will give you in exchange a brass *ficha* token, good for one ride and one transfer. If you opt to transfer, you have to do it at Juárez station, the next stop west of Plaza Universidad, where Lineas 1 and 2 intersect. (Hint: It's best to begin your Guadalajara subway adventure before 9 P.M.; the Tren Ligero goes to sleep by about 11 P.M.)

westbound bus #51A or #51B (from the corner of 16 de Septiembre and Av. La Paz) four blocks south of Parque San Francisco.

For the southeastern suburban handicrafts villages of **Tlaquepaque and Tonalá,** ride the very convenient southbound **TUR 706** (or cheaper but oft-crowded southbound bus #275 diagonal), both accessible at city-center stops along 16 de Septiembre. (If, on the other hand, you catch a **northbound TUR 706** (or #275 diagonal) it will take you to the colorful pilgrimage town of **Zapopan** at Guadalajara's northwest edge.)

Finally, for the northern suburban **Guadalajara Zoo, Selva Mágica amusement park,** and **planetarium** complex, ride **eastbound bus 258A** from the corner of Alcalde and Juan Manuel, two blocks north of the cathedral. (Alternatively, you can access the same destinations via buses #62A and #62D, which run north–south along big thoroughfare Calzada Independencia, beneath Plaza Tapatía.)

For a country ride north into the **Barranca,** the tropical canyon of the Río Santiago (Los Camachos *balneario* bathing spring), ride the **Los Camachos Bus** from its terminal at the Glorieta Normal (Normal Circle) on Alcalde about a mile north of the city center.

If you're going to be riding lots of Guadalajara buses, visit the handy **www.rutasjalisco. com** website, which displays a number of bus routes. Alternatively, stop by a downtown newsstand and buy a copy of the handy bus route guide **Guia de Rutas de Camiones y Midbuses,** published by the bus drivers' alliance, Alianza de Camioneros de Jalisco.

Rental Cars, Guides, and Tours

For longer trips in the suburbs and to destinations around Guadalajara, a rental car is a convenient, but relatively expensive, option. Car rentals are available at the airport (see *Getting There*) or from one of several downtown car rental offices, some of which are clustered at the corner of Niños Héroes and Manzano, near the Hotel Misión Carlton, at the south edge of downtown. There, bargain and shop around among the agencies, including National (tel. 33/3614-7175, 33/3614-7994, or 33/3614-6006) and Alaniz (tel. 33/3614-6353).

As in most metropolitan downtowns, congestion and lack of parking space in the Guadalajara city center make driving an even less desirable option for all but intrepid and experienced drivers. Best walk or ride taxis or buses downtown.

A number of highly recommended guides offer Guadalajara custom tours. Expect to pay about $100 per day, including transportation, or about $50 per day if you supply the car. One of the best persons to inquire about Guadalajara guides is experienced guide **Lynn Mendez,** who staffs the state of Jalisco tourist information office (Paseo Morelos 102, tel. 33/3668-1600 or 33/3668-1601) on Plaza Tapatóa. She strongly recommends professional tour guides **Roberto Arellano** (tel. 33/3657-8376), former president of the Guadalajara Guides Association, **Fernando Mediana** (tel. 33/3654-5957), and **Octavio Estrada** (tel. 33/3632-7306).

Another very well prepared and personable guide is American-Mexican inkeeper Arturo Magaña, co-owner of Quinta Don José in Tlaquepaque (U.S.-Canada toll-free tel. 866/629-3753, Guadalajara tel. 33/3635-7522, fax 33/3659-9315, info@quintadonjose.com, www.quintadonjose.com).

If somehow Arturo's very popular tours are booked up, he recommends a pair of excellent guides: Four stars go to both **Ramiro Roma** (tel./fax 33/3631-4242, cell 044-33/3661-6202 in Guadalajara, or long-distance 33/3661-6202 outside Guadalajara) and **Lino Gabriel González Nuño** (tel. 33/3152-0324, fax 33/3635-4049, emaillinogabriel@hotmail.com, www.mexonline.com/guadalajaratours.htm.), who specializes in customized Guadalajara tours (downtown, shopping in Tlaquepaque and Tonalá, archaeological sites, and more).

If, on the other hand, a hassle-free private group bus tour appeals to you, consult your hotel travel desk, a travel agent, or an experienced agency, such as **Panoramex** (Federalismo Sur 944, tel. 33/3810-5005, 33/3810-5057, 33/3810-5160, or 33/3810-5109, www.panoramex.com.mx) or **Charter Club Tours** in Guadalajara, in the Chapalita neighborhood (Av. San Francisco 3477, tel. 33/3122-1214, info@charterclubtours.com.mx, www.charterclubtours.com.mx). Tour options vary widely, from Guadalajara sights and the Ballet Folklórico to shopping

Red Tapatio Tour buses depart frequently from the street (north side) adjacent to the downtown cathedral.

© BRUCE WHIPPERMAN

in Tonalá and Tlaquepaque. Wider-ranging tours can include regional destinations, such as Mazamitla in the mountains or the monumental Guachimontones pyramids at Teuchtitlán, near Tequila, to as far as Lake Pátzcuaro in Michocán.

Or, alternatively, hop on to one of the red **Tapatio Tour** tour buses that the Jalisco Tourism Secretariat runs frequently every day from the street that runs along the north side of the downtown Cathedral. Get your ticket at the bus. For updated information, call tel. 33/3613-0887 or toll-free 01-800/002-2287, visit www.tapatiotour.com.mx, or drop by the Jalisco tourism information desk, at Morelos 102 behind the Teatro Degollado.

WEST AND NORTH

For longer than anyone can remember, the march of Guadalajara's history has always pointed west. Nuño de Guzmán, Guadalajara's conquistador, hurried west after pacifying the Valle de Atemajac where Guadalajara now spreads. Later, explorers, mission fathers, governors, and the crowd of settlers that followed them did the same. To most Guadalajarans, the east represented the old and the settled. The west represented opportunity.

That's still true. Guadalajara's last hundred year of history has been largely marked by waves of westward development. A glance at a map of metropolitan Guadalajara reveals successive rings of peripheral thoroughfares—Avenida López Mateos and the northern and southern *circunvalación* boulevards built during the 1950s, Avenida Patria during the 1970s,

and now the *periférico* that now, at the beginning of the 21st century, marks the border between city and country.

Within those expanding western boundaries, new tree-shaded neighborhoods were founded, beginning around 1900, when moneyed merchant and professional families began building stylish, landscaped mansions along broad boulevards beyond the old colonial town's western edge.

Most of those mansions still line the streets of the earliest western district, known as the *colonias antiguas,* now part of the Minerva-Chapultepec district that spreads west from the old city boundary, marked by Avenida Federalismo. In the Minerva-Chapultepec district, many of those old houses are still occupied by descendants of the first families—some as residences,

© BRUCE WHIPPERMAN

HIGHLIGHTS

◖ **Rectoría de la Universidad de Guadalajara:** Inside the central hall, the neoclassic rectory houses a pair of grand murals – the contemplative *Man* and the starkly arresting *The People and Their Leaders* (page 71).

◖ **Templo Expiatorio:** The neo-Gothic Temple of Atonement has a brilliantly luminous stained-glass interior and a thrice-daily revolving mechanical procession of the Twelve Apostles high on its monumental facade (page 71).

◖ **Los Arcos:** Climb the monument for a panoramic Guadalajara vista and a refreshment at the rooftop café. Be sure to take a look at the mural that lines the staircase (page 74).

◖ **Bosque Los Colomos:** Escape the city hubbub at Guadalajara's get-away-from-it-all forest park. Picnic, bird-watch at the Lake of the Birds, botanize at the Canyon of the Serpent, stroll the Japanese Garden, or jog the trails to your heart's content (page 75).

◖ **Guadalajara Zoo:** Spend a relaxing afternoon strolling Guadalajara's world-class zoo, where you'll find rarely seen species culled from the ocean's blackest depths, the Amazon's remotest jungle, Kenya's breeze-swept Masai Mara, and the East Indian island that the Komodo dragon calls home (page 75).

◖ **Expo Guadalajara:** Explore inside and most likely you'll be rewarded by one of the Expo's many dozens of annual expositions. A multitude of booths display variations on one theme, ranging from books and computers to jewelry and shoes (page 94).

◖ **El Iztepete Archaeological Zone:** A few reconstructed low pyramids and soil permeated by tiny shards of volcanic glass give hints of the uses that ancient Mexicans

made of this huge – but largely unexplored – complex of ceremonial platforms, avenues, ball courts, and dwellings (page 95).

◖ **Basílica de Nuestra Señora de Zapopan:** Visit Guadalajara's beloved Virgin of Zapopan in her basilica home. Every October 12, hundreds of thousands of Guadalajarans escort her from her temporary resting place, at the downtown Guadalajara cathedral, back to Zapopan (page 110).

◖ **Museo Huichol Wirrarica:** This excellent museum of indigenous Huichol arts, crafts, and customs is worth a visit. Next door, continue to the Museo de la Virgen, fascinating for its exhibits of pilgrim-donated gifts and the Virgin's miracles (page 111).

LOOK FOR ◖ TO FIND RECOMMENDED SIGHTS, ACTIVITIES, DINING, AND LODGING.

WEST AND NORTH

but many as smart restaurants and shops that decorate the east–west thoroughfares.

Later, during the 1960s and 1970s, a checkerboard of development spread west, south, and north, notably in the southwest-side Plaza del Sol–Chapalita neighborhood. The Plaza del Sol shopping-convention-luxury hotel complex achieved phenomenal success, side by side with the charming tree-shaded Chapalita residential village-within-a-city.

Minerva-Chapultepec

The Minerva-Chapultepec marks the beginning of the new Guadalajara that spread west from the city center around 1900. Today, a casual look around shows that the Minerva-Chapultepec has matured gracefully. Although it's still mostly a residential suburb of grand homes set in flowery, tree-shaded gardens, the Minerva-Chapultepec now hosts a trove of stylish restaurants and night clubs, relaxing outdoor cafés, glittering shopping malls, art galleries, and designer shops that cater to the district's mostly well-heeled residents.

PLANNING YOUR TIME

See the sights of the Minerva-Chapultepec district (best in the morning) Tuesday–Sunday, when they are most likely to be open. After breakfast, start at the **Rectoría** of the University of Guadalajara to see its pair of Orozco murals, and continue to the adjacent **Museo de las Artes** (one hour). Continue one block south to the **Templo Expiatorio** to admire the glorious stained-glass windows and the mechanical procession of the Twelve Apostles at 9 A.M., noon, and 6 P.M. (half hour).

Continue east to the **Los Arcos** monumental arch, climb to the top and enjoy the airy view, then continue to the **Casa Museo José Clemente Orozco,** the maestro Orozco's former studio-home, now a venue for exhibitions of the work of new local artists (one hour).

While you're in the Minerva-Chapultepec, be sure to enjoy at least lunch or dinner at one of the excellent local restaurants. Arguably the best of all is **Restaurant Sacramonte,** which is especially pleasant for lunch. Also, for perhaps the best Mexican food in town,

try **Restaurant Tequila** for either lunch or dinner. For pure showplace atmosphere, go to **Restaurant Santo Coyote** for dinner. Actually, all of your evening dining for a one-week Guadalajara stay could be enjoyed in the Minerva-Chapultpec, by visiting the three restaurants above, plus **Polibio, Ma Come No, Luscherly, Pierrot,** and **Tinto y Blanco.**

ORIENTATION

Main boulevards anchor the Minerva-Chapultepec district, from its eastern boundary at **Avenida Federalismo** on the downtown side to the **Minerva Fountain and Traffic Circle** on the west side. **Avenida Vallarta** (the continuation of downtown Avenida Juárez), the district's backbone artery, runs (motor traffic one-way west) past the **University of Guadalajara,** continuing past dozens of upscale businesses, restaurants, and banks, and the **Centro Magno** shopping center before passing under the **Los Arcos** monumental arch and around the Minerva Circle.

North and south of Avenida Vallarta run eastbound Avenidas Pedro Moreno and López Cotilla, similarly decorated by stately residences, exclusive shops, and stylish restaurants. Major arteries **Avenida Mexico** and **Avenida Niños Héroes** define the district's northern and southern edges, respectively.

The Minerva-Chapultepec district's major north–south business-restaurant avenues are, moving west, **Avenida Chapultepec, Avenida Americas** (which switches to Avenida Unión south of Avenida Vallarta), and **Avenida López Mateos,** which circles the Minerva Fountain, forming the district's western boundary.

SIGHTS
🚺 Rectoría de la Universidad de Guadalajara

Let the brilliant white marble Rectory of the University of Guadalajara on Avenida Vallarta, on the south side, a few blocks west of Federalismo, be your starting point. The grand neoclassic edifice was designed in large part by noted architect Rafael Urzúa and erected in 1918. Originally intended as the Jalisco state legislature, it became part of the university during the mid-1930s.

In the *paraninfo* (so-called for the mysterious paranormal incidents said to have occurred there) lecture hall (tel. 33/3134-1678, open Mon.–Sat. 10 A.M.–9 P.M.) celebrated muralist José Clemente Orozco crafted a pair of monumental works between 1936 and 1939. Spreading across the cupola overhead, *Man*—as creator, thinker, questioner, investigator, and celebrator—displays the master's contemplative side. In contrast, above the stage spreads *The People and Their Leaders,* in which a fire-ringed crowd confronts the evils of militarism, brutality, and false science.

Museo de los Artes

Inside the rectory, behind the lecture hall (there's also a south-side entrance on Avenida López Cotilla) is the Museo de los Artes (López Cotilla 930, tel. 33/3134-1664, open Tues.–Sun. 10 A.M.–6 P.M.). Six galleries (two with temporary exhibits, four with permanent) display paintings, sculptures, and graphic arts, both traditional and modern.

🚺 Templo Expiatorio

Across López Cotilla from Museo de las Artes, find the monumental Templo Expiatorio (Temple of Atonement) (open daily 7 A.M.–9 P.M.). The temple commenced in 1897 by Italian architect Adamo Boari, who is celebrated for the Palace of Fine Arts in Mexico City. Although the soaring neo-Gothic facade and its towering 25-bell carillon are impressive enough, the radiant contemporary French stained-glass windows inside are the main attraction. Besides Biblical themes, one of the glass panes is, interestingly, of architect Ignacio Díaz Morales, who finished the interior construction in 1972 (and who is buried in the Grand Crypt beneath the sacristy behind the altar). The bells, accompanied by a mechanical procession of the Twelve Apostles, toll daily at 9 A.M., noon, and 6 P.M.

Centro Magno

For more worthwhile sights, walk, take a taxi, or ride the refreshingly antique **Par Vial electric trolley bus** (four short blocks north along Independencia) west two miles to Centro Magno shopping center, at the corner of Vallarta and Lope de Vega. If nothing else, take a table in the ground-floor Starbucks, order a refreshment, and relax and enjoy the soaring indoor space around you.

The Centro Magno is one of three recent complexes (including Gran Plaza, on Vallarta farther west, and Centro Pabellón, on Avenida Patria, northwest) built within a multifloored roofed structure around a single towering

Templo Expiatorio is famous for its brilliant stained-glass windows.

© BRUCE WHIPPERMAN

WEST AND NORTH

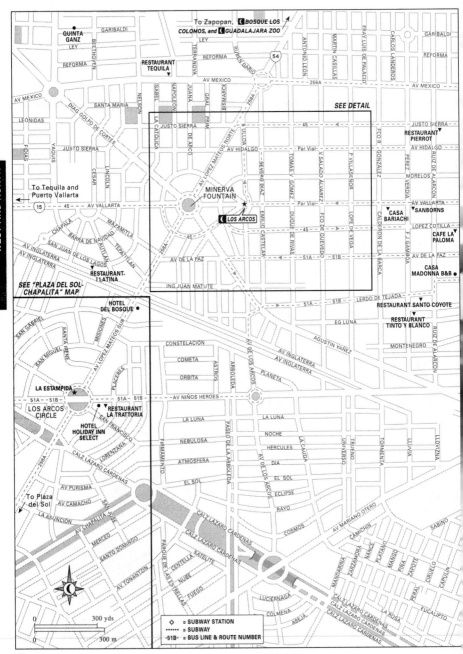

To Zapopan, **◖BOSQUE LOS COLOMOS, and ◖GUADALAJARA ZOO**

QUINTA GANZ

GARIBALDI

LEY

REFORMA

RESTAURANT TEQUILA

GARIBALDI

REFORMA

AV MEXICO

AV MEXICO

SANTA MARIA

SEE DETAIL

LEONIDAS

JUSTO SIERRA

RESTAURANT PIERROT

AV HIDALGO

FIDIAS

JUSTO SIERRA

AV HIDALGO

MORELOS

To Tequila and Puerto Vallarta

MINERVA FOUNTAIN

AV VALLARTA

AV VALLARTA

SANBORNS

◖LOS ARCOS

CASA BARIACHI

LOPEZ COTILLA

CAFE LA PALOMA

RESTAURANT LATINA

AV DE LA PAZ

AV DE LA PAZ

CASA MADONNA B&B

SEE "PLAZA DEL SOL-CHAPALITA" MAP

ING JUAN MATUTE

LERDO DE TEJADA

RESTAURANT SANTO COYOTE

HOTEL DEL BOSQUE

EG LUNA

RESTAURANT TINTO Y BLANCO

CONSTELACIÓN

AGUSTIN YANEZ

MONTENEGRO

COMETA

AV INGLATERRA

ORBITA

AV NIÑOS HEROES

LA ESTAMPIDA

LA LUNA

LA LUNA

51A — 51B

LOS ARCOS CIRCLE

RESTAURANT LA TRATTORIA

NEBULOSA

NOCHE

HOTEL HOLIDAY INN SELECT

HERCULES

DIA

ATMÓSFERA

CALZ LAZARO CARDENAS

EL SOL

EL SOL

To Plaza del Sol

AV PURISIMA

ECLIPSE

AV CAMACHO

RAYO

LA ASUNCIÓN

COSMOS

AV CHAPALITA

MERCED

SANTO DOMINGO

AV TONANTZIN

CALZ LAZARO CARDENAS

PARQUE DE LAS ESTRELLAS

SATELITE

NUBE

FUEGO

LUCIERNAGA

COLMENA

ABEJA

CALZ LAZARO CARDENAS

0 300 yds	◇ = SUBWAY STATION
0 300 m	••••• = SUBWAY
	-51B- = BUS LINE & ROUTE NUMBER

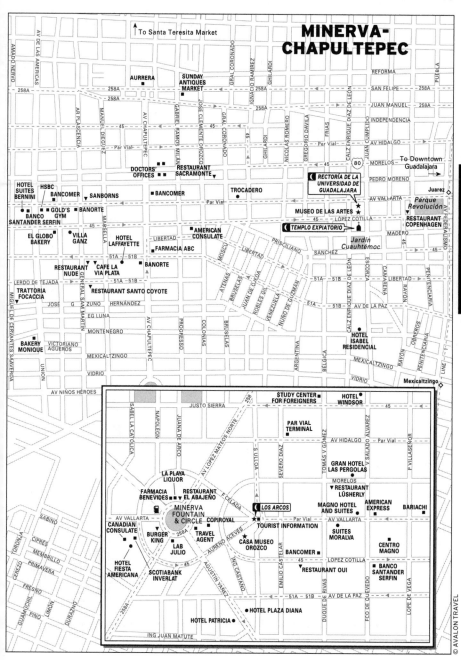

© AVALON TRAVEL

atrium. These are *the* places to be seen, especially among working- and middle-class youth. Exit on the north, Avenida Vallarta side, where a few blocks west, in the direction of traffic flow, rises Los Arcos.

Los Arcos

This neo-Roman triumphal arch was erected 1939–1941, on what was, at the time, the country edge of Guadalajara. Inside the south pedestal entry door, find the bilingual information office of **City Tourism** (tel. 33/3616-9150 or 33/3615-1182, open Mon.–Fri. 9 A.M.–7 P.M., Sat.–Sun. 9 A.M.–5 P.M.). Be sure to pick up a copy of the excellent *Points of Interest* fold-out brochure, which describes Guadalajara walking tours.

Los Arcos is more than a monument. In addition to the tourism office, it houses temporary art exhibits and an unusually frank **mural,** illustrating the best and worst of Guadalajara, halfway up the south-side staircase. Climb the three flights to the upper floor **café** to enjoy the sweeping views, both east and west along Avenida Vallarta. On the east side, Centro Magno rises before the far-off downtown skyline, while on the opposite side, traffic circles around the Minerva Fountain in front of the shining glass tower of the Hotel Fiesta Americana.

Casa Orozco

Walk over to the **Museo Casa Taller José Clemente Orozco** (Museum, House, and Workshop of José Clemente Orozco), a half block southwest of Los Arcos (27 Aurelio Aceves, tel. 33/3616-8329, open Tues.–Sat. 10 A.M.–6 P.M., Sun. 10 A.M.–3 P.M.), adjacent to the intimate neighborhood plaza, decorated with a statue of the great muralist.

After Orozco's death in 1949, his wife, Margarita Valladares, modified the house that they had built a few years earlier, and opened it as a memorial to her late husband, in 1951. The house is now administered by the Centro Cultural Cabañas, which maintains it as an exhibition showcase for the works of noted local artists.

Minerva Circle and Fountain

Traffic flows around the grand Minerva Circle, constructed in the mid-1950s during the term of Governor Agustín Yañez. If you prefer safety to chance, it's best to hire a taxi to deposit you on the rose-decorated inner circle curbside, where you can appreciate the helmeted Roman goddess Minerva (equivalent to Greek goddess Athena) close up. Minerva, the goddess of wisdom, with spear and shield ready, guards the city's western gate. In the front (west) side, at the statue's feet, the inscription translates to "Justice, Wisdom, Strength, the Custodian of this Loyal City."

Estampida Sculpture

Not nearly so well known, but equally monumental, is the nearby dramatic bronze sculpture of a pack of stampeding wild horses. Find it by following Avenida López Mateos about a half mile southwest to the Los Arcos traffic circle, at the intersection of Circunvalación A. Yañez (see

The Goddess Minerva guards Guadalajara's western gateway, the Glorietta Minerva (Minerva Circle).

the Holiday Inn high-rise on the east side). The sculpture is on the circle's west side.

◖ Bosque Los Colomos

Guadalajara's "get away from it all" park, comparable in concept to New York's Central Park or Golden Gate Park in San Francisco, started out as a source for Guadalajara's municipal water during the late 1800s. Now the Bosque Los Colomos (north entrance at Av. Patria 1805, tel. 33/3641-7633, open daily 9 A.M.–7 P.M.) is a playground for picnicking families, joggers, soccer and tennis players, and horseback riders (rentals available). Furthermore, nature lovers enjoy strolling in and around the Bosque's especially lovely **Japanese Garden** (Jardín Japonés), **Lake of the Birds** (Lago de los Aves), and lush **Canyon of the Serpent** (Cañon del Serpiente). The Bosque ("Forest") is the long-term project of a club of dedicated volunteers, the **Grupo Guardabosque** (Forest Preservation Group). For more information, drop by their office (Av. El Chaco 3200, tel. 33/3641-3804),

at the Bosque's south entrance, where the horses and the athletic facilities are.

Getting There: The Bosque Los Colomos is at the Minerva-Chapultepec's northwest edge. The best way to get there is by taxi ($5). By car, follow Avenida Las Americas, from its intersection with Avenida Vallarta, north about 2.3 miles (3.7 km) to divided Avenida Montevideo (at the big golf course on the right). Turn left (west), and continue two long blocks, and turn right. In a half block, turn left onto El Charco and continue west about three more blocks to the Bosque south entrance.

◖ Guadalajara Zoo

The world-class Zoológico Guadalajara (Paseo del Zoológico 600, tel. 33/3674-1827, www .zooguadalajara.com, open Wed.–Sun. 10 A.M.–5 P.M., holidays open daily same hours, $6 adults, $3 kids), north of downtown (about 15 minutes by car, 25 minutes by bus), is well worth a visit.

Set in an airy, lush, 125-acre natural park, the zoo maintains Mexico's most important

The Guadalajara Zoo is home to more than 2,000 animals.

© BRUCE WHIPPERMAN

collection of animals, numbering more than 2000 individuals in about 350 species. Its numerous attractions include **Marine Lair,** an interactive computer and ocean-species center; **Secrets of Tropical Life** African jungle, home to snakes large and small; the **Komodo Reserve,** with Latin America's only Komodo dragon; and **Masai Mara Safari,** a 15-acre recreation of the African savannah, where elephants, zebras, and giraffes run free. Don't miss strolling to the downhill, north end of the park, where you'll be rewarded with a panoramic vista of Guadalajara's great semitropical **Huentitán** gorge of the grand Río Santiago-Lerma, Mexico's longest river.

Get There by taxi (from downtown, about $5), or **northeast-bound bus 258A** from the corner of Alcalde and Juan Manuel, two blocks north of the downtown cathedral. Alternatively, you can go via buses #62A or #62D, which run northeast along broad thoroughfare Calzada Independencia, beneath Plaza Tapatía.

By car, from the downtown Libertad Market, follow divided thoroughfare Calzada Independencia northeast about three miles (five km), where you pass through the big *periférico* intersection. Continue north another four or five blocks to the signed Guadalajara Zoo, Selva Mágica (Magic Jungle) amusement park, and planetarium complex entrance on the right.

ENTERTAINMENT AND EVENTS
Nightlife

The owners of Restaurant Casa Bariachi also operate **Bariachi** ("Here we pay for the mariachis") entertainment bar (Av. Vallarta 2308, tel. 33/3616-9180, open nightly 6 P.M.–3 A.M.). Lately they've been setting aside Wednesday nights for sing-alongs, and "Mexican Nights" on Tuesdays and Thursdays (all the tequila you can drink, women $3, men $6).

Restaurant Santo Coyote's owners invite you to join them in their new effort, **Restaurant Nude** (López Cotilla 1582, corner of General San Martín, tel. 33/3616-5248 or 33/3616-5411, open Mon.–Sat. 1 P.M.–1 A.M.). Not

that you actually have to show up nude, but you will get the opportunity to join the other beautiful people who are flocking to see and be seen. Step inside and enter an ultra Hollywood retro world of towering columns, flowing white curtains, and walls decorated with photographs of modestly nude females. The food is likewise modestly innovative California-style fusion fare, such as Thai tacos (actually a misnomer, $5), romaine lettuce with peanut sauce ($6), Mystery (pork loin with potato, $8), and more. If you're hungry, it's probably best simply to stop in for appetizers and continue on for serious eating somewhere else. They feature live medium-to-high-volume techno beat music Tuesday–Saturday starting around 9 P.M.

One of the Minerva-Chapultepec's most popular and longstanding clubs is restaurant-bar **Peña Cuicalli** (1988 Niño Héroes, tel. 33/3825-4690, open Tues.–Sun. from around 6 P.M.), famous for nightly jazz, rock (Wednesdays), Latin folk, and blues programs. The music customarily begins around 9 P.M. and heats up by 11 P.M.

Cinema

Minerva-Chapultepec has plenty of movies, starting with multiscreen **Cinepolis** (Av. Vallarta 2445, about four blocks east of Los Arcos, tel. 33/3630-3940), in the Centro Magno shopping center. Other popular cinema complexes are in the shopping centers, such as the Plaza del Sol (Multicinemas del Sol, at Mariano Otero 2397, tel. 33/3122-9035), Centro Magno (Cinepolis Centro Magno, Av. Vallarta 2425, tel. 3630-3940) and at Gran Plaza (Cinepolis La Gran Plaza, Av. Vallarta 3959, tel. 33/3122-5657). For screening programs, see the Arts and Entertainment section of the *Guadalajara Colony Reporter*).

SPORTS AND RECREATION
Walking and Jogging

Open walker- and jogger-friendly spaces are scarce in the Minerva-Chapultepec district. Nevertheless, if you're in need of a jogging workout you might consider the two-mile-long grassy strip that divides south-side

JORGE NEGRETE AND THE GOLDEN ERA OF MEXICAN FILM

Late at night, in the lobbies of small Mexican hotels, the TV often keeps flickering after everyone has retired to their rooms. The audience is usually only the lobby clerk and maybe a friend or a night-owl guest. They sit, transfixed by an old film of the 1940s or 1950s, frequently featuring handsome, resolute men in *sombreros* and lovely, brave señoritas. The reason is clear: These old films' crisp dialogues, rapid-fire action, and fine, often artful photography are irresistible. Not unlike the fans of the American Movie Classics TV channel, Mexicans remain drawn to these old films, from an epoch known as the golden era of Mexican film.

Although Mexican filmmaking got started around 1900, it didn't really flower until after World War II, with a new generation of actors and directors inspired by Russian director Sergei Eisenstein and American John Ford. Perhaps the most prominent of Mexican golden era directors was "Indio" Fernández, who, collaborating with cinematographer Gabriel Figueroa, made such classics as *La Perla* (The Pearl), *La Malquerida* (The Unloved Woman), *Flor Silvestre* (Wildflower), and the *Rebelión de los Colgados* (Rebellion of the Hanged).

Directors notwithstanding, it is the actors whom the public remembers: such unforgettables as María Felix, Dolores del Río, Silvia Pinal, Pedro Armendáriz, Pedro Infante, and Jorge Negrete. Of them all, none was more loved than Jorge Negrete, the Charro Cantante (Singing Cowboy). Although directors loved to place him in Jalisco *rancho* dramas and romances, such as *Ay Jalisco, No Te Rajes* (Jalisco, Do Not Destroy Yourself) and *Hasta Que Perdió Jalisco* (Until He Loses Jalisco), Negrete sometimes broke out of the cowboy mold for other roles, such as the historical *En Tiempos de la Inquisición* (In the Times of the Inquisition).

A mold he never broke out of, however, was that of leading man. And as he did on the celluloid, he often fell in love with his leading lady in private. Between 1937 and 1953 Negrete made 45 films and repeatedly dashed the hopes of his millions of Mexican female fans by marrying three of his leading ladies: Elisa Christy in 1938, Gloria Marín in 1941, and María Felix in 1952.

Although Negrete was capable of singing operatic arias and invariably sang in all of his films, he is remembered as much for his dramatic performances and his droll, mildly self-deprecating film persona as for his vocal renditions. His mild pathos on screen was more than matched by the sadness of his personal life. Negrete will nevertheless long be remembered for the heartfelt verses that he sang of his love for his homeland: "Dear beautiful Mexico . . . If I die far away . . . let them say that I am sleeping . . . that they may return me to you."

Jorge Negrete, the man for whom everything was not enough, died in Los Angeles, California, of cirrhosis of the liver, on December 5, 1953, at the age of 41.

WEST AND NORTH

Calzada Lázaro Cárdenas west of its intersection with Avenida Niños Héroes.

Otherwise, take a taxi from the Minerva Circle about three miles north to **Bosque Los Colomos,** Guadalajara's prime walking, jogging, and horseback-riding zone. (Enter at either the park's north side, Av. Patria 1805, tel. 33/3641-7633, or the south side, El Charco 3200, open daily 9 A.M.–7 P.M.). For more details, see *Bosque Los Colomos* earlier in this chapter.

Gyms and Swimming

Workout gyms are relatively plentiful in Guadalajara's affluent west-side neighborhoods. In Minerva-Chapultepec, you have the option of a **Gold's Gym** on Av. Vallarta (Av. Vallarta 1791, tel. 33/3630-2221 and 33/3616-0419, south side of the street, three blocks west of Chapultepec).

For a gym with a **swimming pool,** walk or take a taxi to the big **World Gym** fitness center (Jesús Garcia 804, corner of Miguel Ángel de Quevedo, tel. 33/3640-0704 or 33/3640-0576, open Mon.–Fri. 6:30 A.M.–10 P.M., Sat. 5:30 A.M.–5 P.M., closed Sun.). Follow López Mateos north from the Minerva Circle; after about a mile, turn left at Garcia; continue two blocks to the corner of Quevedo.

If your hotel doesn't have a pool, you can always ride a taxi to the popular **Balneario Lindo Michoacán** (Río Barco 1614, corner of González Gallo, tel. 33/3635-9399, open daily 9 A.M.–6 P.M.), southeast of downtown.

SHOPPING AND SERVICES
Outdoor Markets

Shopping is one of the Minerva-Chapultepec residents' prime diversions. Among the most colorful shopping venues are the outdoor markets that bloom locally on weekends. Two of them, the **Antique Market** (sometimes known as the Thieves' Market—secure your purse and pockets) and the **Santa Teresita Market** (which offers a little bit of everything except food), happen in the Minerva-Chapultepec vicinity on Sunday, just a few blocks apart. Find the Antiques Market spread along north-side east-west Avenida Mexico, centering around

Calle Ramos Millan. From there, simply head north along Ramos Millan several blocks, to the corner of Herrera and Cairo, marked by the beloved Santa Teresita church, on the left. Both markets are likely to be set up and running by at least 10 A.M., rain or shine.

Shopping Plazas and Warehouse Stores

Three shopping plazas—one mid-scale and two upscale—provide convenient Minerva-Chapultepec shopping opportunities. The mid-scale option is **Plaza Mexico** (Av. Mexico, at the north end of Av. Chapultepec). The anchor is giant **Aurerra** (tel. 33/3813-2049, open daily 8 A.M.–9 P.M.), a Kmart-style general store/supermarket that sells everything, including produce, meat, and groceries.

Farther west and south, multistory upscale **Centro Magno** (tel. 33/3630-1113 or 33/3630-1772) rises prominently between east-west Avenidas Vallarta and López Cotilla, midway between Avenida Americas and the Minerva Circle. However, lacking a department store anchor, a bank, or even a drugstore, the Centro Magno's success seems to rest on the plethora of youth-oriented designer shoe, clothes, sports, and jewelry boutiques that fill its four (basement, ground, first, and second) floors. The second, highest, floor is given over nearly completely to the youthful crowds that flock to the 15-screen cinema complex, the score of fast-food outlets, and the big video game arcade.

In contrast, the larger **Gran Plaza** (tel. 33/3563-2900), on the south side of Avenida Vallarta about a mile west of the Minerva Circle (accessible by bus #45), provides more diverse shopping opportunities. Like the Centro Magno, Gran Plaza has four floors, with the upper level devoted mainly to a cinema multiplex, fast-food restaurants, and a big video game parlor.

Multistory shop-lined arcades radiate from the central atrium to department stores **Sears** (tel. 33/3669-0210, open daily 11 A.M.–8:45 P.M.) on one side and **Fábricas de Francia** (tel. 33/3660-0212, open daily 11 A.M.–8:30 P.M.) on the other. At the bottom-floor end of a third arcade is **Sanborns** restaurant, book and magazine store, and upscale gift emporium (tel. 33/3122-5947, open daily 7:30 A.M.–midnight).

The Gran Plaza's only bank, with ATM, is **Bancomer** (tel. 33/3614-5314, open Mon.–Fri. 8:30 A.M.–4 P.M.), facing Avenida Vallarta, on the ground floor. Other useful ground-floor outlets are **Radio Shack** (tel. 33/3122-3715, open daily 10 A.M.–9 P.M., **Laboratorios Julio** photo and camera (open Mon.–Sat. 10 A.M.–8:30 P.M., Sun. 11:30 A.M.–7:30 P.M.), and **McDonald's** (33/3122-7733, open Mon.–Thurs. 7 A.M.–10 P.M., Fri.–Sun. 7 A.M.–11:30 P.M.).

Bottom-floor **information kiosks** list a swarm of mostly upscale in-house outlets: about 60 shoe stores, 60 women's clothing boutiques, seven men's clothing stores, four perfume stores, four sporting goods *(deportes)* stores, three women's undergarments *(ropa íntima)* stores, three jewelry stores *(joyerías),* three opticians *(opticas),* a drugstore, a travel agency, a natural foods *(tienda naturista)* store, Internet access, and more.

Gran Plaza has attracted American **warehouse chains** to locate nearby. Just west of Gran Plaza, on Avenida Vallarta's south side, is **Price Club** (tel. 33/3629-8245, open daily 7 A.M.–10 P.M., **Wal-Mart** (tel. 33/3673-2451, open daily 7 A.M.–11:30 P.M.), and **Sam's Club** (tel. 33/3629-8245 or 33/3673-2323, open daily 7 A.M.–10 P.M.).

ACCOMMODATIONS

The Minerva-Chapultepec district offers a wide variety of comfortable lodgings to suit many tastes and budgets. They vary from budget one-nighters to luxury high-rises, from garden cottage complexes to deluxe bed-and-breakfasts. What they all have in common are safe, established neighborhoods close to shops, restaurants, and transportation.

Under $50

Surprisingly, the elite neighborhood near Los Arcos monument and the Minerva Circle offers an authentic budget alternative in the **Hotel Windsor** (Salado Álvarez 131, Guadalajara,

Jalisco 44600, tel. 33/3615-7790, 33/3616-7561, $23–32), between Avenida Mexico and Justo Sierra. Although the Hotel Windsor has seen better times and is now plain and a bit tattered around the edges, an elegant marble-floored lobby attests to its former glory. Nevertheless, it offers the basics: a quiet residential street front and 18 clean rooms of varying sizes, all with double beds, drapes, a bit of furniture, and bath with hot water. Be prepared for bare-bulb lighting, however. Rooms have fans and cable TV, but credit cards are not accepted.

Two blocks southeast from the Minerva Circle, along Avenida Agustín Yañez, budget travelers might consider the bare-bones 16-room **Hotel Patricia** (Circunvalación Agustín Yañez 2745C, Guadalajara, Jalisco 44100, tel./fax 33/3616-3180, $30–40). You get a plain, worn but clean enough bare-bulb room with bath, near shops, good restaurants, and right on the 51A-51B bus line. For more quiet, get a room away from the busy street front.

Or go about two miles west of the Minerva Circle on Avenida Vallarta, south side, to **Hotel Nuevo Vallarta** (Av. Vallarta 3999, Zapopan, Jalisco 45040, tel./fax 33/3121-2095 or 33/3121-0017, $33–43). Here you have a basic but decent 26-room lodging, stacked in three stories with accommodations opening onto motel-style outdoor walkways. The rooms themselves are plainly furnished but clean, with either one king-size or two double beds and hot shower-baths, cable TV, fans, and phone (local calls $0.50).

$50-100

Check out the very reliable **Hotel Isabel Residencial** (J. Guadalupe Montenegro 1572, Guadalajara, Jalisco 44100, tel./fax 33/3826-2630, info@hotelisabel.com, www.hotelisabel.com, $63–65). The Isabel offers a relaxing garden setting at moderate rates. Its immaculate 1960s-era amenities—comfortably furnished semideluxe rooms with phones, small blue pool, popular coffee shop, and parking—have long attracted a loyal following of Guadalajara return travelers, students, and businesspeople. Its coffee shop usually bustles with residents and local merchants and professionals during breakfast and lunch hours. If the hotel has a drawback, it's the general atmosphere, which the desk staff reflects, with YMCA-like institutional coolness. On the other hand, the 51A and 51B buses (less than 10 minutes to the city center) run along Libertad, two blocks north of the hotel. The Isabel's 50 rooms come with a/c, cable TV, ceiling fans, and some wheelchair access. Discounts for long-term rentals (10 percent for one week, 25 percent for a month) are customarily available.

If you're interested in an economical apartment setting, consider the conveniently located **Magno Hotel y Suites** (Av. Vallarta 2452, Guadalajara, Jalisco 44100, toll-free in Mexico tel. 01-800/368-3200, or tel. 33/3615-2062, fax 33/3616-3817, reservahotel@terra.com.mx, www.magnohotel.com.mx, $60–68, drops to $30–38 for monthly rental), diagonally across Avenida Vallarta from Centro Magno shopping plaza. This self-styled "economical business hotel" offers six floors of about 100 kitchenette semideluxe (but some worn) apartments, furnished with sofas, carpets, drapes, floor-to-ceiling windows, private balconies, modern-standard baths, and king-size (or two double) beds. Room rates include TV, phone, fans, and parking; credit cards are accepted, but there is no pool.

Circle around to the quiet block directly behind Magno Hotel y Suites to the lively, popular, and reasonably priced four-star **⟨ Gran Hotel Las Pergolas** (The Arbors) (Morelos 2244, Guadalajara, Jalisco 44100, toll-free in Mexico tel. 800/713-9615, tel. 33/3615-0088 or 33/3630-0629, fax 33/3630-0576, reservaciones@pergolas.com.mx, www.pergolas.com.mx, $75, drops to $45 with monthly rental). Downstairs, the open-air polished marble lobby leads past the coffee shop and nightclub-bar to an invitingly intimate tropical inner pool-patio. Upstairs, the 158 deluxe rooms, all with modern-standards baths, are very clean and comfortably furnished with pastel-toned king-size (or two double) beds, carpets, and drapes. Rooms vary, especially baths; look at more than one. Rates include

satellite TV, air-conditioning, parking, and basketball and volleyball courts; credit cards are accepted. This hotel, which operates in cooperation with the University of Guadalajara, is a popular conference site and houses many foreign students who study at the nearby Centro de Estudios Para Extranjeros (Foreign Student Study Center).

Moderately priced, comfortable, and modern one- and two-bedroom apartments are available at dignified high-rise **Hotel Suites Bernini** (Vallarta 1881, Guadalajara, Jalisco 44150, toll-free Mexico tel. 01-800/362-8200, tel./fax 33/3615-2418, 33/3616-6736, or 33/3616-0858, suitesbernini@hotelsuitesbernini.com, www.hotelsuitesbernini.com, $75–100, drops to $40–50 with monthly rental), on busy Avenida Vallarta at the corner of Unión. The approximately 50 semideluxe kitchenette apartments are comfortably furnished with wall-to-wall carpets, drapes, living-dining room, and king-size (or two double) beds. To minimize street noise, choose a suite on an upper floor. All have fans, cable TV, and parking, but there's no pool and desk services are minimal.

Many visitors who prefer a deluxe, full-service, but reasonably priced, hotel choose the **⟨ Hotel Laffayette** (La Paz 2055, Guadalajara, Jalisco 44160, tel. 33/3615-0252, toll-free in Mexico tel. 01-800/362-2200, fax 33/3630-1112, ventas@laffayette.com.mx, www.laffayette.com.mx, $60–100). The Laffayette offers the advantage of plush amenities, a leafy, semi-residential upscale neighborhood, and close proximity to Avenida Chapultepec shops, cafés, restaurants, and transportation. Inside the front door you enter a cool green interior with a bar and restaurant compactly tucked around a plush, inviting lobby. Doors lead outside to a tranquil, tropical pool-patio. Upstairs, the 189 rooms are luxuriously furnished and decorated with navy blue wall-to-wall carpets and white walls, with pastel blue bedspreads. Asking rates include air-conditioning, cable TV, parking, restaurant, live music every night except Sunday, two downstairs event rooms seating 50 and 100, and credit cards accepted.

Skip about three miles west to the south side of Avenida Vallarta, a few blocks west of the Gran Plaza shopping mall, and consider the very worthy four-star (**Hotel Malibu** (Av. Vallarta 3993, Zapopan, Jalisco 45040, tel. 33/3121-7782 or 33/3122-2556, tel./fax 33/3122-3192, Mexico toll-free tel. 01-800/365-2500, malibu@cybercable.net.mx, www.hotelmalibu. com.mx, $85–110), a deluxe but moderately priced (and handy) option for folks driving or busing in along Highway 15. The hotel is attractively built around an inviting pool-patio and a small grove of magnificent tropical trees. Builders have arranged the 175 rooms in two sections, a low-rise two-story tier and an airy tower section. Rooms in both are comfortable, but the dim lighting in the low-rise tier can make the rooms appear dark and uninviting. Take a look for yourself, and if the lighting isn't satisfactory, opt for better illumination, privacy, and the balcony view of a tower section room. They're attractively decorated in whites and soothing creams and comfortably furnished in modern style, with double beds and marble shower baths. All rentals include breakfast, two kids under 12 free, air-conditioning, phone, cable TV, restaurant, secure interior parking, in-house wireless Internet, and a lobby bar with live music Thursday–Sunday. Moreover, there's a car rental (tel. 33/3122-3316 or 33/3122-1354) out front, and Gran Plaza shopping center and Wal-Mart, Sam's Club, and Price Club on Avenida Vallarta nearby.

The Magno Hotel y Suites owners also operate the similarly well-located, nine-story, deluxe **Suites Moralva** (Av. Vallarta 2477, Guadalajara, Jalisco 44100, tel. 33/3615 1845 or 33/3615-4804, $100, drops to $60 with monthly rental), diagonally west across the street. Here you can enjoy your own deluxe view apartment, with floor-to-ceiling drapes and sliding glass doors, leading to a panoramic vista terrace. Soft couches, designer lamps, wall-to-wall carpets, and two comfortable bedrooms, one king-size, the other with two double beds, complete the attractive picture. Rooms house up to four people, and include bathroom, kitchenette, a/c, and cable TV.

For a different, but equally luxurious, option, go about five blocks along Avenida López Mateos southwest from the Minerva Circle to the (**Hotel del Bosque** (Av. López Mateos Sur 265, Guadalajara, Jalisco 45000, toll-free in Mex. tel. 01-800/326-7783, tel./fax 33/3121-4700, ventas@hoteldelbosquegdl. com, www.hoteldelbosquegdl.com, $75–130). The 75 rooms encircle a lovely inner garden, sheltered by magnificent shade trees and adjoining a large blue designer pool-patio. Next to the lobby, diners enjoy the view from a cool, graceful restaurant. The rooms come in deluxe and standard (semideluxe) grades, all spotless and comfortably furnished in light pastels, with reading lamps, soft beds, and marble baths. Standard rooms have one double bed, tile floors, and ceiling fans. Deluxe rooms improve upon this with two double beds, marble floors, and air-conditioning; some accommodations have kitchenettes for the same price. Long-term rates may be negotiable. All rooms come with cable TV, phones, restaurant, pool, inside parking, and credit cards accepted.

Yet another good, moderately priced option is the **Hotel Plaza Diana** (Circunvalación Agustín Yañez 2760, Guadalajara, Jalisco 44130, toll-free in Mexico tel. 800/248-1001, tel. 33/3540-9700, fax 33/3540-9715, reservaciones@hoteldiana.com.mx, www.hoteldiana.com.mx, $95), directly across Yañez from Hotel Patricia. The Plaza Diana, which caters especially to business travelers, offers luxurious amenities for lower rates than its competitors towering nearby. Past the reception and plush lobby, restaurant, and bar, elevators rise to five floors of 150 rooms, in standard, deluxe, and junior suite grades. The smallish standard-grade rooms are comfortably furnished with king-size beds and shiny marble tub baths. Deluxe rooms have about the same, but with two double beds and a larger bath. One entire floor is reserved for nonsmokers. Rates include air-conditioning, cable TV, phone (local calls $0.40), and parking, pool, sauna, exercise room, and business center. Credit cards are accepted.

WEST AND NORTH

For something quite different, go to the **Trocadero** (1188 Cotilla, Guadalajara, Jalisco 44160, Mexico toll-free tel. 800/813-2333, tel./fax 33/3120-1416, www.villaganz.com, $80–100), across from the Alliance Francaise on the north side of Cotilla. A savvy European-born owner has converted a large family house into a comfortable, seven-unit lodging, offering clean, spacious rooms, attractively furnished with shiny hardwood furniture and large baths with showers. A quiet rear garden patio, usable by all guests, and all king-size beds except a double in one suite, are desirable pluses. Two kids under 12, accompanied by parents, are free. Lower longer-term rental rates may be available. Amenities include daily maid service, cable TV, phone, private bath, a/c, and fans, but street parking only.

About a mile northwest of the Minerva Circle, the country club–like **Suites Residenciales Margarita** (Eulogio Parra 3190, P.O. Box 1-1881, Guadalajara, Jalisco 44670, tel. 33/3641-6363, fax 33/3641-6837, margaritasuites@megared.net.mx, www.publinet.tv/paginas/margarita, $110, drops to $65 with monthly rental) is set in green, luxuriously spacious grounds. Past the gate you'll find 38 ranch-style cottages with carports dotting a grassy park. The units are clean, semideluxe, and comfortably appointed with ceiling-to-floor drapes, white walls, shiny tile floors, and modern dark-wood furniture. Units include a carpeted living room with fireplace, dining area, kitchenette with stove and refrigerator, and one bedroom with two double beds and a bathroom with tub shower. Extras include a pool patio, luxuriously nestled on a scenic canyon hillside, and a clubhouse with a meeting salon and hotel desk service. Rooms include cable TV, phone, and credit cards accepted. Get there from the Minerva Circle by following Diagonal Golfo de Cortés a total of nine blocks, past the another circle, to an intersection with Avenida Aztecas. Follow Avenida Aztecas from the intersection's north side three blocks; turn right at Eulogio Parras and, after half a block, turn left at the entrance gate.

$100-200

For a luxurious combination of charm and elegance, consider **Casa Madonna** (Lerdo de Tejada 2308, Guadalajara, Jalisco 44150, tel./fax 33/3615-6554, reserva@megared.net.mx, $150–200) at the corner of Cervantes. Casa Madonna is a 1920s-vintage Spanish-style family house, restored to a graceful posada-style garden hotel. Most of Casa Madonna's guests start their days with breakfast on the garden veranda, and on cool winter nights, they end the day over glasses of cabernet and port around a cozy fireplace. The six rooms, actually spacious suites, named Bugambilia, Girasol, Obelisco, El Nido, Tabachines, and the Suite Madonna, each with unique decor, are all you would expect, blooming with plants, colorful old-world tile, and shiny, deluxe bathrooms. All come with cable TV, a/c, ceiling fan, phone, in-house wireless Internet, restaurant service, and credit cards accepted.

About a mile west of the Minerva Circle, on the south side of Avenida Vallarta, find the **Hotel Camino Real** (Av. Vallarta 5005, Guadalajara, Jalisco 45040, Mexico toll-free tel. 01-800/903-2100, U.S. and Canada toll-free tel. 800/7CAMINO (800/722-6466), tel. 33/3134-2424, fax 33/3134-2404, guadalajara@caminoreal.com.mx, www.caminoreal.com/guadalajara, $180–250), the queen of Guadalajara luxury hotels. In contrast to its high-rise local competitors, the Camino Real spreads through a luxurious park of lawns, pools, and shady tropical verdure. Guests enjoy tastefully appointed bungalow-style units opening onto semiprivate pools and patios. Rates include cable TV, phone, four pools, tennis court, a nearby golf course, two restaurants, and a lobby bar with nightly live music. Additionally, the hotel offers the "Camino Real Club," a 35-unit super-luxurious executive section, with breakfast included, for about $250. An adjacent convention complex can accommodate meetings from 50 to 1,000 participants.

Back north of the Minerva Circle stands the **Quinta Ganz** (Ángulo 3047, Fracc. Monraz, Guadalajara, Jalisco 44670, tel. 33/3120-1416, www.villaganz.com, $180, drops to $80 with monthly rental), operated by the same owner as Trocadero. Ten attractively furnished, modern two-story townhouse-style apartments cluster in a leafy garden compound with a swimming pool common to all units. In each unit downstairs, find the living room, dining room, and kitchen; upstairs, two bedrooms and a bath. Add about $20 to the daily rate, $10 to the monthly rate, per extra person. All with daily maid service, phone, cable TV, and fans. Laundry service is available but extra. Get to Quinta Ganz from the Minerva Circle by following Diagonal Golfo de Cortés, the street that radiates northwest from the Minerva Circle's northwest side. Continue seven blocks to a traffic circle; follow the circle counterclockwise to Avenida Juan Palomar Arias at its north side. Continue along Arias four blocks; turn right at Ángulo and continue one and a half blocks to Quinta Ganz, on the right.

Switching to the truly grand, cross to the west side of the Minerva Circle to the high-powered business **Hotel Fiesta Americana** (Aurelio Aceves 225, Guadalajara, Jalisco 44100, tel. 33/3818-1400, fax 33/3330-3671, www.fiestaamericana.com.mx, $160–300). From the reception, a cool, carpeted lobby spreads beneath a light, lofty atrium. Adjacent corridors lead to an entire shopping and service center, including a travel agent, gift shop, bank, Canadian consulate, British Trade Office, and much more. The hotel's lavish in-house business facilities include a big deluxe business-negotiation center with several private rooms, all communication facilities, secretarial help, an executive lounge with complimentary snacks and drinks, and an entire convention center accommodating more than a thousand participants. The approximately 400 plush view rooms and suites are furnished in pastel tones, with soft couches, huge beds, and all-luxury amenities. Rates include tennis courts, spa, restaurants, pool, and sundeck.

Over $200

A few blocks south, At the corner of Avenida López Mateos and Avenida Niños Héroes,

business travelers often opt for the American-style high-rise **Holiday Inn Select** (Av. Niños Héroes 3089, Guadalajara, Jalisco 44520, Mexico toll-free tel. 01-800/009-9900, U.S. and Canada toll-free tel. 800/465-4329, tel. 33/3122-2020, fax 33/3647-7778, reservaciones@hisguadalajara.com, www.hisguadalajara.com.mx, $200–330). The approximately 225 accommodations come in select, junior suite, and master suite grades. Select rooms are luxurious and comfortable, the junior suites add more space and more extras, including two telephones (one in the bathroom). Master suites have a living room with separate bedroom, two TVs, and two bathrooms, one with a spa tub. Moreover, business travelers can choose a room on one of three executive floors, with complete communication and secretarial services and a relaxing executive lounge with daily canapés, coffee, cocktails, and wine. Hotel amenities include exercise room, pool, parking, event salons accommodating up to 800, restaurant, coffee shop, sushi bar, live music evenings in the lobby bar Monday–Saturday, and credit cards accepted. Ask for a commercial or longer-term rate.

The owner of the Trocadero and Quinta Ganz lodgings also offers **Villa Ganz** (López Cotilla 1739, Guadalajara, Jalisco 44160, Mexico toll-free tel. 01-800/813-2333, tel./fax 33/3120-1416, reservaciones@villaganz.com, www.villaganz.com, $220–330), an old-world-elegant mansion converted to a suite-style garden hotel. All 10 suites, both upstairs and down, are luxuriously furnished with king-size beds, plush carpets, and designer lamps and bedspreads. Rates include cable TV, telephone, wireless Internet access, a/c, fans, parking, and continental breakfast. Special weekly, monthly, and promotional rates may be available. You may also reserve Villa Ganz through the luxury Mexico Boutique Hotels agency (Mexico toll-free 01-800/508-7293, U.S.-Canada toll-free tel. 800/728-9098, www.mexicoboutiquehotels.com).

Trailer Parks

RVers can choose from at least a pair of

Guadalajara greater metropolitan area trailer parks. On the southern extension of Avenida López Mateos Sur, the very pleasant **San José del Tajo Resort Trailer Park** (P.O. Box 31-442, Guadalajara 45051, tel. 33/3686-1738, www.ontheroadin.com/interior/sanjosedeltajo_campo.htm, $18), about a mile from the Santa Anita Country Club and Golf Course, remains a favorite among RV travelers. Its very adequate facilities include many shady spaces with all hookups, toilets, showers, pool, clubroom, and tennis court. Rentals run about $18/day, $150/week, $400/month, and about $13 per day for a three-month stay. They also rent **apartments** from about $50. Find it on the southern extension of Avenida López Mateos Sur (Highways 15, 54, and 80) freeway, about three miles (five km) south of the *periférico*. Exit the freeway at the Gigante department store intersection and continue south along the local lateral lane that parallels the freeway. Soon, turn right at the San José del Tajo entrance sign. On the freeway northbound, find the same entrance about a half mile (one km) north of the Santa Anita village exit.

About a half hour farther southwest, you might certainly enjoy a stay in the trailer park at **Chimulco** warm springs bathing resort (tel. 387/778-0014, www.chimulcotrailerpark.com, $18 per day, $400 per month) in Villa Corona, off of Highway 80. For more details, see the *Chimulco* section in the *Guadalajara Getaways* chapter.

FOOD

The Minerva-Chapultepec district is famous for food, a legacy of its legion of fine restaurants. Visitors can also choose between dozens of more modest but worthy coffee shops, espresso cafés, and bakeries tucked behind and between the showplaces.

Breakfast, Cafés, and Bakeries

The Minerva-Chapultepec district abounds in coffee shops and coffeehouses, especially along Avenidas Union-Americas and Chapultepec and the neighboring side streets.

What many satisfied customers like about **Sanborns** coffee shops is that they know exactly what to expect: long hours, shiny plates and silverware, cool air-conditioned ambience, and a moderately priced selection of soups, salads, hearty breakfasts ($3–10), and lunch and dinner plates ($4–12). You have three Sanborns to choose from in the Minerva-Chapultepec district. The first (1600 Vallarta, tel. 33/3615-5894 and 33/3615-1034, open daily 24 hours) at the northeast corner of General San Martín, also includes a large magazine and gift shop that carries everything from paperback novels and perfume to handicrafts and handkerchiefs.

Two other Sanborns, also on Avenida Vallarta, serve the Minerva-Chapultepec vicinity. The second is a few blocks farther west (at the southeast corner of Gamboa, tel. 33/3615-5894, open daily 24 hours). The other Sanborns is at **Gran Plaza,** on Av. Vallarta two miles farther west (tel. 33/3122-5947, open daily 7:30 A.M.–midnight).

A good independent coffeehouse choice is a half block west of the Laffayette Hotel: try **La Vía Plata** (The Silver Way) deli-café (at La Paz 2121, tel. 33/3615-5102, open daily except Sunday 4:30–11:30 P.M.). Balmy afternoons and evenings are especially enjoyable here, while enjoying your cappuccino, sandwich, or salad ($2–7).

Even more popular, especially evenings, is **La Paloma** (The Dove) (López Cotilla 1855, tel. 33/3630-0091, open daily 8 A.M.–12:30 A.M.) at López Cotilla on the southwest corner of Cervantes. Pick a table and join the mostly 20- and 30-ish crowd on the open-air veranda while enjoying your pick of a short but tasty menu of breakfasts, soups, salads, sandwiches ($3–7), and dinner plates ($4–12).

A good, but pricey, place for light refreshment and people-watching while shopping or sightseeing is **Starbucks** (Av. Vallarta 2425, tel. 33/3616-9013, open daily 7:30 A.M.–10 P.M., coffee, pastry, sandwich, $2–6). Find it tucked at street level inside the Centro Magno shopping center, about four blocks east of the Los Arcos monument.

You needn't do without your heart's de-

© BRUCE WHIPPERMAN

WEST AND NORTH

Excellent pastries are delights of a visit to Guadalajara.

light of delectable **pastries** in the Minerva-Chapultepec district. Most renowned are **El Globo** (López Cotilla 1749, a block east of Unión, tel. 33/3616-6408, open for takeout only, daily 7:30 A.M.–10 P.M.), and **Monique** (at Unión 410, four blocks south of La Paz, tel. 33/3615-6851, open daily 8 A.M.–10:30 P.M.).

Traditional Mexican

Start at **℄ Restaurant Sacramonte** (Av. Pedro Moreno 1398, tel. 33/3825-5447, open Mon.–Sat. 1 P.M.–12:30 A.M., Sun. 1–7 P.M.), at the northeast corner of Colonias, a block north of Vallarta, where a billowing ceiling and soothing old-style trumpet-free afternoon mariachi serenades set the tone for this gourmet party in progress. The festive ambience notwithstanding, the continuously innovative *mexicana vieja* (old Mexican) menu (entrées $8–25, most around $15) is what draws the faithful mid- to upper-class crowd of Tapatíos here. The mariachis play Tuesday–Saturday 1:30–5 P.M. Live piano solos continue afterwards; relaxed atmosphere, fine for kids. Res-

ervations highly recommended, credit cards accepted.

℄ Restaurant Tequila (at Av. Mexico 2916, corner of Nelson, tel. 33/3640-3440 or 33/3640-3110, open Mon.–Sat. 12 noon–midnight, Sun. noon–7 P.M.), formerly La Destilería, easily ranks among Guadalajara's best Mexican-style restaurants. With all of the *faux* overhead piping and steel beams (to resemble a tequila distillery), Restaurant Tequila may look like a Chili's or a Señor Frog's, but it's the real thing. A look at the menu reveals a glossary of traditional Mexican cooking, including house specialties such as *cuitlacoche* (cooked corn fungus, appetizer $5), *barbacoa de hoyo* ("pit" barbecued goat wrapped in agave leaves, $10), *molcajete* (lava rock bowl of steaming fowl or meat, with *chorizo* sausage, shallots, *nopal* cactus leaves, cheese, and avocado, all in broth, $12); all orders served with the traditional hot, covered *tortillero* platter of corn tortillas. Credit cards accepted.

Restaurant El Abajeño (corner of Av. López Mateos and Av. Vallarta, tel. 33/3630-2113, open Mon.–Sat. 1–11 P.M., Sun. 1–9 P.M.), on the north side of the Minerva Circle, is a credibly authentic branch of the long-time Guadalajara institution. Temporarily abandon your diet and pick from *antojitos:* Try garlic mushrooms in butter or *enchiladas verdes* ($4 or $7), *sopa de tortilla* ($4), fondues (with bacon, $8), pork loin *(lomo)* with guacamole ($10), or chicken with *mole poblano* ($10). Who needs dessert?

Mariachis (with trumpets) play afternoons 3–6 P.M., and the more restful trumpet-free guitar and violin quintet performs evenings after 7 P.M. (call ahead for programs and schedules). Credit cards accepted.

Nouveau Mexican

All roads seem to lead to **(C Restaurant Santo Coyote** (Lerdo de Tejada 2379, tel. 33/3616-6978, open Mon.–Sat. 1 P.M.–1 A.M., Sun. 1–11 P.M.), Guadalajara's little corner of Hollywood in the suburbs, on Lerdo de Tejada at the southeast corner of Gamboa. (Although the food is good enough, the atmosphere—a galaxy of hanging lanterns glimmering from beneath a village of luxurious thatched *palapas,* all enclosing an idyllic pond and garden—keeps the crowds coming. The food is nouveau Mexican at its best. Some entrées, such as *panela a la vinagretta* and *arrachera* ($14), you might find exotic, while others, such as a big plate of luscious baby-back ribs ($13), you won't. But there are lots more good choices ($12–25); reservations recommended, credit cards accepted.

Despite its name, **(C Restaurant Oui** (a block west of Centro Magno at López Cotilla 2171, tel. 33/3615-0614, open Mon.–Sat. 8 A.M.–midnight, Sun. 8 A.M.–4 P.M.) does not feature French food, but rather refined Mexican-international. Enter the dark but elegantly masculine, shiny brass and glass dining room; overhead glows an artful stained-glass cupola, while all around, floor-to-ceiling windows look out upon an invitingly green and tropical exterior garden patio. Subdued live music (classical quartet mornings, piano afternoons, jazz quintet evenings) completes the elegant picture. The service and food are no less than you would expect. Enjoy breakfast choices from waffles and omelets to steak and *huevos rancheros* ($5–9). For lunch, try a tasty fishburger or a rich vegetable soup and tuna salad ($5–10). For dinner, pick from many fish, fowl, and meat entrées—especially beef filets—that round out the menu ($8–15). Credit cards accepted.

If you're in the mood for some truly innovative all-Mexican fare, try nouveau cuisine restaurant **(C Polibio** (Av. Mexico, corner of Polibio, about a mile northwest of the Minerva Circle, tel. 33/3121-1102, open Mon.–Sat. 1:30 P.M.–1 A.M., Sun. 1:30–6 P.M.). The atmosphere, modern and refined, furnishes a pleasantly appropriate setting for its delicious offerings. The specialties, such as fried *jamaica* flowers ($6), *albondigas* (meatballs) in *mole poblano* ($8), and *cuitlacoche* (black corn fungus) lasagna with cilantro ($7), are excellent. Reservations are highly recommended anytime.

Italian

Guadalajarans enjoy an abundance of excellent Italian food. A relatively moderately priced, very good Italian choice is **Trattoria Focaccia** (Av. La Paz 2308, corner of Cervantes, tel. 33/3616-8710 or 33/3616-6170, open Mon.–Sat. 2 P.M.–midnight, Sun. 2–6 P.M.). All the ingredients are in place: a salad bar ($5) or, if you choose, an *antipasti* bar for about the same price. Entrées include plenty of pastas, such as *fettuccine a la griglia* (grilled, $10), or pizzas such as *quattro stagioni* (four cheeses, $12), all washed down with a bottle of good *chianti classico* ($20).

For another very good, moderately priced Italian option, go to **Restaurant La Trattoria di Pomodoro** (Av. Niños Héroes 3051, 33/3122-1817, tel. 33/3793-1111, open Mon.–Sat. 1 P.M.–midnight, Sun. 1–9 P.M.), about a mile southwest of the Minerva Circle, a block east of the Holiday Inn Select. "La Trattoria," as it's locally known, remains popular with its largely middle- and upper-class patrons for its cool, refined atmosphere, crisp service, and reliable menu. A good way to proceed is to skip the so-so complimentary salad bar and go for the antipasto bar ($4), a scrumptious selection that often includes eggplant parmesan, roasted zucchini, pickled artichokes, and spinach *torta*. As for entrées, pasta is the specialty: spaghetti, linguini, fettuccine, fusilli, lasagna, and ravioli in many styles, such as *arrabiata, pomodoro,* and primavera ($6–10). Other choices include chicken in white wine sauce, beef brochette, *scallopini a la Marsala,* shrimp in garlic, and fish fillet ($6–14). Wines include an excellent all-Italian selection, plus some solid Domecq and Cetto Baja California reds and whites. Credit cards accepted.

On the Minerva-Chapultepec's north side, find 【 **Restaurant Ma Come No** (Av. Americas 302, corner of Manuel Acuña, about a mile north of Av. Vallarta, tel. 33/3615-4952, open Mon.–Sat. 1:30 P.M.–12:30 A.M., Sun. 1:30–8 P.M.), with arguably the best Italian food in Guadalajara. The dining room, with an open-air section out front, rises from a handsomely rustic tiled floor, past whitewashed brick walls, to wide *cantera* stone arches supporting a massive beamed ceiling, leaving the impression of a Tuscan country inn. Decor notwithstanding, the simply excellent food, served with a minimum of pretension, is the main event here. First, try the salad bar, which, for a mere $3, gets you antipasti such as duck roll, frittata, and mushrooms marinated with bean sprouts. Next, choose from the menu of pastas, pizzas (thick-crusted and yummy), grilled meats, and seafood ($8–16). Credit cards accepted.

Alternatively, opt for the refined, upper-middle class **Italiannis** (ground floor of Centro Magno shopping center, tel. 33/3616-2387, open Mon.–Sat. 1:30 P.M.–midnight, Sun. 1 P.M.–10 P.M.) for professionally prepared and presented salads, soups ($3–6), pizza, and pasta ($4–10).

German-Swiss

Walk through the front door at 【 **Restaurant Luscherly** (two blocks north of Vallarta at Duque de Rivas 5, southeast corner of Morelos, tel. 33/3616-2988, open Mon. and Wed.–Sat. 1 P.M.–midnight, Sun. 1–7 P.M., closed Tues.) and let the checkered tablecloths, flower boxes, half-timbered walls, and carved wooden balconies transport you to Switzerland. The menu

only enhances the impression. Here you can escape Mexico completely, with delicious choices such as onion soup ($5), *salade mimosa* (hard-boiled egg and lettuce in vinaigrette, $6), and *bratwurst mit rosti nach Berner* (Bern-style veal sausage with hash browns, $10). If those won't suffice, read through their long list of beef, shrimp, fish, crepes, and more ($8–16).

Steak and Barbecue

Form a party and visit the festive ambience of **El Gordo Steak** (Fat Man Steakhouse) (Av. Terranova 1244, open daily 1:30–11 P.M., tel. 33/3642-0127 and 33/3642-9280, reservations recommended). Enter and let yourself be seemingly transported to another, more traditional world, where old rancho-style candelabras, whirling ceiling fans, and garlands of *calabazas* and tropical vines set the stage, while hearty food provides the main event. First, a small mountain of traditional Mexican *botanas* (appetizers) keeps you content while you're waiting until the main course arrives. Although specialties are mostly steaks, either Mexican or American-style cuts ($10–18), plenty more—salads, soups, and lighter Mexican specialties ($4–10)—is available for the diet-conscious.

At **Casa Bariachi** (2221 Av. Vallarta, corner of Calderón de la Barca, tel. 33/3616-9900 or 33/3615-0029, open Mon.–Sat. 1 P.M.–3 A.M., reservations recommended), you can enjoy *mucho* mariachi entertainment (starting at 3:30 P.M.) with your salad bar ($5), barbecued beef and chicken ($8), and dessert ($3). Very popular and a good place to rub shoulders with American and Canadian resident expatriates.

Fusion/Eclectic

A few blocks south of Avenida Vallarta, **Restaurant Vinería Tinto y Blanco** (Av. Francisco Javier Gamboa 255, southwest corner of Guadalupe Zuño, tel. 33/3615-9535, open Mon.–Sat. 1 P.M.–1:30 A.M.) has an owner whose mission is to introduce wine to Guadalajara. Furthermore, he seems to be getting it right, with a custom wine bar that dispenses any one of a dozen fine varietals while at the same time keeping them out of contact with air. Get a copy of his wine-tasting schedule before you leave.

Next, take a look at the menu. Start, for example, with arugula, betabel (beet), and grapefruit salad with a honey-mustard dressing ($7), continue with *pasta fusilli* in tomato sauce ($12), accompanied by a glass of Chilean Santa Carolina merlot ($5). Finish up with a slice of apple strudel ($4) that will melt in your mouth. Credit cards accepted.

French

At **(Restaurant Pierrot** (Justo Sierra 2355, tel. 33/3630-2087 or 33/3615-4758, open Mon.–Sat. 1:30 P.M.–12:30 A.M.), four blocks north of Vallarta, diners rediscover why French cooking is world-renowned. Start out with *salade de cresson de fontaine* (watercress, $6), continue with *soupe à l'oignon gratinée* ($5), and finish off with *filet de porc normandie* ($15), washed down with the good Spanish house wine ($5), all accompanied by the lilting piano strains of "La Vie en Rose." *C'est magnifique!* Credit cards accepted.

Vegetarian

Vegetarians can regain their equilibrium at **Restaurant Zanahoria** (Carrot) (Americas 332, tel. 33/3124-6000 or 33/3616-6161, 33/3615-8710, open daily except Tues. 8 A.M.–7 P.M.). Eat healthy with your fill of good salads and soups ($3–6), and hearty vegetable entrées such as spicy baked eggplant, squash-stuffed tamales, and avocado-tomato tacos ($5–8).

INFORMATION AND SERVICES
Banking

Start in the Avenida Chapultepec neighborhood, near the corner of Avenida Vallarta, where banks, all with ATMs, are plentiful. Nearby is long-hours **HSBC** (Chapultepec 65, tel. 33/3630-4260 or 33/3630-4264, open Mon.–Sat. 8 A.M.–7 P.M., second location at Av. Vallarta 1835, south side of street, tel. 33/3616-0164 or 33/3616-0191, open Mon.–Fri. 8 A.M.–7 P.M., Sat. 8 A.M.–3 P.M.). A few blocks farther south is **Scotiabank Inverlat** (Chapultepec

324 Sur, tel. 33/3616-6951, 33/3616-6961, or 33/3615-1110, open Mon.–Fri. 9 A.M.–5 P.M., second location at Hotel Fiesta Americana, open Mon.–Fri. 9 A.M.–5 P.M.).

American Express (Av. Vallarta 2440, northeast corner of Salado de Álvarez, tel. 33/3818-2325, fax 33/3616-7665, open Mon.–Fri. 9 A.M.–6 P.M., Sat. 9 A.M.–1 P.M.). It offers full American Express services, including all AmEx credit card services, travelers checks sales and exchange, cash advances, check cashing with AmEx card, and all travel agency services.

Post and Telecommunications

If you need to go to a regular government post office, it's best to visit the small, efficient branch in the Chapalita district (Av. Tepeyac near the corner of Av. de las Rosas, tel. 33/3121-4004, open Mon.–Fri. 8 A.M.–7 P.M., Sat. 9 A.M.–1 P.M.), about a mile southwest of the Minerva Circle.

For **telephones,** use your hotel room phone, or save money by using a widely available yellow-and-blue telephone (Ladatel) card at a public telephone.

Internet connection is commonly available in the Minerva-Chapultepec. However, Internet stores come and go like the breeze. If your hotel doesn't offer in-house Internet, ask your desk clerk for a current location. On the other hand, a very likely spot for an Internet store is Centro Magno, where, at this writing, there is **Internet Puro** (tel. 33/3630-1988, open Mon.–Sat. 10 A.M.–10 P.M.).

Consulates

The **U.S. consulate** (Progreso 175, tel. 33/3268-2100 or 33/3268-2200, service hours for American citizens Mon.–Fri. 8–11 A.M.) is between Cotillo and Libertad, a block east of Av. Chapultepec.

The **Canadian consulate** (Aurelio Aceves 225, local 31, west side of the Minerva Circle, tel. 33/3615-6215, fax 33/3615-8665, open Mon.–Fri. 8:30 A.M.–2 P.M. and 3–5 P.M.) is in the Hotel Fiesta Americana. In emergencies, after business hours, call the Canadian embassy in Mexico City (toll-free tel. 01-800/706-2900).

Other countries maintain Guadalajara consular offices. For specifics, see *Consulates* in the *Downtown* chapter.

Additionally, the **British Commercial Office** maintains a local headquarters (tel. 33/3630-4357 or 33/3630-4358, open Mon.–Thurs. 8:30 A.M.–3:30 P.M., Fri. 8:30 A.M.–1:30 P.M.) at the Hotel Fiesta Americana, ground floor, on the west side of the Minerva Circle.

Drugstores and Minimarts

Along Chapultepec, you'll find several drugstores stocked with everything from bandages and soda pop to stationery and basic groceries. Try **Farmacia ABC** (northeast corner of La Paz and Chapultepec, tel. 33/3826-4742, open Mon.–Sat. 7:30 A.M.–11 P.M., Sun. 8 A.M.–10 P.M.).

On the Minerva Circle's north side, you'll find **La Playa** minimart and liquor store (tel. 33/3615-0636, open Mon.–Sat. 9 A.M.–10 P.M., Sun. 9 A.M.–5 P.M.). The modest offering includes good wines, both room temperature *(templada)* and chilled; liquors; and mixers.

Next door, at the corner of Diagonal Mar de Cortés, is **Farmacia Benevides** (tel./fax 33/3630-5755, open daily 8 A.M.–midnight), with a little bit of everything, including film and development, plenty of over-the-counter remedies, a pharmacist, toiletries, and some snacks.

Photography

At the south side of the Minerva Circle is **Laboratorios Julio** photo and camera store (tel. 33/3630-4564, open Mon.–Fri. 9:30 A.M.–2:30 P.M. and 4–7:30 P.M., Sat. 10 A.M.–3 P.M.). Being a branch of the big Guadalajara chain, it offers virtually all photography services, including in-store one-hour development, together with some supplies, still and video cameras, and popular film.

Travel Agents

Also at the Minerva Circle's south side is **Turiservicios** (tel. 33/3615-7800, fax 33/3616-

4694, open Mon.–Fri. 9 A.M.–7 P.M., Sat. 10 A.M.–1 P.M.). Full-service offerings include bus and air tickets, tours, and car rentals.

Viajes Internacional del Camino (tel. 33/3818-1400, ext. 3089, tel./fax 33/3615-1066, open Mon.–Fri. 9 A.M.–7 P.M., Sat. 9 A.M.–5 P.M.) is inside the Hotel Fiesta Americana.

Community Organizations

At least three community organizations, the **American Society of Jalisco,** the **International Friendship Club,** and the **American Legion Post 3,** welcome participation by Guadalajara newcomers. For specifics, see the *Plaza del Sol–Chapalita* section later in this chapter.

Spanish Language Instruction

On the Minerva-Chapultepec's north side, the **Vancouver Language Center** (Bernardo de Balbuena 60, tel. 33/3615-7074 or 33/3615-4773, vlc@study-mexico.com, www.study-mexico.com) offers moderately priced intensive or part-time instruction.

Also in the Minerva-Chapultepec, the University of Guadalajara's very professional **Centro de Estudios Para Extranjeros** (Study Center for Foreigners) (Tomás V. Gómez 125, P.O. Box 1-2130, Guadalajara, Jalisco 44100, tel. 33/3616-4399, fax 33/3616-4013, cepe@corp.udg.mx, www.cepe.udg.mx) conducts an ongoing program of cultural studies for visitors.

Volunteers at the American Society of Jalisco (see the *Plaza del Sol–Chapalita* section) offer economical ($5/hr.) small-group Spanish lessons.

HEALTH AND EMERGENCIES
Medical Services

For routine medications, consult the on-duty pharmacist at one of the many Minerva-Chapultepec drugstores, especially on Avenida Chapultepec, Avenida Americas, Avenida Vallarta, and around the Minerva Circle. (See the *Drugstores and Minimarts* section for details.)

If you need a doctor, follow your hotel's

recommendation, or choose from the list of highly recommended doctors and hospitals in the *Local Medical Services* section of the *Essentials* chapter.

Alternatively, you can pick a doctor from the several (general practitioner, traumatologist, orthopedist, gynecologist, oral surgeon, urologist, proctologist) who maintain Minerva-Chapultepec offices (Av. Morelos 1558, half block east of Av. Chapultepec, tel./fax 33/3826-0101).

You might also visit the highly recommended ear-nose-throat and allergy specialist Dr. Yolanda Sahagún Muñoz (Reforma 1758, tel. 33/3615-4452 or 33/3616-4706, consultation hours Mon., Wed., and Fri. 5:30–7:30 P.M.). Call ahead for an appointment.

For a medical **ambulance,** call your hotel desk or one of the hospitals that offer ambulance services, such as **Hospital Méxicano-Americano** (Av. Colomos 2110, ambulance tel. 33/3642-7152, 24-hour emergency room tel. 33/3648-3333, ext. 271).

Police and Fire

Guadalajara and its suburban districts maintain good fire and police infrastructure. For police and fire emergencies, dial the emergency number 080. Alternatively, you may contact the Municipal Police by dialing tel. 3668-0800 within Guadalajara. Similarly, contact the fire department by dialing locally tel. 3619-5155.

GETTING AROUND

Taxis present a convenient option for navigating Guadalajara's western suburbs. Tariffs customarily run $2–8, depending on the length of trip. **Rental cars** are also a convenient but more expensive option, best for savvy independent travelers who want to cover lots of ground quickly. See the *Rental Cars, Guides and Tours* section in the *Downtown* chapter for more options.

If you're going to be doing a lot of independent traveling by car or bus in Guadalajara, get a copy of the very reliable **Guia Roji Red Vial Ciudad de Guadalajara** city map. They are available at bookstores and Sanborns restaurants.

A number of useful **bus lines** connect Minerva-Chapultepec district points. (About 80 of these lines are mapped out on the very useful www.rutasjalisco.com website.) Most of the Minerva-Chapultepec sights are accessible on foot via the quiet, diesel-free **Par Vial** east–west electric trolley bus line. It traces a westward route from the north-side downtown corner of Alcalde, going west along Calle Independencia, left at Barcenas/8 de Julio, continuing south three blocks to Juárez/Vallarta, turning right and continuing west all the way to the Los Arcos monument. From there, the Par Vial turns right and continues north two blocks to Hidalgo, turns right again and continues east all the way back to downtown Alcalde.

Access both Minerva-Chapultepec and the far western suburb along Avenida Vallarta past the Minerva Circle via east–west **line 45.** From the downtown south-side corner of 16 de Septiembre and Madero, ride west along Madero; at Pavo, turn north to Morelos, then continue west; at Ramírez, go north to Justo Sierra and continue west to López Mateos, passing the Minerva Circle, then go west along Vallarta, passing the Gran Plaza shopping center (and Price Club, Wal-Mart, and Sam's Club), continuing to the line's far western terminal. Return east via Avenida Vallarta, continuing east past the Los Arcos monument, along López Cotilla, passing the Centro Magno shopping center, and continuing east, crossing 16 de Septiembre at Prisciliano Sánchez and Plaza San Francisco.

Access the Minerva-Chapultepec south side via east–west **lines 51A and 51B,** whose routes are identical in both the downtown and Minerva-Chapultepec districts. Begin at the downtown southwest corner of Libertad and 16 de Septiembre. Ride south a few blocks, turning west at La Paz, continuing to A. Yañez, two blocks south of the Minerva Circle. Here the bus continues southwest to the Chapalita neighborhood. Return from A. Jañez, at the corner of Lerdo de Tejada, continuing west, turning north at Chapultepec, turning east at Libertad, and continuing downtown to 16 de Septiembre. (For the Chapalita route variations, see the *Plaza del Sol–Chapalita* section.)

Plaza del Sol-Chapalita

Western Guadalajara's development really picked up steam when workers laid out **Plaza del Sol,** Latin America's first U.S.-style shopping mall, in 1969. A decade later, city leaders parlayed Plaza del Sol's phenomenal popularity with another big new project next door—Expo Guadalajara, Latin America's largest convention and exposition center. Expo Guadalajara's subsequent unparalleled success echoed that of Plaza del Sol.

Now, modernized and enlarged, Expo Guadalajara regularly hosts a growing battalion of big commercial events—books, jewelry, furniture, electronics, fashion, and textiles shows—that has attracted many millions of buyers and sellers from all over the world.

As part and parcel of Plaza del Sol–Expo Guadalajara, investors built a diadem of fine hotels and restaurants to accommodate the steady stream of Plaza del Sol–Expo Guadalajara visitors.

Despite their proximity, the tree-shaded neighborhoods—Ciudad del Sol, Rinconada del Sol, Jardines del Bosque, and Chapalita—neighboring Plaza del Sol have remained as planned: quiet refuges, apart from the busy boulevards that bring the shoppers and business visitors.

One of the most charming of these petite business-residential neighborhoods is **Chapalita,** centered scarcely a mile from Plaza del Sol. Over the years, Chapalita has grown quietly and gracefully into a suburban village that's home for middle-class Guadalajaran families and a generation of Canadian and Americans who came, saw, and decided to stay.

PLANNING YOUR TIME

You can view the Plaza del Sol–Chapalita sights easily in a few hours, including the Iztepete archaeological zone.

Start with a brief stroll through the Plaza del Sol (half hour), then continue on foot or by short taxi ride to Expo Guadalajara (half hour). Continue to the Chapalita Circle and

the Sor Juana monument, the plant nursery, and Sandi Bookstore (one hour). Finally, bus or drive southwest to El Iztepete archaeological zone (one hour).

ORIENTATION

Compass directions are only marginally useful around the Plaza del Sol–Chapalita neighborhood, since the main streets run like a spider's web of diagonally intersecting threads.

The district's major traffic artery is **Avenida López Mateos,** a divided boulevard that runs diagonally (and mainly underground) southeast–northwest across most of the entire metropolitan area. It continues southwest, passing the Minerva Circle, and, within two miles, bisects the Plaza del Sol–Chapalita district, leaving quiet Chapalita on its northwest flank and bustling Plaza del Sol and Expo Guadalajara on its southeast side. Expo Guadalajara, bordering another southwest diagonal boulevard, **Avenida Mariano Otero,** lies a half mile to the northeast of Plaza del Sol.

The Plaza del Sol–Chapalita district's southern boundary is marked by the **intersection of Avenida López Mateos and Mariano Otero,** while its northern extremity is marked by northwest–southeast expressway **Calzada Lázaro Cárdenas.** Additionally, a pair of roughly parallel east–west business streets, **Avenidas Tepeyac and Guadalupe,** begin where they cross Calzada Lázaro Cárdenas and run west through the heart of the Chapalita neighborhood.

SIGHTS
Plaza del Sol

Let the Plaza del Sol, on Avenida López Mateos Sur a bit more than a mile (or two km) southwest of the Minerva Circle, be your first sightseeing stop. A visionary idea for Mexico at the time it was conceived during the late 1960s, Plaza del Sol became (and remains) immensely popular. The reason is clear: In contrast to the high-end youth-oriented plazas that

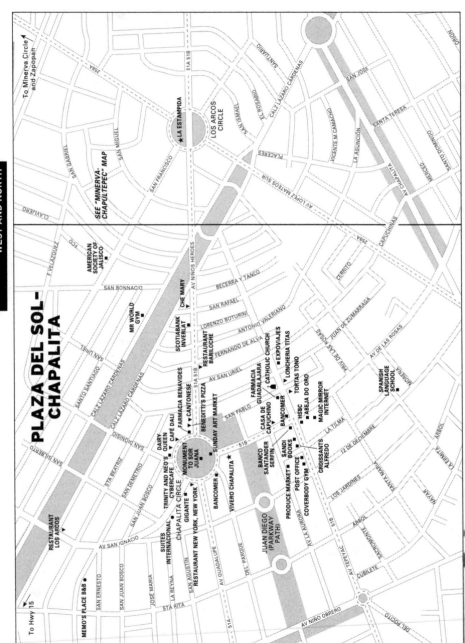

PLAZA DEL SOL– CHAPALITA

To Minerva Circle and Zapopan

To Hwy 15

SEE "MINERVA-CHAPULTEPEC" MAP

★ LA ESTAMPIDA

LOS ARCOS CIRCLE

RESTAURANT LOS ARCOS ▼

MEMO'S PLACE B&B ●

AMERICAN SOCIETY OF JALISCO ■

MR WORLD GYM ■

CHE MARY ▼

SCOTIABANK INVERLAT ■

RESTAURANT BARILOCHE ■

FARMACIA BENAVIDES ■

CANTONESE ▼

CAFE DALI ▼

DAIRY QUEEN ▼

BENEDITTI'S PIZZA ▼

SUNDAY ART MARKET

MONUMENT TO SOR JUANA

TRINITY AND NEO'S CYBERCAFE ▼

CHAPALITA CIRCLE

GIGANTE ■

BANCOMER ■

SUITES INTERNACIONAL ■

RESTAURANT NEW YORK, NEW YORK ▼

VIVERO CHAPALITA ★

FARMACIA GUADALAJARA ■

CATHOLIC CHURCH ■

EXPOVIAJES ■

LONCHERIA TITAS ▼

TORTAS TONO ▼

MAGIC MIRROR INTERNET ■

ABEJA DO ORO ■

HSBC ■

BANCOMER ■

CASA DE CAPUCHINO ■

SANDI BOOKS ■

BANCO SANTANDER SERFIN ■

PRODUCE MARKET

POST OFFICE

COVERBODY GYM ■

CROISSANTS ALFREDO ■

SPANISH LANGUAGE SCHOOL ■

JUAN DIEGO (PARKWAY PATH)

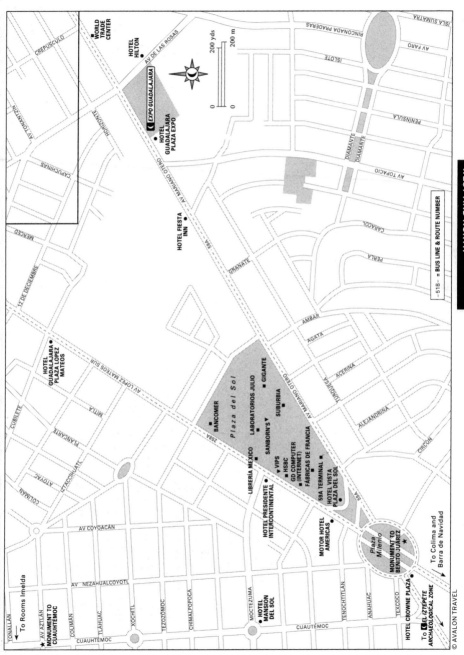

WEST AND NORTH

© AVALON TRAVEL

mushroomed during the 1990s, Plaza del Sol is full of locally owned stores—department, drug, book, clothing, sports, and much more—useful to a big cross section of Guadalajarans.

◖ Expo Guadalajara

Since it opened in 1987 as the largest exposition center in Latin America, Expo Guadalajara (Mexico toll-free tel. 01-800/813-3000, Av. Mariano Otero 1499, tel. 33/3343-3000, fax 33/3343-3030, www.expo- guadalajara.com or www.operadoradeferias.com, daily 9 A.M.–8 P.M.) has maintained leadership among both its national and international counterparts, in both attendance and occupancy rates. It hosts more than 120 events annually, including some of the most important industry-wide exhibitions in Mexico.

Designed to international standards, Expo Guadalajara was built on a single level and spreads over an area about a fifth of a mile (300 meters) on a side. It has kept pace with international design standards, instituting an award-winning quality control system in 1992 and enlarging and modernizing its facilities. Presently, about 500,000 square feet (45,000 square meters) in nine flexible modules can handle 50,000 visitors a day and accommodate expositions from small to gigantic. Furthermore, Expo Guadalajara goes a long way toward minimizing the planning and organizing hassles with its convenient one-level design, with 15 loading gates (which can accommodate 65 tractor-trailers simultaneously) that open directly to the exhibition floor.

A 75,000-square-foot (7,000-square-meter) auditorium was added in 2002. To that, add a plethora of telecommunications and office services and private negotiating facilities, plus a dozen coffee shops, snack bars, and a pair of fine restaurants, all of which contribute to making Expo Guadalajara an excellent setting for seeing, exhibiting, buying, and selling.

Nearly daily, a huge squadron of booths buzz with activity in the main exhibition hall. If you're lucky, maybe you'll catch one of the big fairs, such as fashion (January and July), ice cream (February), computers (March), handicrafts (June), furniture (September), jewelry (October), or books (November). Stop by the convenient food court *(zona gastronómica)* in the middle of the complex for a light meal or refreshment.

To reach Expo Guadalajara from Plaza del Sol, walk northeast along Avenida Mariano Otero, the street that borders the "back" (east) side of Plaza del Sol. After about six long blocks, after Hotel Expo Guadalajara, you'll reach Expo Guadalajara, at the corner of Avenidas de las Rosas and Mariano Otero. Turn right and enter Expo Guadalajara via the plaza on the immediate right.

Chapalita Circle

From Expo Guadalajara, walk or taxi about seven blocks northwest along Avenida de las Rosas (passing the Chapalita district's petite commercial hub, at the corner of Avenida Tepeyac) to the Chapalita Circle, at the intersection of Avenida Guadalupe and Avenida de las Rosas. The Chapalita Circle, scenic focus of the Chapalita neighborhood, is a shady, grassy island park, from which radiate a number of jacaranda-, palm-, and mango-shaded neighborhood streets.

The circular park itself, perfect for a picnic, centers around an abstract, gilded sculpture representing the celebrated 18th-century poet-nun **Sor Juana Inés de la Cruz,** an early Latin American feminist. A collection of organizations and individuals, who have awarded a prize in Sor (Sister) Juana's honor since 1993, erected the sculpture in 1996. The Chapalita Circle is the site of regular community activities: The **Zapopan Municipal Band** performs on Wednesday and Thursday afternoons, and local artists exhibit and sell their works at an **art fair** Sundays starting around 10 A.M.

Vivero Chapalita

Carefully cross back over busy Avenida Guadalupe to Avenida de las Rosas, at the south side of Guadalupe Circle. There, you'll find Vivero Chapalita (Chapalita Nursery) (Av. de las Rosas 825, cell tel. 044-33/3156-2771, open Mon.–Sat. 9:30 A.M.–7 P.M., Sun. 11 A.M.–6 P.M.). Here you can see why Guadalajara is such a gardener's delight. The plants seem to like the weather as much as the people do. Whether temperate or tropical, all the favorites—azaleas, ferns, rubber plants, oranges, lemons, petunias, banana, cactus, bamboo, bromeliads—and dozens more thrive here.

From the nursery, see the results of all this gardening ferment by strolling along the tree-lined garden parkway lane **Juan Diego,** which heads from the south side of the nursery. Walk west, past the houses set back behind sweeping (luxurious for Mexico) green lawns, swathed with regally tall shade trees. For about a mile (to the end, marked by busy Avenida Niños Obrero, and back), stroll and enjoy the calm, the cooling breeze, the birdsong, and flash of butterfly wings in the shade beneath the great rubber *(hule),* mango, pine, and eucalyptus trees.

◖ El Iztepete Archaeological Zone

The important El Iztepete archaeological zone (open daily 9 A.M.–5 P.M., no facilities) is eas-ily accessible from the Plaza del Sol–Chapalita district. By taxi or car, simply drive southwest along Avenida Mariano Otero, about two miles (three km) past the *periférico* (peripheral boulevard) to the Iztepete parking lot on the right. Alternatively, ride the 59A bus, southbound, from the stop on Avenida Mariano Otero, on the east ("back") side of Plaza del Sol shopping center, to the Iztepete stop just past the *periférico.*

Walk through the entrance gate and begin looking along the path for some of the glistening, jet-black volcanic glass shards, the source of the label "El Iztepete" ("Hill of Obsidian").

Most archaeologists who excavated this site, beginning with José Corona Núñez, in 1954, now believe that El Iztepete was probably both a ceremonial-pilgrimage center and commercial meeting ground for both working and bartering for obsidian. People probably gathered from all over western Mexico both to pay homage to the gods and obtain obsidian, prized for decorative and practical purposes—cutting tools, knives, hunting implements, and weapons.

© BRUCE WHIPPERMAN

Many archaeologists believe that El Iztepete Archaeological Zone was once an important ceremonial and trade center.

Climb the reconstructed ceremonial stairway to the summit of the main (and only excavated) mound, a height of about 20 feet (six meters) above the surrounding fields. Look toward the horizon, opposite the *periférico,* for the hulking, truncated silhouette of the active **Cerro Colli** volcano several miles to the southwest.

In the foreground, the approximately 15-acre brushy field occupies the core of a much larger archaeological zone that extends over a 10-square-mile (25-square-kilometer) irregular area to the south, southeast, and northwest. Also in the foreground, look for the three other brush-covered mounds, including a suspected ball court about 150 yards south, all yet to be excavated.

Back at the main mound, excavations have revealed that the present construction, dating from around A.D. 900, represents the third and final construction that overlays, like the peels of an onion, two earlier lower platforms, dating from around A.D. 1 and A.D. 400. Some archaeologists believe that the earliest two constructions, especially their stairways and rectangular substructures, show strong Teotihuacán influences.

ENTERTAINMENT AND EVENTS
Nightlife

Around the Plaza del Sol, the hotels are the most reliable entertainment sources. Nearly all of them have nightly live music at their lobby bars; at least two—the **Hotel Crowne Plaza** and the **Hotel Presidente Intercontinental**—have full-blown nightclubs.

The Chapalita Circle also offers nighttime diversions. Enjoy the live music at **Restaurant New York, New York** Friday–Saturday 10 P.M.–midnight. Alternatively, top-pick Argentine **Restaurant Bariloche,** four blocks east of the Chapalita Circle, offers a nightclub-style tango show Friday–Saturday starting at 9:30 P.M.

Cinema

Plaza del Sol has a pair of **movie theater** options. Try either the five-screen **Multicinema** at Plaza del Sol (tel. 33/3630-3940) or the 12-screen **Cinemark** complex (Av. López Mateos 3333B, corner of Mariano Otero, tel. 33/3634-0509) at the underground Milenio shopping plaza, a few blocks south.

Art and Music

Chapalita offers some regularly scheduled community entertainment. Start at the Chapalita Circle and enjoy the **band concert** Wednesday and Thursday afternoons. Sundays, bring a picnic lunch and stroll around the Chapalita Circle and enjoy perusing the **artists' market** offerings 10 A.M.–5 P.M.

SHOPPING
Plaza del Sol

The perennially popular Plaza del Sol (tel. 33/3630-3940) is one of Guadalajara's prime shopping grounds. Variety, the secret to Plaza del Sol's success, is immediately visible at the Plaza's two main entrances: on the west side, on Av. López Mateos (buses 258A and 258 from downtown, plus numbers 359, 59, 640, and 358) , and on the east side, on Av. Mariano Otero (bus 59A). At each entrance, directory kiosks list the possibilities: shoe and women's clothing boutiques, about a dozen each; plus many jewelry, baby, ice cream, and gift boutiques. Finally, you'll find some banks (all with ATMs), travel agencies, pharmacies, electronics, a copy shop, bookstore, *(papelerías)* (stationers), and *traje de baño* (swimsuit) shops.

Specific locales include department stores Suburbia, Fábricas de Francia, and El Nuevo Mundo, Gigante supermarket, G. D. Computer, Levis, Laboratorios Julio photo store, Federal Express, Jantzen, and Sony. Fast-food options include Burger King, Subway, and Dairy Queen. For restaurants, choose among Pizza Hut and coffee shops Sanborns and VIPs.

Some stores are especially useful, such as the excellent book and magazine store **Librería Mexico** (just inside the López Mateos entrance, tel. 33/3121-0114, open daily 8:30 A.M.–9:30 P.M.), with dozens of English-language magazines, including *Time, Newsweek, USA Today,* and the Miami *Herald* newspaper.

For **Internet access,** go to G. D. Computer (open Mon.–Sat. 11 A.M.–7 P.M., Sun. 11 A.M.–3 P.M.).

Outdoor Markets

Sunday is the big day at the **artists' market** (Chapalita Circle, intersection of Avenidas Guadalupe and de las Rosas) and the **Antiques** and **Santa Teresita** markets (see *Outdoor Markets* earlier in this chapter for details).

On Friday, go (via bus 51B) about two miles farther west along Tepeyac and visit the big **clothes market** (known locally as the *tianguis del sol*) on Avenida Copernicus between Avenidas Tepeyac and Moctezuma. Dedicated lovers of outdoor markets venture even farther, to the country-style Thursday **Santa Anita Market,** in Santa Anita village, west of Avenida López Mateos, about four miles (seven km) south of the *periférico.*

SPORTS AND RECREATION
Walking and Jogging

Among the airiest Expo Guadalajara–Plaza del Sol walking and jogging locations is the unique panoramic-view **jogging track** atop the Hotel Guadalajara Plaza Expo.

Otherwise, the shady Chapalita neighborhood affords some walking and jogging opportunities. The grassy fields at the **Ciudad de Niños** (between Av. Guadalupe and Av. Tepeyac, two blocks west of Av. Niño Obrero) and the **Club de Leones** (a few blocks farther west, at the corner of Tepeyac and Prado Tabachines) appear ideal for jogging.

Another pleasant close-in walking and jogging space is the shady three-block **Juan Diego** parkway lane, which heads from the south side of the Vivero Chapalita nursery. Walk or jog west for about a half mile.

Gyms and Swimming

If you're staying in one of the facility-rich Expo Guadalajara–Plaza del Sol hotels—namely, the Hilton, Guadalajara Plaza Expo, Presidente Intercontinental, and Mansión del Sol—simply go to the exercise gym for a workout. If you're content with swimming for exercise, all of the Expo

Guadalajara–Plaza del Sol hotels recommended (except the Mansión del Sol) have pools.

Alternatively, Chapalita has a number of gyms. One of the better ones is **Mr. World Gym** (Lázaro Cárdenas 3454, tel. 33/3121-1166, open Mon.–Fri. 8 A.M.–8 P.M., Sat. 8 A.M.–5 P.M.), across from the parkway from the Calle San Rafael corner. You'll find a variety of fitness machines, a sauna, aerobics classes, and much more.

The newly remodeled rehabilitation center, **Mundo Físico** (San Francisco 3376, tel. 33/3123-2828, open Mon.–Fri. 8 A.M.–8 P.M., Sat. 8 A.M.–3 P.M.), in the block just west of the American Society's headquarters, is strongly recommended by the American Society of Jalisco. Mundo Físico offers a plethora of facilities, including two heated swimming pools (one outdoor, one indoor), paddle tennis, squash, handball, a fitness gym with professional trainers, sports medicine, steam room, sauna, spa, water aerobics, natural food café, and more. Day use runs about $15; fees for all-inclusive programs start at about $100 per month.

ACCOMMODATIONS

With some exceptions, the hotels around both Expo Guadalajara and Plaza del Sol are high-rise deluxe lodgings catering to business travelers. As a group, they're strong on business services, meeting facilities, and the luxury amenities that their prices reflect.

Chapalita, by contrast, is a residential village-within-a town, whose residents offer a sprinkling of apartment, bed-and-breakfast, and room lodgings for visitors.

Under $100

Budget-minded travelers have a solid option in the old standby **◖ Motel Las Americas** (López Mateos Sur 2400, Guadalajara, Jalisco 45050, Mexico toll-free tel. 01-800/849-2178, tel. 33/3915-9600, tel./fax 33/3631-4415, $62/day, $50/15 days, $40/30 days). The 100 rooms are distributed in two wings: the original garden wing, built around an inner pool-patio, and the newer tower wing, with private balcony views. The garden rooms are smaller and older, but nevertheless clean and comfortable. Natural light is limited, however. For privacy, drapes must be drawn, since the room windows face outside walkway corridors. In the tower section, rooms are newer, larger, and more private. Guests in the upper-level (especially the third and fourth story) rooms enjoy their own balconies with airy views overlooking the surrounding neighborhood and the billowing clouds above the serrated, southwest mountain horizon.

The prices are certainly right. All rooms include air-conditioning, cable TV, coffee shop, two pools, three meeting rooms, and parking.

The **Hotel Guadalajara Plaza López Mateos** (Av. López Mateos Sur 2128, Guadalajara, Jalisco 45050, Mexico toll-free tel. 01-800/363-4500, U.S or Canada toll-free tel. 888/223-7646, tel. 33/3208-4400, fax 33/3122-1703, $90) is several blocks (about a quarter mile) west of Expo Guadalajara. A smallish but inviting lobby area welcomes guests; the adjacent lobby bar provides live music, and a deluxe restaurant offers good breakfasts, lunches, and dinners. The hotel's 142 rooms and suites gracefully enclose a tranquil, tropical pool-garden. In a pair of two-story neocolonial wings, the 30 "royal" suites, all with living rooms, are elegantly adorned in soft greens and reds.

The 112 standard rooms, in a seven-story view high-rise wing, are tastefully decorated in earth-toned pastels with splashes of blue and black. All accommodations include deluxe bathroom with shower, cable TV, phones, and parking included; credit cards are accepted.

Guests have the use of a modest business center, with meeting rooms, bilingual secretarial services, fax, copier, and Internet connection ($0.10/minute, bring your own laptop). For events and business conferences, two salons, accommodating up to 400 people, are available.

The **Hotel Vista Plaza del Sol** (Av. López Mateos Sur 2375, Guadalajara, Jalisco 45050, Mexico toll-free tel. 01-800/361-3300, U.S. and Canada toll-free tel. 800/882-8215, tel. 33/3880-0600, fax 33/3880-0610, www.vistahotel.com, $90), seems to be trying hard, especially for family and business travelers. Don't let the cramped downstairs lobby-restaurant-bar area put you off. Business travelers should instead go upstairs and take a look at the 37-room, two-suite executive floor, with staffed business center, providing phones, printer, fax, and computers with Internet access, plus continental breakfast, free afternoon drinks, and free shuttle transportation to Expo Guadalajara. Family travelers have access to a pool and coffee shop downstairs, special events for families, and a five-minute walk to the movie theaters, fast-food restaurants, and stores at Plaza del Sol. Rooms come with cable TV, air-conditioning, and parking.

The **Hotel Howard Johnson Las Torres Plaza** (Calz. Lázaro Cárdenas 1060, U.S. and Canada toll-free tel. 800/IGOHOJO (800/446-4656), Guadalajara toll-free tel. 01-800/366-6900, tel. 33/3810-3535, fax 33/3810-4686, reserhojogdl@megared.net.mx, www.hojoguadalajara.com.mx, $90) caters especially to business clients in the south-side industrial section about two miles southwest of the Plaza del Sol. You get about what you get back home, nine floors of 125 comfortable standard-grade semideluxe air-conditioned rooms, a step above Motel 6 (for more quiet, get a room facing away from the noisy expressway). Rooms on the more deluxe executive floor have plusher carpets and soft easy chairs. Guests may enjoy the use of a modest business center (check first to see if it's up and running) and a compact but attractive lobby, a sports bar, and a coffee shop. Conference facilities, in the basement, consist of five meeting rooms, accommodating 40–200 participants.

$100-200

Ideally located right next door to Guadalajara Expo convention center is the very worthy **⟨ Hotel Guadalajara Plaza Expo** (Mariano Otero 3261, Guadalajara, Jalisco 45050, tel. 33/3669-0215, Mexico toll-free tel. 01-800/363-4500, U.S. and Canada toll-free tel. 888/223-7646, fax 33/3122-2850, $105). It offers a plethora of super-deluxe amenities for relatively modest south-of-the-border prices. Enter and continue past the reception to the elegantly carpeted and flower-decorated lobby. Upstairs, elevators rise to seven floors of 204 plush rooms, adorned with soft quilted floral bedspreads and carpeted and draped in dark earth tones. On the top floor, guests enjoy a panoramic-view pool sundeck, an exercise gym, and a professionally designed soft-surface jogging track. Guests have use of a downstairs business center, with secretarial services, computer, fax, copier, and negotiating and conference rooms for 10–120 people. Rooms include phone, cable TV, two kids free with parents, safety deposit boxes at desk, restaurant, lobby sports bar, live music in the lobby Wednesday, Thursday, and Friday, credit cards accepted, and special rooms for the handicapped.

For outstanding luxury option, go to the ◖ **Hotel Crowne Plaza** (Av. López Mateos Sur 2500, Guadalajara, Jalisco 45050, tel. 33/3634-1034, Mexico toll-free tel. 01-800/365-5500, U.S. and Canada toll-free tel. 800/227-6963, fax 33/3631-9393, www.crowneplaza.com, $120), just past the traffic circle at the Plaza del Sol's southern edge. Stroll into the lobby and feast your eyes on the immaculate, polished interior, where nothing, not even a single bit of dust, seems to mar the gracious, old-world ambience. Farther on, in the interior garden, the impression continues, next to the broad green lawn and manicured flower beds, beneath the great shady trees and beside the gracefully curving blue swimming pool.

The 289 accommodations—suites at the garden level, rooms in a high-rise wing—are as deluxe as you would expect, tastefully adorned, with marble baths, tub showers, and garden-view windows or private city-vista balconies, and including many luxury extras.

Business accommodations are equally lavish, including a special "Plaza Club" executive floor, with continental breakfast, afternoon hors d'oeuvres, shoe shine, and private check-in and check-out.

The list goes on. Business conference options include 13 possible meeting-exhibition

rooms, accommodating 10–800 people. Entertainment and recreation facilities feature an excellent deluxe restaurant, coffee shop, lobby bar with nightly live music, a nightclub, billiard room, a full gymnasium, big pool, and tennis court. Ask for a commercial or weekend package discount.

Two blocks south along Mariano Otero, consider the smaller, deluxe four-star **Hotel Fiesta Inn** (Av. Mariano Otero 1550, Guadalajara, Jalisco 45055, tel. 33/3669-3200, Mexico toll-free tel. 01-800/504-5000, fax 33/3669-3247, www.fiestainn.com, $140). This efficient branch of the well-managed Fiesta Americana chain combines a business- and family-friendly atmosphere with downstairs coffee shop, modest business center and meeting rooms, gym, pool, and comfortable deluxe rooms and suites upstairs. Commercial rates may be available by prior reservation.

The intimate, boutique ◖ **Hotel Mansión del Sol** (Av. Moctezuma 1596, Guadalajara, Jalisco 45050, tel. 33/3647-4762, Mexico toll-free tel. 01-800/715-9339, fax 33/3647-9447, www.lamansion-delsol.com, $130) is tucked in the upscale neighborhood a few blocks west of Avenida López Mateos. A quick look downstairs—polished oak paneling, plush Persian carpets, antique Chinese tapestries, elegant guest-only restaurant—begins to reveal the gracious amenities of this distinguished small hotel.

The 22 spacious rooms expand the impression, with handsomely masculine hardwood paneling, king-size beds, soft carpets, and roomy, deluxe shower baths. Designed with the business client in mind, the rooms additionally provide a big work desk with 24-hour in-room Internet access.

Guests have the use of a small business center, including bilingual secretarial service and all communication and copy services at no extra charge. Furthermore, after a hard day of shopping or negotiating, you can work out in the small but deluxe gym, steam in the sauna, or simply relax in the sun in the lush, tropical exterior patio garden. All rooms include big continental breakfast, afternoon snack, parking, credit cards accepted, valet parking, but no pool.

Find the **Hotel Presidente Intercontinental** (López Mateos Sur and Moctezuma, Guadalajara, Jalisco 45050, tel. 33/3678-1234, Mexico toll-free tel. 800/690-9352, U.S. and Canada toll-free tel. 800/327-0200, fax 33/3678-1222, www.ichotelsgroup.com, $185–300) right across López Mateos (via pedestrian bridge) from the Plaza del Sol and a five-minute taxi ride to Expo Guadalajara.

Beyond the airy, light lobby-atrium, decorated by a grand flowing fountain, guests enjoy a pair of good restaurants and relax to live music in the lobby bar early evenings and a nightclub until the wee hours. Furthermore, business clients have the use of a well-equipped business center, with bilingual secretarial services, all communication services, and negotiating rooms. A big in-house conference-exhibition center accommodates up to 1,600 participants.

Upstairs, 414 luxuriously furnished rooms and suites, including an exclusive "Club Intercontinental" business floor, provide a host of amenities. The business floor is the plushest, with its own private lounge with complimentary canapés and drinks, in-room printer, wireless Internet connection, VCR, newspaper, laundry and shoe-shine service. All rooms include pool, spa, gym, parking, and credit cards accepted.

Over $200

At the top of the pecking order is the grand, high-powered **(Hotel Hilton** (Av. de las Rosas 2933, Guadalajara, Jalisco 44540, tel. 33/3678-0510, Mexico toll-free tel. 800/003-1400, U.S. or Canada toll-free tel. 800/445-8667, fax 33/3678-0511, www.hilton.com, $250–300), right across the street from Guadalajara Expo. In its third Guadalajara incarnation, the Hilton chain seems to have gotten it right. Business travelers can have everything under one roof. The big downstairs **business center** has a reception and services area, leading to eight meeting rooms, accommodating 5–40 people, and three interviewing rooms for

2–4 people. On-site bilingual secretarial service and all communications services are readily available. Furthermore, the in-hotel **convention center** can accommodate 20–1,200 in 12 various rooms and an auditorium seating 300 for events, projections, and promotions.

Upstairs, the 450 rooms and suites include an exclusive, self-contained executive floor, with 20 spacious master suites and 11 super-deluxe rooms, free morning continental breakfast and afternoon canapés and cocktails.

All accommodations are super-deluxe, with a computer and fax outlet, satellite TV, safety deposit box, telephones, cable TV, and much more. Kids under 12 stay free with parents. Amenities include two good restaurants, a lobby bar, pool, exercise gym, sauna, and aerobics room.

Bed-and-Breakfast and Apartments

At her **(Bed-and-Breakfast Gloria** (Axayacatl 476, Colonia Chapalita, Guadalajara, Jalisco 45040, tel. 33/3631-9531, fax 33/3632-4185, $28–40) semiretired former Texas resident Gloria Meija offers three spacious rooms, two with shared bath, one with private bath, in a quiet, residential suburban neighborhood convenient to Plaza del Sol. The immaculate, comfortably furnished rooms are all upstairs, where they share a homey sitting room with soft couches and a TV. Two of the rooms open to a sunny deck overlooking the verdant backyard garden. In the kitchen downstairs, Señora Meija serves breakfast to order (fruit, coffee, toast, jam, and eggs) for guests.

If, however, you prefer the privacy of your own apartment, you can have it, at modern-style **Suites Internacional** (San Ignacio 63, Colonia Chapalita, Guadalajara, Jalisco 45040, tel. 33/3122-2625, toll-free Mex. tel. 01-800/718-5536, suitesinternational@yahoo.com.mx, $65/day; $320/wk; $850/mo.). The approximately 24 units, well-maintained inside and out, occupy two floors, next to suburban thoroughfare Avenida San Ignacio. Past the small lobby-reception, the apartments line a central corridor. Inside, they're clean, comfortably furnished, and attractively decorated in 1980s-style, designed for comfortable living, with an efficiency kitchenette, a bedroom with double bed, and shiny shower bath, just two blocks from Chapalita restaurants and shopping.

Finding a Room, Apartment, or House Rental

Some householders in Chapalita rent rooms, apartments, and houses at modest rates. Perhaps the best way to find them is to walk around the neighborhood you like, looking for the Se Renta (For Rent) signs. Another possible rental sources are the classified sections of the *Guadalajara Colony Reporter* and the *El Informador* newspapers. Both are generally available at bookstore Librería Sandi (Tepeyac 718, three doors from the northwest corner of Av. de las Rosas, tel. 33/3121-0863, fax 33/3810-4686, sandibooks@sandibooks .com, www.sandibooks.com, open Mon.–Fri. 9:30 A.M.–7 P.M., Sat. 9:30 A.M.–2 P.M.).

Another useful apartment and house rental source is the rental and real estate agency **Associados Corona Orozco** (La Noche 2249,

Colonia Jardines de Bosque, tel. 33/3122-8484, fax 33/3122-8181, informes@superrenta.com, www.superrenta.com).

Rentals are also listed on the community **bulletin boards** at Librería Sandi and the **American Society of Jalisco** headquarters (San Francisco 3392, tel. 33/3121-2395, open Mon.–Fri. 10 A.M.–2:30 P.M.). (From the north side of Calz. Lázaro Cárdenas, four blocks west of its intersection with Av. Guadalupe, follow Av. San Gabriel one long block north and turn left on to San Francisco. Continue one short block to the headquarters, at the next corner, of Fco. Javier, on the north side, opposite the Colegio Guadalupe.)

FOOD
Plaza del Sol

Around Plaza del Sol, coffee shop **Sanborns Restaurant** (in the Plaza del Sol, open daily about 7:30 A.M.–11 P.M.) is one of the best bets for breakfast or a light meal. Also in Plaza del Sol, try **VIPs,** open about the same hours as Sanborns, for a variation on the same coffee shop

© BRUCE WHIPPERMAN

Plum-like yellow *ciruelas* make a healthy and tasty afternoon snack.

theme. For faster food, try Pizza Hut, Dairy Queen, or Burger King, also in Plaza del Sol.

Hotel coffee shops also offer good options. Best bets for breakfast or lunch are at mid-scale Motel Americas, Hotel Vista del Sol, and Hotel Fiesta Inn, or upscale Hotel Crowne Plaza, Hotel Guadalajara Plaza López Mateos, or Expo Guadalajara Plaza Expo.

If natural food is your thing, go to **La Panza Es Primera** (The Body Comes First) store and restaurant (tel. 33/3123-1847, open Mon.–Sat. 10 A.M.–8:30 P.M. and Sun. 11 A.M.–8 P.M.), in the Plaza del Sol shopping center.

Like the breakfast and lunch options, serious dinner dining around the Plaza del Sol is mostly confined to the hotels, with good gourmet options available at the **Hotel Crowne Plaza,** the **Hotel Mansión del Sol** (only hotel guests and their guests admitted), and the **Hotel Guadalajara Plaza Expo.**

One hotel restaurant, however, the superplush **(Restaurant Belvedere,** at the Hotel Hilton, is outstanding. One look at the Belvedere menu, with French, Italian, and Mexican food rolled into one, gives the clue that you're in for something unusual.

For Mexican, try the appetizers, such as quesadillas with mushroom *cuitlacoche* ($5), *flor de calabaza* ($7), or *sopes estilo Guadalajara* ($6). Or, if you're a truly adventurous eater, go for the deep-fried *gusanos de maguey*—maguey worms ($6). People tell me they're excellent. For Italian, choose from Serrano ham with melon ($5) or *carpaccio di salmone* ($7). For French, go for tricolor soup ($6) or seafood soup *al pernado* ($8). Actually, it's probably best to let the waiter order for you; it seems especially difficult to go wrong at the Belvedere.

Chapalita
BAKERY AND LIGHT MEALS

Chapalita offers more good, local-style options, many of them right near the village-center corner of Tepeyac and Avenida del las Rosas. For baked goods, go to **Croissants Alfredo** (tel. 33/3121-4979, open daily 8 A.M.–9 P.M.).

For breakfast, you have at least two good options: **La Casa de Capuchino,** from Avenida Tepeyac, half a block north on de las Rosas, on the right. Or, another two blocks north, take a booth at coffee shop **Restaurant New York, New York,** right on the Chapalita Circle's west quadrant (Av. San Ignacio 1197, Mon.–Sat. 8 A.M.–midnight, Sun. 8 A.M.–10 P.M., tel.33/3121-2606 or tel.33/3121-8657)

Get your fill of plenty of good juice drinks, yogurt, whole wheat bread and cookies, vitamins, supplements, and more at the **Abeja de Oro** (Golden Bee) (Av. de las Rosas 591, two doors south of Tepeyac, tel. 33/3121-1504, open Mon.–Fri. 8:30 A.M.–8 P.M., Sat. 8:30 A.M.–4 P.M., Sun. 8:30 A.M.–2 P.M.)

For plenty of healthy options, try the relaxing outdoor **(Lonchería Tita's** (Tepeyac 591, tel. 33/3122-9970, open Mon.–Sat. 7:30 A.M.–5 P.M., Sun. 7:30 A.M.–3 P.M.), one block east of the de las Rosas corner, across the street from the church. Pick from a bunch of salads, fruit drinks, and sandwiches, graded according to nutrition: "naturista," with fresh avocado, nuts, lettuce, and tomato, being the

© BRUCE WHIPPERMAN

The best Mexican-style Guadalajara restaurants bake their own tortillas.

healthiest, and "dinosaur," with lots of meat, the least healthy. Other choices include omelets, quesadillas, *tortas,* and much more.

On the other hand, walk across the adjacent lane to **Tortas Tono** (tel. 33/3647-6208, open daily 9 A.M.–4 P.M.) for a *torta,* the Mexican sandwich: typically chicken breast or pork loin, with tomato, lettuce, avocado, and jalapeño pepper (which you can remove, if you prefer) in a hot, crispy *bolillo* (bun).

Around the Chapalita Circle nearby, you can also avail yourself of a choice of **Benedetti's Pizza** (tel. 33/3647-2525, open daily 10 A.M.–11 P.M.), **Dairy Queen** (cell tel. 044-33/3577-5399, open daily noon–9 P.M.), and a modest **Cantonese** food shop (tel. 33/3121-6333, open daily 11 A.M.–11 P.M.).

RESTAURANTS

Find class-act seafood at **❰ Restaurant Los Arcos** (Av. Lázaro Cárdenas 3549, corner of San Ignacio, tel. 33/3122-3719, open Mon.–Sat. 11 A.M.–10:30 P.M., Sun. 11 A.M.–7:30 P.M., morning hours may vary). Los Arcos is one of a chain of 10 that started humbly in Culiacán in Sinaloa and spread all over northwest Mexico. The label "Los Arcos" comes from the 19th-century brick aqueduct (now in ruins) near the original restaurant. Times change, however, and now a flood of local middle- and upper-class customers return to enjoy dozens of impeccably prepared and served fresh choices, from oysters on the half shell and clam chowder *(crema de almeja)* ($5) to stuffed *corbina* fillet and fresh trout *(trucha,* $14). Reservations are recommended for both lunch and dinner; credit cards accepted; family atmosphere.

Move south, along San Ignacio, to the vicinity of the Chapalita Circle, where a number of restaurants offer good choices. For a little bit of everything in an informal family atmosphere, try **❰ Restaurant New York, New York** (Av. San Ignacio 1197, open Mon.–Sat. 8 A.M.–midnight, Sun. 8 A.M.–10 P.M., tel. 33/3121-2606 or 33/3121-8657), right on the Chapalita Circle's west quadrant. You can enjoy professional service and a long list of familiar options, such as hot cakes, waffles, or eggs any style for

breakfast ($4–8), soup (try *tlalpeño,* $4) and a hamburger ($5) for lunch, or starve up for supper and splurge with the salad bar and a T-bone steak ($15). Stay late enough to enjoy the live music Friday–Saturday 10 P.M.–midnight. Credit cards accepted.

Diagonally across the Chapalita Circle, try the **Café Dalí** (Av. Guadalupe 1144, tel. 33/3343-9038, open Mon.–Sat. 8 A.M.–midnight, Sun. 9 A.M.–11 P.M.), where, beneath a surreal faux Salvador Dalí ceiling and wall mural, you can select from a list of fondues, crepes, salads, baguette sandwiches ($4–8), or meat and chicken entrées ($8–15). The many tasty coffees also make this a good spot for breakfast.

For upscale elegance, go four blocks east (toward Calz. Lázaro Cárdenas) to Argentine **❰ Restaurant Bariloche** (Av. Guadalupe 721, tel. 33/3122-4270 or 33/3122-3270, open Tues.–Sun. 8 A.M.–midnight), at the corner of Fernando Alvo de Ixtlilxochitl (eeks-tleel-soh-CHEE-tl). You can start out the morning with your pick from two pages of scrumptious American or Mexican-style breakfasts, from hot cakes and omelets to *huevos rancheros* and *chilaquiles* ($5–12). For lunch and dinner, the emphasis shifts to meat, wine, and entertainment, specializing in gaucho-style barbecue: four stars for *vacioderes* juicy filet ($18), poultry pampa-style ($14), and broiled fresh trout ($16). Lighter eaters can pick from a list of good salads, soups, and pastas. Other pluses include plenty of good Argentine red wines ($15–30) and a brilliant Friday–Saturday tango show, begining at 9:30 P.M. Reservations are recommended anytime for dinner and are essential for the show. Credit cards accepted.

For calm, cool elegance and fine food, go three blocks west (a block before Calz. Lázaro Cárdenas) to **❰ Che Mary** (shay-mah-REE) (Guadalupe 596, corner of San Rafael, tel. 33/3121-2951, open Mon.–Sat. 1 P.M.–midnight, Sun. 1–6 P.M.). Although the restaurant's name appears to promise French cuisine, you will instead enjoy a culinary journey through old Iberia, complete with sentimental country wall scenes and lilting guitar and orchestral melodies in the background. For appetizers, you might start with *esparragos Aranjuez* ($5); for soup, continue with *gazpacho a la Andaluza* (chilled vegetable soup, $6); and for your main course try *robalo a la Vasco* (Basque-style white fish, $16) or prime rib with gravy ($18). After all that, including a good bottle of old-country red or white wine ($15–30), who needs to go to Spain?

INFORMATION AND SERVICES

Many services are available. Around Plaza del Sol, study the kiosk at the Avenida López Mateos entrance and follow the map to the source inside.

A similar abundance of services is available around the Chapalita village corner of Avenida Tepeyac and Avenida de las Rosas. Within a block in any of the four directions, you have three banks with ATMs, Internet access, beauty shop, barber, locksmith, bookstore, laundry and dry cleaners, TV repair, natural food, car repair, pharmacy, and shoe repair.

Tourist Information

English-speaking travel services are available at the highly recommended **Expoviajes** (Tepeyac 487, tel. 33/3122-1455 or 33/3121-1794), about three blocks east of Avenida de las Rosas, past and across Tepeyac from the church.

Banking

Right at the corner of Avenidas Tepeyac and de las Rosas, you have **Bancomer** (tel. 33/3122-3338, open Mon.–Fri. 8:30 A.M.–4 P.M.) on the northeast corner, **Banco Santander Serfín** (tel. 33/3647-0509, open Mon.–Fri. 9 A.M.–4 P.M.) on the northwest corner, and, on the southwest corner, with the longest hours of all, **HSBC** (tel. 33/3647-0391, open Mon.–Fri. 8 A.M.–7 P.M., Sat. 8 A.M.–3 P.M.). Other bank options include another **Bancomer** (on the Chapalita Circle, tel. 33/3122-2241, open Mon.–Fri. 8:30 A.M.–4 P.M., Sat. 10 A.M.–3 P.M.) and, five blocks east of that, **Scotiabank Inverlat** (corner of Guadalupe and Boturini, open Mon.–Fri. 9 A.M.–5 P.M.).

Post and Telecommunications

Chapalita residents enjoy an efficient, up-to-date **post office** (tel. 33/3121-4004, open Mon.–Fri. 8 A.M.–7 P.M., Sat. 9 A.M.–1 P.M.), on Tepeyac, in the second block (past Librería Sandi), west of the Avenida de las Rosas corner. Services include a stamp-dispensing machine (exceptional for Mexico), lots of P.O. boxes, and reliable Mexpost mail service.

Long-hours **Internet access** ($2/hour) is available at **Trinity and Neos Cyber Café** (Av. Guadalupe 1162, local 4, tel. 33/3647-4155, open Mon.–Sat. 9 A.M.–10 P.M., Sun. 11 A.M.–8 P.M.), on the Chapalita Circle's northeast quadrant, by Dairy Queen. Also available are printer, fax, and computer classes.

Laundry

Go to **Laundromat Aguamatic** (tel. 33/3641-7202, open daily 7 A.M.–10 P.M.), on the southeast corner of Av. de las Rosas and Tepeyac.

Photography

Get your film developed and your camera repaired at **Laboratorios Julio** (Guadalupe 1162, local 7, tel. 33/3587-1728, on the Chapalita Circle, open Mon.–Fri. 9 A.M.–8 P.M., Sat. 9 A.M.–7 P.M., closed Sun.). As a branch of the big citywide chain, it offers virtually all photo services, plus in-house quick development, popular films, and some SLR and point-and-shoot cameras and supplies.

Bookstores

Two excellent bookstores serve local residents. In the Plaza del Sol, go to **Librería Mexico** (just inside the López Mateos entrance, tel. 33/3121-0114, open daily 8:30 A.M.–9:30 P.M.), with many dozens of Mexican and U.S. magazines.

In Chapalita, all roads seem to lead to community information center and bookstore **Librería Sandi** (Tepeyac 718, tel. 33/3121-0863, fax 33/3647-4600, sandibooks@sandibooks.com, www.sandibooks.com, open Mon.–Fri. 9:30 A.M.–7 P.M., Sat. 9:30 A.M.–2 P.M.), two doors west (past Banco Santander Serfín) of the Avenida de las Rosas corner.

SOR JUANA INÉS DE LA CRUZ

Sor (Sister) Juana Inés de la Cruz was baptized Juana Inés Ramírez de Abaje in Mexico City, on December 2, 1648. Her remarkable talents began to surface early when she taught herself to read at the age of three. Soon she learned Latin in order to access its broad literature. A natural poet, Sor Juana began writing lyrics of life and love during her latter teenage years as lady-in-waiting to the Mexican viceroy's wife, the Marquesa de Mancera.

Rejecting the option of a life of court intrigue, marriage, and child-rearing, Sor Juana instead chose to follow her intellectual passion by entering the cloister. She first joined the ultra-austere Barefoot Carmelites, but soon quit in favor of the less strict Sisters of San Jerónimo in 1669, at the age of 21.

She was an unusual nun from the outset. Into her cell she eventually packed a 4,000-volume library and a small orchestra of violins, guitars, and lutes. She received a continuous stream of Mexico City intelligentsia and literary collaborators. During her most productive years, the 1670s and 1680s, Sor Juana wrote extensively, in many styles, from sonnets (many of love) to plays (both alone and in collaboration) to a lengthy poem, *Primero Sueño*

(First Dream), outlining her social and political ideas. The wit and charisma of her work earned her the unofficial title of "Mexico's Tenth Muse."

Eventually, however, church authorities couldn't tolerate such a free spirit under their ecclesiastical roof. In her famous defense, *Reply to Sister Philotea of the Cross,* Sor Juana argues for a woman's right to pursue intellectual freedom.

Nevertheless, she heeded the authorities' admonitions and, around 1690, sadly sold her library and musical instruments and gave the proceeds to charity. Returning to a strictly cloistered life, Sor Juana volunteered to nurse victims of an epidemic. Tragically contracting the disease herself, she died in Mexico City on April 17, 1695, at the age of 46.

A considerable body of Sor Juana literature is available in English. Check out *Women in Hispanic Literature: Icons and Fallen Idols*, Beth Miller, editor, 1983; *A Sor Juana Anthology*, Alan Trueblood, 1988; *Sor Juana: Or, the Traps of Faith*, Octavio Paz, 1988; *Plotting Women: Gender and Representation in Mexico*, Jean Franco, 1989; and *Coded Encounters: Writing, Gender, and Ethnicity in Colonial Latin America*, Francisco J. Cevallos-Candau, editor, 1994.

WEST AND NORTH

First, be sure to pick up a copy of the very useful *Guadalajara Colony Reporter* newspaper and the Miami *Herald.* Then browse around and appreciate the best English-language book selection in western Mexico, with a book and magazine selection as complete as your neighborhood bookstore back home. Before you leave, you might be interested in looking over the community bulletin board.

Libraries

Both the **American Society of Jalisco** and the **American Legion Post 3** maintain general English-language libraries. Collections, although heavy on paperback novels, include guidebooks, cookbooks, histories, and travel literature of Mexico.

Community Organizations

At least two local organizations offer assistance to and encourage participation by Guadalajara newcomers. Very welcoming is the **American Society of Jalisco** (San Francisco 3332, tel./fax 33/3121-2395, open Mon.–Fri. 10 A.M.–2:30 P.M., except games day Thurs. 11 A.M.–4 P.M., amsoc@megared.net.mx, www.amsocmexico.com).

Besides a very respectable library, the American Society of Jalisco maintains a small café and clubroom and always tries to have an information volunteer on duty. Among their services (see their website) they offer low-cost Spanish lessons (Mon. and Wed, 11 A.M.) and free aerobics classes (Mon., Wed. and Fri. 9:30 A.M.) and maintain a community bulletin board, especially useful for finding rooms and bed-and-breakfast rentals. They welcome newcomers to their evening social Fri. 7–11 P.M. Watch the Community Calendar pages of the *Guadalajara Colony Reporter* (available at Librería Sandi, or through www.guadalajarareporter.com) for announcements of their social events.

Get to their headquarters from the north side of Calzada Lázaro Cárdenas, two blocks west of its intersection with Avenida Guadalupe, where you follow Avenida San Gabriel one long block north to San Francisco, then turn left (west) and continue one short block to the headquarters, at the corner of Fco. Javier, on the north side, opposite the Colegio Guadalupe.

The American Legion Post 3 (San Antonio 143, Colonia Las Fuentes, tel. 33/3631-1208, www.americanlegionpost3.tripod.com) offers a number of social activites for the English-speaking community. These include a Saturday morning breakfast (9:30–11 A.M.), Sunday afternoon dinner (2 P.M.) and a Thursday evening dinner-dance ("Strut your stuff" 7–11 P.M.). You need not be a veteran or legionnaire to participate.

Get there from Plaza del Sol by continuing south, via car or taxi, along Avenida López Mateos about three miles to Avenida Las Fuentes; turn right and continue two very long blocks to the Las Fuentes traffic circle. Follow San Antonio, one of the streets that radiate, like the spokes of a wheel, from the circle.

Spanish Language Instruction

Guadalajara community organizations, schools, and individuals offer Spanish classes and tutoring. The most moderately priced ($5 per session) are offered by the American Society of Jalisco Monday and Wednesday at 11 A.M.

A neighborhood **Spanish Language School** (Ermita 1443. tel. 33/3121-4774, spanscho@prodigy.net.mx, www.spanschool .com.mx) offers moderately-priced classes. For more information, contact the director, Julia Barra, Mon.–Fri. 8:30 A.M.–1:30 P.M. Get there, from the Avenida de las Rosas–

Tepeyac corner, by walking three blocks south along Av. de las Rosas to Ermita, then one block west.

Experienced Instructor **Barbara Wallace** (tel. 33/3673-2140) regularly conducts Spanish-language classes and offers tutorial service.

For more language study options, see the *Downtown* chapter and the *Minerva-Chapultepec* section of this chapter. You might also look under Instruction in the classified section of *Guadalajara Colony Reporter* newspaper.

Medical Services

For simple remedies, consult the on-duty pharmacist at one of the several local pharmacies. For example, in Plaza del Sol, try **Farmacia ABC** (in Zone B, local 13, tel. 33/3647-4839, open daily 8 A.M.–10 P.M.).

In Chapalita, go to the **24-hour Farmacia Guadalajara** (Av. Tepeyac, one block east of Av. de las Rosas, next to the church, tel. 33/3121-2580 or 33/3121-2581), with an

Chapalita's Petite Park at Guadalupe Circle features a monument to Sister Juana Inés de la Cruz, an early Mexican feminist.

© BRUCE WHIPPERMAN

on-duty pharmacist, an extensive selection of over-the-counter medications, and some grocery and deli items to boot.

For a doctor, follow your hotel's recommendation, inquire at the American Society of Jalisco, or consult one of the several highly recommended doctors listed under *Local Medical Services* in the *Essentials* chapter at the end of this book.

GETTING AROUND

Of course, taxis are always convenient, but if you need to save money, handy buses run frequently through the Plaza del Sol–Chapalita district. The *Minerva-Chapultepec* map shows bus routes. Very useful is **line 258A,** which connects downtown with the Plaza del Sol and beyond. From the downtown corner of Alcalde and San Felipe, two blocks north of the cathedral, the 258A runs west along San Felipe and its western extension, Avenida Mexico. At Avenida López Mateos, the bus turns left, southwest, and runs past Plaza del Sol, continuing past Avenida Patria, where it returns by virtually the same route.

For the Chapalita–downtown connection, ride either **bus 51A** or **51B.** Both buses start at the downtown corner of Libertad and 16 de Septiembre and continue west along La Paz, to A. Yañez. They turn left, south, at Yañez, to Niños Héroes. There, they turn right, west, and continue west along Guadalupe to the Chapalita Circle, at the intersection of Avenidas de las Rosas and Guadalupe. At the Chapalita Circle, they trace different routes. The 51A continues west on Guadalupe all the way to its terminal at the west *periférico*. The 51B heads south a block to Tepeyac, where it turns right, west, and continues west along Tepeyac, turning left at Avenida Patria and right at Avenida El Colli, continuing all way to its terminal at Colonia El Colli past the *periférico*. Both buses return by the same routes, except at A. Yañez eastbound, they continue east along Lerdo de Tejada to Chapultepec, where they turn left, north, for two blocks to Libertad, where they turn right, east, and continue downtown to 16 de Septiembre.

Zapopan

The midsize provincial town of Zapopan (sah-POH-pahn) is one of Guadalajara's best-kept secrets. It is the *cabercera* (headquarters) of a spreading 345-square-mile (895-square-kilometer), fabulously productive *municipio* (township, municipality) with a population well over one million and more than sixfold the land area of the *municipio* of Guadalajara.

A glance at a detailed map of the Guadalajara metropolitan zone (see the front page map in this book) reveals that much of Guadalajara's upscale western suburb is actually part of the Zapopan *municipio*. Within its jurisdiction, Zapopan encompasses the metropolitan area's three top shopping plazas, the Plaza del Sol, Gran Plaza, and Plaza Patria, and a big fraction of Guadalajara's super-deluxe hotels, including three of the top four: the Crowne Plaza, Presidente Intercontinental, and Camino Real. Add to that the burgeoning new Zapopan industrial parks, from Avenida López Mateos Sur (Motorola, Kodak) to Belén in the north (Interlub, Bardahl Oil), and the hundreds of thousands of acres of fertile corn and cattle hinterland and you have the fifth-richest *municipio* in Mexico, producing a larger peso gross product than any one of several entire Mexican states.

PLANNING YOUR TIME

Zapopan in-town sights are well worth the few hours that they require. Start at the **Basílica de Nuestra Señora de Zapopan** (half hour) then continue to the **Museo Huichol Wirrarica** and the Museo de la Virgen (one hour). See the mural in the Zapopan town hall and the town market (half hour), then stroll downhill, through the Plaza de las Americas, to Zapopan's neo-baroque **entrance arch.**

If you have an extra day, venture to Zapopan's out-of-town sights, which include the grand tropical **canyon of the Río Santiago,** viewable at the famously tall **Cola del Caballo** waterfall, or also canyon-view *balneario* **Los Camachos** water park; venerable **Ixcatán** colonial-era town and church, lovely old

Hacienda Santa Lucia, and **Huaxtla** village warm springs and traditional healing site. It's best to arrange a guided tour for all of this.

HISTORY

It requires a look at history to understand how all this came about. Once upon a time, Zapopan was a small rural town, with miles of country separating it from the center of power and wealth in Guadalajara. At that time, Zapopan people were much more concerned with corn and cattle than politics and power. Zapopan's municipal leaders looked to their western hinterland, home of their patrons, the rich *hacendados* who tended cattle on huge swaths of valley and mountain territory.

Meanwhile, Guadalajara's prosperous investors gradually pushed development westward; they bought great tracts of land, which they filled with the streets, homes, and businesses that inexorably overflowed the west side, from south to north, engulfing the small town of Zapopan.

Nevertheless, old Zapopan lives on, home to those who quietly adhere to the old-Mexico values that are reflected by their credo that Zapopan is the "Land of Friendship, Work, and Respect." And as part and parcel of their traditions, Zapopan people proudly continue to welcome the multitudes of faithful who arrive to pay their respects to the miraculous Virgen de Zapopan.

The Virgin of Zapopan

Although the early history of Zapopan (Place of the Zapote Trees) as a settlement of the mystery-draped Chicomoztoc people, is uncertain, the origin of Zapopan's miraculous Virgin is not. The Virgin, considered to be the very founder of the town, was first known as the "Virgin of the Pacification" because, probably more than anyone or anything else, she was responsible for extinguishing the fiery rebellion known as the Mixtón War.

The story begins with Antonio de Segovia,

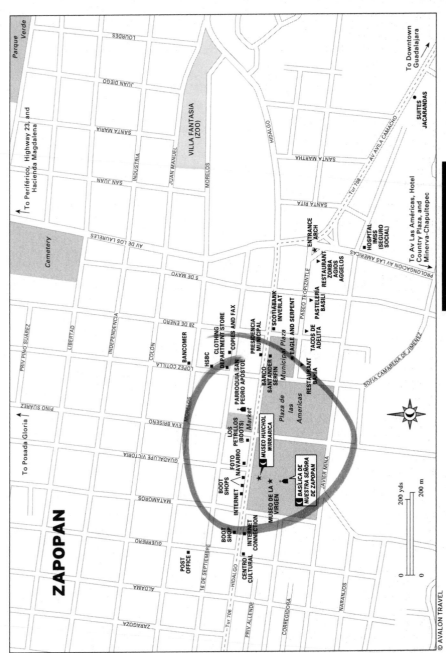

WEST AND NORTH

ZAPOPAN

Parque Verde

To Periférico, Highway 23, and Hacienda Magdalena

LOURDES

JUAN DIEGO

SANTA MARIA

INDUSTRIA

SAN JUAN

JUAN MANUEL

VILLA FANTASIA (ZOO)

MORELOS

HIDALGO

To Downtown Guadalajara

SUITES JACARANDAS

AV AVILA CAMACHO

SANTA MARTHA

Tur 706

SANTA RITA

To Av Las Américas, Hotel Country Plaza, and Minerva-Chapultepec

Cemetery

AV DE LOS LAURELES

5 DE MAYO

ENTRANCE ARCH

HOSPITAL IMSS (SEGURO SOCIAL)

PROLONGACIÓN AV LAS AMÉRICAS

PASEO TEOPIZINTLE

RESTAURANT ZONBA AGIOS AGGELOS

PASTELERIA BASILI

PRIV PINO SUÁREZ

LIBERTAD

INDEPENDENCIA

28 DE ENERO

COLON

BANCOMER

HSBC

CLOTHING DEPARTMENT STORE

COPIES AND FAX

SCOTIABANK INVERLAT

PRESIDENCIA MUNICIPAL

EAGLE AND SERPENT

TACOS DE ADELITA

LOPEZ COTILLA

PARROQUIA SAN PEDRO APÓSTOL

BANCO SANTANDER SERFIN

Municipal Plaza

PINO SUÁREZ

To Posada Gloria

MORELOS

EVA BRISEÑO

Market

LOS PETRILLOS (BOOTS)

Plaza de las Americas

RESTAURANT BAHIA

GUADALUPE VICTORIA

FOTO NAVARRO

MUSEO HUICHOL WIRRARICA

BOOT SHOPS

INTERNET

MUSEO DE LA VIRGEN

BASILICA DE NUESTRA SEÑORA DE ZAPOPAN

JAVIER MINA

SOFÍA CAMARENA DE JIMENEZ

MATAMOROS

GUERRERO

BOOT SHOP

INTERNET CONNECTION

200 yds

200 m

ALDAMA

POST OFFICE

16 DE SEPTIEMBRE

CENTRO CULTURAL

HIDALGO

Tur 706

0

0

PRIV ALLENDE

ZARAGOZA

CORREGIDORA

NARANJOS

© AVALON TRAVEL

a poor Jesuit missionary friar, who had come from Michoacán around 1530, carrying a corn-paste figurine that had been thought miraculous by his indigenous converts in Michoacán. He continued his mission in Jalisco for 10 years, converting the local people with the humble image, which he carried on his chest.

In 1541, alarmed and saddened by the Mixtón rebellion's carnage and destruction, friar Antonio traveled north to the rebellion's crucible, in remote country north of Guadalajara. There, on December 8, 1541, and with nothing more than the frail figure tied to the front of his robe, Segovia confronted a hostile band of natives near the town of Apozol, in the mountains about 50 miles (80 km) north of Zapopan. Segovia's sermon must have been powerful, for soon the natives began seeing a mysterious, brilliantly overpowering light radiating from the figure. Eventually captivated by the Virgin's power, the natives fell to their knees and surrendered their arms. The word spread and within weeks the Mixtón War was over.

Father Segovia brought the miraculous Virgin south to the nearest settlement, at Zapopan, where the local townspeople accepted her as their own, on December 8, 1542, one year exactly after the original miracle. The very same miraculous figure, now called the Virgin of Zapopan, is feted in a grand procession of many hundreds of thousands of Guadalajarans every October 12.

GETTING ORIENTED

The heart of Zapopan is small, easy to know, and accessible on foot. The town's axis runs east-west, from the welcoming entrance arch on the east side. Uphill, west, past the arch, visitors stroll beside the sidewalk restaurants of the **Paseo Teopizintle** and the flag-decorated **Plaza de las Américas,** finally arriving at the towering **Basílica de Zapopan** that shelters Zapopan's beloved patron.

The commercial heart of town concentrates along a single street, Avenida Hidalgo, that similarly runs east–west, a block north of the basilica. Besides the usual commercial establishments, along Hidalgo you'll also find

the **municipal plaza,** the *presidencia municipal* (town hall), the **Parroquia San Pedro Apóstol,** and the town **market.**

SIGHTS
Basílica de Nuestra Señora de Zapopan

Arrive first at the soaring baroque basilica (begun in 1690, finished in 1730), home of the beloved Virgin of Zapopan. The volcanic stone facade's richly ornate style is called "plateresque" because it resembles the scroll designs first found on elaborate 17th-century silver-plated tableware.

Inside the basilica, the legendary image, one of the beloved "three sister" virgins (see the sidebar *The Three Sisters of Jalisco* in the *Guadalajara Getaways* chapter), has enjoyed generations of popularity so enormous that it must be seen to be believed. Local folks, whenever they happen by, often stop to say a prayer (or at least make the sign of the cross as they pass) in front of the cathedral gate. Some faithful crawl the

Upwards of a million folks a year visit the Virgin of Zapopan at her basilica.

© BRUCE WHIPPERMAN

length of the sanctuary to pay their respects to the diminutive blue-and-white figure. The adoration peaks during the **Romería** procession, on October 12, when a crowd of many hundreds of thousands accompanies the Virgin of Zapopan (affectionately known as "La Generala") from the downtown Guadalajara cathedral home to Zapopan, where she stays October 13–May 20.

◖ Museo Huichol Wirrarica

Exit the basilica, turn left a few steps, and have a look inside the small but excellent adjacent Museo Huichol Wirrarica (Huichol Museum Wirrarica) (tel. 33/3636-4430, open Mon.–Sat. 9:30 A.M.–1:30 P.M. and 3–6 P.M., Sun. 10 A.M.–2 P.M.), founded in 1961 by Franciscan friar Ernesto Loera. The Huichol, who call themselves the Wirraritari ("people who inhabit places of thorny plants"), are among the most resistant to modernization of Mexico's indigenous peoples. For centuries they have retired to their high homeland strongholds in mountainous Nayarit and Jalisco and fought off conversion and Mexicanization. As a result, their traditions remain strong. (See the sidebar *The Huichol.*)

Don't miss the fine examples of Huichol Indian handicrafts in the adjoining museum shop. Sale items include eerie beaded masks, intriguing yarn paintings, and *ojos de dios* (God's eyes) yarn sculptures. For more information on Huichol history and traditions, purchase the excellent English language pamphlet *Wirraritari.*

Museo de la Virgen

Don't miss the very interesting Museum of the Virgin, next to the Huichol Museum, open approximately the same hours. You'll find mementos and excellent, detailed exhibits of the Virgin of Zapopan's history.

Plazas, Town Hall, Church, and Market

From the basilica, walk downhill, east, two blocks along Hidalgo to the broad **civic plaza,** on the north (left) side of the street, flanked by

dignified old-world-style municipal offices and banks. Just above street level, contemplate the dramatic eagle and the serpent bronze sculpture. It represents the story, preserved in ancient records, of the founding of the Aztec capital of Tenochtitlán in the Valley of Mexico in 1325. After wandering over western Mexico for generations, the Aztecs came upon what soothsayers had predicted: an eagle with a serpent in its beak, at the very spot where they should build their capital.

Continue north across Hidalgo to the *presidencia municipal* (town hall) and take a look at the 1970 mural *The Universal Revolution,* in three panels, by muralist Guillermo Chávez Vega.

The center panel depicts a young woman in red pointing toward the future, while around her, giant hands reach out for goals not yet realized. Independence and revolution heroes Hidalgo, Madero, Villa, Zapata, Carranza, Obregón, Calles, and Cárdenas stand guard. In the left panel a nude woman, surrounded by doves of peace and the muralist's heroes Ho Chi Minh, Fidel Castro, Vladimir Lenin, and Karl Marx all preside. Finally, on the mural's right side, another nude woman, with the wings of an angel, represents the spirit of freedom, triumphing over capitalist villains, including Napoleon, who ruthlessly substitute machines for man.

Continue uphill along Hidalgo, across Emiliano Zapata, one block to the parish church **Parroquia San Pedro Apóstol,** finished in 1819. Inside is a notable painting, the *Baptism of Jesus,* by the renowned 17th-century painter Juan Correa.

Continue uphill behind the church to the colorful local **market** (corner of Pino Suárez and Hidalgo), festooned with fruit stalls and *fondas* brimming with steaming pots of *guisados* (stews), piles of hot tamales, and *cazuelas* (clay pots) of savory chiles rellenos.

Return south across the civic plaza to the spreading **Plaza de las Americas,** marked by the lineup of the 28 flags of all the American republics. Turn downhill and stroll past the sidewalk restaurants along Paseo Teopizintle (named for the Aztec god of corn).

THE HUICHOL

Because the Huichol have retained more of their traditional religion than perhaps any other group of indigenous Mexicans, they offer a glimpse into the lives and beliefs of dozens of now-vanished Mesoamerican peoples.

Although many have migrated to Western Mexico towns and cities such as Tepic and Guadalajara, several thousand Huichol remain in their ancestral heartland – roughly 100 miles (160 km) northwest of Guadalajara as the crow flies. They cultivate corn and raise cattle on 400 *rancherías* in five municipalities not far from the winding Río Altengo valley: Guadalupe Ocotán in Nayarit, Tuxpan de Bolaños, San Sebastián Teponahuaxtlán, Santa Catarina, and Huejuquilla El Alto in Jalisco.

Although studied by a procession of researchers since Carl Lumholtz's seminal work in the 1890s, the remote Huichol and their religion remain enigmatic. As Lumholtz said, "Religion to them is a personal matter, not an institution, and therefore their life is religion – from the cradle to the grave, wrapped up in symbolism."

Hints of what it means to be Huichol come from their art. Huichol art contains representations of the prototype deities – Grandfather Sun, Grandmother Earth, Brother Deer, Mother Maize – that once guided the destinies of many North American peoples. It blooms with tangible religious symbols, from green-faced Grandmother Earth (Tatei Urianaka) and the dripping Rain Goddess (Tatei Matiniera) to the ray-festooned Grandfather Sun (Tayau) and the antlered folk hero Brother Kauyumari, forever battling the evil sorcerer Kieri.

The Huichol are famous for their use of the hallucinogen peyote, their bridge to the divine. The humble cactus – from which the peyote

© BRUCE WHIPPERMAN

Cuadras (rectangular yarn paintings) depict the important figures (such as antlered hero Kauyumari and the demon Kieri at the bottom border) of the Huichol pantheon.

"buttons" are gathered and eaten – grows in the Huichol's Elysian land of Wirikuta, in the San Luis Potosí desert 300 miles (480 km) east of their homeland, near the town of Real de Catorce.

To the Huichol, a journey to Wirikuta is a dangerous trip to heaven. Preparations go on for weeks and include innumerable prayers and ceremonies, as well as the crafting of feathered arrows, bowls, gourds, and paintings for the gods who live along the way. Only the chosen – village shamans, temple elders, those fulfilling vows or seeking visions – may make the journey. Each participant in effect becomes a god, whose identity and very life are divined and protected by the shaman en route to Wirikuta.

Entrance Arch

Farther downhill you'll pass the gushing, monumental fountain supported by a squad of kneeling, naked cherubs, and arrive at Zapopan's neo-baroque entry arch at the bottom of the hill. Erected generations ago in memory of the city's indigenous founders, the arch abounds with symbolism: the god and goddess of corn in the side niches; at the top center, Diana the Huntress, and above her, at the summit, an eagle, guardian of all. The arch was the work of architect Guillermo González Ibarra and his wife, María del Carmen Rabago, who sculpted the reliefs and statues that adorn the arch's sides and facade.

Sights Outside of Town

Good roads lead from Zapopan town to its spreading rancho and mountain hinterland, famous for the **Barranca**, the 2,000-foot-deep canyon of the Río Santiago. At the viewpoint **Mirador Dr. Atl** (past San Isidro, around Km 15, Saltillo Highway 54), motorists stop to admire the canyon vista and the waterfall **Cola del Caballo** (Horse's Tail) as it plummets hundreds of feet to the river below.

Past that, a small paradise of springs decorates the lush canyonland. First comes **Los Camachos** (Km 17, tel. 33/3122-4034, open daily 8 A.M.–6 P.M.), a forest and mountain-framed *balneario* (bathing park) with pools and restaurants; a few miles farther along is the hot spring bathing complex **Balneario Nuevo Paraíso** (Km 24).

About a half mile farther (follow the left side road from the highway) stop at **Ixcatán,** ancient village of *arrieros* (mule-drivers), whose animals for centuries carried charcoal here for sale.

Admire the picturesque old town **church,** graced by a quaint, triple-arched belfry, with a trio of old bronze bells, two inscribed with the dates of 1834 and 1791; the third is illegible, but it probably dates from around 1700. The lintel over the entrance bears inscriptions of 1691 and 20th of November 1726, presumably marking the beginning and end of construction. Before leaving, examine the stones in the church's front yard, which bear map-like

inscriptions, speculated to be directions to safe havens during the Mixtón War, which blazed around these parts in 1541–1542.

Get to the Barranca from the Guadalajara city center by tour, car, or taxi via Highway 54, the Saltillo-Zacatecas highway, which heads northward along Avenida Alcalde from the city-center cathedral. Bus riders can go via the "Los Camachos" bus #S-165 (which continues to Ixcatán and which leaves the Normal Circle, on Avenida Alcalde about a mile north of the downtown cathedral, about every hour from 5 A.M. until the early afternoon).

Alternatively, from the Zapopan basilica, take a taxi or ride an Ixcatán-labeled bus from Avenida Hidalgo, or drive north, easiest along Avenida Laureles main boulevard, nine blocks north of the basilica, to the *periférico*. Turn right (east) and continue about a mile to signaled San Isidro side road, the northerly extension of Avenida José María Pino Suárez. Turn left and continue straight ahead, about five miles (eight km), through the lush green San Isidro canyon country home development and golf course, to Saltillo Highway 54, where you should turn left and continue a few miles to Los Camachos (Km 24) and the Ixcatán sign (Km 25).

Hacienda Santa Lucia

West of town, the venerable Hacienda Santa Lucia (Calle Juan Manuel Ruvalcaba 139, Santa Lucia, Zapopan 45200, tel./fax 33/3897-0788, haciendasantaluciai@prodigy.net.mx) is the most accessible of Zapopan's several old country haciendas. At its largest extent during the 1800s, it encompassed around 60,000 acres of wheat, corn, and cattle. Now, it still encloses a very respectable 10,000 acres; and moreover its Zaragoza family owners welcome visitors (on specified weekdays or by appointment) and are renting out its beautiful garden for weddings and parties.

The hacienda's features include a crumbling former company store, the "Taberna" former mescal factory, and an elaborate family chapel, with baroque Spanish *retablo* and saint, Santa Lucia, brought from Italy. For more information, contact the hacienda directly, in Spanish.

Get there from Zapopan downtown by private tour or taxi, via the road to Tesistán, Avenida Hidalgo's western extension, past the *periférico* eight miles (about 12 km) to Tesistán. After passing the Tesistán plaza and church, turn left on (another) Avenida Hidalgo and continue another half mile (one km) to the hacienda, at the Santa Lucia village plaza. By bus, similarly go from Avenida Hidalgo via bus S-160 to Nextipac, which passes through Tesistán and Santa Lucia.

Huaxtla Village and Warm Springs

If you start early enough, on the same day as a visit to Hacienda Santa Lucia you can continue to Huaxtla, the semitropical canyon-slope village famous for its curative *aguas termales* (warm springs), open daily 9 A.M.–5 P.M. The paved but narrow and steep access road affords magnificent views of the lush tropical Barranca (canyon of the Río Santiago).

At Huaxtla village itself, great old *higuera* (wild fig) trees shade a big bathing pool of blue-tinted (from natural sulfur) warm spring water. The people are friendly and welcoming. Bring a picnic and enjoy the afternoon.

Get there from downtown Zapopan via the road to Tesistán (as described under *Hacienda Santa Lucia*). But, about six miles (10 km) past the *periférico,* turn right (or left, if doubling back from Hacienda Santa Lucia) on to the road to Colotlán, Highway 23. After approximately another 10 miles (16 km; if the main highway descends into the canyon, turn around—you went too far) and follow a narrow paved side road to the right. Continue, enjoying the airy canyon vistas, another approximately five miles (eight km) to Huaxtla village and the springs.

ENTERTAINMENT AND EVENTS

Zapopan people stick close to home, relying upon friends and family for most entertainment. Families, especially on Friday and Saturday evenings, enjoy strolling along the **Paseo Teopizintle,** Zapopan's favorite people-

Huaxtla villagers welcome visitors to come and soak in their therapeutic warm sulfur spring.

watching ground, and listening to the strolling mariachi bands.

Religious Festivities

Excitement peaks at Zapopan's yearly country religious festivals. Church-linked neighborhood clubs, called *mayordomias,* organize a list of events—processions, *mañanintas* (early masses), barbecues, dances, carnival rides and games, food stalls—that highlight each religious festival.

If you're in the Zapopan vicinity at certain times, join the festivities at the local church: January 18, fireworks at the Zapopan basilica; May 20, departure of the Virgin from the Zapopan basilica; July 25, Santiago (St. James) festival in Nextipac, Santa Ana Tepatitlán, and San Juan de Ocotán; July (last Sunday), Virgen del Refugio festival, in El Batán; August 15, fair of the Virgen de la Asunción, in La Experiencia; September 8, festival of the Señora de Loreto, in Santa Ana Tepatitlán; October (third Sunday), festival of Santo Domingo, in Tesistán;

November 22, festival of Santa Cecilia, in Tesistán; December 1–8, festival of the foundation of Zapopan, in Zapopan; December 12, festival of the Virgin of Guadalupe, everywhere.

The one festival that you won't be able to avoid noticing if you're present on October 12, **La Romería de la Virgen de Zapopan**, is a grand stroll of a million Guadalajara merrymakers and dozens of dance troupes who accompany the Virgin from the Guadalajara cathedral to the Zapopan basilica.

SPORTS AND RECREATION

Greater Guadalajara's prime walking, hiking, jogging, and horseback-riding ground, **Bosque Los Colomos** (tel. 33/3641-7633, open daily 9 A.M.–7 P.M.), is only 1.5 miles due south from Zapopan. Bring a picnic and romp, ride, run, or relax to your heart's content.

Park extras include a Japanese garden, bird lake, and big cactus garden. The closest Colomos entrance is at Avenida Patria 1805, on the park's north side. (For more details, see the *Bosque Los Colomos* section in the *Minerva-Chapultepec* section, earlier in this chapter.)

Golf

Zapopan golf enthusiasts enjoy the 18-hole **Las Cañadas Country Club** course (tel. 33/3685-0363 or 33/3685-0412, open 7 A.M.–6 P.M.). Greens fees run about $55 weekdays, $75 Saturday and Sunday. Arrive early for breakfast, or relax afterward at the restaurant. Get there by car or taxi via the *periférico* northwest of Zapopan. At the intersection of the *periférico* and the highway to Tesistán, turn right, east, and continue about a mile to the signaled **road to San Isidro,** the northerly extension of Zapopan Avenida José María Pino Suárez. Turn left (north) and continue straight ahead, winding about five miles (eight km) through the lush green San Isidro country home development and golf course. The driveway is on the left.

SHOPPING
Downtown Zapopan

For general shopping, you can get much of what you need on Avenida Hidalgo downtown.

For fruit, vegetables, and groceries, go to the municipal **market** a block downhill and north of the basilica, at the corner of Hidalgo and Eva Briseño; in the block adjacent to the basilica there are pharmacies and a photography shop, **Foto Navarro** (Hidalgo 88, tel. 33/3365-7890, open Mon.–Sat. 10 A.M.–8 P.M.). In the same block, you'll also find good **boot shops,** such as Los Potrillos (Hidalgo 12, tel. 33/3208-4633, open Mon.–Sat. 10 A.M.–8 P.M., Sun. 10 A.M.–6 P.M.) that continue the Zapopan rural *vaquero* (cowboy) tradition, catering to both cowboys and cowboy wannabees. A block north of Hidalgo, behind the *presidencia municipal,* you'll find a small photocopy shop.

General **handicrafts** are available at small stores and stalls on Paseo Teopizintle (open daily 10 A.M.–8 P.M.), just downhill from the sidewalk restaurants. Select from a modest all-Zapopan assortment, including candles and candlesticks, wooden knickknacks, glassware, corn husk dolls (like the Virgin of Zapopan), religious art, tiles, and much more.

Plaza Patria

For lots more general shopping opportunities, go to Plaza Patria (tel. 33/3641-3094), about a mile southwest of downtown Zapopan along Avenida Ávila Camacho, at the boulevard intersection of Avenida Patria. Built in the 1970s and now aging, Plaza Patria nevertheless still rivals Plaza del Sol in popularity, with a swarm of stores—many women's clothes, shoes, jewelry, fast-food restaurants, department stores Fábricas de Francia and Suburbia, banks, such as Banamex (tel. 33/3673-0406 or 33/3673-0579), travel agent Van Gogh (tel. 33/3642-2071 or 33/3642-2072), 24-hour Farmacia Guadalajara (tel. 33/3641-2617 or 33/3641-2670; call 33/3818-1818 for delivery), and much more.

ACCOMMODATIONS
Under $50

Hotels are a bit scarce around Zapopan town. Travelers on a tight budget who want to soak in the Zapopan's small-town Mexico ambience, might opt for an overnight at basic **Pension**

Akim Pech (Pino Suárez 127, tel. 33/3633-0319, $20–30), a couple of blocks away from the downtown bustle. The approximately dozen plain but clean bare-bulb rooms on three floors come with hot water shower baths, TV, fans, and parking.

$50-100

A couple of steps up the economic scale is the nearby three-star **Suites Jacaranda** (Av. Ávila Camacho 880, Zapopan, Jalisco 45160, tel. 33/3656-3840, fax 33/3656-3072, $50–75), about three blocks southeast of the Zapopan entrance arch. This is a good lodging for families, with a dozen comfortable two- and three-bedroom kitchenette apartments. Moreover, prices are right, and include fans, phone, TV, and parking. Call ahead for availability.

By far the best in-town lodging is four-star **Hotel Country Plaza** (Av. Américas 1170, Zapopan, Jalisco 45160, tel. 33/3208-4633, toll-free Mexico tel. 01-800/021-6023, fax 33/3656-2522, www.countryplaza.com.mx), about five blocks south of the Zapopan entrance arch. Guests enjoy refined upscale amenities, including a good restaurant up front and, beyond the reception, an airy atrium with a pool, whirlpool tub, and exercise room tucked at the far end. Business visitors have available four meeting rooms accommodating up to 300 and three negotiating rooms accommodating about 10 people each.

Three stories of about 100 rooms in increasing order of luxury—standard, superior, junior suite, and "country" suite—enclose the atrium. All are deluxe, comfortable, and decorated in soothing pastels, with modern-standard bathrooms. All rooms come with air-conditioning, phones, cable TV, in-house wireless Internet, small pool, travel agent, shop, and parking. Credit cards accepted.

For quiet, old-world-style luxury, choose the 🄲 **Hacienda La Magdalena** (Km 1.7 Carretera Tesistan-Colotlan, Jalisco 46200, tel. 33/3897-0392, U.S. direct tel. in Spanish 619/866-3087, reservaciones@haciendalamagdalena.com, www.historichaciendainns.com, $150), about six miles north of Zapopan

town. You may also reserve through the Historic Hacienda Inns association (tel. direct in English from the U.S. and Canada 608/561-4068, admin@historichaciendainns.com).

Here, you can bask in the luxury of an historic early-18th century hacienda, strolling its lush garden grounds, relaxing in the shade of its tiled, plant-decorated corridors, enjoying gourmet home-cooked meals, cozying up with a good book by its warm lounge fireplace, and sleeping like a baby in a soft, quilted, queen-sized bed in a distinguished master suite with private terrace, shiny tile-decorated bath. Other amenities include a library, botanical garden, massage (at extra cost), wireless Internet access, and much more.

From Zapopan get there via the Carretera a Tesistan, Hwy. 23. From the Zapopan arch, head north along the Las Laureles boulevard to the *perifírico*. Continue straight ahead 4.9 miles (7.9 km) and turn right at the Carretera a Colotlán. Continue about another mile (1.1 km) to the hacienda entrance gate.

FOOD

Nearly all of Zapopan's better cafés and restaurants line the Paseo Teopizintli, the strolling plaza downhill east, between the basilica and the entrance arch.

Grecian

Downhill right next to the arch is the Grecian-owned and -operated 🄲 **Restaurant Zorba Agios Aggelos** (just uphill from the Zapopan entrance arch, tel. 33/3833-1131, open daily 8 A.M.–11 P.M.), the popular *taverna* meeting ground of Guadalajara's Grecian community. Take a seat beneath one of the shady umbrellas out front and let the impression grow that you've been transported to some Grecian island halfway around the world. The menu—*gyros* and falafel, *moussaka*, kabobs, *dolmas* (stuffed grape leaves, $4–15), and *retsina* wine ($20)—completes the fantasy. Stop by for guitar melodies Wednesday, jazz Thursday, and line dancing Friday and Saturday evenings 7 P.M.–midnight. Credit cards accepted.

Mexican

For Mexican fare, stroll uphill about a block, to **Tacos de Adelita** (corner of 28 de Enero, tel. 33/3675-8730, open daily 11 A.M.–11 P.M.) local-style taco haven. It offers a short menu of scrumptious *antojitos,* including six varieties of tacos (three for $2), many kinds of tortas ($2–3), and drinks.

Seafood

For good seafood, go uphill another half block to the cluster of sidewalk eateries, the best of which is **Restaurant La Bahía** (open daily approximately 8 A.M.–7 P.M.). Pick from a long menu of many styles of seafood—*almejas* (clams), *ostiones* (oysters, $8), *pulpo* (octopus, $6), *camarones* (shrimp, $7), *cangrejo* (crab, $8), *calamare* (squid, $6) and fish ($5–8)—prepared many ways.

Top the evening off by returning a block downhill to **Pastelería Basili** (tel. 33/3165-5205, open daily 8 A.M.–midnight) and enjoy coffee with your choice of dessert.

INFORMATION AND SERVICES
Tourist Information

Lots of Zapopan information is available at the municipal tourism office (Plaza Concentro, Av. Vallarta 6503, tel. 33/3110-0754 or 33/3110-0759, fax 33/3110-0383, turismo@zapopan.gob.mx, www.zapopan.gob.mx, open Mon.–Fri. 8 A.M.–7:30 P.M.), just inside (east of) the *periférico.* Find them at upstairs offices G13 and G14. Telephone or email ahead to verify office hours. Be sure to get a copy of the handy, detailed bilingual *Guide to Tourist Attractions and Services.*

Banking

Banks, all with ATMs, are well represented. Find them in the business district adjacent to and north of the municipal plaza. Best is long-hours **HSBC** (Hong Kong Shanghai Banking Corporation) (López Cotilla between Morelos and 16 de Septiembre, tel. 33/3636-8945, open

Mon.–Sat. 8 A.M.–7 P.M.). Alternatively, try **Banco Santander Serfin** (Mon.–Fri. 9 A.M.–4 P.M.), on the municipal plaza across from the *presidencia municipal;* or **Bancomer,** at the corner of López Cotilla and Morelos, same hours.

Post and Internet

Get stamps and mail letters at the local post office, on Moctezuma near the corner of 16 de Septiembre, a block north of Hidalgo. For **Internet** connection, try the small store on the north side of Hidalgo (Hidalgo 156, open 9 A.M.–10:30 P.M.), a block west of basilica facade.

HEALTH AND EMERGENCIES

For routine medications, consult the on-duty pharmacist at one of the downtown Zapopan pharmacies. If you need a doctor, follow your hotel's recommendation, or choose from the list of highly recommended doctors and hospitals with ambulance services in the *Local Medical Services* section of the *Essentials* chapter.

For **police** in an emergency telephone the Zapopan police station (tel. 33/3836-3636). In case of **fire,** dial the fire station *(bomberos)* (tel. 33/3633-4389), or call the police.

GETTING THERE

Get to Zapopan from downtown Guadalajara via local **TUR 706** air-conditioned bus (runs northwest all the way from Tonalá through Tlaquepaque to downtown Guadalajara), running north along 16 de Septiembre, then Alcalde to the Normal Circle. From there, the bus northwest along Avenida Ávila Camacho, past the Zapopan entrance arch, then uphill west along Hidalgo. It returns southeast along virtually the same route.

By taxi or car, from the downtown cathedral, follow Avenida Alcalde a mile north to the Normal Circle, to Avenida Manuel Ávila Camacho, which diagonals northwest at the Normal Circle. Continue about three miles along Ávila Camacho to Zapopan, marked by the monumental entrance arch on the left.

WEST AND NORTH

TLAQUEPAQUE AND TONALÁ

Guadalajara visitors flock to the southeast-side towns of Tlaquepaque and Tonalá to buy the renowned handicrafts that these towns' many hundreds of family factories produce. Although Tlaquepaque and Tonalá are each headquarters of their respective sprawling *municipio* (township or municipality), the core village centers, arguably Mexico's most important handicrafts sources, are the main attractions.

About five miles (eight km) southeast of downtown, Tlaquepaque (tlah-kay-PAH-kay), although completely surrounded by the Guadalajara metropolis, is nevertheless separate, with its own church, town hall, comfortable accommodations, many good restaurants, and locally owned shops and businesses close by the old village *jardín* (town square).

Although replete with village charm, Tlaquepaque is not sleepy. Visitors swarm in by day to stroll and shop and by night to savor the delicious snacks and delight in the bright mariachi folkloric dance entertainments for which Tlaquepaque is famous.

On the other hand, Tonalá, another five miles farther east, at Guadalajara's country edge, retains a measure of its drowsy rural past. Nevertheless, an initial glance inside a few of its multitude of handicrafts shops reveals Tonalá's mission. Behind the street-side adobe and brick walls, thousands of Tonalá people are hard at work. Their labor and know-how are the source of Tonalá's celebrated ceramic stoneware and its renowned papier-mâché and brass, in human, animal, and floral designs.

HIGHLIGHTS

◖ Museo Regional de la Cerámica de Tlaquepaque: As you stroll the main Tlaquepaque shopping street, Independencia, be sure to stop in to see this museum's prize-winning ceramics collection and the fine, for-sale examples at the shop (page 124).

◖ El Parián: For an afternoon or evening of pure Mexican entertainment, take a table at El Parián to savor some good country specialties and kick back to the heel-tapping, trumpet-ringing rhythms of the folkloric dance and mariachi music show (page 126).

◖ Avenida Independencia: Be sure to visit some of the showplace shops here, such as quirky Sergio Bustamante or Agustín Parra, for unabashedly monumental baroque reproduction (page 127).

◖ Tlaquepaque Factory Shops: Los Cirios features candles as art and Vidrios Soplados is a good place to learn about the wonders of glassblowing (page 131).

◖ Statue of Cihualpilli: In Tonalá's town plaza, see the remarkable bronze statue of the queen who resisted the Spanish invasion in 1530 (page 144).

◖ Museo Regional Tonallán: This museum is a community effort to illuminate the history and practice of Tonalá crafts, with crafts-making exhibitions and dramatic and musical productions (page 145).

◖ Tonalá Factory Shops: Be sure to follow at least part of this tour, stopping in the factory shops that welcome visitors, such as the Vidrios Jimon glass factory and Galería Bernabe and Artesanías Erandi for fine ceramics (page 149).

LOOK FOR ◖ TO FIND RECOMMENDED SIGHTS, ACTIVITIES, DINING, AND LODGING.

Some Tlaquepaque artisans use their house facades to display their style.

HISTORY

With only five miles separating them, Tlaquepaque and Tonalá share virtually the same history. Most historians agree that the early tribes of the eastern Atemajac Valley, the **Cocas** and **Tecuexes** (tay-KWAY-shays), whose traditions reflected much of the ancient Toltec heritage, were ruled by monarchs whose seat was located at present-day Tonalá. The original name, Tonallán (toh-nah-YAHN, Place of the Rising Sun) reflected its preeminence. The sun, long a popular Tonalá decorative theme, was at the center of the preconquest religion, a faith probably similar to that of the present-day Huichol people. (See the sidebar *The Huichol* in the *West and North* chapter.)

Tonallán's dominance, as source of local military, political, and, consequently, religious authority, probably also led to its strong ceramics tradition. Early Spanish missionaries labeled Tonalá as a "factory of paganism," because every house seemed to be a workshop where family members spent their working hours crafting pottery images of their gods.

Just prior to the Spanish conquest, an underage child-heir named Xuchitzín (Precious Flower) became Tonalá's ruler. Consequently, a distinguished relative, Lady Tzapotzingo (Fruit of the Zapote), was chosen to temporarily take charge as Cihualpilli (queen). According to tradition, Cihualpilli (see-wal-PEE-yee) was a benign and wise ruler who encouraged arts and crafts, including a renowned metalworking factory, famous for gold jewelry.

Tlaquepaque

Tlaquepaque was once a sleepy village of potters miles from the old Guadalajara town center. Attracted by the quiet of the country, rich families built Tlaquepaque mansions during the 19th century. Now, entrepreneurs have moved in and converted them into restaurants, art galleries, and showrooms, stuffed with quality Tonalá and Tlaquepaque ceramics, glass, metalwork, and papier-mâché.

PLANNING YOUR TIME

For most visitors, the main diversion of Tlaquepaque is strolling the main shopping streets of Independencia and Juárez, and seeing and selecting from the fabulous array of handicrafts offered by the many attractive shops. Along the way, you should visit the **Museo Nacional de la Cerámica de Tlaquepaque**

A circular bronze sculpture depicting Tlaquepaque history marks the town center intersection of Avenida Independencia and Avenida Madero.

(half hour), stroll through the town *jardín* and its pair of venerable churches (half hour), and look around inside **El Parián** restaurant and entertainment center. Also walk a few blocks north and west to the lovely old convent, now **Centro Cultural del Refugio** cultural center and art gallery (half hour). Then devote the rest of your time to perusing the handicrafts shops and enjoying the fare of Tlaquepaque's several good restaurants. At least one evening, enjoy dinner and the folkloric dance and mariachi show (Wed., Sat., and Sun. at 3:30 and 9 P.M.) at **El Parián.** This itinerary will take at least most of a day and evening, and as much as three days or even more.

ORIENTATION

Tlaquepaque's primary axes are east–west **Avenida Independencia** and north–south **Avenida Madero,** which intersect at a grand bronze, street-level sculpture, flanked by the pink, portaled **El Parián** restaurant/mariachi/folkloric dance entertainment center on the southeast corner and the *jardín* plaza with a bandstand on the northwest. Stand (or imagine standing) by the sculpture and diagonally face the *jardín*. Avenida Madero runs north, on your right, and on your left, pedestrian shopping mall Avenida Independencia heads west. On the *jardín*'s far left (west) side, past the bandstand, rises the venerated **Santuario de la Soledad,** while on the *jardín*'s north side rises the popular **Parroquia San Pedro** (parish church).

SIGHTS
Old Tlaquepaque

Much of Tlaquepaque's charm flows from its village ambience, which allows most everything to easily be reached on foot. Start at the town center, by the bronze sculpture, at the intersection of Avenidas Madero and Independencia. Since you can't avoid them, you might as well check out the offerings of the regiment of **handicrafts stalls** up and down the streets. For other **economical handicraft choices,** visit the basement floor of the town-center **market** (a half block west of the *jardín,* on Independencia, enter just past Banamex). Shops and stalls offer wide assortment, especially the very economical and atttractive low-fired brown-glazed plates and flower-decorated bowls.

After that, head to the west side of the *jardín* (named in honor of *insurgente* Miguel Hidalgo), to the beloved old **Santuario de Nuestra Señora de la Soledad.** The Augustinian monastic order, which began construction in 1742 and finished in 1813, dedicated it to the Virgin of Solitude.

Around the crucifix-shaped nave, see the graphic prints of all the stations of the cross. Up front, in the left transept, pay your respects to **La Inmaculada,** the Virgin of the Immaculate Conception, and in the right transept, the **Virgin of Guadalupe.** In the center, above the altar, on an austere Gothic stone *retablo,* the Virgin of Solitude reigns from beneath her gilded cupola, while at the tip-top of the *retablo,* the omnipresent Eye of God surveys all.

If you have time, see if the *sacristan* (keeper of the church) is around. Ask him to show you inside the sacristy *(sacristía)* behind the altar (offer a donation). Inside you'll find the more precious paintings, including the noted *Jesus Visiting the Home of Mary and Martha in Bethany,* dating from 1685.

Walk to the *jardín*'s adjacent north side, to the **Parroquia San Pedro,** Tlaquepaque's busy parish church, modified extensively since its construction around 1700. After a few minutes wandering through its beautifully restored interior, head into the courtyard, through the door at the nave's north (left) side. Enjoy the preciously detailed miniature pageant of dozens of Bible stories, from Noah and the Ark and Rachel at the well to Jesus on the Mount and Paul on the road to Damascus.

Casa Histórica

Cross the *jardín* to the Independencia pedestrian mall and head right (west) a block to

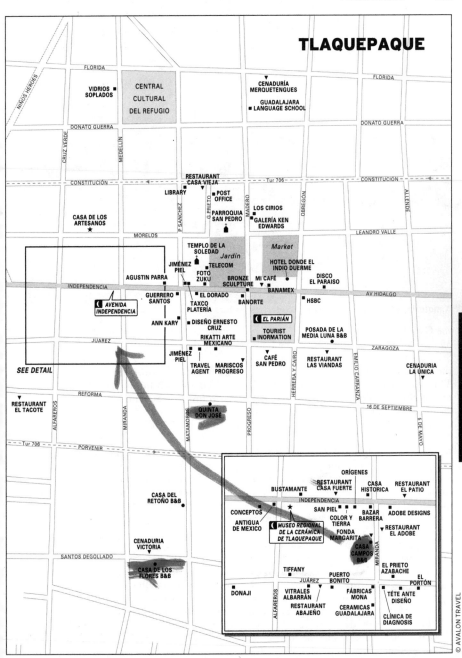

TLAQUEPAQUE

FLORIDA

VIDRIOS SOPLADOS

CENTRAL CULTURAL DEL REFUGIO

CENADURÍA MERQUETENGUES

GUADALAJARA LANGUAGE SCHOOL

FLORIDA

NIÑOS HEROES

DONATO GUERRA

CRUZ VERDE

MEDELLIN

DONATO GUERRA

CONSTITUCIÓN

Tur 706

CONSTITUCIÓN

ALLENDE

RESTAURANT CASA VIEJA

LIBRARY

P. SANCHEZ

G. PRIETO

POST OFFICE

PARROQUIA SAN PEDRO

MADERO

LOS CIRIOS

GALERÍA KEN EDWARDS

OBREGON

CASA DE LOS ARTESANOS ★

MORELOS

LEANDRO VALLE

TEMPLO DE LA SOLEDAD

Jardín

Market

HOTEL DONDE EL INDIO DUERME

JIMÉNEZ PIEL

AGUSTIN PARRA

TELECOM

FOTO ZUKU

BRONZE SCULPTURE

MI CAFÉ

DISCO EL PARAISO

INDEPENDENCIA

AV HIDALGO

AVENIDA INDEPENDENCIA

GUERRERO SANTOS

EL DORADO

BANAMEX

TAXCO PLATERÍA

BANORTE

HSBC

ANN KARY

DISEÑO ERNESTO CRUZ

EL PARIÁN

RIKATTI ARTE MEXICANO

TOURIST INORMATION

POSADA DE LA MEDIA LUNA B&B

JUAREZ

JIMÉNEZ PIEL

ZARAGOZA

SEE DETAIL

TRAVEL AGENT

MARISCOS PROGRESO

CAFÉ SAN PEDRO

HERRERA Y CAIRO

RESTAURANT LAS VIANDAS

EMILIO CARRANZA

CENADURIA LA ÚNICA

RESTAURANT EL TACOTE

REFORMA

ALFAREROS

MIRANDA

MATAMOROS

QUINTA DON JOSÉ

PROGRESO

16 DE SEPTIEMBRE

5 DE MAYO

Tur 706

PORVENIR

CASA DEL RETOÑO B&B

CENADURIA VICTORIA

SANTOS DEGOLLADO

CASA DE LOS FLORES B&B

Detail

ORÍGENES

BUSTAMANTE

RESTAURANT CASA FUERTE

CASA HISTORICA

RESTAURANT EL PATIO

INDEPENDENCIA

CONCEPTOS

ANTIGUA DE MEXICO

SAN PIEL

COLOR Y TIERRA

BAZAR BARRERA

ADOBE DESIGNS

MUSEO REGIONAL DE LA CERÁMICA DE TLAQUEPAQUE ★

FONDA MARGARITA

RESTAURANT EL ADOBE

CASA CAMPOS B&B

MIRANDA

TIFFANY

PUERTO BONITO

EL PRIETO AZABACHE

EL PORTÓN

JUAREZ

DONAJI

ALFAREROS

VITRALES ALBARRÁN

RESTAURANT ABAJEÑO

FÁBRICAS MONA

CERAMICAS GUADALAJARA

TÉTE ANTE DISEÑO

CLÍNICA DE DIAGNOSIS

TLAQUEPAQUE AND TONALÁ

A motorized San Francisco-like trolley ferries visitors around on a Tlaquepaque town tour.

the Casa Histórica (Independencia 208, tel. 33/3659-0238 or 33/3659-0243, open Mon.–Sat. 10 A.M.–6 P.M., Sun. 10 A.M.–4 P.M.), on the northwest corner of Contreras Medellín. This late colonial mansion is typical of the manor houses built by rich Guadalajarans in Tlaquepaque during the 19th century. This one is especially notable, for here, on June 13, 1821, Guadalajara municipal and royal authorities signed on to the revolutionary Plan de Iguala of national independence leader General Agustín. Seeing the writing on the wall, royalist Governor-General José Cruz quickly withdrew, thus making Guadalajara independent of Spain months before the rest of Mexico.

The present owners bid the public welcome. Stroll the spacious inner patio, shaded by what appears to be the majestic grandfather of all *hule* (rubber) trees. Around the patio's periphery a few potters craft the ceramic vases, jars, and bowls for sale back by the entrance door.

Before you leave, don't miss the shop (on the left before you head out the front door), which exhibits fetching nativity figurines

(nacimientos) and charmingly romantic porcelain statuettes.

Museo Regional de la Cerámica de Tlaquepaque

For a further treat, cross the street to the Regional Museum of Ceramics (Independencia 237, tel. 33/3635-5404, open Tues.–Sun. 10 A.M.–6 P.M.). The building itself is historically significant, being the former home of infamous *hacendado* Francisco Velarde, who was a close associate of the notorious President Santa Anna and who later collaborated with the French imperialists, a crime for which he was executed by republican authorities during the 1860s.

Times change, however, and now his former house brims with super-fine examples of Jalisco ceramics and other handicrafts. Examination of all the outstanding examples in the eight galleries constitutes a mini-education in fine Jalisco handicrafts, from *bruñido* and blown glass to *petatillo* and papier-mâché. A ninth gallery displays fine for-sale examples of all the above and much more.

Casa de los Artesanos

One block north of Independencia is the Casa de los Artesanos (Morelos 288, tel. 33/3657-3846, open Mon.–Fri. 9 A.M.–7 P.M., also open Sat. 9 A.M.–6 P.M. and Sun. 10 A.M.–2 P.M. during certain seasonal festivals), between Cruz Verde and Medellín. A dozen rooms display the handiwork of the more than 100 members of the Tlaquepaque artisans' guild. You can see nearly the entire range of possible handicrafts—furniture, both in wood and iron, intricate basketry, shining blown glass, fetching papier-mâché animals, baroque angels, handsome stonework, oil paintings, and colorful stoneware. Moreover, all of it is for sale, and if you don't see exactly what you want, you can go to the source, using the address/telephone list of all the contributing artisans.

Centro Cultural del Refugio

Continue north on Medellín two blocks to Tlaquepaque's gem, the Centro Cultural del Refugio (Donato Guerra 164, tel. 33/3652-7036 or 33/3652-7037, open daily 9 A.M.–8 P.M.), which occupies the entire square block between Medellín and P. Sánchez. One hint that you're in for something special is the line of majestic, ancient *higuera* (wild fig) trees along the block.

The graceful old building's history reflects the last century and a half of Mexico's history. Built in 1859, it was a hospital run by the Hermanas de Caridad (Sisters of Charity), who were exiled by the republican government in 1874. The Josephine sisters took over and continued it as a hospital until 1935. Later, renamed the Hospital Refugio, it was operated privately by the brothers Castiello Fernández del Valle until 1979. The city inaugurated it as the Casa de la Cultura in 1985 and has since used it for a busy schedule of artistic and cultural education, exhibitions, events, and performances.

The **theater** is past the east entrance, at Donato Guerra 160, where the line of trees ends. See the bulletin board just inside. The ticket office is on the right. For more information,

A lazy afternoon sun illuminates the halls at Centro Cultural del Refugio.

© BRUCE WHIPPERMAN

TLAQUEPAQUE AND TONALÁ

ask at the ticket office for a copy of *Refugiarte*, the center's monthly magazine *(revista mensual)*, that customarily lists exhibitions, performances, and art and music classes.

If you have more time, wander around inside the gracefully restored interior. Pause in the lovely portaled lime-tree garden and take a look at the temporary exhibitions.

If you're interested in enrolling in classes (guitar, accordion, painting, ceramics, papier-mâché, dance, photography, and much more), walk east, then north, around the Medellíin corner, to the **Museo Panteón Panduro** (Medellín 194, tel. 33/3635-7036, ext. 2008, open Tues.–Sun. 10 A.M.–6 P.M.) for more information.

ENTERTAINMENT AND EVENTS
Just Wandering Around

Afternoon and evening strolls around Tlaquepaque's central *jardín* yield a bounty of old-Mexico entertainment, especially during holidays and weekends. First are the food

MEXICAN HAT DANCE

Mexican folk celebrations usually blend indigenous and Spanish tradition. In dance, the Spaniards' contribution was the *jarabe* (for "sweet," as in syrup) courtship dance of ancient, perhaps even pre-Christian European origin.

Of the many regional Mexican *jarabes,* the most celebrated is the Jarabe Tapatío (Tapatío referring to its Jalisco origin), popularly known in the United States as the Mexican Hat Dance. It is traditionally performed to the captivating rhythms of nine consecutive *sones* (melodies). The dancers, men often in fancy *charro* braid and sombreros, and women in peasant blouses and colorful, full *poblana* skirts, tap with heel and toe around each other, while never touching, and always keeping proper distance.

After several minutes, the performance climaxes, accompanied by the melody "La Paloma" (The Dove), with the man, his back straight, hands clasped behind, following his partner as she eludes him, prancing gingerly around his sombrero's ample brim.

In the finale, the dancers turn toward the audience and dance to and fro, accompanied by the saucy melody of "Diana," to the shouts and whistles of the audience.

Such traditional staged performances are invariably tame compared to the spontaneous rancho celebrations. Away from city constraints, people kick back and join sizzling, hours-long *jarabe* fiestas, accompanied by mariachis and singing by the excited participants and onlookers.

Folkloric dancers at Tlaquepaque's prime entertainment venue, El Parián, nearly always perform the Jarabe Tapatío on Wednesday, Friday, and Saturday afternoons and evenings.

© BRUCE WHIPPERMAN

The Mexican Hat Dance originated in the Guadalajara countryside.

stalls, where, for starters, you can choose from hot dogs, popcorn, sweet corn, sweet fruit *aguas,* and chilled coconut juice. Then stroll along the rows of **handicrafts and trinket stalls.** Bargain for good deals, especially in leather wallets, belts, purses, and $3 "silver diamond rings."

El Parián

For restful, sit-down entertainment, take a seat inside the adjacent block-square, porticoed El Parián entertainment garden. Order your favorite *antojitos* (such as tamales, tacos, and enchiladas) and enjoy the afternoon or evening shows (mariachi instrumental and folkloric dance Wed., Sat.,

and Sun. at 3:30 and 9 P.M.). For more details, see the *Food* section, later in this chapter.

Festivals

Tlaquepaque overflows with events and entertainment during the annual **Feria San Pedro Tlaquepaque,** lasting about two and a half weeks, beginning June 15. Concurrently with the Tlaquepaque National Ceramics Fair and the San Pedro *patronal* religious festival, the community puts out a stupendous creative effort, a two-week schedule of daily plays, films, concerts, recitals, art exhibits, poetry readings, and much more. All of this peaks around the

Parroquia San Pedro on the *jardín,* on the day of St. Peter and St. Paul, June 29. A few days later, the excitement peaks again, at the awarding of the national ceramics prizes at the Centro Cultural del Refugio. For more information and a complete schedule, pick up the June issue of *Refugiarte,* the Tlaquepaque city cultural magazine, at the Centro Cultural del Refugio office (Donato Guerra 160, tel. 33/3652-7036 to -7039, fax 33/3639-5205).

SPORTS AND RECREATION

Tlaquepaque visitors are usually too busy strolling and shopping, and local people are too busy working, for much formal sports and recreation. Nevertheless, some opportunities do exist.

Gyms and Swimming

America's Gym (2492 Barragán, tel. 33/3635-8208, open daily 6 A.M.–10 P.M.), on the northwest side of town, has exercise machines and provides aerobics classes for both day guests and members.

For swimming, it's best to stay at **Villa del Ensueño, Quinta Don José,** or **Hotel Tapatío,** all of which have pools large enough for lap swimming workouts.

Alternatively, taxi 15 minutes to the **Atlas Country Club** ($12 round-trip; see the *Golf and Tennis* section) and spend the afternoon at the pool ($5 admission per person).

Golf and Tennis

Greater Guadalajara has a number of excellent golf courses. Closest to Tlaquepaque is the **Atlas Country Club** (tel. 33/3689-2620), which also rents tennis courts to the public and welcomes visitors to use their big pool ($5 per person), off the airport–Chapala highway (golf club entrance is on the northbound side of the freeway by the big SCI electronics plant), 1.1 miles (1.8 km) south of the *periférico.*

Serious tennis enthusiasts often stay at the Hotel Tapatío, which has nine clay courts, four of which are night-lit. Villa del Ensueño does have a playable but cramped tennis court that is okay, at least for volleying. Bring your own racquets and balls, however.

SHOPPING

Most of Tlaquepaque's handicrafts shops lie along the east–west **Avenida Independencia** pedestrian mall and the parallel bustling business street **Avenida Juárez,** a block south. Although most Tlaquepaque shops do not manufacture what they sell, a few of them do, and they invite visitors into their workshops.

◖ Avenida Independencia

The four-block stretch of Avenida Independencia from Avenida Niños Héroes on the west to the *jardín* is arguably Guadalajara's most pleasantly relaxing shopping ground. A tranquil automobile-free ambience allows carefree strolling and unfettered handicrafts browsing opportunities.

Consequently, many (but not all) of the shops are decidedly upscale. Nevertheless, careful looking and sharp bargaining can yield prizes—furniture, jewelry, sculpture, ceramics, glassware, papier-mâché, leather—at a fraction of North American and European prices.

(Some of the more exclusive shops, claiming to have fixed prices, turn up their noses at bargaining. But bargaining is such a strong Mexican tradition that you might nevertheless achieve success by making them an offer they cannot refuse. At least ask for a discount—*descuento.* For bargaining tips, see *Shopping* in the *Essentials* chapter.)

Start your shopping tour at **Ricardo Preciado Conceptos** (Independencia 281, midway between Av. Niños Héroes and Calle Cruz Verde, tel. 33/3639-4103, fax 33/3635-4169, conceptosrp@megared.net.mx, open Mon.–Sat. 10 A.M.–8 P.M., Sun. noon–6 P.M.), on the west side. Inside, you'll find an innovative array of art-for-furniture. One main theme is ironwork, from practical tables and chairs to whimsical motorcycles and animal sculptures, pieced together from discarded machine and electronics parts. Also find lots of innovative rustic wood furniture, resembling something out of seventh-century Europe.

A half block east, at the southwest corner of Independencia and Alfareros, **Antigua de Mexico**

Shop-lined Avenida Independencia is a traffic-free paradise for fine, reasonably priced handicrafts.

© BRUCE WHIPPERMAN

(Independencia 255, tel. 33/3639-2997, fax 33/3659-4471, open Mon.–Fri. 10 A.M.–2 P.M. and 3–7 P.M., Sat. 10 A.M.–6 P.M.) specializes in new baroque-style gilt wood reproductions, and a multitude of furnishings, including gleaming chandeliers, elegant candelabras, designer glassware, graceful paper flower displays, a choir of angel and cherub statuettes, and much more. Antigua de Mexico is doubly distinguished, being both a former convent and one of the few studios in Mexico to manufacture fine 17th-century-style furniture.

Cross Alfareros and continue a few doors east and across the street to **Sergio Bustamante** (Independencia 238, tel. 33/3639-5519, www.sergiobustamante.com.mx, open Mon.–Sat. 10 A.M.–7 P.M., Sun. noon–4 P.M.), an upscale outlet for the famous sculptor's arresting, whimsical studies in juxtaposition. Bustamante supervises an entire Guadalajara studio-factory of artists who put out dozens of reproductions on human, animal, and vegetable themes. Prices seem to depend mainly on size; gold rings and silver bracelets

may go for as little as $200, while a two-foot humanoid chicken may run $2,000. Don't miss the restroom.

A half block farther east, leather is seemingly sacred at **San Piel** (Saint Leather) (Independencia 225A, tel. 33/3659-6582, open Mon.–Sat. 10 A.M.–7 P.M., Sun. 10:30 A.M.–6:30 P.M.). Items, all made at the owner's Guadalajara factory, include supple jackets, stylish purses, luggage large and small, bags and briefcases, belts, and more. Combat the high asking prices by offering half the marked price. If you can't get what you want, try its sister store, a half block east, at Independencia 186C.

Right next door, earth tones set the mood at **Mueble y Ambiente** (Furniture and Ambience) (Independencia 225, tel./fax 33/3635-3505, open Mon.–Sat. 10:30 A.M.–7 P.M., Sun. 11 A.M.–5 P.M.). Here, the exquisite rules, from pastel-hued lampshades to one-of-a-kind hand-wrought museum-quality cabinets and tables, from fine hardwood to rattan *(tule)*. The finest pieces run $2,000 and up; make offers or ask for a *descuento*.

A few doors farther east, **Orígenes** (Independencia 211, tel./fax 33/3343-2629, scorigenes@hotmail.com, open Mon.–Sat. 10 A.M.–7 P.M.) displays a fascinating collection of folk crafts mostly from Africa and Asia. The assortment borders upon the fantastic, from animal-motif vases and larger-than-life calabashes to delicate basketry and brilliant art-to-wear dresses.

Descend a few doors farther east and a few steps down the economic scale to **Bazar Barrera** (Independencia 205, tel./fax 33/3635-1961, elmesondelabuelo@hotmail.com, open Mon.–Sat. 10 A.M.–7 P.M., Sun. 10 A.M.–5 P.M.) and pick from a huge selection of all-Mexico handicrafts. Whatever you've always wanted will probably be here: paper flowers, copperware, a bust of your favorite Mexican president, pewter, papier-mâché parrots, onyx eggs, nativity sets, tile country scenes, Talavera-style ceramics—and on and on.

Continue east across the street and step into the airy and chic warehouse of mid-scale **Adobe Designs** (Independencia 195, corner of Miranda, tel. 33/3639-8954 or 33/3657-2405, adobe1996@yahoo.com, open Mon.–Fri. 10 A.M.–7 P.M., Sat.–Sun. 11 A.M.–7 P.M.). Browse the eclectic, carefully selected array, including handsome rustic tables and chairs, resort wear, designer candles-as-furniture, fine ironwork, and earth-toned lamps from all over Mexico and the world. (Don't miss the exquisite **Restaurant El Adobe**, perfect for a mid-shopping lunch break; find it at the rear of the store (see the *Food* section for details).

Just next door (east) stand a pair of interesting small glassware-ceramics stores. First comes **Lamparas y Detalles** (Independencia 181, tel. 33/3635-7415, open Mon.–Sat. 10 A.M.–7 P.M., Sun. 11 A.M.–7 P.M.), outlet of Tiffany-style lamps, Talavera-style ceramics, paintings in baroque-style art, gilded picture frames, and much more.

Next door, enter **Arte en Vidrio** (Art in Glass) (Independencia 177, tel./fax 33/3635-1212, arteenvidrio@gmailcom, open Mon.–Sat. 10 A.M.–7 P.M., Sun. noon–4 P.M.) for all the glass tableware—tumblers, pitchers, vases, and more—that you're ever likely to want.

A few doors east and across the street, **La Casa Canela** (Independencia 163, tel. 33/3635-0768, fax 33/3657-6758, open Mon.–Fri. 10 A.M.–2 P.M. and 3–7 P.M., Sat. 10 A.M.–6 P.M., Sun. 11 A.M.–3 P.M.) takes pride in its museum-quality religious art, furniture, paper flowers, pottery, blown glass, table settings of classic Tlaquepaque and Tonalá stoneware, and much more.

Guadalajara's king of baroque reproductions is **Agustín Parra** (Independencia 154 and 158, on the north side of the street, tel. 33/3657-8530, tel./fax 33/3657-0316, www.agustin-parra.com.mx, open Mon.–Sat. 10 A.M.–2 P.M. and 3–7 P.M.) Find a treasury of new baroque-style art, including rococo-framed religious paintings and scrolly gilded chairs and tables, and a grand, golden 15-foot $500,000 *retablo* (altarpiece) for your family chapel. (Delivery is extra.) While you're inside the store, be sure to visit the small museum that exhibits the papal chair that President Vicente Fox commissioned and Parra crafted, for the visit of Pope John Paul II in 2002.

Across the street, at the southwest corner of P. Sánchez, the shop of **Jesú Guerrero Santos** (Independencia 155, tel./fax 33/3659-7373, open Tues.–Sat. 10:30 A.M.–2 P.M. and 3–7 P.M.) displays a minimuseum of elegant, lovingly crafted art. The artist's singularly eclectic collection tends toward the extravagantly traditional, in manifold manifestations, from silvery tea sets and exquisite porcelain tureens to preciously flowered vases and Porfirian-motif spice jars.

Around the corner, a half block south on P. Sánchez, don't miss the **Ann Kary** shop, detailed in the *Tlaquepaque Factory Shops* section.

Back on Independencia, silver jewelry is well-represented at **Platería Taxco** (at Independencia 148, northeast corner of P. Sánchez, tel./fax 33/3639-6894, open Mon.–Sat. 10:30 A.M.–7:30 P.M., Sun. 11 A.M.–4 P.M.). Here you can buy reasonably priced Taxco silver without having to travel all the way to the source. The source, the savvy Torres family, of Taxco, Guerrero, has come to Tlaquepaque instead. Choose from their very bountiful

(Sterling .925 pure) array, which sells by weight, at the reasonable rate of about $1 per gram. If they don't have exactly what you want, they'll make it to order for you.

Across the street, you get your choice of the grand, the rustic, and even the medieval, at **Galería El Dorado** (Independencia 145, tel. 33/3635-3834, tel./fax 33/3635-3626, open Mon.–Sat. 10:30 A.M.–7:00 P.M., Sun. 11 A.M.– 6:30 P.M.). Here, furniture reproductions grab most of the attention. Wander along the aisles and admire the chests, tables, dressers, cabinets, and chandeliers, which appear to have materialized from Camelot. Bring your truck, or hire a shipper.

Avenida Juárez

Although few, if any, of the Avenida Juárez shops are as spectacularly upscale as some of the shops on Independencia, many excellent handicrafts, bargainable to very reasonable prices, can be the reward of concentrated effort here. Begin a half block east of Avenida Matamoros and work your way west.

Start on the south side of the street at **Rikatti Arte Mexicano** (Juárez 131A, tel. 33/3343-7233, fax 33/3343-7234, www.rikatti.com, open Mon.–Sat. 10 A.M.–3 P.M. and 4–7:30 P.M.), for a lovingly selected and displayed small museum of decorative art. Although the glassware (gleaming goblets, statuesque vases, bright mirrors) first catches your eye, the entire collection (elegant lamps, fetching animal-motif purses, one-of-a-kind tables and chairs, and much more) must be seen to be appreciated.

Cross Juárez to leather store **El Prieto de Azabache** (Juárez 138, tel./fax 33/3639-7997, fax 33/3639-5281, open Mon.–Sat. 10 A.M.– 8 P.M., Sun. 11 A.M.–6 P.M.). It offers loads of fine leather jackets, coats, boots, purses, and women's sandals at relatively high asking prices. If you find something you want, make offers or ask for a discount (and don't buy until you comparison shop across the street).

For the finest leather goods selections, cross to the south side, to **Jiménez Hermanos Piel** (Juárez 145, near the corner of Matamoros, tel./fax 33/3635-1194, www.jimenezpiel.com,

open Mon.–Sat. 10 A.M.–7 P.M., Sun. 11 A.M.– 2:30 P.M.). You can admire a supple selection of jackets, purses, wallets, belts, backpacks, and much more. What's even better is that they are experts in made-to-order goods. Be prepared with a sample (or at least a drawing) of what you want. With 30 years in the business behind them, Jiménez Hermanos Piel backs up their goods with a lifetime guarantee.

A block farther west, check out the attractively quirky **Teté Ante Diseno** (Juárez 173, tel. 33/3635-7965, open Mon.–Sat. 10 A.M.– 7:30 P.M.). Enter, passing a huge, rusted iron cauldron, weathered stone statues, and a giant copper vat, to showrooms inside filled with mostly new (but appealing) antique reproduction sideboards, dressers, china cabinets, and chandeliers. Some pieces, such as a medieval-looking astronomical armillary sphere, sundial, baroque cherubs, and madonnas with child, appear to be genuine antiques (*antiguidades*). If you're seriously interested, bring an antiques expert if you're not one yourself.

Continue west to the southwest corner of Miranda and treat yourself to **Fábricas Mona's** big fabric shop (Juárez 205, tel. 33/3635-6681 or 33/3659-1715, fax 33/3659-3112, monas@prodigy.net.mx, open Mon.–Sat. 10 A.M.–6:30 P.M., Sun. 11 A.M.– 2:30 P.M.). Wander through this wonderland of textiles, mostly hand-woven and hand-embroidered, from all over Mexico, with much from Oaxaca. You'll find shelf after shelf of tablecloths, napkins (*servilletas*), throw rugs (*tapetes*), serapes, vests, *huipiles*, skirts (*faldas*), shirts (*camisas*), blouses (*blusas*), pillowcases (*fundas*), curtains (*cortinas*), and a miniwarehouse of fabric by the roll.

A few doors farther west, check out **Puerto Bonito** (Juárez 223, tel. 33/3639-4110, open Mon.–Sat. 10 A.M.–7 P.M., Sun. 11 A.M.– 3 P.M.). Find a treasury of baroque reproductions, from fine table settings and Tlaxcala and Talavera pottery to candelabras and gilded wooden angels and horses.

Tiffany-motif glass fanciers will appreciate a pair of nearby shops. First find **Vitrales Albarran** (south side of Juárez midway between

Miranda and Alfareros, tel./fax 33/3635-7037, vitralesalbarran@hotmail.com, open Mon.–Sat. 9 A.M.–7 P.M., Sun. 11 A.M.–3 P.M.). Although they do have some items on display, they specialize in fine lampshades and other stained-glass pieces to order.

By contrast, **Tiffany** (Juárez 248, tel./fax 33/3639-0464, open Mon.–Sat. 10 A.M.–7 P.M., Sun. 11 A.M.–4 P.M.), across the street and a half block west, carries a lovely, extensive inventory and will also make to order. Pick from a whole ceiling of gorgeous chandeliers and lamps and shelves of glittering fine table lamps (the antiqued brass bases of which are imported from the United States).

For yet another treat, continue west a half block past Alfareros to **Donaji** textiles shop (Juárez 291A, open Mon.–Sat. noon–7 P.M., Sun. noon–4 P.M.), a little corner of Oaxaca in Tlaquepaque. Get your fill of Oaxaca textiles, including fine wool *tapetes* (serape-rugs) from Teotitlán del Valle, fetching *huipiles* from San Pedro Amusgos, richly embroidered wedding dresses from San Antonio Castillo Velasco, intricate embroidery *(bordado)* from all over, blankets *(mantas),* baby clothes, and tablecloths *(manteles).*

🍷 Tlaquepaque Factory Shops

Begin your factory tour on the west side and continue generally east. Start one block west of Niños Héroes, at the backyard ironwork shop of **Roman Gutierréz Muro** (Moctezuma 2657), on the far west side a half block north of Independencia. Within the ramshackle but well-equipped compound, personable Roman can fashion a remarkably clever and diverse range of ironwork, from scroll-like tables and chairs to ingenious animals and flowers. See the samples and the photo catalog. Or show him a sketch of what you want and he'll probably be able to make it readily, for a reasonable price. Call (in Spanish) 33/3659-0526 for an appointment.

One of Tlaquepaque's most renowned handicrafts producers is **Vidrios Soplados** (Blown Glass) (Medellín 179, between Florida and D. Guerra, tel./fax 33/3659-1790, cearturperez@hotmail.com, Mon.–Fri. 8 A.M.–2 P.M. and Sat.

8 A.M.–noon) The factory, in the north-central town quarter, is open for walk-in visitors. Enter the small street-front store, decorated with clutches of lustrous glass *esferas* (glass spheres), tableware, vases, figurines, and much more. Continue to the fascinating workshop in the big rear yard, where workers bend, twist, blow, and mold red-hot globs of glass into gleaming works of art. The store is open Mon.–Sat. 8 A.M.–3 P.M.

Return east along Independencia, turn south (right) at Miranda, and continue past Juárez a few doors to **Cerámicas Guadalajara** (Miranda 60, tel. 33/3635-5981, fax 33/3657-6486, www.cegualtla.com, open Mon.–Sat. 10 A.M.–2 P.M. and 4–7 P.M., Sun. 11 A.M.–3 P.M.), on the right (west) side of the street. Although it manufactures and stocks a seeming galaxy of fetching examples, Cerámicas Guadalajara will also make any design or style to order. For example, homey sayings, small or large murals, address plates, names—whatever your heart desires—in brilliant, high-fired glazed color.

TLAQUEPAQUE AND TONALÁ

© BRUCE WHIPPERMAN

Los Cirios candle workshop is a highlight of a Tlaquepaque factory shops tour.

Back on Juárez, continue east a block, then left (north) to pewter *(peltre)* showroom and factory **Ann Kary** (Matamoros 28, tel./fax 33/3659-7739 or 33/3659-6292, www.annkary.com.mx, open Mon.–Fri. 9 A.M.–6 P.M., Sat. 9:30 A.M.–5 P.M.). Traditional European pewter is made of tin, alloyed with other metals, such as nickel, but Ann Kary's ware, a vast collection of decorative metal bowls, plates, crucifixes, picture frames, and much more, is of aluminum. Ask to visit the shop in the rear, where workers put the finishing touches on the pieces.

Candles are the mission of the compact **Los Cirios** factory store (Madero 70, tel. 33/3635-2426, fax 33/3635-5456, www.loscirios.com.mx, open daily 8 A.M.–6 P.M.), a block north of the *jardín.* Continue through the Galería Ken Edwards up front to the Los Cirios part of the store at the left rear. You'll find a garden of candles, many huge, in innovative shapes—cones, cubes, cylinders, and more—and in a rainbow of bright colors. Watch the fascinating ongoing work of creation in the workshop, adjacent to the displays. (Also, don't miss the adjacent **Ken Edwards** stoneware store while you're there. Better still, if you have time, visit the Ken Edwards factory store in Tonalá.)

For more visitable factory stores, inquire at the **Casa de los Artesanos** (288 Morelos, between Cruz Verde and Medellín, a block north of Independencia, tel./fax 33/3657-3846, open Mon.–Fri. 9 A.M.–7 P.M.).

ACCOMMODATIONS

Tlaquepaque visitors enjoy a sprinkling of comfortable lodgings. Guadalajara visitors, attracted by Tlaquepaque's rewarding shopping, its good restaurants, and its quietly picturesque neighborhood lanes, are increasingly choosing Tlaquepaque as a deserving destination in itself.

Some Tlaquepaque innkeepers have merged the North American bed-and-breakfast tradition with the Mexican *posada* style of accommodation for those visitors who appreciate the best of both worlds. All Tlaquepaque bed-and-breakfasts are within easy walking distance of the town center.

Under $50

Budget travelers will appreciate the **Hotel La Posada de la Media Luna** (Inn of the Half Moon) (Juárez 36, San Pedro Tlaquepaque 45500, tel. 33/3635-6054, fax 33/3657-7631, info@hotellamedialuna.com, www.hotellamedialuna.com, $27–46), centrally located just a block east of El Parián and the plaza. The owners, with bright paint and lots of savvy, have turned something potentially humdrum into an attractive lodging, elevated away from the noise and bustle on busy Calle Juárez downstairs. Eighteen rooms line both sides of a long, sunny upstairs patio, invitingly decorated with potted plants and canopy-shaded tables for breakfast and relaxation. The rooms themselves are clean and simply but comfortably furnished with pastel bedspreads, rustic wooden furniture, and some reading lamps. Baths are likewise clean and well maintained, with hot-water showers. Prices include fans, cable TV, and continental breakfast. Credit cards accepted, but no parking.

Budget travelers who want to be in the middle of the action often choose the **Donde El Indio Duerme** (Where the Indian Sleeps) (Independencia 74, San Pedro Tlaquepaque 45500, tel. 33/3635-2189, ramindio@prodigy.net, www.indiosleep.com, $32). Choose from about a dozen clean, brightly decorated rooms with bath around a tranquil inner fountain patio, with shaded tables and chairs, for breakfast and socializing. Rates include breakfast, fans, reading lamp, and hot water shower-baths.

$50-100

Youthful architect Eslya Panduro's life project was to transform her former family home into a Tlaquepaque bed-and-breakfast, just three blocks south of the town center. Her successful result was the ◖ **Casa del Retono** (Matamoros 182, Tlaquepaque, Jalisco 45500, tel./fax 33/3587-3989, 33/3639-6510, or 33/3635-7636, info@lacasadelretono.com.mx, www.lacasadelretono.com.mx, $47–75). She offers eight rooms and one suite, all lovingly decorated in bright rainbow hues, each with shiny, up-to-date bath, adorned with flowery tiles. Rooms carry individual names, such as Guerrero, Tamaulipas, and Jalisco, so guests can savor the pleasure of their favorite Mexican state to sleep in.

Downstairs, besides soaking up the tranquility of the spacious, tree-shaded back yard, guests enjoy an inviting dining/living room for a generous continental buffet breakfast and afternoons and evenings lingering over coffee and conversation. Room rates include portable fans, TV, telephone, and credit cards accepted.

At the **Hotel Quinta Don José** (Reforma 139, Tlaquepaque, Jalisco 45500, tel. 33/3635-7522, fax 33/3659-9315, Mexico toll-free tel. 01-800/700-2223, U.S. and Canada toll-free tel. 866/629-3753, info@quintadonjose.com, www.quintadonjose.com, $85–145), personable American-Mexican owner Arturo Magaña and his charming wife Estela have converted a spacious, architecturally designed family house into a relaxed bed-and-breakfast inn, just two blocks south of the town center. They offer 15 comfortable accommodations, rooms and suites, all tucked around a lovely garden and a beautiful blue (but unheated) lap swimming pool. They have added a small restaurant, and a comfortable bar and sitting area where guests enjoy socializing after a hard day seeing the sights.

The suites are all lovingly decorated with plenty of gorgeous tile; fetching handicrafts; colorful, heirloom-quality, hand-sewn bedspreads; and polished rustic wooden furniture. Alternatively, guests can choose from eight comfortable, invitingly furnished rooms at moderate rates. Four of the suites open onto the pool-patio. The rooms are very invitingly decorated and comfortable. All lodgings include a generous full breakfast buffet and a load of extras, including cable TV, fans and deluxe a/c, free laundry service, wireless Internet connection, bus and airport pickup, secure parking, and credit cards accepted.

Over $100

Shift east several blocks to the south-central part of town, four blocks south of Independencia, to **Casa de las Flores** (Santos Degollado 175, San Pedro Tlaquepaque, Jalisco 45500, tel. 888/582-4896, tel./fax 33/3659-3186, toll-free VONAGE.com line, infor@casadelasflores.com, www.casadelasflores.com, $100–111), on quiet side street. Enter and pass through a flowery garden of bright bougainvillea, fragrant roses, and jacaranda to a trellis-shaded patio, where guests enjoy a complete hot breakfast in the morning and coffee and conversation around a cozy fireplace on cool winter nights. The friendly, knowledgeable hosts, Stan Singleton (from Davis, California) and José Gutiérrez, offer to arrange tours for their guests.

A few steps past the patio, arrive at the modern stucco, two-story, seven-room lodging complex. Guests enjoy spotless, comfortable, marble-floored rooms, attractively decorated with crafts and polished handmade wooden furniture. The seven accommodations are distributed between standard room (two double beds), junior suite (one queen-size bed and living room), deluxe room (two queen-size beds), and master suite (two queen-size beds). Add about $18 per additional person per night. Four rooms have a/c and fans, three have fans only. All have modern-standard baths. With parking and credit cards accepted, but no pool.

The refined **Villa del Ensueño** (Florida 305, San Pedro Tlaquepaque, Jalisco 45500, tel. 33/3635-8792, Mexico toll-free tel. 01-800/777-8792, U.S. toll-free tel. 800/220-8689, fax 33/3659-6152, ensueno1@prodigy.net.mx, www.villadelensueno.com, $102–140), tucked six blocks from the town center in the northwest downtown quarter, is just about evenly split between a pair of branches on opposite sides of its quiet neighborhood side street. Guests at the approximately 30-unit complex, formerly a pair of 19th-century villas, enjoy rooms artfully nested along sunny bougainvillea-draped balcony walkways and intimate fountain patios. Two heated pools, a whirlpool tub, breakfast room adjoining a sunny veranda, and an intimate bar with soft couches are all available for guest relaxation.

Staff gladly offer advice regarding sights, restaurants, and tours. A knowledgeable hotel desk manager is available 24 hours for help and advice. An in-house driver with a Chevrolet van is available for transportation and tours for up to seven people at a reasonable hourly rate.

All rooms and suites are both immaculate and attractively neocolonial, with rustic red-tiled floors, wall art, bed lamps, floor-to-ceiling drapes, and shiny tiled baths. Standard, deluxe, two-bedroom deluxe, and suites all come with a/c and fans, full hot breakfast, parking, and credit cards accepted. You can also book through U.S. agent Kief Adler (P.O. Box 1080, Agoura Hills, CA 91376, U.S. toll-free tel. 800/220-8689, fax 818/597-0637).

Little appears to have been spared in lifting the **Hotel Casa Campos** (Francisco de Miranda 30A, Tlaquepaque, Jalisco 45500, tel. 33/3838-5296 or 33/3838-5297, fax 33/3838-0798, hotelcasacampos@yahoo.com, www.hotelcasacampos.com, $105–145) from a 19th-century family house to a modern-standard bed-and-breakfast inn. Ideally located just a half block south of the town center, the Casa Campos, built around an intimate central patio, blooms with elegant neo-colonial embellishments, from finely sculpted stonework and elaborate hand-carved doors to handcrafted wooden furniture and bright Talavera tile highlights.

The hotel's six comfortable accommodations line the upstairs patio-view corridor. They are exquisitely decorated in dark Porfirian-era tones, which, combined with the need to draw the curtains for privacy on the corridor, makes the room lamps necessary for light much of the time. All rooms come with a/c, cable TV, phones, wireless Internet connection, the excellent restaurant Sandwiches and Friends, parking, continental breakfast, credit cards accepted, but no pool.

Five-star landmark resort **Hotel El Tapatío** (Carretera a Chapala 4275, Km 6.50, Tlaquepaque, Jalisco 45588, tel. 33/3837-2929, fax 33/3635-6664, Mexico toll-free tel. 01 800/361-8000, U.S. and Canada toll-free tel. 800/327-1847, ventas@hotel-tapatio.com, www.hotel-tapatio.com, $180–250), reigning over its own airy hilltop estate, about ten minutes by taxi south of Tlaquepaque, seems perfect for visitors who crave (or maybe deserve)

space, facilities, and luxury. You can have it all, including two restaurants, bars, live music nightly, nine clay tennis courts, exercise gym, running track, disco, and heated outdoor swimming pool with kiddie pool. Rooms are spacious, deluxe, clean, and comfortable. Lower-price promotions and packages that include buffet breakfast are often available for the asking. All lodgings come with airy private balcony, air-conditioning, phone, two kids free with parents, satellite TV, baby-sitting (at extra charge), shops, travel agent, extensive business and meeting facilities, parking, and more.

FOOD
Food Stalls, Market *Fondas*, and Cafés
You could enjoy a week of delicious, inexpensive food right around the Tlaquepaque *jardín*. Food stalls begin opening daily around noon, are most active 5–8 P.M., and close around 10 P.M.; Saturday and Sunday are busiest.

Many of the food-stall options are rich and fatty, but understandably popular. Best-liked seem to be heaping bowls of french fries, smothered in chopped hot dogs. If that's not enough, go for *chicharrones* (deep-fried pork rinds), fried bananas, hamburgers, and deep-fried-on-the-spot potato chips.

As for drinks, the fresh fruit *aguas* (waters) are yummy, such as sweet dark red *jamaica* (hah-MAI-kah), *horchata* (rice milk, sugar, and spices), and *fresa* (strawberry—red and fruity). If you prefer, two or three *jugo* (HOO-goh) (juice) stands supply fresh orange, apple, *sandía*(watermelon), *zanahoria* (carrot), pineapple, and many more fresh juices. For dessert, pick up two or three of the yummy cakes, pies, custards, and cheesecakes for sale on tables around the *jardín*'s northwest side.

For healthier (and more typically Mexican) budget-priced ($2–5) meals, go to the *fondas* (permanent food stalls) inside the market, across the street from the *jardín*'s northeast corner (of Madero and Leandro Valle). Choose from dozens of offerings, including savory stews (*guisados* and *birrias*), tamales, *chiles rellenos*,

© BRUCE WHIPPERMAN

Elote (sweet corn) is a big seller on the Tlaquepaque town plaza.

chicken in *mole,* and loads more. Remember: If it's steaming, it's safe. Although rarely necessary anymore, douse salads in plenty of lime *(limón)* juice as a precaution.

Probably the busiest street-front taco action in Tlaquepaque takes place at the stalls on Progreso (Avenida Madero's southern continuation), a block south of the *jardín.* Dedicated teams put out dozens of tacos a minute in many varieties (three for $2) for a throng of enthusiastically hungry customers.

Continue south three blocks and turn right a block and a half to the local favorite, **Cenaduría Victoria** (Santos Degollado 182, in front of the house, open daily 6–9 P.M., $3–4), on the north side of the street between Miranda and Matamoros. Victoria, who started out by serving whatever she would have fixed for her family, has gotten so popular that she opened a small restaurant.

For excellent coffee and tasty light meals, go to refined **Café San Pedro** (Juáez 85, tel. 33/3639-0616, open daily 8:30 A.M.– 10:30 P.M.), on the south, quiet side of the

Parián. Take an outside table and enjoy a cup of coffee (rich café Americano, $1.50), many good salads (Caesar, tuna $3.50), omelets ($3– 4), and much more.

El Parián

Several independent café-restaurants serve the multitude of tables that surround the interior patio of El Parián, diagonally (southeast) across the Madero-Independencia intersection from the *jardín.* Every evening, families crowd in for the free mariachi entertainment; food is just a sideshow.

Nevertheless, competition keeps standards up and prices down. Among the better options seems to be **Salon Monterrey** (open daily around 11 A.M.–1 A.M., $4–10), on the west (Avenida Progreso) side. A long menu of Mexican favorites—such as shrimp *al gusto,* chicken in *mole* sauce, *pozole,* hamburgers, spaghetti, and much more satisfies the customers. Mariachis stroll weeknights, and folkloric music and dance shows go on Wednesdays, Saturdays, and Sundays beginning at 3:30 and 9 P.M.

International-Style Restaurants

Good restaurants sprinkle the Tlaquepaque downtown blocks. They divide themselves by their patronage: international versus local. Near the Avenida Independencia pedestrian mall, restaurants cater to the mostly well-heeled international and upper-class Mexican shopping tourists and wholesale buyers. Most restaurants consequently depend on street traffic and open later, around noon, and close by around 9 P.M. A few do serve breakfast, from around 9 A.M., and suppers until around 11 P.M.

Starting on the west side and moving east, first find **Restaurant Casa Fuerte** (Independencia 224, tel. 33/3639-6481, open daily noon–8 P.M., music Wed.–Sun. 3–6 P.M., credit cards accepted), just past the corner of Cruz Verde. Step inside to an airy inner patio where, afternoons, a trio plays, while ceiling fans whir softly and water trickles musically into the courtyard fountain. A hearty, innovative Mexican-international menu (soups, salads, Mexican specialties, seafood, poultry, and meat, $5–12) completes the attractive picture.

A block farther, consider the tourist shopper's long-time favorite **Restaurant El Patio** (Independencia 186, tel. 33/3635-1108, open daily 9 A.M.–9 P.M., credit cards accepted). You can start your shopping tour early with familiar breakfast choices of eggs, hot cakes, French toast, and much more. Lunch is the main event, when the shaded, relaxing courtyard atmosphere and a tasty menu of soups, salads, beef, chicken, and fish ($5–12) keep the customers coming year-round. For a splurge, order one of the huge Mexican *antojitos* platters ($20), enough for five.

Just past the next corner, enter the Adobe Designs handicrafts store, and continue through the spacious interior to Tlaquepaque's class-act **Restaurant El Adobe** (Independencia 195, tel. 33/3657-2792, open daily 12:30–7 P.M.). The restaurant's blithe, lively atmosphere creates a relaxing counterpoint to a hard morning of Tlaquepaque bargaining. Nouveau Mexican cuisine reigns. For starters, try Mexican stuffed wontons ($5), continue with mushroom soup or passion salad ($5–7), and keep going with macaroni in mescal sauce

or cheese-stuffed chicken breast ($10–13), and finish with one of the excellent espresso coffees ($3). A flute, guitar, and bass trio plays 2:30–6 P.M. Credit cards accepted.

For something light and delicious, enter the cool, refined interior of **Sandwiches and Friends** (Miranda 26A, tel. 33/3838-5296, open daily 7 A.M.–10:30 P.M.), where the savvy owners bring out the best in fresh, simple ingredients: sandwiches (a baker's dozen, including American cheeseburger, German Black Forest ham and gouda cheese, Italian pepperoni sausage and mozzarella cheese, $3–5); soups (cream of cauliflower, Azteca, *caldo de res* vegetable beef, $3); and salads (green, *caprese,* Greek, and more, $4–5); and hearty Mexican plates (such as savory beef fillet, with plenty of refried beans, veggies, and tortillas on the side, $5).

For seafood, all local roads seem to lead to **Mariscos Progreso** (Progreso 80, a half block south of El Parián, tel. 33/3639-6149, open daily 11 A.M.–8 P.M., credit cards accepted). Owners bring in the crowds with mariachis, a relaxing patio atmosphere, and simply good shrimp, fish, octopus, squid, clams, and oysters in many styles ($5–12).

Two blocks north of Independencia, on Guillermo Prieto (the one-block street running north from the *jardín*'s northwest corner), **Restaurant Casa Vieja** (Guillermo Prieta 99, tel. 33/3657-6250, open daily 8:30 A.M.–10 P.M., credit cards accepted) seems to be trying harder, with both breakfast and late evening dinner. In the patio of a genuine *casa vieja* (old house), savor the 18th-century rustic garden atmosphere while enjoying a selection of innovative Jalisco dishes. Start out with *ensalada Adam y Eva* (spinach with sesame, pecan, apple, and cheese, $6), continue with *lomo de Santa Clara* (roast loin of pork smothered in mild red chile sauce with bits of *nopal* leaves and potatoes, $15), and finish with fried ice cream ($5) and cappuccino.

For seafood and fine cuts, many Tlaquepaque visitors like **Restaurant Río San Pedro** (Juárez 300, tel. 33/3659-6136 or 33/3838-0959, open daily 8 A.M.–10 P.M., credit cards accepted), at the west end of Juárez, a half block before Niños Héroes. The menu names the favorites of local innkeepers, such as Casa de las Flores and Villa del Ensueño. These include roasted chicken breast in curry and coconut sauce ($8), fish fillets with shrimp ($9), and steaks ($9). Finish off with apple strudel ($3) and cappuccino ($2).

Local-Style Restaurants

These eateries, patronized largely by local middle- and working-class families, are sprinkled mostly around the north, west, and south edges of downtown. Plenty of free fixings mark a good traditional Mexican eatery: Before your main course arrives, you should at least be served an assortment of salsas along with a plate of *totopos* (chips), often accompanied by small plates of green onions, radishes, and pickled chiles. Many of these restaurants operate as *cenadurias,* customarily open only for *cena* (supper), late afternoons and evenings.

Tasty *cenas* (suppers) are the tradition at **Cenaduría Los Merequetengues** (may-ray-kay-TAYNG-gays) (Florida 83, tel. 33/3639-3814, open Mon.–Sat. 7 P.M.–midnight, Sun. 2–10 P.M.), east of the corner of Madero, three blocks north of the *jardín.* This is the place where you find out if your favorite Mexican restaurant back home cooks Mexican food the way it's supposed to be done. A local family runs a simple, clean establishment, invitingly decorated with sentimental old-Mexico country scenes. (Don't let the old Gepetto—of Pinocchio fame—in the corner scare you; he's a wooden, although startlingly realistic, dummy.)

Turn to the wall menu for dozens of tasty choices, from *sopes* (tortillas topped with spiced meat and vegetables), enchiladas and *flautas* (beef, chicken, cheese, or *verdes), tacos dorados, pozole,* and much more ($3–6).

For professional service and Mexican food at its refined best, take a shady open-air table at class-act **Restaurant A Casa** (Juárez 95, across from El Parián, south side, tel. 33/3635-7190 or 33/3659-3236, open daily 9 A.M.–7 P.M., $5–8). Here, late lunch/early dinner is the main event, with deliciously fresh ingredients

that you've probably never heard much about, such as salsa from *chiles serranos,* tacos de *cochinita pibil (pulled pork), ensalada de ejotes altinas* (green bean salad), *vacio parillada* (grilled flank steak), and much more.

Eat well for less with a *comida casera* (homestyle) afternoon meal at tranquil, refined **Restaurant Las Viandas** (Juárez 27, a block west of El Parián, tel. 33/3659-6296 or 33/3838-3236, open daily 8:30 A.M.–5:30 P.M.). Here you could dine every afternoon and never get bored, since the menu changes daily. Three-course set *comidas* (1–5 P.M.) go something like this: hearty *sopa flor de calabaza* (squash flower) soup, tasty broth-cooked rice, a small baked potato, and beef short ribs in a savory sauce— all for $4. Additionally, they offer plenty of delicious morning breakfasts ($2.50–4), and beef and chicken burgers ($2), salads ($3), and sandwiches ($2–3) all day.

Continuing clockwise around to the east side of town to the hands-down Tlaquepaque local favorite, **Cenaduría La Única** (The Only One) (east side of 5 de Mayo between 16 de Septiembre and Zaragoza, tel. 33/3635-1004, open. Tues.–Fri. 6 P.M.–midnight, Sat.–Sun. 5 P.M.–midnight), founded in 1963, continues its good work into the present. Mountains of *antojitos* keep the local folks coming: *pozole* (hominy, in savory broth, topped with chicken or pork, onions, and cabbage, $4), *torta ahogada* (salsa-dipped chicken or pork, vegetable, and avocado on a big *bolillo* roll, $3), burritos, *flautas,* hot dogs, and hamburgers ($3–5).

Continue to the southwest side and up the economic scale a notch to **Restaurant El Abajeño** (Juárez 231 between Miranda and Alfareros, tel. 33/3635-9097, open daily noon–10 P.M., credit cards accepted). This worthy local representative of the long-time Guadalajara chain brings in the crowds, especially on weekends, with mariachis and a rich country Mexican menu. Choices include *antojitos* (such as garlic mushrooms in butter or *enchiladas verdes,* $3–5), soups (especially *sopa de tortilla,* $5), and entrées ($8–14), including fondues (with bacon), pork loin (*lomo,* with guacamole), and chicken (with *mole poblano*).

INFORMATION AND SERVICES
Tourist Information

The most accessible city tourist information source is the booth *(módulo)* (intersection of Progreso and Juárez, open at least Mon.–Fri. 9 A.M.–3 P.M., Sat.–Sun. 10 A.M.–2 P.M.), on Juárez at El Pariáan's southwest corner. The official city tourism office is **Sub-Dirección de Turismo y Artesanías** (Juárez 238, second floor on the west side, between Cruz Verde and Medellín, tel. 33/3635-7050, 33/3635-2318, 33/3635-2320, or 33/3635-2321, turismotlaquepaque@hotmail.com, open Mon.–Fri. 9 A.M.–3 P.M.).

Banking

At least three banks, all with ATMs, serve the Tlaquepaque town center. Most are along Hidalgo-Independencia, near the *jardín*. For the longest banking hours, go to **Hong Kong Shanghai Banking Corporation** (HSBC) (corner of Hidalgo, just east of El Parián, open Mon.–Sat. 8 A.M.–7 P.M.). On the other side of the street, a half block west, you'll find popular **Banamex** (Hidalgo 88, tel. 33/3636-1701, open Mon.–Fri. 9 A.M.–4 P.M., Sat. 10 A.M.– 2 P.M.). Another half block west, across from El Parián, is **Banorte** (Independencia 115A, corner of Progreso, tel. 33/3635-3515, open Mon.– Sat. 9 A.M.–4 P.M., Sat. 10 A.M.–2 P.M.).

Library

Tlaquepaque's modest municipal library *(biblioteca)* (tel. 33/3639-4363, open Mon.–Fri. 8 A.M.–7:30 P.M.) is at the southeast corner of P. Sánchez and Constitución. A highlight of its (nearly all Spanish) collection is the hard-to-get *Los Indios de Mexico* five-volume set, by Fernando Benítez, cat. 972.0098 B43. Get there by walking west from the *jardín* along Independencia one block to Sánchez, then right (north) two blocks to the corner of Constitución.

Guides and Tours

A very well-prepared and personable guide is American-Mexican innkeeper Arturo Magaña, owner of Quinta Don José in Tlaquepaque (tel. 33/3635-7522, U.S.-Canada toll-free tel. 866/629-3753, fax 33/3659-9315, info@quintadonjose.com, www.quintadonjose.com).

If somehow Arturo's very popular tours are booked up, he recommends a pair of excellent guides: Four stars go to both **Ramiro Roma** (tel./fax 33/3631-4242 or cell tel. 044-33/3661-6202 in Guadalajara, or long-distance tel. 01-33/3661-6202 outside Guadalajara), with accommodation for up to six persons in his late-model van; and well-informed, English-speaking, licensed **Lino Gabriel González Nuño** (Azapozalco 757, Suite 17, Tlaquepaque, Jalisco 45625, tel. 33/3152-0324, cell tel. within Guadalajara 044-33/3195-6315, fax 33/3330-1292, linogabriel@hotmail.com, www.mexonline.com/guadalajaratours.htm), who is available for local and greater Guadalajara tours. He would probably be very helpful in bargaining with shopkeepers for the best prices. He also has a comfortable sedan for touring.

Photography

Tlaquepaque's town-center photo shop is the professionally owned and operated **Photo Studio Kolor Zuku** (Independencia 136, open Mon.–Sat. 10 A.M.–8 P.M., Sun. 10 A.M.– 2 P.M.), a half block west of the *jardín*. Services include one-hour color development, black-and-white development and printing, transparencies, camera repair, enlargements, and some for-sale film and equipment, including point-and-shoot and SLR cameras.

POST AND COMMUNICATIONS

The Tlaquepaque telecommunications office and post office are both on Guillermo Prieto, the short street that runs north from the *jardín*'s northwest corner. Telecom (Guillermo Prieto 29, open Mon.–Fri. 8 A.M.–7 P.M., Sat.– Sun. 9 A.M.–noon) services include telephones, public fax (33/3635-0980), money orders, and Internet access ($2/hour). A half block farther north is the *correo* (Guillermo Prieto 88, tel. 33/3635-0503, open Mon.–Fri. 8 A.M.–3 P.M., Sat. 9 A.M.–1 P.M.).

Shipping Agencies

For a local shipping agency to package and send your purchases safely home, try **Sebastián Exports** (Independencia 299A, west end, a half block before Niños Heroes, tel./fax 33/3657-7282).

HEALTH AND EMERGENCIES
Medical Services

Tlaquepaque has pharmacies, a hospital with an emergency room, a medical specialty clinic, and individual doctors' offices. For routine remedies, consult the on-duty pharmacist at **Farmacia Benavides** (Independencia 70, right in the middle of the town, tel. 33/3635-2137, open daily 8 A.M.–midnight).

For nonemergency medical consultations, there's **Hospital Providencia** (Niños Heroes 29, east side of street between Juárez and Reforma, tel. 33/3639-5155 or 33/3637-8735, Mon.–Sat. 8 A.M.–2 P.M. and 4–8 P.M.).

Alternatively, try the **Hospital de Diagnosis** specialist clinic (Juárez 199, corner of Miranda, tel. 33/3659-4457), with Dr. Jose Jesus Vasquez in charge, and many specialists on 24-hour call.

In a medical emergency, ask your hotel desk to get you a taxi (tel. 33/3635-0662) or ambulance (Red Cross tel. 33/3613-1550 or 33/3614-5600) to the 24-hour emergency room at Tlaquepaque Hospital Providencia.

Police and Fire

For police and fire emergencies, call emergency tel. 066 or the Tlaquepaque police at 33/3635-2045 or 33/3635-8828.

GETTING THERE

Get to Tlaquepaque from downtown Guadalajara by taxi (about $5) or ride the often crowded city bus 275 diagonal (look for Tlaquepaque scrawled on the front window) or, better, the air-conditioned TUR (Turquoise) 706 bus from stops along downtown north–south Avenida 16 de Septiembre. The buses continue southwest for about three miles (five km) to the big **Puente Artesanal** Tlaquepaque entrance arch over Avenida Barragán, just before the Avenida Niños Héroes traffic circle. The Avenida Independencia pedestrian shopping mall is on the left (east) side, one block past (south of) the traffic circle.

By car, from the center of town, the key is to get to the entrance to Tlaquepaque from Guadalajara, marked by a soaring arch over the southeast end of Boulevard General Marcelino Garcia Barragán. Driving south along downtown Avenida 16 de Septiembre, at Plaza San Francisco, turn left at Calzada Revolución, the street that runs just behind the San Francisco church. Mark your odometer.

Continue 1.1 miles (1.8 km) and turn right at main thoroughfare Calzada del Ejército. After two short blocks, turn left at Barragán and continue 1.7 miles (2.8 km) to the arch. Park and walk straight ahead (careful crossing the traffic circle) about 100 yards to the Avenida Independencia pedestrian mall.

Although local buses or your own wheels can get you to Tlaquepaque, crowds of bus commuters and congested city streets increase the desirability of a **local guide or tour.** Contact your hotel travel desk, a travel agent, or a well-equipped agency such as Panoramex (Federalismo Sur 944, tel. 33/3810-5057 or 33/3810-5005, www.pan-oramex.com.mx), which conducts reasonably priced bilingual tours daily from the city center.

If you're doing lots of independent or car traveling, get the very reliable **Guia Roji Red Vial Ciudad de Guadalajara** city street map. It's available at Sanborns restaurants.

Tonalá

About five miles farther southeast past Tlaquepaque, Tonalá reigns over its sprawling *municipio* (pop. 350,000) of towns, factories, farms, and ranches. When the Spanish arrived in 1530, Tonalá was dominant among the small chiefdoms of the Atemajac Valley. Tonalá's queen and her royal court were adorned by the glittering handiwork of an honored class of silver and gold crafters. Although the Spaniards carted off the valuables, the dominance of Tonalá craftsmanship remains today. Most handicrafts sold in Tlaquepaque are actually made in Tonalá.

To the visitor, nearly everyone in Tonalá seems to be making something. Tonalá family patios are piled with their specialties, whether it be pottery, stoneware, brass, or papier-mâché.

Besides the daily host of visitors shopping for souvenirs, gifts, and home decorations, resolute professional buyers frequent Tonalá's small handicrafts factories, negotiating for wholesale lots of merchandise for shipment all over Mexico and the rest of world.

PLANNING YOUR TIME

As in Tlaquepaque, Tonalá's main sights are its many attractive handicrafts shops, and especially the several **factory shops** that welcome visitors. Along your stroll, near the town plaza, be sure not to miss the **Santuario del Sagrado Corazón de Jesús** (Sanctuary of the Sacred Heart of Jesus), the adjacent *palacio municipal,* the bronze **statue of Cihualpilli,** and the beloved old **Parroquia de Santiago** (one hour total).

A few blocks farther, on the north side of town, be sure to stop by the **Museo Regional Tonallán** and **Museo National de la Cerámica** (one hour). Spend the rest of your time, probably most of a day or more, visiting handicrafts shops and stopping for lunch and perhaps supper

© BRUCE WHIPPERMAN

On Sunday and Thursday market days, handicrafts street stalls bloom all over Tonalá.

THE CONQUEST OF TONALLÁN

The arrival of the Spanish, in the person of Nuño de Guzmán and his small army, on March 25, 1530, changed Tonallán forever. The Tonallán ruler, Cihualpilli, after consultation with her ruling council, decided to receive the Spaniards on friendly terms. Nevertheless, a rebellious group of her subjects attacked Guzmán's forces, who retaliated, forcing Cihualpilli, her court, and bodyguards to retreat to their fortified hilltop, north of town, now named Cerro de la Reina (Queen's Hill), but in those days called "Bellybutton Hill" because of its shape.

After a fierce siege, Spanish steel and cannon finally slashed a bloody path to the hilltop, and Guzmán's forces captured Cihualpilli. She and her people, however, remained unrepentant.

Tonalá's official history recounts that, at a mass gathering, Cihualpilli's subjects angrily screamed at the Spanish conquistadors: "To arms! To arms! Enemy! Betrayer!" Guzmán, exasperated, grabbed the captive Cihualpilli by the hand and drew his sword, declaring, "Here you will die, woman." With both innocence and defiant heroism she answered, "You are a warrior and should not hesitate, since I am only a woman, with no fear, standing by your side."

Spaniards who later narrated the conquest of Tonallán wrote that the Tonallán people were "faithful as lambs in peace, and ferocious as lions in war."

While the passage of time has softened the memory of their battle against Spanish arms, storytellers have mythologized the war to a struggle between an apparition of Santiago (Apostle St. James) as a warrior upholding the

© BRUCE WHIPPERMAN

The image of Father Sun is a Tonalá ("Place of the Rising Sun") icon that predates the Spanish conquest.

Spanish (and therefore God's) cause against the idolaters. Still, today the sick and lame make the most of the myth, begging alms in the name of Santiago.

Local folks breathe new life into the legend every July 25, Santiago's feast day, in Tonalá's traditional dance, La Danza de los Tastoanes. Excitement peaks as ferociously masqueraded participants reenact the part of the indigenous defenders *(tastoanes)*, evading the sword swipes of a horseback-mounted Santiago.

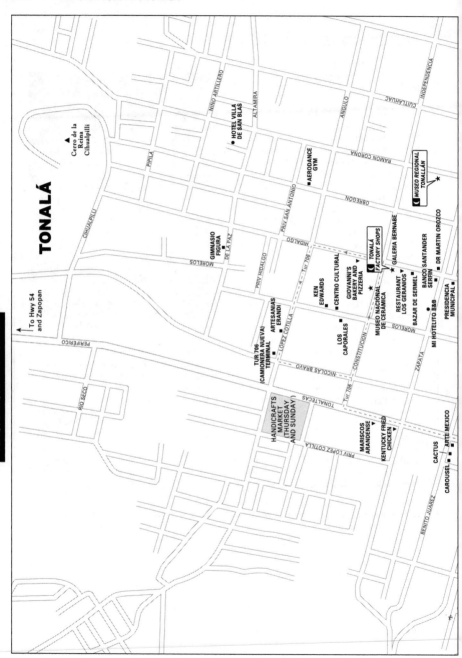

TONALÁ

To Hwy 54 and Zapopan

Cerro de la Reina Cihualpilli

HOTEL VILLA DE SAN BLAS

AERODANCE GYM

MUSEO REGIONAL TONALLÁN

GIMNASIO FIGURA DE LA PAZ

CENTRO CULTURAL

KEN EDWARDS

GIOVANNI'S BAKERY AND PIZZERIA

TONALÁ FACTORY SHOPS

GALERIA BERNABE

MUSEO NACIONAL DE CERAMICA

RESTAURANT LOS GERANIOS

BANCO SANTANDER SERFIN

DR MARTIN OROZCO

BAZAR DE SERMEL

MI HOTELITO B&B

PRESIDENCIA MUNICIPAL

LOS CAPORALES

ARTESANIAS ERANDI

TUR 706 (CAMIONERA NUEVA) TERMINAL

HANDICRAFTS MARKET (THURSDAY AND SUNDAY)

MARISCOS ARANDENSE

KENTUCKY FRIED CHICKEN

CACTUS

ARTE MEXICO

CAROUSEL

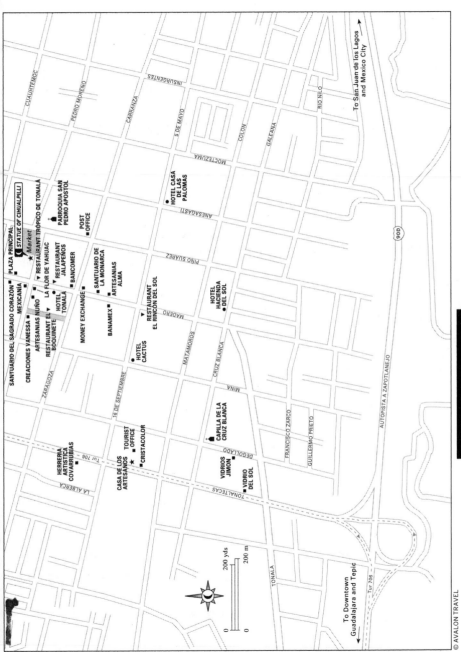

© AVALON TRAVEL

at **Restaurant El Rincón del Sol** or other good Tonalá restaurants.

ORIENTATION

Tonalá's easy-to-follow street grid and small size make it simple to explore on foot. The center of town is the **Plaza Principal,** at the intersection of east–west **Calle Benito Juárez** and north–south **Calle Francisco Madero** (which becomes Calle Hidalgo north of Juárez).

Stand (or imagine standing) at the corner of Juárez and Madero and face north. Straight ahead is Calle Hidalgo, usually decorated with the *tianguis* (awnings) of handicrafts sellers. To the right (east) is the Plaza Principal and central *kiosco* (bandstand). In the building farther to the right, bordering the plaza, is the town **market.**

Across Juárez, on your left, rises the white, spired facade of the venerable **Santuario del Sagrado Corazón de Jesús.** Half a block farther north, on the left side of Hidalgo, stands the dignified, colonnaded *palacio municipal* (town hall).

SIGHTS
Santuario del Sagrado Corazón de Jesús

This 1899 reconstruction of an earlier church makes a good starting point. Dramatic paintings of all the stations of the cross decorate the nave walls. Up front, a lovely modern *retablo* rises behind the altar, with an image of Jesus on a throne of billowing clouds, draped in a cape of gold. Above him, his words, *Venid todos a mi* (All come to me) summon the faithful. Finally, before you leave, pay your respects to the Virgen de la Misericordia (Virgin of the Merciful) in the chapel to the right of the nave.

Palacio Municipal

Let Tonalá's *palacio municipal,* next to the church, be your next stop. Notable art works decorate its interior corridors. To the left after you enter, at the right foot of the stairway, admire the large *bruñido*-technique ceramic tile plaque, commemorating the arrival of the Spanish on March 25, 1530. The plaque's cen-

tral and lower portions illustrate the Cerro de la Reina and the sun god, Tonatiu.

Climb the stairs and see the shiny copper doors, emblazoned with the sun god, in the balcony corridor. Continue along the right-side corridor to the large blue-gray ceramic wall plaque that memorializes the battle on the hill, the Cerro de la Reina, between the Tonalá fighters and the Spanish. (See the sidebar *The Conquest of Tonallán.*)

Back downstairs, continue straight ahead from the foot of the stairs, just past the patio corner, on the right, to admire the ceramic jars, fine examples of native Tonalá *bruñido* and *petatillo* techniques.

◖ Statue of Cihualpilli

Outside, cross Hidalgo east and enter the Plaza Principal. To the right of the Porfirian-era 1890 bandstand stands a dramatically Olympian bronze statue of Tonalá's legendary queen, hurling a spear as if it were a javelin. Although the

Queen Cihualpilli led her subjects in a fierce last-ditch battle against Spanish guns and steel.

statue depicts a Tarzanesque woman of about age 20, Cihualpilli was a widow of about 40 at the time of her people's battle with conquistador Nuño de Guzmán in 1530. (See the sidebar *The Conquest of Tonallan.*)

Parroquia de Santiago

Continue east a half block along the plaza's south side to the landmark parish church and ex-convent Parroquia de Santiago. The present building, started by the Augustinian friars around 1625, was their home until 1799, when the local "secular" (as opposed to monastic) clergy replaced them and finished rebuilding the original church in 1813.

The interior is replete with religious symbolism. Moving clockwise around the nave, first find a painted stucco image of Santiago (St. James), looking like Jesus, with sword in hand, mounted atop his traditional white horse. Next to him, San Rafael, following Jesus's charge to become "a fisher of men," sits with a fish in his left hand. Above the altar is the Sacred Heart of Jesus, and below that, elevated just a step above the nave floor, is the original 1630 *cantera* stone baptismal font. Finally, step through the nave's right-hand side door (with keystone dated 1744) and take a turn around the cloister of the Augustinian ex-convent.

◖ Museo Regional Tonallán

Make the regional museum (Ramón Corona 73, tel. 33/3683-2519, open Mon.–Fri. 9 A.M.–3 P.M.), one block east and two blocks north of the Santiago parish church, your first north-side stop. Appropriately housed in a rustic old-Tonalá adobe, the museum's mission is to interpret the history and demonstrate the practice of Tonalá crafts. Artisans exhibit their technique, displays illustrate historical events, masters exhibit their finished work, and local people stage dramatic productions on a stage beneath the traditional sun symbol of Tonalá.

Museo Nacional de la Cerámica

Next, walk a fraction of a block north and turn left (west) at Independencia and continue three blocks (past Hidalgo, where Independencia changes to Constitución) to the Museo Nacional de la Cerámica (Constitutción 104, tel. 33/3283-4765 or 33/3683-0971, open Tues.–Fri. 10 A.M.–5 P.M., Sat.–Sun. 10 A.M.–3 P.M.). Ten exhibition rooms on two floors display super-fine examples of ceramics from all over Mexico. After feasting your eyes on the many luscious examples, from Oaxaca's lustrous San Bartolo blacks and brilliant Atzompa reds to Michoacán's rich Uruapan green and Tonalá's gorgeous *petatillo,* pick out your favorites for sale in the shop.

Cerro de la Reina

Finally, if you have an extra hour, make a pilgrimage (six blocks north along Hidalgo) to the Cerro de la Reina (Queen's Hill), originally known as Cerro del Ombligo (Bellybutton Hill). Stroll to the summit and enjoy the airy panorama of the surrounding Valle de Atemajac.

This hilltop was the setting for the final bloody battle between the Spaniards and Cihualpilli and her people in 1530. Nearby, a statue depicts the queen embracing the True Cross. Other statues dramatize the queen's fierce, spear-brandishing guardian warriors. If it's open, take a look around inside the hilltop chapel, built in honor of the Virgin of Guadalupe, of locally quarried volcanic stone.

Although ordinarily quiet, this hilltop bustles with activity on Holy Saturday, the day before Easter Sunday. As part of the combined National Handicrafts Fair and the Tonalá Festival of the Sun, dancers reenact the battle with the Dance of the Tastoanes, and pilgrims trace the stations of the cross.

Capilla de la Cruz Blanca

Later, if you have time during your Tonalá shopping tour, visit the Capilla de la Cruz Blanca (Chapel of the White Cross), the spot where the Spaniards celebrated Guadalajara's first mass, on March 25, 1530. Find it at the corner of Calles Cruz Blanco and Degollado, four blocks south and two blocks east of the main town plaza.

TAKING PICTURES OF PEOPLE

Like most folks everywhere, typical Guadalajara people on the street rarely appreciate strangers taking their pictures. The easiest route to overcoming this is a local friend, guide, or even a willing interpreter or bystander who can provide an introduction. Lacking that, you'll need to be at least semifluent in Spanish in order to introduce yourself or say something funny to break the ice.

A useful way to go is to offer to send them a copy of their picture. If they accept, make sure that you follow through. If for some reason the picture doesn't come out, at least send them a picture of you, explaining what happened.

Although it's becoming less common, some country people still believe that they might lose their soul if they let you take their picture. In such a case, humor again might help (or perhaps offering to let them take a picture of you first).

Markets are wonderful picture-taking places, but also pose challenges. Vendors are often resistant, to the point of hostility, if you try to take their picture behind their sumptuous pile of tomatoes or stack of baskets. The reasons aren't hard to understand. They're grumpy partly because sales are probably disappointing, and, since they have to stay put, they probably feel used. Buying something from them might go a long way toward soothing their feelings.

Under all circumstances, please do not offer to pay people for the privilege of taking a their picture. It will be a shame if you do, because they're going to be thinking money whenever they see tourists. Instead, turn the photo session into a person-to-person exchange by offering to send them a copy of their picture.

As for church picture-taking, remember that churches are places of worship, and not museums. Don't be rude and try to take pictures of people at the altar. Moreover, churches are usually dark inside, and, unless you have a flash-suppress option or an unusually high-speed camera, your flash will disturb worshippers.

Be considerate when taking photos of people.

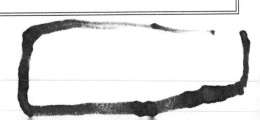

FESTIVALS

Tonalá's hardworking people take time out to whoop it up during three big local yearly festivals. For more information and event schedules, watch for street posters or contact Tonalá's Turismo information office.

The Tonalá year heats up early, with the Mardi Gras–like **Carnaval,** which climaxes on Shrove Tuesday (six weeks and five days before Easter Sunday and the day before Ash Wednesday). Besides plenty of music, street dancing, floats, and carnival rides and games, dancers delight the crowd as they poke fun at the former Spanish colonials in the **Los Viejitos** (Little Old Ones) traditional dance.

Tonalá's year peaks again in the joint municipal **Fiesta del Sol** (Festival of the Sun) and the **Feria Nacional Artesanal** (National Handicrafts Fair), during the two weeks preceding Easter Sunday. The town overflows with events, including a daily handicrafts street market, expositions of Jalisco and national handicrafts, all-Jalisco handicrafts competitions, demonstrations of technique by master craftspeople, float parade, bands, literary and artistic performances, sports events, carnival games, fireworks, cockfights, and, finally, a pilgrimage of the stations of the cross on the Saturday before Easter Sunday.

Tonalá's other big annual blowout, the **Fiesta de Santiago** (St. James), sometimes known as the **Fiesta Pagana,** or Pagan Festival, culminates on July 25 with the not-to-be-missed **Dance of the Tastoanes.** In Tonalá's unique reenactment of the conquest, a mounted Santiago swings his sword against a troupe of fearsome masked *tastoanes* (indigenous warriors). The local crowd of onlookers, whipped to excitement by drumbeats and the staccato rhythm of indigenous flutelike *chirimias,* roars with delight as the defending *tastoanes* fiercely persist, beneath Santiago's punishing charges and blows.

SPORTS AND RECREATION
Walking and Jogging

Tonalá's quiet back streets (away from the crowded main plaza area) are excellent for walking. For example, start at the southeast-side corner of Anesagasti and Matamoros, and walk north gradually uphill, a total of one mile (1.6 km) to the top of the 200-foot (60-meter) **Cerro de la Reina.**

If that's not enough exercise, jog some laps around the Cerro de la Reina's breezy summit park. Each full circuit will amount to approximately a quarter mile.

Golf, Tennis, and Swimming

Tonalá has few, if any, close-by public sports facilities. However, the Atlas Country Club, on the airport road a mile south of the *periférico,* has a big swimming pool, tennis courts, and an 18-hole golf course usable by the public for a moderate fee. (See *Sports and Recreation* in the *Tlaquepaque* section.)

SHOPPING

Right at the source, Tonalá is an unexcelled shopping ground. For super bargains and *mucho* holiday excitement and color, visit the **Thursday and Sunday** *tianguis* (market), which spreads over half the town, four blocks east from the west-side Avenida Tonaltecas, past the Tonalá main plaza.

During any day of the week, mounds of attractive handicrafts are available in the dozens of shops around Tonalá's central plaza corner of north–south Avenida Hidalgo-Madero and east–west Avenida Juárez.

The two shopping tours covered here can be done singly or in succession. The shortest requires a couple of hours around the plaza. It continues for an approximately four-hour loop that takes in several of the renowned factory stores that welcome visitors.

Shops near the Plaza

Attractive handicrafts shops dot **Avenida Francisco Madero,** from a couple of blocks south of the main plaza to a couple of blocks north (where Avenida Madero has become Avenida Hidalgo). Browse the shops, starting at the southern end and wandering gradually north.

Start at **Carrusel** (Madero 88, tel. 33/3683-1986, open Mon.–Sat. 10 A.M.–7 P.M., Sun.

TLAQUEPAQUE AND TONALÁ

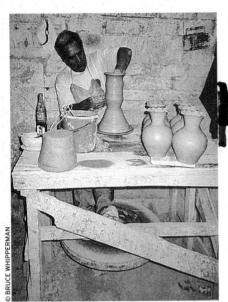

The elegant design of Tonalá's ceramics begins in the gentle but skillful hands of master craft workers.

© BRUCE WHIPPERMAN

10 A.M.–4 P.M.), on the west side of the street. The owners specialize in the rustic but decorative, such as merry-go-round horses, quixotic Don Quixotes, and chandeliers.

Continue north to **Artesanías Alma** (Madero 75, tel./fax 33/3683-0547, open Mon.–Fri. 10 A.M.–7 P.M., Sat.–Sun. 10 A.M.–3 P.M.). Select from a wide range of metalware, from sculpted horses and rhinos to bright mother moon mirrors and jeweled lamps, and much, much more.

A few doors farther north, find **Artesanías Rústicos Lagarto** (Alligator) (corner of Madero and Zaragoza, tel./fax 33/3683-1230, open Mon.–Sat. 10 A.M.–7 P.M., Sun. 10 A.M.–3:30 P.M.). Choose from a broad assortment of attractively rustic pre-Columbian ceramic figurines, vases, and masks (especially handsome for wall decorations), and plenty of glass, including shiny solid spheres and gems. (You might also visit their second branch, at 57A Zaragoza, a half block west.)

Also at Zaragoza, be sure to detour a half block west (left) to the shady mall-like **Pasaje El Santuario** (Sanctuary Passage), which connects from Zaragoza north with Juárez. Along the way, stop to soak in the passing scene at **El Boquinete** restaurant. While there, be sure to check out **El Santuario** (cell tel. 044-33/3456-7676, open Mon.–Sat. 10 A.M.–6:30 P.M., Sun. 10 A.M.–3:30 P.M.), a clothing stall across the aisle from the café. Choose from oodles of attractive Guadalajara cotton resort wear and embroidered skirts, blouses, dresses, shirts, and *huipiles,* all from Oaxaca. (See more at their main store, Creaciones Vanesa, at 87 Juárez.)

Moving north from the passageway to Juárez, find **Artesanías Nuño** (Juárez 59, tel. 33/3683-0011, open Mon.–Sat. 10 A.M.–7:30 P.M., Sun. 10 A.M.–5 P.M.) to the right, a few doors before the town plaza corner. Pick from a fetching menagerie, including parrots, monkeys, flamingos, and toucans, in papier-mâché, brass, and ceramics; bargain for very reasonable buys.

Continue to the plaza corner, and **La Mexicanía** (Hidalgo 13, tel. 33/3683-0152, open Mon.–Sat. 10 A.M.–7 P.M., Sun. 11 A.M.–3 P.M.), at the northwest corner of Juárez. In the many years that I've been coming to Tonalá, La Mexicanía has prospered and expanded, by virtue of its diverse, all-Mexico collection. This is heaven for Mexico handicrafts lovers. If you've wanted a particular item—a weaving or a *huipil* from Oaxaca, a jaguar mask from Guerrero, a guitar from Michoacán, an ironwood sailfish from Sonora, a Huichol indigenous yarn painting, or a Guanajuato papier-mâché clown—they've got it.

A block and half farther north, be sure to visit **El Bazar de Sermel** (Hidalgo 67, tel. 33/3683-0010, fax 33/3683-0160, sermelsa@prodigy.net.mx., open Mon.–Fri. 9 A.M.–6:30 P.M., Sat. 9 A.M.–2:30 P.M., Sun. 10 A.M.–3 P.M.). Here, master craftspersons have stretched the Tonalá papier-mâché tradition to the ultimate. Stop in and pick out the life-size flamingo, pony, giraffe, or zebra you've always wanted for your living room.

Continue a few doors north to **Galería Bernabe** factory store (Hidalgo 83, tel.

33/3683-0040, tel./fax 33/3683-0877, www.galeriabernabe.com, open Mon.–Fri. 9 A.M.–7 P.M., Sat.–Sun. 8 A.M.–3 P.M.). Celebrated founder of the 200-year-old *petatillo* (little petal) double-fired technique, Bernabe specializes in intricate, fetching animal and plant designs in black, green, and white. Some of the best pieces are reminiscent of fine ancient Chinese ceramics. Offerings vary, from glistening vases, pitchers, and bowls to gorgeous table settings for a dozen or more. If you can't find exactly what you want, they'll create your own design to order.

◖ Tonalá Factory Shops

With your handicrafts appetite whetted by the excellent **Galería Bernabe,** continue (north half a block, turn left at Cotilla, then right at Morelos) to **Los Caporales** big factory store (Morelos 155B, tel./fax 33/3683-0312, fax 33/3683-1184, info@ceramicacaporales.com, www.ceramicacaporales.com, open Mon.–Fri. 9 A.M.–6 P.M., Sat. 10 A.M.–2 P.M.). Los Caporales specializes in glistening, high-fired *cor-*

cho-technique ware, from decorative animal figurines to utilitarian plates, bowls, and vases. Past the rear of the showroom, tour the factory, where workers begin with humble clay that they mix, mold, smooth, paint, glaze, and finally fire into handsome works of art.

Continue north, across the street, to **Ken Edwards** store and factory (Morelos 184, tel./fax 33/3683-0313, kentonala@yahoo.com, open Mon.–Fri. 9:30 A.M.–6 P.M., Sat. 10 A.M.–2 P.M.). Founder Ken Edwards, elaborating on the intricate high-fired *petatillo* stoneware, gained international renown during the 1970s and 1980s. He turned his operation over to present owner Pedro Velasco and moved to Guatemala, but his tradition lives on, in the irresistible heirloom animal and floral design table settings that the factory produces.

No Tonalá factory tour would be complete without a visit to **Artesanías Erandi** (López Cotilla 118, tel. 33/3683-0253, fax 33/3683-0871, ventas@erandi.com, www.erandi.com, open Mon.–Fri. 10 A.M.–7 P.M., Sat. 10 A.M.–2 P.M.), a half block farther north (turn left on

© BRUCE WHIPPERMAN

A factory tour reveals the humble clay origin of Tonalá's fine ceramics.

TLAQUEPAQUE AND TONALÁ

Cotilla). You're at the source of the much-imitated high-fired Erandi style, known all over Mexico and much of the developed world. Step into the rear factory and view craftspeople putting life into the fetching motifs—curled-up cats, preening ducks, bearded men in the moon.

Next, for something different, head west a block to divided Avenida Tonaltecas, turn left (south), and continue three blocks to the woodcrafts and furniture stores, at the southwest corner of Avenida Juárez.

First comes **Rústica Alameda** (Juárez 237, tel./fax 33/3683-1479, open Mon.–Sat. 10 A.M.–7 P.M., Sun. 10 A.M.–5 P.M.). The all-rustic selection, made at their factory nearby, includes chairs, tables, sideboards, chandeliers, and rocking horses. If you don't find what you want, they'll make it for you.

Next, head across the street, where you can check out a number of stores. These include **Mi Viejo Mexico** (Juárez 240B); **Rústicas Tequila,** next door; and **Muebles Rústicos** (Juárez 246, tel./fax 33/3683-1772), a few doors west. Select from a big array of utilitarian couches, cabinets, tables, small desks, bar stools, bedsteads, and much more, at both retail and wholesale prices. All are open approximately Monday–Saturday 10 A.M.–7 P.M., Sunday 10 A.M.–5 P.M.

A block and a half farther south, fine ironwork is king at **Herrería Artistica Covarrubias** (Tonaltecas 106, tel./fax 33/3683-2420, open Mon.–Sat. 9 A.M.–6 P.M., Sun. 11 A.M.–4 P.M.). The showroom (be sure to see the factory in back) gleams with nearly everything that can be crafted from iron—tables, chairs, cabinets, shelves, benches, chandeliers—and also brass and copper. If you don't see it here, take a look at the catalog and special order what you've always wanted.

Continue another half block south to what appears to be the glass capital of Tonalá, **Cristacolor Export** (Tonaltecas 200, tel. 33/3683-0665, fax 33/3683-0668, crista-color@att.net.mx, open Mon.–Fri. 10 A.M.–6 P.M., Sat.–Sun. 10 A.M.–4 P.M.), with a huge (public-inaccessible) factory looming behind the street-front store. Although they produce a small mountain of wholesale glassware daily, they do sell directly to the public, with discounts of up to 10 percent for purchases of $1,000 or more. The showroom displays a huge assortment of fetching blue, green, red, and crystal-clear colorless glassware tumblers, goblets, pitchers, bowls, and wine glasses.

Continue to another pair of glass factories. Two blocks farther south, find **Vidrios del Sol** (Av. Tonaltecas 281, tel. 33/3683-1015, fax 33/3683-2632, open daily 10 A.M.–7 P.M.). Step inside and pick from a rainbow of decorative glass, from whales to cocktail stirrers to silver glass spheres and hurricane lampshades. Don't be put off by the dust that covers everything; they're too busy selling to clean it off.

Circle the block (continue south a half block, left at Avenida Tonalá, and left again at Santos Degollado) to **Vidrios Jimon** (open Mon.–Sat. 9 A.M.–6 P.M., Sun. 11 A.M.–4 P.M.), in the middle of the block. Out front, the factory, which you shouldn't miss, sounds like a volcano from the roar of the gas-fired ovens inside. Enter through the store, which displays a shiny, multicolored array of mirrored glass balls.

ACCOMMODATIONS

Tonalá has a sprinkling of modest (all under $50 double) but recommendable hotels. Although initially built to accommodate the platoons of professional buyers who visit Tonalá year-round, these hotels are now increasingly serving the needs of visitors who appreciate Tonalá as a destination in its own right. Make advance reservations, especially for the Saturday and Wednesday nights before the big Sunday and Thursday outdoor *tianguis* markets.

Under $25

Tonalá's most picturesque lodging, the **Hotel Villas Don Blas** (Cerrada Altamira 10, Tonalá, Jalisco 45400, tel. 33/3683-2588, villasdonblas@tonala.org, $20–50) is tucked on a quiet, north-end lane. A labor of love for its on-site owners, Rafael Ángel and his American wife, Diana Romo, Villas Don Blas is named in honor of Rafael's late father.

After several years of building, Rafael's monument has blossomed. He's a stonemason, and it shows. The easily worked local volcanic stone, called *cantera,* decorates the facade in a feast of Renaissance columns, arches, window sills, and downspouts.

The elegantly quirky decorations extend to the rooms. The most attractive and light lodgings are upstairs, above a cool garden corridor-patio. Most accommodations are spacious, with at least two double beds, reading lamps, and rustic handmade wooden furniture. Baths, with sinks (some of which are mounted on classic stone pedestals of Rafael's design) are uniquely attractive.

Get there from the main plaza, corner of Juárez, by walking north along Hidalgo five blocks; turn right at de la Paz, continue three short blocks, turn left at uphill lane Cerrada Altamira, and continue a half block to the hotel on the right.

Right in the middle of downtown action is the newcomer best-buy **(Mi Hotelito Bed and Breakfast** (E. Zapata 76, Tonalá, Jalisco 45400, tel. 33/3683-2176, hotelito@ tonala.com.mx, www.tonala.com.mx/miho-telito, $23–37), between Morelos and Hidalgo, just a half block west of the town plaza. Mi Hotelito owners are trying harder, offering 16 immaculate white-walled and tiled-floor rooms and suites on two (ground and upstairs) floors. Amenities include reading lamp, shiny shower baths, ceiling fans, continental breakfast and comfy downstairs sitting room around a fireplace. Since the downstairs rooms open directly on to the sitting room, reserve a room upstairs for more quiet and privacy. Some rooms lack exterior windows: have a look before you pay.

$25-50

Just two blocks from the town center, the plain, last-resort **Hotel El Cactus** (Javier Mina 153, Tonalá, Jalisco 45400, tel. 33/3683-2176 or 33/3683-2914, $25–30), on Mina between 16 de Septiembre and Matamoros, may have a room when no else does. Owned and operated by the blown-glass artisan-owners of nearby Tienda Cactus, the hotel's nine rooms line opposite sides of a dim interior corridor. Rooms are basic but clean and acceptable for a night or two, and come with shaded reading lamps, cable TV, Internet access, fans, and parking.

Find the cheerier **Hotel Hacienda del Sol** (Cruz Blanca 44, Tonalá, Jalisco 45400, tel./ fax 33/3683-0275, 33/3683-5141 or 33/3683-5142, reserve@hotelhaciendadelsol.com, www. hotelhaciendadelsol.com, $28–40) four blocks directly south of the town center. Hotel guests, many of whom are Mexican and international wholesale buyers, enjoy a spacious inner courtyard leading upstairs to about 30 clean and comfortable modern-style rooms. Furnishings include one king-size or two single or two double beds and attractively tiled, up-to-date bathrooms with shower. Extras include handcrafted furniture, designer bed lamps, rustic wall art, and fax and Internet access. Rates include fans, telephone, cable TV, and credit cards accepted.

The centrally located, long-time, but now renovated **Hotel Tonalá** (Madero 22, Tonalá, Jalisco 45400, tel./fax 33/3683-0595 or 33/3683-4892, reservations@hoteltonala.com, www.hoteltonala.com, $35–42), with an entry doubling as a cut-rate art gallery, stands just a half block south of the main plaza. The 22 milk-white-walled, tiled-floor rooms, which line both side of a long corridor, come with fans, TV, hot-water bath, parking, and restaurant downstairs.

Two blocks east and two blocks south of the town center, the **(Hotel Casa de las Palomas** (Anesagasti 125, corner of Cinco de Mayo, tel./fax 33/3683-5542 or 33/3683-5543, reserve@casadelaspalomas.com, www. casadelaspalomas.com, $38–47) caters to both tourists and business clientele. Past the small front lobby, the hotel's two upper floors of 22 rooms line walkways that overlook an inner parking courtyard. Little has been spared to make the rooms attractive and comfortable, including creamy pastel bedspreads, rustic-chic tile floors, designer reading lamps, and modern standard bathrooms. The hotel's only apparent drawback is the noise and exhaust from the cars in the parking courtyard. Alleviate this problem by reserving a third-floor room. All rooms come with satellite TV, fans, Internet access, and parking.

FOOD
Food Stalls

Dive into Mexico by savoring the steaming offerings of the *fondas* (permanent food stalls) in the market, on the main plaza just east of the bandstand. Select from many choices, from flavorful *pozoles* (savory hominy and pork or chicken soup with fresh-cut onions and cabbage, $2–3) and *guisados* and *birrias* (flavorful barbecued beef, lamb, and goat, $2–4) to rich *chiles rellenos,* quesadillas, tamales, *moles* ($2–5), and loads more. Remember: hot (preferably steaming) food is invariably safe. As a precaution, best drench uncooked vegetable salads in plenty of *limón* (lime) juice.

American-Style Restaurants

For pizza and snacks ($5–8) try **Giovanni's Pizzeria** (103 Hidalgo, tel. 33/3683-0303, open daily 11 A.M.–9:30 P.M.), a block and a half north of the *palacio municipal.*

Take a comforting food retreat from Mexico at **Kentucky Fried Chicken** ($3–6), on westside thoroughfare Avenida Tonaltecas, corner of Emiliano Zapata (three blocks west of the main plaza).

For snappy hamburger, hot-dog, and sandwich-style counter service, go to **El Tropico de Tonalá** (Madero 15), a few doors south of the town plaza.

Mexican-Style Restaurants

Mexican country-style restaurants provide relaxing respites for visitors after a hard morning of shopping among Tonalá's seemingly endless displays of attractive pottery, *petatillo,* and papier-mâché.

Moving across town from south to north, first try **Restaurant El Rincón del Sol** (16 de Septiembre 61, tel. 33/3683-1989 or 33/3683-1940, open daily 8:30 A.M.–10 P.M.), at the southwest corner of Madero, two blocks south of the main plaza. In a relaxing hacienda-style

patio setting, kick back and savor Tonalá food at its most typical best, along with live mariachi music Monday–Saturday 7–10 P.M. and Sunday 3–6 P.M. House specialties include beef filets ($8–12), fondue with chorizo ($6), quesadillas with *cuitlacoche* (cooked black corn fungus with mushrooms, $4), cream of carrot soup, and salad (green or chef, $3–5). Afterward, continue to the long list of cocktails, wines, tequilas, brandies, and rums ($3–6). Credit cards accepted.

One block north, step inside the shoppers' reliable standby, **Restaurant Jalapeños** (Madero 23, tel. 33/3683-0344, open daily 8 A.M.–9 P.M.), a block south of the main plaza. Newly installed air-conditioning makes the hot days cool and comfortable. Here you can choose from the long menu of *típica* Mexican specialties, heavy on beef, light on salads and chicken. For a simple meal, go for the tortilla soup ($4), followed by tuna salad (*ensalada de atún,* $4). For something more typical, try the hearty *platón tonalteca,* a big plate of quesadillas, fish tacos, guacamole, chips, and refried beans ($8). Credit cards accepted.

In contrast, **◖ Restaurant Los Geranios** (Hidalgo 69, tel. 33/3383-0486, open Sun.–Fri. 11 A.M.–5 P.M.), a half block north of the plaza, offers a short but Mexican-gourmet menu in a relaxingly refined atmosphere. Operated by the artisan-proprietors of Bazar Sermel next door, Los Geranios specializes in light, innovative, Mexican-style lunch and early supper specialties. For example, start with onion soup or green salad ($4), continue with a plate of enchiladas or maybe chicken *en mole* ($4–6), and finish with flan custard for dessert ($3). Credit cards accepted.

Yet another cool spot for a break or meal is the airy restaurant **◖ El Boquinete** (Pasaje Santuario, tel. 33/3683-5839, www.elboquinete.com, open daily 8 A.M.–9 P.M.), in the shopping passageway that runs north–south from Zaragoza to Juárez, a half block west of Madero. Fine for a drink or meal, the long menu includes professionally prepared and served breakfasts, lunches, and dinners—from pancakes and omelets to salads, hamburgers, Mexican specialties, steaks, fish fillets, and much more ($4–12).

Large seafood eatery **Restaurant Arandense** (Tonaltecas 69 between Independencia and Zapata, tel. 33/3683-5349, open daily 10 A.M.–6:30 P.M.), three blocks west of the plaza, is a locally popular spot to relax for lunch, especially during the Thursday and Sunday open markets. Open-air, family atmosphere, strolling mariachis, and good fresh seafood and *típica* favorites, such as *arrachera* (marinated grilled beef strips, $8), keep the customers streaming in.

INFORMATION AND SERVICES
Tourist Information
On the west side, just north of the Cristacolor glass factory, is Tonalá's generally helpful **Turismo** (Av. Tonalteca 140 Sur, tel./fax 33/3284-3092 or 33/3284-3093, www. tonala.gob.mx/turismo, open Mon.–Fri. 9 A.M.–3 P.M.).

Banking
Three downtown banks, all with ATMs, serve Tonalá customers. Moving from south to north on Madero-Hidalgo, start at **Banamex** (Madero 83, tel. 33/3683-2056, open Mon.–Fri. 9 A.M.–4 P.M.). A half block north and across the street, find **Bancomer** (tel. 33/3683-0070, open Mon.–Fri. 8:30 A.M.–4 P.M.). Finally, three blocks farther north, is **Banco Santander Serfín** (corner of Zapata, open Mon.–Fri. 9 A.M.–4 P.M., Sat. 10 A.M.–2 P.M.).

Travel Agents and Guides
For your air and bus tickets, car rental, hotel reservations, and more, go to **Agencia de Viajes Alfa** (Hidalgo 60, tel. 33/3683-1334, alfa@att.net.mx, open Mon.–Fri. 9 A.M.–3 P.M., and 4–7 P.M., Sat. 9 A.M.–3 P.M.). Alternatively, try **Viajes Tonalá** (Javier Mina 166, tel. 33/3683-1416 or 33/3602-5151, viajestonala@hotmail.com, open Mon.–Fri. 10 A.M.–2 P.M. and 4–6 P.M., Sat. 10 A.M.–2 P.M.).

A number of experienced guides are available for Tonalá sightseeing and shopping. English-speaking Ramo Ramirez is especially recommended, as is well-informed **Lino Gabriel Nuño.** For details, see the *Tlaquepaque* section.

Packing and Shipping
Several Tonalá agencies pack and ship purchases. On the north side, try **Promart** (Privada del Cajón 69, tel. 33/3683-1434, fax 33/3683-2380, promart@prodigy.net.mx, open Mon.–Fri. 9 A.M.–6 P.M.). Get there, from the *palacio municipal,* by walking north on Hidalgo two blocks to López Cotilla. Walk one more short block and turn right on Privada San Antonio, then left on Privada del Cajón.

Laundry
Get your laundry done at **Lavandería Cihualpilli** (Morelos 140A, open Mon.–Sat. 8:30 A.M.–8 P.M., Sun 9 A.M.–3 P.M.), at the corner of Constitución.

COMMUNICATIONS
Post and Telecommunications
The Tonalá post office *(correo)* (Pino Suárez 39, open Mon.–Fri. 9 A.M.–3 P.M., Sat. 9 A.M.–1 P.M.) is a half block south of Parroquia Santiago, a block east of the plaza.

Email, Internet, telephone, and fax service is available at **Instituto MG** (Hidalgo 39, tel. 33/3683-1765, open Mon.–Sat. 8 A.M.–9 P.M.) on the north side of the *palacio municipal.*

Newspaper
Pick up a copy of the information-packed *Guía Tonalá* local newspaper for a load of informative hotel, restaurant, shopping, and service advertisements and interesting historical articles (in Spanish). Free copies are generally available in stores, restaurants, and hotels around town. Alternatively, get a copy at its editorial office (Pedro Moreno 39A, tel. 33/3683-2752, open Mon.–Fri. 9 A.M.–2 P.M. and 4–7 P.M.). Find it on the block that runs along the north side of the Parroquia Santiago Apóstol parish church, a block east of the plaza.

HEALTH AND EMERGENCIES
Medical Services

For routine medications, go to one of Tonalá's many pharmacies. Try **Farmacia Benevides** (Morelos 44, tel./fax 33/3683-3966, open daily 8 A.M.–midnight), on the block behind the *palacio municipal*, or visit family medicine practitioner Dr. Mario Martín Orozco at his **Farmacia Homeopático** (Homeopathic Pharmacy) (Hidalgo 39, office hours at the pharmacy are Mon.–Fri. 4–8 P.M., Sat. 11 A.M.–2 P.M.), a half block north of the plaza.

If you need to consult a specialist, go to the small, centrally located, 24-hour **Hospital de la Cruz** (Independencia 44, tel. 33/3683-2780). For example, associated with this hospital are dermatologist Dra. Norma Aceves Montes, urologist Dr. Hugo Álvarez, gynecologist Dra. Maria Elena Mariscal Rubio, opthalmologist Dr. Elvia Castellanos Bala, and several others.

Alternatively, you can follow your hotel's recommendation, or in a medical emergency, ask your hotel to get a taxi or ambulance (Red Cross tel. 33/3613-1550 or 33/3614-5600) to either their closest recommended hospital or the 24-hour emergency room at Tlaquepaque Hospital Providencia in Tlaquepaque (tel. 33/3639-5155 and 33/3637-8735). Or have the ambulance take you to the highly recommended **Hospital Méxicano-Americano** (in Guadalajara, a 25-minute drive in an emergency) at north-side Avenida Colomos 2110.

Police and Fire

For the Tonalá police, dial 33/3284-3038, 33/3284-3039, 33/3284-3040, or 33/3284-3041. For the firefighters *(bomberos),* call 33/3691-2675 or 33/3691-2676.

GETTING THERE

Get to Tonalá from downtown Guadalajara by taxi (about $10) or ride the air-conditioned TUR (Turquoise) 706 bus or the oft-crowded **city bus 275 diagonal** (look for Tlaquepaque or Tonalá scrawled on the front window), from stops along downtown north–south Avenida 16 de Septiembre. The bus continues southeast along boulevards Revolución, then Barragán, about three miles (five km), passing under the big Puente Artesanal Tlaquepaque entrance arch and continuing along Avenida Corregidora in Tlaquepaque, past the new Central Bus Station, continuing another two miles to Tonalá. Get off at north–south main street Avenida Francisco Madero and walk a few blocks north to the Tonalá central plaza, at the corner of east–west Avenida Benito Juárez.

By car, from either Guadalajara's west side or the city center, get to Tonalá via cross-town expressway Calzada Lázaro Cárdenas. From the west side, connect to Lázaro Cárdenas via Avenida López Mateos south; likewise, from downtown, connect via Calzada Gobernador Curiel, the southern prolongation of Calzada Independencia.

Traveling east on Calzada Lázaro Cárdenas, follow the Tonalá (and Zapotlanejo and Mexico City) signs to Highway 90 Autopista Zapotlanejo–Mexico City and turn off right at the Tonalá exit. Turn left (north), crossing over the freeway. After one long block, turn right (east) onto four-lane Avenida Tonalá. After three more blocks you'll be at north–south Avenida Francisco Madero, where you should park somewhere and walk the three or four blocks north to the Tonalá town plaza, at the corner of Madero and Benito Juárez.

Although local buses or your own wheels can get you to Tonalá, crowds of bus commuters and congested city streets increase the desirability of a **tour or local guide.** Contact your hotel travel desk, a travel agent, or a reliable, well-equipped agency such as Panoramex (Federalismo Sur 944, tel. 33/3810-5057 or 33/3810-5005), which conducts reasonably priced bilingual tours daily from the city center.

For individual guide recommendations, see *Information and Services* in the *Tlaquepaque* section and *Tours, Guides, and Courses* in the *Essentials* chapter.

LAKE CHAPALA

Guadalajara's appeal overflows its metropolitan boundaries. For more than a century, Guadalajara city folks have been drawn to Lake Chapala for the cooling onshore breezes, strolls along the peaceful shoreline, the healing warmth of its thermal springs, and breezy boat rides to mid-lake Alacranes (Scorpions) Island for good afternoon whitefish dinners. Since around 1900, a number of well-to-do Chapala visitors have built lakeshore mansions and spent summers living the good life while enjoying the lake view.

All of Lake Chapala's residents pride themselves on their lake's brilliant sunsets, its quiet country ambience, and its famously temperate weather. Formed by gigantic earth movements millions of years ago, the lake, Mexico's largest, was originally much larger. In ancient times, Lake Chapala spread far beyond its present cu-cumber-shaped 50- by 20-mile (80- by 30-km) basin south of Guadalajara.

Now rounded, gentle mountains shelter the sprinkling of small towns and villages that decorate the shoreline. Chapala's sleepy, rural, southern lakeside contrasts with the northern shore, which, as a holiday and weekend retreat for Guadalajara families, is now also home to a sizable colony of American and Canadian retirees. The 10-mile procession of petite, picturesque towns—Chapala, Chula Vista, San Antonio, La Floresta, Ajijic, San Juan Cosala, and others—scattered along the northern shore have collectively become known as the Chapala Riviera. A stream of visitors and an abundance of resident talent and resources sustain good restaurants and hotels as well as fine shops that offer the works of an accomplished community of artisans and artists.

© BRUCE WHIPPERMAN

HIGHLIGHTS

◖ Ajijic Town Plaza: A visit to the Ajijic plaza can include a stop at the ancient Chapel of the Virgin of Santiago and the Church of San Andrés (page 161).

◖ Neill James Library and Garden: The Lake Chapala Society oversees this library and its lovely gardens. Combine your visit here with a browse through the many inviting shops and art galleries awaiting nearby (page 161).

◖ Ajijic Lakeshore: Walk out onto the Ajijic pier in the late afternoon to enjoy the sunset view over the lake. Be sure to see the textile offerings of the several indigenous women weavers in front of the Restaurant Posada Ajijic (page 162).

◖ Chapala Pier: In Chapala town, stroll past crafts stalls, watching the boats and people and enjoying the breeze and the airy lake views, while walking out to the antique lighthouse at the end of the pier (page 163).

◖ Isla de Mezcala: Hire a boat tour to this historic mid-lake island and national monument. If you have time on the return trip, stop for lunch at one of the restaurants on neighboring Isla de los Alacranes (page 163).

◖ Hotel Villa Montecarlo: Spend a lazy afternoon on the grounds of this elegant hotel in Chapala, relaxing in the warm-spring pool, sunning, reading, enjoying a picnic, strolling, enjoying the lake view, and maybe even playing a set of tennis (page 166).

◖ Quinta Quetzalcoatl: It would be fun to spend an overnight at this unique bed-and-breakfast. Or, try to arrange a tour of the hotel, including some of their very unique rooms and lush gardens, when the friendly English owners, Rob and Lorrie Cracknell, are on-site. They enjoy talking about their experiences and the history of D.H. Lawrence's stay at the hotel (page 166).

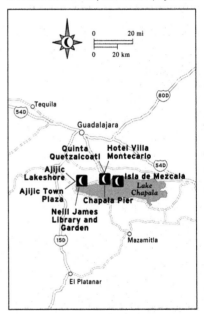

LOOK FOR ◖ TO FIND RECOMMENDED SIGHTS, ACTIVITIES, DINING, AND LODGING.

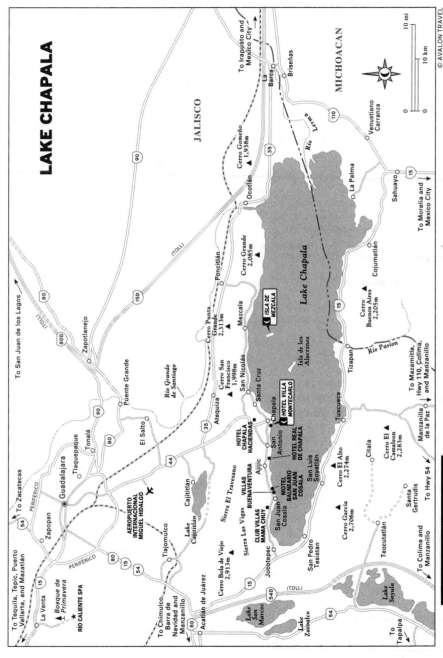

LAKE CHAPALA

© AVALON TRAVEL

LAKE CHAPALA

PLANNING YOUR TIME

You can easily idle away two days at leisure, exploring Ajijic and Chapala, the heart of the Chapala Riviera. Spend your first day exploring **Ajijic.** Include the town plaza, the garden of the Neill James Library, the many attractive Ajijic handicrafts shops and art galleries, and the Lake Chapala shore by the Ajijic pier. Have lunch and dinner (with perhaps evening live music and dancing) at a couple of Ajijic's several good restaurants (Hotel La Nueva Posada, Melanie's, Joanna's).

On your second Lake Chapala day, explore **Chapala town.** Be sure to include the Chapala town plaza and market, the pier and lakefront, the restored rail station and museum, and the Braniff mansion, where you can enjoy lunch at Restaurant Los Cazadores (three hours). After lunch, at the Chapala pier, go on a boat tour to Isla de los Alacranes and Isla de Mezcala (three hours). Return to Ajijic in early evening for dinner (La Bodega) and entertainment.

If you have a day or two more, you could enjoyably spend the first of them at one of the warm spring resorts (Hotel Balneario San Juan Cosala or Villas Buenaventura Cosala) relaxing by the pool or hot tub and strolling the San Juan Cosala village and lakeshore, perhaps extending your stay overnight. On a fourth day, you might return to Ajijic or Chapala to pursue individual interests, such as horseback riding, tennis or golf (Chula Vista Country Club, Hotel Villa Montecarlo), or handicrafts, art, or bric-a-brac browsing in Ajijic (Galería de Paola, Barbara's Bazaar) and fine dining (Bruno's, Telares, Pedro's).

HISTORY

Bands of hunter-gatherers, attracted by the lake basin's trove of fish, game, and wild fruits and grains, may have occupied Lake Chapala's shores as early as 10,000 B.C. Interestingly, they probably used the strategy of driving wild animals into the lake, where they could be subdued more easily. The Museo de Paleontología in downtown Guadalajara displays remains of a number of species, such as antelope, camel, horse, and a very complete mammoth, all unearthed at likely hunting grounds near the prehistoric lakeshore.

Recorded history began for Lake Chapala during the 1400s, when a tribe known as the "Cocas," after victorious campaigns against Purépecha (Tarascans) of Michoacán, established themselves at Cutzatlán (now San Juan Cosala) on Chapala's northwest shore. Under King Xitomatl, Cutzatlán flourished. A flurry of new towns, such as Axixic (now Ajijic), Xilotepec (now Jocotepec), and later Chapala (around 1500), were established.

An Intriguing Mystery

In contrast to Ajijic, the origin of the name "Chapala" remains a fascinating unsolved puzzle. Every scholar seems to have a different explanation. It's tempting to believe that the name has something to do with grasshoppers, which the Aztecs called *chapulín.* Another possibility stems from the name Chapa, a local chief at the time of the conquest. The name also might originate with *chapalac,* which translates as "wet place." On the other hand, the word *chapaltlán* (place of many pots) provides the most intriguing explanation of all. It seems that warriors of the Coca tribe used to sanctify themselves by ritually splattering the blood of their vanquished battlefield victims on themselves. Later, as a ceremonial substitute for their own bodies, they sprinkled the victims' blood on small clay jars and figurines, which they tossed into the water at the Chapala lakefront as offerings to their lake god. Fishing nets still bring in little ceramic human forms or animals from the lake bottom.

Conquest, Colonization, and Modern Times

The Spanish, in the person of Captain Alonso de Avalos and a platoon of soldiers, arrived in the early 1520s. Impressed by the Spanish armor, guns, and horses, the Cocas offered little resistance. Franciscan padres arrived soon afterwards, baptized the Cocas's chief Andrés Carlos and, not insignificantly, named their new Ajijic church San Andrés.

It was not long before Ajijic and Chapala, the Chapala Riviera's best-known towns, began to assume their present characters. The

THE BATTLE OF MEZCALA

Lake Chapala was the stage of a renowned heroic drama played out during the Mexican War of Independence (1810-1821). The struggle centered on the small, half-mile-long island of Mezcala, located mid-lake about six miles east of Chapala town. There, for four continuous years (1812-1816), a determined battalion of *insurgente* guerrillas held off the best the royal Spanish army and navy could throw at them.

The rebels' principal players were Marcos Castellanos, a fiery local priest, and José Santana, an indigenous village leader who, by heroic example, eventually became the rebel commander. On the Spanish side, General José de la Cruz directed the several thousand royalist soldiers deployed around the lakeshore; his subordinate officer, José Navarro, led the day-to-day campaign against the insurgents.

The rebels – a thousand armed men, plus women and children – retreated to the island in late 1812. There they fortified their island with walls, ditches, and sharp underwater stakes. By day, they grew fruits and vegetables and manufactured their own shot; by night, they resupplied themselves at friendly shoreline farms and by raiding lakeshore garrisons.

In June 1813, both sides were ready for battle. Royalist commanders, having accumulated a small army of troops, acres of supplies, and boats carried over the mountains all the way from San Blas, demanded the Mezcala rebels surrender. "Let blood run first!" the rebels answered.

Blood did run, freely, for three years. Hundreds on both sides fell, as the tide of battle swept from island to shore and back again. In late 1816, many rebels, suffering from a two-year blockade, were sick and starving. General de la Cruz was meanwhile weary of wasting lives and resources in a futile attempt to dislodge the rebels. Santana, negotiating for the rebels, bargained for a full pardon, including repaired farms, supplies, and seeds for his men, and a good church position for Castellanos. To his surprise, de la Cruz accepted.

In November 1816 the rebels left the island, inspiring others to fight on for the *independencia* they finally achieved five years later.

curative springs around Ajijic (in Nahuatl "the place where water overflows") have long attracted travelers and settlers to the lakeshore. Spanish colonists arrived early, in 1530, when the Saenz family was awarded rights of *encomienda* to the labor of the local people. Their establishment, the Hacienda de Cuije, prospered, manufacturing *mescal* liquor for generations. During the 1910 revolution, the local *campesinos* divided its holdings into a number of small *ejidos* that tried several schemes, including coffee production and gold refining, with mixed results. In 1938, new managers converted the old main house into a hotel, the Posada Ajijic, which now lives on as a picturesque, lakeshore restaurant.

During the twilight decade of President Porfirio Díaz's 34-year rule, Lake Chapala began to surge as a tourist destination. Many rich foreigners, encouraged by government laissez-faire policies, were living in Mexico. One of them,

Septimus Crow, came and developed hot springs and lakeshore land around Chapala town. He raved about Chapala to his wealthy friends, who came and also built sumptuous homes. President Díaz, who visited in 1904 and several years thereafter, opened the floodgates. Dozens of millionaire families soon moved to Chapala. One such was Alberto Braniff, of the famous airline family. In 1906 he bought a fancy lakeshore Victorian mansion, which remains gracefully preserved as the El Cazador restaurant.

The fame of Lake Chapala spread. Improved transportation—first trains, then cars and airplanes—brought droves of visitors from the United States, Canada, and Europe by the 1940s. Soon, Ajijic, with its picturesque cobbled lanes, quiet lakeshore ambience, and bargain prices, enticed a steady stream of U.S. and Canadian retirees to stay. Their lovely restored colonial homes and bougainvillea-adorned gardens still grace Ajijic and its surroundings today.

OF WHITEFISH AND WATER HYACINTHS

On the scale of geologic time, lakes are momentary features of the landscape. Mother Nature, having created lakes in the first place, immediately sets out to drain them, evaporate them, or pack them with silt. Plants encroach on their shores until, finally, they're filled and forgotten. Such natural forces are particularly consequential for a shallow lake, such as Lake Chapala, which, although large in area, typically averages only about 15 or 20 feet (5-6 meters) deep.

In recent years nature has not intruded upon Lake Chapala nearly as much as people have. Factories, towns, and farms are demanding an ever-greater share of the lake's most significant source, the Río Lerma, which trickles through four states before entering Lake Chapala's eastern end. Without care, it may simply dry up.

Most of the same upstream culprits who demand more water are also major polluters. The resulting contamination does double harm, both shrinking the fish population and increasing the plague of water hyacinth plants.

The delicious whitefish *(pescado blanco)*, which comprises a number of species of the genus *Chirostoma,* once flourished in both Lake Chapala and Lake Pátzcuaro in Michoacán. But, as at Pátzcuaro, the Chapala whitefish catch has declined steadily since the 1960s, when yearly hauls in excess of 2,000 tons were routine.

The water hyacinth, *Eichornia crassipes,* a native of South America, was introduced into Lake Chapala long ago for the beauty of its purple blossoms and brilliant green leaves. It has since burgeoned into a three-pronged menace. Besides blocking the navigation of fishing boats, canoes, and tourist launches on great swaths of the lake's surface, the hyacinth kills fish by decreasing water oxygen and encourages mosquitoes and other disease carriers to breed beneath its floating mass.

The water hyacinth, or *lirio* as it's known locally, has defied attempts at eradication. Authorities gave up trying to kill it with chemicals; a more benign solution involved the introduction of manatees, which officials hoped would make quick work of the hyacinth. Unfortunately, hungry local fisherfolk made quicker work of the manatees. In recent years a few mechanical harvesters have operated on the lake, pathetically scratching away at the nightmarishly swelling vegetable expanse.

Huge floating hyacinth beds, which appear as solid green fields when viewed near the shore, cover areas varying from as little as a few percent to as much as a fifth of the lake's surface. For a few weeks, as winds from the west prevail, the *lirio* beds drift and clog the eastern shore, only to reverse direction after the winds change, a few weeks or months later.

While whitefish fingerlings from a government lakeshore hatchery are repopulating the lake, whitefish from commercial ponds reduce the pressure on the lake fishery. Meanwhile, government eco-scientists are studying both the *lirio* and the whitefish at a local laboratory. And if the Consortio Nacional de Agua, a four-state Lake Chapala blue-ribbon commission, continues to move effectively to manage water use and curb pollution, Lake Chapala may yet find its way back to health.

The Chapala Riviera

Chapala and Ajijic are the Chapala Riviera's most-visited towns. Chapala (pop. about 10,000), at the Highway 23 freeway terminus from Guadalajara, is both the main business center and a weekend picnic spot for Guadalajara families. Ajijic (ah-HEE-heek, pop. about 5,000), by contrast, is the scenic, artistic, and tourist center, retaining the best of both worlds—picturesque rustic ambience *and* good, reasonably priced restaurants and hotels.

The paved lakeshore highway runs about five miles (eight km) west to Ajijic from Chapala, through the tranquil retirement communities of Chula Vista (marked by the golf course on the uphill side), San Antonio, and La Floresta. From Ajijic, the route continues another five miles past lakeshore vineyards and gardens to San Juan Cosala village and hot springs resort. About five miles farther on, you reach Jocotepec, the lake's west-end commercial center, just before arriving at the Morelia–Guadalajara Highway 15 junction.

Eight miles (13 km) west of Chapala, San Juan Cosala has long been famous and popular for its therapeutic hot springs. Moreover, the San Juan Cosala lakeshore is often much more visible and picturesque than in Ajijic and Chapala. Owing to the steeper San Juan Cosala shoreline, the lakeshore recedes only a few yards for a drop of a foot in lake level, while in Ajijic and Chapala, a corresponding drop of one foot causes the very gently sloping lakeshore to recede 100–200 yards to a distant, water-lily-clogged beachfront.

On the opposite, eastern side of Chapala town, the lakeshore is much less developed. The road, which runs east as Paseo Corona from the Chapala lakefront, is paved for about five miles to San Nicolas (pop. about 1,000). After that, it changes to gravel, passing small inlets and tiny isolated cliff-bottom beaches en route to sleepy Mezcala (12 mi, 19 km, 30 minutes from Chapala).

SIGHTS

Ajijic Town Plaza

At the Ajijic town plaza, take a look inside the old (ca. 1540) Chapel of the Virgin of Santiago on the north (uphill) edge of the plaza. From the opposite side of the plaza, head east one block to the baroque San Andrés parish church, founded during the mid-1500s and completed in 1749.

For nine days during Ajijic's late-November **Fiesta of San Andrés,** the church's spreading front courtyard and surrounding streets overflow with food stands, carnival rides, pitch-penny games, fireworks, and folk dancing. Moreover, Ajijic's **Semana Santa** (pre-Easter week) celebration at this same spot is becoming renowned for its elaborately costumed, three-day reenactment of Jesus's trial and crucifixion.

Neill James Library and Garden

From the San Andrés church, head downhill along Castellanos; after two blocks, turn right at 16 de Septiembre. Not far, at #16, on your left, will be the Neill James Library (Calle 16 de Septiembre 16A, two blocks above the lakeshore and a block east of Colón, in Ajijic tel. 376/766-1140, fax 376/766-4685, open Mon.–Sat. 10 A.M.–2 P.M.), a good work of the Lake Chapala Society and a delight for quiet contemplation. It shares its lovely garden with the adjacent Spanish-language library (open Mon.–Sat. 10:30 A.M.–1 P.M. and 3–5 P.M.). Before you leave, look over the notices of local performances, exhibits, and fiestas on the walkway bulletin board between the two buildings.

If you visit the Neill James Library in winter, you might be able to join an informative tour of Ajijic's lovely homes and gardens. Lake Chapala Society volunteers conduct the programs regularly and give the donations (customarily, about $10 per person) to charitable causes,

LAKE CHAPALA

such as the Jocotepec School for the Deaf. Call the Lake Chapala Society (tel. 376/766-1140) for more information.

Continue a half block west along 16 de Septiembre to the corner of Morelos, where you'll enjoy browsing through the excellent **arts and crafts shops** clustered here.

Note: Although Calle Morelos has a different name, it is actually the downhill continuation of Colón. Ajijic streets change names midtown. Streets that run parallel to the lakeshore change names at the Colón-Morelos line. Streets that run perpendicular to the lakeshore change names at the Constitución-Ocampo line.

◖ Ajijic Lakeshore

Continue another block downhill to the Ajijic lakeshore dock. You can relax, perhaps enjoy a refreshment, and take in the scene. Late afternoons, a gentle breeze often cools the lakeshore. Overhead, great white clouds billow above blue mountains bordering the far shoreline. On the beach by the pier, fishermen mend their nets, while at the beach's uphill edge, a few *indigena* women in native costumes weave their colorful wares beneath the great trees that shelter the **Restaurant Posada Ajijic.**

The restaurant is the present incarnation of the Hacienda de Cuije, founded here by the Saenz family in 1530. In 1938, Englishman Nigel Millet turned the building into a hotel, the Posada Ajijic. By the 1970s, the Posada Ajijic was attracting a loyal clientele, which included a number of artists, writers, and film stars such as Elizabeth Taylor and Charles Bronson. New owners, the Eager family of Vancouver, Canada, took over in 1975 and stayed until 1990, when they moved to their new hotel nearby. The current proprietors, who operate it exclusively as a restaurant, remodeled the Posada Ajijic to its present state of rustic elegance.

The showplace **Hotel La Nueva Posada,** which the Eager family built in 1990, is a gorgeous neocolonial creation at the foot of Donato Guerra. It spreads from its intimate, art-decorated lobby through an airy, romantic terrace restaurant, climaxing in a verdant, semitropical lake-view garden.

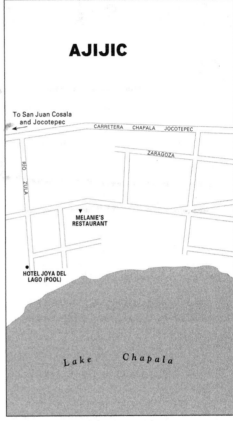

AJIJIC

To San Juan Cosala and Jocotepec

CARRETERA CHAPALA JOCOTEPEC

ZARAGOZA

RIO ZULA

▼ MELANIE'S RESTAURANT

● HOTEL JOYA DEL LAGO (POOL)

Lake Chapala

Chapala Town Plaza and the Church of St. Francis Assisi

In Chapala town, start your walk beneath the great shady trees in the old town plaza, three blocks from the lakefront, on main street Avenida Francisco I. Madero. Stroll south, downhill, toward the lake, a block and a half, to the town church. Although dedicated to St. Francis of Assisi when founded in 1538, the church wasn't completed for more than 200 years. Inside rest the venerated remains of Padre Miguel de Bolonia, one of the pioneer local Franciscan missionaries. He was probably instrumental in building the 16th-century former hermitage (now merely a crumbling foundation) on Cerro San Miguel, the hill that

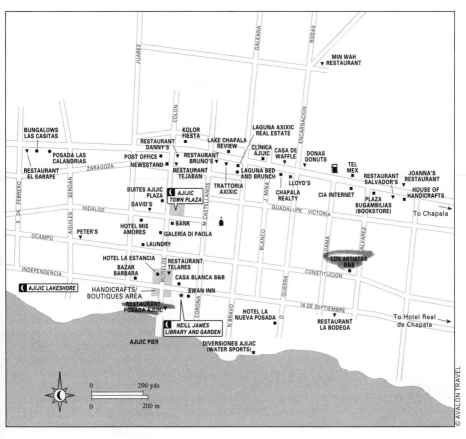

rises just west of town. A white summit cross marks the spot.

◖ Chapala Pier

Cross lakefront Paseo Corona, past the handicrafts stands, to the municipal pier. In good times, the adjacent anchorage is free of *lirio* (water hyacinths). Otherwise, boaters must frequently chop a navigation path through the thick green vegetable carpet. From the pier, a number of excursions are possible, from a one-hour ride along the lakeshore to extended lake and island tours. These could include a two-hour visit to Isla de los Alacranes (Scorpion Island), with its regional-food restaurants and bird-watching, or to Mezcala (Isla Presi-

dio), with its ruins and bird-watching, for four hours. Rental rates run about $17 hourly per boat while running, $13 hourly while waiting.

◖ Isla de Mezcala

This tree-shaded island is often the high point of a leisurely (3–5 hours) Lake Chapala outing. It's the site of a fierce, see-saw struggle between royalist forces and insurgent guerrilla fighters during Mexico's bloody 1810–1821 War of Independence. Besides its idyllic location, cooling breezes, and bird-watching opportunities, in a one hour stroll visitors can explore the entirety of the small (200 yards long) island, including the ruins of the old fort that was so tenaciously defended by the guerrillas for four years

(1812–1816). You can hire a tour boat at the Chapala pier. Rental rates customarily run about $17 hourly per boat (capacity about 10 passengers), $13 per hour while waiting. On holidays, you may be able to ride a *colectivo* (shared) boat for much less, maybe $10 per person. Bring food and drinks as none may be available on the island. Allow for three hours round trip. Add about two hours for the lunch stop at Isla Alacranes. (For more historic details of Isla Mezcala, sometimes known as Isla Presidio, see the sidebar *The Battle of Mezcala*.)

The Braniff Mansion

Head back from the Chapala pier and turn right (east) along lakefront boulevard Paseo Corona. You'll immediately see the big Victorian Braniff mansion on the left, now the Restaurant Cazadores (open daily 8 A.M.–5 P.M.). Drop in for lunch or a drink to relax and enjoy the passing scene from the mansion veranda.

Step inside and admire what amounts to an informal museum of Porfiriana, from the original silk wallpaper to patriarch Alberto Braniff's white-bearded portrait (which bears an uncanny resemblance to revolutionary president Venustiano Carranza).

Parque Cristiana

If you continue east four or five blocks, past the curio stands lining the lakefront walkway, you'll reach spreading green Parque Cristiana, one of Mexico's most complete public parks. Appropriately built for the droves of Sunday visitors, Cristiana has a children's playground, a picnic area, good public tennis courts, and a big swimming pool, all available for modest fees.

Chapala Rail Museum

Continue another block east past the *parque;* you'll see the restored (in bright yellow) former train station (corner of Calle Martínez and Av. Cristiana, tel. 376/765-7424, open Mon.–Sat. 10 A.M.–6 P.M., Sun. 10 A.M.–3 P.M.). Officially the Centro Cultural Gonzales Gallo, it's named in honor of a former Jalisco

The Braniff Mansion (now operated as Restaurant Cazadores) is fine for a relaxing sightseeing lunch break.

LAKE CHAPALA

© BRUCE WHIPPERMAN

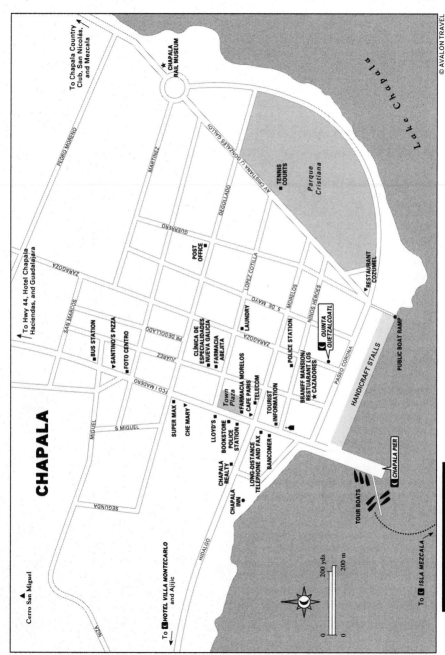

LAKE CHAPALA

Lake Chapala

CHAPALA

Cerro San Miguel

CHAPALA RAIL MUSEUM

To Chapala Country Club, San Nicolás, and Mezcala

To Hwy 44, Hotel Chapala Haciendas, and Guadalajara

To HOTEL VILLA MONTECARLO and Ajijic

To ISLA MEZCALA

PEDRO MORENO

MARTINEZ

AV CRISTIANA (J GONZALES GALLO)

ZARAGOZA

SAN MARCOS

S MIGUEL

MIGUEL

SEGUNDA

HIDALGO

INZA

FCO I MADERO

JUAREZ

IN DEGOLLADO

DEGOLLADO

GUERRERO

LOPEZ COTILLA

5 DE MAYO

MORELOS

NIÑOS HEROES

ZARAGOZA

PASEO CORONA

Parque Cristiana

TENNIS COURTS

POST OFFICE

RESTAURANT COZUMEL

PUBLIC BOAT RAMP

BUS STATION
SANTINO'S PIZZA
FOTO CENTRO

CLÍNICA DE ESPECIALIDADES
NUEVA GALICIA
FARMACIA ABEJITA

LAUNDRY

POLICE STATION

QUINTA QUETZALCOATL

SUPER MAX
CHE MARY

Town Plaza

FARMACIA MORELOS
CAFE PARIS
TELECOM

TOURIST INFORMATION

BRANIFF MANSION/
RESTUARANT LOS CAZADORES

HANDICRAFT STALLS

LLOYD'S
BOOKSTORE
POLICE STATION

LONG-DISTANCE TELEPHONE AND FAX
BANCOMER

CHAPALA REALTY

CHAPALA INN

CHAPALA PIER

TOUR BOATS

200 yds
200 m
0
0

governor. The building, now handsomely painted and polished, is a lovely gem-like reminder of days gone by, set in a grassy green lakeview park. Lately it's been both a showcase for temporary art exhibits and a stage for community events. Plans include adding historical displays of Chapala's colorful past, when the station was the bustling arrival and transfer point for Guadalajara's vacationing elite.

◖ Hotel Villa Montecarlo

Back west, at the downtown traffic intersection and signal on Madero, a block uphill from the church, Avenida Hidalgo heads west along the lakeshore toward Ajijic. Follow it about six blocks to view an inextricably connected pair of Chapala fixtures, one as famous as the other is notorious. The famous one is Hotel Villa Montecarlo (tel. 376/766-2120, see the *Accommodations* section for more details), adjacent to the lake, with spreading, parklike grounds. Facilities inside, which the public can enjoy for a fee of about $6 per day, include flowery green lakeview grounds, tennis courts, picnic areas, and pools, one of which is fed by a natural underground hot spring.

The subterranean hot water gathers along an earth fault that runs from the adjacent hillside, beneath the highway and hotel grounds. Earth movement along the fault causes the notorious 50-yard-long "hump" in the highway adjacent to the hotel. The pesky mound once defied all attempts to alter its growth. Citizens of Chapala, irritated by hump-caused traffic jams, long petitioned local government for a solution. Engineers, after many proposals, widened the road and installed underground drains. Hopefully, this will not upset the natural balance and interfere with the hot spring for which the Hotel Villa Montecarlo was built in the first place.

◖ Quinta Quetzalcoatl

Friendly English owners Rob and Lorrie Cracknell are bullish about the history of Quinta Quetzalcoatl (Calle Zaragoza 307, tel./fax 376/765-3653, see the *Accommodations* section for more details). Their hotel brochure announces Quinta Quetzalcoatl as "the home

The elegantly restored former Chapala Rail Museum now hosts the work of noted local artists.

LAKE CHAPALA UP AND DOWN

© BRUCE WHIPPERMAN

Lake Chapala residents breathed a sigh of relief when the lake filled to its historic level.

Of all the many threats to Lake Chapala, the most serious is that the lake may one day dry up completely. No problem, optimists say. They point out that Lake Chapala nearly dried up in 1955 but recovered in the 1970s, flooding Chapala town streets under two feet of water for weeks. Nevertheless, in the summer of 2001, Lake Chapala's level dropped ominously, to its lowest in living memory: so low that its shoreline receded a quarter mile from the Chapala town dock and lighthouse.

Although people disagree on the gravity of the problem, virtually everyone agrees that the drying of Lake Chapala would be a manifold tragedy. Besides the demise of the beautiful shimmering lakeshore sunsets, the lake's temporizing effect on weather would be erased, resulting in hotter summers and colder winters. More immediate would be the loss of easy irrigation for lakeside farms and water for Guadalajara's people and industries.

And therein may lie a major part of the problem. According to government data, since the city of Guadalajara began drawing water from Lake Chapala during the 1970s, the lake level steadily dropped about 18 feet (6 meters). From other perspectives, during the last quarter of the 20th century, the lake lost seven-eighths of its total water volume, a shrinkage of its surface area by 40 percent, and a reduction of its average depth from about 22 feet (7 meters) in the mid-1970s to a mere 4 feet (1.4 meter) in the summer of 2001.

Fortunately, however, that scary episode has (at least temporarily) ended, with abundant rains in 2006 and 2007, when residents rejoiced as the lake regained its historic levels once again. This happy state continues at this writing.

Although people can cross their fingers and hope that abundant rainfall will continue to maintain Lake Chapala's historic level, more is clearly necessary in the long term. Hopefully, resolute regional and federal leadership will soon produce the conservation measures necessary to save this precious resource.

of author D. H. Lawrence while writing *The Plumed Serpent* in 1923." Their enthusiasm is justified: Quinta Quetzalcoatl (Inn of the Plumed Serpent) is elegantly lovely, with seven luxuriously furnished rooms and suites within an acre of manicured tropical garden grounds. The hotel is a real showplace, as much a museum as a lodging.

Rob and Lorrie's five attractively unique rooms are all decorated around a theme, such as Lady Chatterly's Lover honeymoon suite, Carriage House, Las Mañanitas, and D.H. Lawrence Suite. Ask for a tour of the hotel and grounds, and be sure to inquire after the fine wall paintings by owner Rob, and much more. Sorry, no kids under 18.

ENTERTAINMENT AND EVENTS
Watching the Sunset

As many locals do, start off your Lake Chapala evening in proper style by enjoying the sunset (5:30–6:30 P.M. in the winter, an hour later in summer). An excellent spot to ensure that you don't miss something spectacular is the Ajijic pier at the foot of Colón. The Chapala pier offers a similarly panoramic prospect.

Cruises

Evening lake cruises offer another possibility. While at the Chapala pier, ask the boatmen about a *crucero de puesta del sol* (sunset cruise). In Ajijic, seasonal onboard parties *(fiestas a bordo)* leave by lake cruiser from the beach, at the foot of Donato Guerra by the Hotel La Nueva Posada, on weekends around noon and 4 P.M.

Additional special cruises, when passengers can enjoy both the sunset and the full moon shimmering on the lake, depart around 4 P.M. from the same point on dates when the moon is full.

Music and Dancing

A major exception to the generally quiet nights around Ajijic and Chapala occurs at the Ajijic **Hotel La Nueva Posada** bar (tel. 376/766-1444), with a live combo for dancing Saturdays 8–10:30 P.M. Find it at the lakeshore, foot of

© BRUCE WHIPPERMAN

Chapala Pier is a great place to watch the sunset.

Donato Guerra, four blocks east, two blocks downhill from the central plaza.

At **La Bodega** restaurant-bar in Ajijic (16 de Septiembre 124, tel. 376/766-1002, open daily noon–10:30 P.M.), good times also roll nightly. Programs vary, from harp and Latin dance music to mariachis and progressive jazz. Get there from the highway gas station; go straight downhill (along Aldama) four blocks and turn left.

Another lively spot is **Melanie's** restaurant (Ocampo 151, tel. 376/766-4253 or 376/765-2753, melanies1@prodigy.net.mx, food served Wed. and Fri.–Mon. noon–around 11 P.M.), with live oldies but goodies Wednesday and Friday–Sunday from around 7:30 P.M., and cards and dominos every night. Melanie's is three blocks downhill from the highway, six blocks west of the Ajijic plaza, inside the Hotel Danza del Sol.

Hotel Chapala Haciendas (at Kilometer 40, Carretera Guadalajara-Chapala, Chapala, Jalisco 45900, tel. 376/765-2720), a five-minute drive uphill from downtown Chapala along the highway to Guadalajara, entertains patrons with Armando's piano-guitar-drum combo in the hotel restaurant, Saturdays 7–11 P.M. The restaurant is open daily for breakfast, lunch, and dinner.

Also popular is **Club Hidalgo** (Calle Hidalgo 10, tel. 376/766-3831), with live oldies but goodies for dancing, food, and sometimes a variety show Tuesday–Sunday 5–7 P.M.; $10 cover at door (food and drinks served Tuesday–Sunday 1–9 P.M.).

Salvador's Restaurant (Plaza Bugambilias shopping center, tel. 33/3776-2301, Mon., Wed., Fri. and Sat. 7 A.M.–8 P.M., Thurs. 7 A.M.–3:30 P.M., and Sun. 7 A.M.–5:30 P.M.) also has become an entertainment spot, with live music afternoons and evenings Wednesday–Sunday; times vary.

For more entertainment suggestions, such as concerts, plays, and art exhibitions, see the informative Mark Your Calendar section in the widely available English-language monthly *El Ojo del Lago.*

Fiestas

Occasional local festivals quicken the ordinarily drowsy pace of Lake Chapala life. Jocotepec, at the lake's west end, kicks off the year in early January with the two-week fiesta **El Señor del Monte.** The fiesta's origin is local—an image of Jesus on the Cross, originally carved from the branches of a *guaje* tree, is believed miraculous because it was seen either glowing or burning (depending on which account you believe). Nevertheless, folks make plenty of the legend, with a swirl of events including masses, processions, bullfights, and cockfights, all accompanied by a continuous carnival and fair. The celebration peaks on the third Sunday of January, when downtown is awash with merrymakers thrilling to the boom, roar, and flash of a grand fireworks display.

The local North American community joins in the party, usually in early to mid-February, with a big, for-charity **Chili Cookoff.** (The 2008 event, the 30th annual, occurred Feb. 14, 15, and 16.) Past cookoffs have included "Las Vegas Lounge" gambling-for-charity ta-

bles; a "Mexican Night" with music, dancing, and a "Miss Chili Cookoff" pageant; and finally, chili judging and awards, with plenty left over for everyone. For information, visit www.mexicanchilicookoff.com, or contact *El Ojo del Lago* newspaper (P.O. Box 279, Chapala, Jalisco 45900, tel. 376/765-3676 or 376/765-2877, fax 376/765-3528, ojodellago@laguna.com.mx).

Merrymaking continues with **Carnaval** (Mardi Gras) dancing and parades before Ash Wednesday, the first day of Lent, usually in late February. On several subsequent Fridays, rockets boom high over town and village streets, as image-bearing processions converge for special masses at local churches. This all culminates in **Semana Santa** festivities, notably in Ajijic, where local people, in full costume, reenact Jesus's ordeal.

The hubbub resumes in Chapala around October 4, with the climax of the fiesta of the town patron, **San Francisco.** Townsfolk dance, join processions, watch fireworks, ride the Ferris wheel, and pitch pesos. Later, party animals can enjoy more of the same during Ajijic's **Fiesta of San Andrés** during the last nine days of November.

SPORTS AND RECREATION
Walking, Jogging, and Bicycling

The airy Lake Chapala shore is the best spot for a stroll or a jog. It's best to get out early or late to avoid the heat of the day. In Ajijic, try the beach by the pier (foot of Colón), where several hundred yards of level, open sand invite relaxing walking and running. In Chapala, the lakefront boardwalk or the grassy perimeter of Parque Cristiana on lakefront Avenida Ramón Corona, a few hundred yards east of the church, offers similar opportunities. Alternatively, you might join company with the many local folks who bike, jog, and walk along the paved bicycle path *(pista)* that parallels the Chapala–Ajijic highway.

Swimming

Although Lake Chapala's shallowness (which keeps bottom mud stirred up) and hyacinth-clogged shorelines make it uninviting, hotel pools remain an option. In Chapala, the uphill **Hotel Chapala Haciendas** (tel. 376/765-2720, go by taxi, $2) has an inviting, medium-size, but unheated pool. Most luxurious, however, is the big lake-view pool at the **Hotel Villa Montecarlo** (tel. 376/765-2120, $6 adult, $3 child), whose palm-treed grounds and natural hot spring are open for public day use. Call ahead to see if the big pool is open.

In Ajijic, an equally luxurious swimming possibility exists at the beautiful lakefront pool at the **Hotel Real de Chapala** (tel. 376/766-0007), where, for the price of a poolside lunch, you can enjoy a swim. Another good swimming opportunity is available at the **Hotel Balneario San Juan Cosala** hot spring resort (tel. 387/761-0302, $8 adult, $4 child), where spring-fed lake-view pools are available for public use.

Probably the best local **lap swimming** (open daily 8 A.M.–7 P.M., $3 per person) spot is at the **Hotel Joya del Lago**, on Calle Río Zula, on the far west side of town. Get there by taxi, car, or foot about one mile west of Ajijic town center. From the highway, turn toward the lake at Calle Río Zula (at the Hotel Danza del Sol sign) and continue about three long blocks downhill, to Hotel Joya del Lago, on the right.

Tobolandia water slide park (open Tues.–Sun. 10 A.M.–6 P.M., $9 adult, $4 child) is a favorite with kids, with two big, warm-water swimming pools, water slides, picnic ground, restaurant, and more. Find it on the Chapala–Ajijic highway, a block west of the signalled intersection of the Guadalajara cutoff road.

Boating

Although winds and currents often push mats of pesky water hyacinths on to Lake Chapala beaches, lake access is possible at certain times and locations. If so, nothing else will stop you from floating your kayak, or your sailboard, on the lake.

If you want to launch your own boat, and the lake is high enough, use the **public boat ramp** at the end of Paseo Corona (in front of all the restaurants, about four blocks east of the Chapala pier). Alternatively, you can probably launch your boat on the beach, at the foot of Avenida Colón in Ajijic.

Golf

Local enthusiasts enjoy a pair of nine-hole golf courses. The **Chula Vista Country Club** greens (tel. 376/766-2515 or 376/766-2281) carpet the intimate valley that spreads uphill from the highway, midway between Chapala and Ajijic. Play starts daily at 8 A.M.; the last round begins not long after 3 P.M. The nine-hole greens fee runs about $30 weekdays, $40 weekends, plus caddy, $8. A clubhouse bar and restaurant serves food and refreshments.

Golfers enjoy similarly good conditions at the nine-hole **Chapala Country Club** (tel. 376/763-5136 or 376/763-5138, greens fee $25–40), overlooking the lake near San Nicolas, about five miles (eight km) east of Chapala.

Tennis

Private tennis courts are available day and night at the Chula Vista Country Club (tel.

The far end of the Chapala Pier is usually crowded with boats offering tours around the lake.

376/766-2515, $3 per hour days; $6 per hour nights), the Hotel Villa Montecarlo in Chapala (tel. 376/766-2120, $6 per day), and the Hotel Real de Chapala (tel. 376/766-0007, in Ajijic, $6 per hour days, $14 per hour nights). Cheaper public tennis courts are available at Parque Cristiana in Chapala.

Horseback Riding

Guided horseback rides and rental horses ($10 per hour) are available daily at the corner of Avenidas Camino Real and Camino del Lago, in La Floresta subdivision, a block west of the Hotel Real de Chapala.

SHOPPING

In Ajijic you have at least a couple of close-to-the-source handicrafts options: the woven art of a number of indigenous women at the lakeshore, and the Jalisco state **Casa de las Artesanías** (House of Handicrafts) (tel. 376/766-0548, open Mon.–Fri. 10 A.M.–6 P.M., Sat. 10 A.M.–4 P.M., Sun. 10 A.M.–2 P.M.). Watch for the sign on the highway as you're entering Ajijic, heading west, from Chapala, just after the big white roadside sculpture on the left. Jalisco handicrafts—shiny Tlaquepaque red and blue glass and fine painted stoneware, fanciful painted pottery figures, cute papier-mâché and pottery animals from Tonalá, charming nativity sets, bright paper flowers—fill the gallery.

On Colón, a half block downhill from the Ajijic plaza, be sure to step into the **Galería de Paola** (Colón 11, tel. 376/766-1010, fax 376/766-2572, open Mon.–Sat. 10 A.M.–2 P.M. and 4–6 P.M., Sun. 11 A.M.–2 P.M.), the labor of love of owner-photographer María de Paola Blum. You can peruse downstairs and upstairs and be entertained by her eclectic gallery of carefully chosen sculptures, paintings, photos, handicrafts, many books, and artistic odds and ends.

Several more interesting Ajijic shops cluster another block downhill, near the corner of Morelos (Colón's downhill continuation) and 16 de Septiembre. Among the best is **Mi México** (Morelos 8, corner of 16 de Septiembre, tel. 376/766-0133, open Mon.–Sat. 10 A.M.–

6 P.M., Sun. 11 A.M.–3 P.M.), the life project of its expatriate owners. Their collection seems to include a little bit of everything handmade from all over Mexico and the world: paintings, jewelry, Guadalajara resort wear, block-printed cottons, and Javan batiks.

Ready-to-wear clothes are a specialty of **Opus Boutique,** across the street (Morelos 15, tel. 376/766-1790, loiscugi@laguna.com. mx, open Mon.–Sat. 10 A.M.–6 P.M., Sun. 11 A.M.–3 P.M.). The inventory blooms with attractive, comfortable resort wear—dresses, slacks, skirts, blouses—and some Indonesian batiks, jewelry, and small paintings.

Cross to the adjacent (southwest) corner of 16 de Septiembre and Colón to **La Flor de la Laguna** (Morelos 17, tel. 376/766-1037, open Mon.–Sat. 10 A.M.–6 P.M., Sun. 10 A.M.–2 P.M.), offering a bright kaleidoscope of Mexican handicrafts. Its assortment includes glistening papier-mâché parrots, a rogue's gallery of masks, and a fetching menagerie of nativity sets, yarn dolls, and much more in leather, wood, brass, copper, and cotton.

At the corner, turn west along the prolongation of 16 de Septiembre (which has changed to Independencia), a half block from the Morelos corner, to **Bazar Barbara** (7A Independencia, tel. 376/766-1824, open Mon.–Fri. 10 A.M.–2 P.M. and 3–5 P.M., Sat. 10 A.M.–4 P.M.). Here the collector-owner has acquired so many odds and ends—furniture, old refrigerators, antiques, books, and bric-a-brac—that he (his name is not Barbara) had to have a place to put them. "If you're looking for something, you'll find it there," one resident passerby told me.

Finally, at the Ajijic lakeshore, be sure to take a look at the attractive hand-woven art: wool rugs, serapes, blankets, and more, that a number of indigenous women make and sell, adjacent to the Restaurant Posada Ajijic.

In Chapala, try the stalls that line the lakefront walkway, beginning at the Chapala pier. Look for good bargains in Oaxaca wool weavings, Jocotepec serapes, Tonalá pottery and papier-mâché, Guadalajara huaraches, Paracho (Michoacán) guitars, Santa Clara del Cobre

(Michoacán) copperware, and dozens more colorful items brought from all over Mexico.

ACCOMMODATIONS

The Chapala Riviera offers a wide range of lodgings, from luxury lakeview hotels and friendly motellike complexes to intimate bed-and-breakfasts. Although both Ajijic and Chapala have plenty of colorful old-Mexico atmosphere, Ajijic is quieter and more picturesque, and consequently has most of the better lodgings. Rates depend strongly upon availability and season; unless stated otherwise, the lodging figures given below approximate winter high-season rates. Summer low-season (May–October) prices will customarily be 10–30 percent lower.

Ajijic
UNDER $50

Some of Ajijic's most economical lodgings are on the highway, especially convenient for drivers. Only a couple of blocks east of the town center signal, the Laguna Real Estate office marks the location of its 【 **Laguna Bed and Brunch.** Reserve through Laguna Real Estate (Carretera Chapala-Ajijic 24 Oriente, Ajijic, Jalisco 45920, tel. 376/766-1174 or 376/766-1186, fax 376/766-1188, lagunarealty@prodigy.net.mx, www.lagunamex.ocm/bnb, $35/day, $225/week). Four comfortable rooms with bath, an adjacent cheery breakfast room/living room/lobby, and a partially shaded outside patio keep a steady stream of satisfied customers returning year-round. Extras are king-size beds, a shelf of thick paperbacks, and sofas for reading and socializing. Hearty breakfasts are included with lodgings. By day, you can make inquiries or access Laguna Bed and Brunch through the real estate office or by telephone. With your key, you can get in anytime through the residential entrance at Zaragoza 29 Oriente, behind the real estate office, one block downhill from the highway.

Also on the highway is the **Posada Las Calandrias** (at Carretera Chapala-Jocotepec 8 Poniente, P.O. Box 76, Ajijic, Jalisco 45920, tel. 376/766-1052, $37–65/day, $180–300/week, $250–350/month), about two blocks west of the town signal. Many folks with cars and RVs like the motel-style setup and the reunions with fellow Ajijic long-timers. The 25 clean, comfortably furnished but plain one- and two-bedroom apartments include living room, kitchen, ceiling fans, and plenty of daily company around a blue pool and sundeck adjacent to the parking lot. By night, residents relax on their front porches, enjoying the balmy evenings while visiting and playing cards; later some might stroll down the street together for dinner at a favorite restaurant. All rentals include TV, but no fans (bring your own) and only weekly maid service. Get your winter season (November–April) reservations in early.

If you can't get in at Posada Las Calandrias, try the neighboring **Bungalows Las Casitas** (Carretera Chapala-Jocotepec 20 Poniente, Ajijic, Jalisco 45920, tel. 376/766-1145, $45/day, $230/week), a few doors farther west. About two dozen simply but comfortably furnished apartments surround a pool and sundeck by the parking lot. The friendly winter residents are mainly North American retirees. All units are one bedroom and have kitchens, living rooms, ceiling fans, maid service, and satellite TV. Discounts may be available during May–July and September–November low seasons.

$50-100

On Colón by the Ajijic plaza, close to everything, is **Ajijic Plaza Suites** (Colón 33, Ajijic, Jalisco 45920, tel. 376/766-0383, ajijichotel@yahoo.com, www.ajijichotel.com, $50). The small, sometimes busy lobby leads to a long, sunny, leafy apartment-lined inner patio. The savvy owners Patricia and Jeremy Lusch (who also offer tours) have packed a lot into a small space. They offer a dozen spruced-up one-bedroom units with tasteful, colorful Mexican-style decor (but with windows that face the patio and thus need curtains drawn for privacy at night). Rentals include breakfast, phone, maid service, satellite TV, VCR, small pool and patio right next to their restaurant, and limited wheelchair access. Credit cards are accepted.

Two blocks downhill and a block east, at the **Hotel Casa Blanca** (16 de Septiembre 29, Ajijic, Jalisco 45920, tel. 376/766-4440, info@casablancaajijic.com, www.casablancaajijic.com, $59–69), a savvy Lebanese-Mexican owner has transformed a large family home and inner patio into an attractive, compact inn. He offers eight accommodations, each with two beds for up to four people; four of them have kitchenettes, with double hot plate electric stoves, microwave oven and refrigerator. Up to a 20 percent discount is available for weekly rentals, 50 percent for monthly, all including continental breakfast. Amenities include a café with coffee and snacks, large shady rear patio, some balcony terraces, high speed Internet access, laundry, cable TV, and ground floor wheelchair access.

Back, a half block west, of the Ajijic plaza, the renovated **Hotel and Restaurant Mis Amores** (Hidalgo 22, Ajijic, Jalisco 45920, tel./fax 376/766-4640, fax 376/766-4641 or 376/766-4642, info@misamores.com, www.misamores.com, $60–80) continues to attract a cadre of loyal returnees. The front entry leads you into an inviting fountain courtyard, past breakfast tables set beneath a shady side portico to a manicured tropical garden, with the six rooms set artfully to one side. They are lovingly decorated in earth tones and pastels, embellished with flowers hand-painted on the walls, and hung with original oils and watercolors. Rooms include ceiling fans, queen- and king-size beds, modern-standard decorator-tile bathrooms, telephones, and large-screen TVs. Rates include full breakfast.

One of Ajijic's loveliest accommodations is **Los Artistas** (Constitución 105, Ajijic, Jalisco 45920, tel. 376/766-1027, fax 376/766-1762, artistas@laguna.com.mx, www.losartistas.com, $60–90), on the east side of town. Owners Kent Edwards and Linda Brown's lovingly tended accommodations are arranged around the edge of a flowery rear garden. Rooms, some with king-size

beds, all with attractively tiled and fitted baths, are artfully furnished with weavings, paintings, and sculpture. Rooms vary; if possible, take a peek before picking. Rates include breakfast, parking, and a lovely pool, but neither credit cards nor travelers checks are accepted. Reserve early, especially for the winter season. Find it about five blocks east of main street Colón.

Ajijic's **Hotel La Nueva Posada** (Donato Guerra 9, P.O. Box 30, Ajijic, Jalisco 45920, tel. 376/766-1344, 376/766-1444, or 376/766-1460, fax 376/766-2049, nuevaposada@prodigy.net.mx, www.mexconnect.com/mex/rest/nueva/index.html, $65–100), on the east-side lakeshore, is so popular that prospective winter guests make reservations far in advance. Its Canadian owners have spared little in embellishing the hotel's colonial-style decor. Past the lobby, an elegant but comfortable bar provides nightly piano entertainment, and a romantic, airy terrace-restaurant leads to a verdant, semitropical lake-view garden. The 17 hotel accommodations vary from poolside rooms to upstairs view suites. All are immaculate and tastefully decorated, in rustic-chic Mexican style, with original watercolor art and native crafts. Rooms include full breakfast, ceiling fans, and parking. There are four roomier, more private garden villa-apartments with kitchenette across the street. Ask for a promotional low-season or long-term discount; credit cards are accepted (although you get a 10 percent discount if you pay cash).

The exquisite **Swan Inn** (16 de Septiembre 18, Ajijic, Jalisco 45920, tel. 376/766-2354 or 376/766-0917, swaninnajijic@hotmail.com, www.swaninnajijic.com, $75–140) is in the quiet downhill neighborhood right next to the Neill James Library and garden. Guests have a choice of six rooms, two *casitas* (cottages), and a two-bedroom, two-bath guest house, all in a magnificent, manicured garden compound, embellished by venerable shade trees, a cactus garden, and a heated lap pool and patio. Rates include full breakfast, with fans and satellite TV in the lounge area. Owners invite folks to visit their "tavern" for a look-see.

The local deluxe, resort-style accommodation is the plush **Hotel Real de Chapala** (Paseo del Prado 20, Ajijic, Jalisco 45920, tel. 376/766-0007 or 376/766-0014, fax 376/766-0025, reservasrealdechapala@yahoo. com, www.realdechapala.com/ing, $90–100) in the choice La Floresta neighborhood, just east of Ajijic. Except for Christmas and Easter holidays and weekends, the hotel, operated by the Universidad Autonoma de Guadalajara, is minimally occupied and consequently very quiet. Its lavish facilities—a spreading lakefront park, big blue pool, night-lit tennis courts, volleyball, soccer field, billiard room, table tennis, and bars and restaurants—are often unused. Weekends are more lively; guests, mostly middle- and upper-class Guadalajarans, enjoy seasonal live combo music Friday and Saturday evenings, and mariachis and folkloric dance on Sunday. The 85 spacious, luxurious rooms and suites (40 of which have lake and mountain views) come with ceiling fans, queen-size beds, satellite TV, parking, and limited wheelchair access. Credit cards are accepted.

Chapala
UNDER $50
Guests at the **Hotel Chapala Haciendas** (Km 40, Carretera Guadalajara-Chapala, Chapala, Jalisco 45900, tel./fax 376/765-2720, $27–42, seventh day free) enjoy a high hillside setting, five minutes' drive or taxi ($2) uphill from the Chapala lakeshore. Its lush country lakeview location, inviting pool and patio, friendly family management, and reasonable prices explain the Chapala Hacienda's continuing popularity with both foreign and Mexican vacationers. Breakfast, sunrise view, piano bar, and live oldies-but-goodies music Saturday 7–11 P.M. are popular traditions in the hotel's homey restaurant. The 20 rooms, in rows facing a flower garden and panoramic lake views, are simply but attractively furnished, with rustic high-beamed rattan ceilings. (If you're planning on using the pool, check to see if it's being maintained; sometimes during low occupancy it becomes green, although at this writing, it was clear and blue.)

$50-100
Back in town, about six blocks west along Chapala's main lakeshore street, the family-friendly resort **Hotel Villa Montecarlo** (Hidalgo 296, Chapala, Jalisco 45900, tel./fax 376/765-2120 or 376/765-2024, fax 376/765-3366, $63) basks in palm-treed, lakeview grounds. The site, originally developed because of its hot spring, is now owned and operated by the University of Guadalajara. The natural setting—lush green lawns overlooking the lake's mountain- and cloud-framed expanse—sets the tone. When not gazing at the view, guests can soak in the natural warm pool, cool off in another, play some tennis, or enjoy a drink at the bar or a meal in the restaurant. The two-story, motel-style lodging tiers occupy only one side of the grounds and consequently avoid cluttering the views. The rooms are furnished in 1960s institutional semideluxe style, open to airy balconies, many with lake vistas. They include parking, cable TV, and many extras, but no phones or fans.

One of Chapala town's most gracefully tranquil lodgings is the **◖ Lake Chapala Inn** (23 Paseo Ramón Corona, Chapala, Jalisco 45900, tel. 376/765-4786 or 376/765-4809, fax 376/765-5174, chapalainn@laguna.com.mx, www.mexonline.com/chapalainn.htm, $75), on the lakeshore promenade west of the pier. This former mansion, now bed-and-breakfast, retains a good measure of its gracious old-world ambience, with a light, spacious living room, a well-stocked library, and an elegant dining room. Upstairs, the several rooms are immaculate, spacious, and comfortably appointed with polished 1930s-era furniture and large, spotless bathrooms. Guests additionally enjoy an airy, shaded lake-view veranda ideal for quiet relaxation. Rates include breakfast, heated lap pool, and parking, but no phones or TV. The owners also rent a pair of adjacent newly decorated three-bedroom, two-bath houses with kitchens and lakeview balconies for about $315 per week. **◖ Quinta Quetzalcoatl** (Calle Zaragoza 307, P.O. Box 286, Chapala, Jalisco 45900, tel./fax 376/765-3653, qq@ac-commodationslakechapala.com, www.accommodationslakechapala.com, $75–110) includes seven luxuriously furnished rooms and suites (including the Lady Chatterly's Lover honeymoon suite, Carriage House, Las Mañanitas, and D.H. Lawrence Suite) within an acre of manicured tropical garden grounds (See description of hotel and gardens in the preceding Sights section.).

Amenities include fans (but no a/c), cable TV, hot water bathrooms, king or queen-size beds, some private patios, some kitchenettes, an intimately lovely small pool and patio, wireless Internet access, and a restaurant exclusively for guests in a regal dining room.

San Juan Cosala
$50-100
Right on the lakefront in San Juan Cosala, the major hotel is the **Motel Balneario San Juan Cosala** (P.O. Box 181, Chapala, Jalisco 45900, tel. 387/761-0302, fax 387/761-0222, $75–90) whose complex of several big blue pools and a water slide is a weekend and holiday magnet for Mexican families. Although the main

pools and facilities are open to the public for a moderate fee ($10 for adults, $5 kids), the hotel reserves some pools and gardens for hotel guests only. Other hotel amenities include hot tub, massage, natural vapor sauna, and volleyball, basketball, and tennis courts. The rooms, while not luxurious, are comfortably furnished with two double beds and have airy, private garden patios, which, from the second floor, have lake views. If you prefer peace and quiet, it's best to book your stay during the calm, relatively unoccupied midweek period. Breakfast is included.

OVER $100
A sprinkling of small, comfortable hotels dot the Lake Chapala shoreline west of Motel Balneario San Juan de Cosala. The quietly luxurious **Villas Buenaventura Cosala** (Km 13.5, Carretera Ajijic-San Juan Cosala, Jalisco 45820, tel. 387/761-0303 or 387/761-0202, fax 387/761-0364, hotelvbc@laguna .com.mx, www.hotelvbc.com, $110–200) is among the best. The owners seem to have

Motel Balneario San Juan Cosala's pools perch right above the lakeshore.

© BRUCE WHIPPERMAN

LAKE CHAPALA

successfully bridged the gap between family and adult needs, with a small village of about 20 rooms, suites, and bungalows artfully placed around an intimate garden of natural hot spring water pools. Accommodations vary from simply but harmoniously decorated rooms to suites with private jetted tub and king-size beds to two-bedroom, two-bath family kitchenette bungalow apartments. Decorations—rustic tile floors and polished wood highlights, reading lamps, soft pastel bedspreads and drapes—are thoughtfully selected. Facilities include therapeutic natural sulfur-water pools, varying from warm to hot, a recreation room for teenagers, small playground for tots, and sauna, or *temazcal* (indigenous ceremonial hot room), and massage and spa treatments for adults at extra cost. All rooms come with fans, cable TV, and parking, but no dogs allowed. Promotions customarily include third night free and/or discounts (to $450) for weekly rentals (except for July, August, Christmas, and Easter vacations).

Long-Term Rentals

Many agents rent Chapala-area apartments, houses, and condos. Among the busiest is **Coldwell Banker-Chapala Realty** (Hidalgo 223, Chapala, Jalisco 45900, tel. 376/765-2877 or 376/765-3676, fax 376/765-3528, chapala@infosel.net.mx or axixix@infosel.net.mx, www.chapala.com), in downtown Chapala. Or visit its Ajijic office (tel. 376/766-1152, fax 376/766-2124, axixic@infosel.net.mx), on the highway at #38, about three blocks east of the Colón signal.

Alternatively, check out the offerings of **Ajijic Rentals** (Colón 1, Ajijic, Jalisco 45920, tel. 376/766-1716 or 376/766-4272, fax 376/766-0967, rentals@prodigy.net.mx, www.ajijicrentals.com). You might also consult with local rental wizard **Beverly Hunt** (24 Oriente, tel. 376/766-1174 or 376/766-1186, fax 376/766-1188, lagunarealty@prodigy.net.mx, www.lagunamex.com), at Laguna Real Estate, in front of the Laguna Bed and Brunch, on the highway, east side.

For more rental possibilities, look through the classifieds section of the local news magazine *Ojo del Lago,* or take a look at the bulletin board at the Lake Chapala Society's Neill James Library (on Calle 16 de Septiembre, a block east of main street Colón, open Mon.–Sat. 10 A.M.–2 P.M.). If you can't find a copy of *Ojo del Lago,* drop by the Coldwell Banker-Chapala Realty office in Chapala or Ajijic.

FOOD

A resident brigade of discriminating diners has led to the unusually high standards of successful cafés and restaurants, especially in Ajijic.

Ajijic
BREAKFAST

In Ajijic, all roads seem to lead to **Danny's Restaurant** "Best Breakfast in Ajijic" (on the lakeshore highway, corner of Colón, tel. 376/766-2222, open daily 8 A.M.–2 P.M.). Hot breakfasts (eggs, hash browns, and toast, $3), hamburgers ($3), Mexican specialties ($3–5), bottomless cups of coffee, and plenty of friendly conversation long ago ensured Danny's local following.

Also on the highway, about three blocks east, try the morning innovative "breakfasts and newspapers" offerings of the **Casa de Waffle** (Carretera Chapala-Jocotepec #75, tel. 376/766-1946, open daily 8 A.M.–4 P.M.), about four blocks east of Colón, near the gas station. Choices include pancakes and strawberries, cheese omelet with hash browns, *huevos rancheros,* and much, much more ($3–5).

Another good choice is **David's** (21 Hidalgo, a half block west of the Ajijic plaza, tel. 376/766-3074, open daily 8 A.M.–4 P.M.), for savory coffee and American breakfasts ($3–5).

The **Laguna Bed and Brunch** (Carretera Oriente #24, tel. 376/766-1174, daily 8 A.M.–noon) offers hearty country breakfasts. This includes a choice of entrées (scrambled eggs, omelets, pancakes, french toast, hash browns, and more), plus fruit, rolls, apple-bran muffins, and coffee or tea for about $4. On Sundays they add biscuits, sausage and gravy, and blintzes and crepes. Get there from the highway through Laguna Real Estate, or through Laguna Bed and Brunch's front door, a block downhill from the highway at Zaragoza 29 near the corner of Galeana.

CASUAL DINING

In Ajijic, starting on the highway, east side (and moving west and downhill toward the lake), first comes **((Joanna's Restaurant** (118 A Blv. La Floresta, on the highway, three blocks east of the gas station, tel. 376/766-0437, open Tues.–Sat. noon–8 P.M., Sun. noon–6 P.M.), whose bona fide claim of "authentic German cuisine" seems a marvel, two continents and an ocean away from Luneborg, where Joanna was born. But remarkable it is—from the *gemischecter fruhling salat* (with *hausdressing,* $6) to the *reibekuche* (potato pancakes) and *mandel forelle* (rainbow trout, $12) to the scrumptious apple strudel ($5). Find Joanna's in a suburban house, set back from the north side of the street.

Two blocks west, plain good food at very reasonable prices draws a flock of local Americans and Canadians to coffee-shop-style **Salvador's** (88 Carretera Oriente, tel. 33/3776-2301, open Mon., Wed., Fri., and Sat. 7 A.M.–8 P.M., Thurs. 7 A.M.–3:30 P.M., and Sun. 7 A.M.–5:30 P.M.), at the highway-front of the Plaza Bugambilias shopping center. Besides a very familiar American-style breakfast, lunch, and dinner menu, owner Salvador offers a big $5 Sunday brunch and specialties of the day, such as roast beef, lasagna, and stuffed rainbow trout ($5–7).

Next comes **La Trattoria de Axixic** (Carretera Oriente #30, tel. 376/766-3796, open Mon.–Sat. noon–10 P.M., Sun. noon–8 P.M.), a spacious (but dark in the daytime) restaurant/bar, also on the highway, lake side, at the corner of Galeana. Here, the happy mixture of folks—kids, retirees, Mexicans, Americans, Canadians—is both a cause and effect of the amiable atmosphere. The food—pizzas, pastas, salads, fish, chicken, steaks ($4–12)—is crisply served and tasty. Desserts, which include carrot cake and apple, chocolate, or banana cream pie ($2–5), are a specialty.

Next door, the friendly and celebrated owner/chef of **((Restaurant Bruno's** (Carretera Oriente #20, tel. 376/766-1674, Fri.–Sun. 2:30–8:30 P.M.) is so popular that, even though open only weekends, he manages to achieve success. Bruno, who also sometimes waits on tables, puts out an innovative repertoire of mostly Italian- and Chinese-style dishes at lunchtime, and good old reliables such as barbecued ribs or chicken for dinner ($8–12). He buys his food fresh daily, and in quantities calculated so that nothing will be left over. By 6 P.M. on a busy day, he begins to run out of food. Arrive early for a full choice. Reservations are strongly recommended.

Off the Ajijic town plaza, on Hidalgo, a half block west of the bank, you'll find **David's** restaurant/snack shop/café (Hidalgo 21, tel. 376/766-3074, open daily 8 A.M.–4 P.M.), whose friendly owners' specialties are house-roasted coffee, home-baked fruit pies, and gourmet soups and sandwiches.

FINE DINING

Diners seeking elegance enjoy a number of excellent Ajijic options. Many regulars pick the refined **Restaurant Telares** (on Colon about a block and a half downhill from the Ajijic town plaza, tel. 376/766-0666 or 376/766-0428, open Tues.–Sun. 11 A.M.–8 P.M.). Patrons have a choice of seating, either in the sunny central patio/garden or in the shady surrounding veranda. Likewise, they have plenty of options in the long menu of tasty appetizers, soups and salads, and expertly prepared continental-style meat, seafood, and pasta entrées ($8–20). Reservations are strongly recommended.

Soft lighting, live background guitar melodies, and an airy stone-arched dining room terrace set the romantic tone of restaurant **((La Rusa** (9 Donato Guerra, tel. 376/766-1344, open daily 8 A.M.–9 P.M.), at the Hotel La Nueva Posada. The menu of mesquite-broiled fish, chicken, ribs, and steaks garnished with delicious broiled vegetables ($8–18) provides the successful conclusion. Reservations are strongly recommended.

Equally festive and nearby is the class-act

LAKE CHAPALA

family-run restaurant 🄲 **La Bodega** (16 de Sept. 124, just east of Morelos, tel. 376/766-1002, open daily noon–10 P.M.), which attracts customers when others do not. Live nightly guitar and vocal music and a solid Italian-Mexican-Asian fusion menu (Caesar salad $4, fusilli with tuna and olives $6, chicken fajitas $8, Thai curried chicken $6) keep the customers coming.

For a relaxing lunch or sunset-view dinner, try the landmark lakefront **Restaurant Posada Ajijic** (at the foot of Colón, tel. 376/766-0744, open Mon.–Thurs. noon–10 P.M., Fri.–Sat. noon–1 A.M., Sun. noon–8 P.M.). Once a hacienda, later a hotel, the Posada Ajijic restaurant now rests in comfortable old age beneath a grove of towering eucalyptus trees. Inside, the dining room, furnished in colonial-style leather and wood, spreads beneath rustic beamed ceilings to lakeview windows. Service is crisp, and the soups, salads, sandwiches ($4–6), and entrées (chicken, fish, steak, $6–14) are tasty and professionally presented. A trio plays live music for dancing Tuesday and Thursday–Saturday evenings.

For a treat, go to **Pedro's** on the southwest side of town (Ocampo 71, tel. 376/766-4747, open Tues.–Sat. noon–8:30 P.M.) at the corner of Ocampo and Aquiles Serdán. Here, personable chef and Toronto native Peter Palmer lives his bliss creating delicious menus. When I was there he was featuring breast of chicken smothered in pistachio cream sauce ($8), Grecian-style shish kebabs ($9), smoked loin of pork with fresh spring tomato sauce ($8), and red snapper almondine ($9). For something special, bring a party of friends to sample all 10 courses of a fixed-price ($15 per person) dinner (reserve with Peter a few days ahead of time).

Chapala
BREAKFAST

A good place to start the day is at **Cafe Paris** (on Madero, corner of Hidalgo, tel. 376/765-5353, open daily 8:30 A.M.–11 P.M.), right in the center of town. Sunny morning (and shady afternoon) sidewalk tables and tasty offerings attract a loyal local and foreign clientele. The menu features breakfasts ($3–6), soups, salads, sandwiches ($3–6), Mexican plates ($4–7), and beer, wine, and espresso.

CASUAL DINING

Across the street and uphill a block, open-air *palapa* **Che Mary** (430 Madero, Mon.–Thurs. 7 A.M.–5 P.M., Fri.–Sat. 7 A.M.–8 P.M.) offers a reliably tasty, moderately priced menu.

Back on the opposite side of Madero, the baked offerings of **Santino's Pizza** (Madero 467A, tel. 376/765-2360, open daily 1–10 P.M.), three blocks up the street from the Chapala plaza, are equally good onsite or delivered.

FINE DINING

The **Restaurant Los Cazadores** (on Paseo Ramón Corona, across the street from the Chapala Pier, tel. 376/765-2162, open daily 1–8 P.M.) is equally good for lunch or dinner. Located in the historic Braniff mansion, the restaurant offers both a touch of class and relaxing, front veranda seating, ideal for taking in the lakefront street scene. Choose from a long menu of tasty, very recognizable international and Mexican favorites (tortilla soup $3, shrimp cocktail $7, red snapper $7, filet mignon $8). Before you leave, step inside for a look at the collection of polished Porfiriana that adorns the mansion's venerable silk-covered walls.

Also on Corona, four blocks east of Los Cazadores and overlooking the lakeshore, is Chapala's favorite seafood eatery, longtime **Restaurant Cozumel** (Paseo Corona 22A, tel. 377/765-4606, open Tues.–Sun. noon–10 P.M.). Highlights include live music and Wednesday and Friday specials (such as chicken cordon bleu and surf and turf, $10–12), in addition to a long menu, usually including stuffed crab and squid ($10–12), Alaskan crab ($18), scallops ($12), lobster ($18), frog legs ($10), and steaks ($10–16). Reservations are recommended (and mandatory for the Wednesday special).

Elote (sweet corn) and *nieve* (ice cream) add to the Chapala Pier's festive atmosphere.

© BRUCE WHIPPERMAN

GROCERIES

In Ajijic, smart shoppers go to **Super El Torito** (at Plaza Bugambilias, on the highway, east side, tel. 376/766-2202, open daily 7:30 A.M.–9 P.M.) for a wide selection of fresh veggies, fruit, meat, groceries, and a small but good English-language newsstand.

Super Lake (tel. 376/766-0174, open daily 8 A.M.–8 P.M.), midway between Ajijic and Chapala, enjoys equal popularity. It offers a wide choice of groceries, vegetables, and fruits, plus many frozen foods, a deli, and a soda fountain. Also available are magazines and newspapers, including *USA Today* and the Miami *Herald* and the informative local monthly *El Ojo del Lago.* Find it in San Antonio, on the lake side of the highway.

In Chapala, you can get most of your basic groceries at **Super Max** (Francisco Madero 378, tel. 376/765-5500, open Mon.–Sat. 8 A.M.–9 P.M., Sun. 8 A.M.–3 P.M.), on the west side of the street about a block uphill from the town plaza. For fresh fruits and vegetables, it's best to go to the town market, on the east side of the Chapala plaza.

INFORMATION AND SERVICES
Tourist Information

The small Chapala office of Jalisco state tourism (Madero 407, upper level, tel./fax 376/765-3141, open Mon.–Fri. 9 A.M.–5 P.M., Sat. 9 A.M.–1 P.M.) is downtown, near the lakefront, and across the street from the banks. During regular hours the staff will answer questions and give out brochures and maps. For information (in Spanish) after hours, call the tourism information number (tel. 1-800/363-2200).

In Ajijic, one of handiest information sources is the friendly **Laguna Real Estate** (24 Carretera Oriente, tel. 376/766-1174, open Mon.–Sat. 9 A.M.–5 P.M.).

Banking

In both Chapala and Ajijic, bank-rate money exchange, travelers checks, and prompt service in English are available at **Lloyd's** (seguros@lloyd.com.mx, www.lloyd.com.mx): in Chapala (Madero 232, across from the town plaza, tel. 376/765-4750 or 376/765-3598, fax 376/765-4545); in Ajijic (Carretera Oriente #40, tel. 376/766-3110, 376/766-3111, 376/766-3112, or 376/766-3113, fax 376/766-3115), on the highway, east side of the town center, across the street from the gas station. Lloyd's, moreover, offers financial and investment services. Both branches are open Monday–Friday 9 A.M.–5 P.M.

Conventional banks, all with ATMs, are well represented in Chapala, all near the corner of Hidalgo (the Ajijic highway) and main street Madero. Moving uphill, first comes long-hours **HSBC** (tel. 376/765-4110, open Mon.–Fri. 8 A.M.–7 P.M., Sat. 8 A.M.–3 P.M.). Two doors farther, find **Bancomer** (tel./fax 376/765-4515, open Mon.–Fri. 8:30 A.M.–4 P.M.). After bank hours, use the banks' automated teller machines or the small *casas de cambio,* around the corner from Bancomer, to change money until about 7 P.M.

In Ajijic, change your American or Canadian cash or travelers checks at the plaza-front **Bancomer** (southwest corner of Hidalgo and Colón, tel. 376/766-2300, open Mon.–Fri.

8:30 A.M.–4 P.M.). After hours, use the bank's ATM or go to the hole-in-the-wall *casa de cambio* Epsilon Divisas (28 Colón, across from the plaza, tel. 376/766-2213, open Mon.–Sat. 8:30 A.M.–5 P.M., Sat. 8:30 A.M.–4 P.M.).

Post and Communications

You can have everything—express mail, fax, long-distance phone, Internet connection, message center, copies, office services, and even a Nuevo Laredo, Texas, mailbox—at **Mailboxes, Etc.** (Carretera-Jocotepec 144, tel. 376/766-0647, fax 376/766-0775, www.chapala.com/mailboxes.html, open Mon.–Fri. 9 A.M.–6 P.M., Sat. 9 A.M.–2 P.M.), on the highway in San Antonio, which is halfway between Ajijic and Chapala.

The Chapala town **post office** *(correo)* (open Mon.–Fri. 9 A.M.–4 P.M., Sat. 9 A.M.–1 P.M.) is on Degollado, near the corner of Guerrero, two blocks uphill from the town plaza and four short blocks east of main street Madero.

In Ajijic, the small *correo* (tel. 376/766-1888, open Mon.–Fri. 8 A.M.–3 P.M.) is on the highway, a half block west of the town stoplight.

The Chapala *telecomunicaciones* (open Mon.–Fri. 9 A.M.–3 P.M.)—money orders, public fax)—is a half block east of Madero, at the corner of Morelos and the town plaza.

For economical long-distance telephone in both Chapala and Ajijic, it's best to use the **street telephones,** operable by the easily purchased Ladatel telephone cards (look for blue and yellow signs at groceries and pharmacies).

In Ajijic, a number of **Internet** stores are available. For example, C.I.A. (Café Internet Ajijic) (tel. 376/766-3626, open Mon.–Fri. 8:30 A.M.–4:30 P.M., Sat. 9 A.M.–2 P.M.), with a plethora of services—Internet connection, color photo printing, copies—serves soup and sandwiches to boot. It's on the highway, east side, across from Telmex and the gas station.

Books, Newspapers, and Library

The best bookstore in Chapala is **Libros y Revistas de Chapala** (Madero 230, tel. 376/765-6990, open daily 9 A.M.–5 P.M.), across from the plaza. Its extensive stock includes racks of English paperback books and dozens of American popular magazines and newspapers, such as *USA Today* and the Miami *Herald.* It also stocks several Mexico maps and some guidebooks.

Ajijic's best bookstore is in the Bugambilias shopping center (on the highway, east side, tel. 376/766-4319, open Mon.–Sat. 9 A.M.–5 P.M., Sun. 9 A.M.–2 P.M.), next to Tonito grocery. It stocks many U.S. magazines, some guidebooks, maps, and paperback novels.

The **Neill James Library** (Calle 16 de Septiembre a block east of main street Colón, open Mon.–Sat. 10 A.M.–2 P.M.), the good work of the charitable Lake Chapala Society, stands in its flowery showplace garden two blocks downhill from the Ajijic town plaza. Its broad all-English loan collection includes many shelves of classic and contemporary literature, donated by Ajijic residents. In the corridor outside the library, an informative bulletin board and community calendar details local cultural, civic, and social events.

While at Lake Chapala, be sure to pick up a free copy of the superb local monthly *El Ojo del Lago.* Its lively pages are packed with details of local exhibits, performances, and cultural events; pithy articles of Mexican lore and nearby places to visit; and even interesting advertisements. If you can't find a copy, either drop by the Chapala office (Av. Hidalgo 223, by Coldwell Banker-Chapala Realty, tel. 376/765-3676, fax 376/765-3528, ojodellago@laguna.com.mx, www.chapala.com/chapala/ojo.html), or the Ajijic office (38B Carretera Oriente, tel. 376/766-1152) on the highway about two blocks east of the Colón traffic signal.

Also worth a look is the likewise gratis *Chapala Review* monthly magazine, stuffed with thoughtful, locally-focused columns, historical and cultural articles, and handy advertisements. If you can't find a copy, drop by their office (Carretera Oriente #17-3, upstairs, tel. 376/766-4200, review@laguna.com.mx, www.chapalareview.com) on the highway, in Ajijic.

Civic Organizations

The Lake Chapala Society, a volunteer civic organization, welcomes visitors at its information desk (open Mon.–Sat. 10 A.M.–2 P.M.), at the society's Neill James Library headquarters (Calle 16 de Septiembre 16A, two blocks above the lakeshore and a block east of Colón, in Ajijic, tel. 376/766-1140, fax 376/766-4685, lakesoc@prodigy.net.mx, www.lakechapalasociety. org). The Society invites newcomers to sign up and take part in their extensive schedule of social events and activities, from great books discussions and digital camera lessons to Spanish classes and eye doctor visits. For more information, see the Lake Chapala Society's section in the *El Ojo del Lago* newspaper.

Conservation-minded local citizens have banded together to form **Amigos del Lago** (Friends of the Lake). Besides local educational projects, such as lakeshore trash cleanup and tree planting, they are also pursuing a focused political action campaign to restore Lake Chapala to its former magnificence. They invite participation by all folks interested in aiding their efforts. For more information, contact the Amigos del Lago (at this writing, temporary) office (Zaragoza 23, Ajijic, Jalisco 45920, tel. 376/765-5755, tel./fax 376/766-0282, info@ amigosdelago.org, www.amigosdelago.org).

Tours and Guides

Check out the services of **Charter Club Tours** (tel. 376/766-1777), in Ajijic, at Plaza Montana, by the Colón highway signal, or in Guadalajara, (Av. San Francisco 3477, in Chapalita, tel. 33/3122-1215, info@charterclubtours.com. mx, www.charterclubtours.com.mx). Itineraries vary and include downtown Guadalajara sights, the Ballet Folklórico, shopping in Tonalá and Tlaquepaque, or an around–Lake Chapala jaunt. Wider-ranging tours can include regional destinations, such as Mazamitla in the mountains, the distillery town of Tequila, or the monumental Guachimontones pyramids at Teuchtitlán in the west.

You might also check out English-speaking naturalist and guide Jeremy Lusch, who follows his bliss either leading visitors on trips or arranging Guadalajara-region sightseeing and nature excursions. Contact him at the lodging he operates, Hotel Plaza Suites Ajijic (Colón 33, Ajijic, tel. 376/766-0383, ajijichotel@ yahoo.com, www.ajijichotel.com).

One of the best local travel agencies is **Viajes Vikingo** (Carretera Oriente #54, upstairs, tel. 376/766-0936 or 376/766-0104, fax 376/766-1058, aramirezochoa@hotmail.com, Mon.–Fri. 9 A.M.–6 P.M., Sat. 9 A.M.–1 P.M.), at Plaza Bugambilias in Ajijic.

Consulates

The closest U.S. consul is in Guadalajara (Progreso 175, about a mile west of the city center, service hours for American citizens Mon.–Fri. 8 A.M.–11 P.M., tel. 33/3268-2100 and 33/3268-2200). In a genuine emergency, call 33/3826-5553. The American consul occasionally visits the Chapala area. The visitation schedule is usually posted on one of the bulletin boards at the Ajijic library of the Lake Chapala Society, on Calle 16 de Septiembre.

The Guadalajara **Canadian consulate** (Aurelio Aceves 225, local 31, near the intersection of Avenidas López Mateos and Vallarta, about three miles west of the city center, tel. 33/3615-6215, fax 33/3615-8665, open Mon.–Fri. 8:30 A.M.–2 P.M. and 3–5 P.M.) is in the Hotel Fiesta Americana. In emergencies, after business hours, call the Canadian consulate in Mexico City (toll-free tel. 01-800/706-2900).

Real Estate Agents

The long list of local real estate agencies that sell and rent properties includes the reliable **Coldwell-Banker Chapala Realty** (Hidalgo 223, Chapala, tel. 376/765-2877, fax 376/765-3528, www.chapala.com). Alternatively, visit their Ajijic office (Carretera Oriente #38, about three blocks east of the Colón signal, tel. 376/766-1152, fax 376/766-2124).

Also very experienced and worthy is **Laguna Real Estate** (#24 Oriente, tel. 376/766-1174, fax 376/766-1188, laguna@ laguna.com.mx, www.lagunamex.com), on the highway in Ajijic.

LAKE CHAPALA

Handicrafts and Spanish Instruction

Jalisco state **Casa de las Artesanías** (House of Handicrafts) offers pottery, painting, weaving, and other courses in handicrafts. For more information call 376/766-0548, or drop into their Ajijic gallery (open Mon.–Fri. 10 A.M.– 6 P.M., Sat. 10 A.M.–4 P.M., Sun. 10 A.M.– 2 P.M.), on the highway as you're entering from Chapala, just after the big white roadside sculpture on the left.

The **Lake Chapala Society** sponsors a busy ongoing Spanish-language instruction program. Classes are chiefly small group, encompassing five graduated skill levels, in three yearly sessions: January–March, May–July, and September–November. The fee runs about $40 per session. For information, visit www.lakechapalasociety.org or email spanish-program@lakechapalasociety.org, telephone 376/766-1140, or drop by the Society's Ajijic headquarters (see *Civic Organizations*).

If you want more intensive instruction, the Lake Chapala Society recommends **Profesora Beatriz Siliceo** (see-lee-SAY-oh), who offers Spanish instruction at her school (Independencia 153, P.O. Box 764, Ajijic, Jalisco 45920, tel. 376/766-2276, spanlang2@prodigy.net.mx, langteach123@yahoolcom.mx) in San Antonio (midway between Ajijic and Chapala). She offers a wide range of instructional options, from regular to intensive, and individual to small group.

Medical Services

Both Chapala and Ajijic have well-equipped small private hospitals, with 24-hour ambulance service and English-speaking specialists available for both regular and emergency consultations. Among the most highly recommended is the **Núcleo Médico y Dental de Especialidades de Chapala** (Hidalgo 796, Riberas del Pilar, tel. 376/765-4805), halfway between Chapala and Ajijic.

In Ajijic you can go to the **Clínica Ajijic** (33 Oriente, four blocks east of Colón, tel. 376/766-0662 or 376/766-0500), on the highway.

If you get sick in Chapala, contact your hotel desk or the **Clínica de Especialidades Nueva Galicia** (Juárez 563A, tel. 376/765-2400), around the northeast plaza corner. General practitioner Dra. Adela Macias Vengas offers services, on-call 24 hours.

If you prefer homeopathic treatment, go to **Farmacia Abejita** (Little Bee) (Juárez 559, corner of L. Cotilla, tel. 376/765-2266, open Mon.–Wed. and Fri. 9 A.M.–2 P.M. and 4–8 P.M., Sat. and Thurs. 9 A.M.–2 P.M., closed Sun).

For medicines and routine advice, the best-supplied Chapala-area pharmacy is **Hector's Farmacia Morelos** (421 Madero, south corner of the plaza, tel. 376/765-4002, open 8:30 A.M.–8:30 P.M. except Sun. and Thurs., when hours are 8:30 A.M.–3:30 P.M.). In Ajijic, get your medicines and drugs from **Farmacia Cristina** (Plaza Bugambilias, on the highway, about six blocks west of the town center, tel. 376/766-1501, open daily 8 A.M.–9 P.M.).

Police

For emergencies in Chapala, call or go to the police station (on Madero, near the town plaza, tel. 376/765-4444 or 376/765-2819). In Ajijic, contact the police at the *presidencia municipal* (on Colón by the plaza, tel. 376/766-1760).

GETTING THERE
By Car or RV

The town of Chapala is about 33 miles (53 km), about an hour, south of the Guadalajara city center by Highway 44. See the *Lake Chapala and Vicinity* map.

If you're connecting with Lake Chapala directly to or from Tepic or Puerto Vallarta, use the Guadalajara *periférico* (peripheral city-center bypass). This links the Chapala Highway 44 directly with the westside Tepic–Puerto Vallarta leg of Highway 15.

To or from southern destinations of Barra de Navidad, Colima, and Manzanillo, route yourself south of Guadalajara along the lake's northwest shore via Highway 15's Jocotepec–Acatlán de Juárez leg. Around Acatlán de Juárez, pay close attention to turnoff signs. They'll guide your connection from Highway 54D *cuota au-*

topista (toll freeway) (Colima and Manzanillo) or two-lane Highway 80 (Barra de Navidad).

By Bus

The main Lake Chapala bus station is in Chapala downtown on Madero at M. Martínez, about three blocks uphill from the town plaza. The red-and-white second-class buses of **Autotransportes Guadalajara-Chapala** (tel. 376/765-2212), connect about every half hour with the Guadalajara downtown old terminal (Camionera Antigua) until about 9:15 P.M. Other red-and-white departures connect about every half hour with both Jocotepec and San Nicolas, and every hour with Mezcala.

GETTING AROUND
By Car or RV

Generally light traffic makes your automobile the most convenient way to explore Lake Chapala. Car rentals are available either directly at the Guadalajara airport (Hertz, Avis, Budget, Optima, and more) or through a Lake Chapala travel agent such as Viajes Vikingo

(tel. 376/766-0966 or 376/766-0104, fax 376/766-1058).

Drivers who want to avoid Chapala town traffic do so via the **bypass road** *(libramiento)*, which forks from Highway 23 two miles uphill from Chapala. The *libramiento* continues for four miles, joining the lakeshore highway about a mile east of the center of Ajijic.

By Minibus

Local minibuses run frequently from curbside across from the Chapala bus station (about six blocks uphill from the lake, along main street Francisco I. Madero) and, a block from the lake, from the Chapala town center at the corner of Hidalgo and Francisco I. Madero. Most frequent is the westbound bus, which heads along the lakeshore to Ajijic and San Juan Cosala and back, and which will stop anywhere along the road. Other lakeshore destinations (departing from inside the terminal) include Jocotepec about every half hour 5 A.M.–8:30 P.M., and San Nicolas about every half hour eastbound 7 A.M.–7 P.M.

GUADALAJARA GETAWAYS

A trove of delightful surprises await visitors ready to explore Guadalajara's fascinating country hinterlands. Along your adventure trail, you can discover what many Guadalajarans already have discovered, in just one, two, or three hours by road from the city. Starting in the northeast and moving clockwise around the *Guadalajara Getaways* map, you'll first find **San Juan de los Lagos,** home of the fabulously adored **Virgin of San Juan de los Lagos,** a humble but miraculous corn-paste figurine that rescued a small girl from death. To the south of Guadalajara is the picturesque, pine-shadowed mountain villages of **Mazamitla** and **Tapalpa,** sprinkled with comfortable country lodgings and replete with tasty homemade sweets, hearty local-favorite meals, and a long menu of hiking, horseback riding, camping, boulder climbing,

bicycling, and more. Next you'll find relaxing warm spring resorts, such as **Chimulco,** favorite of families, tenters, and RVers, and the **Hotel Rio Caliente Spa,** a quietly exclusive haven of warm pools for soaking, healing spa treatments, and hiking and wildlife-viewing in the surrounding pristine **Bosque de Primavera** (Forest of Spring). **Guachimontones,** an archaeological park of monumental two-thousand-year-old pyramids, is next to cool **Balneario El Rincón,** a crystal-clear spring-fed lake and campground; nearby, the elegant but relaxed and flower-bedecked **Hotel Hacienda El Carmen** awaits. The distillery town **Tequila** is the source of its world-famous namesake liquor, and the rustic **Magdalena** village, nearby, is renowned for the glistening opal jewelry that its mines produce.

HIGHLIGHTS

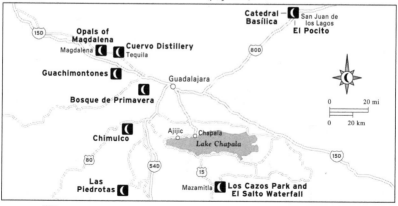

◖ Catedral Basílica: Visit the cathedral basilica of the miraculous Virgen de San Juan de los Lagos. Linger and peruse the fascinating swarm of religious souvenir stands in front of the basilica (page 189).

◖ El Pocito: This shrine in San Juan de los Lagos features a room festooned with gifts and mementos brought by the Virgin's multitude of yearly visitors (page 189).

◖ Los Cazos Park and El Salto Waterfall: In Mazamitla, explore this private park and take a guided horseback ride through the surrounding pine-tufted forest. Vigorous visitors might want to leave the horses behind and take the exercise themselves by doing the walk on foot (page 194).

◖ Las Piedrotas: From Tapalpa, drive, taxi, or hike the four miles to the Big Rocks – fine for wandering, wondering, climbing, and possible overnight camping (page 205).

◖ Chimulco: Bring the whole family to splash in natural spring-water pools and enjoy a picnic afterward in the adjacent shady park.

Stay overnight in a bungalow or at the RV park (page 212).

◖ Bosque de Primavera: Enjoy a swim and a picnic at one of the *balnearios* (bathing springs), such as Las Tinajitas or El Bosque. Arrive prepared to camp in the pine-scented forest on the bank of the steaming Río Caliente (page 214).

◖ Guachimontones: Explore this ancient monumental ceremonial complex and enjoy the lake view from atop the pyramids, and a picnic and swim in the cool, crystalline waters of nearby Balneario El Rincón (page 215).

◖ Cuervo Distillery: In Tequila, do a morning tour through the renowned liquor factory and museum and enjoy lunch at the neighboring Fonda Cholula restaurant (page 222).

◖ Opals of Magdalena: Make your first Magdalena stop at this store and defacto opal museum, chock full of glistening opal jewelry and handicrafts. Followed it with lunch at top-pick Fonda Lupita restaurant and (if prearranged) a tour of the Magdalena opal mines (page 227).

LOOK FOR ◖ TO FIND RECOMMENDED SIGHTS, ACTIVITIES, DINING, AND LODGING.

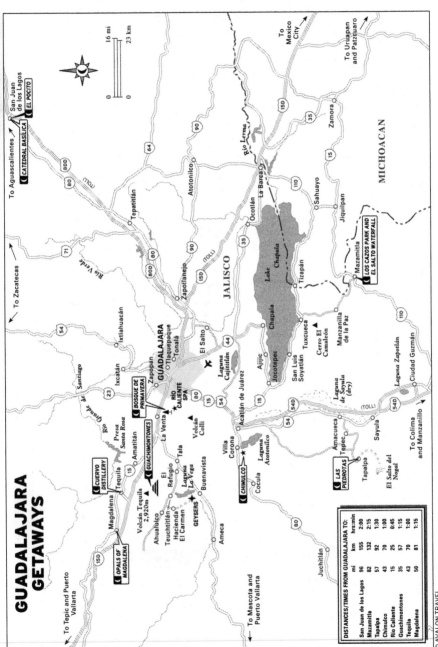

GUADALAJARA GETAWAYS

DISTANCES/TIMES FROM GUADALAJARA TO:	mi	km	hrs:min
San Juan de los Lagos	96	155	2:00
Mazamitla	82	132	2:15
Tapalpa	57	92	1:30
Chimulco	43	70	1:00
Rio Caliente	15	25	0:45
Guachimontones	35	57	1:15
Tequila	43	70	1:00
Magdalena	50	81	1:15

© AVALON TRAVEL

PLANNING YOUR TIME

The several getaway destinations described in this chapter are reachable from either downtown Guadalajara or Lake Chapala in an average drive of about two-and-a-half hours for the farthest (San Juan de los Lagos and Mazamitla) and one to one-and-a-half hours for the closest (Río Caliente Spa, Bosque de Primavera, and Tequila). All of the getaways are fine for a day trip (as long as you get started by around 9 A.M.) or an overnight, or, even better, a two-night stay that allows a day for getting oriented and a second day for relaxing and lingering.

If you have only one day, you could probably spend it most profitably on a west-side excursion, starting early, stopping at one of the warm springs *balnearios* (such as Cañon de Las Flores) in the Bosque de Primavera for a picnic and swim and continuing on to Tequila for the Cuervo distillery tour and early dinner (at Fonda Cholula).

At some getaways with lots to do, such as Tapalpa, Río Caliente Spa/Bosque de Primavera, or Guachimontones/Hacienda El Carmen/Tequila/Magdalena combined, you could spend an enjoyable three or four nights, or even a week.

The getaways are arranged clockwise, beginning with San Juan de los Lagos in the northeast and moving around the regional map to Magdalena in the far west.

San Juan de los Lagos

The renown of San Juan de los Lagos (pop. about 50,000) springs from the faith of the many hundreds of thousands of devotees who flock annually to worship the Virgin of San Juan de los Lagos. She is one of a trio of miraculous Virgins (see the sidebar *The Three Sisters of Jalisco*) who have captured the faith and compassion of tens of millions of Mexicans.

For the discerning visitor, a trip to San Juan de los Lagos can be an eye-opening journey into an old Mexico—of devoted crowds, favorite traditional foods and sweets, festoons of religious trinkets—still vibrant and a wonder to experience despite 100 years of modernization and oft-hostile antireligious federal policies.

HISTORY

The first Spaniards bypassed the village of Mezquititlán (Place of Mesquite), the Tecuexe indigenous village site of present-day San Juan de los Lagos. A need arose, however, after the devastation and suffering of the Mixtón War. Missionaries came to heal and convert the starving and sick.

Fray Miguel de Bolonia built a chapel, refuge, and hospital at the village that, in 1542, he had christened as San Juan Bautista de Mezqui-

titlán. Soon thereafter, the chapel acquired a figurine of the Virgin of the Immaculate Conception, humbly fashioned of native canes.

Three generations later, in 1623, that very image gained fame for restoring the life of a seven-year-old girl, daughter of itinerant circus folk. The figure's fame skyrocketed, attracting hosts of visitors and a pile of offerings. In 1633, authorities decided to establish a local township to handle the crowds of pilgrims and administer the donations. Being in the district of Santa María de los Lagos, the authorities named the town San Juan de los Lagos, after St. John the Baptist.

During the colonial period, the town and municipality, buoyed by the constant pilgrim influx and its rich agricultural hinterland, prospered. In 1810, San Juan de los Lagos leaders were among the first to embrace the insurgency of revolutionary priest Miguel Hidalgo, who was received enthusiastically when he passed through in early 1811.

In the aftermath of the Revolution of 1910, the strong Catholic faith of local people came into conflict with the anticlerical provisions of the revolutionary Constitution of 1917. When President Plutarco Calles (1924–1928)

THE THREE SISTERS OF JALISCO

In all of Mexico, only the Virgin of Guadalupe exceeds in adoration the all-Jalisco trio – the "Three Sister" Virgins of Talpa, Zapopan, and San Juan de los Lagos. Yearly they draw millions of humble Mexican pilgrims who bus, walk, hitchhike, or, in some cases, crawl to festivals honoring the Virgins. Each Virgin's popularity springs from some persistent, endearing legend. The Virgin of Talpa defied a haughty bishop's efforts to cage her; the Virgin of Zapopan rescued Guadalajara from war and disaster; the Virgin of San Juan de los Lagos restored a dead child to life.

Talpa, Zapopan, and San Juan de los Lagos townsfolk have built towering basilicas to shelter and honor each Virgin. Each small and fragile figurine is draped in fine silk and jewels and worshipped by a continuous stream of penitents. During a Virgin festival the image is lifted aloft by a platoon of richly costumed bearers and paraded to the clamor, tumult, and cheers of a million or more of the faithful.

Even if you choose to avoid the crowds and visit Talpa, Zapopan, or San Juan de los Lagos on a nonfestival day, you'll soon see that the hubbub continues. Pilgrims come and go, bands and mariachis play, and curio stands stuffed with gilded devotional goods crowd the basilica square.

© BRUCE WHIPPERMAN

The Virgin of Zapopan joins the Virgin of Talpa and the Virgin of San Juan de los Lagos to form the Three Sisters of Jalisco.

attempted to zealously enforce the law, the people of San Juan de los Lagos and the surrounding "Los Altos" upland region mounted a fiercely disciplined guerrilla campaign, killing federal troops and harassing officials.

When federal troops executed their leader, Anacieto González Flores, in April 1927, the guerrillas, known as "Cristeros," crying *¡Viva Cristo Rey!,* mounted a full-scale war. Federal authorities responded with a brutal, scorched-earth policy, burning farms and crops, killing livestock, and moving all the country people into concentration camps in towns. Deprived of food and support, the guerrillas nevertheless kept fighting, but with diminished vigor, until 1935.

ORIENTATION

Let San Juan's twin-steepled **basilica** be your reference. Standing on the front steps, with the basilica facade behind you, you'll be facing west, with the main plaza (Plaza Principal) in front of you. The east–west street running to your right is Rita Pérez de Moreno; the one to your left is Juárez. Running north–south, on the far side of the plaza, Hidalgo runs to the right past Moreno, while Guerrero, Hidalgo's southward extension, runs left, south, past the plaza. Running east–west, one block north of Moreno, is Independencia, while on the south side, one block south of Juárez, Porvenir runs likewise east–west.

SIGHTS
◖ Catedral Basílica

Climb the stairs and pass beneath the rose-tinted volcanic stone facade of the basilica, officially known as the Catedral Basílica Santuario de la Virgen de San Juan de los Lagos. In addition to the approximately 10 daily masses, the faithful flock inside continually, resting in the pews, pausing up front to pay their respects, and kneeling to pray for the Virgin to grant a wish.

She reigns above all, in a shiny silver case, flanked by glittering marble and gold, beneath the all-seeing Eye of God. In a room to the left of the altar, be sure to view the displayed mass of mute testimony—pictures, letters, clothing, bouquets—from the Virgin's followers.

Back outside, wander through the ranks of stalls along Moreno on the basilica's north side and behind, to the east, along Juárez. The abundance is staggering: embroidery, sombreros, serapes, religious goods—pious angels, baby Jesuses, gilded portraits of Jesus and San Juan—and a small mountain of old-fashioned sweets, from dates and *rollos* (fruit rolls) of tamarind and guava *(guayaba)* to *rompope* (guava eggnog) and coconut candy.

Be sure not to miss the *milagro* stands at the foot of the basilica front steps. The faithful buy the diversely shaped metal charms—dogs, cats, horses, legs, hands, babies, men, women—for making requests (by pinning the token to the robe) of their patron saint.

◖ El Pocito

Despite its petite size, El Pocito (poh-SEE-toh, The Little Well) is San Juan's most endearing and not-to-be-missed pilgrimage stop. From the basilica front, walk west along Moreno three blocks (passing the larger but less notable Chapel of the Retablo of the Virgin on the right at block two), west to the chapel yard, at the north-side corner of Primavera. The chapel, officially La Capilla del Primer Milagro (The Chapel of the First Miracle), shelters El Pocito, where the Virgin worked her wonder in 1623.

The story began when the seven-year-old daughter of an itinerant circus master died

In a typical year, a million pilgrims visit the Catedral Basílica in San Juan de los Lagos.

from a fall from a trapeze. The next day, the people were about to bury her, when Ana Lucía, an indigenous woman who for many years had been the custodian of the chapel and its humble cane figurine of the Virgin of Immaculate Conception, placed the Virgin on the girl's breast, and she amazingly came to life. The girl left with her father and his circus troupe, Ana Lucía lived on for 20 more years, finally passing away at age 110, and ever-increasing multitudes of pilgrims came to visit the Virgin year after year.

Be sure to visit the room, the former hospital, outside, to the north of the chapel, where wall pictures dramatize the Virgin's story and the modest belongings—knitted booties, caps, dresses, gloves—of children whose parents asked the Virgin to protect them decorate the walls.

ENTERTAINMENT AND EVENTS

Although the continual crowds and the plaza-front trinket stalls seem to make San Juan's

At the chapel at El Pocito pilgrims can read the miraculous story of the Virgin of San Juan de los Lagos.

basilica-front blocks appear like a nonstop party, several local fiestas periodically ratchet the excitement up to a near-fever pitch.

Fiestas

The excitement peaks during a pair of winter *ferias.* The entire month of December amounts to a continuous party, beginning December 1–8, when hundreds of thousands of merrymakers crowd in for the **Fiesta de la Inmaculada Concepción de la Santísima Virgen.** (Come if you enjoy crowds, and make your hotel reservations very early.)

Concurrently, December 1–12, the parish church, Parroquia de San Juan Bautista, celebrates the **Virgin of Guadalupe** with carnival games, traditional dances, processions, floats, masses, food, and fireworks.

During Christmas, **Navidad,** people crowd in to celebrate December 20–25 with plenty of food, fireworks, and Las Posadas processions around the town.

The second *feria* kicks off with the **Fiesta**

de la Virgen de Candelaria, January 23–February 2, highlighted by processions and traditional dances. These include La Presentación del Niño Jesús al Templo and the Danza de los Cristianos y Moros, a thinly disguised reenactment of the conquest of Mexico.

During Passover (Pasqua) and Easter Week (Semana Santa), celebration peaks again with reenactments of the passion, death, and resurrection of Jesus on the days just before Easter Sunday.

The Virgin returns to the focus once again, August 1–15, with the **Fiesta de la Asunción,** the celebration of the ascent of the Virgin Mary into heaven.

ACCOMMODATIONS

San Juan de los Lagos has a swarm of hotels, some good, some bad, but most indifferent. Unfortunately, demand has driven prices up and kept quality down. Several are nevertheless recommendable. Prices quoted are the normal, nonfiesta rates; expect increases of 10–30 percent during times of high occupancy.

Under $50

Uphill, three blocks east of the basilica, start at the worthy budget option **Posada Andrea** (Plazuela de Romo 4, San Juan de los Lagos, Jalisco 47000, tel. 395/785-0663, $30). Past the small reception and lobby, the 36 rooms in three floors are modern, clean, and simply but comfortably furnished. Some rooms are a bit dark, however. Look at more than one before moving in. Rates include shower bath, fan, TV, and parking.

Larger **Hotel Primavera** (Primavera 13, San Juan de los Lagos, Jalisco 47000, tel. 395/785-1506, fax 395/785-2220, www.hprimavera.com, $45), downhill, is well located on a quiet back street, three blocks due west of the basilica plaza. The Primavera offers four floors of 50 comfortably furnished clean rooms, with color-coordinated bedspreads, shiny tile floors, drapes, and well-maintained bathrooms. Rooms vary in size, with one to three beds. Rooms come with fans and TV. Other amenities include parking, elevator, and a restaurant. Credit cards accepted.

In exchange for a plaza-front location, you get more for your money at the (C Hotel **Balha Grande** (Begnino Roma 75, San Juan de los Lagos, Jalisco 47000, tel. 395/785-4606 or 395/785-4607, fax 395/785-4108, hotbalgran@redial.com.mx, $45), two blocks north and two blocks east of the plaza. Past the attractive (but low-ceilinged) lobby and the modern coffee shop/restaurant in the back, an elevator and stairs lead to four floors of about 60 upstairs rooms and suites. They are simply but comfortably furnished with cool white walls and attractive floral bedspreads, with fixed wall reading lamps, air-conditioning, fans, TV, white tile floors, and shiny shower baths. Get a room away from the street for more tranquility. Parking is included.

$50-100

Move three blocks west to the northwest plaza corner and the big, ideally located, plaza-front **Hotel Posada Arcos** (Rita Pérez de Moreno y Hidalgo, San Juan de los Lagos, Jalisco 47000, tel./fax 395/785-1580, $60). The four floors of 140 rooms and suites, arranged in tiers around a central atrium, are not well arranged with respect to privacy or noise. Windows of most rooms (which look out on tiled, and therefore noisy, atrium corridors) must have their drapes drawn for privacy. (Get one of the quieter, more private rooms with windows facing outward toward the plaza.) Rooms are clean and comfortable, but many are not particularly well maintained. Make sure that everything works before you move in. Rates include air-conditioning, TV, phones, and a reliable restaurant. Credit cards are accepted.

Back uphill to the east, a block past the Hotel Balha Grande, at the corner of Begnino Roma and Matamoros, stands the posh highrise (C Hotel **Estancia Real** (Begnino Roma 95, San Juan de los Lagos, Jalisco 47000, tel./fax 395/785-2524, 395/785-5100, or 395/785-5101, Mexico toll-free tel. 01-800/714-4496, estancia-real@redial.com.mx, $60), queen of local hotels. Builders have taken maximum advantage of the uphill site to provide pan-

oramic westward (sunset) views of the basilica and surrounding downtown. Rooms are arranged in about eight floors, around an airy inner atrium. All are deluxe and attractively decorated with plush carpets, large beds, and luxury bathrooms. Additionally, guests in the suites, on the building's southwest corner, enjoy magnificent views, soft couches, elegantly carved interior stone columns and arches, and large whirlpool bathtubs. All rooms come with air-conditioning, cable TV, phone, parking, and a restaurant. Credit cards accepted.

Among the many other local hotels, the moderately priced, centrally located **Hotel Roma** (Vicente Guerrero 26, tel. 395/785-1783 or 395/785-2536, Mexico toll-free tel. 01-800/710-2536, $40) is highly recommended, as is the good-value deluxe **Hotel Quinta Cesar** (Juárez 99, tel. 395/785-5551, toll-free Mex. tel. 01-800-614-5467, www.quintacesar.com.mx, $55), with continental breakfast and a/c. Other centrally located standbys that you might check out in an emergency are **Hotel Fanny** (Independencia 2, tel. 395/785-4343, $30), **Hotel Diana** (Diana 6, south side of the basilica, tel. 395/785-2009 or 395/785-1558, $32) **Hotel Frances** (Independencia 3, tel. 395/785-0195 or 395/785-4343, $35).

FOOD
Food Stalls and Juice Bars

The market *fondas* (food stalls) are probably the best food choice for your money around the main plaza. Find them on the upper floor of the market, in the block diagonally northwest of the main plaza. Look around and choose from dozens of savory *guisados* (stews) of chicken, pork, lamb, or beef, as well as rice, tamales, *chiles rellenos,* and much more. Remember, if *fonda* food is steaming hot, it's wholesome.

Also in the market, stop at one of the *jugerías* (juice bars) for your choice of delicious orange *(naranja)*, pineapple *(piña),* strawberry *(fresa),* apple *(manzana),* or banana *(plátano)* juice *(jugo).*

Natural Foods

For natural vitamins, minerals, teas, cereals, and more, go to **Rincón Naturista San Juan** (Fortuna 109, tel. 395/785-3249, open Mon.–Sat. 10 A.M.–3 P.M. and 5–8 P.M., Sun. 10 A.M.–3 P.M.), on the north–south lane a short block east of the basilica's back side.

Casual Dining

Of the acceptable choices around the main plaza, consider the colorful, low-end open-air **Restaurant Imelda** (open daily 8 A.M.–7 P.M.), at the northwest corner of Guerrero and Independencia, a block north of the plaza's northwest corner. Here you have approximately the same options as at the market *fondas*—eggs and pancakes for breakfast, soups, sandwiches, stews, chicken, *chiles rellenos,* and more ($2–4). You can get about the same at the more sophisticated, mid-scale **Restaurant Señorial** (tel. 395/785-1270, open daily 8 A.M.–7 P.M.) on Guerrero, at plaza-front, facing the basilica.

Hotel Restaurants

For a more refined atmosphere, try the hotels. The **Restaurant Veranda** (open daily 8 A.M.–9 P.M., tel. 395/785-1580), in the plaza-front Hotel Posada Arcos, on the corner of Rita Pérez de Moreno and Hidalgo, seems to offer the best restaurant combination of food, atmosphere, and service. Glistening white plates and blue tablecloths set the stage. The very recognizable menu—hamburgers, hot dogs, onion soup, omelets ($2–5), and many entrées, including fish, chicken, and steak ($4–10)—provides the tasty conclusion.

The restaurants at both the **Hotel Balha Grande** and **Hotel Estancia Real** provide similarly refined atmospheres and familiar, reliable food choices.

INFORMATION AND SERVICES
Tourist Information

Get your questions answered at the local office of **Jalisco Turismo** (Segovia 10, tel./fax 395/785-0979, open Mon.–Fri. 9 A.M.–5 P.M.), on the south side of the street at the corner of Fortuna, one short block directly behind the basilica.

Banking

A few banks dot the downtown streets. For long hours and an ATM, go to **Hong Kong Shanghai Banking Corporation** (HSBC) bank (Moreno 37, tel. 395/785-0010, open Mon.–Fri. 8 A.M.–7 P.M., Sat. 8 A.M.–3 P.M.), two blocks east of the basilica.

Communications

To make a local or long-distance telephone call, buy a Ladatel phone card and use it at the many public street telephones. Answer your email or connect to the Internet at Café Mundo Virtual, on Independencia, upstairs, a few doors west of Hidalgo.

HEALTH AND EMERGENCIES
Medical Services

For routine remedies, consult the pharmacist on duty at one of several pharmacies. Try the **Farmacia Guadalajara** (tel. 395/785-3510 or 395/785-3624, Mon.–Sat. 9 A.M.–9 P.M., Sun. 9 A.M.–7 P.M.), on Independencia, between Hidalgo and Zaragoza, one block directly north of the main plaza.

Alternatively, go to the very professional 24-hour pharmacy at the **Clínica San José** (Plazuela de Romo 2, tel. 395/785-1581 or 395/785-2727). Find it by following Moreno four blocks east of the basilica front to Plazuela de Romo, the short block that diagonals left from Moreno.

If you need a doctor, follow your hotel's recommendation, or call the Clínica San José, which has many specialists on call.

For **emergency medical care,** have a taxi take you to the 24-hour emergency room of the Hospital Seguro Social (tel. 395/785-1777), on the Guadalajara highway, a half mile east of downtown.

Police and Fire

Contact the *policía* downtown, at the city hall *(presidencia municipal)* on Segovia, directly behind the basilica (tel. 395/785-0730). In case of fire, call the *bomberos* (Santa Rosa 12, tel. 395/785-4666).

GETTING THERE
By Car

Get to San Juan de los Lagos by car, via four-lane toll expressway Highway 80D. From the center of Guadalajara, follow expressway Calzada Lázaro Cárdenas east. Follow the Highway 90 (Tonalá–Zaplotanejo–Mexico City) signs. Continue about 10 miles (16 km) to the Highway 80D *cuota* (toll) turnoff to Tepatitlán–San Juan de los Lagos–Lagos de Moreno. Continue north another 72 miles

(116 km) an hour and a half to San Juan de los Lagos.

By Bus

From the Central Camionera Nueva (New Central Bus Station) in downtown Guadalajara, many of the bus companies provide first- or luxury-class service to San Juan de los Lagos. These include: Omnibus de Mexico (*módulo 6*, tel. 33/3600-0184 or 33/3600-0469); Estrella Blanca (Turistar, Transportes del Norte, Transportes Chihuahuenses) (*módulo 7*, tel. 33/3679-0404); or ETN (*módulo 2*, tel. 33/3600-0501). (For more details, see *Getting There and Around* in the *Downtown* chapter.)

Mazamitla

Mazamitla (elev. 7,280 feet/2,220 meters) is a village of deep traditions and picturesque back streets that nestle on the side of a lush, pine-tufted mountainside. Lately, Mazamitla has managed to attract the new, *because* of what's old. In the beginning, a few well-to-do Guadalajarans began coming, attracted by Mazamitla's hearty country food, handicrafts, and fresh, pine-scented air. Now the hillsides are dotted with weekend cabins in the woods, a few rustic-chic developments, and some knotty pine *posadas* for the middle- and upper-class city folks who flock in on holidays and weekends.

For much more information about Mazamitla (in Spanish, however), visit www.mazamitla.org.mx.

HISTORY

Mazamitla (pop. about 12,000) straddles the boundary between the Purépecha (Tarascan) culture of Michoacán and the Nahuatl (Aztec) culture of Jalisco. Although the name Mazamitla ("place where arrows for deer-hunting are made") is of Nahuatl origin, Purépecha influence is locally evident. A number of introduced plants, such as avocados, and local street and *barrio* names, such as Charandas,

Charácuaro, Coporo, and Huricho are native to Michoacán culture.

The earliest records place Nahuatl-speaking people living in the vicinity by at least 1165. Later, in 1481, the army of the Purépecha emperor invaded and subdued Mazamitla, en route to the prized salt beds of dry Lago de Sayula.

Purépecha influence was overrun by the Spanish, scarcely a year after their victory over the Aztec empire. In 1522, Spanish captains Alonso de Ávalos and Cristóbal Juan Rodriguez Villafuerte arrived in Mazamitla with a company of soldiers and cavalry. Local people peaceably accepted the authority of the Spanish king and Catholic baptism, sheltering themselves beneath the fold of the Virgin Mary and Saint Christopher. Legal recognition followed with the founding of the town, officially San Cristóbal de Mazamitla, on March 27, 1537, under the authority of Viceroy Antonio de Mendoza.

ORIENTATION

The steps of the town parish church, the **Parroquia de San Cristóbal,** built in 1940, are a good spot to get your bearings. With the church facade behind you, you're looking north, toward the main plaza bandstand (kiosco). Behind that is the north plaza-front street, which becomes Allende, west (left, downhill) from the plaza and Reforma, east (right, uphill) from the plaza. Main north–south streets are Juárez on your right and Gómez Farias on your left (which become, respectively, 16 de Septiembre and Hidalgo, north of the plaza).

SIGHTS
Around Mazamitla Plaza

The main plaza is a fine spot for strolling, enjoying the sunshine, and relaxing in general. A choice vantage point for taking it all in is the second-story front porch balcony of the **Posada Alpina,** on the plaza's north side.

It's also fun to escape the plaza bustle and explore nearby, where antique adobe houses decorate the back lanes. Start directly on the plaza's east side, at the restored **Palacio Yarín** (Cuauhtémoc 2, corner of Juárez). You can see another interesting old house, north two blocks and west another two blocks, at the corner of Galeana and Mina, by the market and the woodcrafts shops.

While you're downhill, stroll south along Galeana two blocks to the market, at the corner of Allende, where vendors offer piles of colorful jicama, cilantro, *platanos,* and mangos and mounds of stark white *cal* (lime) for soaking and softening corn kernels.

A third lovely old adobe house, more easily viewable because it's being run as a hotel, is the **Casa Cortijo Azul,** two blocks south of the plaza, at the corner of Guillermo Prieto.

◖ Los Cazos Park and El Salto Waterfall

Beyond the downtown, streets give way to paths that lead to Mazamitla's scenic outdoors. Be sure to include the pine-studded Los Cazos private park (open daily 9 A.M.– 5 P.M.) that surrounds El Salto waterfall. The waterfall delicately cascades about a hundred feet down a rocky, verdant cliff to a petite crystal pool, which is a popular wading spot for tots and teenagers. From there, hike out

© BRUCE WHIPPERMAN

The Mazamitla parish church presides over the town plaza.

on foot or travel by horseback along shady pathways, enjoying the pine-scented air, watching for rabbits and squirrels, listening for the woodpeckers. You may glimpse an occasional hawk or vulture soaring overhead. Bring a picnic and spend the whole afternoon enjoying the outdoors.

Get there by walking south on Juárez a few blocks from the plaza; at the dead-end street, turn right and continue three blocks and turn left at Paseo los Cazos. Continue about three long blocks, past an intersection, to the horse rental station. Past another long downhill block is the entrance to El Salto park, on the right. Pay the entrance fee and continue past a restaurant and picnic tables. Follow the trail downhill through the pine-shaded grounds to the scenically precipitous rock-wall waterfall.

ENTERTAINMENT AND EVENTS
Fiestas

Although Mazamitla always seems busy, excitement peaks during annual town festivals, when

MAZAMITLA

To Restaurant La Troje, Quinta del Bosque, Gas Station, Bus Station, Guadalajara and Colima

DOMÍNGUEZ

L VICARIO

MOCTEZUMA

GALEANA

HIDALGO

16 DE SEPTIEMBRE

HISTORIC HOUSE

J MINA

TENOCHTITLÁN

VIAJES INTERNACIONAL

PANADERÍA EL MOLINO

VIAJES MONARCA

COMPUCLICK INTERNET

GROCERIES

LONG-DISTANCE TELEPHONE

FLECHA AMARILLA BUS

HOTEL CABAÑAS COLINA DE LOS RUISEÑORES

Market

RESTAURANT POSADA MAZAMITLA

HOTEL POSADA ALPINA

DOCTOR

CONSERVAS ELENA

MADERO

FOOD STALLS

PHARMACY

ALLENDE

PORTAL REFORMA

REFORMA

HANDICRAFT STORES

HOSTAL DEL CIERVO ROJO

KIOSK

BANCO SANTANDER SERFIN

TOURIST INFORMATION

Plaza

WIKI TAU

CUAUHTÉMOC

M CÁRDENAS MATA

GÓMEZ FARÍAS

PARROQUIA DE SAN CRISTÓBAL

JUÁREZ

PALACIO YARÍN

PINO SUÁREZ

AQUILES SERDÁN

G PRIETO

PASTELERÍA GLORIA

CASA CORTIJO AZUL

0   60 yds
0   60 m

To Hotels Paraíso Ranas, Monteverde ◖LOS CAZOS PARK AND EL SALTO WATERFALL

© AVALON TRAVEL

hotel reservations are especially recommended. Check with the Mazamitla tourism office for details and schedules.

The festival year heats up early with the **Fiestas Taurinas,** February 17–27, with *charreadas* (rodeos), *jaripeo* (bull-roping), livestock auctions, judging and prizes, fireworks, and plenty of country food.

Enthusiasm peaks again March 27–30, with the **Founding of Mazamitla** festival, centering around the plaza, with speeches, band concerts, dance, dramatic and athletic performances, a crafts fair, and fireworks.

Processions, special masses, carnival games, food, and fireworks around the church mark the patronal **Fiesta de San Cristóbal** during the last week of July.

The September 13–17 national **Fiestas Patrias** (Patriotic Festivals) culminate with the reenactment of Father Hidalgo's *Grito de Dolores* by the Mazamitla *presidente* (mayor) at the plaza-front *presidencia municipal*.

Mazamitla's festival year comes to a joyful conclusion with the **Fiesta Guadalupana** (Festival of the Virgin of Guadalupe) December 3–12. Mazamitla people celebrate their indigenous and colonial heritage by dressing up and parading in *traje* (ancestral tribal dress) and *ropa típica* (colonial traditional dress), and enjoying lots of old-fashioned food treats, performing traditional dances, especially the *Danza del Garrotazo,* and oohing and aahing as fireworks paint the sky with showers of red, white, and green over the plaza.

Horseback and Hiking Excursions

From the horse rental station, rent a horse with guide to lead you on a local excursion. These might include **Los Cazos** private park (El Salto waterfall, arroyos, creek, one hour, $5), **El Tabardillo** panoramic viewpoint (two hours, $8), or all the way to the summit of **El Tigre** mountain (elev. 8,990 feet/2,740 meters), an eight-mile, four-hour round-trip, elevation gain 1,710 feet, 520 meters (four hours, $17). (If you enjoy the exercise like I do, skip the horse and hire a guide for about half the above prices.)

SHOPPING
Handicrafts

Woodcrafts are a Mazamitla specialty. Local creativity in wood appears nearly boundless, inspiring a host of woodcrafts: fetching wooden clocks, diminutive log houses and flower carts, animals (owls, raccoons, bears), picture frames, and much more decorate the shelves of plaza-front shops. Near the plaza's northeast corner of Hidalgo and 16 de Septiembre, try **Artesanías del Bosque** (Forest Handicrafts) (Reforma 2, local 1, tel. 382/538-0132, just uphill from the plaza's northeast corner, open daily 10 A.M.–8 P.M.); **Artesanías Conchita** (Reforma 4, tel. 382/538-0800, open daily 9 A.M.–6 P.M.), two doors uphill; **Sima Artesanías** (Reforma 3B, open daily 9 A.M.–6 P.M.), across the street; and **Artesanías Julio Emmanuel** (16 de Septiembre 2, open daily 9 A.M.–6 P.M.), around the corner.

Trinkets

For something quite different, step back into the 1960s at **Wik-Tau** (the Huichols' Bird of the Sun) shop, (at the plaza's southeast corner of Juárez and Cuauhtémoc, tel. 382/538-1137, open Wed.–Mon., 8 A.M.–2 P.M. and 4–9 P.M.). The friendly, bearded owner offers a wide and unusual selection, from water pipes and T-shirts to brass Buddhas and Huichol God's eyes.

ACCOMMODATIONS

Mazamitla has about two dozen hotels, mostly knotty pine cabin–style, built to accommodate the visitors who flock in on weekends and holidays, when reservations are necessary. Other times you will probably have your pick of the choicest rooms for cut-rate prices (ask for a *descuento*). Of the dozen-odd hotels that I inspected, I can recommend several.

Under $25

Walk two blocks south of the plaza to the antique **Casa Cortijo Azul** (Juárez 10, Maza-

Any place is a good place to do business in Mazamitla.

© BRUCE WHIPPERMAN

mitla, Jalisco, 49500, tel. 382/538-0068, $15–25), at the corner of Juárez and Guillermo Prieto. Enter the tranquil interior garden patio, once the center of family life, now a restful spot for guests to read and relax. The hotel is old and in need of some repairs. Pluses, however, include bright hand-embroidered bedspreads, hand-hewn wood floors, fireplaces, massive beamed ceilings, and friendly female management. Look at some rooms and pick what suits you. The price is certainly right.

Back at the town center stands the **Posada Alpina** (Portal Reforma 8, Mazamitla, Jalisco 49500, tel./fax 382/538-0104, $24–35), on the plaza's north side (opposite the church). Past the reception and pleasantly airy patio restaurant, stairs rise to the 17 rooms, most arranged around the interior balcony corridor, overlooking the patio. They are attractively furnished with brightly painted walls, wood-beamed ceilings, and polished wooden and tile floors. Rear rooms, away from the busy plaza-front, are quieter and more private. One pleasant extra here is the rustic wooden porch upstairs in front, with seats and tables for relaxing and enjoying the plaza view below. Rates include hot water shower baths, some king-size beds, parking, and credit cards accepted.

$25-50

On the west (downhill) edge of town (follow Allende about five blocks south of the plaza), consider **Hotel Cabañas Colina de los Ruiseñores** (Hill of the Nightingales) (Allende 50, Mazamitla, Jalisco 49500, cell tel. 044-33/3494-1210 from Guadalajara, tel. 33/3494-1210 from anywhere else in Mexico, $18–36). Personable on-site owner Guillermo Arias Mori and his wife have built a collection of about 20 artfully designed, quaintly rustic accommodations in a two-floor wing overlooking an inviting garden. Although rooms vary in details, they have polished tile floors, shaded reading lamps, attractive hand-loomed bedspreads, fireplaces, and lots of fragrant knotty pine throughout.

A half block uphill (east) from the plaza, find the graceful, old-world, former family home ◖ **Hostal del Ciervo Rojo** (House of

The Casa Cortijo Azul, one of Mazamitla's historic houses, operates as a hotel.

© BRUCE WHIPPERMAN

the Red Deer) (Reforma 18, Mazamitla, Jalisco 49500, tel. 382/538-0129, $40–50). Airy verandas, a flowery garden, and a refined living room/lobby with a piano and fireplace set the tone. Owners offer two antique-adorned suites and three comfortable rooms, all with heat (a very desirable winter option) and up-to-date bathrooms. The rooms are furnished with king-sized beds, the suites with two double beds and private parlors.

Other moderately priced lodgings that appear promising are the **Posada Las Charandas** (Obregón 2, tel./fax 382/538-0254, $27), on the south side at the end of Madero; **Hotel Loma Bonita** (Calle Loma Bonita, two blocks west of Hotel Monteverde, tel. 382/538-0500 or 382/538-1117, $45); **Cabañas d' Nellys** (Zapata 26, two blocks uphill from the church, tel. 382/538-0093, $50). (For many more lodging choices, visit www.mazamitla.org.mx).

$50-100

At the south end of Juárez, about four blocks

south of the plaza, you reach a sign and a driveway that leads downhill a hundred yards to the rambling, pine-studded grounds of **Paraíso de las Ranas** (Paradise of the Frogs) (Privada de la Sanja #5, Mazamitla, Jalisco 49500, tel. 382/538-1536, Guadalajara tel. 33/3650-3433 or 33/3650-3436, robertoi@elparaisodelasranas.com.mx, www.elparaisodelasranas.com.mx, $50–100). A glance around reveals a small village of about 15 wood and stucco cabins scattered on a tree-shaded hillside. Within all this, owner Roberto Paniagua maintains a forested park, including a small farm of fighting cocks, ducks, and a regiment of frogs in a big pond. To enjoy this place you have to be okay with the roosters crowing and the frogs singing, but it seems a small payment to make for such a charmingly bucolic atmosphere.

The cabins themselves are equally quaint—knotty pine throughout, slightly rickety, but appealing. They appear to be fine for either families or couples who enjoy (and are prepared to put up with) the unusual. Units vary but are generally spacious and airy, with big living rooms with soft couches, beamed ceilings, and fireplaces, but mostly bare-bulb lighting. Stairs and ladders lead to second-floor bedrooms and lofts and at least one bathroom. Kitchens are basic, with utensils, stove, and refrigerator. Some of the cabins have inviting exterior patios with barbecues, picnic tables, and lawn furniture for relaxing. On weekends, add about 25 percent to tariffs.

For something deluxe yet rustic in the woods, continue farther south, a total of about eight blocks south of the plaza, to **Cabañas Monteverde** (Chavarría y Constitución, Mazamitla, Jalisco 49500, tel. 382/538-0150, Guadalajara reservations line tel. 33/3616-1060, toll-free Mex. tel. 01-800/777-1060, tel./fax 382/538-0049, fax 33/3615-6812, www.monteverde.com.mx, $65–160). Inside the gate and past the reception office, pine-shaded lanes wind through a complex of about 60 cabins sprinkled through inviting, parklike, pine-shadowed grounds. Tucked beneath the trees you'll find a restaurant, plus tennis, volleyball,

and basketball courts and a small soccer *("futbol rápido")* field for guest use.

Accommodations come in three sizes: small (studio), for around two adults and two kids; medium, with bedrooms, for four adults and four kids; and large, with bedrooms, accommodating about six adults and six kids. Most accommodations are single-storied and attractively furnished, with dark, wood-paneled walls, but with light streaming in through large windows that look out on lovely forest vistas. The medium units are more luxurious, with high-beamed ceilings, fireplaces, soft couches, and fully furnished kitchenettes.

Rancho Epenche

On the other hand, get away from it all at Rancho Epenche (from Mazamitla cell tel. 044-33/3171-5518, Guadalajara area tel. 33/3171-5518, toll-free Mexico tel. 01-800/500-4446, ranchoepenche@hotmail.com, $45–120), a working ranch and *finca* (farm) about 12 miles (20 km) west of Mazamitla that invites visitors. The Sánchez family, owners and managers, split their time between milking cows, growing corn and tomatoes, tending their peach and quince orchards, and looking after their guests. Their Rancho Epenche, originally built around 1890, still retains the rustic red-tile roof, high ceilings, and spacious rooms of yesteryear. Like many Jalisco ranches and haciendas, the Rancho Epenche served as a hideout for anti-government rebels during the bloody Cristero rebellion of the 1920s. Nevertheless, present-day guests find its six clean, attractively rural rooms (with hand-hewn wooden furniture and embroidered bedspreads) quite comfortable. Linger a couple of days, hiking or mountain-biking the surrounding hills, playing volleyball or badminton, milking a cow, or simply kicking back with a thick novel about Mexico. Rooms all come with private hot water shower baths and include three meals.

For more information, visit www.historichaciendainns.com/epencheeng.html, website of the association Historic Haciendas and Inns of western Mexico. You may also book Rancho Epenche through the association office (Gua-

HACIENDAS AND COUNTRY INNS

A recently established network of historic haciendas and country inns is providing opportunities for visitors to get out into the countryside, breathe the fresh air, and appreciate some of the delights of rural Jalisco. The effort is not unlike similar efforts in Spain, Portugal, and other countries with large numbers of underutilized historic palaces, estates, and castles.

Facilities include comfortably furnished accommodations with baths, often with amenities, such as restaurant, swimming pool, terrace, chapel, and, in some cases, a whole working ranch to wander. Activities can include trips to local sites of interest, such as lakes, waterfalls, and pilgrimage shrines. More vigorous activities can include hiking, cycling, kayaking, horseback riding, mountain climbing and rappelling, and volleyball. At least one of the haciendas offers lessons in the arts of charrería, such as horseback riding, bull roping, and bull riding (jaripeo) for men, and, for women, horseback riding, or escaramuza, feats of sidesaddle horseback riding.

The network extends all over the state of Jalisco, presently in five haciendas or ranchos, and six casas rurales. They are located, moving counterclockwise from the west, at Zapopan, Ahualulco, Etzatlán, Mascota, and Ayutla; to the south at Tapalpa, Sayula, Ajijic, and Mazamitla; and, to the northeast, at Lagos de Moreno. Three of them, the Hacienda El Carmen, in Ahualulco, La Casona de Manzona, in Tapalpa, and Rancho Epenche, are recommended in the Getaways chapter, while one of them, Hacienda Magdalena, is recommended in the Zapopan section of the West and North chapter.

For information and bookings for all of them contact the Historic Haciendas and Inns of Jalisco association (Guadalajara tel. 33/3632-5413, U.S. tel. 1-608/461-4053, admin@historichaciendainns.com, www.historichaciendainns.com).

---

dalajara tel. 33/3632-5413, U.S. tel. 608/561-4053, admin@historichaciendainns.com).

Get there from Mazamitla southeast (downhill) by bus or car along Highway 110. After about five miles (eight km), pass through Cofradia and continue about two miles (three km) farther, where you turn right onto the side road to Epenche Grande village. After another five miles, pass through the village and continue south (on the road to Tamazulapan) about another mile to the Rancho Epenche driveway on the left.

FOOD

Among Mazamitla's prime attractions are its hearty country specialties. At the top of the list is el bote, a bountiful broth of chicken, beef, and pork with vegetables and condiments, simmered in pulque; el sanchocho, morsels of vinegar-marinated mango, jicama, and carrots; menguiche, sour cream seasoned with onion, pepper, green chile sauce, and cilantro, and eaten with totopos (tortilla chips).

Drinks include a yummy ponche (punch) of blackberry, capulín, and the cherry-plum-like ciruela; and a wine of quince, atole, and honey.

All of the above are served up at a squadron of clean food stalls (fondas), at the town market, corner of Galeana and Allende, a block downhill from the town plaza's southeast corner.

Restaurants

You can get most of the above and more starting right on the main plaza. For example, try the restaurant in the **Posada Alpina** (Portal Reforma 8, north side of the plaza, tel. 382/538-0104, open Mon.–Fri. 8:30 A.M.–8 P.M., Sat. 8:30 A.M.–9 P.M., and Sun. 8:30 A.M.–6 P.M.), probably the best spot for breakfasts ($4). Besides local specialties, it offers a very recognizable list of soups, sandwiches ($2–3), and entrées ($5–8).

Equally well located a half block west (near the northwest plaza corner) and trying just as hard is **Restaurant Posada Mazamitla** (Hidalgo 2, tel. 382/538-0608, open daily 8 A.M.–6 P.M.). Besides the traditional *el bote* ($6) all day Sunday, they continue the rest of the week with *pacholas de metate* ($7), *costillitas con chile* (baby back ribs in chile sauce, $8), and *carne en adobo* (beef, slow-simmered in a rich, mild, dark *mole* sauce, $10).

Probably the most popular restaurant in Mazamitla is **La Troje** (Galeana 53, tel. 382/538-0070, open daily 9 A.M.–7:30 P.M.), five blocks north of the plaza, across from the *gasolinera*. Choose from a long menu of many local specialties, including *filete gaucho* with garlic shrimp ($10); *arrachera* (marinated steak, $12); *chile poblano* with shrimp, bathed in sauce ($10); and stir-fried vegetable *fajitas* ($8). (Unfortunately, the crush of weekend crowds lowers the food and service standards at La Troje; go midweek if at all possible.)

My best Mazamitla restaurant pick is relative newcomer **❰ Restaurant Quinta del Bosque** (Prolongacion V. Guerrero, tel. 382/538-0969, open Sun.–Thurs. 1–9 P.M., Fri.–Sat. 1–11 P.M.). Find it directly on the northwest edge of town, on the road to Guadalajara, west (downhill) from the gas station two blocks. In a refined, rustic-chic setting, you can enjoy the best of Mazamitla's hearty local cuisine: *papas bravas,* roasted small potatoes with cilantro and mild green chile sauce ($2); cheese and cream ($2); and *peincillo de res,* rib steak on a hot iron plate with roasted baby onions ($10); all served with a bottomless basket of piping hot corn tortillas. For lighter eating, you might select a delicious soup and/or salad and scrumptious barbecued chicken ($5–8).

Groceries, Baked Goods, and *Conservas*

Abarrotes Casa Chávez (Portal Reforma 10, tel. 382/538-0016, open daily 9 A.M.–10 P.M.), beneath the portal on the plaza's north side, by the Posada Alpina, stocks a supply of basic staples and canned goods.

For a bakery, try **El Molino** (16 de Septiembre 17, tel. 382/538-0131, open daily 9 A.M.–10 P.M.), a block north of the plaza (best get there before noon); or **Pasteleria Gloria** (Aquiles Serdán 14, tel. 382/538-0542), a block south and a block west of the church.

Conservas (canned fruits, jellies, and jams) are a Mazamitla old-time specialty. Check out **Conservas Elena** (Reforma 7B, open daily 9 A.M.–6 P.M.), a half block east of the plaza's northeast corner, or **Conservas Ema** (Allende 35, tel. 382/538-0118, open daily 9 A.M.–9 P.M.), four blocks west of the plaza's northwest corner, a block uphill from the Hotel Cabañas Colina de los Ruiseñores.

INFORMATION AND SERVICES
Tourist Information and Communications

Staff will answer your questions at Mazamitla's small city tourist information office (at the plaza's northwest corner, tel. 382/538-0230, open Mon.–Fri. 9 A.M.–3 P.M., Sat. 10 A.M.–2 P.M. and 4–6 P.M., Sun. 10 A.M.–4 P.M.).

Mail letters and buy stamps at Mazamitla's *correo* (post office) (Hidalgo 30, tel. 382/538-0440, open Mon.–Fri. 9 A.M.–3 P.M.), on the far north side, a block east of the gas station.

As for telephones, buy a Ladatel telephone card and use it in one of the several public telephones around the plaza. Alternatively, go to the small *larga distancia* (public long-distance phone office) (open daily 8 A.M.–9 P.M.), on 16 de Septiembre 8, a half block north of the plaza's northeast corner.

Find an **Internet** connection at **Compuclik** (Galeana 18B, tel. 382/538-0214, open daily 10 A.M.–9 P.M.), a block west and a half block north from the plaza's northwest corner.

Banking

Mazamitla's bank, **Banco Santander Serfín** (tel. 382/538-0590, open Mon.–Fri. 9 A.M.–4 P.M.), with ATM, is conveniently located beneath the plaza's west-side portal.

Travel Agents

Get your air tickets, hotel reservations, cabaña rentals, and more at **Viajes Internacional** (Galeana 14, tel./fax 382/538-0580, open Mon.–Sat. 9 A.M.–3 P.M. 4–7 P.M.); or **Viajes Monarca** (Galeana 3, tel. 382/538-0394, open Mon.–Sat. 9 A.M.–2 P.M., 5–8 P.M.), across the street and next to the Flecha Amarilla hole-in-the wall bus station. (Get there from the plaza's northwest corner by walking one block west to Galeana, then turn right, north.)

HEALTH AND EMERGENCIES
Medical Services

For routine remedies, see the pharmacist or doctor on duty at a pharmacy. Try kindly Dr. Lorenzo Nuño Barrios at his small pharmacy (16 de Septiembre 6, tel. 382/538-0127, open Mon.–Sat. 8 A.M.–2 P.M. and 4–8 P.M.), a half block north of the plaza's northeast corner. If he's not available, go to **Farmacia de la Sierra** (Hidalgo 1, northwest corner of the plaza, tel. 382/538-0034, open daily 9 A.M.–2 P.M. and 4–9 P.M.).

In a medical emergency, follow your hotel recommendation, or have a taxi take you to the local **Seguro Social Hospital** (tel. 382/538-0350), on Xochitl near the gas station, six blocks north of the plaza.

Police and Fire

For both police and fire emergencies, contact the police station, at the *presidencia municipal,* west side of the plaza (tel. 382/538-0202).

GETTING THERE
By Car

From Guadalajara, follow Avenida López Mateos Sur to the Highway 15 right turnoff (watch for Highway 15 Jocotepec/Morelia/Mexico City signs), about 15 miles (25 km) or half hour south of the *periférico* (peripheral boulevard). Continue another 33 miles (55 km), passing Jocotepec and Soyatlán, along the southwest lakeshore another hour to Tuxcueca. At the Mazamitla sign, turn right and continue another 26 miles (42 km), or 45 minutes, uphill via Manzanilla to Mazamitla.

By Bus

Mazamitla is conveniently accessible by first-class **Autotransportes Mazamitla** buses, from Guadalajara's Nueva Central Camionera, *módulo* 2. Buses customarily depart daily, every 30 minutes, from about 7:15 A.M. until about 6 P.M. Be sure to call for schedule confirmation (tel. 33/3600-0733).

From the Mazamitla bus station, on 16 de Septiembre four blocks north of the plaza, buses return to Guadalajara daily, approximately every 30 minutes, from about 4:30 A.M. until about 6:30 P.M. Call for confirmation (tel. 382/538-0410).

Alternatively, **Flecha Amarilla** runs buses to and from Guadalajara (last bus leaves Mazamitla around 7 P.M.) from a tiny station (Galeana 5), just north of the Allende corner, a block south of the plaza.

Tapalpa

Tapalpa (pop. 16,000, elev. 6,780 feet/2,060 meters) seems to have been able to combine the best of both worlds. From a distance, the entire village—completely of adobe-walled, tile-roofed houses clustered around a proud old church—appears like a vision of colonial Mexico. Move closer, however, and, instead of old-world country folks, you see mostly city people in shorts and T-shirts, strolling the plaza, sampling homemade sweets, and relaxing in plaza-front eateries, enjoying the country cooking for which Tapalpa is famous.

HISTORY
In the Beginning
Although archaeological evidence indicates that Tapalpa's first settlers may have been of Otomi origin, the later, preconquest indigenous residents were Nahuatl (Aztec language) speakers, tributaries to the kingdom of Sayutlán (present-day Sayula). Records show that they paid their tribute mainly with textile dyes, taken from local plants, and pottery, exuberantly decorated with the bright mineral pigments extracted from nearby deposits. Thereby Tapalpa's original name, Tlapalpan, or Land of Colors, was born.

Moreover, archaeologists have uncovered a swarm of treasured remains—jadeite, onyx, terra cotta, and stone petroglyphs—that suggest that Tapalpa was once an important ceremonial center.

The Spanish arrived in 1523; quickly the Tapalpa people accepted baptism, and Franciscan missionaries put up the first big church in nearby Atacco in 1533. They taught the local people to plant and husband groves of peaches and avocados and began building the present Tapalpa church, Templos San Antonio, in 1535.

Colonial and Modern Times
During the colonial era, Tapalpa drew Spanish colonists for its mineral wealth—iron, mercury, silver, and gold. Settlers founded bronze and

Tapalpa drowses in the warm light of the afternoon sun.

© BRUCE WHIPPERMAN

ironworks in the nearby locality, still known as the Ferrería de Tula (Tula Ironworks), although products once manufactured, such as iron grillwork and bronze bells, have long ceased being made there.

Paper, another noted local product, was made at the La Constancia paper mill, the ruins of which still stand west of town. Built in 1840, La Constancia was the first paper factory in Latin America; it continued operating until the turbulence of the 1910 revolution shut it down.

The Tapalpa municipality has taken three generations to recover from the devastation and depopulation suffered during the 1910 revolution and the succeeding 1925–1930 "Cristero" rebellion. The resulting destruction and anarchy left Tapalpa open to the ravages of guerrillas and bandits, such as the notorious Pedro Zamora, whose gang burned the town three separate times, leaving terror and misery in their wake.

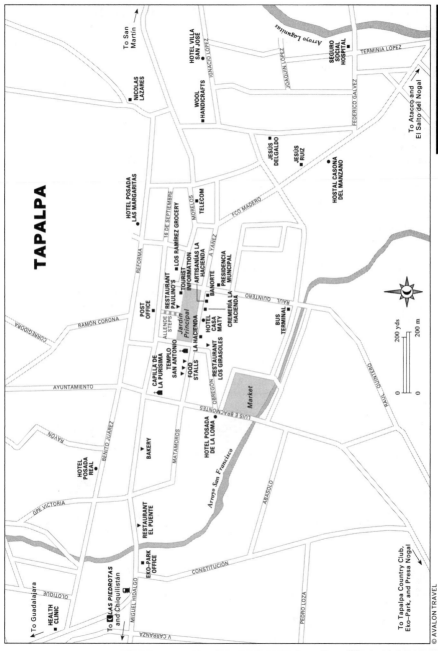

TAPALPA

To San Martín

HOTEL VILLA SAN JOSÉ

Arroyo Lagunillas

SEGURO SOCIAL HOSPITAL

TERMINIA LÓPEZ

NICOLAS LAZARES

IGNACIO LÓPEZ

JOAQUÍN LÓPEZ

FEDERICO GALVEZ

To Atacco and El Salto del Nogal

WOOL HANDICRAFTS

JESÚS DELGALDO

JESÚS RUIZ

HOSTAL CASONA DEL MANZANO

HOTEL POSADA LAS MARGARITAS

16 DE SEPTIEMBRE

MORELOS

ECO MADERO

TELECOM

REFORMA

CORREGIDORA

RAMÓN CORONA

POST OFFICE

ALLENDE STEPS

RESTAURANT PAULINO'S

LOS RAMÍREZ GROCERY

TOURIST INFORMATION

ARTISANÍAS LA HACIENDA

A YÁNEZ

BANORTE

PRESIDENCIA MUNICIPAL

RAÚL QUINTERO

Jardín Principal

HOTEL CASA MATY

LA HACIENDA

CREMERÍA LA HACIENDA

CAPILLA DE LA PURÍSIMA

TEMPLO SAN ANTONIO

FOOD STALLS

RESTAURANT LOS GIRASOLES

OBREGÓN

BUS TERMINAL

AYUNTAMIENTO

RAYÓN

BENITO JUÁREZ

BAKERY

MATAMOROS

LUIS E BRACAMONTES

Market

HOTEL POSADA DE LA LOMA

Arroyo San Francisco

RAÚL QUINTERO

GPE VICTORIA

HOTEL POSADA REAL

RESTAURANT EL PUENTE

ABASOLO

CONSTITUCIÓN

To Guadalajara

OLOTIQUE

MIGUEL HIDALGO

EKO-PARK OFFICE

LAS PIEDROTAS and Chiquilistán

HEALTH CLINIC

V CARRANZA

PEDRO LOZA

To Tapalpa Country Club, Eko-Park, and Presa Nogal

0   200 yds

0   200 m

© AVALON TRAVEL

But those bad old times have now faded to barely a memory. One glance around the automobile-free, invitingly picturesque main plaza reveals that enterprising Tapalpa residents have entered a new, prosperous era, with a host of businesses—pharmacies, groceries, creameries, hotels, restaurants, and handicrafts shops—that serve the influx of visitors.

ORIENTATION

The **Allende steps** on the west side of the **Jardín Principal** are a good place to get yourself oriented. Standing on the steps, facing downhill, you're looking south. On your right (west) side, stand the venerable Templos San Antonio (in two sections). On your far left, Quintero runs north uphill from between the **presidencia municipal** and the bank, on the *jardín*'s southeast corner. Also on your left is the *jardín* bandstand, and behind it, to the south, the former street, now pedestrian mall portal, Matamoros, which runs east–west along the *jardín*'s south-side shop fronts.

SIGHTS IN TOWN
Jardín Principal

Savvy planners have transformed the Jardín Principal into a relaxing, traffic-free strolling ground. Take a look into the *jardín*'s pair of recently restored old churches, the Templos San Antonio (in two parts, one with a distinguished dome, 1535) and the **Capilla de la Purísima** (behind, dating from 1555).

Around the *Jardín*

After wandering around the *jardín,* stroll around and sample the goodies for sale beneath the Matamoros portal. Sweets shops and creameries offer stacks of *conservas* (jam), such as *durazno* (peach) in ceramic jars, sugary bonbons, rolls of chewy tamarind, *rompope* (guava eggnog), guava-nut cookies, and plenty of white cheese.

Later, take a table on the airy balcony-front of the **Restaurant Paulino's** (north side, by the Allende steps), order a drink or an *antojito* lunch, and take in the *jardín* scene below.

Tapalpa's Allende steps afford a fine view of the town plaza.

© BRUCE WHIPPERMAN

SIGHTS OUT OF TOWN

Interesting attractions beckon to visitors with the time to venture a few hours beyond the town limits.

⟨ Las Piedrotas

Not-to-be-missed is Las Piedrotas (the Big Rocks), easily reached by car or on foot, about three miles (five km) west of town. Along the way (at mile 1.2, km 1.9) you pass the ruins of the 1840 **La Constancia** paper mill on the right, and a quarter mile farther a private trout farm, stocked and ready for fishing.

Las Piedrotas, however, are the main attraction. As you approach from a distance they resemble a family of giant mushrooms in the process of sprouting from the ground. On the top of a mountain, where such rocks would be a dime a dozen, Las Piedrotas wouldn't be worth a mention, but bulging where they are, they present an extraordinary contrast to their bucolic cow pasture surroundings.

Las Piedrotas are a favorite with families, especially with preteens and teenagers who delight in climbing their friendly slopes and exploring their many mysterious niches, overhangs, and passageways. After gazing for a spell at their rounded, tan forms it's not hard to begin imagining animal forms—especially seals, whales, and walruses—among the giant, rounded boulders. Bring a picnic and spend the day; add camping gear and stay overnight.

Get there by car, taxi, or on foot via the rough but passable road to Chiquilistán that forks left, when heading out of town, from the southern extension of Hidalgo, six blocks west from the Allende steps, just before the gas station.

El Salto del Nogal

Jalisco's highest waterfall, El Salto del Nogal (The "Jump" of the Nogal), cascades a spectacular 344 feet (105 meters) in two stages into a pool at the bottom of its *barranca* (gorge). It's an impressive sight, especially during the high-water summer season. From Tapalpa, the waterfall is about nine miles (15 km), the last mile on foot, down a (dry-season negotiable with care) dirt canyon-side trail. You can get there

© BRUCE WHIPPERMAN

The giant Las Piedrotas rocks make for friendly climbing.

following my directions below or asking for a guide at the tourist information office. In any case, you'll probably need to hire a taxi, drive your own car, or hike the nine miles south. Rustic cabañas at the top of the falls can provide you a roof and a bed for an overnight.

Get there by car, minibus, or hired taxi along the road to Atacco. Follow Calle Madero (one block east of the *jardín*) south. Mark your odometer. Continue over the Tapalpa River bridge at the edge of town a total of 1.7 miles (2.7 km) to Atacco. Take a look at the communal spring and swimming pool (two blocks to the right, in the Atacco town center). This might be an inviting place to cool off, if soap suds are not mucking up the water. Nevertheless, it's still an interesting spot, if only to watch the crowd of kids splashing happily in the water.

Continue south a couple of blocks through Atacco and turn right at the Cascada del Molino sign. At mile 5.0 (km 8.0) at the El Salto sign, turn right on to a side road. Continue through Barranca del Refugio village at mile 5.7 (km 9.2). At mile 8.1 (km 13.0) arrive at the gate to restaurant Cascada del Molino and El Salto del Nogal waterfall. The restaurant is open seasonally: Christmas, Easter, and some weekends. Check with the Hotel Posada Las Margaritas (16 de Septiembre 81, tel. 343/432-0799) whose owner operates the Cascada de Molino for confirmation. The driveway meanders a few hundred yards downhill to the canyon-edge parking lot, the cabañas, and a few snack stalls.

A path continues down into the gorge another 1.2 miles (1.9 km) to the Río Nogal 600 feet below. Interesting **historical sites** dot the canyon and river bottom. Along the trail, look for the ruins of the former *taberna* (mescal factory), source of the once-famous "Barranca" mescal; also note the *monasterios* (caves) where the Cristero guerrilla fighters hid out. Also keep an eye peeled for the ruins of some of the seven former flour mills *molinos de trigo* that used to operate along the river but were destroyed by the disastrous 1917 flood.

La Presa del Nogal

An easier, albeit less spectacular, excursion is to the reservoir La Presa del Nogal, about five miles (eight km) southwest of town. If the water level is high (most likely during the summer rainy season), the reservoir affords opportunities for fishing, kayaking, canoeing, and camping along its lush green shoreline. Bring your own equipment.

Get there from the town *jardín,* via north–south Calle Bracamontes (also known as the road to San Gabriel). Follow Matamoros past the church, two blocks to Bracamontes, and turn left. Set your odometer. After about three miles (five km), pass the Tapalpa Country Club driveway/road on the right. Continue past a couple of signs, the first at about mile 3.5 (km 5.5) and another a fraction of a mile (about one km) farther. Finally, turn left at about mile 4.5 (km 7.2) at the entrance road to a big fenced-in development. Continue over a bridge, curving gradually left around the lakeshore a few hundred yards to lake access, on the left, just before the dam.

Eko-Park Tapalpa

Get your fill of so-called "extreme" sports at Tapalpa's hottest new attraction, Eko-Park, a 1500-acre forested fun ground, designed for working off your excess adrenalin. You can choose between the "extreme" rappelling, "gotcha" bungie jumping, forest-canopy riding, escalading (ropeless rock climbing—or the more ho-hum varieties—mountain biking, off-roading via four-wheeled ATV, archery, horseback riding, and overnight tenting. Sorry, you have to be at least 11 years old to participate. Tariffs begin at about $50 for a half day. For more information, stop by the Eko-Park office, on Hidalgo, about a block past the gas station as you enter town, or call their Guadalajara office (tel. 33/3817-8083), email the Eko-Park Tapalpa director (leticia@ekopark.com.mx or paulina@ekopark.com.mx), or visit www.ekopark.com.mx.

Get there by following the directions above, to Presa de Nogal, except, about a half mile past the Tapalpa Country Club gate, turn at the Eko-Park entrance on the right.

ENTERTAINMENT AND EVENTS
Fiestas

Tapalpa's hardworking residents throw several big annual shindigs. The year starts on a high note with the local **Fiesta de la Virgen de Guadalupe,** which features traditional *mañanitas* masses, dressing up and parading, and folk dancing, and peaks in a big fireworks blowout on January 13.

Two days later, people have barely had time to catch their breath when the **Fiesta Charro-Taurina** begins on January 15 with *charreadas* (rodeos), *corridas de toros* (bullfights), and popular dances in the *jardín,* culminating with fireworks on January 20.

A week before Easter, local potters get their big chance to sell their wares in the **Feria de Domingo de Ramos** (Fair of Palm Sunday), when the *jardín* and the surrounding streets are decked out with riots of colorful for-sale ceramics.

The first Saturday of July, seemingly half the town joins a pilgrimage for the **Fiesta de la Virgen de la Defensa,** in which townsfolk take turns carrying the Virgin home to Tapalpa all the way from the town of Juanacatlán.

In the **Fiestas Patrias,** September 13–16, the whole town seems to heat up, with rodeos, parades of townsfolk on horseback in *charro* (gentleman cowboy) dress, decorated floats, the reenactment of the *Grito de Dolores* by the mayor at the *presidencia municipal,* and fireworks.

SHOPPING
Handicrafts

Tapalpa craftspeople continue their ancient handicrafts tradition to the present day. Local products include hand-painted pottery, brightly painted papier-mâché, wool, hand-woven serapes, *tapetes* (tapestries and throw rugs), *morrales* (backpacks), *alfombras* (carpets), and *colchas* (bedspreads).

Town-center shops sell some or all of the above. Start right on the *jardín,* at **Artesanías La Hacienda** (Matamoros 7, tel. 343/432-0194,

© BRUCE WHIPPERMAN

Bargaining for Tapalpa handicrafts *es la costumbre* (is customary).

open Mon.–Tues. and Thurs.–Sat. 9 A.M.–3 P.M. and 5–8 P.M., and Sun. 9 A.M.–5 P.M.), upstairs, on the southeast side of the *jardín* next to the bank. Pick from a host of what Tapalpa has to offer: practical woodcrafts (picture frames, spice racks, religious plaques), medium-fired red clay ceramics (appetizer trays, bowls, vases, casseroles, table settings, flower pots), and homemade *conservas* (jams and jellies).

For more woodcrafts, go to **Artesanías Charly** (Hidalgo 125, tel. 343/432-0806, open Fri.–Wed. 9 A.M.–3 P.M. and 5–8 P.M.), the shop of Carlos and Geña Vásquez. At the source, prices are lowest and the quality highest. Tell them what you want and they'll make it to order (or will find someone who will).

Another good handicrafts source is the shop at the **Restaurant Los Girasoles** (Obregón 110, tel. 343/432-0458, open Mon.–Sat. 10 A.M.–9 P.M. and Sun. 10 A.M.–7 P.M.). They offer an exceptional all-Mexico assortment in addition to some local baskets and woolen *quechquemitls* (capes).

Others sell handicrafts right out of their cottage factory shops. Among the more noted are Nicolas Lizares (leatherwork), Jesús Ruíz (woodcarving), Jesús Degaldo (wool), and the *familia* Aguilar (ceramics), in the village of Rosa de Castilla, south of Atacco. Ask for more suggestions and access details at the tourist information office.

ACCOMMODATIONS

Tapalpa has comfortable hotels, some with *chimeneas* (fireplaces), a welcome plus in sometimes cool Tapalpa. Best arrive with a reservation, especially on weekends, holidays, and during fiesta times. On the other hand, during the quieter mid-week (Sun.–Thurs.), by simply asking, you can often get a 10–20 percent discount below the prices listed below.

$50-100

A good choice is the uphill (east side) **Hotel Posada Las Margaritas** (16 de Septiembre 81, Tapalpa, Jalisco 49430, tel./fax 343/432-0799,

$42–170). The owners offer eight immaculate, rustic-chic accommodations, lovingly decorated with bright wall paintings to match the room themes, such as *colibri* (hummingbird), *palomas* (doves), or *uvas* (grapes). Three rooms offer king-size beds for two; four larger kitchenette "villas" sleep four; and a grand multibedroom kitchenette "villa" sleeps 12. All come with parking and a good restaurant next door, but no fireplaces.

On the opposite, Guadalajara, end of town, the newish **Hotel Posada Real** (Juárez 229, Tapalpa, Jalisco 49430, tel./fax 343/432-0589, reservaciones@realtapalpa.com, www.realtapalpa.com, $45–90) offers an attractive neo-rustic colonial-style alternative (a block above Hidalgo and about four blocks west of the *jardín*). The 20 compactly arranged, clean, comfortably furnished rooms come with up-to-date baths, parking, and credit cards accepted.

Most popular of all is the comfortable plaza-front **Hotel La Casa de Maty** (Matamoros 69, Tapalpa, Jalisco, 49430, tel./fax 343/432-0189, $75), where you can have it all: 14 semideluxe rooms, with fireplaces and terraces, overlooking a leafy rear patio garden that stair-steps down to a rear veranda patio with a solarium-enclosed hot tub (very welcome in sometimes cool Tapalpa) for guest use. Kids enjoy a recreation room with video games downstairs, adults a billiards room upstairs. All rooms come with parking, good restaurant, and credit cards accepted.

The best of Tapalpa's in-town lodgings is the distinguished **[C Hostal la Casona de Manzano** (Madero 84, Tapalpa, Jalisco 49430, tel. 343/432-1141 or 343/432-0767, hostallalcasonademanzano@yahoo.com.mx, www.historichaciendainns.com, $80–130), on the quiet southeast side of town. Hostess Luz María Manzano offers 9 beautifully appointed TV- and phone-free suites, all with shiny, modern-standard baths, fireplace, large, fluffy-quilted beds, soft lamps, and polished Porfirian-period furniture. Downstairs, guests gather around the living room fireplace or snuggle up with a good book in one of the house's relaxing alcoves. Amenities include parking, Internet access, and complimentary home-cooked breakfast on the view veranda.

If all the above lodgings are full, Tapalpa has more good hotel choices to check out, all at budget-to-moderate rates: **Posada La Hacienda** (Matamoros 7, tel. 343/432-0193, $20–30), with 19 rooms; **Hotel Posada La Loma** (Bracamontes 197, tel. 343/432-0168, $35) with 32 rooms; **El Mesón de Ticuz** (privada Pedro Loza 555, tel. 343/432-0351, pandolom@hotmail.com, $65), with 19 rooms and restaurant-bar, includes breakfast; and **Villa San José** (Ignacio T. López 91, tel. 343/432-0431, fax 343/432-0397, $70), with 21 rooms.

Tapalpa Country Club

Deluxe accommodations with lots of sports extras are available about three miles (follow Calle Bracamontes) south of town at the Tapalpa Country Club (Km 5.5, Carretera Tapalpa–San Gabriel, Tapalpa, Jalisco 49430, tel. 343/432-432-0710 or 343/432-0720, Mexico toll-free tel. 01-800/713-7030, fax 343/432-0753, reservaciones@tapalpacountry.com, www.tapalpacountry.com, $110). Guests enjoy high-beamed-ceiling hillside suites, private valley-view patios, up-to-date bathrooms, and fireplaces (wood included). Kids under 12 free, with cable TV, golf course, tennis courts, volleyball, and credit cards accepted.

FOOD

Tapalpa is well known for *borrego al pastor* (barbecued lamb, shepherd style), served up at restaurants, both along the road into town and in town itself. Another favorite is *tamales de acelga* (chard), available locally in season.

Favorite local drinks include the yummy *ponche de granada* (pomegranate punch) and *rompopes* (eggnogs) of guava, almond, or pine nuts.

Milk caramel candies, *conservas* (jam), canned fruit, guava egg nog, and much more are for sale in Tapalpa.

© BRUCE WHIPPERMAN

Groceries, Creameries, and Bakeries

Get nearly all the goodies you need right on the *jardín*. Start with the **Cremería La Hacienda** (Matamoros 11, tel. 343/432-0258, open Mon.–Tues. and Thurs.–Sat. 8 A.M.–9 P.M., Sun. and Wed. 4 P.M.–9 P.M.), five doors from the corner bank. Pick from a selection of basic groceries and a few deli items (hot dogs and cheese) in a refrigerated case. For what you can't get at the *cremería*, continue next door to **Minisuper Perigrina** (Pilgrim) (Matamoros 13, open daily 8 A.M.–2:30 P.M. and 4–9 P.M.).

For dessert, try **Dulcería del Centro** (Matamoros 9, open daily 8 A.M.–2:30 P.M. and 4–9 P.M.), for a big selection of party goods and traditional sweets, including peanut brittle and *jericaya* (brown sugar and milk) candy.

Get your fresh baked goods at **Panadería Dona Tere** (Hidalgo 207, tel. 343/432-0531, open daily 9 A.M.–6 P.M.), two and a half blocks south (past Bracamontes) of the Allende steps. The rich selection includes whole wheat bread *(pan integral)*, pasta, cookies, cakes, pies, donuts, and much more.

For hearty budget snacks and meals, check out the **food stalls**, on Matamoros, south end of the plaza, downhill side of the church. Choose from crispy home-fried potato chips, hot *churros* (long donuts), creamy yogurt, *birria* pit-barbecued lamb and goat, and tacos galore.

Restaurants

One of the most relaxing restaurants in town is the airy tourist favorite 【 **Restaurant Paulino's** (Allende 69, tel. 343/432-0109, open Fri.–Wed. 9 A.M.–10 P.M.), overlooking the *jardín,* on the Allende steps. Pick from an all-Mexican menu of eggs, French toast, or pancakes for breakfast ($3–5), and *antojitos,* such as *chiles rellenos, enchiladas al la Tehuacán,* quesadillas, tamales, and smoked pork chops for lunch or dinner ($4–10).

Alternatively, head across the *jardín,* to Tapalpa's reliable standby restaurant, in the **Hotel La Casa de Maty** (Matamoros 69, tel. 343/432-0189, open daily 8 A.M.–10 P.M.). Within the refined, high-ceilinged, dark, wood-paneled dining room, patrons pick from a very recognizable and professionally prepared and served menu of soups and salads ($4–6), pastas, meats, fish, and fowl ($5–12).

For traditional specialties, try the highly recommended, refined 【 **Restaurant Los Girasoles** (Sunflowers) (Obregón 110, tel. 343/432-0458, open Mon.–Thurs. 10 A.M.–9 P.M., Fri.–Sat. 9 A.M.–11 P.M., Sun. 9 A.M.–7:30 P.M.), a half block downhill from the *jardín*-front church. Owner-chef Genny Cisneros specializes in healthy cuisine: soups, salads, and pastas ($4–10). Her special treats include *tamal acelga* (chard-stuffed tamale, $4) and *chile Girasoles* (a fresh chile, baked with a banana on the outside and cheese on the inside, $7).

Also highly recommended is **Restaurant El Puente** (Hidalgo 324, tel. 343/432-0435, open daily 2–6 P.M.), three and a half blocks south of the Allende steps. Like many Tapalpa restaurants, it specializes in *borrego al pastor* (lamb, shepherd style).

Out on the Guadalajara highway, 1.5 miles (2.5 km) out of town, stop by country-style open-air restaurant **Borrego la Sierra** (Kilometer 2.5 Carretera Tapalpa-Guadalajara, tel. 343/432-0664), for good *birria* and *borrego al pastor*. (The schedule varies; call to check.)

Alternatively, a third of a mile (a half km) farther, try the equally popular pine-shadowed restaurant **El Árbol de la Culebra** (Kilometer 3.0 Carretera Tapalpa-Guadalajara, tel. 343/432-0143, open Sat.–Sun. and holidays from around noon until dark).

INFORMATION AND SERVICES
Tourist Information

Get your questions answered at the Tapalpa **Turismo** (tourist information office) (Portal Morelos 1, tel. 343/432/0650, or leave a message at tel. 343/432-0471, open Mon.–Fri. 9 A.M.–3 P.M., Sat. 10 A.M.–2 P.M., Sun. 10 A.M.–2 P.M.), right on the *jardín's* northwest corner, at the corner of Quintero and Morelos.

Banking

Change money at **Banorte** (tel. 343/432-0715 or 343/432-0705, Mon.–Fri. 9 A.M.–4 P.M., Sat. 10 A.M.–2 P.M.), with ATM, at the southeast *jardín* corner of Quintero and Matamoros.

Post and Communications

For telephone, use your Ladatel card at one of the several public telephones around the *jardín.* Otherwise, use the public telephone and fax at **Las Ramírez** grocery store (Morelos 2, corner of Quintero and Morelos, open daily 8 A.M.–9:30 P.M.).

Mail postcards and buy stamps at the Tapalpa *correo,* on Hidalgo, across the street from the top of the Allende steps.

HEALTH AND EMERGENCIES
Medical Services

If you get sick, consult with Dr. Ruben Lozana Montes de Oca at his pharmacy, **Farmacia del Centro** (tel./fax 343/432-0357, open daily 8:30 A.M.–9:30 P.M.) on Matamoros, south side of the *jardín.*

Alternatively, consult with Dr. Ignacio Gonzales at **Farmacia Tapalpa** (Morelos 5, tel. 343/432-0473), a few doors east of the *jardín.*

A third option is to go to the Tapalpa 24-hour **Centro de Salud** (Juan Gil Preciado 15, tel. 343/432-0363), on the Guadalajara highway out of town, on the right, about a block past the gas station.

Police and Fire

In case of either police or fire emergencies, contact the police station (tel. 343/432-0008), at the *presidencia municipal.*

GETTING THERE
By Car

From Guadalajara, follow Avenida López Mateos Sur about 17 miles (27 km), about a half hour, south of the *periférico* (peripheral boulevard) to the old Highway 54 *(libre)* Acatlán–Sayula–Colima south turnoff. Continue along old Highway 54 another 34 miles (55 km) south to Amacueca. Turn right at the Tapalpa-signed intersection, and follow the signs uphill another 20 miles (32 km) to Tapalpa.

If you have an extra hour for the return trip, take the scenic route by turning left at Frontera, about 6 miles (10 km) downhill from Talpa. Continue over a picturesque, pine-shadowed pass to Atemajac de Brizuela, another 15 miles (25 km). Turn right at the Guadalajara sign and continue downhill, to Highway 54 *(libre)* at Zacoalco, where you turn left, north, toward Guadalajara.

By Bus

Tapalpa-bound **Autotransportes Sur de Jalisco** buses leave from the Guadalajara Camionera Central Vieja (Old Central Bus Terminal). At least 10 direct buses depart approximately hourly between about 6 A.M. and 4:30 P.M. Call for confirmation (tel. 33/3600-0346).

Return to Guadalajara from the Tapalpa bus stop (Matamoros 129), on Quintero, one long block south downhill from the *jardín* (just south of the *jardín* across Matamoros from the church). Guadalajara-bound buses run about every hour 6 A.M.–6 P.M.

Chimulco and Bosque de Primavera

The Guadalajara region's natural warm springs continue to soothe the tired and sick as they have for millennia. Warm springs resorts Chimulco and Río Caliente are outstanding, albeit very different, examples.

Chimulco is a family-friendly, mid-scale resort, with bungalows and trailer park, within a private park of swimming pools, water slides, and curative sulfur water baths about an hour and a quarter south of Guadalajara.

In contrast, Río Caliente is an upscale but low-profile, unpretentious, private hot-spring retreat for adults, set in the pristine Bosque de Primavera forest about an hour west of Guadalajara.

◖ CHIMULCO

Chimulco (Place of Vapors) was a sacred healing ground of the indigenous Chimulhucanes people for untold generations before the arrival of the Spanish, who established nearby Villa Corona (pop. 16,000, elev. 4,610 feet/1,405 meters) around 1550.

Sights and Activities

Inside the entrance gate a quarter mile off Highway 80, Chimulco (day-use fee $8 adults, kids half price) offers a wealth of aquatic delights. Naturally healing warm sulfur water feeds a half dozen pools. Children head straight toward the big, kids-only pool, complete with bouncy music; Willy the Whale; a pretend lighthouse that spews jets of water; water slides, both straight and super twisty; and a "lazy man" river inner-tube run.

Meanwhile, adults enjoy therapeutic jet water massage, smaller private pools, a private night pool, plenty of space, and tennis courts.

Additional facilities for everyone to enjoy include a shady picnic ground, with barbecues and

The Chimulco Balneario offers warm-water pools, playgrounds, a trailer park, bungalows, restaurants, and a store.

© BRUCE WHIPPERMAN

benches, and adjacent shallow Lake Atotonilco, which, at high water, becomes a ripe fishing ground from the shoreline or your own boat.

Accommodations and Food

Spend an overnight or a week at 〔 **Bungalows Chimulco Spa** (tel. 387/778-0014 or 387/778-0209, fax 387/778-0161, Guadalajara tel. 33/3616-9393, fax 33/3616-9696, chimulco2000@hotmail.com, www.chimulco.com. mx., $55–80) in one of the clean, comfortable kitchenette bungalows beneath a shady grove on the quiet side of the complex. They come in two sizes: one bedroom, with living-dining room, kitchenette, and bath, sleeping two adults and two kids; and larger two-bedroom versions, sleeping four adults and four kids.

The adjacent shady **trailer park** (33/3362-8568, Guadalajara tel. 33/3362-8568, www. chimulcotrailerpark.com, $18/night, $400/ month if you pay in advance), part of the Chimulco Spa, has about 50 spaces, concrete pads, and all hookups. Amenities include 20-amp hookups, many pull-through spaces, laundry, barbecue grills, and much more.

As for food, you could either bring your own (shop at the on-site minimart or at stores in Villa Corona across the highway), eat in the on-site restaurant/snack bar, or check out several decent local restaurants.

Neighboring Facilities

Chimulco is just one of a number of Villa Corona water-park complexes. Very worthy of consideration is the similarly lavish **Agua Caliente** (Km 56, tel. 387/778-0784 or 387/778-0785, Guadalajara tel. 33/3616-3249, fax 387/778-0202, info@aguacaliente.com. mx, www.aguacaliente.com.mx), in its own large lakeside park, including a shady campground ($12/night) and bungalows ($75–110), just south of Highway 80, about a quarter mile west of Chimulco.

Getting There
BY BUS
At the downtown Guadalajara Camionera Central Vieja, catch one of the several daily "Servicios

Coordinados" (Flecha Amarilla, tel. 33/3619-4533) Villa Corona–bound buses. Or from the suburban Camionera Central Nueva, go by either Flecha Amarilla subsidiary lines (*módulo* 1, tel. 33/3600-0770, or 33/3600-0526); or by allied lines Autocamiones del Pacífico and Transportes Cihuatlán (*módulo* 4, second-class tel. 33/3600-0076, first-class tel. 33/3600-0598). (For more information on bus lines, see *Getting There and Around* in the *Downtown* chapter.)

BY CAR
From Guadalajara, follow Avenida López Mateos Sur about 16 miles (26 km) south of the *periférico* (peripheral boulevard), where you turn right off the expressway onto Highway 80 (Melaque–Barra de Navidad direction), west. Continue approximately another 7 miles (11 km) to Villa Corona, where you turn left (westbound) at the Chimulco sign.

RÍO CALIENTE
The boiling-hot Río Caliente (Hot River) gurgles from its subterranean cliff-side source and steams downhill through the Bosque de Primavera (Forest of Spring) preserve, sustaining local warm-spring *balnearios* along the way. Closest to the source is Río Caliente Spa, on whose land the spring bubbles forth.

Sights and Activities
From the Hotel Río Caliente Spa, trails lead out, lacing the Bosque de Primavera. They follow the river from the source downhill, or lead uphill through the lush pine-oak woodlands that coat this still-active volcanic wonderland.

Although frequented by weekend day-trippers, the trails are nearly empty on weekdays, when you'll probably have the Bosque de Primavera pretty much to yourself. Along the paths, if you're quiet and patient, you might glimpse any one of a hundred bird species, from hawks (*halcones*) and vultures (*zopilotes*) to colorful orioles, dainty vermilion flycatchers, and golden vireos. Mammals that you might see along the trail include deer, armadillos, wildcats, and the piglike wild *jabalí*.

Río Caliente Spa

The Río Caliente Spa (Bosque de Primavera, La Venta, Jalisco 45221, tel./fax 33/3151-0887, riocal@aol.com, www.riocaliente.com, $175 per person) is a tranquil village of brick cottages nestled beside and above the steaming Río Caliente, which gushes, steaming hot, from a nearby cliff bottom. The approximately 50 spartan-chic accommodations, each with its own fireplace, are enclosed in attractively rustic brown brick walls, with shiny tile floors, comfortable beds, handmade wooden furniture, and immaculate shower baths.

Single occupancy rates begin at about $175/day, $1150/week; double occupancy $160/day and $1070/week per person, including taxes and all meals and many activities. Spa treatments are extra (although customary one-week special packages, including some spa treatments, run as low as about $1,100/wk per person, double occupancy).

The rates include three hearty (largely meatless, but delicious) macrobiotic buffet meals with plenty of choices (cereal, eggs, hash browns, and coffee for breakfast; split pea soup, tossed salad, and fish tacos for lunch or dinner). No alcoholic beverages or smoking is allowed in common rooms or lodging rooms.

Lodging and food are only the beginning at Río Caliente Spa. Guests (who are largely college-educated upper-middle-class Americans and Canadians, usually about twice as many women than men) can choose a full schedule at no extra cost. Activities include hikes, yoga, water exercise, steam room, tai chi, and professionally led workshops, such as "Journal Writing" or "Relationships, Work, and Self Esteem."

Other services, such as mud wrap, pedicure, massage, facial, dermabrasion, antiaging medical therapies, horseback riding, and shopping and sightseeing trips are available at extra cost.

Alternatively, guests can opt simply to relax, read, or converse in the patio by the spa's outdoor swimming pools and the two secluded nude bathing pools.

Some people have described Río Caliente Spa as more a retreat than a spa. If you're planning on bringing a big designer wardrobe and working out half the day on the treadmill or stair-step machine, this place is not for you. Hiking and swimming takes the place of machines, noise is kept to a minimum, and food is plentiful but healthfully low in fat, refined sugar, and salt.

For reservations from outside of Mexico (mandatory in winter, recommended all times), information, and brochure, contact the spa's North American agent, (P.O. Box 897, Millbrae, CA 94030, tel. 800/200-2927 or 650/615-9543, fax 650/615-0601). Either outside or inside Mexico, you may also contact Río Caliente Spa directly. *Credit cards are not accepted* at the spa, although American personal checks and travelers checks are.

Guadalajara travelers can reach the Río Caliente Spa most easily by airport taxi. The spa has a system for guests to get together and share transportation. By car or bus from Guadalajara, or from Highway 15 (via Tepic and Tequila) eastbound, see *Bosque de Primavera*.

◖ BOSQUE DE PRIMAVERA

The Río Caliente Spa is only a small, albeit important, part of the Bosque de Primavera. The Bosque de Primavera itself is a communally owned reserve for public use and enjoyment. It stretches over dozens of square miles of forest, river, and mountain, not far west of Guadalajara's metropolitan edge.

Camping is allowed with your own equipment for a small fee, and three local-style *balnearios* (bathing resorts) line the warm Río Caliente, all accessible along the entrance road. Use the following access directions to guide your arrival.

By car or bus, follow Highway 15 west, exit the four-lane highway by turning left (westbound) at La Venta village, marked on the highway by Bosque de Primavera and Cañon de las Flores signs, 7.1 miles (11.5 km) west of the *periférico*. Set your odometer.

Follow the Cañon de las Flores signs through the village, straight ahead (south) about four blocks, then right (west) another four blocks, then left (south) again. At mile 0.8 (km 1.3) you arrive at the **Balneario Cañon de las Flores** (tel. 33/3151-0160, 374/741-0160, open daily 9 A.M.–8 P.M., adults $3, parking $2) on the left, with warm pools, water toboggan, restaurant, picnic ground, and playground equipment. If there's a rope across the road, ask them to let you pass (which they're obligated to do) and continue a fraction of a mile farther to the sign and right-hand dirt road leading to the **Balneario Las Tinajitas** (Bosque de Primavera, Kilometer 20, tel. 33/3617-2656, open daily 9 A.M.–8 P.M.), about the same facilities and prices as Cañon de las Flores.

A glance at the handsome pine grove around you is a clue that you are in the Bosque de Primavera pine-oak forest. Camping is allowed most anywhere. Take care not to start a forest fire, and clean up your camp.

Continue ahead; at mile 2.1 (km 3.3) you arrive at a gate where, to continue, you have to pay about $0.50 to an attendant. At the same spot, a dirt road heads right, through the pines downhill to the river and the rustic **Balneario El Bosque** (open Fri.–Sun. 8 A.M.–6 P.M., $1 per person).

Continue ahead; at mile 2.9 (km 4.7), the road splits. Take the left fork for the Río Caliente Spa gate a quarter of a mile farther. The right fork continues to the river and some informal riverside camping and picnic spots.

By bus, get to Bosque de Primavera via second-class **Transportes Ceocuitatlan** (tel. 33/3619-3989 or 33/3619-8891, ext. 106) buses, which connect west from the downtown Camionera Central Vieja, *sala* A. (See *Getting There and Around* in the *Downtown* chapter.) Ask the driver to let you off at La Venta, then taxi or walk from the highway.

Guachimontones and Hacienda El Carmen

Although crystal-clear, spring-fed bathing ponds and pools, a hot spring and steaming geyser, and a graceful colonial-era working hacienda hotel are reasons enough to venture a hour's drive west of Guadalajara, the monumental conical pyramids, locally known as the Guachimontones (wah-chee-mon-TOH-nays), are where most visitors head first.

GUACHIMONTONES

The Guachimontones archaeological site spreads more than 100 acres over the rocky hillside about three miles north of the small town of Teuchtitlán (tay-oosh-teet-LAHN). I was especially lucky to meet, by chance, one of the principal archaeological investigators, Professor Phil Weigand of the Colegio de Michoacán, when I first visited the site in the spring of 2003. He summarized what he and his colleagues, notably Professor Efrain Cárdenas, also of the Colegio de Michoacán, had uncovered since they initiated excavations in 1998. By comparing Guachimontones pottery finds with pottery found at other west Mexico sites,

Professor Weigand and his colleagues believe that the earliest constructions at Guachimontones date from around the beginning of the Christian era.

Subsequently, Guachimontones's early builders added as many as four layers of new construction over the old, until the site was abandoned, most likely after around A.D. 400. By that time, the total complex encompassed at least 10 conical pyramids, the largest around 100 feet (30 meters) in height and double or triple that in diameter. Other identified structures include at least two ball courts (one very long, at 260 feet/80 meters) and numerous courtyards, stone walls, staircases, and avenues—in aggregate, amounting to at least two dozen separate ceremonial complexes.

Although excavations at many such sites in Mexico have often uncovered regal tombs, the Guachimontones pyramids excavated so far have yielded few, if any, human remains. Nevertheless, one of the most intriguing finds at Guachimontones was of a five-pound (1.8-kg) meteorite, which apparently

GETAWAYS

© BRUCE WHIPPERMAN

The most unusual remains at the Guachimontones archaeological complex are several monumental conical pyramids.

had been enshrined as an object of veneration, atop one of the ceremonial platforms. Moreover, investigators have uncovered evidence of two fires that razed the site. The first occurred early in its history; the second, later, probably around the time the site was abandoned (since the remains of the fire were not cleared).

Exploring the Site

The most recognizable of Guachimontones's monumental but mostly unreconstructed architecture is the largest pyramid, which has been partially restored to its original conical form. Dozens of circular steps ring the pyramid and culminate at the summit. Viewed from there, a spreading valley panorama reveals the spring-fed ponds of Balneario El Rincón, Teuchtitlán town in the mid-foreground, beyond that the shimmering surface of reservoir Laguna de la Vega, and, on the far misty purple horizon, the cloud-capped ramparts of the Sierra Madre.

Several other lesser but similarly conical

pyramid complexes, some reconstructed, most not, are scattered in the immediate foreground, both up- and downhill. You may be able to make out the general layout of each, ringed by a patio, which in turn is surrounded by another ring of smaller conical platforms.

In 1998, Professors Wiegand and Cárdenas found that the principal pyramid had been extensively looted. Robbers had dug into the heart of the structure via a trench that amounted to about a quarter of the volume of the entire original pyramid, and which required several workers months to fill in about 13,000 cubic yards of earth for the restoration. (For more details and updates on the continuing Guachimontones investigations, visit www.carbon.cudenver.edu/~cbeekman/research/SAA2004.html. Also, for a portfolio of lovely photos and many more details on Guachimontones and other regional archaeological finds, check out Richard Townsend's *Ancient West Mexico: Art and Archaeology of the Unknown Past.* (See *Suggested Reading* at the end of this book.)

BALNEARIO EL RINCÓN

On the way back downhill from Guachimontones, turn left at the signed side road and enjoy a visit to these lovely local bathing springs, ponds, and pools, especially refreshing on a warm day.

It's tempting to speculate that this gorgeously relaxing spot was the original attraction that led to the building of the Guachimontones ceremonial complex in the first place. It's easy to imagine an extended village of hundreds of *jacales* (thatched-roofed indigenous houses), homes of a community of thousands who tended a lush patchwork of fields, irrigated by the bounty of the year-round spring water.

Enter the gate ($3 per car) and you'll see the natural crystal-pure source still welling up and filling a half dozen crystal-clear pools and ponds. An old-fashioned water slide provides unlimited child's play, while a park offers picnic tables, spreading shady trees, and plenty of room for kids to run around after splashing in the water.

As for food and facilities, two or three down-home-style open-air restaurants serve plenty to eat and drink, including barbecued fish, chicken, meat, and frog dinners. Moreover, a shady **campground** ($5 per car overnight) has space for a squadron of small RVs (no hookups) and tents. This place is more likely to be crowded Saturdays, Sundays, and holidays, and quiet on weekdays.

Accommodations and Food

If you're not camping in the Balneario El Rincón, the **Hacienda El Carmen** (see below) provides comfortable old-Mexico bed-and-breakfast-style resort accommodation. Otherwise, check out the moderately priced **Hotel Las Fuentes** (Km 12, Carretera El Refugio-Ahualulco, Teuchtitlá, Jalisco, tel. 384/733-0162 or 384/733-0366, or cell 044-384/733-0548, add 01 if you're dialing long distance, hotellasfuentes@prodigy.net.mx, $25–35), on the south side of the highway, atop the hill a mile or so, Guadalajara direction, east of Teuchtitlán. There you'll find about a dozen motel-style, sparely furnished but clean rooms.

a springwater pool at Balneario El Rincón

Amenities include hot-water shower baths, fans, and a blue swimming pool on the breezy view hillside behind the hotel.

For food, besides the Balneario El Rincón and the few local-style eateries and taco stands around the plaza in Teuchtitlán, you might try one of the relaxing lake-view restaurants (Monte Carlo, Soky, and Naútico; watch for signs on the highway) overlooking the Laguna de la Vega, about a mile, Guadalajara direction, east of Teuchtitlán. The best of the lot appears to be El Naútico, right on the lakeshore. The restaurants are best visited from morning to mid-afternoon, before the mosquitoes come out. Consequently, they close around sundown, especially on weekdays.

Services and Getting There

Teuchtitlán (pop. 3000) offers a modicum of services, including post and Telecom offices, pharmacies, a private doctor or two, a public health center, and police, all around or near the plaza, a few blocks north of the highway. For more services, such as a bank and ATM, specialized doctors, and a travel agent, continue another eight miles (about 12 km) west to the local *municipio* (county seat) **Ahualulco** (pop. about 15,000).

By bus, get to Guachimontones and Balneario El Rincón from the Guadalajara old bus station (Camionera Central Vieja). Go by second-class **Transportes Guadalajara-La Vega-Cocula** (tel. 33/3650-3033), via the Ahualulco-bound bus.

By car, from Guadalajara, follow Highway 15 (Avenida Vallarta) west, 11 miles (18 km) beyond the *periférico* (peripheral expressway) to the left (signed Tala or Ameca) turnoff. Continue another 10 miles (16 km) to a point a fraction of a mile past Tala. There, at the sign to Ahualulco, turn right and continue another 7.5 miles (12 km) to Teuchtitlán and turn right at the town entrance road. Note your odometer at the highway. After a few blocks, pass the town plaza on the right. After 0.4 mile (0.6 km) from the highway, turn right where the road surface changes to dirt. Continue two blocks, then turn left. At

0.7 mile (1.1 km) pass the driveway to Balneario El Rincón on the right. Continue straight ahead, winding uphill about another mile, to Guachimontones, a total of about 30 miles (48 km) from the *periférico* (or about 35 mi/56 km from downtown Guadalajara).

HACIENDA EL CARMEN

After a hard day climbing the Guachimontones pyramids, enjoy the best of old Mexico at the gracefully beautiful Hacienda El Carmen (Kilometer 58, Carretera Guadalajara-Etzatlan, tel./fax 33/3656-9436, 33/3733-0110, or 33/3633-1771, Mex. toll-free tel 01-800/561-4053, hotel@hdaelcarmen.com, www.haciendaelcarmen.com.mx, $130–320, adults only), a few miles west of Guachimontones. Although of much more recent origin than the Guachimontones themselves, the hacienda's history nevertheless dates way back to 1569, when royal authorities deeded the property to Don Francisco Merodio de Velasco. Subsequent owners began construction of the present buildings in 1728 and named their estate the Hacienda Santa María de Miraflores. During the late colonial and early republican era the hacienda began to be known as the Hacienda El Carmen because, beginning in 1803, its profits were donated to support the El Carmen convent in Guadalajara until the convent was forced to close in 1856. The name has continued into recent times, when new owners Dr. Joaquin Baeza and his wife, Señora Serrano Zermeño de Baeza, restored their hacienda to its present gorgeous condition.

The accommodations at Hacienda El Carmen are luxuriously traditional and spacious, with big beds (either two doubles or a king-size), lacy curtains and bedspreads, and polished wood, brass, and tile throughout. Midweek (Sun.–Thurs.) rates for 21 junior suites begin at around $130 without food, $220 with all food and beverages included. Weekend rates for the same run about $200 and $320, respectively. Larger master suites cost about 20 percent more. The hacienda offers reduced group and business rates. Two conference halls can accommodate up to 500 people.

You can get more information and reserve Hacienda El Carmen through the Historic Haciendas and Inns website (www.historichaciendainns.com).

Get to Hacienda El Carmen by either bus or car, by following the directions for Guachimontones above, except that you continue past Teuchtitlán west another four miles (six km) to the signed side road to the hacienda on the left, about 39 miles (63 km) from downtown Guadalajara.

Optionally, the hacienda provides round-trip Guadalajara airport or downtown transfers for about $90 per person, minimum of two people.

Amenities and Activities

Hacienda guests enjoy a serenely regal setting of spacious green lawns, fountains, flowery verdure, high-ceilinged, antique-embellished rooms, and elegantly long, arched corridors. Guests who crave activity can have it, with mountain biking, golf (six holes), horseback rides ($12), lap swimming in the big pool, soaking in the hot tub, warming up in the sauna, or sallying out on guided tours as far as downtown Guadalajara ($30–60).

Evenings can be filled with leisure at the bar, lingering over dinner in the regal dining room, enjoying cards, dominos, or backgammon, browsing the library, or viewing the moon, planets, and nebulae through the hacienda telescope.

Let yourself be pampered by a complete menu of spa services, including massage and aromatherapy ($20–60), facials, exfoliation, mud bath, and traditional *temazcalli* sweat lodge ($25–45).

AMARILLO HOT SPRING AND GEYSERS

Lovers of the Mexican outback hankering for small off-highway adventure might enjoy a visit to the Amarillo hot spring and the petite (but fiercely boiling) geysers (known locally as Agua Caliente). Your destination will be the very modest rancho of the *familia* Alfonso Pérez, past the village of Amarillo, about five miles (eight km), a half hour by car, south of the Hacienda El Carmen.

The easiest travel option is by guided tour, if you're a guest of the hacienda ($40), or with your own wheels (half day, 10 miles round-trip), or on foot (all day, take good walking shoes, water, sunscreen, and a hat).

Upon arrival, you'll find a rickety working ranch, with tree-shaded corrals of goats and cows, pecking and scratching chickens, and a concrete-lined pool of warm but murky spring water. For a small fee, you can join the locals soaking in the pool. Be sure to bring your bathing suit. (If not, go in your clothes. Nude bathing is a definite local no-no.) A trail leads a quarter mile farther (the kids will lead you), through a shady mesquite grove, to the source: two or three small, steam-spurting geysers.

No additional facilities are available. Be prepared with your own food and drinks. The shady grove and the bucolic (albeit hardscrabble) ambience is not without charm. You may want to stay overnight. Ask if it's okay to camp there: *¿Es bueno acampar aquí?* Offer to pay (perhaps around $5) for the privilege.

Get there from the Hacienda El Carmen. If driving, set your odometer. A block or two past the hacienda, in the hacienda village, take the left fork (road to Amarillo). Continue 1.9 miles (3.1 km) to Amarillo village (pop. about 1,000). Turn right just after entering the village. After a couple of blocks, at the plaza-park at mile 2.0 (3.2 km), turn left. Continue about a half mile to a cemetery, where you turn right, at mile 2.6 (4.2 km). At mile 2.8 (4.5 km), cross over the railroad track. Continue nearly a mile; at the fork at mile 3.6, turn left. Continue a bit more than a mile to the ranch and hot spring at mile 4.9 (7.9 km).

Tequila

The ranks of cactuslike plants that spread over the valleys and hills an hour's drive west of Guadalajara are the source of the tradition that has propelled the name of the country town of Tequila (pop. 35,000) to worldwide renown.

That seemingly humble source, the leathery and spiny **blue agave,** cousin of the so-called "century plant," of Mexico and the southwest United States, is harvested and processed for its sugary *aguamiel* (honey water) juice that is distilled into the fiery liquor, known everywhere as tequila.

HISTORY
In the Beginning

Although the fermented alcoholic drink, called *pulque,* is part of indigenous Mexican tradition, liquor distillation is not. *Pulque,* like its distant American relatives, Budweiser beer, California wine, and Japanese sake, contains only the modest percentage of alcohol (usually 5–15 percent) obtainable directly from fermentation.

To get stronger stuff, you have to boil (technically, "distill") the alcohol away from the water. And there's where the Spanish came into the picture. Hernán Cortés introduced liquor distillation into Mexico with the conquest, in 1521.

Colonial Mexican distillers made *ron* (rum) and *aguardiente* (white lightning) from sugarcane, and *mezcal* (in some places, known as *raicilla*) from the juice of agave and agavelike plants. Finished products of all such distilled liquors contain sharply increased alcohol levels, as much as 45–50 percent (90–100 proof). Nowadays, commercial liquors made in Mexico and the United States generally contain a standard 38 percent (76 proof) alcohol level.

Local Developments

The history of the town of Tequila corresponds closely with that of the Cuervo and Sauza families, who were prominent pioneer liquor distillers. It was about a century after the 1656 founding of the town of Tequila that José Antonio de Cuervo settled and began distilling *mezcal* locally in 1758. In 1795, his son, José María Guadalupe de Cuervo, obtained an exclusive governmental license to distill *"el vino mezcal de tequila,"* the forerunner of present-day tequila.

In 1873, Cenobio Sauza de Madrigal established a local distillery and began competing with the Cuervos. Subsequently, both the Cuervos and Sauzas won international awards for their products, whose purity and uniquely clean taste gained renown among a growing number of liquor aficionados, especially in the United States.

ORIENTATION

Tequila is not a large town, and most attractions can be reached within a few blocks of the main plaza. Get your bearings by standing on the sidewalk adjacent to the west, or plaza, side

Tequila town church

© BRUCE WHIPPERMAN

TEQUILA

As local liquor production rocketed upward, reaching millions of cases per year during the 1970s, Sauza, Cuervo, and several other eminent regional liquor manufacturers became concerned that any distilled spirit could be labeled "tequila." In 1977, they cemented international appellation-of-origin agreements that limited the name "tequila" to liquors distilled only from juice made up of at least 51 percent by weight of locally grown blue agave plants.

The 51 percent minimum notwithstanding, the finest tequilas continued to be made from 100 percent agave juice. By the 1990s, tequila had become so popular that demand was far outstripping the supply of the slow-growing local blue agave. By 2000, despite thousands of newly planted acres, connoisseur-grade 100 percent blue agave tequila, like many fine California or French varietal wines, was routinely selling for hundreds of dollars a bottle.

All tequila is not the same. Manufacturers produce authentic tequila in three grades: **blanco, reposado,** and **añejo.** Tequila *blanco*, although conforming to the minimum requirements to be labeled "tequila," is not aged. To pass muster, however, it must be double distilled to crystal clarity, have a rich taste that is unmistakably of agave, and consist of 38 percent alcohol (76 proof) by volume.

Further processing begins with good tequila *blanco* and transforms it through care and aging. Tequila *reposado* (rested) is aged a minimum of two months in either French or American oak barrels. During the process, the liquor acquires a light straw color that should sparkle with flashes of gold when finished. Additionally, good *reposados* exhibit light floral and fruit aromas, with soft, pleasing hints of toasted wood.

Increased care and longer aging distinguish the finest tequila *añejo*, which must be aged a minimum of 12 months, preferably in French oak barrels. Depending upon barrel time, the liquor takes on a medium to dark amber shade that should sparkle with flashes of red to bright copper. Oxygen penetrating through the barrel during the aging process leads to a fine soft taste and rare, rich aromas, resulting in a liquor excellent for after-dinner consumption. Some manufacturers are pushing the process even further, producing ultra-fine tequilas aged five years or more, which retail for upwards of $400 a bottle.

© BRUCE WHIPPERMAN

The highest-quality tequila liquor begins with the cactus-like blue agave plant that grows in great ranks around Guadalajara.

of the main town church, **La Parroquia de la Purísima Concepción.** With your back to the church, you'll be looking west. Calle Juárez, immediately in front of you, runs both north and south of the church. On your right, plaza-front street Vicente Albino Rojas runs east–west along the plaza's north flank, while Avenida Sixto Gorjon runs along the plaza's south flank. On the far side of the plaza, Calle Ramón Corona borders the plaza's west flank, while, from the plaza's far west side, Calle José Cuervo runs west, away from you, past the Cuervo liquor distillery, restaurant, and handicrafts gallery, on the left.

SIGHTS IN TOWN
◖ Cuervo Distillery

Your first Tequila stop should be **Cuervo Distillery "La Rojena"** (on Calle Cuervo, at the town plaza's southwest corner, tel. 374/742-2170, Guadalajara tel. 33/3134-3300 or 33/3134-3368, fax 33/3134-3347, tours@cuervo.com.mx, www.mundocuervo.com). Via guided tour, view the operations of the venerable (1873) distillery. The raw materials are *piñas,* the pineapple-shaped hearts of the blue agave plants, shorn of their long, blue-green leaves. Pass the big cooker ovens where the *piñas* are digested and then pressed for their sweet *aguamiel* juice. Next, the juice is fermented in big vats, then distilled in gleaming copper kettles, and finally barreled, aged, and bottled. The tour ends in the long exit hall, decorated with the big Gabriel Flores 1969 mural that dramatizes the role of Tequila in the march of Mexican history.

The tours, in both English and Spanish, are conducted hourly, Monday–Saturday 10 A.M.– 4 P.M., and three times on Sunday, at 11 A.M., noon, and 1 P.M. Arrive early and buy your ticket (adults $7, students $5, kids under 12 free) ahead of time, at the counter, inside the handicrafts gallery, at the east end (near the street corner).

Afterward, take a look around the multiroom **handicrafts gallery** (open daily 9 A.M.–5 P.M.) with many fine for-sale examples of Jalisco ceramics, textiles, jewelry, and more. You might also stop for a drink, snack, or lunch at the adjacent Cuervo restaurant

(Fonda Cholula, see the *Restaurants* section), open daily 9 A.M.–6 P.M.

National Museum of Tequila

From the distillery, walk south a block along west plaza-front street Ramón Corona to the National Museum of Tequila (Ramón Corona 12, corner of Luis Navarro, tel. 374/742-0012, 374/742-2410, open Tues.–Sun. 10 A.M.– 5 P.M.). Rooms of excellent displays illustrate the early history of Mexican alcoholic beverages, especially *pulque* (interestingly represented by the rabbit hieroglyph) and agave culture.

Sauza Museum

Make your last museum stop on the plaza's north side, a few doors east of Corona, at the interesting Sauza Museum (Albino Rojas 22, tel. 374/742-0247, open Mon.–Fri. 10 A.M.– 2 P.M., Sat.–Sun. 10 A.M.–5 P.M.). The museum is housed in the *recinto* (reception hall) of the former Sauza family house. It's the life project of the Sauza family, currently including Sylvia Sauza, daughter of tequila patriarch Francisco Javier Sauza and granddaughter Helena Erickson Sauza and grandson Guillermo Erickson Sauza. They supervise the family museum and the associated shop, La Tiendita.

Inside the museum, wander the rooms of Sauza memorabilia, including oil paintings, historical photographs, antique distillation equipment, charming old promotional posters and calendars, and a handsome silver and braid *charro* outfit, presented by renowned Mexican singing cowboy actor Pepe Guizar.

Although Francisco Javier Sauza sold his big local distillery and Sauza brand to the Domecq Spanish wine conglomerate in 1976, Guillermo Erickson Sauza has recently restored the century-old Sauza family distillery, La Fortaleza (for "fortitude"), not far from the town plaza. In 2002 he began producing his own "Los Abuelos" brand of fine tequila. He welcomes visitors and conducts tours by appointment. Contact him in advance by email (abuelo@losabuelos.com). For Guillermo's history of Sauza and his restored distillery, visit www.tequilasource.com/losabuelos. At the bottom

© BRUCE WHIPPERMAN

An ancient crushing mill is a prominent exhibit at the National Museum of Tequila.

of the web page, click on the "Sauza Family Museum–Tequila Jalisco" link for more information about the museum.

SIGHTS OUT OF TOWN

If you have a second day, the Tequila area offers at least two worthwhile nearby excursions.

Hacienda San José

Visit the Hacienda San José del Refugio, now preserved as both museum and working distillery of the celebrated Herradura tequila firm, in the town of Amatitán, on Highway 15 not far east of Tequila. Visits are by guided tour only and include an introductory video, the hacienda chapel, and the working Herradura tequila factory.

In-house guides conduct tours hourly Monday–Friday 9 A.M.–3 P.M. Entrance fee is $7 per person. For more information, call the hacienda tour office (in Spanish, tel. 374/745-1100, cristinadelgadillo@herradura.com.mx).

Get there from Tequila via old Highway 15 *(libre)*, seven miles (11 km) east of Tequila. At the west (Guadalajara) side of Amatitán, just before the highway climbs the hill, turn left at the side lane that you can see continuing beneath the railroad bridge. Continue to the ex-hacienda gate within a few hundred yards, on the right. (From Guadalajara, turn right, just after old Highway 15 *(libre)* has finished its winding, downhill descent, just before Amatitán.)

You can also visit the Hacienda San José via the **Tequila Express** Saturday rail excursion from downtown Guadalajara (about $75 per adult). It's a complete party, including the museum and distillery tour, plus a Mexican buffet and a folkloric show. Get your tickets from the Guadalajara Chamber of Commerce or Ticketmaster. For more details, see *Entertainment and Events* in the *Downtown* chapter.

Balneario La Toma and Balneario El Paraíso

Perched on the tropical edge of the **Barranca** (Canyon) of the Río Santiago, Balneario La Toma affords a chance to appreciate and enjoy Tequila's great outdoors. The *balneario* (bathing spring), with three big, spring-fed pools, a cave waterfall, picnic tables, snack restaurants, and panoramic semitropical canyon views, is famously popular. For maximum peace and tranquility, avoid crowded Saturday, Sunday, and holiday afternoons. The *balneario* is 15 minutes by car or taxi west of Tequila.

For a change of scene, drive or stroll the road downhill from La Toma about a quarter mile to rustic **Balneario El Paraíso.** It offers basic facilities, tropical tranquility, a cool, spring-fed bathing pool, and a bit of space for camping beneath a shady tropical hillside mango grove (with all the free mangoes you can eat in May and June). Bring insect repellent.

Get there by taxi, car, or bus (to Magdalena) via old Highway 15 *(libre);* follow the main Tequila old Highway 15 northwest from the crossing (at the monumental statue of the *agavero*—agave cutter).

By car, set your odometer at the statue. At mile 1.9 (km 3.0), at the top of the hill, make a sharp right from Highway 15 at the bar El Texano sign. Continue along the graded dirt road, past a school at mile 2.7 (km 4.2). Soon, at the next fork, turn right for Balneario La Toma, or left for Balneario El Paraíso, which you'll find, on the right, at mile 3.0 (km 4.9).

ENTERTAINMENT AND EVENTS
Fiestas

Local *barrios* celebrate their respective patron saints often and well, with carnivals, food, processions, masses, and fireworks. If you enjoy ceremony and revelry, arrive for the **Fiesta de Santa Cruz,** May 1–3; the **Fiesta de la Señora de la Asunción,** August 1–15; the **Fiesta de San Francisco,** September 27–October 4; or the **Fiesta de la Purísima Concepción,** December 8.

Patron saints notwithstanding, Tequila people also celebrate a pair of unique nonreligious festivals. First, on June 24, everyone goes overboard in a communal smashing of traditional clay *cantaritos* (tequila jugs).

The festival year peaks with the **National Tequila Fair,** November 30–December 12.

The town becomes awash with celebrations, starting with the crowning of a tequila queen, and then, successively, manufacturers' exposition of products, rodeos, parade and floats, cockfights, mariachi serenades, carnival games, all topped off by a fireworks *spectaculo.*

SHOPPING
Handicrafts

Make your first Tequila shopping stop at **La Tiendita** (22 Albino Rojas, tel. 374/742-0247, open Mon.–Fri. 10 A.M.–2 P.M., Sat.–Sun. 10 A.M.–5 P.M.), the shop of the Sauza Museum, on the north side of the plaza. Choose from shelves and counters full of all-Mexico handicrafts, individually selected by Sauza family head, Sylvia Sauza, and her daughter and store manager, Helena Erickson Sauza.

A few doors to the west, at the corner, check out the handicrafts offerings of **Regalos Palomar,** (open Mon.–Fri. 10 A.M.–6 P.M., Sat.–Sun. 10 A.M.–4 P.M.), then go to **Cuervo Restaurant and Shopping Center** (tel. 374/742-2170, open daily 9 A.M.–6 P.M.) at the plaza's west side to look through the **handicrafts gallery.** Most of the offerings are both very fine and expensive.

ACCOMMODATIONS
Under $25

Tequila overnighters have their choice of a few modest but recommendable hotels. Right next to the plaza church and small but colorful town market, consider the worthy **Hotel San Francisco** (Vallarta 10, Tequila, Jalisco 46400, tel. 374/742-1757, $17–22). Here you have your basic, clean, small-town hotel, with eight upstairs rooms, plainly but comfortably furnished, with bedspreads and drapes and well-maintained hot-water shower bath.

A few blocks east, along the main street, check out the **Posada del Agave** (Sixto Gorjon 83, Tequila, Jalisco 46400, tel. 374/742-0774, $22–28). Brand-new in 2004, the hotel's rooms sparkle with shiny designer tile floors, color-coordinated bedspreads and drapes, shaded reading lamps, and shiny, 1990s-standard baths. Smart designers located the rooms in two floors, away from the busy street-front. Rooms come with TV, fan, and telephone.

Out on the highway, a few blocks northwest of the main town crossing, stands the **Hotel María Isabel** (Carretera Internacional 63, Tequila, Jalisco 46400, tel. 374/742-1592, $20–44). The María Isabel offers a selection of about six accommodations, ranging from rooms to three-bedroom suites. The good news is that they're light and immaculate, with attractively rustic bedsteads, dressers, and bedspreads, and hot-water shower baths. Unfortunately, reading lamps are lacking, and the hotel fronts the noisy highway. Bring earplugs. In addition to standard rooms, two-bedroom suites sleep up to four, and three-bedroom suites sleep up to six.

$25-50

Probably the best hotel in town is the newish **Hotel Plaza Jardín** (José Cuervo 13, Tequila, Jalisco 46400, tel. 374/742-0061, 374/742-4000, or 374/742-4001, plaza.jardin@hotmail.com, www.hotelplazajardin.com, $29–50), right on the plaza. Three stories (no elevator, however) of rooms surround a tranquil inner patio. They're furnished simply but comfortably in *anejo* (aged tequila) browns and tile. Guests in the upper-level front rooms enjoy plaza and mountain views from private balconies. An airy upstairs patio features a small rooftop pool and kiddie pool. Amenities include fans, cable TV, and a small restaurant, good for breakfast, downstairs.

FOOD
Food Stalls, Bakeries, and Groceries

Get your fill of hearty country cooking at the food stalls *(fondas)* on Albino Rojas, behind the plaza church. Get there early, when food is fresh and hot.

Plenty of fruits, veggies, groceries, and baked goods are available in the town **market,** in the alley off of Vallarta, just north of the Hotel San Francisco and east of the plaza church. Alternatively, you can get about the same at the several bakeries *(panaderías)* and grocery stores *(abarroterias)* on the main ingress street, Sixto Gorjon.

Restaurants

Tequila visitors enjoy a sprinkling of recommendable restaurants. For breakfast, the restaurant at the Hotel Plaza del Jardín is fine for tasty omelets, french toast, pancakes, fresh fruit, orange juice, and coffee ($1–5).

The best restaurant in town is probably the **Restaurant Real Marinero** (92 Juárez, tel. 374/742-12794, open daily 10 a.m.–11 p.m.), a block north of the plaza's northeast corner, behind the church. Here, you'll find plenty of *ceviche* (raw fish marinated in lime or lemon juice)options ($3–5) and a choice of shrimp, octopus, oyster, and clam cocktails ($4–8). Continue with soups ($3–5), fish fillets in eight styles, and pizza ($5–10).

Second choice goes to the Cuervo Restaurant, **Fonda Cholula** (59 Ramón Corona, tel. 374/742-2170, open daily 9 a.m.–8 p.m.), across Corona from the Cuervo distillery. Choose from a menu of yummy *comida poblano* (country-style) specialties, such as *chile en nogada* (mild, sweet, stuffed fresh chile, $7); *pacholas Doña Lepe* (savory grilled ground meat patties with all the fixings, $9); and *alambres de la fonda* (ham, beef, bacon, whole onions, and green pepper brochette, $9).

A more local, recommendable restaurant choice, away from the plaza tourist hubbub, is **Carnes Guadalajara** (Sixto Gorjon 111, open daily 9 a.m.–8 p.m.), three blocks into town from the Highway 15 crossing. A friendly, hardworking proprietor specializes in country specialties, such as *birria de agave* (barbecued lamb served in agave leaves, *carnes en su jugo* (stewed beef meat in its juice), and barbecued steaks ($5–10). Vegetarians can always order a vegetable omelet *(omelet de verduras),* a mixed salad *(ensalada mixta),* or pasta smothered in tomato sauce *(salsa de tomate)* ($3–6).

For maximum relaxation while dining, first choice goes to refined open-air **Restaurant Campestre Mariscos El Mar II** (Km 2.8, Carreterra Tequila-Magdalena, tel. 374/742-2121, open Sun.–Thurs. noon–8 p.m., Fri.–Sat. noon–10 p.m.), on the old Hwy. 15, northwest of town. Enjoy the freshest and best from the coast ($5–12). Extras include playground equipment for kids and a panoramic canyon view. Get there by car or taxi, via Highway 15, 1.8 miles (2.8 km) northwest of the main Tequila highway crossing. Find it on the right at the crest of the hill.

INFORMATION AND SERVICES
Tourist Information

The Tequila **Turismo** tourist information office (tel. 374/742-0159, open Mon.–Fri. 9 A.M.–5 P.M.) is in the *presidencia municipal,* at the southwest corner of the main plaza, across Corona from the Cuervo distillery. If it's closed, you might get your question answered at the information booth that's often open on the town plaza, or the tour ticket counter inside the Cuervo complex, at the plaza's southwest corner.

Banking

Choose among three banks, all with ATMs, around the Tequila plaza. Start at **Banorte** (tel. 374/742-2314, open Mon.–Fri. 9 A.M.–5 P.M.), at the northwest plaza corner of Albino Rosas and Ramón Corona; or go two blocks south and one block east to **Bancomer** (tel. 374/742-1690, open Mon.–Fri. 8:30 A.M.–4 P.M.), at the northwest corner of Juárez and J. Rodríguez de Hilar; or **Banamex** (Sixto Gorjon 115, tel. 374/742-0092, open Mon.–Fri. 9 A.M.–4 P.M.), a few blocks east (Guadalajara direction) from the church.

Post and Communications

The Tequila *correo* (post office) (Juárez 4, tel. 374/742-0457) is on the plaza; the Telecom (Juárez 4, tel. 374/742-0085) has public telephone, fax, and money orders next door. For long-distance telephone after hours, buy a Ladatel card at a pharmacy or grocery store and use it in one of the several plaza-front public telephones, or use the public telephone and fax at the **Super Farmacia del Centro,** on the plaza, north side (Albino Rojas, open daily 9 A.M.–8 P.M.).

Connect to the **Internet** at **Ciber Café,** at the northeast plaza corner, behind the church (open daily 10 A.M.–9 P.M.).

Travel Agent

Get your air tickets at travel agent **Tequi Tours** (Sixto Gorjon 35, tel. 374/742-2331), at the north side of street, between Degollado and Bravo.

HEALTH AND EMERGENCIES
Medical Services

For simple remedies, consult the physician or pharmacist on duty at one of several local pharmacies, such as **Super Farmacia del Centro** (Albino Rojas, north side of the plaza, open daily 9 A.M.–8 P.M.).

For a doctor in a hurry, follow your hotel's advice, or have a taxi take you to the **Hospital Seguro Social** (Sixto Gorjon 225, tel. 374/742-0138).

Police and Fire

In a police or fire emergency, contact the police headquarters at the *presidencia municipal,* on the plaza's south side (tel. 374/742-3519).

GETTING THERE
By Bus

A number of bus lines serve the town of Tequila from Guadalajara's suburban Camionera Central Nueva. Lines serving western destinations, such as **Transportes Pacífico** (tel. 33/3600-0211), in the terminal's *módulo* 4, have second-class departures that stop in Tequila.

Alternatively, go by second-class **Transportes Ceoquitatlán** (tel. 33/3619-3989) bus from the downtown Guadalajara Camionera Central Vieja.

By Car

From Guadalajara, drive west along either Avenida Vallarta or Calzada Lázaro Cárdenas. Continue west, Tepic direction, along old Highway 15 (*libre,* one hour total) or Highway 15D *cuota* (toll, 40 minutes) to Tequila, about 37 miles (60 km) west of the Guadalajara *periférico.* A monumental statue, *El Agavero* (The Agave Cutter), on the left, marks the town entrance intersection at Avenida Sixto Gorjon.

Magdalena

Like most Mexican towns, Magdalena's history stretches back long before the arrival of the Spanish. The present town coincides with the preconquest Tecuexe town of Xuchitepec (Hill of Flowers), undoubtedly referring to the high hill, Cerro Norte, north of town, which during the summer rainy season usually sports a coat of colorful wildflowers.

HISTORY
In the Beginning

Old Xuchitepec was a tributary of the chiefdom of Etzatlán (a still-important town, 15 miles south). Xuchitepec people once lived on two islands in a now-dry lake (which paradoxically they had to evacuate because of floods), west of the present town.

The Spanish, in the person of Francisco Cortés de Buenaventura, Hernán Cortés's nephew, arrived in 1524. Buenaventura's company of cavalry and foot soldiers caught the Xuchitepec chief, Goaxicar, unprepared. Goaxicar fled with his warriors, leaving his daughter behind, with no choice but to accept baptism, taking the name of Magdalena, which became synonymous with the town. Later, Franciscan padres built a convent and a church, which they dedicated with the name Santa María Magdalena de Xuchitepec.

ENTERTAINMENT AND EVENTS
Fiestas

Although life usually goes on quietly in Magdalena, folks do rev up for a few festivals, when hotel reservations are mandatory. Excitement builds with special masses, carnival rides, procession, and food during the **Fiesta de Santa María Magdalena,** July 17–22.

The fiesta year peaks during the combined **Feria Nacional de Ópalos** (National Opal Fair) and the **Fiesta del Señor de los Milagros,** September 15–29. Local people go all out, with pilgrimages, cultural and sports events, a popular dance, float parade, mariachi serenades, *mojigangos* (stilt-mounted dancing effigies), grand opal and handicrafts expositions, and plenty of food.

SHOPPING
Buying Opals

Although the September 15–29 National Opal Fair is the best time to buy local opals, jewelry, and handicrafts, a number of shops are open year-round near the town plaza. Of the three or four plaza-front shops, one of the best-established seems to be **Ópalos y Artesanías Mexicanas** (Corona 31, tel. 386/744-0708 or 386/744-0085, open daily 9 A.M.–2 P.M.), on the plaza's west side.

Another worthy plaza-front shop is **Opalos Xochitl** (Juárez 20, tel. 386/744-0589, open Mon.–Sat. 10 A.M.–3 P.M. and 5–7 P.M., Sun. 10 A.M.–2 P.M.), on the north side. Choose from an eclectic assortment, including unmounted opals, along with a trove of attractive rings, necklaces, and brooches, plus a distinctive collection of black volcanic obsidian statuettes.

Besides the shops, individuals—the men who usually hang out on the plaza's west side—sell opals. However, in order to deal with them, you must either have a command of Spanish or ask a friend who does to bargain for you. Moreover, experts warn that opals, especially if recently mined, may change colors until they mature long enough for their hydrated water content to stabilize. For this reason, it's safest to buy from an established dealer who can furnish you with a bona fide guarantee of authenticity.

◖ Opals of Magdalena

Ópalos de Magdalena (Independencia 115, tel./fax 386/744-0447, info@opalosdemexico.com.mx, www.opalosdemexico.com.mx, open Mon.–Sat. 10 A.M.–8 P.M., Sun. 10 A.M.–2 P.M.), three blocks east of the town plaza, is a museum and store. It's is the family enterprise of personable Javier López Ávila, whose

© BRUCE WHIPPERMAN

Magdalena opals are valuable by virtue of the hard labor required to hammer them from solid rock.

rooms enjoy eastward views of the green silhouettes of the Tequila volcano and Cerro Norte. Rates are right, and include fans and TV. Arrive with a reservation, especially during the opal festival, during the last two weeks of September.

A pair of emergency-only hotels serve truckers and midnight drop-in guests at the east end of town, on old Highway 15 *(libre)*, near the entrance from the toll Highway 15D. The best of the pair is probably the loosely managed motel-style **Magdalena Inn** (Km 73, Carretera 15, Magdalena, Jalisco 46470, tel. 386/744-0983, $13–20), at the far eastern edge of town. Rooms are clean but plain and may need some basic maintenance, such as light bulbs. Make sure everything's working and in place before moving in. For less truck noise, get one of the rooms at the back of the parking lot, farthest from the highway.

Last choice goes to the **Quinta Minas** (M. Ávila Camacho 450, tel. 386/744-0560, $18–28), with 25 rooms, west of the toll Highway 15D entrance, across from the hospital.

mission is to promote Magdalena opals. He's doing an effective job of it, judging from his shop's wealth of jewels in dozens of forms, including jet-black opal turtles, sparkling silver and gold necklaces, shimmering bracelets, and handsome statuettes.

As part of his enterprise, Javier also arranges **tours** and packages for visiting local opal mines. Visits can include lodging, guide, and transportation to view both the opal diggings and the nearby *tumbas de tiro* (bottle-shaped tombs) of Huitzizilipan.

ACCOMMODATIONS
Under $25

Magdalena has only a few hotels. First choice goes to the town-center **Hotel El Ópalo** (Allende 36, Magdalena, Jalisco 46470, tel. 386/744-0118, fax 386/744-0069, $13–25). The three floors of 28 rooms, around a quiet inner courtyard, are plain but clean and comfortably furnished with large beds and tile and shower baths. Guests in some upper-floor

FOOD
Food Stalls

Hearty, economical meals—especially *guisados* (stews) and *birrias* (pit barbecued lamb or goat), tamales, enchiladas, and *chiles rellenos*—are available at the downtown market *fondas* (permanent food stalls) just east of the plaza-front church.

Beginning around 6 P.M., evening action centers around a number of **taco and snack stands** that set up at curbside on Mina, the street behind the plaza-front church.

Restaurants

A single family seems to have cornered the Magdalena restaurant trade, with a trio of restaurants, all named "Lupita," after the founder. The 1920 original, **Fonda Lupita** (Independencia 26, tel. 386/744-0142, open daily 7:30 A.M.–11 P.M.), on the main highway ingress street, a block northeast of the town plaza, is still the best,

THE OPAL STORY

No evidence exists that Magdalena's original inhabitants knew of the riches in opals buried beneath their land. Nevertheless, opals, those prized multihued stones, were well-known in preconquest Mexico. Historical data indicate that the Aztec nobility treasured opals for ornamentation from at least A.D. 1200. They called them *vitzitziltecpal* (the hummingbird stone) for their shimmering colors, akin to the hummingbird's flashing plumage.

Although the conquest erased the knowledge of the old Aztec mines, opals were rediscovered in Mexico's Querétaro state in 1840 and in Magdalena, by prospector Alfonso Ramírez, in 1957. Although the rush that led to Magdalena's 1965-1975 "opal fever" has subsided, plenty of opals are sold locally in town shops and by street sellers who station themselves on the west side of the town plaza. The excitement that opals arouse is justified.

Opals, which come in all colors of the rainbow, plus jet black and milky white, are prized for their uniquely enchanting iridescence. Their colors are due to various trace minerals. If an opal were pure, its color would merely mimic the colorless transparency of glass, which, like opal, is composed of nearly pure silicon dioxide, the same as silica sand and quartz.

Opals differ slightly from quartz or glass, however, because they contain a few percent by weight of loosely bound (hydrated) water. The opal's water content is both a blessing and a curse. The presence of water gives opals their unique shimmer, but at the same time, it makes them more fragile than most precious stones. Opals must retain their water content or their beauty will be destroyed. Experts recommend that owners of opals keep them away from flame and store them under water occasionally to preserve their beauty.

---

however. The local protocol is to check inside the kitchen (right up front) and see what's cooking for the day. You'll often find Magdalena country specialties such as rich *caldo de res con verduras* (beef-vegetable soup), *carne con chile* (beef or pork chile stew, $4), or *chicharron con chile* (delicious but fatty deep-fried pork rinds in chile, $4). Also, they'll usually be offering a another local specialty, *jocoque:* a milk product, somewhere between yogurt and cheese.

For a variation on the same menu, also try **Lupita II** (Manuel Ávila Camacho 382, tel. 386/744-0330, open daily 7:30 A.M.–8 P.M.), a half mile east on the continuation of the same main street.

Alternately, go to rival **Restaurant Evangelina** (Ramón Corona 47, open daily 8 A.M.–10:30 P.M.), across the street from the plaza's northwest corner. You can enjoy breakfast (omelet or *huevos al la mexicana,* $3, with toast and coffee) or carne asada (grilled beef, $5), quesadilla ($3), or *camarones al gusto* (shrimp as you like them, $5).

INFORMATION AND SERVICES

Change money at **Bancomer** (tel. 386/744-0050, open Mon.–Fri. 8:30 A.M.–4 P.M.), with ATM, diagonally across from the plaza's northwest corner.

Mina, the street that runs behind the church, has a travel agent, **Agencia de Viajes Narsam** (tel. 386/744-0717, open Mon.–Sat. 9 A.M.–2 P.M. and 4–7 P.M.).

Next door, get development service, film, and other photo supplies at **Magdalena Photo Radio** (Mina 11, open Mon.–Sat. 9 A.M.–9 P.M., Sun. 9 A.M.–2 P.M.).

POST AND COMMUNICATIONS

Find the Magdalena *correo* (post office) on the highway, about four blocks west of the town plaza (Ávila Camacho 7, tel. 386/744-0230, 386/744-0234, open Mon.–Fri. 9 A.M.–3 P.M.).

The *larga distancia* (public long-distance telephone) and fax (and maybe Internet connection) is located in the corner shoe store *(zapatería)* (open daily 9 A.M.–9 P.M.), on the plaza-front north side, across the street from the taxi stand.

MEDICAL SERVICES

For medical consultation, see internist Alfonso Islas Rivera, M.D. (Independencia 102A, cell tel. 044-33/3449-5379), about three blocks east of the plaza, south side of the street, across from Ópalos de Magdalena.

If Dr. Rivera isn't available at his office, you may find him (or another doctor) at the **Hospital Regional** (M. Ávila Camacho 435), with a 24-hour emergency room, on the highway, east of downtown.

GETTING THERE

Get to Magdalena, by either car or bus via Transportes Ceocuitatlaán, by virtually the same directions as for Tequila (see *Tequila,* earlier in this chapter). Simply drive an additional 10 miles (16 km) farther west past Tequila from Guadalajara.

BACKGROUND

The Land

Guadalajara (pop. 3.5 million), western México's grand capital, is blessed with a sunny, springlike climate and fertile soils, born from the host of ancient volcanoes that dot its region. Go to any high place in the city on a clear day and you'll see these volcanoes as humps and hillocks rising from the broad Atemajac Valley ("place where the waters divide among the rocks") that surrounds the metropolis.

One of the most prominent of these is the still-active **Volcán Colli** (Volcano of the Gods, approx. 7,500 feet/2,300 meters), jutting up beyond the city's southwest suburb. Shift your view westward to the far horizon, and on a clear day you'll see the rugged mass of **Volcán Tequila**

(9,580 feet/2,920 meters), with a rounded plug picturesquely topping its summit. Continue your survey by reversing your view to the opposite horizon and look for the dark, brooding massif of **Cerro Gordo** (Fat Mountain, 8,760 feet/2,670 meters) on the eastern horizon and the **Cerro las Gallinas** (Mountain of the Hens, 8,301 feet/2,530 meters) to the far southeast.

Rivers and lakes likewise feature prominently in Guadalajara's list of geographical surprises. Hidden south of the city, beyond the ridge, marked on its western side by high peak **Cerro Bela del Viejo** (9,710 feet/2,960 meters), spreads the broad expanse of **Lake Chapala,** Mexico's largest lake. Hidden to the west of Lake Chapala,

© BRUCE WHIPPERMAN

a number of lesser lakes, including **Laguna de Sayula, Laguna San Marcos,** and **Laguna Atotonilco,** decorate the landscape. Although in 2002–2003, Lake Chapala receded to record low levels, it recovered, giving hope to residents that authorities will prevent it from suffering the same fate as very shallow lakes Sayula and San Marcos, now nearly always dry.

The fate of Lake Chapala is strongly tied to that of another of Guadalajara's natural wonders, the **Río Lerma-Santiago.** Mexico's longest river, the Lerma-Santiago rises in the mountains west of Mexico City and flows westward through six states—Mexico, Querétaro, Michoacán, Guanajuato, Jalisco, and Nayarit—finally emptying into the Pacific Ocean north of San Blas.

Despite its long meandering journey, the Lerma-Santiago's crucial juncture is in Jalisco, not far southeast of Guadalajara, where, known as the Lerma upstream and appearing as a mere drainage canal at La Barca town, it empties into Lake Chapala. Then, at Ocotlán, only about 15 miles to the northwest, the river, thenceforth known as the Santiago downstream, flows out of the lake and meanders northwest through the Atemajac Valley.

In the southeast city outskirts, at **El Salto** (The Jump), the river drops in rainy years as a foaming, brown waterfall. El Salto also marks the beginning of another of the river's episodes: the **Barranca,** or, more formally, the **Grand Canyon of the Río Santiago.** The river's channel, starting as a mere crease in the Atemajac Valley at El Salto, quickly grows to a magnificent verdant gorge. It's conveniently viewable from points (like the Guadalajara Zoo) on the north edge of town, a district locally known as Huentitán. The viewer's eye follows an airy panorama down the canyon slope, dropping steeply to the tropical river bottom far below, then rising on the far north side to towering ramparts topped by high oak- and pine-studded ridges.

Even more spectacular is the descent into the canyon itself (easiest by car or bus via Saltillo Highway 54—see the *Zapopan* section in the *West and North* chapter). As the elevation diminishes, the air becomes warmer and noticeably more humid; hanging vines and riots of tropical verdure cover the slope. The experience climaxes with the bountiful green mango, banana, and citrus groves that carpet both sides of the river at canyon bottom.

Climate

Historical evidence indicates that Spanish colonial authorities encouraged settlement in Guadalajara both for its easy access and its dry, temperate climate. A legion of latter-day visitors and residents still enjoy Guadalajara's famously balmy two-season climate, with the rainy season coming in summer and early fall, and the dry season in winter and spring.

Guadalajara's winter (December–February) days will usually be mild and springlike, climbing to around 75°F (24°C) by noon, with nights dropping to a temperate 45°F (5°C). Winter visitors should pack a sweater or light jacket: During cold snaps, Guadalajara's nighttime temperatures occasionally drop to near freezing.

April, May, and June, before the rains, are customarily Guadalajara's warmest months, with highs around 90°F (32°C). July, August, and September temperatures are moderated by the rains. Mornings are typically bright, warming to the low 80s (28°C). By afternoon, clouds sometimes gather and bring short, occasionally heavy thundershowers. Later the clouds usually part, the sun dries the pavements, and the temperature cools to a balmy 70°F (21°C)—perfect for strolling.

Moreover, the Guadalajara region is blessed with a diversity of microclimates. As most everywhere in Mexico, elevation rules the climate. If, on a Guadalajara winter day, you hanker for some warmth, simply travel 30 minutes downhill along Highway 54 north to the tropical canyon bottom of the Barranca and bask in the heat of perpetual summer—or get the same effect three hours south in Colima or Manzanillo, or four hours west in Puerto Vallarta.

Conversely, if on a warm June day you crave a spell of cool mountain breezes, simply travel two hours south to Jalisco's high mountain country—here you'll enjoy the fresh, pine-scented air and warm glow of an evening wood fire.

Flora and Fauna

The Guadalajara region's strongly distinct two-season (dry and wet) climate has fostered a highly diverse and tenacious array of native animal and plant species. In the metropolitan zone, however, benign conditions—including human hands and abundant year-round irrigation water—have nurtured nonnative plants that otherwise could not survive the region's November–May drought. Thus, many neighborhoods—especially in the leafy suburbs west of the downtown center—comprise a de facto botanical garden of exotics from all over the world. In a single afternoon stroll in a suburban neighborhood, a plant lover might recognize dozens of tropical and temperate varieties, such as sago palm, coconut, bamboo, orchids, roses, elms, maples, firs, California redwood, eucalyptus, ginkgo, bananas, begonias, azaleas, and more.

NATURAL VEGETATION ZONES

Outside of urban and agricultural districts, plants have evolved on their own. Eons of adaptation to wet and dry, sun and shade, and competition from animals and other plants have nurtured the natural cover of the Guadalajara region. Botanists recognize at least 14 major vegetation zones in Mexico, five of which lie within the Guadalajara region. Most often, travelers pass by long stretches of these zones, seeing only thickets, forests, and fields, without understanding what they're seeing. However, a little advance knowledge of what to expect can blossom into recognition and discovery, transforming the humdrum into the extraordinary.

Directly along the Guadalajara regional highways, travelers often pass long sections of the three most common vegetation zones: pine-oak forest, mesquite grassland, and tropical deciduous forest.

Pine-Oak Forest

Along the mountain highways (notably west of Guadalajara along the old, nontoll, two-lane Highway 15 toward Tequila and Magdalena, and south along Highway 80 toward Barra de Navidad), agricultural land gives way to temperate pine-oak forest, the Guadalajara region's most extensive vegetation zone. Here, many of Mexico's 112 oak and 39 pine species thrive. Oval two-inch cones and foot-long drooping needles (three to a cluster) make the **pino triste,** or sad pine *(Pinus lumholtzii)*, appear in severe need of water. Unlike many of Mexico's pines, it produces neither good lumber nor much turpentine, although it *is* prized by guitar makers for its wood.

Much more regal in bearing and commercially important are the tall **Chihuahua pine** *(Pinus chihuahuana)* and **Chinese pine** *(Pinus leiophylla)*. Both with reddish bark and yellow wood, they resemble the ponderosa pine of the western United States. You can tell them apart by their needles: the *pino prieto* (Chihuahua pine) has three to a cluster, while the *pino Chino* (Chinese pine) has five.

Pines often grow in stands mixed with **oaks,** which fall into two broad classifications—*encino* (evergreen, small-leafed) and *roble* (deciduous, large-leafed)—both much like the oaks that dot California hills and valleys. Clustered on their branches and scattered in the shade, *bellota* (acorns) distinctly mark them as oaks. The **Bosque de Primavera** is the most accessible and diverse pine-oak forest preserve in the Guadalajara region (see the *Getaways* chapter).

Mesquite Grassland

Although many outlying districts have been tamed into farmland, much of the country northeast of Guadalajara (notably along Highway 80 between Tepatitlán and San Juan de los Lagos) exhibits the landscape of the mesquite grassland vegetation zone, similar to the semiarid plateau land of the U.S. Southwest.

Despite its sometimes monotonous roadside aspect, the mesquite grassland nurtures surprisingly exotic and unusual plants. Among the most interesting is the **maguey** (mah-GAY), or century plant, so-called because it's said to bloom once, then die, after 100 years of growth—although its life span is usually closer to 50 years. The maguey and its cactuslike (but not true cacti) *Agave* relatives **(mescal, *lechugilla,* and sisal)** each grow as a roselike cluster of leathery, long, pointed, gray-green leaves, from which a single flower stalk eventually blooms.

Century plants themselves, which can grow as large as several feet tall and wide, thrive either wild or in cultivated fields in rank and file like a botanical army on parade. These fields, of the **blue agave** subspecies, are prominently visible from National Highway 15 west of Guadalajara. They are eventually harvested, crushed, fermented, and distilled into fiery 80-proof tequila, the most renowned of which comes from the town of Tequila on old Highway 15.

Watch for the mesquite grassland's **candelilla** *(Euphorbia antisyphillitica),* an odd cousin of the poinsettia, also a Mexico native. In contrast to the poinsettia, the *candelilla* resembles a tall (two- to three-foot) candle, with small white flowers scattered upward along its single vertical stem. Abundant wax on the many pencil-sized stalks that curve upward from the base is useful for anything from polishing your shoes to lubricating your car's distributor.

Equally exotic is the **sangre de drago**— 'blood of the dragon'—*(Jatropha dioica),* which also grows in a single meaty stem, but with two-inch-long lobed leaves and small white flowers. Break off a stem and out oozes a clear sap, which soon turns blood red.

Tropical Deciduous Forest

In well-watered lower-altitude areas, the pine-oak forest grades into tropical deciduous forest. This is the "friendly" or "short-tree" forest, blanketed by a tangle of summer-green leaves that fall in the dry winter to reveal thickets of branches.

Excursions by jeep or foot along shaded, off-highway tracks through the tropical deciduous forest can bestow delightful jungle scenes. During the rainy summer in the tropical deciduous forest's most verdant reaches, you might see vine-strewn thickets overhanging your path like a scene from some lost prehistoric world, where at any moment you expect a dinosaur to rear up.

Actually, the biological realities here are nearly as exotic. A four-foot-long green iguana, looking every bit as primitive as a dinosaur, sunbathes on a rock. Nearby, a spreading, solitary **strangler fig** *(Ficus padifolia)* stands, draped with hairy, hanging air roots (which in time plant themselves in the ground to support the branches). Its Mexican name, *matapalo* (killer tree), is gruesomely accurate: strangler figs often entwine themselves in death embraces with less aggressive tree-victims.

Other, more benign trees show bright fall reds and yellows, which blossom during the late winter with brilliant flowers—spider lily, cardinal sage, pink trumpet, poppylike yellowsilk *(pomposhuti),* and mouse-killer *(mala ratón)*—that swirl in the wind like cherry-blossom blizzards.

Nevertheless, unwary travelers must watch out for the poison oak–like *mala mujer* (evil woman) tree. The oil on its large five-fingered leaves can cause an itchy rash.

You can reach stretches of tropical deciduous forest easily, right at the edge of the Guadalajara city limits, either at the north end of **Guadalajara Zoo** (see the *West and North* chapter) or along Highway 54 downhill, past the village of Ixcateopan. At both of these spots, you can look down on to the lush (summer-green) coat of tropical deciduous forest that coats the Canyon of Réo Santiago, locally known as the Barranca.

Cloud Forest

Adventurous visitors who travel to certain remote, dewy mountainsides above 7,000 feet (2,134 meters) can explore the plant and wildlife community of the cloud forest. The Sierra Manantlán, a roadless de facto wilderness southeast of Autlán, Jalisco, and west of Colima city, preserves such a habitat. There, abundant cool fog nourishes forests of glacial-epoch remnant flora: tree ferns and lichen-draped pines and oaks, above a mossy carpet of orchids, bromeliads, and begonias.

High Coniferous Forest

The Guadalajara region's rarest, least accessible vegetation zone is the high coniferous forest, which swathes the slopes of lofty peaks, notably the Nevado de Colima (elev. 14,220 feet/4,335 meters) on the Jalisco-Colima border. This pristine alpine island, accessible only on horseback or by foot, nurtures stands of pines and spruce, laced by grassy meadows, similar to the higher Rocky Mountain slopes in the United States and Canada. Reigning over the lesser species is the regal **Montezuma pine** *(Pinus montezumae),* distinguished by its long, pendulous cones and rough, ruddy bark, reminiscent of the sugar pine of the western United States.

For many more details of Mexico's feast of roadside plants, see M. Walter Pesman's delightful *Meet Flora Mexicana* (unfortunately out of print, but major libraries may have copies). Also informative is the popular paperback *Handbook of Mexican Roadside Flora,* by Charles T. Mason Jr. and Patricia B. Mason.

WILDLIFE

Despite continued habitat destruction—forests are logged, wetlands filled, rivers dammed—great swaths of the Guadalajara region still abound with wildlife. Common in the temperate pine-oak forest highlands are mammals familiar to U.S. residents: mountain lion (puma), coyote, fox *(zorro),* rabbit *(conejo),* and badger *(tejón).*

However, the tropical deciduous forests are home to fascinating species normally seen only in zoos north of the border. The reality of this dawns on travelers when they glimpse something exotic, such as raucous, screeching swarms of small green parrots rising from the roadside, or an armadillo or coati crossing the road in front of their car or bus.

Population pressures have nevertheless decreased wild habitats, endangering many previously abundant animal species. If you are lucky (and quiet) as you hike a remote forest trail, you may get a view of the endangered striped cat, the **ocelot** *(tigrillo),* or its smaller relative, the **margay.** On such an excursion, if you are really fortunate, you may hear the chesty roar or catch a glimpse of a jaguar, the fabled *el tigre.*

El Tigre

Each hill has its own *tigre,* says a Mexican proverb. With black spots spread over a yellow-tan coat, sometimes stretching more than six feet (two meters) and weighing 200 pounds (90 kg), the typical jaguar resembles a muscular spotted leopard. Although hunted since prehistory and now endangered, the jaguar lives on in the Guadalajara region. It hunts along thickly forested stream bottoms and foothills. Unlike the mountain lion, the jaguar will eat any game. Jaguars have even been known to wait patiently for fish in rivers and to stalk beaches for turtle and egg dinners. If they have a favorite food, it is probably the piglike wild peccary, *jabalí.* Experienced hunters agree that no two jaguars will have the same prey in their stomachs.

Although humans have died of wounds inflicted by cornered jaguars, there is little or no hard evidence that they eat humans, despite legends to the contrary.

Armadillos, Coatis, and Bats

The cat-sized armadillos are mammals that act and look like opossums but carry reptilianlike shells. If you see one, remain still, and it may walk right up and sniff your foot before it recognizes you and scuttles back into the woods.

A common inhabitant of the tropical deciduous forest is the raccoonlike coati *(tejón, pisote).* In the wild, coatis like shady stream banks, often congregating in large troops of 15–30 individuals. They are identified by their short brown or tan fur, small round ears, long nose, and straight, vertically held tail. They make endearing pets; the first coati you see may be one on a string offered for sale at a local market.

Mexican bats *(murciélagos)* are widespread, with at least 126 species compared to 37 in the United States. In Mexico, as everywhere, bats are feared and misunderstood. As sunset approaches, many bat species come out of

© BRUCE WHIPPERMAN

Coatimundis make congenial family pets.

their hiding places and flit through the air in search of insects. Most people, sitting outside enjoying the early evening, will mistake their darting silhouettes for those of birds, who, except for owls, do not generally fly at night.

Bats are often locally called *vampiros*, even though only three relatively rare Mexican species actually feed on the blood of mammals (nearly always cattle) and birds.

The many nonvampire Mexican bats carry their vampire cousins' odious reputation with forbearance. They go about their good works, pollinating flowers, clearing the air of pesky gnats and mosquitoes, ridding cornfields of mice, and dropping seeds, thereby restoring forests.

BIRDS

Despite the city environment, plenty of birds make the Guadalajara metropolitan area their home. Lots of these are kin to the familiar temperate species—busy woodpeckers *(pájaro carpintero)*, soaring turkey vultures *(zopilotes)* and hawks *(halcones)*, scurrying banded quail

(codorniz), solitary mottled owls *(tecolotes)*, and lots of hummingbirds *(colibris)*.

Reservoirs and marshy ground in suburban and adjacent agricultural areas provide habitats for water birds, such as egrets and herons *(garzas)*, especially the large, long-necked snowy egret and its even larger cousin, the majestic great blue heron. Other familiar waterborne residents—black cormorants and their cousins, the snake-necked anhingas—and also the dark brown lily-walkers *(jacanas)*, stalk, nest, and preen in local lagoons and wetlands.

In forest zones, especially in semitropical lower-altitude habitats, the choices include most of the above plus exotic species seen only in U.S. and Canadian zoos. These include several varieties of small parrots, such as the lilac-crowned parrot and the Mexican parrotlet, and a number of spectacular species, such as the mountain trogon *(Trogon mexicanus)*, sometimes known as the *pájaro bandera* (flag bird) for its red, white, and green coloration, identical to the Mexican flag. Nearly as spectacular is the yellow-breasted kiskadee flycatcher *(Pitangus sulpuratus)*, known locally as the "Luis" bird because it seems to call this name (with a Spanish accent, of course) repeatedly.

REPTILES AND AMPHIBIANS
Snakes and Gila Monsters

Mexico has 460-odd snake species, the vast majority shy and nonpoisonous; they will get out of your way if you give plenty of warning. In Mexico, as everywhere, poisonous snakes have been largely eradicated in city and tourist areas. In brush or forest habitats, carry a stick or a machete and beat the bushes ahead of you while watching where you put your feet. When hiking or rock-climbing in the country, don't put your hand in niches you can't see into.

The most venomous of Mexican snakes is the **coral snake** *(coralillo)*, which occurs as about two dozen species, all with multicolored bright bands that always include red. Although relatively rare, small, and shy, coral

Although endangered, *garrovos* (iguanas) still can be found in semitropical lowland zones of the Guadalajara region.

© BRUCE WHIPPERMAN

snakes occasionally inflict serious, sometimes fatal bites.

More aggressive and generally more dangerous is the Mexican **rattlesnake** *(cascabel)* and its viper relative, the **fer-de-lance** *(Bothrops atrox)*. About the same in size (up to six feet) and appearance as the rattlesnake, the fer-de-lance (which confines itself to tropical forest habitats) is known by various local names, such as *nauyaca, cuatro narices, palanca,* and *barba amarilla.*

It is potentially more hazardous than the rattlesnake because it lacks a warning rattle.

The Gila monster (confined in Mexico to northern Sonora) and its southern tropical relative, the yellow-spotted, black **escorpión** *(Heloderma horridum),* are the world's only poisonous lizards. Despite its beaded skin and menacing, fleshy appearance, the *escorpión* only bites when severely provoked. Even then, its venom is rarely fatal.

History

Once upon a time, perhaps as early as 40,000 years ago, the first bands of hunters, possibly paddling rafts, kayaks, or canoes along the coastline or trudging overland following the great game herds, crossed from Siberia to the American continent. They drifted southward, many of them eventually settling in the lush highland valleys of Mexico.

Among the earliest human remains found in the Guadalajara region are 10,000-year-old arrowheads in the seminal Clovis style (of the earlier remains, found at Clovis, New Mexico). Much later, perhaps around 5000 B.C., these early people began gathering and grinding the seeds of a hardy grass that required only the summer rains to thrive. After generations of selective breeding, *teocentli* (sacred seed), the grain that we call maize or corn, led to prosperity.

Early local residents left evidence of their growing sophistication. Ceramic jugs with handles, artfully decorated vases, and animal-, plant-, and human-motif figurines, between 1,500 and 2,500 years old, have been unearthed near Cerro El Tecolote, San Marcos, and Zacoalco, not far west of Guadalajara.

EARLY MEXICAN CIVILIZATIONS

With abundant food, settlements grew and leisure classes arose—artists, architects, warriors, and ruler-priests—all of whom had time to think and create. Using a calendar, they harnessed the constant wheel of the firmament to life on earth, defining the days to plant, harvest, feast, travel, and trade. Eventually, grand cities arose.

Teotihuacán

Teotihuacán, with a population of perhaps 250,000 in the beginning centuries of the Christian era, was one of the world's great metropolises. Its epic monuments still stand not far north of Mexico City: the towering Pyramid of the Sun at the terminal of a grand, 150-foot-wide ceremonial avenue facing a great Pyramid of the Moon. Along the avenue sprawls a monumental temple-court surrounded by scowling, ruby-eyed effigies of Quetzalcoatl, the feathered serpent god of gods.

Its inhabitants gradually abandoned Teotihuacán mysteriously around A.D. 650, leaving a host of former vassal states to tussle among themselves. The Guadalajara region's people— notably the Tecuejes and Cocas, but also the Huicholes, Nahuas, and Purépechas—were among these. **Iztepete,** one of their most monumental constructions yet uncovered, stands at Guadalajara's southwest edge. Recent excavations indicate that it was an early ceremonial site with distinct Teotihuacán architectural influence, built in several stages, starting around the beginning of the Christian era.

The Aztecs

Among the several civilizations that flowered in Mexico following the fall of Teotihuacán were the Aztecs, a collection of seven aggressive subtribes that migrated, beginning around A.D. 1100, from a mysterious western land of Aztlán (Place of the Herons) into the lake-filled valley that Mexico City now occupies.

The Aztecs survived by being forced to fight for every piece of ground they occupied. Within a century, the Aztecs' dominant tribe, whose members called themselves the "México," had clawed its way to dominion over the Valley of Mexico. With the tribute labor that their emperors extracted from local vassal tribes, the México, beginning around A.D. 1325, built an imperial capital, Tenochtitlán, on an island in the middle of the valley-lake. From there, Aztec armies, not unlike Roman legions, marched out and subdued kingdoms for hundreds of miles in all directions. They returned with the spoils of conquest: gold, brilliant feathers, precious jewels, and captives, whom they sacrificed by the thousands as food for their gods.

Among those gods they feared was Quetzalcoatl—tradition held that he was bearded and fair-skinned. This turned out to be a remarkable, fateful coincidence. When the bearded, fair-skinned Castilian **Hernán Cortés** landed on Mexico's eastern coast on April 22, 1519, it happened to be the very year that legends said Quetzalcoatl would return.

THE CONQUEST

Although a generation had elapsed since Columbus founded Spain's West Indian colonies, returns had been meager. Scarcity of gold and of native workers, most of whom fell victim to European diseases, turned adventurous Spanish eyes westward once again, toward rumored riches beyond the setting sun.

Preliminary excursions piqued Spanish interest, and Cortés was commissioned by Spanish governor Diego Velázquez to explore further. Cortés, then only 34, had left his Cuban base in February 1519 with an expedition of 11 small ships, 550 men, 16 horses, and a few small cannons. By the time he landed in Mexico, he was burdened by a murderous crew. His men, mostly soldiers of fortune hearing stories of the great Aztec empire west beyond the mountains, had realized the impossible odds they faced and became restive.

Cortés, however, cut short any thoughts of mutiny by burning his ships. As he led his grumbling but resigned band of adventurers toward the Aztec capital of Tenochtitlán, Cortés played Quetzalcoatl to the hilt, awing local chiefs. Coaxed by **Doña Marina** (Malinche), Cortés's native translator-mistress, local chiefs began to add their warrior-armies to Cortés's march against their Aztec overlords.

Moctezuma, Lord of Tenochtitlán

Once inside the walls of Tenochtitlán, the Aztecs' Venice-like island-city, the Spaniards were dazzled by gardens, animals, gold and palaces, and a great pyramid-enclosed square where tens of thousands of people bartered goods gathered from all over the empire. Tenochtitlán, with perhaps a quarter of a million people, was the grand capital of an empire more than equal to any in Europe at the time.

But Moctezuma, the lord of the empire,

MALINCHE

Hernán Cortés may have become a mere historical footnote if it hadn't been for Doña Marina (whom he received as a gift from a local chief). Doña Marina, speaking both Spanish and native tongues, soon became Cortés's interpreter, go-between, and negotiator. She persuaded a number of important chiefs to ally themselves with Cortés against the Aztecs. Clever and opportunistic, Doña Marina was a crucial strategist in Cortés's deadly game of divide and conquer. She eventually bore Cortés a son and lived in honor and riches for many years, profiting greatly from the Spaniards' exploitation of the Mexicans.

Latter-day Mexicans do not honor her by the gentle title of Doña Marina, however. They call her Malinche, after the volcano – the ugly, treacherous scar on the Mexican landscape – and curse her as the female Judas who betrayed her country to the Spanish. *Malinchismo* has become known as the tendency to love things foreign and hate things Mexican.

was unsure if Cortés was really the returned Quetzalcoatl—he was frozen by fear and foreboding. He quickly found himself hostage to Cortés, then died a few months later, during a riot against Spanish greed and brutality. On July 1, 1520, on what came to be called *el noche triste* (the sad night), the besieged Cortés and his men broke out, fleeing for their lives along a lake causeway from Tenochtitlán, carrying Moctezuma's treasure. Many of them drowned beneath their burdens of gold booty, while the survivors hacked a bloody retreat through thousands of screaming Aztec warriors, finally reaching the safety of the lakeshore.

A year later, reinforced by a small fleet of armed sailboats and 100,000 native warrior-allies, Cortés retook Tenochtitlán. The stubborn defenders, led by Cuauhtémoc, Moctezuma's nephew, fell by the tens of thousands beneath a smoking hail of Spanish grapeshot. But the

Aztecs refused to surrender, forcing Cortés to destroy the city in order to take it.

The triumphant conquistador soon rebuilt the city in the Spanish image; Cortés's cathedral and main public buildings—the present *zócalo,* or central square, of Mexico City—still rest upon the foundations of Moctezuma's pyramids.

NEW SPAIN

With the Valley of Mexico firmly in his grip, Cortés sent his lieutenants south, north, and west to extend the limits of his domain. Alonso de Ávalos commanded the first expedition to the present region of Guadalajara; later, in 1524, Cortés sent his cousin, Francisco Cortés de Buenaventura, in charge of a company of soldiers and cavalry, to pacify the chiefdom of Xalisco, west of Guadalajara (in the present state of Nayarit). The Spanish later converted the name to Jalisco ("place built on the surface of sand"), which later became the name of the present-day Mexican state.

Within a few years, most of Mexico—a realm several times the size and population of old Spain—was under Cortés's control. His conquest now consolidated, Cortés, in a letter to King Charles V, christened his empire "New Spain of the Ocean Sea."

The Missionaries

While Cortés and his conquistador officers subjugated the native people, missionaries began arriving to teach, heal, and baptize them. A dozen Franciscan brothers impressed the natives and conquistadors alike by trekking the entire 300-mile stony path from Veracruz to Mexico City in 1523. Missionary authorities generally enjoyed a sympathetic ear from Charles V and his successors, who earnestly pursued Spain's Christian mission, especially when it dovetailed with its political and economic goals.

Trouble in New Spain

Increasingly after 1525, the crown, through the Council of the Indies, began to wrest power away from Cortés and his lieutenants, many of whom had been granted rights of *encomienda:* taxes and labor of an indigenous district. From the king's point of view, tribute pesos collected by *encomenderos* from their indigenous serfs reduced the gold that would otherwise flow to the crown. Moreover, many *encomenderos* callously enslaved and sold their native wards for quick profit. Such abuses, coupled with European-introduced diseases, began to reduce the native population at an alarming rate.

No region of New Spain suffered more from Spanish depredations than the west. In the latter 1520s, with New Spain seemingly secure, Cortés returned to Europe for three years, leaving one of his senior officers, **Nuño Beltrán de Guzmán,** in charge in Mexico City.

It quickly turned out that Guzmán had plans of his own. He wasted no time aggrandizing himself and his friends by attacking and burning villages and selling the natives into slavery. Alarmed by word of Guzmán's excesses, the king dispatched a new royal *audiencia* (executive-judicial panel) to take control from Guzmán. Seeing the writing on the wall, Guzmán cleared out beforehand, three days before Christmas in 1529. He was in command of a small renegade army of adventurers bent upon finding new riches in western Mexico.

Guzmán first encountered the natives of the Valley of Atemajac and their queen at Tonalá, in the eastern suburb of present-day Guadalajara. Though **Cihualpilli** and her subjects resisted Guzmán's brutality with a stiff armed resistance from their hilltop stronghold—now called Cerro de la Reina (Hill of the Queen), at the north edge of Tonalá—they were no match for Spanish armor and cannons. They surrendered after a bloody siege. Guzmán and his men celebrated their victory at Guadalajara's first mass, on March 25, 1530.

The Many Guadalajaras

As soon as he had pacified the Valley of Atemajac, Guzmán began looking for a settlement site to name after his old hometown, Guadalajara, back in Spain. The first settlement called Guadalajara was founded on January 5, 1532, about 55 miles (90 km) to the north, near Nochistlán, in present-day Zacatecas state.

But the local natives, the seminomadic Caxcanes, refused to work and rebelled. With no laborers to do the work, the ragged band of Spanish settlers and their military escort trudged back south across the Río Santiago canyon to Tonalá in 1533.

Guzmán, however, wanted Tonalá, the richest town in the valley, for himself, and sent the colonists back north across the river, to Tlacotlán, where their refounded Guadalajara lasted until 1541. Although the settlers didn't know it at the time, the crown, on November 8, 1539, granted Guadalajara the rank of city, complete with the coat of arms that the city retains to the present day.

By 1541, however, Guzmán was gone, having been arrested in the mid-1530s by a powerful and incorruptible new viceroy, **Antonio de Mendoza,** and sent back to prison in Spain. Rebellious natives again sent Guadalajara's mere 200 tattered settlers fleeing Tlacotlán, back to the Valley of Atemajac, where, near the exact center of modern Guadalajara, they founded their city for the final time on February 14, 1542.

The Mixtón War

Although Nuño de Guzmán was gone, his cruel legacy remained in the hatred and resentment that his brutality had raised among the native peoples of western Mexico. Deadly rebellion, led by Caxcane chief Tenamaxtli, broke out in 1540 and led to slaughter, pillage, and retribution on both sides. The uprising radiated from the Cerro de Mixtón, an impenetrable maze of ridges and deep canyons, in the present municipality of Apozol, about 60 miles (100 km) north of Guadalajara. From there, native guerrilla bands attacked Spanish settlers and garrisons, retiring to their Mixtón hideaways with impunity, leaving terror and destruction in their wake.

Viceroy Mendoza, alarmed at the death in battle of Pedro de Alvarado (the conqueror of Guatemala), took personal command of Spanish forces in January 1541. Mendoza, arguably

the best viceroy that New Spain ever had, managed to secure a truce within a year. He was greatly aided by the apparition of the **Virgin of the Pacification,** a mysterious figure swathed in a brilliant light, witnessed by a throng of rebellious natives who were so awestruck that they laid down their arms. The very same miraculous figure, now called the Virgin of Zapopan, is feted in a grand procession of many hundreds of thousands of Guadalajarans every October 12.

COLONIAL GUADALAJARA

In 1542, the Council of the Indies, through Viceroy Mendoza, promulgated its liberal New Laws of the Indies. They rested on high moral ground: The only Christian justification for New Spain was the souls and welfare of the native Mexicans. Slavery was outlawed, and the colonists' *encomienda* rights over land and the native peoples were eventually to revert to the crown.

Despite near-rebellion by angry colonists, Mendoza and his successors kept the lid on New Spain. Although some *encomenderos* held their privileges into the 18th century, chattel slavery of native Mexicans was abolished in New Spain 300 years before Abraham Lincoln's Emancipation Proclamation.

Meanwhile, with peace established, colonists and missionaries streamed west from Mexico City to found new settlements around Guadalajara and Zacatecas. Others continued west, to Santiago de Compostela (in present-day Nayarit), north to Culiacán, and south to Colima.

In 1548, recognizing western Mexico's growing importance, colonial authorities created **Nueva Galicia,** a domain that encompassed a vast western territory, including the present-day states of Jalisco, Nayarit, Colima, Aguascalientes, and parts of Zacatecas, San Luis Potosí, Sinaloa, and Durango. Nueva Galicia's governing *audiencia,* originally headquartered in Compostela, was shifted to Guadalajara in 1560.

Although peace reigned, sleepy Guadalajara grew only slowly at first. *Audiencias* came, served, and went; newcomers put down roots; friars built country churches; and the original settlers' rich heirs played while their indigenous charges labored.

Expansion to the Californias

In the 1700s, exploration and expansion accelerated Nueva Galicia's growth. Missionaries pushed north; Jesuit fathers Eusebio Francisco Kino and Juan Maria Salvatierra established a string of missions on both coasts of the Gulf of California. Guadalajara's merchants benefited as their town, no longer the end of the road to nowhere, became a supply hub for a burgeoning western domain.

Propelled by British, French, and Russian pressure in the north Pacific, the Spanish established a new port and Pacific naval headquarters in 1768 at San Blas, on the coast west of Guadalajara. After the king expelled the Jesuits in 1767, Spanish colonial authorities asked the Franciscans, led by **Padre Junípero Serra,** to revitalize the Jesuit mission. They answered the call, using Guadalajara as their supply center and San Blas as their jumping-off point, sailing north to found dozens of mission settlements as far north as San Francisco, in Alta California, by 1800.

Guadalajara's growing population demanded more and better goods; entrepreneurs responded with dozens of small new factories to supply textiles, leather, soap, and liquor. Increased commerce led to construction of better roads and bridges to connect Guadalajara with Colima, San Blas, and Mexico City. The ferment raised Guadalajara from a backwater of 6,000 souls in 1703 to a bustling city of 35,000 a century later.

The immigration influx overtaxed existing facilities and led to the construction of two of Guadalajara's most distinguished institutions: the **Hospital of Belén** and the **Hospicio Cabañas,** respectively promoted by Bishops Antonio Alcalde and Juan Cruz Ruíz de Cabañas. (Both institutions, now known as the Hospital Civil and the Centro Cultural Cabañas, respectively, continue their benevolent missions.)

The Church

Religious activity in colonial Mexico was rigorously confined to Catholic rites. An active Inquisition watched vigilantly for any straying brethren, be they errant Protestants or Jews, or native Mexicans covertly worshipping their old gods.

Nevertheless, the church had carried out its original compassionate Christian mission. It had protected the native Mexicans from the colonists' excesses, taught them useful trades, and moderated their toil. As a result, the native population, which by 1600 had sunk to a mere 10 percent of the original numbers, had doubled by 1800. Moderate prosperity even allowed for a few luxuries. Indigenous folks looked forward to feast days, when they would dress up, parade their patron saint, drink *pulque,* dance in the plaza, and ooh and aah at the fireworks.

The church profited from the rosy status quo. The biblical tithe—one-tenth of everything earned—filled clerical coffers. By 1800, the church owned half of Mexico.

Furthermore, both the clergy and the military were doubly privileged. They enjoyed the right of *fuero* (exemption from civil law) and could only be prosecuted by ecclesiastical or military courts.

Despite its faults, Spain's Mexican Empire, by most contemporary measures, was prospering in 1800. The Indian labor force was both docile and growing, and the galleons carried increasing tonnage of silver and gold across the Atlantic to Spain. The authorities, however, failed to recognize that Mexico had changed over 300 years.

Criollos, the New Mexicans

Nearly three centuries of colonial rule gave rise to a burgeoning population of more than a million criollos—Mexican-born, pure European descendants of Spanish colonists, many rich and educated—to whom power was denied.

High government, church, and military office had always been the preserve of a tiny minority of *peninsulares*—whites born in Spain.

THE VIRGIN OF GUADALUPE

Conversion of Mexico's native population to the Catholic religion was sparked by the vision of Juan Diego, a humble farmer. On the hill of Tepayac north of Mexico City in 1531, Juan Diego saw a brown-skinned version of the Virgin Mary enclosed in a dazzling aura of light. She told him to build a shrine in her memory on that spot, where the Aztecs had long worshipped their "earth mother," Tonantzín. Juan Diego's brown virgin told him to go to the cathedral and relay her instruction to Archbishop Zumárraga.

The archbishop, as expected, turned his nose up at Juan Diego's story. The vision returned, however, and this time Juan Diego's virgin realized that a miracle was necessary. She ordered him to pick some roses at the spot where she had first appeared to him (a true miracle, since roses previously had been unknown in the vicinity) and take them to the archbishop. Juan Diego wrapped the roses in his rude fiber cape, returned to the cathedral, and placed the wrapped roses at the archbishop's feet. When he opened the offering, Zumárraga gasped: Imprinted on the cape was an image of the virgin herself – proof positive of a genuine miracle.

In the centuries since Juan Diego, the brown virgin – La Virgen Morena, or Nuestra Señora La Virgen de Guadalupe – has blended native and Catholic elements into something uniquely Mexican. In doing so, she has become the virtual patroness of Mexico, the beloved symbol of Mexico for *indígenas*, mestizos, *negros*, and criollos alike.

Virtually every Guadalajara-region town and village celebrates the cherished memory of their Virgin of Guadalupe on December 12. This celebration, however joyful, is but one of the many fiestas that Mexicans, especially the *indígenas*, live for. Each village holds its local fiesta in honor of their patron saint, who is often a thinly veiled sit-in for a local preconquest deity. Themes appear Spanish – Christian vs. Moors, devils vs. priests – but the native element is strong, sometimes dominant.

Pope John Paul II, in the summer of 2002, journeyed to Mexico to perform a historic gesture. Before millions of joyous faithful, on July 31, 2002, the frail pontiff elevated Juan Diego to sainthood, thus making him Latin America's first indigenous person to be so honored.

Criollos could only watch in disgust as unlettered, unskilled *peninsulares,* derisively called *gachupines,* "wearers of spurs," were boosted to authority over them.

Mestizos, Indígenas, and African Mexicans

Upper-class luxury existed by virtue of the sweat of Mexico's mestizo (mixed), *indígena* (native), and *negro* laborers and servants. African slaves were imported in large numbers during the 17th century after typhus, smallpox, and measles epidemics wiped out most of the *indígena* population. Although African Mexicans contributed significantly (crafts, healing arts, dance, music, drums, and marimba), they had arrived last and experienced discrimination from everyone.

INDEPENDENCE

Although the criollos stood high above the mestizo, *indígena,* and *negro* underclasses, that seemed little compensation for the false smiles, deep bows, and costly bribes that *gachupines* demanded. By 1800 the republican revolutions in the United States and France had spilled over all the way to Guadalajara. Revolutionary ferment had led to higher aspirations, notably by rich criollo merchants and professionals, who were ripe for rebellion.

The chance for change came during the aftermath of the French invasion of Spain in 1808, when Napoléon Bonaparte replaced Spain's King Ferdinand VII with his brother Joseph. Most *peninsulares* backed King Ferdinand VII; most criollos, however, talked and dreamed of independence. One such group, urged on by a firebrand parish priest, acted.

El Grito de Dolores

"¡Viva México! Death to the gachupines!" cried **Father Miguel Hidalgo** passionately from the church balcony in the Guanajuato town of Dolores on September 16, 1810, igniting action. A mostly *indígena*, machete-wielding army of 20,000 coalesced around Hidalgo and his compatriots, Ignacio Allende and Juan Aldama. Their ragtag force raged out of control around Guanajuato, massacring hated *gachupines* and pillaging their homes.

The insurgency quickly spread to Guadalajara, where, on November 11, 1810, an irregular force led by Hidalgo's compatriots, Manuel Hidobro and José "El Amo" Antonio Torres, overwhelmed the small royalist garrison. Hidalgo arrived two weeks later and pushed his insurgency by organizing a revolutionary local government, eliminating royal taxes, reiterating the abolition of slavery, and urging the publication of Latin America's first revolutionary newspaper, *El Depertador Americano,* by Francisco Severo Maldonado, on December 20, 1810.

Emboldened, Hidalgo (now "Generalisimo") marched on Mexico City. But, unnerved by stiff royalist resistance west of the city, Hidalgo retreated and regrouped east of Guadalajara. Although its numbers had swollen to 80,000, Hidalgo's poorly equipped and ill-trained army was no match for the disciplined, 6,000-strong pursuing royalist force of General Felix Calleja. Hidalgo suffered a disastrous defeat at Calderón Bridge on a tributary of the Río Lerma-Santiago, not far east of Guadalajara, on January 17, 1811. He fled north toward the United States, but was soon apprehended, defrocked, and executed. His head and those of his comrades hung from the walls of the Guanajuato granary for 10 years in compensation for the slaughter of 138 *gachupines* by Hidalgo's army.

Meanwhile, as Calleja pacified the Guadalajara region, his lieutenant, General José de la Cruz, marched north and retook Zacate-

cas; Calleja captured and executed rebel commander "El Amo" Torres. Later, Cruz's forces erased the last pockets of resistance around Lake Chapala.

The 10-Year Struggle

Other *insurgentes* carried on the fight. A mestizo former student of Hidalgo, **José María Morelos,** led a revolutionary shadow government in the present states of Guerrero and Oaxaca for four years until he was apprehended and executed in December 1815.

As Morelos's compatriot, **Vicente Guerrero,** continued a war of attrition, a new government in Spain approved a new, liberal constitution that radically reduced the king's authority. Mexican conservatives, with the royal rug thus pulled out from beneath their feet, began linking with the Mexican insurgents. In February 1820, Guerrero and criollo royalist Brigadier Agustín de Iturbide announced the Plan de Iguala, promising the renowned Trigarantes (Three Guarantees)—Independence, Catholicism, and Equality—which their united army would enforce.

As royalist resistance gradually melted away, Nueva Galicia became independent before New Spain, when, on June 13, 1821, royalist Brigadier Pedro Celestino Negrete, with the influential backing of Bishop Cabañas, signed on to the Plan de Iguala in Tlaquepaque. Nueva Galicia's military commander, General de la Cruz, fled, and local authorities formally declared independence. On September 21, 1821, Iturbide rode triumphantly into Mexico City at the head of his army of Trigarantes. Mexico was independent at last.

The Rise and Fall of Agustín I

Iturbide, crowned Emperor Agustín I by the bishop of Guadalajara on July 21, 1822, soon lost his charisma. In a pattern that became sadly predictable for generations of topsy-turvy Mexican politics, an ambitious garrison commander issued a *pronunciamiento,* or declaration of rebellion, against him; old revolutionary heroes endorsed a plan to install a republic. Iturbide, his braid tattered and brass tarnished, abdicated in February 1823.

Guadalajarans, led by businessman Luis Quintanar, became the first to declare statehood—'the free and sovereign state of Xalisco'—on June 16, 1823, before the federal republic was even formed. Finally, on January 31, 1824, the new national congress in Mexico City followed with the act of Mexican federation that conferred statehood upon "Jalisco."

Prisciliano Sanchéz became Jalisco's first constitutional governor. He and his immediate successors initiated liberal programs to broaden political and religious freedoms, lower taxes, stimulate commerce, limit church and military special privileges, and create Guadalajara's first public institution of higher education, the Instituto de Ciencias del Estado (State Scientific Institute).

The Disastrous Era of Santa Anna

Despite well-intentioned attempts at reform, independence had solved little except to expel the *peninsulares*. With an illiterate populace and no experience in self-government, Mexicans began a tragic 40-year love affair with a fantasy: the general on the white horse, the gold-braided hero who could save them from themselves.

Antonio López de Santa Anna, the eager 28-year-old military commander of Veracruz whose *pronunciamiento* had pushed Iturbide from his white horse, maneuvered to gradually replace him. Meanwhile, throughout the late 1820s the federal government teetered on the edge of disaster as the presidency bounced between liberal and conservative hands six times in three years. During the last of these upheavals, Santa Anna jumped to prominence by defeating an abortive Spanish attempt at counterrevolution in Tampico in 1829. Santa Anna was called "The Victor of Tampico."

In 1833, the government was bankrupt; mobs demanded the ouster of conservative President Anastasio Bustamante, who had executed the rebellious old revolutionary hero, Vicente Guerrero. Santa Anna issued a *pronunciamiento* against Bustamante; Congress obliged, elevating Santa Anna to "Liberator of the Republic" and naming him president in March 1833.

Santa Anna would pop in and out of the presidency like a jack-in-the-box 10 more times before 1855. First, he foolishly lost Texas to rebellious Anglo settlers in 1836; then he lost his leg (which was buried with full military honors) fighting the emperor of France.

Santa Anna's greatest debacle, however, was to declare war on the United States with just 1,839 pesos in the treasury. With his forces poised to defend Mexico City against a relatively small 10,000-man American invasion force, Santa Anna inexplicably withdrew. United States marines surged into the "Halls of Montezuma," Chapultepec Castle, where Mexico's six beloved Niños Héroes cadets fell in the losing cause on September 13, 1847.

In the subsequent Treaty of Guadalupe Hidalgo, Mexico lost two-fifths of its territory—the present states of New Mexico, Arizona, California, Nevada, Utah, and Colorado—to the United States. Mexicans have never forgotten; they have looked upon gringos with a combination of awe, envy, admiration, and disgust ever since.

For Santa Anna, however, enough was not enough. Called back as "His Most Serene Highness" and elevated to president for the 11th and last time in 1853, Santa Anna financed his final extravagances by selling off a slice of what later became southern New Mexico and Arizona for $10 million: the Gadsden Purchase.

Jalisco liberals, however, had seen enough. They formulated the "Plan of Ayutla" to remove Santa Anna, preparing to storm Guadalajara in August 1855. Santa Anna, however, preempted their plan and cleared out forever. Guadalajara federal authorities gave up without a fight, opening the door for a liberal sweep that vaulted Santos Degollado into the Jalisco governorship.

Fortunately for Guadalajarans, the turbulence and destruction of the Santa Anna years had largely spared Guadalajara. Since independence, the city had finished important public works, added new factories and businesses, and grown from a population of 47,000 in 1822 to 68,000 by 1856.

REFORM, CIVIL WAR, AND INTERVENTION

Despite the demise of Santa Anna, Mexico still suffered from a severe political split. While conservatives searched for a king to replace Santa Anna, liberals plunged ahead with three controversial reform laws: the **Ley Juárez, Ley Lerdo,** and **Ley Iglesias.** These *reformas,* augmented by a new Constitution of 1857, directly attacked the privilege and power of Mexico's landlords, clergy, and generals. The reforms abolished *fueros* (the separate military and church courts), reduced huge landed estates, and stripped the church of its excess property and power.

Conservative generals, priests, *hacendados* (landholders), and their mestizo and *indígena* followers revolted; President Comonfort attempted a coup d'état. In response, liberals elevated Vice President **Benito Juárez** to the presidency, but conservative forces sent Juárez and his government fleeing to Guanajuato, then Guadalajara.

Guadalajara, teetering between liberal and conservative control, turned out to be an insecure perch for Juarez's government. Thanks to the help of his ministers and his liberal Guadalajara friends, Juárez barely escaped assassination, then arrest, by fleeing with his ministers to Manzanillo, then on to safe haven in Veracruz. There, Juárez ran the government while the War of the Reform (not unlike the U.S. Civil War) raged in the countryside. Finally, Juárez's victorious liberal armies captured Guadalajara for the last time, on November 3, 1860, then paraded triumphantly in Mexico City on New Year's Day, 1861.

Juárez and Maximilian

Benito Juárez, the leading *reformista,* had won the day. Like his contemporary, Abraham Lincoln, Juárez—of pure Zapotec Indian blood—overcame his humble origins to become a lawyer, a champion of justice, and the president who held his country together during a terrible civil war. Also like Lincoln, Juárez had little time to savor his triumph.

After President Juárez suspended debt payment, Imperial France invaded Mexico in January 1862. At the end of two costly years of fighting, the French pushed Juárez's liberal army into the hills, occupying Guadalajara from January 1864 until December 1866. In Mexico City, the French installed the king whom Mexican conservatives thought the country needed. Austrian Archduke Maximilian and his wife Carlota were crowned emperor and empress of Mexico in June 1864.

The well-meaning but naive Emperor Maximilian I was surprised that some of his subjects resented his presence. Meanwhile, Juárez refused to yield, stubbornly performing his constitutional duties in a somber black carriage one jump ahead of the French occupying army. The climax came in May 1867, when Juarez's forces besieged and defeated Maximilian's army at Querétaro. Juárez, giving no quarter, sternly ordered Maximilian's execution by firing squad on June 19, 1867.

Peace reigned in Jalisco, but not for long. A native rebellion—not unlike the colonial-era Mixtón War—led by indigenous leader Manuel Lozada (the "Tigre de Álica"), spread from Nayarit to Jalisco. It was finally stopped at the outskirts of Guadalajara by General Ramón Corona on January 28, 1873.

THE PORFIRIATO, REVOLUTION, AND STABILIZATION

Juárez worked day and night at the double task of reconstruction and reform. He won reelection but died, exhausted, in July 1872.

The death of Juárez, stoic partisan of reform, signaled hope to Mexico's conservatives. They soon got their wish: General **Don Porfirio Díaz,** the "Coming Man," was elected president in 1876.

Pax Porfiriana

Don Porfirio is often remembered wistfully, as old Italians remember Mussolini: "He was a bit rough, but, dammit, at least he made the trains run on time."

Although Porfirio Díaz's humble Oaxaca mestizo origins were not unlike Juárez's, Díaz was not a democrat. When he was a general, his officers took no captives; when he was president, his country police, the *rurales,* shot prisoners in the act of "trying to escape."

"Order and Progress," in that sequence, ruled Mexico for 34 years. Foreign investment flowed into the country; new railroads brought the products of shiny factories, mines, and farms to modernized Gulf and Pacific ports. Mexico balanced its budget, repaid foreign debt, and became a respected member of the family of nations.

Most Guadalajarans united around Díaz's policies. The city enjoyed a long-deserved rest. Telephone service arrived in 1882, electric lights in 1884, and electric streetcars in 1907. Presidential aspirant Ramón Corona, elected Jalisco's governor in 1887, promoted the railroad, which arrived from Mexico City in 1888 (and was finally completed, via Colima, to Manzanillo in 1909).

Corona's liberal social agenda, which included universal public elementary education, was cut short by his assassination in 1889. Nevertheless, Guadalajara continued booming, reaching a population of 100,000 by 1900.

In retrospect, President Díaz's "Order and Progress" had come at a high human price. He allowed more than a hundred million acres—one-fifth of Mexico's land area (including most of the arable land)—to fall into the hands of his friends and foreigners. Poor Mexicans suffered the most. By 1910, 90 percent of the *indígenas* had lost their traditional communal land. In the spring of 1910, a smug, now-cultured and elderly Don Porfirio Díaz anticipated with relish the centennial of Hidalgo's Grito de Dolores.

¡No Reelección!

Porfirio Díaz himself had first campaigned on this slogan. It expressed the idea that the president should step down after one term. Although Díaz had stepped down once in 1880, he had gotten himself reelected for 26 consecutive years. In 1910, **Francisco I. Madero,** a short, squeaky-voiced son of rich landowners, opposed Díaz under the same banner.

Madero campaigned in Guadalajara twice before Díaz had him jailed before the balloting. But even after Díaz had been declared the winner, Madero refused to quit. From a safe platform in the United States, he called for a revolution to begin on November 20, 1910.

Villa and Zapata

Not much happened, but soon the millions of poor Mexicans who had been going to bed hungry began to stir. In Jalisco, *maderistas* Enrique Estrada, Luis Moza, and Domingo Arriega organized guerrilla bands that harassed federal troops. In Chihuahua, followers of **Francisco (Pancho) Villa,** an erstwhile ranch hand, miner, peddler, and cattle rustler, began attacking the *rurales,* dynamiting railroads, and raiding towns. Meanwhile, in the south, horse trader, farmer, and minor official **Emiliano Zapata** and his *indígena* guerrillas were terrorizing rich *hacendados* and forcibly recovering stolen ancestral village lands. Zapata's movement gained steam and by May had taken the Morelos state capital, Cuernavaca. Meanwhile, Madero crossed the Rio Grande and joined with Villa's forces, who took Ciudad Juárez.

The *federales* (government army troops) began deserting in droves, and on May 25, 1911, Díaz submitted his resignation.

As General Victoriano Huerta (Madero's deputy) put Díaz on his ship of exile in Veracruz, Díaz confided, "Madero has unleashed a tiger. Now let's see if he can control it."

The Fighting Continues

Emiliano Zapata, it turned out, was the tiger Madero had unleashed. Meeting with Madero in Mexico City, Zapata fumed over Madero's go-slow approach to the "agrarian problem," as Madero termed it. Madero tried to negotiate with Zapata, but government forces, led by Huerta, attacked Zapata's guerrillas as they were getting ready to lay down their arms. By November, Zapata had denounced Madero. "*¡Tierra y Libertad!*" (Land and Liberty!) the Zapatistas cried, as they renewed their fiery rebellion in the south. During 1912, a number of serious anti-Madero revolts broke out, which Madero appointed Huerta to quell. But in February 1913, Huerta double-crossed Madero. Backed by his troops, Huerta forced Madero to resign on February 18, 1913, immediately got himself appointed president, then ordered Madero murdered four days later.

The rum-swilling Huerta ruled like a Chicago mobster; general rebellion, led by the "Big Four"—Villa, Álvaro Obregón, Venustiano Carranza in the north, and Zapata in the south—soon broke out. Although Guadalajara was not occupied by revolutionary forces until mid-1914, increasing numbers of radicals and homeless refugees began living in the city's streets, forcing rich residents to flee to their west-side suburban homes.

Eventually, on July 8, 1914, forces of Generals Obregón, Rafael Buelna, Lucio Blanco, and Manuel M. Dieguez decisively defeated Huerta's forces north of Guadalajara and entered the city in triumph. Pressed by the rebels on all sides and refused U.S. recognition, Huerta fled into exile in late July 1914. Dieguez, installed as governor for the second time, immediately declared state support for secondary education, fixed minimum wages and work standards, and required a Sunday work holiday and cash payment of wages.

Fighting sputtered on for three more years as authority seesawed between Obregón and Carranza's Constitutionalist faction on one hand and Zapata and Villa on the other. Finally Carranza, who ended up controlling most of the country by 1917, got a convention together in Querétaro to formulate political and social goals. The resulting Constitution of 1917, while restating most ideas of the Reformistas' 1857 constitution, additionally prescribed a single four-year presidential term, advocated labor reform, and subordinated private ownership to public interest. Every village had a right to communal *ejido* land, and subsoil wealth could never be sold away to the highest bidder.

The Constitution of 1917 was a revolutionary expression of national aspirations and, in retrospect, represented a social and political agenda for the entire 20th century. In modified form, it has lasted to the present day.

Obregón Stabilizes Mexico

On December 1, 1920, General Álvaro Obregón legally assumed the presidency of a Mexico still bleeding from 10 years of civil war. Although a seasoned revolutionary, Obregón was also a pragmatist who recognized that peace was necessary to implement the goals of the revolution. In four years, Obregón managed to put down a number of rebellions (one of which included Jalisco governor Dieguez), disarmed a swarm of warlords, executed hundreds of *bandidos,* obtained U.S. diplomatic recognition, assuaged the worst fears of the clergy and landowners, and began land reform.

All this set the stage for the work of **Plutarco Elías Calles,** Obregón's secretary of the interior and handpicked successor, who won the 1924 election. Aided by peace, Mexico returned to a semblance of prosperity. Calles brought the army under civilian control, balanced the budget, and shifted Mexico's revolution into high gear. New clinics vaccinated millions against smallpox, new dams irrigated thousands of previously dry acres, and campesinos received millions of acres of redistributed land.

Meanwhile, Guadalajara was solidifying its position as Mexico's second city. In 1927, crews completed the Guadalajara rail link with the U.S. California and Arizona border. Built by Americans, it was later nationalized and named the Ferrocarril del Pacífico (Pacific Railroad). It opened the gate for the burgeoning Guadalajara–United States trade that continues today.

The Cristero War

By single-mindedly enforcing the agrarian, pro-labor, and anticlerical articles of the 1917 constitution, Calles made many influential enemies. The clergy, infuriated by the government's confiscation of church property, closing of monasteries, and deportation of hundreds of foreign priests and nuns, issued a pastoral letter, in July 1926, refusing to perform marriages, baptisms, and last rites. Riots broke out, especially in Guadalajara, where a violent confrontation erupted when soldiers tried to evict a group of Catholic rebels—'Cristeros'—who had barricaded themselves in the downtown Sanctuary of Guadalupe.

The Cristero rebellion climaxed most violently in Jalisco's conservative upland "Los Altos" region around Tepatitlán, San Juan de los Lagos, and Lagos de Moreno, not far northeast of Guadalajara. One of the leading Cristeros was Victoriano Ramírez ("El Catorce"), whose followers began to wage a deadly shoot-and-run guerrilla war upon federal troops. After a series of bloody skirmishes, federal troops initiated a ruthless scorched-earth policy, forcing rural populations to concentrate in towns, burning crops and farms, and killing and confiscating livestock.

Eventually the Cristero guerrillas, weak from hunger and without ammunition, surrendered. In mid-1929, church officials and federal authorities were able to negotiate a peace settlement.

Calles, who started out brimming with revolutionary fervor and populist zeal, became increasingly conservative and dictatorial. Although he bowed out peaceably in favor of Obregón (the constitution had been amended to allow one six-year nonsuccessive term), Obregón was assassinated two weeks after his election in 1928. Calles continued to rule for six more years through three puppet-presidents: Emilio Portes Gil (1928–1930), Pascual Ortíz Rubio (1930–1932), and Abelardo Rodríguez (1932–1934).

For 14 years since 1920, the revolution had first waxed, then waned. With a cash surplus in 1930, Mexico skidded into debt as the Great Depression deepened and Calles and his cronies lined their pockets. In blessing his minister of war, General Lázaro Cárdenas, for the 1934 presidential election, Calles expected more of the same.

Lázaro Cárdenas, President of the People

The 40-year-old Cárdenas, former governor of Michoacán, immediately set his own agenda, however. He worked tirelessly to fulfill the social prescriptions of the revolution. As morning-coated diplomats fretted, waiting in his outer office, Cárdenas ushered in delegations of campesinos and factory workers and sympathetically listened to their petitions.

In his six years of rule, Cárdenas moved public education and health forward on a broad front, supported strong labor unions, and redistributed 49 million acres of farmland, more than any president before or since.

Cárdenas's resolute enforcement of the constitution's **Artículo 123** brought him the most renown. Under this pro-labor law, the government turned over a host of private companies to employee ownership and, on March 18, 1938, expropriated all foreign oil corporations.

In retrospect, the oil corporations, most of which were British, were not blameless. They had sorely neglected the wages, health, and welfare of their workers while ruthlessly taking the law into their own hands with private police forces. Although Standard Oil cried foul, U.S. President Franklin Roosevelt did not intervene. Through negotiation and due process, the U.S. companies eventually were compensated with $24 million, plus interest. In the wake of the expropriation, President Cárdenas created Petróleos Mexicanos (Pemex), the national oil corporation that today continues to run all Mexican oil and gas operations.

Although the 1930s were by and large a time of rebuilding, Guadalajara still suffered from the ideological split aggravated by the Cristero War. The dispute broke out at the state-financed University of Guadalajara, where leftists demanded that socialist philosophy should rule university policies and curriculum. Governor Sebastián Allende took office in April 1932, facing a violent student strike that forced him to close the university for a year.

Meanwhile, he and his successor, Evarardo Topete, continued an ambitious road-building plan to connect Guadalajara with paved highways south, west, and east, with Barra de Navidad, Tequila, and the state of Michoacán.

Manuel Ávila Camacho, the "Believer"

Manuel Ávila Camacho, elected in 1940, was the last general to be president of Mexico. His administration ushered in a gradual shift of Mexican politics, government, and foreign policy as Mexico allied itself with the U.S. cause during World War II. Foreign tourism, initially promoted by the Cárdenas administration, ballooned. Good feelings surged as Franklin Roosevelt became the first U.S. president to officially cross the Rio Grande when he met with Camacho in Monterrey in April 1943.

In both word and deed, moderation and evolution guided President Camacho's policies. *"Soy creente"* ("I am a believer"), he declared to the Catholics of Mexico as he worked earnestly to bridge Mexico's serious church-state schism. Land policy emphasis shifted from redistribution to utilization as new dams and canals irrigated hundreds of thousands of previously arid acres. On one hand, Camacho established IMSS (Instituto Mexicano de Seguro Social), and on the other he trimmed the power of labor unions.

As WWII moved toward its 1945 conclusion, both the United States and Mexico were enjoying the benefits of four years of governmental and military cooperation and mutual trade in the form of a mountain of strategic minerals that had moved north in exchange for a similar mountain of U.S. manufactures that moved south.

Meanwhile, in Guadalajara, a pair of progressive governors, Marcelino Garcia Barragan (1943–1947) and Jesús González Gallo (1947–1953) pushed the modernization of Guadalajara: a west-side industrial park (including the now-renowned Guadalajara Arch, **El Arco**) and widening east-west Avenida Vallarta–Juárez and north-south Avenida 16 Septiembre–Alcalde.

CONTEMPORARY MEXICO AND GUADALAJARA
The Mature Revolution

During the decades after WWII, beginning with President **Miguel Alemán** (1946–1952), a moderate, Mexican politicians gradually honed their skills of consensus and compromise as their middle-aged revolution bubbled along under liberal presidents and sputtered haltingly under conservatives. Doctrine required that all politicians, regardless of stripe, be "revolutionary" enough to be included beneath the banner of the PRI (Partido Revolucionario Institucional), Mexico's dominant political party.

To date, Mexico's revolution hadn't been very revolutionary about women's rights. The PRI didn't get around to giving Mexican women, hundreds of thousands of whom fought and died during the revolution, the right to vote until 1953.

Adolfo Ruíz Cortínes, Alemán's secretary of the interior, was elected overwhelmingly in 1952. He fought the corruption that had crept into government under his predecessor, continued land reform, increased agricultural production, built new ports, eradicated malaria, and opened a dozen automobile assembly plants.

Women, voting for the first time in a national election, kept the PRI in power by electing liberal **Adolfo López Mateos** in 1958. Resembling Lázaro Cárdenas in social policy, López Mateos redistributed 40 million acres of farmland, forced automakers to use 60 percent domestic components, built thousands of new schools, and distributed hundreds of millions of new textbooks. *"La electricidad es nuestra"* ("Electricity is ours"), Mateos declared as he nationalized foreign power companies in 1962.

Despite his left-leaning social agenda, unions were restive under López Mateos. Protesting inflation, workers struck; the government retaliated, arresting Demetrios Vallejo, the railway union head, and renowned muralist David Siquieros, former communist party secretary.

Despite the troubles, López Mateos climaxed his presidency gracefully in 1964 as he opened the celebrated National Museum of Anthropology, appropriately located in Chapultepec Park, where the Aztecs had first settled 20 generations earlier.

During the decade of the 1950s, Guadalajara doubled its population, to about 850,000, as waves of migrants from the countryside flocked to new factory jobs in the city. Guadalajara's new metropolitan status was underlined by the appointment of Guadalajara's archbishop, José Garibi Rivera, as Mexico's first cardinal. Meanwhile, a handful of conservation-conscious citizens in 1955, worried that Lake Chapala had sunk to its lowest level in memory, breathed a sigh of relief when the lake recovered a few years later.

Elected in 1964, dour, conservative President **Gustavo Díaz Ordaz** immediately clashed with liberals, labor, and students. The pot boiled over just before the 1968 Mexico City Olympics. Reacting to a student rebellion, the army occupied the National University; shortly afterwards, on October 2, government forces opened fire with machine guns on a downtown protest, killing or wounding hundreds of demonstrators.

Guadalajarans were fortunate to escape much of the violent social ferment of the 1960s. As the city's population passed the one million mark, optimistic investors pushed up Guadalajara's first two skyscrapers, the Hilton Hotel (now the Hotel Misión Carlton) and Condominios Guadalajara, planned to anchor a shiny new financial center on the south edge of downtown. Concurrently, confident developers promoted and built Latin America's first U.S.–style mall, Plaza del Sol, in Guadalajara's west-side suburb. Although the downtown financial center never prospered, Plaza del Sol was (and still is) a huge success.

Maquiladoras

Despite its serious internal troubles, Mexico's relations with the United States were cordial. President Lyndon Johnson visited and unveiled a statue of Abraham Lincoln in Mexico City. Later, Díaz Ordaz met with President Richard Nixon in Puerto Vallarta.

Meanwhile, bilateral negotiations produced the **Border Industrialization Program.** Within a 12-mile strip south of the United States–Mexico border, foreign companies could assemble duty-free parts into finished goods and export them without any duties on either side. Within a dozen years, a swarm of such plants, called *maquiladoras,* were humming as hundreds of thousands of Mexican workers assembled and exported billions of dollars worth of shiny consumer goods—electronics, clothes, furniture, pharmaceuticals, and toys—worldwide.

In the 1970s, following Mexico's improved transportation network, *maquiladora* construction shifted to Mexico's interior, arriving in Guadalajara in 1975. The first four plants—harbingers of things to come—were all electronics: Motorola, General Instruments, Unisys, and TRW.

The 1974 discovery of gigantic new oil and gas reserves along Mexico's Gulf Coast added fuel to Mexico's already rapid industrial expansion. During the late 1970s and early 1980s, billions in foreign investment financed other major developments—factories, hotels, power plants, roads, airports—all over the country.

Economic Trouble of the 1980s

The negative side of Mexico's industrial expansion was the huge dollar debt required to finance it. President **Luis Echeverría Alvarez** (1970–1976), diverted by his interest in international affairs, passed Mexico's burgeoning financial deficit to his successor, **José López Portillo.** As feared by some experts, a world petroleum glut during the early 1980s burst Mexico's ballooning oil bubble and plunged the country into financial crisis. When the 1982 interest came due on its foreign debt, Mexico's largest holding company couldn't pay the $2.3 billion owed. The peso plummeted more than fivefold, to 150 per U.S. dollar. At the same time, prices doubled every year.

But by the mid-1980s, President **Miguel de la Madrid** (1982–1988) was working hard to get Mexico's economic house in order. He sliced government and raised taxes, asking rich and poor alike to tighten their belts. Despite getting foreign bankers to reschedule Mexico's debt, de la Madrid couldn't stop inflation. Prices skyrocketed as the peso deflated to 2,500 per U.S. dollar, becoming one of the world's most devalued currencies by 1988.

Despite the economic trouble, optimism still reined in Guadalajara. Having seen the population of their metropolis double again to more than two million in the previous decade, Guadalajarans initiated a civic construction project of visionary proportions—**Plaza Tapatía**—which architect Ignacio Díaz Morales conceived to unify the downtown into a grand strolling ground. But there was bad news that developers tried to minimize: Upwards of 10 square commercial blocks, including dozens of noteworthy historic buildings (including the popular bullring), had to be torn down despite the protests of Guadalajarans.

Salinas de Gortari and NAFTA

Public disgust with official corruption led to significant opposition during the 1988 presidential election. Billionaire Partido Acción Nacional (PAN) candidate Michael Clothier and liberal National Democratic Front candidate Cuauhtémoc Cárdenas ran against the PRI's Harvard-educated technocrat Carlos Salinas de Gortari. The vote was split so evenly that all three candidates claimed victory. Although Salinas eventually won the election, his showing, barely half of the vote, was the worst ever for a PRI president.

Salinas, however, seemed to be Mexico's "Coming Man" of the 1990s. His major achievement—despite significant national opposition—was the North American Free Trade Agreement (NAFTA), negotiated in 1992 by him, U.S. president George Bush, and Canadian prime minister Brian Mulrooney.

Rebellion in Chiapas, Disaster and Assassination in Guadalajara

On the very day in early January 1994 that NAFTA took effect, rebellion broke out in the poor, remote state of Chiapas. A small but well-disciplined campesino force, calling itself Ejército Zapatista Liberación Nacional (Zapatista National Liberation Army—EZLN—or "Zapatistas") captured a number of provincial towns and held the former governor of Chiapas hostage.

Earlier, back in Guadalajara, the 1990s had started off on a positive note, with the Ibero-American summit of 19 Latin American heads of state, plus Portugal and Spain in July 1991.

Soon, however, a pair of tragedies struck the city. On April 22, 1992, gasoline leaking into the street drains ignited a horrific explosion that blew six miles of city pavements, cars, buildings, and people into the air, killing 200 and injuring thousands. Scarcely a year later, assailants gunned down Guadalajara's cardinal, Juan Jesús Posada Ocampo, along with four other victims, at the Guadalajara airport. Although the streets have been repaired and city officials swear such an explosion will never occur again, Cardinal Posada Ocampo's killers have never been brought to justice.

To further complicate matters, Mexico's already tense 1994 drama veered toward tragedy. While Salinas de Gortari's chief negotiator, Manuel Camacho Solis, was attempting to iron out a settlement with the Zapatista rebels, PRI presidential candidate Luis Donaldo Colosio, Salinas's handpicked successor, was gunned down just months before the August balloting. However, instead of disintegrating, the nation united in grief; opposition candidates eulogized their fallen former opponent and later earnestly engaged his replacement, stolid technocrat **Ernesto Zedillo,** in Mexico's first presidential election debate.

In a closely watched election unmarred by irregularities, Zedillo piled up a solid plurality against his PAN and Partido Revolucionario Democrática (PRD) opponents. By perpetuating the PRI's 65-year hold on the presidency, the electorate had again opted for the PRI's familiar although imperfect middle-aged revolution.

New Crisis, New Recovery

Zedillo, however, had little time to savor his victory. Right away he had to face the consequences of his predecessor's shabby fiscal policies. Less than a month after he took office, the peso crashed, losing a third of its value just before Christmas 1994. A month later, Mexican financial institutions, their dollar debt having nearly doubled in a month, were in danger of defaulting on their obligations to international investors. To stave off a worldwide financial panic, U.S. president Clinton, in February 1995, secured an unprecedented multibillion-dollar loan package for Mexico, guaranteed by U.S. and international institutions.

At the same time, the Zedillo government gained momentum in addressing the Zapatistas' grievances in Chiapas, even as it decreased federal military presence, built new rural electrification networks, and refurbished health clinics. Moreover, Mexico's economy began to improve. By mid-1996, inflation had slowed to a 20 percent annual rate, investment dollars were flowing back into Mexico, the peso had stabilized at about 7.5 to the U.S. dollar, and Mexico had paid back half the borrowed U.S. bailout money.

Zedillo's Political Reforms

In the political arena, although the justice system generally left much to be desired, a pair of unprecedented events signaled an increasingly open political system. In the 1997 congressional elections, voters elected a host of opposition candidates, depriving the PRI of an absolute congressional majority for the first time since 1929. A year later, in early 1998, Mexicans were participating in their country's first primary elections—in which voters, instead of politicians, chose party candidates.

Although President Zedillo had had a rough ride, he entered the twilight of his 1994–2000 term able to take credit for an improved economy, some genuine political reforms, and relative peace in the countryside. The election of 2000 revealed, however, that the Mexican people were not satisfied.

End of an Era: Vicente Fox Unseats the PRI

During 1998 and 1999 the focal point of opposition to the PRI's three-generation rule had been shifting to relative newcomer Vicente Fox, former president of Coca Cola Mexico and former PAN governor of Guanajuato.

Fox, who had announced his candidacy for president two years before the election, seemed an unlikely challenger. After all, the minority PAN had always been the party of wealthy businessmen and the conservative Catholic right. But blunt-talking, six-foot-five Fox, who sometimes campaigned in *vaquero* boots and a 10-gallon cowboy hat, preached populist themes of coalition building and "inclusion." He backed up his talk by carrying his campaign to hardscrabble city *barrios,* dirt-poor country villages, and traditional outsider groups, such as Jews.

In a relatively orderly and fair 2000 election, Fox decisively defeated his PRI opponent Fernando Labastida, 42 percent to 38 percent, while PRD candidate Cárdenas polled a feeble 17 percent. Fox's win also swept a PAN plurality (223/209/57) into the 500-seat Chamber of Deputies lower house (although the Senate remained PRI-dominated).

Nevertheless, in pushing the PRI from the all-powerful presidency after 71 consecutive years of domination, Fox had ushered Mexico into a new, more democratic era. Furthermore, despite stinging criticism from his own ranks, **President Zedillo,** whom historians were already praising as the real hero behind Mexico's new democracy, made an unprecedented early appeal for all Mexicans to unite behind Fox.

Vicente Fox, President of Mexico

Wasting little time getting started, President Fox first headed to Chiapas to confer with indigenous community leaders. Along the way, he shut down Chiapas military bases and removed dozens of military roadblocks. Back in Mexico City, he sent the long-delayed **peace plan,** including the **indigenous bill of rights,** to Congress. Zapatista rebels responded by journeying en masse from Chiapas to Mexico City, where, in their black masks, they addressed Congress, arguing for indigenous rights. Although by mid-2001, Congress had passed a modified version of the negotiated settlement, and the majority of states had ratified the required constitutional amendment, indigenous leaders condemned the legislation plan as watered down and unacceptable, while proponents claimed it was the best possible compromise between the Zapatistas' demands and the existing Mexican constitution.

On the positive side, by mid-2002, Vicente Fox could claim credit for cracking down on corruption and putting drug lords in jail, negotiating a key immigration agreement with the United States, keeping the peso stable, clamping down on inflation, and attracting a record pile of foreign investment dollars.

Furthermore, Fox continued to pry open the door to democracy in Mexico. In May 2002, he signed Mexico's first **freedom of information act,** entitling citizens to timely copies of all public documents from federal agencies. Moreover, Fox's long-promised **Transparency Commission** was taking shape. In July 2002, federal attorneys were taking unprecedented action. They were questioning a list of 74 former government officials, including ex-president Luis Echeverría Alvarez, about their roles in government transgressions, notably political murders and the University of Mexico massacres during the 1960s and 1970s.

But Mexico's economy, reflecting the U.S. economic slowdown, began to sour in 2001, losing a half million jobs and cutting annual growth to 2.5 percent, down from the 4.5 percent that the government had predicted. In the July 7, 2003, congressional elections, voters took their frustrations out on the PAN and gave its plurality in the Chamber of Deputies to the PRI. When the dust settled, the PRI total had risen to 225 seats, while the PAN had slipped to 153. The biggest winner, however, was the PRD, which gained more than 40 seats, to a total of about 100.

Fortunately, by 2004, the Mexican economy, reflecting that of the United States, was beginning to turn around. Exports to the United States soared to record levels in the spring of 2004. Finally, in 2005, with his term nearly spent, critics were increasingly claiming that Fox was a lame-duck president running out of time to accomplish what he promised. But Fox, despite a hostile opposition-dominated congress that almost continuously blocked his legislative proposals, could claim some accomplishments. During his first four years, he had pushed through gains in indigenous rights, national reconciliation and government transparency, drug enforcement, U.S.-Mexico immigration policy, social security reform, housing, and education. Moreover, in addition to nurturing a recovering economy, Fox had kept the peso strong against the dollar and clamped the lid on inflation.

The Election of 2006

During the first half of 2006, as Vicente Fox was winding down his presidency, Mexicans were occupied by the campaign to elect his successor. Most headlines went to the PRD candidate, the mercurial leftist-populist Andres Manuel López Obrador, former mayor of Mexico City. Trying hard not to be upstaged was the steady, no-nonsense PAN candidate, Harvard-educated centrist-conservative Felipe Calerón, a leading light of President Fox's cabinet. Also, veteran politico Robert Madrazo carried the banner for what appeared to be a resurgent PRI. But, after a half year of mudslinging and angry debates over the major election issues of drug-related mayhem, killings and kidnappings, police and judicial corruption and inefficiency, and lack of jobs for impoverished workers, Madrazo's initial popularity faded, narrowing the contest to a bitter neck-and-neck race between Calderón and Obrador.

On Sunday, July 2, 2006, 42,000,000 Mexicans cast their ballots. In an intensely monitored election marred by few irregularities, unofficial returns indicated that voters had awarded Calderón a paper-thin plurality. Four days later, after all returns were certified, the Federal Electoral Institute announced the official vote tally: only about 22 percent for Madrazo, with the remaining lion's share divided nearly evenly, with 38.7 percent going to Obrador and 39.3 percent to Calderón. This result, the Federal Electoral Institute ruled, was too close to declare a winner without a recount.

Besides the close Obrador-Calderón vote, the election results revealed much more. Not only were the 32 electoral entities (31 states and the Federal District) divided equally, with 16 going to Obrador and 16 to Calderón, the vote reflected a nearly complete north-south political schism, with virtually all of the 16

PAN-majority states, including Jalisco and Guadalajara, forming a solid northern bloc, while the 16 PRD-voting states did the same in the south. Furthermore, the election appeared to signal a collapse of PRI power; with no state (nor the Federal District) giving either a majority or a plurality to Madrazo.

Election Aftermath

A howl of protest came from Obrador and his PRD followers after the election results were announced. They demanded a complete recount of all 42,000,000 ballots. They claimed the PAN had stolen the election. After weeks of hearing the PRD arguments for (and PAN counter-arguments against) ballot fraud, the Federal Election Institute announced (in agreement with virtually all independent observers) that the election was essentially clean, and the recount would be limited only to the questionable ballots. These amounted to about 9 percent of the total, all mostly in the Calderón-majority states.

After a month exhaustively examining the suspect ballots, the Supreme Election Tribunal, an impeccable panel of federal judges, found that the recount shifted the margin by only a few thousand votes away from Calderóon to Obrador. On September 6, the Federal Electoral Institute declared Calderóon the president-elect by a margin of about 240,000 votes, or a bit more than one half of a percent of the total vote.

Obrador and his supporters screamed foul even louder and pushed their obstructionist tactics to an outrageous climax when a handful of PRD senators and deputies made such a ruckus during a joint session of the federal legislature that they prevented the President of Mexico, for the first time in history, from delivering his annual state of the union address.

Mexican voters were not amused. National polls showed that more than two-thirds of Mexicans disapproved of the PRD's protest behavior. By October, many of the PRD's leaders agreed, further isolating Obrador and his rump government to a footnote in Mexican history. Mexico's new democracy, given a gentle shove forward ten years earlier by President Ernesto Zedillo and nurtured for six more years by Vicente Fox, seemed to have again surmounted a difficult crisis and emerged stronger.

An important result of the 2006 election, initially overshadowed by the intense struggle over the presidential vote, was the federal legislative vote, in which PAN emerged as the biggest winner by far. The final results showed that voters had given PAN candidates strong pluralities of 206/127/106 over the PRD and PRI, respectively, in the 500-seat federal Chamber of Deputies, and 52/29/33 in the 128-seat Senate, with the remainder of seats scattered among minor parties. This result may bode well for Mexican democracy. With some cooperation (most likely from the PRI), Felipe Calderón may be able to use his party's pluralities to further the national political and economic reform agenda that Vicente Fox promised six years earlier, but could only partially deliver.

Felipe Calderón Takes Charge

As he prepared for his December 1, 2006, inauguration, Felipe Calerón not only appeared to be moving ahead with many of his predecessor's original proposals, but he also seemed to be reaching out to the PRI and the PRD with some new ideas. These, although containing much of PAN's pro-business, pro-NAFTA ideas, also appeared to borrow considerably from the liberal-populist agenda of Obrador and the PRD and produce the much-needed cooperation that President Fox didn't receive.

Mexico's new president wasted no time in tackling his country's thorniest problems. He immediately launched a no-holds-barred attack on Mexico's drug trade, the cause of hundreds of thousands of Mexican addicts and thousands of yearly drug-related murders and kidnappings. Right off the bat, Calderón fired all of Mexico's state police chiefs, then sent in the army to smash hundreds of drug factories, jailing a small army of suspects and uprooting thousands of acres of drug crops.

Simultaneously, Calderón began to chip away at Mexico's rusty economic system. His first priority was to prod his fellow citizens to pay a fair share of taxes, which customarily amount to only about a tenth of Mexico's gross domestic product, compared to about one-third for the United States and Europe. Mexico sorely needs the money, for improved education, health, and infrastructure, as well as to put a halt to Mexico's increasing dependence on oil export revenues.

For his decisive actions, by mid-year 2007, Felipe Calderón's national approval ratings rocketed to a robust 65 percent, boding well for Mexico's continuing efforts to attain a just and prosperous motherland for all its citizens.

Economy and Government

THE ECONOMY
Post-Revolutionary Gains

By many measures, Mexico's 20th-century revolution appears to have succeeded. Since 1910, illiteracy has plunged from 80 percent to 10 percent, life expectancy has risen from 30 years to nearly 70, infant mortality has dropped from a whopping 40 percent to about 2 percent, and, in terms of caloric intake, Mexicans are eating about twice as much as their forebears at the turn of the 20th century.

Decades of near-continuous economic growth account for rising Mexican living standards. The Mexican economy has rebounded from its last three recessions due to several factors: plentiful natural resources, notably oil and metals; diversified manufacturing, such as cars, steel, petrochemicals, and electronics; steadily increasing tourism; exports of fruits,

Mexicans often take second and third jobs to make ends meet.

vegetables, and cattle; and its large, willing, low-wage workforce.

Recent governments, moreover, have skillfully exploited Mexico's economic strengths. The Border Industrialization Program has led to millions of jobs in thousands of *maquiladora* factories, from Tijuana to the mouth of the Rio Grande to Mexico City and Guadalajara. Foreign trade, a strong source for new Mexican jobs, has burgeoned since Mexico joined the General Agreement on Tariffs and Trade (GATT) in 1986 and NAFTA in 1994. As a result, Mexico has become a net exporter of goods and services to the United States, its largest trading partner. Belt-tightening measures brought inflation down and foreign investment has been flowing into Mexico—especially Guadalajara—since 1996. And benefits from the devalued peso, such as increased tourism and burgeoning exports, have contributed to a generally improving economy for the 10-year 1997–2007 period.

Guadalajara remains one of the stars of the Mexican economy, especially in electronics. From 2000 to 2006, yearly electronics exports from Guadalajara skyrocketed from $8 billion to more than $25 billion, confirming Guadalajara's claim to being the "Silicon Valley of Latin America." Scores of big electronics factories, with heavyweight names such as Hewlitt-Packard, NEC, Texas Instruments, Intel, Kodak, SCI, and IBM, dot Guadalajara's industrial landscape.

Contemporary Economic Challenges

Despite huge gains, Mexico's Revolution of 1910 is nevertheless incomplete. Improved public health, education, income, and opportunity have barely outdistanced Mexico's population, which has increased nearly sevenfold—from 15 million to 107 million—between 1910 and 2006. For example, although the literacy rate has increased, the actual number of Mexican people who can't read, some 10 million, has remained about constant since 1910.

Moreover, the land reform program, once thought to be a Mexican cure-all, has long been a disappointment. The *ejidos* of which Emiliano Zapata dreamed have become mostly symbolic. The communal fields are typically small and unirrigated. *Ejido* land, constitutionally prohibited from being sold, cannot serve as collateral for bank loans (except under special circumstances). Capital for irrigation networks, fertilizers, and harvesting machines is consequently lacking. Communal farms are typically inefficient; the average Mexican field produces about *one quarter* as much corn per acre as a U.S. farm. Mexico must accordingly use its precious oil dollar surplus to import millions of tons of corn—originally indigenous to Mexico—annually.

The triple scourge of overpopulation, lack of arable land, and low farm and factory income has driven millions of campesino families to seek better lives in Mexico's cities and young men to seek work north of the border. Since 1910, Mexico has evolved from a largely rural country, where 70 percent of the population lived on farms, to an urban nation, in which more than 70 percent of the population lives in cities. Fully one-fifth of Mexico's people now live in Mexico City.

Nevertheless, the future appears bright for many privately owned and managed Mexican farms, concentrated largely in the northern border states. Exceptionally productive, they typically work hundreds or thousands of irrigated acres of crops, such as tomatoes, lettuce, chiles, wheat, corn, tobacco, cotton, fruits, alfalfa, chickens, and cattle, just like their counterparts across the border in California, New Mexico, Arizona, and Texas.

Staples—wheat for bread, corn for tortillas, milk, and cooking oil—are all partially imported and consequently expensive for the typical working-class Mexican family, which must spend half or more of its income (typically $500 per month) for food. Inflation, which fortunately has been kept modest, to an approximate 5 percent per year, since around 2000, compounds the problem, particularly for the millions of families on the bottom half of Mexico's economic ladder.

Although average gross domestic product

figures—about $8,000 per capita—place Mexico above nearly all other developing nations' averages, in reality the numbers are misleading. Historically, the richest one-fifth of Mexican families earn about 10 times the income of the poorest one-fifth. A relative handful of people own a large hunk of Mexico, and they don't seem inclined to share any of it with the less fortunate. As for the poor, the typical Mexican family in the bottom one-third income bracket often owns neither car nor refrigerator; nor do the children finish elementary school.

GOVERNMENT AND POLITICS
The Constitution of 1917

Mexico's governmental system is rooted in the Constitution of 1917, which incorporated many of the features of its reformist predecessor of 1857. The 1917 document, with amendments, remains in force. Although drafted at the behest of conservative revolutionary Venustiano Carranza by his handpicked Querétaro "Constitucionalista" congress, it was greatly influenced by Álvaro Obregón and generally ignored by Carranza during his subsequent three-year presidential term.

Although many articles resemble those of its United States model, the Constitution of 1917 contains provisions developed directly from Mexican experience. Article 27 addresses the question of land. Private property rights are qualified by societal need; subsoil rights are public property, and foreigners and corporations are severely restricted in land ownership. Although the 1917 constitution declared *ejido* (communal) land inviolate, 1994 amendments allow, under certain circumstances, the sale or use of communal land as loan security.

Article 23 severely restricts church powers. In declaring that "places of worship are the property of the nation," it stripped churches of all title to real estate, without compensation. Article 5 and Article 130 banned religious orders, expelled foreign clergy, and denied priests and ministers all political rights, including voting, holding office, and even criticizing the government.

Student political protest is alive and well at the University of Guadalajara.

Article 123 establishes the rights of labor: to organize, bargain collectively, strike, work a maximum eight-hour day, and receive a minimum wage. Women are to receive equal pay for equal work and be given a month's paid leave for childbearing. Article 123 also establishes social security plans for sickness, unemployment, pensions, and death.

On paper, Mexico's constitutional government structures appear much like their U.S. prototypes: a federal presidency, a two-house congress, and a supreme court, with their counterparts in each of the 31 states and the Federal District. Political parties field candidates, and all citizens vote by secret ballot.

Mexico's presidents, however, enjoy greater powers than their U.S. counterparts. They can suspend constitutional rights under a state of siege, can initiate legislation, veto all or parts of bills, refuse to execute laws, and replace state officers. The federal government, moreover, retains nearly all taxing authority, relegating the states to a role of merely administering federal programs.

Although ideally providing for separation of powers, the Constitution of 1917 subordinates both the legislative and judicial branches, with the courts being the weakest of all. The supreme court, for example, can only, with repeated deliberation, decide upon the constitutionality of legislation. Five separate individuals must file successful petitions for writs *amparo* (protection) on a single point of law in order to affect constitutional precedent.

Jalisco's government reflects the federal model. By secret ballot, voters in 20 state electoral districts elect the governor, several of the governor's cabinet, and the 40 deputies of the unicameral legislature. Legislative candidates must be a minimum 21 years of age, not hold executive or judicial office, and have been a Jalisco resident for two years.

Democratizing Mexican Politics

Reforms in Mexico's stable but top-heavy "Institutional Revolution" came only gradually. Characteristically, street protests were brutally put down at first, with officials only later working to address grievances. Dominance by the PRI led to widespread cynicism and citizen apathy.

Change began slowly in the late 1980s and picked up steam with the election of PRI presidential candidate Ernesto Zedillo. Following his 1994 inaugural address, in which he called loudly and clearly for more reforms, President Zedillo quickly began to produce results. He immediately appointed a respected member of the PAN opposition party as attorney general—the first non-PRI cabinet appointment in Mexican history. Other Zedillo firsts were federal senate confirmation both of supreme court nominees and the attorney general, multiparty participation in the Chiapas peace negotiations, and congressional approval of the 1995 financial assistance package received from the United States. Zedillo, moreover, organized a series of precedent-setting meetings with opposition leaders that led to a written pact for political reform and the establishment of permanent working groups to discuss political and economic questions.

Perhaps most important was Zedillo's campaign and inaugural vow to separate both his government and himself from PRI decision-making. He kept his promise, becoming the first Mexican president in as long as anyone could remember who did not choose his successor.

Guadalajara's post-millennium politics led the national trend, with a succession of four PAN governors, Alberto Cárdenas (1988–1994, 1994–2000), Ramírez Acuña (2000–2006), and Emilio Gonzalez Marques (2006–2012.) At the same time opposition PRD and Green parties gained minority footholds in the state legislature. Although the July 2003 elections produced a PRI majority in the state legislature, the 2006 elections reversed that by electing PAN majorities to both the Jalisco state legislature and the Guadalajara city council.

A New Mexican Revolution

Finally, in 2000, like a Mexican Gorbachev, Ernesto Zedillo—the man most responsible for Mexico's recent democratic reforms—

watched as PAN opposition reformer Vicente Fox swept his PRI from the presidency after a 71-year rule. Despite severe criticism from within his own party, Zedillo quickly called for the country to close ranks behind Fox. Millions of Mexicans, still dazed but buoyed by Zedillo's statesmanship and Fox's epoch-making victory, eagerly awaited Fox's inauguration address on December 1, 2000.

He promised nothing less than a new revolution for Mexico and backed it up with concrete proposals: reduce poverty by 30 percent with a million new jobs a year from revitalized new electricity and oil production; a Mexican Silicon Valley in Guadalajara; and free trade between Mexico, all of Latin America, and the United States and Canada. He promised justice for all, through a reformed police, army, and the judiciary. He promised conciliation and an agreement with the Zapatista rebel movement in the south, including a bill of rights for Mexico's native peoples. With all of Mexico listening, Fox brought his speech to a hopeful conclusion: "If I had to summarize my message today in one sentence, I would say: Today Mexico has a future, but we have lost much time and wasted many resources. Mexico has a future, and we must build that future starting today."

It was truly a bold vision, and five years later, nearing the twilight of his six-year term, Fox could only claim partial success. He admitted that the path to democracy, which he believes cannot be reversed, would continue to be messy and difficult. His unfinished agenda therefore will remain a challenge to future Mexican presidents, especially his successor Felipe Calderón, who in his brief but emphatic inauguration speech on December 1, 2006, vowed to continue Mexico's difficult but nonreversable march toward a truly just, democratic, and prosperous homeland for all Mexican people.

The People

Let a broad wooden chopping block represent Mexico; imagine hacking it with a sharp cleaver until it is grooved and pocked. That fractured surface resembles Mexico's central highlands, where most Mexicans, divided from each other by high mountains and yawning *barrancas,* have lived since before history.

The Mexicans' deep divisions, in large measure, led to their downfall at the hands of the Spanish conquistadors. The Aztec empire that Hernán Cortés conquered was a vast but fragmented collection of tribes. Speaking more than a hundred mutually alien languages, those original Mexicans viewed each other suspiciously, as barely human barbarians from strange lands beyond the mountains. Even today the lines Mexicans draw between themselves—of caste, class, race, wealth—are mostly the result of the realities of their mutual isolation.

DEMOGRAPHICS
Population Growth
The Spanish colonial government and the Roman Catholic religion provided the glue that, over 400 years, has welded Mexico's fragmented people into a burgeoning nation-state. Although Mexico's population in recent years has increased steadily, this has not always been so. Historians estimate that European diseases, largely measles and smallpox, wiped out as many as 25 million—perhaps 95 percent—of the *indígena* population within a few generations after Cortés stepped ashore in 1519. Consequently, the Mexican population dwindled to a mere one million inhabitants by 1600. It wasn't until 1950, four centuries after Cortés, that Mexico's population had recovered to its preconquest level of 20 million.

After 1950, reflecting a typical developing nation birthrate of 7–8 children per woman, Mexico's population zoomed upward, more than quadrupling, to around 90 million by 1990. But during the millennium decade, increased education, affluence, and greater political and social freedom for women reduced the birthrate to 2–3 children per woman. Reduced fertility and emigration consequently slowed Mexico's population growth, to about 1 percent annually, to a total of about 107 million in 2006.

By contrast, Guadalajara's metropolitan-zone population increased more sharply, from about 2.65 million in 1990 to around 4 million in 2006, and continues to zoom upward by about 8 percent per year. While this growth rate is about several times the national average, it mostly reflects an influx from the country to the city, rather than a high birthrate.

POPULATION GROUPS
Mestizos, *Indígenas*, Criollos, and African Mexicans
Although by 1950 Mexico's population had recovered, it was completely transformed. The mestizo, a Spanish-speaking person of mixed blood, had replaced the pure Native American, the *indígena* (een-DEE-hay-nah), as the typical Mexican.

The trend continues. Perhaps three of four Mexicans (and Guadalajarans) would identify themselves as mestizo: that class whose part-European blood elevates them, in the Mexican mind, to the level of *gente de razón*—people of "reason" or "right." And there's the rub: The *indígenas* (or, mistakenly but much more commonly, Indians), by the usual measurements of income, health, or education, squat at the bottom of the Mexican social ladder.

The typical *indígena* family lives in a small adobe house in a remote valley, subsisting on corn, beans, and vegetables from their small, unirrigated *milpa* (cornfield). They usually have chickens, a few pigs, and sometimes a cow, but no electricity; their few hundred dollars a year in cash income isn't enough to buy even a small refrigerator, much less a truck.

The typical mestizo family, on the other hand, enjoys most of the benefits of the 20th century. They usually own a modest concrete

The Trique-speaking women from Oaxaca are typical of the many indigenous folks who flock to Guadalajara to sell handicrafts.

house in town. Their furnishings, simple by developed-world standards, will often include an electric refrigerator, washing machine, propane stove, television, and old car or truck. The children go to school every day, and the eldest son sometimes looks forward to college.

Sizable *negro* communities, descendants of 17th-century African slaves, live in the Gulf states and along the Guerrero–Oaxaca Pacific coastline. Last to arrive, the *negros* experience discrimination at the hands of everyone else and are integrating very slowly into the mestizo mainstream.

Above the mestizos, a tiny criollo (Mexican-born white) minority, a few percent of the total population, inherits the privileges—wealth, education, and political power—of their colonial Spanish ancestors.

Indígena Language Groups

The Maya speakers of Yucatán and the aggregate of the Nahuatl (Aztec language) speakers of the central plateau are Mexico's most numerous *indígena* groups, totaling about two and a half million (one million Maya, a million and a half Nahua).

Official figures, which show that the Guadalajara region's indigenous population amounts to a mere 1 percent of the total, are misleading. Official counts do not measure the droves of transient folks—migrants and new arrivals—who sleep in vehicles, shanty towns, behind their crafts stalls, and with friends and relatives. Although they are often not listed on census and voting rolls, you will see them in Guadalajara, especially around the Libertad Market downtown, laden with their for-sale fruit or handicrafts: men in sombreros and scruffy jeans, women in homemade full-skirted dresses with aprons much like your great-great-grandmother may have worn.

Immigrants in their own country, they flock to Guadalajara from hardscrabble rural areas of the poorest states, often Michoacán, Guerrero, and Oaxaca. Although of pure native blood, they will not acknowledge it or will even be insulted if you ask them if they are *indígenas*. It would be more polite to ask them where they're from. If from Michoacán, they'll often speak Tarasco (more courteously, say Purépecha: poo-RAY-pay-chah); if from Guerrero, the answer will usually be Nahuatl. Oaxaca folks, on the other hand, will probably be fluent in a dialect of either Zapotec or Mixtec. If not one of these, then it might be Chinantec, Mazatec, Mixe (MEE-shay), Chatino, Trique, or any one of a dozen others from Oaxaca's crazy-quilt of language.

As immigrants always have, they come seeking opportunity. If you're interested in what they're selling, bargain with humor. And if you err, let it be on the generous side: Like anyone, they'd prefer to walk away from a sale rather than lose their dignity.

The Huichol and Cora

In contrast to the migrants from the south, the Huichol and their northerly neighbors, the Cora, are native to the Guadalajara region. Isolated and resistant to Mexicaniza-

INDIGENOUS POPULATIONS

The 2000 government census totals were:

State	Indigenous Population (Over Five Years of Age)	Total Population (Over Five Years of Age)	Percent of Total
Nayarit	37,200	769,000	4.8
Jalisco	39,300	5,323,000	0.7
Sinaloa	49,700	2,130,000	2.3
Colima	2,900	421,000	0.7
Michoacán	121,800	3,342,000	3.6
Guerrero	367,100	2,572,000	14.3
Oaxaca	1,120,300	2,924,000	38.3

The same government sources tabulate indigenous peoples by language groupings. Although such figures are probably low, the 2000 figures revealed significant populations in many areas:

GUADALAJARA REGION

Language	Group Population	Important Centers
Cora	15,600	Nayarit (Acaponeta)
Huichol	27,900	Nayarit-Jalisco (Santiago Ixcuintla, Huejuqilla)
Nahua	8,100	Jalisco (Ciudad Guzmán)
Purápecha (Tarasco)	3,000	Southern Jalisco (Zamora)

NEIGHBORING STATES AND REGIONS

Language	Group Population	Important Centers
Tepuan	17,000	Sinaloa-Durango
Purépecha (Tarasco)	111,000	Michoacán (Pátzcuaro)

tion, about 30,000 Huichol (and about half as many Cora) farm, raise cattle, and hunt high in their Sierra Madre mountain homeland, which extends northerly and easterly from the foothills northwest of Guadalajara. Although the Cora's traditional territory intermixes with the Huichol's at its southern limit, it also spreads northward, between the foothills and the 6,000-foot-high Sierra Madre Occidental valleys, to the Nayarit-Durango border.

The Huichol, more so than all *indígena* groups, have preserved their colorful dress and religious practices. Huichol religious use of hallucinogenic peyote and the men's rainbow-tinted feathered hats and clothes are renowned. (For more, see the sidebar *The Huichol,* in the *West and North* chapter.)

Arts and Culture

TRADITIONAL DRESS

Country markets are where you're most likely to see people in traditional dress. And although virtually no men in the Guadalajara region wear the white cottons of yesteryear, nearly all men throughout Mexico wear the Spanish-origin straw sombrero (literally, "shade-maker") on their heads.

Country women's dress, by contrast, is more colorful. It can include a *huipil* (long, sleeveless dress) embroidered in bright floral and animal motifs and a handwoven *enredo* (wraparound skirt that identifies the wearer with a locality). A *faja* (waist sash) and, in winter, a *quechquemitl* (shoulder cape) complete the ensemble.

RELIGION

"God and Gold" was the two-pronged mission of the conquistadors. Most of them concentrated on gold, while missionaries tried to shift the emphasis to God. They were hugely successful; about 90 percent of Mexicans profess to be Catholics.

Catholicism, spreading its doctrine of equality of all people before God and incorporating native gods into church rituals, eventually brought the *indígenas* into the fold. Within a hundred years, nearly all native Mexicans had accepted the new religion, which raised the universal God of humankind over local tribal deities.

The miraculous **Virgin of Guadalupe,** who led to the conversion of millions of indigenous Mexicans during early colonial times, is Mexico's virtual patron saint, and is central to Mexican Catholicism. For the Virgin's story, see the sidebar *The Virgin of Guadalupe.*

FESTIVALS AND EVENTS

Guadalajarans love to party, so much so that parties (fiestas) are institutionalized. There seems to be a celebration—saint's day, country agricultural fair, old-fashioned small-town circus and carnival, pilgrimage, rodeolike *charreada*—occurring somewhere in and around Guadalajara every day.

Urban families watch the calendar for midweek national holidays that create a *puente,* or "bridge," to the weekend and allow them to squeeze in a three- to five-day mini-vacation. Visitors should likewise watch the calendar. Such holidays (especially Christmas and pre-Easter week) can mean packed buses, roads, and hotels, especially in town and around beach resorts.

Campesinos, on the other hand, await their local saint's day (or holy day). The name of the locality often provides the clue: in Santa Cruz de las Flores, just west of Highway 15/54/80, a few miles south of the city limits, expect a celebration on May 3, El Día de la Santa Cruz (Day of the Holy Cross). People dress up in their traditional best, sell their wares and produce in a street fair, join a procession, get tipsy, and dance in the plaza.

Guadalajara's biggest party is the month-long

© BRUCE WHIPPERMAN

The testimonies of pilgrims fill the walls at El Pocito in San Juan de los Lagos.

JUAN RULFO

Juan Rulfo, celebrated leading light of 20th-century Latin American literature, was a child of Jalisco country landholders, made destitute by the ravages of both the 1910-1917 revolution and the 1926-1929 Cristero rebellion. He was deeply marked by the destruction and terror born of both conflicts. His mother died and his father and a number of relatives were assassinated while he was still a child. Bereft of close family, young Juan grew up in an orphanage and with relatives. He studied law briefly in Guadalajara but moved to Mexico City in 1935 to pursue a writing career.

Bleakness, sadness, and violence pervade his few major works. He began to write short stories during the 1940s and collected them into his first important publication, *El Llano en Llamas* (The Burning Plain), published in 1953 and translated into English in 1967. Each narrative, typically of seemingly simple country people, is uniquely crafted, but each contains the common thread that blends them into Rulfo's view of the universal human condition.

Rulfo's acknowledged masterpiece, *Pedro Páramo*, published in 1955 and repeatedly revised, in 1959, 1964, and 1980, established his renown. The author, thinly disguised as the protagonist, Juan Preciado, fulfills his moth-er's dying request by returning to his shadowy Jalisco hometown, Comala, in search of his father.

In recognition of his literary accomplishments, Rulfo was asked to become an advisor to the Mexican Writer's Center, during which time he influenced a new generation of writers, such as Carlos Fuentes and Octavio Paz. Recognition rained down upon him: notably, the prestigious Xavier Urrutia prize in 1956, the National Prize of Letters in 1970, and the Spanish Prince of Asturias prize in 1983.

Despite the acclaim, Rulfo remained moody and remote. In a rare interview, in 1966, asked why he didn't bother to teach any writing classes, he answered, "I have no facility with words."

Rulfo's passion for photography remains one of his lesser-known but nevertheless significant legacies. A few exhibitions have revealed his images, captured between 1940 and 1955, of lonely places and marginalized people that he claimed his written works could not describe. The Juan Rulfo Foundation of Guadalajara archives the bulk of his 6,000 mostly unexhibited images.

Born in Barranca de Apulco, in southwest Jalisco, on May 16, 1918, Juan Rulfo died in Mexico City on January 7, 1986.

Fiestas de Octubre, in which everyone seems to get into the act. The action centers around the downtown Plaza Tapatía, the Hospicio Cabañas, and the Teatro Degollado, starting right off the first few days of October, with the crowning of the festival queen. Every day for four weeks thereafter, the auditoriums and plazas bloom with folkloric dancers, mariachis, athletic events, marching bands, dramatic and classical music and dance performances, and a heap more. For details, visit www.fiestasdeoctubre.com.

The merrymaking peaks on October 12, during the **Fiesta de la Virgen de Zapopan,** when a million Guadalajarans fill the streets in a grand **Romería** (pilgrimage stroll) to accompany their beloved "La Generala" (as the image is popularly known) from the downtown cathedral to her home in the basilica in Zapopan.

In addition to the annual fiestas, Guadalajarans enjoy a steady menu of artistic and cultural events—folkloric and modern dance, symphonic concerts, art expositions, art films, lectures—at locations such as the celebrated **Teatro Degollado** and the **Instituto Cultural Cabañas** on downtown Plaza Tapatía, and the **Teatro Diana** a mile south of the city center. For details, visit www.ticketmaster.com.mx, or see the Arts and Entertainment section of the *Guadalajara Colony Reporter* either via a copy of the newspaper, or by visiting www.guadalajarareporter.com.

Moreover, Guadalajara is brimming with

You know the Mexican Independence Day is near when the Mexican flags begin to appear on street corners.

less formal entertainment, such as mariachi shows, jazz and rock 'n' roll concerts, and oldies-but-goodies dance clubs. For details, pick up a copy of the *Guadalajara Colony Reporter,* and refer to the restaurant and entertainment sections of this book.

BULLFIGHTING

It is said there are two occasions for which Mexicans arrive on time: funerals and bullfights.

Bullfighting is a recreation, not a sport. The bull is outnumbered seven to one, and the outcome is never in doubt. Even if the matador (literally, "killer") fails in his duty, his assistants will entice the bull away and slaughter it in private beneath the stands.

Mexicans don't call it a "bullfight"; it's the *corrida de toros,* during which six bulls are customarily slaughtered, beginning at 5 P.M. (4 P.M. in the winter). After the beginning parade, featuring the matador and his helpers, the *picadores* and the *bandilleros,* the first bull rushes into the ring in a cloud of dust. Clockwork *ter-*

cios (thirds) define the ritual: the first, the *puyazos,* or "stabs," requires that two *picadores* on horseback thrust lances into the bull's shoulders, weakening it. During the second *tercio,* the *bandilleros* dodge the bull's horns to stick six long, streamer-laden darts into its shoulders.

Trumpets announce the third *tercio* and the appearance of the matador. The bull—weak, confused, and angry—is ready for the finish. The matador struts, holding the red cape, daring the bull to charge. Form now becomes everything. The expert matador takes complete control of the bull, which rushes at the cape, past its ramrod-erect opponent. For charge after charge, the matador works the bull to exactly the right spot in the ring—in front of the judges, a lovely señorita, or perhaps the governor—where the matador mercifully delivers the precision *estocada* (killing sword thrust) deep into the drooping neck of the defeated bull.

HANDICRAFTS
Basketry and Woven Crafts

Weaving straw, leaves, palm fronds, and reeds is among the oldest of Mexican handicraft traditions. Five-thousand-year-old mat- and basket-weaving methods and designs survive to the present day. All over Mexico, people weave *petates* (palm-frond mats) that vacationers use to stretch out on the beach and that locals use for everything, from keeping tortillas warm to shielding babies from the sun. Along the coast, you might see a woman or child waiting for a bus or even walking down the street weaving white palm leaf strands into a coiled basket. Later, you may see a similar basket, embellished with a bright animal—parrot, burro, or even Snoopy—for sale in the market.

Like the origami paper-folders of Japan, folks who live around Lake Pátzcuaro have taken basket-weaving to its ultimate form by crafting virtually everything—from toy turtles and Christmas bells to butterfly mobiles and serving spoons—from the reeds they gather along the lakeshore.

Hatmaking has likewise attained high refinement in Mexico. Workers in Sahuayo,

FIESTAS

The following calendar lists notable national holidays and festivals. If you happen to be where one of these is going on, get out of your car or bus and join in! Information on regional fiestas can be found in the destination chapters.

- January 1: **New Year's Day** *¡Feliz Año Nuevo!*
- January 6: **Día de los Reyes** (Day of the Kings; traditional gift exchange)
- January 17: **Día de San Antonio Abad** (decorating and blessing animals)
- January 20-February 2: **Fiesta de la Virgen de Candelaria** (honoring the Virgin with parades, dances, rodeos, cockfights, and fireworks)
- February 2: **Día de Candelaria** (plants, seeds, and candles blessed; procession and bullfights)
- February 5: **Constitution Day** (commemorating the constitutions of 1857 and 1917)
- February 24: **Flag Day**
- February: The week before Ash Wednesday, usually in late February, many towns stage **Carnaval** (Mardi Gras) extravaganzas
- March 19: **Día de San José** (Day of St. Joseph)
- March 21: **Birthday of Benito Juárez,** the revered "Lincoln of Mexico"
- April: **Semana Santa** (pre-Easter Holy Week, culminating in Domingo Gloria, Easter Sunday)
- May 1: **Labor Day**
- May 3: **Día de la Santa Cruz** (Day of the Holy Cross)
- May 3-15: **Fiesta of St. Isador the Farmer** (blessing of seeds, animals, and water; agricultural displays, competitions, and dancing)
- May 5: **Cinco de Mayo** (defeat of the French at Puebla in 1862)
- May 10: **Mothers' Day**
- Third Week in June: **National Ceramics Fair** in Tlaquepaque
- June 24: **Día de San Juan Bautista** (Day of St. John the Baptist; fairs and religious festivals, playful dunking of people in water)

- June 29: **Día de San Pablo y San Pedro** (Day of St. Peter and St. Paul)
- July 20-25: **Fiesta de Santiago** – sometimes known as the **Fiesta Pagana** (Pagan Festival)
- August 1-15: **Fiesta de la Asunción,** especially in San Juan de los Lagos and Tequila
- September 14: **Charro Day** (Cowboy Day; rodeos)
- September 16: **Independence Day** (mayors everywhere reenact Father Hidalgo's 1810 Grito de Dolores from city hall balconies on the night of 15 September)
- Month of October: **Fiestas de Octubre** (multiple festivals – folkloric dance and music, sporting events, literary readings, theater, classical music, and much more)
- October 4: **Día de San Francisco** (Day of St. Francis)
- October 12: **Romería del Virgen de Zapopan** (grand procession accompanies the Virgen of Zapopan to her home basilica in Zapopan)
- November 1: **Día de Todos Santos** (All Souls' Day; the departed descend from heaven to eat sugar skeletons, skulls, and treats on family altars)
- November 2: **Día de los Muertos** (Day of the Dead; in honor of ancestors, families visit cemeteries and decorate graves with flowers and favorite foods of the deceased)
- November 20: **Revolution Day** (anniversary of the revolution of 1910-1917)
- December 1: **Inauguration Day** (national government changes hands every six years: 2006, 2012, 2018)
- December 8: **Día de la Purísima Concepción** (Day of the Immaculate Conception)
- December 12: **Día de Nuestra Señora de Guadalupe** (Festival of the Virgin of Guadalupe, patroness of Mexico)
- December 16-24: **Christmas Week** (week of *posadas* and piñatas; midnight mass on Christmas Eve)
- December 25: **Christmas Day** *¡Feliz Navidad!* (Christmas trees and gift exchange)
- December 31: **New Year's Eve**

Michoacán, near the southeast shore of Lake Chapala, make especially fine sombreros. Due east across Mexico, in Becal, Campeche, workers fashion Panama hats, or *jipis* (pronounced HEE-pees), so fine, soft, and flexible you can stuff one into your pants pocket without damage.

Although Huichol men (from the Guadalajara region and the neighboring state of Nayarit) do not actually manufacture their headwear, they do decorate them. They take ordinary sombreros and embellish them into Mexico's most flamboyant hats, flowing with bright ribbons, feathers, and fringes of colorful wool balls.

Clothing and Embroidery

Although **traje** (ancestral tribal dress) has nearly vanished in large cities such as Guadalajara, significant numbers of Mexican country women make and wear *traje*. Such traditional styles are still common in remote districts of the Guadalajara region and in the states of Michoacán, Guerrero, Oaxaca, Chiapas, and Yucatán. Most favored is the **huipil,** a long, square-shouldered, short- to mid-sleeved full dress, often hand-embroidered with animal and floral designs. Some of the most beautiful *huipiles* are from Oaxaca, especially from San Pedro de Amusgos (Amusgo tribe; white cotton, embroidered with abstract colored animal and floral motifs), San Andrés Chicahuatxtla (Trique tribe; white cotton, richly embroidered red stripes, interwoven with greens, blues, and yellows, and hung with colored ribbons), and Yalalag (Zapotec tribe; white cotton, with bright flowers embroidered along two or four vertical seams and distinctive colored tassels hanging down the back). Beyond Oaxaca, Maya *huipiles* are also highly desired. They are usually made of white cotton and embellished with brilliant machine-embroidered flowers around the neck and shoulders, front and back.

Shoppers sometimes can buy other, less-common types of *traje* accessories, such as a **quechquémitl** (shoulder cape), often made of wool and worn as an overgarment in winter.

The **enredo** (literally, "tangled") wraparound skirt, by contrast, enfolds the waist and legs, like a Hawaiian sarong. Mixtec women in Oaxaca's warm south coastal region around Pinotepa Nacional (west of Puerto Escondido) commonly wear the *enredo,* known locally as the **pozahuanco** (poh-sah-oo-AHN-koh), below the waist, and when at home, go barebreasted. When wearing her *pozahuanco* in public, a Mixtec woman usually ties a **mandil,** a wide calico apron, around her front side. Women weave the best *pozahuancos* at home, using cotton thread dyed a light purple with secretions of tidepool-harvested snails *(Purpura patula pansa),* and silk dyed deep red with cochineal, extracted from the dried bodies of a locally cultivated beetle *(Dactylopius coccus).*

Colonial Spanish styles have blended with native *traje* to produce a wider class of dress, known generally as **ropa típica.** Fetching embroidered blouses *(blusas),* shawls *(rebozos),* and dresses *(vestidos)* fill boutique racks and market stalls throughout the Mexican Pacific. Among the most handsome is the so-called **Oaxaca wedding dress,** in white cotton with a crochet-trimmed riot of diminutive flowers, hand-stitched about the neck and yoke. Some of the finest examples are made in Antonino Castillo Velasco village, in the Valley of Oaxaca.

In contrast to women, only a very small population of Mexican men—members of remote groups, such as Huichol and Cora in the Guadalajara region—wear *traje.* Nevertheless, shops offer some fine men's *ropa típica,* such as serapes, decorated wool blankets with a hole or slit for the head, worn during northern or highland winters, or *guayaberas,* hip-length, pleated tropical dress shirts.

Fine embroidery *(bordado)* embellishes much traditional Mexican clothing, tablecloths *(manteles),* and napkins *(servilletas).* As everywhere, women define the art of embroidery. Although some still work by hand at home, cheaper machine-made factory lace needlework is more commonly available in shops. (Some shops in Tlaquepaque carry embroidery, *traje,* and *ropa típica.* See the *Tlaquepaque and Tonalá* chapter.)

Leather

The Guadalajara region abounds in for-sale leather goods, most of which are manufactured locally or in León and Guanajuato (shoes, boots, and saddles). For unique and custom-designed articles you'll probably have to confine your shopping to the pricier stores; for more usual, though still attractive, leather items, such as purses, wallets, belts, coats, and boots, veteran shoppers find bargains at individual stores in Tlaquepaque, Zapopan, and at Guadalajara's downtown Libertad Mercado, where an acre of stalls offers the broadest selection at the most reasonable prices (after bargaining) in Mexico.

Furniture

Although furniture is usually too bulky to carry back home with your airline luggage, low prices make it possible for you to ship your purchases home and enjoy beautiful, unusual pieces for half the price you would pay—even if you could find them—outside Mexico (including transport).

A number of classes of furniture (*muebles*, MWAY-blehs) are crafted in villages near the sources of raw materials, notably wood, rattan, bamboo, or wrought iron.

Sometimes it seems as if every house in Mexico is furnished with **colonial-style furniture**, the basic design for much of it dating back at least to the Middle Ages. Although many variations exist, colonial-style furniture is usually heavily built. Table and chair legs are massive, usually lathe-turned; chair backs are customarily arrow-straight and often uncomfortably vertical. Although usually brown-varnished, colonial-style tables, chairs, and chests sometimes shine with inlaid wood or tile, or animal and flower designs. Family shops turn out good furniture, usually in the country highlands, where suitable wood is available.

Equipal, a very distinctive and widespread class of Mexican furniture, is made of leather, usually brownish pigskin or cowhide, stretched over wood frames. Factories are centered mostly in Guadalajara and Tonalá, where a number of stores offer examples.

It is interesting that **lacquered furniture,** in both process and design, has much in common with lacquerware produced half a world away in China. The origin of Mexican lacquerware tradition presents an intriguing mystery. What is certain, however, is that it predated the conquest and was originally produced only in the Pacific states of Guerrero and Michoacán. Persistent legends of pre-Columbian coastal contact with Chinese traders give weight to the speculation, shared by a number of experts, that the Chinese may have taught the lacquerware art to the Mexicans many centuries before the conquest.

Today, artisan families in and around Pátzcuaro, Michoacán, and Olinalá, Guerrero, carry on the tradition. The process, which at its finest resembles cloisonné manufacture, involves carving and painting intricate floral and animal designs, followed by repeated layering of lacquer, clay, and sometimes gold and silver to produce satiny, jewel-like surfaces.

A few villages produce furniture made of plant fiber, such as reeds, raffia, and bamboo. In some cases, entire communities, such as Ihuatzio (near Pátzcuaro) and Villa Victoria (west of Toluca) have long harvested the bounty of local lakes and marshes as the basis for their products.

Wrought iron, produced and worked according to Spanish tradition, is used to produce tables, chairs, and benches. Ruggedly fashioned in a riot of baroque scrollwork, they often decorate garden and patio settings. Several colonial cities, notably Tonalá and Tlaquepaque in the Guadalajara region, and San Miguel de Allende, Toluca, and Guanajuato, are wrought-iron manufacturing and sales centers.

Glass and Stonework

Glass manufacture, unknown in pre-Columbian Mexico, was introduced by the Spanish. Today, the tradition continues in factories throughout Mexico that turn out mountains of *burbuja* (boor-BOO-hah), bubbled glass tumblers, goblets, plates, and pitchers, usually in blue or green. Finer glass is manufactured around Guadalajara, mostly in Tlaquepaque

© BRUCE WHIPPERMAN

Fine ironwork gates are one of Tlaquepaque's renowned local crafts.

the Huichol's original commercial outlets in Tepic, Nayarit, still market their goods, several Guadalajara-area shops, especially in Tlaquepaque and the Huichol museum in Zapopan (and even commercial Christmas catalogs in the United States) now offer Huichol goods. To the original items—mostly devotional arrows, yarn *cicuri* (God's eyes), and decorated gourds for collecting peyote—have been added colorful *cuadras* (yarn paintings) and bead masks.

Cuadras, made of synthetic yarns pressed into beeswax on a plywood backing, traditionally depict plant and animal spirits, the main actors of the Huichol cosmos. Bead masks likewise blend the major elements of the Huichol worldview into an eerie human likeness, usually of Grandmother Earth (Tatei Nakawe).

Precious Metals and Stones

Gold and silver were once the basis for Mexico's wealth. Spanish conquerors plundered a mountain of gold—religious offerings, necklaces, pendants, rings, bracelets—masterfully crafted by a legion of local blacksmiths and jewelers. Unfortunately, much of that indigenous tradition was lost because the Spanish denied Mexicans access to precious metals for generations while they introduced Spanish methods instead. Nevertheless, a small gold-working tradition survived the dislocations of the 1810–1821 War of Independence and the 1910–1917 revolution. Silver crafting, moribund during the 1800s, was revived in Taxco, Guerrero, principally through the efforts of architect-artist William Spratling and the local community.

Today, spurred by the tourist boom, jewelry making thrives in Guadalajara and other Mexican towns. Taxco, Guerrero, where dozens of enterprises—guilds, families, cooperatives—produce sparkling silver and gold adornments, is the acknowledged center. Many Guadalajara regional shops (notably in Tlaquepaque) sell fine Taxco products—shimmering butterflies, birds, jaguars, serpents, turtles, fish—reflecting pre-Columbian tradition.

One hundred percent pure silver is rarely

and Tonalá, where you can watch artisans blow glass into a number of shapes—often paper-thin balls—in red, green, and blue.

Mexican artisans work stone, usually near sources of supply. Puebla, Mexico's major onyx *(onix)* source, is the manufacturing center for the galaxy of mostly rough-hewn, cream-colored items, from animal charms and chess pieces to beads and desk sets, which crowd curio shop shelves all over the country.

Cantera, a soft, often pinkish or greenish volcanic stone, quarried near Pátzcuaro and Oaxacais, is used similarly.

For a keepsake from a truly ancient Mexican tradition, don't forget the hollowed-out stone *metate* (meh-TAH-teh; corn-grinding basin), or the three-legged *molcajete* (mohl-kah-HAY-teh; mortar for grinding chiles).

Huichol Art

Huichol art evolved from the charms that Huichol shamans crafted to empower them during their hazardous pilgrimages to their peyote-rich sacred land of Wirikuta. Although sold because it's too soft. Silver (sent from processing mills in the north of Mexico to be worked in Taxco shops) is nearly always alloyed with 7.5 percent copper to increase its durability. Such pieces, identical in composition to sterling silver, should bear the mark ".925," together with the initials of the manufacturer, stamped on their back sides. Other, less common grades, such as "800 fine" (80 percent silver), should also be stamped.

If silver is not stamped with the degree of purity, it probably contains no silver at all and is an alloy of copper, zinc, and nickel, known by the generic label "alpaca" or "German" silver. Once, after haggling over the purity and prices of his offerings, a street vendor handed me a shiny handful and said, "Go to a jeweler and have them tested. If they're not real, keep them." Calling his bluff, I took them to a jeweler, who applied a dab of hydrochloric acid to each piece. Tiny, tell-tale bubbles of hydrogen revealed the cheapness of the merchandise, which I returned the next day to the vendor.

Some shops price sterling silver jewelry simply by weighing, which typically translates to about $1.25 per gram. If you want to find out if the price is fair, ask the shopkeeper to weigh it for you.

People prize pure gold partly because, unlike silver, it does not tarnish. Gold, nevertheless, is rarely sold pure (24 karat); for durability, it is alloyed with copper. Typical purities, such as 18 karat (75 percent) or 14 karat (58 percent), should be stamped on the pieces. If not, chances are they contain no gold at all.

Opals, first discovered near Magdalena during the 1960s, are centerpieces for fine for-sale jewelry in Magdalena shops. See the *Magdalena* section of the *Getaways* chapter.

Masks

Spanish and native Mexican traditions have blended to produce a multitude of masks— some strange, some lovely, some scary, some endearing, and all interesting. The tradition flourishes in the strongly indigenous southern Pacific states of Michoacán, Guerrero, Oaxaca, and Chiapas, where campesinos gear up all year for the village festivals—especially Semana Santa (Easter week), early December (Virgin of Guadalupe), and the festival of the local patron, whether it be San José, San Pedro, San Pablo, Santa María, Santa Barbara, or one of a host of others. Every local fair has its favored dances, such as the Dance of the Conquest, the Christians and Moors, the Old Men, or the Tiger, in which masked villagers act out age-old allegories of fidelity, sacrifice, faith, struggle, sin, and redemption.

Although masks are made of many materials—from stone and ebony to coconut husks and paper—wood, where available, is the medium of choice. For the entire year, carvers cut, carve, sand, and paint to ensure that each participant will be properly disguised for the festival.

The popularity of masks has led to an entire made-for-tourist mask industry of mass-produced duplicates, many cleverly antiqued. Examine the goods carefully; if the price is high, don't buy it unless you're convinced it's a real antique.

Alebrijes

Tourist demand has made the zany wooden animals called *alebrijes* (ah-lay-BREE-hays) a Oaxaca growth industry. Virtually every family in the Valley of Oaxaca villages of Arrazola and San Martín Tilcajete runs a factory studio. There, piles of soft *copal* wood, which men carve and women finish and intricately paint, become whimsical giraffes, dogs, cats, iguanas, gargoyles, dragons, and many permutations in between. The farther from the source you get, the higher the *alebrije* price becomes; what costs $5 in Arrazola will probably run about $10 in Guadalajara and $30 in the United States or Canada.

Other commonly available wooden items are the charming, colorfully painted fish carved mainly in the Pacific coastal state of Guerrero, and the burnished, dark hardwood animal and fish sculptures of desert ironwood from the state of Sonora.

© BRUCE WHIPPERMAN

Alebrijes, fantastic wood-carved animals, are made in Oaxaca.

Musical Instruments

Virtually all of Mexico's guitars are made in Paracho, Michoacán (southeast of Lake Chapala, 50 miles north of Uruapan). There, scores of cottage factories turn out guitars, violins, mandolins, *viruelas,* ukuleles, and a dozen more variations every day. They vary widely in quality, so look carefully before you buy. Make sure that the wood is well cured and dry; damp, unripe wood instruments are more susceptible to warping and cracking.

Metalwork

Bright copper, brass, pewter, and tinware; sturdy ironwork; and razor-sharp knives and machetes are made in a number of regional centers. **Copperware,** from jugs, cups, and plates to candlesticks—and even the town lampposts and bandstand—all come from Santa Clara del Cobre, a few miles south of Pátzcuaro, Michoacán.

Although not the source of **brass** itself, Tonalá, in the Guadalajara eastern suburb, is the place where brass is most abundant and

beautiful, appearing as menageries of brilliant, fetching birds and animals, sometimes embellished with shiny nickel highlights.

A few Guadalajara factories craft fine **pewter** (mostly of aluminum instead of the traditionally European copper-tin alloy) plates, trays, candlesticks, bowls, and much more, which they sell at regional outlets, notably in Tlaquepaque.

Be sure not to miss the tiny *milagros,* one of Mexico's most charming forms of metalwork. Usually of brass, they are of homely shapes—a horse, dog, or baby, or an arm, head, or foot—which, accompanied by a prayer, the faithful pin to the garment of their favorite saint whom they hope will intercede to cure an ailment or fulfill a wish. Vendors in front of the Guadalajara-region pilgrimage basilicas of Zapopan and San Juan de los Lagos offer swarms of *milagros.*

Paper and Papier-Mâché

Papier-mâché has become a high art in Tonalá, where swarms of birds, cats, frogs, giraffes, and other animal figurines are meticulously crafted by building up repeated layers of glued paper. The results—sanded, brilliantly varnished, and polished—resemble fine sculptures rather than the humble newspaper from which they were fashioned.

Other paper goods you shouldn't overlook include **piñatas** (durable, inexpensive, and as Mexican as you can get), available in every town market; colorful, decorative, cutout banners (string overhead at your home fiesta) from San Salvador Huixcolotla, Puebla; and *amate,* wild fig tree bark paintings in animal and flower motifs, from Xalitla and Ameyaltepec, in the state of Guerrero.

Pottery and Ceramics

Although the Mexican pottery tradition is as diverse as the country itself, some varieties stand out. Among the most prized is the so-called **Talavera** (or Majolica), the best of which is made in a few family-run shops in Puebla. The names Talavera and Majolica derive from Talavera, the Spanish town from where the tradition migrated to Mexico; prior to that it originated on the Spanish Mediterranean island of Majorca, from a combination of still older Arabic, Persian, Chinese, and African ceramic styles. Shapes include plates, bowls, jugs, and pitchers, hand-painted and hard-fired in intricate bright yellow, orange, blue, and green floral designs. So few shops make true Talavera these days that other, cheaper, look-alike grades made around Guanajuato are more common, selling for one-half to one-third the price of the genuine article.

More practical and nearly as prized is hand-painted **petatillo stoneware** from Tlaquepaque and Tonalá in Guadalajara's southeastern suburbs. Although made in many shapes and sizes, such stoneware is often available in complete dinner place settings. Decorations are usually in abstract floral and animal designs, hand-painted over a reddish clay base.

From the same tradition come the famous **bruñido** pottery animals of Tonalá. Round, smooth, and cuddly as ceramic can be, the Tonalá animals—very commonly doves and ducks, but also cats and dogs and sometimes even armadillos, frogs, and snakes—each seem to embody the essence of its species.

Some of the most charming Mexican pottery, made from a ruddy low-fired clay and crafted following pre-Columbian traditions, comes from western Mexico, especially Colima. Charming figurines in timeless human poses— flute-playing musicians, dozing grandmothers, fidgeting babies, loving couples—and animals, especially Colima's famous playful dogs, decorate the shelves of a sprinkling of shops.

Although most latter-day Mexican potters have become aware of the health dangers of **lead pigments,** some for-sale pottery may still contain lead. The hazard comes from low-fired pottery in which the lead has not been firmly melted into the glaze. Acids in foods such as lemons, vinegar, and tomatoes dissolve the lead pigments, which, when ingested, can eventually result in lead poisoning. In general, the hardest, shiniest pottery, which has been twice fired—such as the high-quality Tlaquepaque stoneware used for dishes—is the safest.

Woolen Woven Goods

Mexico's finest wool weavings come from Teotitlán del Valle and neighboring towns, in the Valley of Oaxaca, less than an hour's drive east of Oaxaca City. The weaving tradition (originally of cotton) carried on by Teotitlán's Zapotec-speaking families dates back at least 2,000 years. Many families still carry on the arduous process, making everything from scratch. They gather the dyes from wild plants and the bodies of insects and sea snails. They hand-wash, card, spin, and dye the wool and even travel to remote mountain springs to gather water. The results, they say, *"vale la pena"* ("are worth the pain"): intensely colored, tightly woven carpets, rugs, and wall hangings that retain their brilliance for generations.

Rougher, more loosely woven blankets, jackets, and serapes come from other parts, notably mountain regions, especially around San Cristóbal de las Casas, in Chiapas; Lake Pátzcuaro, in Michoacán; and Tapalpa, in the Guadalajara region.

© BRUCE WHIPPERMAN

Tonalá is the nearly exclusive source of the celebrated *bruñido* (burnished) style of ceramics.

MEXICAN FOOD

On most Mexican-style menus, diners will find variations on a number of basic themes:

Carnes (meats): Carne asada is grilled beef, usually chewy and well-done. Something similar you might see on a menu is *cecina* (say-SEE-nah), dried salted beef, grilled to a shoe-leather-like consistency. Much more appetizing is **birria,** a Guadalajara specialty. Traditional *birrias* are of lamb or goat, often wrapped and pit-roasted in maguey leaves, with which it is served, for authenticity. In addition to *asada,* meat cooking styles are manifold, including *guisado* (stewed), *al pastor* (spit barbecued), and *barbacoa* (grill barbecued). Cuts include *lomo* (loin), *chuleta* (chop), *milanesa* (cutlet), and *albóndigas* (meatballs).

Chiles rellenos: Freshly roasted green chiles, usually stuffed with cheese but sometimes with fish or meat, coated with batter, and fried. They provide a piquant, tantalizing contrast to tortillas.

Enchiladas and **tostadas:** Variations on the filled-tortilla theme. Enchiladas are stuffed with meat, cheese, olives, or beans and covered with sauce and baked, while tostadas consist of toppings served on crisp, open-faced tortillas.

Guacamole: This luscious avocado, onion, tomato, lime, and salsa mixture remains the delight it must have seemed to its Aztec inventors centuries ago. In nontourist Mexico,

© BRUCE WHIPPERMAN

Mexican food is based on the humble corn tortilla.

it's served sparingly as a garnish, rather than in appetizer bowls as is common in the U.S. Southwest (and Mexican resorts catering to North Americans). (Similarly, in nontourist Mexico, burritos and fajitas, both stateside inventions, seldom, if ever, appear on menus.)

FOOD AND DRINK

Many travelers flock to Guadalajara for the food, and for good reason: Excellent Guadalajara restaurants offer a feast of Italian, French, and Chinese cuisine and a banquet of fresh seafood. Nevertheless, Guadalajara's Mexican-style cooking remains the main attraction. True Mexican food is old-fashioned, home-style fare requiring many hours of loving preparation. Such food is short on meat and long on corn, beans, rice, tomatoes, onions, chiles, eggs, and cheese.

Mexican food is the unique product of thousands of years of native tradition. It is based on corn—*teocentli,* the Aztec "holy food'—called *maíz* (mah-EES) by present-day Mexicans. In the past, a Mexican woman spent much of her time grinding and preparing corn: soaking the grain in lime water, which swells the kernels and removes the tough seed-coat, and grinding the bloated seeds into meal on a stone metate. Finally, she patted the meal into tortillas and cooked them on a hot, baked-mud *comal* (griddle).

Sages (men, no doubt) wistfully imagined that gentle pat-pat-pat of women all over

Moles (MOH-lays): Uniquely Mexican specialties. *Mole poblano,* a spicy-sweet mixture of chocolate, chiles, and a dozen other ingredients, is cooked to a smooth sauce, then baked with chicken (or turkey, a combination called *mole de pavo*). So *típica,* it's widely regarded as the national dish.

Quesadillas: Made from soft flour tortillas, rather than corn, quesadillas resemble tostadas and always contain melted cheese.

Sopas: Soups consist of vegetables in a savory chicken broth and are an important part of both *comida* (afternoon) and *cena* (evening) Mexican meals. *Pozole,* a rich steaming stew of hominy, vegetables, and pork or chicken, often constitutes the prime evening offering of small side street shops. *Sopa de taco,* an ever-popular country favorite, is a medium-spicy cheese-topped thick chili broth served with crisp corn tortillas.

Tacos or **taquitos:** Tortillas served open or wrapped around any ingredient.

Tamales: As Mexican as apple pie is American. This savory mixture of meat and sauce imbedded in a shell of corn dough and baked in a wrapping of corn husks is rarely known by the singular, however. They're so yummy that one *tamal* invariably leads to more tamales.

Tortas: The Mexican sandwich, usually hot meat with fresh tomato and avocado, stuffed between two halves of a crisp *bolillo* (boh-LEE-yoh) or Mexican bun.

Tortillas y frijoles refritos: Cooked brown or black beans, mashed and fried in pork fat, and rolled into tortillas with a dash of vitamin C-rich salsa to form a near-complete combination of carbohydrate, fat, and balanced protein.

BEYOND THE BASICS

Mexican food combinations seem endless. Mexican corn itself has more that 500 recognized culinary variations, all from indigenous tradition. This has led to myriad permutations on the taco, such as *sopes* (with small and thick tortillas), *garnacho* (flat taco), *chilequile* (shredded taco), *chalupa* (like a tostada), and *memela*.

Taking a lesson from California nouvelle cuisine, avant-garde Mexican chefs are returning to traditional ingredients. They're beginning to use more and more chiles – habanero, morón, poblano, jalapeño and more – prepared with many variations, such as *chipotle, ancho, piquín,* and *mulato.* Squash flowers *(flor de calabaza)* and cactus *(nopal)* leaves are increasingly finding their way into soups and salads.

Chefs are often serving the wild game – *venado* (venison), *conejo* (rabbit), *guajalote* (turkey), *codorniz* (quail), armadillo, and iguana – that country Mexicans have always depended upon. As part of the same trend, *cuitlacoche* (corn mushroom fungus), *chapulines* (fried small grasshoppers), and *gusanos de maguey* (maguey worms) are increasingly being added as ingredients in upscale restaurants.

Mexico to be the heartbeat of Mexico, which they feared would cease when women stopped making tortillas.

Fewer women these days make tortillas by hand. The gentle pat-pat-pat has been replaced by the whir and rattle of the automatic tortilla-making machine in myriad *tortillerías,* where women and girls line up for their family's daily kilo-stack of tortillas.

Tortillas are to the Mexicans as rice is to the Chinese and bread to the French. Mexican food is invariably some mixture of sauce, meat, beans, cheese, and vegetables wrapped in a tortilla, which becomes the culinary be-all: the food, the dish, and the utensil wrapped into one.

If a Mexican man has nothing to wrap in his lunchtime tortilla, he will content himself by rolling a thin filling of salsa in it.

Hot or Not?

Much food served in Mexico is not "Mexican." Eating habits, as most other customs, depend upon social class. Upwardly mobile Mexicans typically shun the corn-based *indígena* fare in favor of the European-style food of the Spanish colonial elite: chops, steaks, cutlets, fish, clams, omelets, soups, pasta, rice, and potatoes.

Such fare is often as bland as Des Moines on a summer Sunday afternoon. *No picante*—not spicy—is how the Mexicans describe bland food. *Picante*, then, means spicy. *Caliente*, the Spanish adjective for "hot" (as in "hot water"), never implies spicy, in contrast to English usage.

Although strictly vegetarian cooking is the exception in Mexico, a few macrobiotic restaurants, health-food stores, and organic produce outlets serve Guadalajara region customers.

The simple fact is, meat is such a delicacy for many Mexicans that they can't understand why people would give it up voluntarily. Nevertheless, the typical Mexican menu offers many healthy meatless possibilities, such as beans, guacamole, omelets, savory rice *(arroz)*, rich vegetable soups *(sopas)*, and fruit for dessert.

Bread and Pastries

Excellent locally baked bread is a delightful surprise to many first-time Guadalajara visitors. Small bakeries everywhere put out trays of hot, crispy-crust *bolillos* (rolls) and *panes dulces* (pastries). The pastries range from simple cakes, muffins, cookies, and donuts to fancy fruit-filled turnovers and puffs. Half the fun occurs before the eating: perusing the goodies, tongs in hand, and picking out the most scrumptious. With your favorite dozen or two finally selected, you take your tray to the cashier, who deftly bags everything up and collects a few pesos (two or three dollars) for your entire mouthwatering selection.

Seafood

Early chroniclers wrote that Moctezuma employed a platoon of runners to bring fresh fish 300 miles from the sea every day to his court. Around Guadalajara nowadays, fresh seafood is fortunately much more available: You'll find it in dozens of establishments, from humble downtown fish taco stalls to sophisticated suburban restaurants.

Fruits and Juices

Squeezed vegetable and fruit juices, called *jugos*

(HOO-gohs), are among the widely available delights of Guadalajara. Among the many establishments—restaurants, cafés, and *loncherías*—willing to supply you with your favorite *jugo*, the juice bars *(jugerías)* are the most fun. Colorful fruit piles mark *jugerías*. If you don't immediately spot your favorite fruit, ask; it might be hidden in the refrigerator.

Besides your choice of pure juice, a *jugería* will often serve *licuados*. Into the juice, they whip powdered milk, your favorite flavoring, and sugar to taste, for a creamy afternoon pick-me-up or evening dessert. One big favorite is a cool banana-chocolate *licuado*, which comes out tasting like a milkshake (minus the calories).

Alcoholic Drinks

The Aztecs sacrificed anyone caught drinking alcohol without permission. The more lenient Spanish attitude toward getting *borracho* (soused) has led to a thriving Mexican renaissance of traditional alcoholic beverages: tequila, mescal, Kahlúa, pulque, and *aguardiente*. **Tequila** and **mescal** are both distilled from the fermented juice of the cactuslike maguey plant. While mescal originated in Oaxaca, where the best is still made, tequila originated in the Guadalajara-region distillery town of Tequila. Both tequila and mescal come 76 proof (38 percent alcohol) and up. A small white worm, endemic to the maguey plant, is customarily added to each bottle of factory mescal for authenticity. The best tequilas are distilled exclusively from the scarce blue agave variety of maguey and consequently have become very expensive. (For more details, see the sidebar *Tequila* in the *Getaways* chapter.)

Pulque, although also made from the sap of the maguey, is locally brewed to a small alcohol content between that of beer and wine. The brewing houses are sacrosanct preserves, circumscribed by traditions that exclude women and outsiders. The brew, said to be full of nutrients, is sold to local *pulquerías* and drunk immediately. If you are ever invited into a *pulquería*, it is an honor you cannot refuse.

Aguardiente, by contrast, is the notorious

A TROVE OF FRUITS AND NUTS

Besides carrying the usual temperate fruits, *jugerías* and markets are seasonal sources for a number of exotic varieties.

- **avocado** (*aguacate*, ah-gwah-KAH-tay): Aztec aphrodisiac

- **banana** (*platano*): many kinds – big and small, red and yellow

- *chirimoya:* green scales, white pulp; sometimes called an *anona*

- **coconut** (*coco*): coconut "milk" is called *agua coco*

- **grapes** (*uvas*): August–November season

- *guanabana:* looks, but doesn't taste, like a green mango

- **guava:** delicious juice, widely available canned

- **lemon** (*limón real*, lee-MOHN ray-AHL): uncommon and expensive; use lime instead

- **lime** (*limón*, lee-MOHN): douse salads with it

- *mamey* (mah-MAY): yellow, juicy fruit; excellent for jellies and preserves

- **mango:** king of fruit, in a hundred varieties June–November

- **orange** (*naranja*, nah-RAHN-ha): greenish skin but sweet and juicy

- **papaya:** said to aid digestion and healing

- **peach** (*durazno*, doo-RAHS-noh): delicious and widely available as canned juice

- **peanut** (*cacahuate*, kah-kah-WAH-tay): home roasted and cheap

- **pear** (*pera*): fall season

- **pecan** (*nuez/nueces*): for a treat, try freshly ground pecan butter

- *piña anona:* looks like a thin ear of corn without the husk; tastes like pineapple

- **pineapple** (*piña*): huge, luscious, and cheap

- *pitaya:* red, soft when ripe, fruit of the organ cactus; tastes like a sweet apple

- **strawberry** (*fresa*, FRAY-sah): local favorite

- **tangerine** (*mandarina*): common around Christmas

- **watermelon** (*sandía*, sahn-DEE-ah): perfect on a hot day

- *yaca:* Mexican version of the southeast Asian jackfruit; green, football-sized, and delicious mild taste

- *zapote:* yellow, fleshy fruit; said to induce sleep

- *zapote colorado:* brown skin, red, puckery fruit, like persimmon; incorrectly called *mamey*

fiery Mexican "white lightning," a sugar cane–distilled, dirt-cheap ticket to oblivion for poor Mexican men.

While pulque comes from age-old Indian tradition, beer is the beverage of modern mestizo Mexico. Full-bodied and tastier than "light" U.S. counterparts, Mexican beer enjoys an enviable reputation.

Those visitors who indulge usually know their favorites among the many brands, including, from light to dark: Superior, Corona, Pacífico, Tecate (served with lime), Carta Blanca, Modelo, Dos Equis, Bohemia, Indio, Tres Equis, and Negra Modelo. Nochebuena, a hearty dark brew, becomes available only around Christmas.

Mexicans have yet to develop much of a taste for *vino tinto* or *vino blanco* (red or white table wine), although some domestic vintages (especially of the Baja California labels **Cetto,**

Domecq, and **Monte Xanic** (MON-tay shah-NEEK) are often excellent.

Chocolatl

The refreshing drink *chocolatl,* enjoyed by Aztec nobility, is a remote but distinct relative of the chocolate consumed today by hundreds of millions of people. It was once so precious, chocolate beans were a common medium of exchange in preconquest Mexico. In those days a mere dozen cacao beans could command a present value of upwards of $100 in goods or services. Counterfeiting was rife—entrepreneurs tried to create *chocolatl* from anything, including avocado seeds. Moreover, *chocolatl* was thought to be so potent an aphrodisiac and hallucinogen that its use was denied, under penalty of death, to commoners.

Although intrigued, Europeans were put off by *chocolatl's* bitter taste. Around 1600, a whole shipload of chocolate beans was jettisoned at sea by English privateers who, having captured a Spanish galleon, mistook its cargo for goat dung.

The French soon made *chocolatl* easier to stomach by powdering it; the British added milk; and finally the Swiss, of Nestlé fame, cashed in with chocolate candy. The world hasn't been the same since.

Though *chocolatl* found its way to Europe, it never left Mexico, where hot chocolate, whipped frothy with a wooden-ringed *molinillo* (little mill), is more common now than in Aztec times. In Mexico, chocolate is more than mere dessert—used to spice the tangy *moles* of southern Mexico, it's virtually a national food.

ESSENTIALS

Getting There

BY AIR
From the United States and Canada

Most foreign visitors reach Guadalajara by air. Flights are frequent and reasonably priced. Competition sometimes shaves tariffs down as low as $350 for a Guadalajara round-trip from one of the Guadalajara departure gateways of Sacramento, San Francisco, Oakland, San Jose, Los Angeles, Las Vegas, Phoenix, Tucson, Dallas, Houston, Chicago, and New York.

Air travelers can save lots of money by shopping around. Make it clear to the airline or travel agent you're interested in a bargain. Ask the right questions: Are there special-incentive, advance-payment, night, midweek, business, senior, tour package, or charter fares? Peruse the ads in the Sunday newspaper travel section for bargain-oriented travel agencies. Alternatively, log on to airlines' websites or ticket agencies and look for promotions.

From Europe, Australasia, and Latin America

A few airlines fly across the Atlantic directly to Mexico City. These include **Lufthansa** (www.lufthansa.com), which connects directly from Frankfurt; and **Aeroméxico** (www.aeromexico.com), which connects directly from Paris and

AIRLINES

These air carriers have direct connections between North American gateway cities and Guadalajara. You may be able to save money by booking an air/hotel, or air/hotel/car package.

Aerocalifornia
(tel. 800/237-6225, www.aerocalifornia.com) Flies direct to Guadalajara from Los Angeles, Tijuana, and Tucson.

Aeroméxico
(tel. 800/237-6639, www.aeromexico.com) Flies direct to Guadalajara from Los Angeles, Ontario (CA), Las Vegas, Phoenix, and Atlanta. Also offers flights to Mexico City from San Diego, Tijuana, Boston, Miami, Houston, Dallas, and several others.

Alaska Airlines
(tel. 800/426-0333, www.alaskaair.com) Flies direct to Guadalajara from Los Angeles.

American Airlines
(tel. 800/433-7300, www.aa.com) Flies direct to Guadalajara from Dallas and Los Angeles.

America Trans Air (ATA)
(tel. 800/435-9282, www.ata.com)

Flies direct to Guadalajara from Chicago.

Aviacsa
(tel. 800/967-5263, www.aviacsa.com.mx) Flies direct to Guadalajara from Los Angeles.

Continental
(tel. 800/231-0856, www.continental.com) Flies direct to Guadalajara from Houston. Also flies to Mexico City from Newark.

Delta
(tel. 800/221-1212, www.delta.com) Flies direct to Guadalajara from Los Angeles and Atlanta. Also flies to Puerto Vallarta from Los Angeles and Atlanta and Mexico City from Los Angeles, Dallas, and Atlanta.

Mexicana
(tel. 800/531-7921, www.mexicana.com) Flies direct to Guadalajara from Los Angeles, Sacramento, San Francisco, San Jose, Las Vegas, Tijuana, Portland, and Chicago. Also flies to Mexico City from Denver, New York, Toronto, and San Antonio.

US Airways (formerly America West)
(tel. 800/363-2597, www.usairways.com) Flies direct to Guadalajara from Phoenix. Also flies to Puerto Vallarta from Phoenix.

Madrid. In Mexico City, several connections with the Guadalajara region are available, mostly via Mexicana and Aeroméxico airlines.

From Latin America, Aeroméxico connects directly with Mexico City from Sao Paulo, Brazil; Santiago, Chile; and Lima, Peru. Other Latin American flag carriers also fly directly to Mexico City.

Very few flights cross the Pacific directly to Mexico, except for **Japan Airlines** (www.jal.com), which connects Tokyo to Mexico City via Vancouver. More commonly, travelers from Australasia routinely transfer at Seattle, San Francisco, Los Angeles, or Phoenix for Guadalajara. For more information, consult a travel agent or log on to an airline ticketing website.

For many more arrival and departure details specific to the Guadalajara airport, see *Getting There and Around* in the *Downtown* chapter.

Baggage

Veteran travelers often condense their luggage to carry-ons only. Airlines routinely allow a carry-on (not exceeding 45 inches in combined length, width, and girth) and a purse. Thus relieved of heavy burdens, your trip will become much simpler. You'll avoid possible luggage loss and long baggage check-in lines by being able to check in directly at the boarding gate.

Even if you can't avoid checking luggage, loss of it needn't ruin your trip. Always carry your irreplaceable items in the cabin with you. These should include all money, credit cards, travelers checks, keys, tickets, cameras, passport, prescription drugs, and eyeglasses.

At the X-ray security check, calmly insist that your film and cameras be hand-inspected. Regardless of what attendants claim, repeated X-ray scanning will fog any undeveloped film, especially the sensitive ASA 400 and 1,000 high-speed varieties. The cleverest (although weighty) film option is to use one or two lead-lined film bags, which X-rays cannot penetrate. This, of course, forces hand-inspection.

Insurance

Travelers packing lots of expensive baggage, or those who may have to cancel a nonrefundable flight or tour (because of illness, for example), might consider buying travel insurance. Travel agents routinely sell packages that include baggage, trip cancellation, and default insurance. Baggage insurance covers you beyond the conventional liability limits (typically about $1,000 domestic, $400 international); check with your carrier. **Trip cancellation insurance** pays if you must cancel your prepaid trip, while **default insurance** protects you if your carrier or tour agent does not perform as agreed. Travel insurance, however, can be expensive. **Travel Insurance Services** (800/937-1387, www.travelinsure.com), for example, offers $3,000 of baggage insurance per person for two weeks for about $65. Weigh your options and the cost against benefits carefully before putting your money down. Or contact World Travel Center (tel. 866/979-6753 or 402/343-3621, www.worldtravelcenter.com).

Flight Confirmation

It's wise to reconfirm both departure and return flight reservations, especially during the busy Christmas and Easter seasons. This is a useful strategy, as is prompt arrival at check-in, against getting "bumped" (losing your seat) by the tendency of airlines to overbook the rush of high-season vacationers. For further protection, always get your seat assignment and boarding pass included with your ticket when possible.

BY BUS

Just as air travel rules in the United States, bus travel rules in Mexico. Hundreds of sleek, first-class bus lines with names such as Elite, Turistar, Futura, Omnibus de Mexico, Transportes Pacífico, and White Star (Estrella Blanca) depart the border daily, headed for the Guadalajara region.

Since North American bus lines ordinarily terminate just north of the Mexican border, you must usually disembark, collect your things, and, after having filled out the necessary but very simple paperwork at the Mexican immigration office, proceed on foot across the border to Mexico, where you can bargain with one of the local taxis to drive you the few miles to the *camionera central* (central bus station).

First- and luxury-class bus service in Mexico is much cheaper and often better than in the United States. Tickets for comparable trips in Mexico cost a fraction of their U.S. price (as little as $50 for the Guadalajara trip, compared to $100 for a similar-length trip in the United States).

In Mexico, as on U.S. buses, you often have to take it as you find it. *Asientos reservados* (seat reservations), *boletos* (tickets), and information must generally be obtained in person at the bus station, and credit cards and travelers checks may not be accepted. Neither are reserved bus tickets usually refundable, so don't miss the bus. On the other hand, plenty of buses roll south almost continuously.

Request a reserved seat, if possible, with numbers 1–25 in the front *(delante)* to middle *(medio)* of the bus. Although it's becoming less likely, rear seats are sometimes occupied by smokers, who might try to light up (although on-board smoking is officially frowned upon). At night, you will sleep better on the right side *(lado derecho)*, away from the glare of oncoming traffic lights.

Baggage is generally secure on Mexican buses. Label it, however. Overhead racks are sometimes too cramped to accommodate airline-sized carry-ons. Carry a small bag with your money and irreplaceables on your person; pack clothes and nonessentials in your checked luggage. Although it's not generally necessary, for peace of mind, you might watch the handler put your checked baggage on the bus and watch to make sure it is not mistakenly taken off the bus at intermediate stops.

If your baggage gets misplaced, remain calm. Bus employees are generally competent and conscientious. If you are patient, recovering

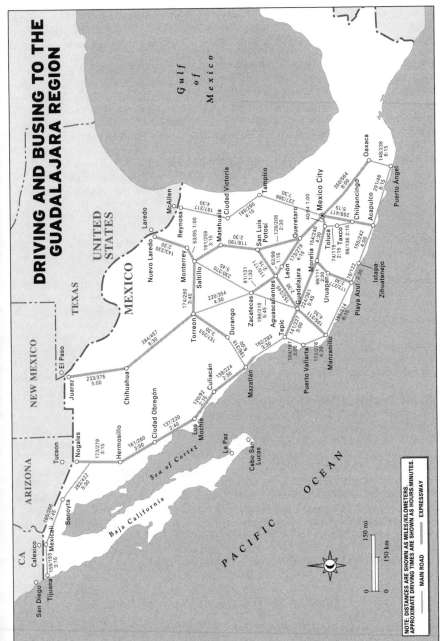

DRIVING AND BUSING TO THE GUADALAJARA REGION

NOTE: DISTANCES ARE SHOWN AS MILES/KILOMETERS.
APPROXIMATE DRIVING TIMES ARE SHOWN AS HOURS:MINUTES.

——— MAIN ROAD   ——— EXPRESSWAY

© AVALON TRAVEL

your luggage will become a matter of honor for many of them. Baggage handlers are at the bottom of the pay scale; a tip for their mostly thankless job is very much appreciated.

Bus Routes to Guadalajara

From California and the West, cross the border to Tijuana, Mexicali, or Nogales, where you can ride one of at least three bus lines along the Pacific coast route (National Highway 15) south to Guadalajara.

Choices include Estrella Blanca (via its subsidiaries, Elite, Transportes Norte de Sonora, Futura, or Turistar), Omnibus de Mexico (via its subsidiary TAP), or independent Transportes del Pacífico. Allow a full day and a bit more (about 30 hours), depending upon connections, for the trip. Carry liquids and food (which might be only minimally available en route) with you.

From the Midwest, cross the border from El Paso to Juárez and head south by way of Chihuahua and Durango by either Estrella Blanca (via subsidiaries Transportes Chihuahuenses or luxury-class Turistar) or independent Omnibus de Mexico. Similarly, from the U.S. Southeast and East, cross the border at Laredo to Nuevo Laredo and ride Transportes del Norte or Turistar direct (or transfer at Monterrey) to Guadalajara.

BY CAR AND RV

If you're adventurous and like going to out-of-the-way places, but still want to have all the comforts of home, you may enjoy driving your car or RV to Guadalajara. On the other hand, cost, risk, wear on both you and your vehicle, and congestion hassles in towns may change your mind.

Mexican Car Insurance

Mexico does not recognize foreign insurance. When you drive into Mexico, Mexican auto insurance is at least as important as your passport. At the busier crossings, you can get it at insurance "drive-ins" just north of the border. The many Mexican auto insurance companies are government-regulated; their numbers keep prices and services competitive.

Sanborn's Mexico Insurance (Sanborn's Mexico, P.O. Box 310, McAllen, TX 78502, tel. 956/686-3601, toll-free 800/222-0158, www.sanbornsinsurance.com), one of the best-known agencies, certainly seems to be trying hardest. It offers a number of books and services, including the *Recreational Guide to Mexico,* a good road map, "smile-by-mile" *Travelog* guide to "every highway in Mexico," hotel discounts, and more. Much of the above is available to members of Sanborn's Sombrero Club.

Alternatively, look into **Vagabundos del Mar** (tel. 800/474-2252, www.vagabundos.com), an RV-oriented Mexico travel club offering memberships that include a newsletter, caravan opportunities, discounts, insurance, and much more.

Mexican car insurance runs from a barebones rate of about $6 a day for minimal $10,000/$50,000 (property damage/medical payments) coverage to a more typical $12 a day for more complete $20,000/$100,000 coverage. On the same scale, insurance for a $50,000 RV and equipment runs about $30 a day. These daily rates decrease sharply for six-month or one-year policies, which run from about $200 for the minimum to $400–1,600 for complete, high-end coverage.

If you get broken glass, personal effects, and legal expenses coverage with these rates, you're lucky. Mexican policies don't usually cover them.

You should get something for your money, however. The deductibles should be no more than $300–500, the public liability/medical payments should be about double the legal minimum ($25,000/$25,000/$50,000), and you should be able to get your car fixed in the United States and receive payment in U.S. dollars for losses. If not, shop around.

A Sinaloa Note of Caution

Although *bandidos* no longer menace Mexican roads (but loose burros, horses, and cattle still do), be cautious in the infamous marijuana- and opium-growing region of Sinaloa state north of Mazatlán. It's best not to stray from

ROAD SAFETY

Hundreds of thousands of visitors enjoy safe Mexican road-trip vacations every year. Their success is due in large part to their frame of mind: Drive defensively, anticipate and adjust to danger before it happens, and watch everything – side roads, shoulders, the car in front, and cars far down the road. The following tips will help ensure a safe and enjoyable trip.

Don't drive at night. Range animals, unmarked sand piles, pedestrians, one-lane bridges, cars without lights, and drunk drivers are doubly hazardous at night.

Don't break speed limits, although they are rarely enforced. Mexican roads are often narrow and shoulderless. Poor markings and macho drivers who pass on curves are best faced at a speed of 40 mph (64 kph) rather than 75 mph (120 kph).

Don't drive on sand. Even with four-wheel-drive, you'll eventually get stuck if you drive either often or casually on beaches. When the tide comes in, who'll pull your car out?

Slow down at the *topes* (speed bumps) at the edges of towns and for *vados* (dips), which can be dangerously bumpy and full of water.

Extending the courtesy of the road goes hand-in-hand with safe driving. Both courtesy and machismo are more infectious in Mexico; on the highway, it's much safer to spread the former than the latter.

Highway 15 between Culiacán and Mazatlán or from Highway 40 between Mazatlán and Durango. Curious tourists have been assaulted in the hinterlands adjacent to these roads.

The Green Angels

The Green Angels have answered many motoring tourists' prayers in Mexico. Bilingual teams of two, trained in auto repair and first aid, help distressed tourists along main highways. They patrol fixed stretches of road twice daily by truck. To make sure they stop to help, pull completely off the highway and raise your hood. You may want to hail a passing trucker to call them for you (tel. 01-800/903-9200, or Mexico emergency number tel. 078 for the tourism hotline).

If, for some reason, you have to leave your vehicle on the roadside, don't leave it unattended. Hire a local teenager or adult to watch it for you. Unattended vehicles on Mexican highways are quickly stricken by a mysterious disease, the symptoms of which are rapid loss of vital parts.

Mexican Gasoline

Pemex, short for Petróleos Mexicanos, the government oil monopoly, markets diesel fuel and two grades of unleaded gasoline: 92-octane premium and 89-octane Magna. Magna (MAHG-nah) is good gas, yielding performance similar to that of U.S.-style "regular or super unleaded" gasoline. (My car, whose manufacturer recommended 91-octane, ran well on Magna.) It runs about $0.70 per liter (or about $2.70 per gallon).

On main highways, Pemex makes sure that major stations (typically spaced about 25 miles apart) stock Magna.

Gas Station Thievery

Although the problem has abated considerably in recent years (by the hiring of female attendants), boys who hang around gas stations to wash windows are notoriously light-fingered. When stopping at the *gasolinera*, make sure that your cameras, purses, and other movable items are out of reach. Also, make sure that your car has a lockable gas cap. If not, insist on pumping the gas yourself, or be extra watchful as you pull up to the gas pump. Make certain that the pump reads zero before the attendant pumps the gas.

A Healthy Car

Preventive measures spell good health for both you and your car. Get that tune-up (or that long-delayed overhaul) *before,* rather than after, you leave.

A *gasolinera* (gasoline station) is not necessary for an unleaded fill-up in Guadalajara's remote country districts.

Carry a stock of spare parts, which will be more difficult to get and more expensive in Mexico than at home. Carry an extra tire or two, a few cans of motor oil and octane enhancer, oil and gas filters, fan belts, spark plugs, tune-up kit, points, and fuses. Be prepared with basic tools and supplies, such as screwdrivers, pliers including Vice-Grip, lug wrench, jack, adjustable wrenches, tire pump and patches, tire pressure gauge, steel wire, and electrical tape. For breakdowns and emergencies, carry a folding shovel, a husky rope or chain, a gasoline can, and flares.

Car Repairs in Mexico

The American big three—General Motors, Ford, and Chrysler—as well as Nissan and Volkswagen are represented by extensive dealer networks in Mexico. Latecomers Toyota and Honda are represented, although to a lesser extent. Getting your car or truck serviced at such agencies is straightforward. While parts will probably be higher in price, shop rates run less

than half U.S. prices, so repairs will generally cost much less than back home.

Repair of other makes is more problematic. Mexico has few, if any, additional Japanese car or truck dealers; and other than Mercedes-Benz, which has some truck agencies, it is difficult to find officially certified mechanics for other Japanese, British, and European vehicles. Parts, moreover, may not be locally available and may take as long as week to have them shipped from the United States.

Many clever Mexican independent mechanics, however, can fix any car that comes their way. Their humble repair shops *talleres mecánicos* (tah-YER-ays may-KAH-nee-kohs) dot town and village roadsides everywhere.

Although most mechanics are honest, beware of unscrupulous operators who try to collect double or triple their original estimate. If you don't speak Spanish, find someone who can assist you in negotiations. *Always* get at least a verbal (better if written) cost estimate, including needed parts and labor, even if you have to write it yourself. Make sure the mechanic understands, then ask him to sign it before he starts work. Although this may be a hassle, it might save you a much nastier hassle later. Shop labor at small, independent repair shops should run $10–20 per hour. For more information, and for entertaining anecdotes of car and RV travel in Mexico, consult Carl Franz's *The People's Guide to Mexico*.

Bribes

Traffic police around Guadalajara sometimes seem to be watching foreign cars with eagle eyes. If they whistle you over, stop immediately or you will really get into hot water. If guilty, say *"Lo siento"* ("I'm sorry") and be cooperative. Although they most likely won't mention it, the officers are sometimes hoping that you'll cough up a $20 *mordida* (bribe) for the privilege of driving away. Don't do it. Although they may hint at confiscating your car, calmly ask for an official *boleto* (written traffic ticket), if you're guilty in exchange for your driver's license (have a copy), which the officers will probably keep if they write a ticket. If after a

DISASTER AND RESCUE ON A MEXICAN HIGHWAY

My litany of Mexican driving experiences came to a climax one night when, heading north from Tepic, I hit a cow at 50 mph head on. The cow was knocked about 150 feet down the road, while my two friends and I endured a scary impromptu roller-coaster ride. When the dust settled, we, although in shock, were grateful that we hadn't suffered the fate of the poor cow, who had died instantly from the collision.

From that low point, our fortunes soon began to improve. Two buses stopped and about 40 men got out to move my severely wounded van to the shoulder. The cow's owner, a rancher, arrived to cart off the cow's remains in a jeep. Then the police – a man and his wife in a VW bug – pulled up. "Pobrecita camioneta," "Poor little van," the woman said, gazing at my vehicle, which now resembled an oversized, rumpled accordion. They gave us a ride to Mazatlán, found us a hotel room, and generally made sure we were okay.

If I hadn't had Mexican auto insurance I would have been in deep trouble. Mexican law – based on the Napoleonic Code – presumes guilt and does not bother with juries. It would have kept me in jail until all damages were settled. The insurance agent I saw in the morning took care of everything. He called the police station, where I was excused from paying damages when the cow's owner failed to show. He had my car towed to a repair shop, where the mechanics banged it into good enough shape so I could drive it home a week later. Forced to stay in one place, my friends and I enjoyed the most relaxed time of our entire three months in Mexico. The *pobrecita camioneta*, all fixed up a few months later, lasted 14 more years.

© BRUCE WHIPPERMAN

If you carry a couple of sturdy spare tires on your Guadalajara road trip you'll at least save time and money, and at most, avoid a disaster.

few minutes no money appears, the officer will most likely give you back your driver's license rather than go to the trouble of writing the ticket. If not, the worst that will usually happen is you will have to go to the *presidencia municipal* (city hall) in Zapopan, Tlaquepaque, or Tonalá, or the *transito* in Guadalajara (motor vehicle department, at the traffic circle-intersection of Alcalde and Circunvalación, about two miles—three kilometers—north of the downtown cathedral) the next morning and pay the $20 to a clerk in exchange for your driver's license.

Highway Routes from the United States

Three main routes head south from U.S. border crossings to Guadalajara. At safe highway speeds, the two western routes (from Nogales, Arizona, and El Paso, Texas, respectively) require a minimum of about 24 hours at the wheel. The eastern route (from either Laredo or McAllen, Texas) is shorter and quicker, requiring one very long day (about 15 hours) behind the wheel. For comfort and safety, many folks allow three full south-of-the-border driving days to Guadalajara via the western routes and two days via the eastern.

All of these routes follow **toll** *(cuota)* expressways, which often parallel the original two-lane nontoll *(libre)* routes. You can avoid some of the tolls (around $60 total to Guadalajara for a passenger car, about double that for big, multiple-wheeled RVs) by sticking to the old *libre* route. However, the one or two days of extra travel time, with the associated hotel and food costs, and the significantly increased road hazards—pedestrians, roadside carts, stray animals, noisy, smoky trucks, and congestion—will, in most cases, not be worth the toll savings.

From the U.S. Pacific coast and points west, follow National Highway 15 (or 15D when it's a four-lane expressway) from the border at Nogales, Sonora, an hour's drive south of Tucson, Arizona. Highway 15D continues southward smoothly, leading you through cactus-studded mountains and valleys that turn into green, lush farmland and tropical coastal plain and forest by the time you arrive in Mazatlán. Watch for the peripheral bypasses *(periféricos)* and truck routes that route you past the congested downtowns of Hermosillo, Guaymas, Ciudad Obregón, Los Mochis, and Culiacán. Between these centers, you can cruise along, via *cuota* (toll) expressways, virtually all the way to Mazatlán.

South of Mazatlán, continue along the narrow (but soon to be replaced) two-lane route to Tepic, where the route forks left (east) as *cuota autopista* (toll expressway) 15D, continuing to Guadalajara.

If, however, you're driving to Guadalajara from the central United States, cross the border at El Paso to **Ciudad Juárez,** Chihuahua. There, National Highway 45D, the *cuota* (toll) multilane expressway, leads you southward through high, dry plains past the cities of Chihuahua and Jiménez. From there continue, by combined Highways 45 and 49, to just north of Gómez Palacio–Torreón. There, bypass the downtown (toward Durango/Fresnillo/Zacatecas) and proceed about 60 miles (100 km) southwest, where you fork south (toward Fresnillo and Zacatecas), continuing along Highways 45 and 49. Bypass Fresnillo and continue south along Highways 45 and 49 to Zacatecas, where you connect with Highway 54 south toward Guadalajara (or, longer but quicker, via Highway 45 via Aguascalientes, thence southwest via speedy expressway 80D to Guadalajara).

Folks heading to Guadalajara from the eastern and southeastern United States should cross the border from either Laredo, Texas, to **Nuevo Laredo,** or McAllen, Texas, to **Reynosa.** Via McAllen, follow either the National Highway 40 nontoll *(libre)* route or the new toll *(cuota)* expressway Highway 40D southwest, which continues to the eastern outskirts of Monterrey. (If via Laredo, do the same via either nontoll Highway 40 or toll expressway 40D.)

Bypass Monterrey (toward Saltillo, west) via expressway Highway 40. At Saltillo, connect to Highway 54 south to Zacatecas, thence south to Guadalajara via two-lane Highway 54 (or more quickly by connecting at Zacatecas, with Highway 45 to Aguascalientes, thence via toll expressway 80D to Guadalajara).

BY TRAIN

Privatization is rapidly putting an end to most passenger train service in Mexico, with the exception of the **Copper Canyon** scenic route. One of the few remaining passenger train rides in Mexico begins with a bus trip or flight south to Chihuahua, where you board the Chihuahua–Pacific Railway train and ride west along the renowned Copper Canyon (Barranca del Cobre) route to the Pacific. Only finished during the early 1960s, this route traverses the spectacular canyonland home of the Tarahumara people. At times along the winding 406-mile (654-km) route, your rail car seems to teeter at the very edge of the labyrinthine Barranca del Cobre, a canyon so deep that its climate varies from Canadian at the top to tropical jungle at the bottom.

The railway-stop village of Creel, with a few stores and hotels and a Tarahumara mission, is the major jumping-off point for trips into the canyon. For a treat, reserve a stay en route to Guadalajara at the Copper Canyon Lodge in Creel. From there, the canyon beckons: Explore the village, enjoy panoramic views, observe mountain wildlife, and breathe pine-scented mountain air. Farther afield, you can hike to a hot spring or spend a few days exploring the canyon-bottom itself. For more information, contact Copper Canyon Hiking Lodges (2741 Paldan St., Auburn Hills, MI 48326, tel. 248/340-7230 or 800/776-3942, www.coppercanyonlodges.com).

Copper Canyon Tours

Some agencies arrange unusually good Copper Canyon rail tours. Among the best is **Columbus Travel** (900 Ridge Creek Ln., Bulverde, TX 78163-2872, tel. 800/843-1060, www.canyon-travel.com), which employs its own resident, ecologically sensitive guides. Trips range from small-group, rail-based sightseeing and birding/natural history tours to customized wilderness rail-jeep-backpacking adventures.

Elderhostel (75 Federal St., 3rd Fl., Boston, MA 02110-1941, tel. 877/426-8056, www.elderhostel.org) has long provided some of the best-buy Copper Canyon options, designed for seniors. Participants customarily fly to Los Mochis on the Pacific coast, then transfer to the first-class Mexican Chihuahua-Pacific train for a four-day canyonland adventure. Highlights include nature walks, visits to native missions, and cultural sites in Cerrocahui village and Creel, the frontier outpost in the Tarahumara heartland. The return includes a comfortable overnight at Posada Barranca, at the canyon's dizzying edge.

Getting Around

BY BUS

The passenger bus is the king of the Mexican road. Dozens of lines with thousands of buses, from luxury Mercedes-Benz leviathans to humble converted school buses, connect virtually every Guadalajara destination, both in the city and its surrounding region.

Intercity Bus Travel

Three distinct levels of intercity service—luxury class, first class, and second class—are generally available. **Luxury-class** (called something like "Primera Plus," depending upon the line) riders enjoy coaches speeding between the major destinations. In exchange for relatively high fares (about $50 for Puerto Vallarta–Guadalajara, for example), passengers enjoy rapid passage and airline-style amenities: plush reclining seats, a (usually) clean toilet, air-conditioning, onboard video, and an aisle attendant.

Second-class buses connect with nearly all of the Guadalajara region's towns and villages.

Although less luxurious, for about two-thirds the price, **first-class** service is frequent and always includes reserved seating. Additionally, passengers enjoy soft reclining cushions and air-conditioning (if it is working). Besides the regular stops at or near most towns and villages en route, first-class bus drivers, if requested, will usually stop and let you off anywhere along the road.

Second-class bus seating is unreserved. In outlying parts of the Guadalajara region, there is even a class of bus beneath second-class, but given the condition of many second-class buses, it seems as if third-class buses wouldn't run at all. Such buses are the stuff of travelers' legends: the recycled old GMC, Ford, and Dodge school buses that stop everywhere and carry everyone and everything to even the smallest villages tucked away in the far mountains. As long as there is any kind of a road, the bus will most likely go there.

Second-class buses are not for travelers with weak knees or stomachs. On long trips, carry food, beverages, and toilet paper. Station food may be dubious, and the toilet facilities may be ill maintained.

If you are waiting for a first-class bus at an intermediate *salida de paso* (passing station), you have to trust luck that there will be an empty seat. If not, your best option may be to ride a more frequent second-class bus.

Often, you will initially have to stand, cramped in the aisle, in a crowd of campesinos. They are warmhearted but poor people, so don't tempt them with open, dangling purses or wallets bulging in back pockets. Stow your money safely away. After a while, you will be able to sit down. Such privilege, however, comes with obligation, such as holding an old woman's bulging bag of carrots or a toddler on your lap. But if you accept your burden with humor and equanimity, who knows what favors and blessings may flow to you in return.

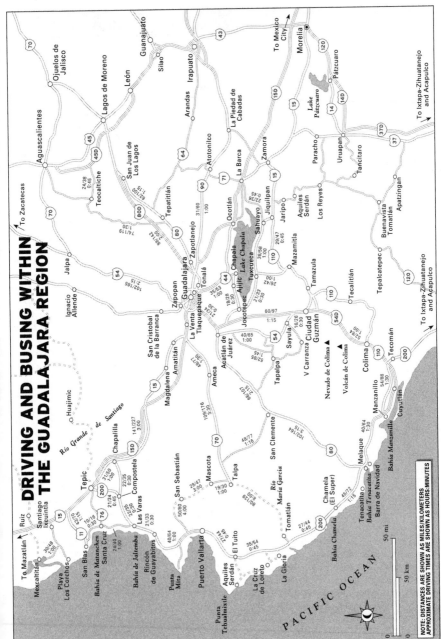

DRIVING AND BUSING WITHIN THE GUADALAJARA REGION

NOTE: DISTANCES ARE SHOWN AS MILES/KILOMETERS
APPROXIMATE DRIVING TIMES ARE SHOWN AS HOURS:MINUTES

© AVALON TRAVEL

Guadalajara Bus Stations

Guadalajara has two long-distance bus stations. Most Guadalajara regional towns and villages are accessible from the second-class **Camionera Central Vieja** (Old Central Bus Terminal), dating from around 1960, in the southeast quarter of the downtown district, a few blocks north of Parque Agua Azul. The complex sprawls over about two square city blocks, bounded by Calles Los Angeles and 5 de Febrero on the north and south, and Calles Michel and Analco on the west and east. A flurry of second-class buses heads out daily, from 6 A.M. until about 9 P.M., to destinations up to about 100 miles (160 km) from downtown.

Longer-distance and luxury- and first-class connections are available at Guadalajara's other major bus terminal, the **Camionera Central Nueva** (New Central Bus Terminal), built around 1990 at Guadalajara's southeast edge, about seven miles (11 km, 20 minutes by taxi) from the city center. From this grand airport-style seven-building complex, hundreds of sleek buses roar away daily to destinations as far away as Mexico City and the U.S. border.

For many more details, both on Guadalajara's central bus stations and specific bus lines and departures, see *Getting There and Around* in the *Downtown* chapter.

Tickets, Seating, and Baggage

Although most Guadalajara long-distance bus lines do not publish schedules or fares, if you speak Spanish you can telephone the bus ticket desk *(taquilla)* or ask someone, such as your hotel desk clerk, to call for you. Only a few travel agents handle bus tickets. If you don't want to spend the time to get a reserved ticket yourself, hire someone trustworthy to do it for you. Another option is to get to the bus station early enough on your traveling day to ensure that you'll get a bus to your destination.

Although major bus lines are accepting credit cards and issuing computer-printed tickets, in small towns reserved bus tickets are still often sold for cash and handwritten, with a specific seat number *(número de asiento),* on the back. If you miss the bus, you lose your money. Furthermore, although some bus lines offer airline-style automated reservations systems, many do not. Consequently, you can generally buy reserved tickets only at the local departure *(salida local)* station. (An agent in Guadalajara, for example, cannot ordinarily reserve you a ticket on a bus that originates in Tepic, 100 miles up the road.)

City Buses

Within the metropolitan area, a welter of privately operated city buses, from shiny air-conditioned models to smoky rattletraps, connect Guadalajara's city neighborhoods. Usually their route destinations will be scrawled on the window. Fares run from about $0.30 (three pesos) up. Although by far the most economical mode of transport, city buses are often crowded. When possible, pay the extra $0.30 and ride one of the air-conditioned buses, which you can recognize because their windows are all closed and they are less likely to be crowded. For routes, see the maps and *Getting Around* sections in the *Downtown* and *West and North* chapters, and *Getting There* in the *Tlaquepaque and Tonalá* chapter.

BY CAR AND RV

Driving a car or RV in Mexico may or may not be for you. Be sure to read the pros and cons in *Getting There* section, earlier in this chapter.

Rental Cars

Car and jeep rentals are an increasingly popular transportation option in Guadalajara. They offer mobility and independence for local excursions. At the Guadalajara airport, the gang's all there, including Alamo, Avis, Budget, Dollar, Hertz, and National, plus several local outfits. (For Guadalajara airport car-rental specifics, see *Getting There and Around* in the *Downtown* chapter.)

Before renting a car, Guadalajara agencies require you to present a valid driver's license, passport, a major credit card, and additionally may require you to be at least 25 years old. Some local companies do not accept credit cards as payment, but do offer lower rates in return.

CAR RENTAL AGENCY TOLL-FREE NUMBERS AND WEBSITES

Alamo	U.S. 800/462-5266, Canada 800/462-5266	www.alamo.com
Avis	U.S. 800/331-1212, Canada 800/879-2847	www.avis.com
Budget	U.S. 800/527-0700, Canada 800/268-9800	www.budget.com
Dollar	U.S. 800/800-4000, Canada 800/800-4000	www.dollar.com
Hertz	U.S. 800/654-3001, Canada 800/654-3001	www.hertz.com
National	U.S. 800/227-7368, Canada 800/227-7368	www.nationalcar.com
Thrifty	U.S. 800/367-2277, Canada 800/367-2277	www.thrifty.com

Base prices of international agencies, such as Hertz, National, and Avis are not cheap. With a 17 percent value-added tax and mandatory insurance, rentals run more than in the United States. The cheapest possible rental car, usually a Japanese- or U.S.-brand, Mexican-made compact, runs $40–60 per day or $250–450 per week, depending on the season. Prices are highest during Christmas and pre-Easter weeks. Before departure, use the international agencies' toll-free numbers and websites for availability, prices, and reservations. During nonpeak seasons, you may save lots of pesos by waiting until arrival and renting a car through a local in-town (as opposed to the airport) agency. Shop around, starting with the agent in your hotel lobby or with the local Yellow Pages (under *"Automóviles, renta de"*).

Car insurance that covers property damage and public liability is a government requirement in Mexico and is therefore an absolute must with your rental car. If you get into an accident without such insurance, you will be in deep trouble—probably jail. Some of your credit cards, such as American Express, Mastercard, and Visa, may offer **free rental car supplemental insurance** as a benefit for renting your car with their card. If so, this allows you to waive the expensive insurance offered by the rental agency and thereby save yourself $15–20 per day. Check carefully with your credit card company.

Driving in Guadalajara

Driving in Guadalajara is similar to driving in a large U.S. city, except you must drive more defensively. Potholes, pedestrians crossing at random points, and aggressive drivers dictate more watchful driving than back home.

If you're going to be doing lots of Guadalajara driving, get a copy (always available at Sanborns gift shop/restaurant) of the very reliable **Guia Roji Red Vial Ciudad de Guadalajara** city map.

A number of boulevards, such as east–west expressways Avenida Lázaro Cárdenas–Avenida Vallarta and north–south Avenida Patria–Avenida López Mateos, have **laterals** (streets running parallel to the main boulevard) for slower traffic or for turnoffs accessing overpasses and underpasses. Be prepared. Watch for signs indicating the turnoffs to the laterals ahead. If you miss the desired turnoff, look for a *retorno* where you can make a U-turn and correct your mistake.

Be aware also that **left turns,** especially on four- or six-lane expressways with laterals, often must be made from the right lateral, and only in response to a green left-turn signal arrow.

Without a lateral, left-turn rules are similar to those in the United States.

BY TAXI

The high prices of rental cars make taxis a viable option for local excursions. Cars are luxuries, not necessities, for many Guadalajara families. Travelers might profit from the Mexican money-saving practice of piling everyone in a taxi for a Sunday outing. You may find that not only will an all-day taxi and driver cost less than a rental car and relieve you of driving, your driver also may become your impromptu guide.

The magic word for saving money by taxi is *colectivo:* a taxi you share with other travelers. The first place in Guadalajara where you'll practice getting a taxi will be at the airport, where *colectivo* tickets are routinely sold from booths at the terminal door.

If, however, you want your own private taxi, ask for a *taxi especial,* which will run about 3–4 times the individual tariff for a *colectivo.*

Your airport experience will prepare you for in-town taxis, nearly all of which have meters, but which many drivers don't like to use. Best insist—*"Metro, por favor"* ("Meter, please")—on using the meter. If the driver refuses, you have the usually easy option of getting another taxi or establishing the price before the ride starts. Bargaining comes with the territory in Mexico, so don't shrink from it, even though it seems a hassle. If you get into a taxi without an agreed-upon price, you are allowing for a more serious and potentially nasty hassle later. If your driver's price is too high, he'll probably come to his senses as soon as you get out to hail another taxi.

You'll find that you don't have to take the more expensive taxis lined up in your hotel driveway. If the price isn't right, walk toward the street and hail a regular taxi.

In town, if you can't find a taxi, it may be because they are waiting for riders at the local stand, called a taxi *sitio.* Ask someone to direct you to it: *"Excúseme. ¿Dónde está el sitio taxi, por favor?"* ("Excuse me. Where is the taxi stand, please?")

Visas and Officialdom

YOUR PASSPORT

Your passport (or birth or naturalization certificate) is your positive proof of national identity; without it, your status in any foreign country is in doubt. Don't leave home without one. **In fact, passport regulations have changed.** Since January 2007, U.S. Immigration rules require that everyone, including U.S. citizens, must present a valid passport in order to re-enter the United States, from Mexico, Canada, and the Caribbean. United States citizens may obtain passports (allow four to six weeks) at local post offices. For-fee private passport agencies can speed this process and get you a passport within a week, maybe less.

ENTRY INTO MEXICO

For U.S. and Canadian citizens, entry by air into Mexico for a few weeks could hardly be easier. Airline attendants hand out tourist permits *(permisos turísticas)* en route and officers make them official by glancing at passports and stamping the cards at the immigration gate. Business travel permits for 30 days or fewer are handled by the same simple procedures.

Furthermore, Mexican immigration rules require that all entering U.S. citizens 15 years old or over must present proper identification—either a valid passport, original (or notarized copy) of either birth certificate, military ID, or state driver's license, while naturalized citizens must show naturalization papers (or a laminated naturalization card) or valid U.S. passport.

Canadian citizens must show a valid passport or original birth certificate. Nationals of other countries (especially those such as Hong Kong, which issue more than one type of passport) may be subject to different or additional regulations. For advice, consult your regional Mexico Tourism Board Office (see the sidebar *Mexico Tourism Board Offices*) or local Mexican consulate. Very complete and up-to-date Mexico visa and entry information for nationals of virtually all of the world's countries, is available at the Toronto, Canada, Mexican Consulate website (www.consulmex.com).

More Options

For more complicated cases, get your tourist permit early enough to allow you to consider the options. Tourist permits can be issued for multiple entries and a maximum validity of 180 days; photos are often required. If you don't request multiple entry or the maximum time, your card will probably be stamped single entry, valid for some shorter period, such as 90 days. If you are not sure how long you'll stay in Mexico, request the maximum (180 days is the absolute maximum for a tourist permit; long-term foreign residents routinely make semiannual "border runs" for new tourist permits).

STUDENT AND BUSINESS VISAS

A visa is a notation stamped and signed on your passport showing the number of days and entries allowable for your trip. Apply for a student visa at the consulate nearest your home well in advance of your departure; the same is true if you require a business visa of longer than 30 days. One-year renewable student visas are available (sometimes with considerable red tape). An ordinary 180-day tourist permit may be the easiest option, if you can manage it.

ENTRY FOR CHILDREN

Children under 15 can be included on their parents' tourist permits, but complications occur if the children (by reason of illness, for example) cannot leave Mexico with both parents. Parents can avoid such red tape by getting a passport and a Mexican tourist permit for each of their children.

Mexico travelers should hurdle all such possible delays far ahead of time in the cool calm of their local Mexican consulate rather than the hot, hurried atmosphere of a border or airport immigration station.

ENTRY FOR PETS

A pile of red tape may delay the entry of dogs, cats, and other pets into Mexico. Be prepared with veterinary-stamped health and rabies certificates for each animal. For more information, contact your regional Mexico Tourism Board (see the sidebar *Mexico Tourism Board Offices*), or your local Mexican Consulate.

DON'T LOSE YOUR TOURIST PERMIT

If you do, be prepared with a copy of the original, which you should present to the nearest federal Migración (Immigration) office (on duty long hours at Guadalajara airport) and ask for a duplicate tourist permit. Lacking this, you might present some alternate proof of your date of arrival in Mexico, such as a stamped passport or airline ticket. Savvy travelers carry copies of their tourist permits while leaving the original safe in their hotel rooms.

CAR PERMITS

If you drive to Mexico, you will need a permit for your car. Upon entry into Mexico, be ready with originals and copies of your proof-of-ownership or registration papers (state title certificate, registration, or notarized bill of sale), current license plates, and current driver's license. The auto permit fee runs about $30, payable only by non-Mexican bank Master-Card, Visa, or American Express credit cards. (The credit-card-only requirement discourages those who sell or abandon U.S.-registered cars in Mexico without paying customs duties.) Credit cards must bear the same name as the vehicle proof-of-ownership papers.

The resulting car permit becomes part of the owner's tourist permit and receives the same length of validity. Vehicles registered in the name of an organization or person other than the driver must be accompanied by a notarized affidavit authorizing the driver to use the car in Mexico for a specific time.

Border officials generally allow you to carry or tow additional motorized vehicles (motorcycle, ATV, another car, large boat) into Mexico, but will probably require separate documentation and fee for each vehicle. If a Mexican official desires to inspect your trailer or RV, go through it with him.

Accessories, such as a small trailer, boat shorter than six feet, CB radio, or outboard motor, may be noted on the car permit and must leave Mexico with the car.

For more details on motor vehicle entry and what you may bring in your baggage to Mexico, you might also consult the AAA (American Automobile Association) *Mexico TravelBook*. See the *Unique Guide and Tip Books* section in *Suggested Reading* at the end of this book.

Since Mexico does not recognize foreign automobile insurance, you must buy Mexican automobile insurance. (For more information on this and other details of driving in Mexico, see *Getting There,* earlier in this chapter.)

BORDER CROSSINGS

Squeezing through border bottlenecks during peak holidays and rush hours can be time-consuming. If possible, avoid crossing 7–9 A.M. and 4:30–6:30 P.M.

Just before returning across the border with your car, park, if necessary, and have a customs *(aduana)* official *remove and cancel the holographic identity sticker that you received on entry.* If possible, get a receipt *(recibo)* or some kind of verification that it's been canceled *(cancelado).* Tourists have been fined hundreds of dollars for inadvertently carrying uncanceled car entry stickers on their windshields.

At the same time, return all other Mexican permits, such as tourist permits and hunting and fishing licenses. Also, be prepared for Mexico exit inspection, especially for cultural artifacts and works of art, which may require exit permits. Certain religious and pre-Columbian artifacts, legally the property of the Mexican government, cannot be taken from the country.

If you entered Mexico with your car, you cannot legally leave without it except by permission from local customs authorities, usually the Ad-uana (Customs House) or the Oficina Federal de Hacienda (Federal Treasury Office).

All returnees are subject to U.S. immigration and customs inspection. Current U.S. rules require U.S. citizens you to have a passport in order to re-enter the United States. Border inspections have become generally more time-consuming since September 11, 2001. The worst bottlenecks are at busy border crossings, especially Tijuana and to a lesser extent, Mexicali, Nogales, Juárez, Nuevo Laredo, and Matamoros, all of which should be avoided during peak hours.

United States law allows a fixed value ($800 at present) of duty-free goods per Mexico returnee. This may include no more than one liter of alcoholic spirits, 200 cigarettes, and 100 cigars. A flat 10 percent duty will be applied to the first $1,000 (fair retail value, save your receipts) in excess of your $800 exemption. You may, however, mail packages (up to $100 value each) of gifts duty-free to friends and relatives in the United States. Make sure to clearly write "unsolicited gift" and a list of the contents and value of each enclosed item on the outside of the package. Perfumes (over $5), alcoholic beverages, and tobacco may not be included in such packages.

Improve the security of such mailed packages by sending them by Mexpost class, similar to U.S. Express Mail service. Even better (but much more expensive), send them by Federal Express or DHL international couriers, which maintain offices in Guadalajara.

U.S. GOVERNMENT CUSTOMS INFORMATION

For detailed information on U.S. customs regulations important to travelers abroad, read or download the useful pamphlet *Know Before You Go,* by visiting the U.S. Customs and Border Patrol website (www.cpb.gov). Click on travel at the bottom of the home page, then scroll down and click on *Know Before You Go.*

For more information on the importation of endangered wildlife products, contact the Fish and Wildlife Service (1849 C. St. NW, Washington, DC 20240, toll-free tel. 800/344-WILD, www.fws.gov).

MEXICO TOURISM BOARD OFFICES

More than a dozen Mexico Tourism Board (Consejo de Promoción Turístico de Mexico) offices and scores of Mexican government consulates operate in the United States, Canada, Europe, South America, and Asia. Mexican Consulates generally handle questions of Mexican nationals abroad, while Mexico Tourism Boards serve travelers heading for Mexico.

For straightforward questions and Mexico regional information brochures, contact the Tourism Board (U.S./Can. tel. 800/44MEXICO or 800/446-3942, Europe tel. 00-800/111-2266, www.visitmexico.com). If you need more details and read a bit of Spanish, you might find visiting www.cptm.com helpful also. Otherwise, contact one of the North American, European, South American or Asian Mexico Tourism Boards directly for guidance.

NORTH AMERICA

From Alaska, Arizona, California, Colorado, Hawaii, Idaho, Montana, Nevada, Utah, Washington, and Wyoming, contact the **Los Angeles** office (1880 Century Park East, Suite 511, Los Angeles, CA 90067, tel. 310/282-9112, fax 310/282-9116, losangeles@visitmexico.com).

From Alberta, British Columbia, Alberta, Saskatchewan, and the Yukon and Northwest Territories, contact the **Vancouver** office (999 W. Hastings St., Suite 1110, Vancouver, B.C. V6C 2W2, tel. 604/669-2845, fax 604/669-3498, mgto@telus.net).

From Arkansas, Colorado, Louisiana, New Mexico, Oklahoma, and Texas, contact the **Houston** office (4507 San Jacinto, Suite 308, Houston TX 77004, tel. 713/772-2581, fax 713/772-6058, houston@visitmexico.com).

From Alabama, Florida, Georgia, Mississippi, Tennessee, North Carolina, Puerto Rico, and South Carolina, contact the **Miami** office (5975 Sunset Drive #305, Miami, FL 33143, tel. 786/621-2909, fax 786/621-2907, miami@visitmexico.com).

From Illinois, Indiana, Iowa, Kansas, Kentucky, Michigan, Minnesota, Missouri, Nebraska, North Dakota, Ohio, South Dakota, and Wisconsin, contact the **Chicago** office (225 North Michigan Ave., 18th Floor, Suite 1850, Chicago, IL 60601, tel. 312/228-0517, fax 312/228-0515, chicago@visitmexico.com).

From Connecticut, Delaware, Kentucky, Maine, Maryland, Massachusetts, New Hampshire, New Jersey, New York, Pennsylvania, Rhode Island, Vermont, Virginia, Washington D.C., and West Virginia, contact the **New York** office (400 Madison Avenue, Suite 11C, New York, NY 10017, tel. 212/308-2110, fax 212/308-9060, newyork@visitmexico.com).

From Ontario, Manitoba, and the Nunavut Territory, contact the **Toronto** office (2 Bloor St. West, Suite 1502, Toronto, Ontario M4W 3E2, tel. 416/925-0704, fax 416/925-6061, toronto@visitmexico.com).

From New Brunswick, Newfoundland, Nova Scotia, Prince Edward Island, and Quebec, contact the **Montreal** office (1 Place Ville Marie, Suite 1931, Montreal, Quebec H3B2C3, tel. 514/871-1052 or 514/871-1103, fax 514/871-3825, montreal@visitmexico.com).

EUROPE

In Europe, travelers may either contact the all-Europe Mexico tourism information (tel. 00-800/111-2266, www.visitmexico.com) or contact the local offices directly.

London (Wakefield House, 41 Trinity Square, London EC3N 4DJ, England, UK, tel. 207/488-9392, fax 207/265-0704, uk@visitmexico.co)

Frankfurt (Taunusanlage 21, D-60325 Frankfurt-am-Main, Deutschland, tel. 697/103-3383, fax 697/103-3755, germany@visitmexico.com)

Paris (4 Rue Notre-Dame des Victoires, 75002 Paris, France, tel. 1/428-69612, 1/428-69613, fax 1/428-60580, france@visitmexico.com)

Madrid (Calle Velázquez 126, 28006 Madrid, España, tel. 91/561-3520, 91/561-1827, fax 91/411-0759, spain@visitmexico.com)

Rome (Via Barbarini 3-piso 7, 00187 Roma, Italia, tel. 06/487-4698, fax 06/487-3630 or fax 06/420-4293, italy@visitmexico.com)

SOUTH AMERICA

Contact the Mexico Tourism Board in Brazil, Argentina, or Chile.

Sao Paulo (Alameda Administrativo, Rocha Azevedo 882, Conjunto 31, Tercer Andador, Sao Paulo, Brazil, 01410-002, tel. 3088-2129, fax 3083-5005, brasil@visitmexico.com)

Buenos Aires (Avenida Santa Fe 920, 1054 Buenos Aires, Argentina, tel. 1/4393-7070, 1/4393-8235, fax 1/4393-6607, argentina@visitmexico.com)

Santiago (Felix de Amesti #128, primer piso, Los Condes, Santiago de Chile, tel. 562/583-8426, fax 562/583-8425, chile@visitmexico.com)

ASIA

Contact the Mexico Tourism Board in either Japan or China.

Tokyo (2-15-1-3F, Nagata-Cho, 2-chome, Chiyoda-ku, Tokyo, Japan 100-0014, tel. 335/030-290, fax 335/030-643, japan@visitmexico.com)

Beijing (San Li Dongwajie 5, Chaoyang 100600, Beijing, Peoples Republic of China, tel./fax 106/532-1717 or 106/532-1744, jamezcua@visitmexico.com)

Conduct and Customs

Behind its modern glitz, Mexico is an old-fashioned country where people value traditional ideals of honesty, fidelity, and piety. Violent crime rates are low; visitors are often safer in Mexico than in their home cities.

Even though four generations have elapsed since Pancho Villa raided the U.S. border, the image of a Mexico bristling with *bandidos* persists. And similarly for Mexicans: Despite the century and a half since the *yanquis* invaded Mexico City and took half their country, the communal Mexican psyche still views gringos (and, by association, all white foreigners) with a combination of revulsion, envy, and awe.

Fortunately, the Mexican love-hate affair with foreigners in general does not necessarily apply to individual visitors. Your friendly *"Buenos días"* or courteous *"por favor"* is always appreciated. The shy smile you receive in return will be your not-insignificant reward.

Tipping

Without their droves of visitors, Mexican people would be even poorer. Deflation of the peso, while making prices low for outsiders, makes it rough for Mexican families to get by. The workers at your hotel typically get paid only a few dollars a day. They depend on tips to make the difference between dire and bearable poverty. Give the *camarista* (chambermaid) and floor attendant a couple of dollars (or 20 pesos) every day or two. And whenever uncertain of what to tip, it will probably mean a lot to someone—maybe a whole family—if you err on the generous side.

In restaurants and bars, Mexican tipping customs are similar to those in the United States and Europe: tip waitstaff and bartenders about 15 percent for satisfactory service.

Alcohol and Drugs

Alcohol often leads to trouble. If, given Mexico's excellent beers, you can't abstain completely, at least maintain soft-spoken self-control in the face of challenges from macho drunks.

Mexican authorities are decidedly intolerant of substances such as marijuana, psychedelics, cocaine, and heroin. Getting caught with such drugs in Mexico usually leads to swift and severe results.

Female Travelers

Your own behavior, despite low crime statistics, largely determines your safety in Mexico. For women traveling solo, it is important to realize that the double standard is alive and well in Mexico. Dress and behave modestly and you will most likely avoid trouble. Whenever possible, stay in the company of friends or acquaintances; find companions for beach, sightseeing, and shopping excursions. Ignore strange men's solicitations and overtures.

Clothing

Visitors should wear bathing suits and brief shorts only at the beach. Nude sunbathing is both illegal in public and offensive to Mexicans. Confine your nudist colony to very private locations.

MACHISMO

I once met an Acapulco man who wore five gold wristwatches and became angry when I quietly refused his repeated invitations to get drunk with him. Another time, on the beach near San Blas, two drunk campesinos nearly attacked me because I was helping my girlfriend cook a picnic dinner. Outside Taxco I once spent an endless hour in the seat behind a bus driver who insisted on speeding down the middle of the two-lane highway, honking aside oncoming automobiles.

Despite their wide differences (the first was a rich criollo, the campesinos were *indígenas*, and the bus driver, mestizo), the common affliction shared by all four men was machismo, a disease that seems to possess many Mexican men. Machismo is a sometimes-reckless obsession to prove one's masculinity, to show how macho you are. Men of many nationalities share the instinct to prove themselves. Japan's *bushido* samurai code is one example.

When confronted by a Mexican braggart, male visitors should remain careful and controlled. If your opponent is yelling, stay cool, speak softly, and withdraw as soon as possible. On the highway, be courteous and unprovoking – don't use your car to spar with a macho driver. Drinking often leads to problems. It's best to stay out of bars or cantinas unless you're prepared to deal with the macho consequences. Polite refusal of a drink may be taken as a challenge. If you visit a bar with Mexican friends or acquaintances, you may be heading for a no-win choice between a drunken all-night *borrachera* (binge) or an insult to the honor of your friends by refusing.

For women, machismo requires even more cautious behavior. In Mexico, women's liberation is long in coming. Few women hold positions of power in business or politics. One woman, Rosa Luz Alegría, did attain the rank of minister of tourism during the former Portillo administration; she was the president's mistress.

Female visitors can follow the example of their Mexican sisters by making a habit of going out in the company of friends or acquaintances, especially at night. Many Mexican men believe an unaccompanied woman wants to be picked up. Ignore their offers; any response, even refusal, might be taken as an encouraging sign. If, on the other hand, there is a Mexican man whom you'd genuinely like to meet, the traditional way is an arranged introduction through family or friends.

Mexican families, as a source of protection and friendship, should not be overlooked – especially on the beach or in the park, where, among the gaggle of kids, grandparents, aunts, and cousins, there's room for one more.

Accommodations

The rates listed in this book are U.S. dollar equivalents of peso prices, taxes included, as quoted by the lodging management at the time of writing. They are intended as a general guide and probably will only approximate the asking rate when you arrive. Some readers, unfortunately, try to bargain by telling desk clerks that, for example, the rate should be $40 because they read it in this book. This is unwise, because it makes hotel clerks and managers reluctant to quote rates, for fear readers might, years later, hold their hotel responsible for such quotes.

To cancel the effect of relatively steep Mexican inflation, rates are reported in U.S. dollars (although, when settling your hotel bill, *you will nearly always save money by insisting on paying in pesos*). To further increase accuracy, estimated low- and high-season rates are quoted whenever possible.

Saving Money

The listed accommodation prices are **rack rates,** the maximum tariff, exclusive of packages and promotions, that you would pay if you walked in and rented an unreserved room for one day. Savvy travelers seldom pay the maximum. Always inquire if there are any discounts, business rates, or packages *(descuentos o paquetes)* (dees-koo-AYN-tohs OH pah-KAY-tays).

For stays of more than two weeks, you'll usually save money and add comfort with an apartment, condominium, or house rental.

Airlines regularly offer air/hotel packages that may save you pesos. These deals often require that you depart for Guadalajara through certain gateway cities, which depend on the airline. Accommodations are usually (but not exclusively) in luxury hotels.

LUXURY HOTELS

Guadalajara has many well-managed, international-class hotels, mostly in the upscale western suburbs, around the Plaza del Sol–Expo Guadalajara complex. A number of these ho-

tels cater especially to businesspeople and convention goers.

Their plush amenities need not be overly expensive. During the right time of year you can sometimes lodge at many of the big-name spots for surprisingly little. While rack rates ordinarily run $150–300, packages, promotions, and business rates can cut these prices significantly.

MODERATE HOTELS

These lodgings vary from scruffy to spick-and-span, from humble to distinguished. Many such hostelries are the once-grand first-class hotels established long before their luxurious international-class cousins mushroomed on Guadalajara's west side. You can generally expect a clean, large (but not necessarily deluxe) room with bath and toilet and even sometimes a private balcony and a pool. Such hotels usually lack the costly international-standard amenities—air conditioning, cable TV, direct-dial phones, tennis courts, gyms, and golf access—of the big luxury resorts. Their guests, however, usually enjoy good service, good food, and a local ambience more charming and personal than many of their five-star competitors.

Booking these hotels is straightforward. All of them may be dialed direct and many have websites, email, and U.S. and Canada toll-free information and reservation numbers.

BED-AND-BREAKFASTS AND GUESTHOUSES

North American–style bed-and-breakfasts are new in Mexico. Bed-and-breakfasts have sprouted in west-side Guadalajara neighborhoods, Tlaquepaque, and on the Lake Chapala north shore where Americans and Canadians have been relocating.

Less common in tourist zones are *casas de huéspedes,* family houses where rooms, usually around an interior patio, are offered to guests. While the facilities, such as baths, are usually shared, the ambience is often friendly and the prices, typically around $30 per day, are right.

APARTMENTS, CONDOMINIUMS, AND HOUSES

For longer stays, many visitors prefer the convenience and economy of an apartment or condominium, or the space and comfort of a house rental. Choices vary, from spartan studios to deluxe suites and rambling homes big enough for entire extended families. Prices depend strongly upon neighborhood and amenities, ranging from about $300 per month for the cheapest to at least 10 times that for the most luxurious.

At the low end, visitors can expect a clean, furnished apartment, convenient to public transportation, in a quiet, middle-class neighborhood. Condominiums—often colloquially named *suites* (soo-EE-tays)—are generally more luxurious and rent for about $1,000 per month. Typically the condos are high-rises with desk services and resort amenities such as pool, hot tub, and sundeck.

House rentals can range from modest suburban bungalows for about $500 per month to rambling villas with pool, garden, cook, maid, and gardener for $3,000 per month.

Finding a Long-Term Rental

In Guadalajara as everywhere, location is the key to finding a good rental. In the city, it's best to concentrate your search in the middle- to upper-class west-side neighborhoods: Minerva-Chapultepec, Providencia, Chapalita, Ciudad del Sol, and Las Fuentes. Also, take a look at Tlaquepaque and the Lake Chapala north-shore communities, beginning with Chapala town and moving west, through San Antonio, La Floresta, Ajijic, San Juan Cosala, and Jocotepec.

A potentially useful Guadalajara rental source is the classified section of the weekly **Guadalajara Colony Reporter** (413 Interamerica Blvd. WH1 PMB5-452, Laredo, TX 78045, or, from Mexico, to Duque de Rivas 254, Colonia Arcos Sur, Guadalajara 444140, Mexico tel. 33/3766-6338, www.guadalajarareporter. com), available by online subscription for $30/year. Alternatively, subscribe by mail by sending a letter—including your name, address, telephone, and, if applicable, email address—and a check or money order for US $45 (for three

months), made out to Nuevas Publicaciones en Ingles de Mexico, S.A. de C.V.

A load of local information, plus several Lake Chapala agency rental listings, usually appears in the monthly Lake Chapala English-language newspaper, **El Ojo del Lago** (Eye of the Lake) (P.O. Box 279, Chapala, Jalisco 45900, Mexico, tel. 376/765-3676, fax 376/765-3528, ojodellago@laguna.com.mx, www.chapala. com). Subscribe by sending a letter—including your name, address, and telephone—with a check or money order payable to the publisher, David Tingen, for US $35 (for six months).

A number of English-speaking **real estate-rental agencies** also maintain (mostly Lake Chapala) rental listings. They may also be able to connect you with a Guadalajara rental agent. Currently very active is the Ojo del Lago's parent, **Coldwell Banker-Chapala Realty** (Hidalgo 223, Chapala, Jalisco 45900, tel. 376/765-2877, fax 376/765-3528, chapala@infosel.net.mx, www. chapala.com), in downtown Chapala. Also active with Lake Chapala rentals is **Ajijic Rentals** (Colon 1, Ajijic, tel. 376/766-1716, fax 376/766-0967, rentals@prodigy.net.mx, www.ajijicrentals. com). Additionally, you might try **Century 21-Vistas Realty** (P.O. Box 281, Chapala, Jalisco 45915, tel./fax 376/766-2612, info@century21accessmex.com, www.century21accessmex.com).

You might also consider **exchanging your home** with a Guadalajara or Lake Chapala homeowner for a set period. A couple of agencies that list Guadalajara area homes for exchange are **Home Exchange** (tel. 386/238-3633, www. homeexchange.com) and **Home for Exchange** (www.homeforexchange.com).

Another potentially useful online-only rental source is the worldwide website **Vacation Rentals by Owner** (www.vrbo.com), which, at this writing, lists four Guadalajara home and apartment rentals and about 20 Chapala-area rentals.

Other potentially very useful rental information sources are the bulletin boards at the **American Society of Jalisco** headquarters and **Sandi Bookstore** (see the *Chapalita* section of the *West and North* chapter), and the **Lake Chapala Society** (see the *Lake Chapala* chapter).

Shopping

Although bargains abound in Guadalajara, savvy shoppers are selective. Steep import and luxury taxes drive up the prices of foreign-made goods such as professional-grade cameras, computers, sports equipment, and English-language books. Instead, concentrate your shopping on locally made items: leather, jewelry, cotton resort wear, Mexican-made designer clothes, and the galaxy of handicrafts for which Mexico is renowned.

Guadalajara is a magnet for buyers of handicrafts. The major sources, the suburban villages of Tlaquepaque and Tonalá, each nurture vibrant traditions with roots in the pre-Columbian past. This rich cornucopia, the product of hundreds of family workshops and factories, fills dozens of shops, not only in Tlaquepaque and Tonalá, but also in the city at large, including the grand Mercado Libertad in downtown Guadalajara and a number of stores and weekly outdoor markets.

Credit cards, such as Visa, Mastercard, and, to a lesser extent, American Express, are widely honored in the hotels and boutiques that cater to well-heeled customers. Although this is convenient, such shops' offerings will be generally higher-priced than those of stores in the older downtown districts that depend more on local trade. Local shops sometimes offer discounts for cash purchases.

OUTDOOR MARKETS

Guadalajarans' irrepressible commercial urge blossoms forth with *tianguis* (Aztec for "awning"), weekly markets in certain neighborhoods of town. They're sure to be set up and running by at least 10 A.M., rain or shine: The **Antique Market,** Sundays, spreads along Avenida Mexico, just west of Avenida Chapultepec; a few blocks north of that, around Avenida Angulo, the **Santa Teresita Market,** also on Sunday, offers a little bit of everything except food.

Also operating on Sunday is the **Artists' Market,** at Chapalita Circle, intersection of Ave-

It's interesting to look around inside of a *papelería* (stationery store) for the old-fashioned goods that "dime stores" used to carry in the U.S.

nidas Guadalupe and de las Rosas; furthermore, in the same southwest quarter of town, is the big Friday **Clothes Market** on Avenida Copernicus, between Avenidas Tepeyac and Moctezuma. Even farther southwest is the country-style Thursday **Santa Anita Market,** in Santa Anita village, west of Avenida López Mateos, about four miles (seven km) south of the *periférico* (peripheral) boulevard. For the markets' locations and other details, see the *Shopping and Services* section of the *West and North* chapter.

Bargaining

Bargaining will stretch your money even farther. It comes with the territory in Mexico and needn't be a hassle. On the contrary, if done with humor and moderation, bargaining can be an enjoyable way to meet (and even befriend) people.

© BRUCE WHIPPERMAN

Huichol handicrafts are customarily on sale on the downtown Guadalajara Plaza de los Fundadores.

The handicrafts market stalls are where bargaining is most intense. For starters, try offering half the asking price. From there on, it's all psychology: You have to content yourself with not having to have the item. Otherwise, you're sunk; the vendor will sense your need and stand fast. After a few minutes of good-humored bantering, ask for *el último precio* (the final price), which, if it's close, just may be a bargain.

SUPERMARKETS AND DEPARTMENT STORES

Several branches of big Mexican chains—**Gigante, Aurrera,** and **Comercial Mexicana**—serve Guadalajara shoppers with everything from groceries and meats and produce to auto tires and baby clothes.

Guadalajara's department stores of choice are **Sears-Roebuck, Fábricas de Francia,** and **Suburbia.** A walk along their calm, air-conditioned aisles seems like a journey back to the 1950s, complete with elevator music and plenty of counter clerks.

SHOPPING MALLS AND WAREHOUSE STORES

Several American-style shopping malls have sprouted in Guadalajara's west-side suburbs since the 1970s. **Plaza del Sol,** on Avenida López Mateos, in the southwest suburb, was the first and remains very successful, anchored by Fábricas de Francia and Suburbia and an eclectic swarm of smaller stores.

Although showing its age, **Plaza Patria,** on Guadalajara's northwest side, at the corner of Avenidas Patria and de las Americas, is still popular, with Fábricas de Francia and Suburbia branches and a brigade of smaller shops.

Guadalajara's hottest new malls are **Centro Magno,** between Avenidas Vallarta and Cotilla in the closer-in Minerva-Chapultepec district, and **Centro Pabellón,** on the far northwest side, corner of Avenidas Patria and Acueducto. With no department store anchors, these enclosed single-building complexes abound with designer boutiques on the lower floors and big youth entertainment complexes—video game arcade, food court, and cinemaplex—on the top floors.

Shoppers can enjoy the best of both worlds at the huge, newish, multistory enclosed **Gran Plaza** mall farther west on Avenida Vallarta, about a mile west of the Minerva fountain and traffic circle. Sears-Roebuck, Fábricas de Francia, a big multiscreen movie complex, a video game arcade, a fast-food court, and a swarm of upscale boutiques divert a legion of young customers.

Gran Plaza has attracted U.S. warehouse chains to locate nearby. West of Gran Plaza, on Avenida Vallarta's south side, is **Price Club, Wal-Mart,** and **Sam's Club,** farther west.

For many more details on most of the above shopping complexes, see the *Shopping and Services* and *Plaza del Sol* sections of the *West and North* chapter.

Tips for Travelers

BUSINESS TRAVELERS

As a growing legion of foreign companies have discovered, Guadalajara is a good place to do business. Although Jalisco is a Mexican leader in jewelry, footwear, clothing and textiles, foreign tourism, and handicrafts, Guadalajara's mushrooming **electronics** industry (more than $US 20 billion exported in 2006) is attracting the most attention. The list of firms operating plants— Hewlett-Packard, Texas Instruments, Intel, Fairchild, Logistix, Tektronics, Motorola, Panasonic, Redwood Systems, IBM, NEC, SCI, Pentex—reads like a who's who list of the high-tech industry.

Meeting Facilities

Guadalajara is ready with world-class resources for business and professional visitors. The ace in the pack is the one-million-square-foot **Expo Guadalajara** (Corner of Av. Lóopez Mateos Sur and Av. de las Rosas, Guadalajara, Jalisco 44540, tel. 33/3343-3000, Mexico toll-free tel. 01-800/813-3000, fax 33/3343-3030, www.expo-guadalajara.com or www.operadoradeferias.com, open daily 9 A.M.–8 P.M.). Guadalajara Expo, a superb place to meet, sell, and buy, was built in 1987 and continuously updated since. Features include a 280,000-square-foot main exposition hall, a smaller 22,000-square-foot special events hall, a fully equipped business center, a swarm of private negotiating rooms, a 75,000-square-foot multiple-use auditorium— accommodating meetings from 200 to 3,000 people—exterior patios, lobbies, a seeming mile of loading docks, a pair of fine restaurants, and a swarm of coffee shops and snack bars.

Expo Guadalajara hosts a continuous menu of meetings and exhibitions. Last year's schedule included more than 150 events, with themes varying from ice cream and furniture to jewelry and books. For more information, visit www.expo-guadalajara.com.

Additionally, Guadalajara offers a host of fine hotel and other smaller meeting venues, ranging from the planetarium and art museums to the Degollado opera house and lovely old haciendas. For more information on all facilities, contact the **Guadalajara Convention and Visitors' Bureau** (Oficina de Visitantes y Convenciones, or OFVC, Av. Vallarta 4095, tel. 33/3122-8711 or 33/3122-7544, fax 33/3122-8707, gdlovc@convencionesgdl.com.mx, www.guadalajaramidestino.com.mx). The bureau is on the upstairs floor in the chamber of commerce building, past Gran Plaza shopping center, south side of the boulevard. Ask for a copy of the excellent bilingual meeting planner's handbook.

Businesspeople may also find the services of the Guadalajara Chamber of Commerce helpful (Av. Vallarta 4095, tel. 33/3880-9090, fax 33/3880-9097, www.canacogdl.com.mx, Mon.–Sat. 9 A.M.–5 P.M.).

Business-Oriented Hotels

A number of Guadalajara luxury hotels that cater especially to business travelers deserve special mention. For their super-comfortable accommodations, private executive floors, extensive in-house business centers, and sizable convention facilities, all for discounted commercial rates, consider the following: Right next to Expo Guadalajara are the American-style **Hilton Guadalajara** and the refined but more relaxed Mexican-style **Guadalajara Plaza Expo.** Within a five-minute taxi ride stand the **Presidente Inter-Continental,** the charmingly intimate 16-room **Mansión del Sol,** and the regal but restful **Crowne Plaza Guadalajara** garden resort. Farther afield, but still within a 10-minute taxi ride, are the more spartan, but still comfortable, midsize **Holiday Inn Select;** the high-rise commercial, at-your-service, **Fiesta Americana;** the relaxed, garden hotel **Camino Real,** queen of Guadalajara hostelries; and the class-act, luxury bed-and-breakfast **Casa Madonna and Villa Ganz.** (For details on all of these good choices, see the *Plaza del Sol* and *Minerva-Chapultepec* sections of the *West and North* chapter.)

TRAVELERS WITH DISABILITIES

Mexican airlines and hotels have become sensitive to the needs of travelers with disabilities. Open, street-level lobbies and large, wheelchair-accessible elevators and rooms are available in many Guadalajara (large deluxe and smaller boutique) hotels. Furthermore, most street-corner curbs accommodate wheelchairs.

United States law forbids travel discrimination against otherwise qualified people with disabilities. As long as your disability is stable and not liable to deteriorate during passage, you can expect to be treated like any passenger with special needs.

Make reservations far ahead of departure and ask your agent to inform your airline of your needs, such as boarding wheelchair or in-flight oxygen. Be early at the gate to take advantage of the preboarding call.

For many helpful details to smooth your trip, get a copy of *Survival Strategies for Going Abroad* by Laura Hershey, published in 2005 by **Mobility International USA** (132 E. Broadway, Suite 343, Eugene, Oregon 97401, voice/TDD tel. 541/343-1284, fax 541/343-6812, www.miusa.org). Mobility International is a valuable resource for many disabled lovers of Mexico, for it encourages disabled travelers with a goldmine of information and literature and can provide them with valuable Mexico connections. They publish a regular newsletter and provide information and referrals for international exchanges and homestays.

Similarly, **Partners of the Americas** (1424 K St. NW, Suite 700, Washington, D.C. 20005, tel. 202/628-3300 or 800/322-7844, fax 202/628-3306, info@partners.net, www.partners.net), with chapters in 45 U.S. states, works to improve understanding of disabilities and facilities in Mexico and Latin America. It maintains communications with local organizations and individuals whom disabled travelers may contact at their destinations.

SENIOR TRAVELERS

Age, according to Mark Twain, is a question of mind over matter: If you don't mind, it doesn't matter. Mexico is a country where whole extended families, from babies to great-grandparents, live together. Elder travelers will benefit from the respect and understanding Mexicans accord to older people. Besides these encouragements, consider the number of retirees already in havens such as Puerto Vallarta, Guadalajara, Lake Chapala, Manzanillo, Oaxaca, and other regional centers.

Certain organizations support and sponsor senior travel. Leading the field is **Elderhostel** (11 Ave. de Lafayette, Boston, MA 02111-1746, toll-free tel. 800/454-5768, www.elderhostel.org). For more information about Elderhostel's special tours, study, homestays, and people-to-people travel programs, visit the Elderhostel website, and/or write for Elderhostel's U.S. and international catalogs. Also see the *Tours, Guides, and Courses* section later in this chapter.

A number of newsletters publicize senior vacation and retirement opportunities. Among the best is the **Mexico File** monthly newsletter that, besides featuring pithy stories by Mexico travelers and news updates, offers an opportunity-packed classified section of Mexico rentals, publications, services, and much more. Subscribe ($39/year) at Simmonds Publications (5580 La Jolla Blvd. #306, La Jolla, CA 92037, tel./fax 858/456-4419 or 800/563-9345 (voice mail), mf@mexicofile.com (information), www.mexicofile.com).

Houston-based Vacation Publications, Inc. offers yet more possibilities. Check out *Travel 50 and Beyond* magazine, with plenty of budget-to-moderate hotel, travel club, tours, cruise, and air flights values for senior travelers. Also useful is the magazine *Where to Retire*. For information, a catalog, and to order, contact Vacation Publications, Inc. (5851 San Felipe St., Ste. 500, Houston, TX 77057, tel. 713/974-6903, www.vacationsmagazine.com).

Some books also feature senior travel opportunities. One of the pithiest is *Unbelievably Good Deals and Great Adventures You Can't Have Unless You're Over 50,* by Joan Rattner Heilman, published by McGraw Hill (2003). Its 200 pages are packed with details of how to get bargains on cruises, tours, car rentals, lodgings, and much, much more.

For seniors with online access (as close as your neighborhood library these days) the **Internet** is a gold mine of senior-oriented travel information. For example, on the Google search engine (www.google.com) home page, I typed in "Senior Travel" and netted more than 90 million responses.

Near the top of the list was the **Transitions Abroad** site (www.transitionsabroad.com), which offers a gold mine of a sub-site (www.transitionsabroad.com/listings/travel/senior) with a load of useful resources, centering around senior traveling and living abroad.

TRAVELING WITH CHILDREN
Bringing the Kids

Children are treasured like gifts from heaven in Mexico. Traveling with kids will ensure your welcome most everywhere. On the beach, take extra precautions to make sure they are protected from the sun.

A sick child is no fun for anyone. Fortunately, clinics and good doctors are available even in most small towns. When in need, ask a storekeeper or a pharmacist, *"¿Dónde hay un doctor, por favor?"* ("¿DOHN-day eye oon doc-TOHR por fah-VOHR?"). In most cases, within five minutes you will be in the waiting room of the local physician or hospital.

Children who do not favor typical Mexican fare can easily be fed with always available eggs, cheese, *hamburguesas,* milk, oatmeal, corn flakes, bananas, cakes, and cookies.

Your children will generally have more fun if they have a little previous knowledge of Mexico and a stake in the trip. For example, help them select some library picture books and magazines so they'll know where they're going and what to expect, or give them responsibility for packing and carrying their own small travel bag.

Be sure to mention your children's ages when making air reservations; child discounts of 50 percent or more are often available. Also, if you can arrange to go on an uncrowded flight, you can stretch out and rest on the empty seats.

For more details on traveling with children, check out *Adventuring with Children* by Nan Jeffrey. (See *Suggested Reading.*)

Family Outings

Guadalajara has plenty of fun places where adults and kids can share a good time. In general, family entertainment spots are more tranquil and relaxing in midweek, in contrast to the crowded weekends and holidays.

Kids enjoy a world-class **zoo and amusement park** (the "Magic Jungle"—Selva Mágica, at the north edge of town, end of Calzada Independencia). Bring a picnic and spend the day tripping along the winding paths, past the yawning crocodiles and snoozing turtles in the reptile house, through the leafy aviary and into the "Heart of Africa." Be sure to make your way to the zoo's airy downhill end, and take a break at a picnic table overlooking the vast green panorama of the canyon of the Río Santiago (here, called the "Barranca de Huentitán").

© BRUCE WHIPPERMAN

Kids love playing around Plaza de Armas in downtown Guadalajara.

Later, exit the zoo's west gate to the adjacent Selva Mágica and enjoy the roller coaster and dozens of other rides, plus slides, hot dogs, and video games. Unfortunately, the nearby planetarium and science center is sorely in need of renovation. (For details, see the *West and North* chapter.)

A number of Guadalajara's parks are fine spots to turn the kids loose. Closest in is **Parque Agua Azul** (corner of González Gallo and Independencia on the south side of downtown), where visitors enjoy plenty of shaded strollable green grassy spaces, plus an orchid house, bird house, butterfly house, and a tropical plant nursery. (See the *Downtown* chapter.)

Families find plenty of space for wandering in northwest-side **Parque Colomos** forest reserve, replete with acres of shade, lawns, creeks, a "Lake of the Birds," a Japanese garden, horseback riding, a cactus garden, and a number of picnic areas. (See the *West and North* chapter.)

Teenagers, on the other hand, might enjoy **Disco Roller** roller rink (which also has a play area for little ones, plus video games and snacks) or **Iceland** ice-skating rink; the admission fee also includes skate rental and free video games. (See the *Downtown* chapter.)

GAY AND LESBIAN TRAVELERS

Although Guadalajara is sometimes known as the "San Francisco of Mexico," the gay male presence in Guadalajara compared to the total flow of Guadalajara visitors is modest; and the lesbian presence is even less apparent. Nevertheless, gay and lesbian travelers generally enjoy a welcome from Guadalajara people, especially in Guadalajara's sprinkling of gay- and lesbian-friendly hotels, restaurants, bars, and entertainment spots.

For Guadalajara specifics, one of the best general gay travel websites is San Francisco–based **www.purpleroofs.com.** Its several pages detail several gay- and lesbian-friendly Guadalajara and Ajijic hotels, plus many more in Puerto Vallarta.

Furthermore, about two dozen lodgings, restaurants, night clubs and services are also advertised in the rather explicit **Gay Guadalajara** (www.gaygdl.com).

For travel agency advice and services, check out **Now Voyager** (4406 18th St., San Francisco, CA 94114, tel. 415/626-1169, toll-free tel. 800/255-6951, www.nowvoyager.com), a reliable San Francisco–based general travel agency that specializes in gay travel. They offer a plethora of services, from tour bookings and air tickets, to travel insurance and hotel reservations.

PROSPECTIVE RESIDENTS

If you're considering pulling up stakes and moving to Guadalajara, help and advice will be easy to find among the many folks who've already done it. First of all, most folks who've moved to Guadalajara (nearly all American and Canadian retirees) will tell you to do it gradually. Try living in Guadalajara for a spell in a rented house or apartment to see if you like it. Get to know people, listen to their stories, and, after six months (or preferably a year to experience all seasons), you'll be ready to make your choice.

In any case, Guadalajara's housing prices are certainly right. Rents for well-located apartments, suites, and houses run about half stateside city prices, for similar amenities. For example, expect to pay about $250 for a studio apartment in a middle-class Guadalajara neighborhood, or about $500 for a semi-deluxe two-bedroom apartment, $600–800 for a large unfurnished house, and $1,000–1,500 for a large luxurious apartment or house in an upper-class neighborhood.

As soon as (or even before) you arrive in Guadalajara, either get copies or visit the websites of the excellent local English-language newspapers, the *Guadalajara Colony Reporter* and the Lake Chapala area *El Ojo del Lago.* Both are chock-full of informative articles, event and organization listings, service advertisements, and real estate and rental listings. They're widely available. (For details on how to get copies, see *Finding a Long-Term Rental* in the *Accommodations* section earlier in this chapter.)

Helpful Local Organizations

Both of the newspapers above list local organizations of friendly folks, most of whom have experienced settling into Guadalajara. One of the best organized is the **American Society of Jalisco** (AMSOC), which furnishes new members with a useful information packet and maintains a library, small café, community information board, and a busy schedule of educational and social events for members. The center is in the Chapalita neighborhood in the Guadalajara western suburb (Av. San Francisco 3332, tel. 33/3121-2395). (For more details, see the *West and North* chapter.)

A similarly helpful Lake Chapala organization is the **Lake Chapala Society** (16 de Septiembre, in Ajijic, tel. 376/766-1140), which can be contacted at its activities center. (For more details, see the *Lake Chapala* chapter.)

Moreover, the **International Friendship Club of Guadalajara** has compiled a handy *Survival Guide to Guadalajara,* packed with useful recommendations, including emergency numbers, doctors, hospitals, services (such as TV repair, plumbing, and carpet cleaning), restaurants, hotels, and much more. Get your copy, customarily on sale for about $3, at the American Society of Jalisco's headquarters. For information on activities and membership in the International Friendship Club, contact former president Adele Vogt (tel. 33/3685-0423 or 33/3685-0445).

Many Guadalajara long-timers swear by the **American Legion,** which functions mostly as a social club and a place to make friends. Both Lake Chapala and Guadalajara have active branches. For example, try the Guadalajara Alvarez Castillo Post 3, which maintains headquarters at San Antonio 143, in the Colonia Las Fuentes (tel. 33/3631-1208; turn right off Avenida López Mateos at Avenida de las Fuentes, about two mi/three km south of Plaza del Sol). You don't have to be a war veteran to be an active member. They hold monthly general meetings and regular dinner-dances, breakfasts, and other events.

Other organizations, such as the **Hash House Harriers, Amigos del Lago** (Friends of the Lake), **Grupo Amigos, Rotary Club, Gamblers Anonymous, Masons,** and **Navy League** cordially invite participation by newcomers. See the community calendar events pages of the *Guadalajara Colony Reporter* and *El Ojo del Lago* for specifics.

Relocation Services

One of the most experienced of the Guadalajara relocation services is **The Relocation Connection** (tel. 33/3686-0067, info@relo.com, www.relomexico.com), whose partners specialize in helping newcomers settle into Guadalajara.

Many satisfied customers testify to the excellence of their services, that can include an introductory seminar, tours of sights and neighborhoods, and reasonably priced consultations and advice on rentals, real estate, hotels, restaurants, organizations, medical care, investments, and much more.

Buying a Home in Guadalajara

Thousands of former U.S. and Canadian residents have happily settled and bought homes in the Guadalajara region. Once you decide to take that step, best get a recommendation of a good real estate agent from your local friends. An agent will explain the details that, while generally similar, do differ in important aspects with the rules for buying a U.S. or Canadian home.

SOCIALLY RESPONSIBLE TRAVEL

Latter-day jet travel has brought droves of vacationing tourists to developing countries largely unprepared for the consequences. As the visitors' numbers swell, power grids black out, sewers overflow, and roads crack under the strain of accommodating more and larger hotels, restaurants, cars, buses, and airports.

Worse yet, armies of vacationers drive up local prices and begin to change native customs. While visions of tourists as sources of fast money replace traditions of hospitality, television wipes out folk entertainment, Coke and Pepsi substitute for fruit drinks, and prostitution and drugs flourish.

Some travelers have said enough is enough and are forming organizations to encourage visitors to travel with increased sensitivity to native people and customs. They have developed travelers' codes of ethics and guidelines that encourage visitors to stay at local-style accommodations, use local transportation, and seek alternative vacations and tours, such as language-study and cultural programs and people-to-people work projects.

For more information, visit a socially responsible website, such as www.greenglobe.org, www.planeta.com, www.tourism-concern.org.uk, and www.sociallyresponsible.org.

Tours, Guides, and Courses

TOURS AND GUIDES

For many Guadalajara visitors, a guided tour offers a hassle-free alternative to sightseeing by car or taxi. Hotels and travel agencies, many of which maintain lobby-front travel and tour desks, offer a bounty of sightseeing options.

A number of highly recommended guides offer Guadalajara custom tours. Expect to pay about $100 per day, including transportation, or about $50 per day if you supply the car. One of the best persons to inquire about Guadalajara guides is experienced guide **Lynn Mendez,** who staffs the state of Jalisco tourist information office (Paseo Morelos 102, tel. 33/3668-1600 or 33/3668-1601), on Plaza Tapatóa. She strongly recommends professional tour guides **Roberto Arellano** (tel. 33/3657-8376), former president of the Guadalajara Guides Association, **Fernando Mediana** (tel. 33/3654-5957), and Octavio Estrada (33/3632-7306).

Another very well prepared and personable guide is American-Mexican innkeeper **Arturo Magaña,** co-owner of Quinta Don José in Tlaquepaque (tel. 33/3635-7522, U.S.-Canada toll-free tel. 866/629-3753, fax 33/3659-9315, info@quintadonjose.com, www.quintadonjose.com).

If somehow Arturo's very popular tours are booked up, he recommends a pair of excellent guides: Four stars go to both **Ramiro Roma** (tel./fax 33/3631-4242, or cell tel. 044-33/3661-6202 in Guadalajara, or long-distance 33/3661-6202 outside Guadalajara); and **Lino Gabriel González Nuño** (tel. 33/3152-0324, fax 33/3635-4049, linogabriel@hotmail.com,

www.mexonline.com/guadalajaratours.htm.), who specializes in customized Guadalajara tours (downtown, shopping in Tlaquepaque and Tonalá, archaeological sites, and much more).

If you're on a tight budget, a private group bus tour might be just the ticket. Contact an experienced agency, such as **Charter Club Tours** (Av. San Francisco 3477, tel. 33/3122-1214) in Guadalajara, in the Chapalita district; or in Ajijic, at Plaza Montana, by the Colón highway signal (tel. 376/766-1777, info@charterclubtours.com.mx, www.charterclubtours.com.mx). Alternatively, contact **Panoramex** (Federalismo Sur 944, tel. 33/3810-5005, 33/3810-5057, 33/3810-5160, or 33/3810-5109, www.panoramex.com.mx). Tour options vary widely, from Guadalajara sights and the Ballet Folklórico to shopping in Tonalá and Tlaquepaque. Wider-ranging tours can include regional destinations, such as Mazamitla in the mountains or the monumental Guachimontones pyramids at Teuchtitlán, near Tequila, to as far as Lake Pátzcuaro in Michoacán.

A very easy and economical option is to hop on to one of the red double-decker tour buses that the Jalisco Tourism Secretariat runs frequently every day from the street that runs along the north side of the downtown Cathedral (at the Rotonda de los Hombres Ilustres). Get your ticket at the bus. For updated information, check with the Jalisco tourism information desk (Morelos 102, tel. 33/3613-0887, toll-free 01-800/002-2287, www.tapatiotour.com.mx), behind the Teatro Degollado.

EDUCATIONAL OPPORTUNITIES

Elderhostel

Elderhostel's rich offerings customarily include a pair of cultural programs in Guadalajara. One focuses on the arts and crafts of colonial Mexico and includes visits to the venerable monuments of downtown Guadalajara, especially Hospicio Cabañas for viewing and discussions of the José Clemente Orozco murals. The tour continues on to Uruapan and Morelia, in Michoacán, where the focus shifts to native and colonial arts and crafts traditions.

A separate frequently offered Guadalajara program, "Language and History of Mexico," provides Elderhostelers with opportunities to hone their language skills in practical encounters and appreciate history in context, while exploring the architectural, art, and craft treasures of Guadalajara and Zacatecas. For details, request the international catalog from Elderhostel (11 Ave. de Lafayette, Boston, MA 02111-1746, toll-free tel. 800/454-5768, www.elderhostel.org).

University of Guadalajara

At a more intensive level, the University of Guadalajara maintains excellent study programs for visitors through its **Centro de Estudios Para Extranjeros** (CEPE, Study Center for Foreigners, Tomás S. V. Gómez 125, P.O. Box 1-2130, Guadalajara, Jalisco 44100, tel. 33/3616-4399 or 33/3616-4382, fax 33/3616-4013, www.cepe. udg.mx). Its extensive offerings range from beginning Spanish language to advanced history, politics, literature, and art. Housing options include homestays with Guadalajara families.

Field Guides Tours

Naturalists enjoy the excellent Field Guides birding tour (800/728-4953, fax 512/263-0117, www.fieldguides.com), centered in wildlife-rich Jalisco and Colima backcountry. Of the 80 endemic Mexican bird species, about 35 have been seen on this tour.

Health and Safety

In Guadalajara, as everywhere, prevention is the best remedy for illness. For visitors who confine their travel to the beaten path, a few common sense precautions will ensure vacation enjoyment.

Resist the temptation to dive headlong into Mexico. It's no wonder that people get sick—broiling in the sun, gobbling peppery food, guzzling beer and margaritas, then discoing half the night—all in their first 24 hours. Give your body time to adjust. Travelers often arrive tired and dehydrated from travel and heat. During the first few days, drink plenty of bottled water and juice, and take siestas.

A good physician can recommend the proper immunizations for your Guadalajara trip. If you are going to stay in town, your doctor may suggest little more than updating your basic typhoid, diphtheria-tetanus, and polio shots.

TRAVELER'S DIARRHEA

Traveler's diarrhea (known in Mexico as "turista" or "Montezuma's Revenge") sometimes persists, even among prudent vacationers. You can suffer turista for a week after simply traveling between California and Philadelphia or New York. Doctors say the familiar symptoms of runny bowels, nausea, and sour stomach result from normal local bacterial strains to which newcomers' systems need time to adjust. Unfortunately, the dehydration and fatigue from heat and travel reduce your body's natural defenses and sometimes lead to a persistent cycle of sickness at a time when you least want it.

Time-tested protective measures can help your body either prevent or break this cycle. Many doctors and veteran travelers swear by Pepto-Bismol for soothing sore stomachs and stopping diarrhea. Acidophilus, the bacteria found in yogurt, aids digestion and is widely available in the United States in tablets. Warm *manzanilla* (chamomile) tea, used widely in Mexico (and by Peter Rabbit's mother), provides liquid and calms upset stomachs. Temporarily avoid coffee and alcohol, drink plenty of *manzanilla* tea, and eat bananas and rice for a few meals until your tummy can take regular food.

Although powerful antibiotics and antidiarrhea medications such as Lomotil and Imodium are readily available over *farmacia* counters, they may involve serious side effects and should not be taken in the absence of medical advice. If in doubt, consult a doctor.

WATER AND FOOD

Although Mexican municipalities have made great strides in sanitation, food and water are still potential sources of germs in the Guadalajara region. It's probably best to avoid local tap water, in preference to bottled water, which needn't be expensive. Groceries and drug stores carry gallon (four liter) bottles for less than $2. More economical still are the large five-gallon *garrafones* ("demijohns" in English) that are routinely delivered to Guadalajara restaurants, hotels, and residences for about $3–4. Hotels, whose success depends vitally on their customers' health, generally provide *agua purificada* (purified bottled water). If, for any reason, the water quality is doubtful, add a water purifier, such as Potable Aqua brand (get it at a camping goods store before departure) or a few drops per quart of water of *blanqueador* (household chlorine bleach) or *yodo* (tincture of iodine) from the pharmacy.

Pure bottled water, soft drinks, beer, and fresh fruit juices are so widely available it is easy to avoid tap water, especially in restaurants. Washing hands before eating in a restaurant is a time-honored Mexican ritual that visitors should religiously follow. The humblest Mexican eatery will customarily provide a basin to *lavar los manos* (wash the hands). If it doesn't, don't eat there.

Hot, cooked food is generally safe, as are peeled fruits and vegetables. Milk and cheese these days in Mexico are generally processed under sanitary conditions and sold pasteurized (ask, *"¿Pasteurizado?"*) and are typically safe. Mexican ice cream used to be both

MEDICAL TAGS AND AIR EVACUATION

Travelers with special medical problems should consider wearing a medical identification tag. For a reasonable fee, **Medic Alert** (P.O. Box 1009, Turlock, California 95381, tel. 209/668-3333, toll-free tel. 888/633-4398, www.medicalert.org) provides such tags, as well as an information hotline that will inform doctors of your vital medical background.

In life-threatening emergencies, the highly recommended **Aeromedevac** (Gillespie Field Airport, 681 Kenney St., El Cajon, CA 92020, tol-free tel. 800/462-0911, from Mexico 24-hr. toll-free tel. 001-800/832-5087, www.aeromedevac.com) provides high-tech jet ambulance service from any Mexican locale to a U.S. hospital for roughly $20,000.

Alternatively, you might consider the similar services of **Med-Jet Assistance** (Birmingham, Alabama, Intl. Airport, 4900 69th St., Birmingham AL, 35206, toll-free U.S. tel. 800/963-3538, www.medjetassistance.com; in emergencies, world-wide, call U.S. tel. 205/595-6626 collect).

bad-tasting and of dubious safety, but national brands available in supermarkets are so much improved that it's no longer necessary to resist Mexican ice cream.

In recent years, much cleaner public water and increased hygiene awareness have made salads—once shunned by Mexico travelers—generally safe to eat in cafés and restaurants in Guadalajara. Nevertheless, lettuce and cabbage, particularly in country villages, are more likely to be contaminated than tomatoes, carrots, cucumbers, onions, and green peppers. In any case, whenever in doubt, douse your salad in vinegar *(vinagre)* or plenty of sliced lime *(limón)* juice, the acidity of which kills bacteria.

SUN PROTECTION

Use a good sunscreen with a sun protection factor (SPF) of 15 or more, which will reduce burning rays to one-fifteenth or less of direct sunlight. Better still, take a shady siesta-break from the sun during the most hazardous midday hours. If you do get burned, applying your sunburn lotion (or one of the "-caine" creams) after the fact usually decreases the pain and speeds healing.

TROPICAL BACKCOUNTRY PRECAUTIONS

Although most of the Guadalajara region lies within the temperate 5,000-foot (1,600-meter)

elevation zone, in some lower-elevation areas, notably in the Barranca north and west of town and the southwest coastal slope, campers and trekkers should exercise precautions. Doctors usually recommend a gamma-globulin shot against hepatitis A and a schedule of chloroquine pills against malaria. While in backcountry areas, use other measures to discourage mosquitoes—and fleas, flies, ticks, no-see-ums, "kissing bugs," and other tropical pests—from biting you. Common precautions include sleeping under mosquito netting, burning *espirales mosquito* (mosquito coils), and rubbing on plenty of pure DEET (dimethyl-meta-toluamide) "jungle juice" mixed in equal parts with rubbing (70 percent isopropyl) alcohol. Although super-effective, 100 percent DEET dries and irritates the skin.

Chagas' disease, spread by the "kissing" (or, more appropriately, "assassin") bug, is a potential hazard in the Mexican tropics. Known locally as a *vinchuca,* the triangular-headed, three-quarter-inch (two cm) brown insect, identifiable by its yellow-striped abdomen, often drops upon its sleeping victims from the thatched ceiling of a rural house at night. Its bite is followed by swelling, fever, and weakness and can lead to heart failure if left untreated. Application of drugs at an early stage can, however, clear the patient of the trypanosome parasites that infect victims' bloodstreams and vital organs. See a doctor immediately if you believe you're infected.

Also while camping or staying in a *palapa* or other rustic accommodation, watch for scorpions, especially in your shoes, which you should shake out every morning. Scorpion stings and snakebites are rarely fatal to an adult but are potentially very serious for a child. Get the victim to a doctor calmly but quickly.

PEDESTRIAN AND DRIVING HAZARDS

The Guadalajara region's rough pavements and "holey" sidewalks might send you to the hospital if you don't watch your step, especially at night. "Pedestrian beware" is especially good advice on Guadalajara's streets, where it is rumored that some drivers speed up rather than slow down when they spot a tourist stepping off the curb.

Driving regional country roads, where slow trucks and carts block lanes, campesinos stroll the shoulders, and horses, burros, and cattle wander at will, requires extra caution, and doubly so at night.

FIRST-AID KIT

At tropical elevations, ordinary cuts and insect bites are more prone to infection and should receive immediate first aid. A first-aid kit with aspirin, rubbing alcohol, hydrogen peroxide, water-purifying tablets, household chlorine bleach or iodine for water purifying, swabs, Band-Aids, gauze, adhesive tape, Ace bandage, chamomile *(manzanilla)* tea bags for upset stomachs, Pepto-Bismol, acidophilus tablets, antibiotic ointment, hydrocortisone cream, mosquito repellent, knife, and good tweezers is a good precaution for any traveler and mandatory for campers.

LOCAL MEDICAL SERVICES

For medical advice and treatment, let your hotel or, if you're camping, the closest *farmacia*, refer you to a good doctor, clinic, or hospital. Many Guadalajara doctors practice like private doctors in the United States and Canada once

did before the onset of HMOs, liability, and group practice. They will often come to you if you request; they often keep their doors open even after regular hours and charge reasonable fees. And remember: *cita* means an "appointment," and *nota* means "receipt."

You will generally receive good treatment at the local hospitals in the Guadalajara region. If, however, you must have an English-speaking American- or Canadian-trained doctor, **IAMAT** (1623 Military Road #279, Niagra Falls, NY 14304, tel. 716/754-4883 or 716/754-4883, or in Canada at 1287 St. Clair Ave. W, Toronto, Ontario M6E 1B8, tel. 416/652-0137, info@iamat.org, www.iamat.org.) maintains a worldwide network of English-speaking doctors. At least two IAMAT medical groups practice in Guadalajara. Contact J. Jaime Ramírez Parra, M.D. (Tarascos 3514-14, Rinconada Santa Rita, tel. 33/3813-0440 or 33/813-1025), or Salvador Vásquez, M.D., with offices next to the Hospital Mexicano Americano (Colomos 2110).

Moreover, Guadalajara's **International Friendship Club** recommends a number of hospitals and English-speaking doctors in its handy *Survival Guide to Guadalajara.* Among Guadalajara doctors, two of the most highly recommended are internists **Dr. Daniel Gil Sánchez** (Torre Médico, Av. Pablo Neruda 3265, tel. 33/3642-0213) and **Dr. Michael Ritota Jr.** (Av. Tarascos 3422, tel. 33/3813-0540).

Others also recommended are cardiologist Dr. Ricardo Ascencio Ochoa (Lacandones 310, tel. 33/3813-0699); general practitioner Dr. Ira Luisa Ceja Martínez (Tarascos 3363, tel. 33/3813-1162 or 33/3813-2046); traumatologist Dr. Oscar Ramírez Macías (Av. López Mateos Norte 328, corner of Av. Mexico, first floor, tel. 33/3648-3405); orthopedist and traumatologist Dr. Cesar Álvarez (Tarascos 3385, tel. 33/3813-0096 or 33/3813-0342); pediatrician Dr. Jaime Unda Gómez (Tarascos 3432-15, second floor, tel. 33/3813-2026, 33/3813-2019, or 33/3813-2090); dentist Dr. Rene Hernández Acevedo (Av. Providencia 2450-202, tel. 33/3642-6300); gynecologist-obstetrician Dr. Rafael Chung Garay (Av. Hidalgo 2380 Ste. 5, tel. 33/3616-2776, cell 044-33/3648-6290).

The International Friendship Club also recommends a number of Guadalajara **hospitals.** Probably the most useful for Americans is the **Hospital Americas** (Av. Americas 932, Guadalajara 44620, tel. 33/3817-3141 and 33/3817-3004). It accepts the coverage of many U.S. HMOs; all staff are U.S.–trained and all hospitalization is in private rooms, with TV, phone, and bathroom.

Additionally recommended are **Hospital Méxicano-Americano** (Av. Colomos 2110, tel. 33/3641-3141, fax 33/3642-6401), with 24-hour emergency room; **Hospital del Carmen** (Tarascos 3435, tel. 33/3813-0025 and 33/3813-0042, emergencies tel. 33/3813-1224) with 24-hour emergency room; **Hospital San Javier** (Av. Pablo Casals 640, Col. Providencia, tel. 33/3669-0222, fax 33/3669-0222, ambulance tel. 33/3616-9616), with 24-hour emergency room; and **Hospital Arboledas** (Av. Nicolás Copernico 4000, tel. 33/3631-3051, fax 33/3631-4450), with 24-hour emergency room.

For many more useful details of health and safety in Mexico, consult Dr. William W. Forgey's *Traveler's Medical Alert Series: Mexico* (Merrillville, IN: ICS Books); or Dirk G. Schroeder's *Staying Healthy in Asia, Africa, and Latin America* (Emeryville, CA: Avalon Travel Publishing, 2000).

POLICE AND FIRE EMERGENCIES

Guadalajara and its suburban districts maintain good fire and police infrastructure. Contact the Guadalajara police through the main switchboard (tel. 33/3838-0808); Federal Highway Police (tel. 33/3629-5078); police in Tlaquepaque (tel. 33/3635-8828 or 33/3345-5900); in Tonalá (tel. 33/3284-3038, 33/3284-3039); in Zapopan (tel. 33/3836-3636, 33/3656-5656, or 33/3633-1010).

For fire emergencies, call the main fire switchboard (tel. 33/1201-7700); the south-side Industrial Zone station (tel. 33/3645-6034 or 33/3645-9593); the north-side Transito station (tel. 33/3823-0833); or east-side district Gigantes-Manuel Ponce (tel. 33/3644-4555 or 33/3644-4479); in Zapopan (tel. 33/3836-3636 or 33/3656-8577); in Tlaquepaque (tel. 33/3635-8828); in Tonalá (tel. 33/3284-3040 or 33/3284-3041).

PACKING CHECKLIST

Use this list as a guide for packing (and actually check it off before walking out the door) to avoid forgetting necessary items.

NECESSARY ITEMS

___ camera, film (expensive in Mexico)
___ clothes, hat
___ comb
___ credit and/or ATM cards, travelers checks, money
___ guidebook, reading books
___ keys, tickets
___ mosquito repellent
___ passport, tourist card, visa
___ prescription eyeglasses
___ prescription medicines and drugs
___ purse, waist-belt carrying pouch
___ sunglasses
___ sunscreen
___ swimsuit
___ toothbrush, toothpaste
___ watch, clock
___ windbreaker

USEFUL ITEMS

___ address book
___ birth control
___ checkbook
___ contact lenses
___ dental floss
___ earplugs
___ first-aid kit
___ flashlight, batteries
___ immersion heater
___ lightweight binoculars
___ portable music player
___ razor
___ travel book light
___ umbrella
___ vaccination certificate

NECESSARY ITEMS FOR CAMPERS

___ camp cup, fork, and spoon
___ collapsible plastic gallon bottle
___ dish soap
___ first-aid kit
___ insect repellent
___ lightweight hiking shoes
___ lightweight tent
___ matches in waterproof case
___ nylon cord
___ plastic bottle, quart
___ pot scrubber/sponge
___ sheet or light blanket
___ single-burner stove with fuel
___ Swiss army knife
___ tarp
___ toilet paper
___ towel, soap
___ two nesting cooking pots
___ water-purifying tablets, iodine, or household chlorine bleach

USEFUL ITEMS FOR CAMPERS

___ coffee, tea, sugar, powdered milk
___ dishcloths
___ hot pad
___ magnetic compass
___ moleskin (Dr. Scholl's)
___ paraffin household candles
___ plastic plate
___ poncho
___ whistle

Information and Services

MONEY
The Peso

Overnight in early 1993, the Mexican government shifted its monetary decimal point three places and created the "new" peso, which subsequently has deflated from its initial value of 3 per dollar to about 11 per dollar. Since the peso value sometimes changes rapidly, U.S. dollars have become a much more stable indicator of Mexican prices; for this reason they are used in this book to report prices. Regardless, you should always use pesos to pay in Mexico—you'll usually end up paying a little less.

Since the introduction of the new peso, the centavo (one-hundredth of a new peso) has reappeared in coins of 10, 20, and 50 centavos. Incidentally, the dollar sign, "$," also marks Mexican pesos. Peso coins, in denominations of 1, 2, 5, 10, and 20, and peso bills of 20, 50, 100, and 200 pesos are common. Since banks like to exchange your travelers checks for a few crisp large bills rather than the often-tattered smaller denominations, ask for some of your change in 50-peso notes. A 200- or 500-peso note, while common at the bank, sometimes looks awfully big to a small shopkeeper, who might be hard-pressed to change it.

Banks, ATMs, and Money Exchange Offices

Mexican banks, like their North American counterparts, have lengthened their business hours. Hong Kong Shanghai Banking Corporation (HSBC) maintains the longest hours: generally Monday–Saturday 8 A.M.–7 P.M. Banamex (Banco Nacional de Mexico), generally the most popular with local people, usually posts the best in-town dollar exchange rate in its lobbies; for example, *"Tipo de cambio: venta 11.615, compra 11.720"* means they will sell pesos to you at the rate of 11.615 per dollar and buy them back for 11.720 per dollar.

ATMs or *cajeros automáticos* (kah-HEY-rohs ow-toh-MAH-tee-kohs) are rapidly becoming the money source of choice in Mexico. Virtu-ally every bank has a 24-hour ATM, accessible (with proper PIN identification code) by a swarm of U.S. and Canadian credit and ATM cards. All ATMs dispense peso notes, while only some dispense U.S. dollars.

Since one-time bank charges for ATM cash are not negligible (typically about $3 per transaction), get as much the money you can (typically about $300 per day) from a single transaction.

Even without an ATM card, you don't have to go to the trouble of waiting in long bank service lines. Opt for a less-crowded bank, such as BBV–Bancomer, Banco Santander–Serfín, Scotiabank Inverlat, HSBCl, or a private money-exchange office *(casa de cambio)*. Often most convenient, such offices often offer long hours and faster service than the banks for a fee (as little as $0.50 or as much as $3 per $100).

Keeping Your Money Safe

Travelers checks, the universal prescription for safe money abroad, are widely accepted in the Guadalajara region. Even if you plan to use your ATM card, purchase some U.S. dollar travelers checks (a well-known brand such as American Express or Visa) at least as an emergency reserve. Canadian travelers checks and currency are not as widely accepted as U.S. travelers checks. European and Asian checks are even less acceptable. Unless you like signing your name or paying lots of per-check commissions, buy denominations of $50 or more.

In Guadalajara, as everywhere, **thieves** circulate among the tourists. Keep valuables in your hotel *caja de seguridad* (security box). If you don't particularly trust the desk clerk, carry what you can't afford to lose in a money belt attached to your front side; pickpockets love crowded markets, buses, and airport terminals where they can slip a wallet out of a back pocket or dangling purse in a blink. In the absence of a money belt or waist pouch, guard against this by carrying your wallet in your front pocket and your purse or daypack (which clever crooks can sometimes slit open) on your front side.

Don't attract thieves by displaying wads of money or flashy jewelry. Don't get sloppy drunk; if so, you may become a pushover for a determined thief.

Don't leave valuables unattended at the beach. Share security duties with trustworthy-looking neighbors, or leave a bag with a shopkeeper nearby.

Investing

Satisfied local investors recommend the services of **Lloyd Investment Funds** (Guadalajara main branch near Plaza del Sol, tel. 33/3880-2000). Other local branches are at Lake Chapala (tel. 376/765-2149 in Chapala; 376/766-3110 in Ajijic). For investment details, visit www.lloyd.com.mx.

COMMUNICATIONS
Telephones

Mexican phones operate more or less the same as in the United States and Canada. Mexican phone numbers have changed frequently in recent years because the Mexican telephone system is growing rapidly. A complete telephone number (in Guadalajara, for example) is generally written like this: 33/3817-2822. As in the United States, the "33" denotes the telephone *lada* (area code), and the "3817-2822" is the number that you dial locally. If you want to dial this number long-distance within Mexico, first dial "01" (like dialing "1" before the area code in the United States), then "33/3817-2822."

When placing a local call to a **cell phone,** you must dial "044" then the area code and local number. Long-distance calls to cell phones do not require that you dial "044" first; you simply dial "01" then the area code and local number.

Nearly all area codes in Mexico have three numbers (such as 322 for Puerto Vallarta or 328 for San Blas). Only three large cities—Guadalajara (33), Mexico City (55), and Monterrey (81)—have two-number area codes. Local phone numbers of Guadalajara, Mexico

City, and Monterrey contain eight digits; all other local phone numbers contain seven.

Direct *larga distancia* (long-distance) dialing is the rule—from hotels, public phone booths, and efficient private Computel telephone offices. The cheapest and often most convenient way to call is by purchasing and using a **Ladatel phone card.** Buy them in 30-, 50-, and 100-peso denominations at the many outlets—minimarkets, pharmacies, liquor stores—that display the blue and yellow Ladatel sign.

In small towns, you must often do your long-distance phoning in the *larga distancia* (local phone office). Typically staffed by a young woman and often connected to a café, the *larga distancia* becomes an informal community social center as people pass the time waiting for their phone connections.

Postal Services

Mexican *correos* (post offices) operate similarly but more slowly and less securely than their counterparts in most parts of the world. Mail services usually include *lista de correo* (general delivery—address letters *"a/c lista de correo"*), *servicios filatelicas* (philatelic services), *por avión* (airmail), *giros* (postal money orders), and Mexpost secure and fast delivery service, usually from separate Mexpost offices.

Mexican ordinary mail is sadly unreliable and pathetically slow. If, for mailings within Mexico, you must have security, use the efficient, reformed, government **Mexpost** (like U.S.P.S. Express Mail) service. For international mailings, check the local Yellow Pages for widely available **DHL** or **Federal Express** courier service.

Telégrafos (telegraph offices), usually near the post office, send and receive *telegramas* (telegrams) and *giros*. *Telecomunicaciones* (Telecom), the new high-tech telegraph offices, add telephone and public fax to the available services.

TIME

The Guadalajara region and all of the state of Jalisco operates on U.S. Central time (although the bordering state of Nayarit, west of Jalisco,

CALLING MEXICO AND CALLING HOME

CALLING MEXICO FROM THE UNITED STATES

To call Mexico direct from the United States, first dial 011 for international access, then 52 for Mexico, followed by the Mexican area code *(lada)* and local number.

Some Guadalajara regional area codes are: Guadalajara, Zapopan, Tlaquepaque and Tonalá 33; San Juan de los Lagos 395; Mazamitla 382; Tapalpa 343; Chapala and Ajijic 376; Tequila 374; and Magdalena 386.

CALLING THE UNITED STATES FROM MEXICO

For station-to-station calls, dial 001 for the United States, plus the area code and the local number. For calls to other countries, ask your hotel desk clerk or see the easy-to-follow directions in the front of the local Mexican telephone directory.

The most economical way to call home from Mexico is to purchase a blue and yellow Ladatel telephone card (in $3, $5, and $10 denominations) and use it in a public telephone (widely available on streets and in restaurants and hotels).

Using your personal telephone credit card or calling collect are other convenient (although much more expensive) ways to call home. Dial 090 for the local English-speaking international operator or contact your U.S. long-distance operator by dialing direct: 001-800/462-4240 for AT&T, 001-800/674-7000 for MCI, or 001-800/877-8000 for Sprint.

Beware of private "Call home collect" telephones installed prominently in airports, tourist hotels, and shops. Tariffs on these phone can run as high as $10 a minute, with a three-minute minimum (which will cost $30 even if you don't talk for three minutes). If you do use such a phone, always ask the operator for the rate, and if it's too high, take your business elsewhere.

operates on U.S. Mountain time). When traveling by highway east from Nayarit into Jalisco toward Guadalajara, set your watch ahead (for example, from 1 P.M. to 2 P.M.).

Mexican businesses and government offices sometimes use the 24-hour system to tell time. Thus, a business that posts its hours as 0800–1700 is open 8 A.M.–5 P.M. When speaking, however, people customarily use the 12-hour system.

ELECTRICITY

Mexican electric power is supplied at U.S.-standard 110 volts, 60 cycles. Plugs and sockets are generally two-pronged, nonpolar (like the pre-1970s U.S. ones). Bring adapters if you're going to use appliances with polar two-pronged or three-pronged plugs. A two-pronged polar plug has different-sized prongs, one of which is too large to plug into an old-fashioned nonpolar socket.

RESOURCES
Glossary

Many of the following words have a socio-historical meaning; some you will not find in the usual English-Spanish dictionary.

abarrotería grocery store

alcalde mayor or municipal judge

alfarería pottery

alfarero, alfarera potter

andando walkway or strolling path

antojitos native Mexican snacks, such as tamales, *chiles rellenos*, tacos, and enchiladas

artesanías handicrafts, as distinguished from artesano, artesana a person who makes handicrafts

audiencia one of the royal executive-judicial panels sent to rule Mexico during the 16th century

ayuntamiento either the town council or the building where it meets

bienes raíces literally "good roots," but popularly, real estate

birria pit-barbequed goat, pork, or lamb—especially typical of Jalisco

boleto ticket, boarding pass

caballero literally, "horseman," but popularly, gentleman

cabercera head town of a municipal district, or headquarters in general

cabrón literally a cuckold, but more commonly, bastard, rat, or S.O.B.; sometimes used affectionately

cacique chief or boss

calandria early 1800s-style horse-drawn carriage, common in Guadalajara

camionera central central bus station

campesino country person; farm worker

canasta basket of woven reeds, with handle

casa de huéspedes guesthouse, often operated in a family home

caudillo dictator or political chief

charro, charra gentleman cowboy or cowgirl

chingar literally, "to rape," but is also the universal Spanish "f- word," the equivalent of "screw" in English

churrigueresque Spanish baroque architectural style incorporated into many Mexican colonial churches, named after José Churriguera (1665-1725)

científicos literally, scientists, but applied to President Porfirio Díaz's technocratic advisers

cofradía Catholic fraternal service association, either male or female, mainly in charge of financing and organizing religious festivals

colectivo a shared public taxi or minibus that picks up and deposits passengers along a designated route

colegio preparatory school or junior college

colonia suburban subdivision/satellite of a larger city

Conasupo government store that sells basic foods at subsidized prices

correo post office

criollo person of all-Spanish descent born in the New World

cuadra a rectangular work of art, such as a painting. Often refers to a Huichol yarn painting. Also a city block.

Cuaresma Lent

curandero, curandera indigenous medicine man or woman

damas ladies, as in "ladies room"

Domingo de Ramos Palm Sunday

ejido a constitutional, government-sponsored form of community, with shared land ownership and cooperative decision making

encomienda colonial award of tribute from a designated indigenous district

estación ferrocarril railroad station

farmacia pharmacy or drugstore

finca farm

fonda food stall or small economical restaurant, often in a traditional market complex

fraccionamiento city sector or subdivision

fuero the former right of clergy and the military to be tried in separate ecclesiastical or military courts

gachupín "one who wear spurs"; a derogatory term for a Spanish-born colonial

gasolinera gasoline station

gente de razón "people of reason"; whites and mestizos in colonial Mexico

gringo once-derogatory but now commonly used term for North American whites

grito impassioned cry, as in Hidalgo's *Grito de Dolores*

hacienda large landed estate; also the government treasury

hidalgo nobleman; called honorifically by "Don" or "Doña"

indígena indigenous or aboriginal inhabitant of all-native descent who speaks his or her native tongue; commonly, but incorrectly, an Indian *(indio)*

jardín literally garden, but often denoting a town's central plaza

jejenes "no-see-um" biting gnats, especially around mangrove jungle wetlands.

judiciales the federal or state "judicial," or investigative police, best known to motorists for their highway checkpoint inspections

jugería stall or small restaurant providing a large array of squeezed vegetable and fruit *jugos* (juices)

juzgado the "hoosegow," or jail

larga distancia long-distance telephone service, or the *caseta* (booth) where it's provided

licenciado literally "licensed"; more commonly an academic degree (abbr. Lic.) approximately equivalent to a bachelor's degree

lonchería small lunch counter, usually serving juices, sandwiches, and *antojitos* (Mexican snacks)

machismo, macho exaggerated sense of maleness; person who holds such a sense of himself

mescal alcoholic beverage distilled from the fermented hearts of maguey (century plant)

mestizo person of mixed European/indigenous descent

milpa native farm plot, usually of corn, squash, and beans

mordida slang for bribe; literally, "little bite"

palapa thatched-roof structure, often open and shading a restaurant

Pemex acronym for Petróleos Mexicanos, Mexico's national oil corporation

peninsulares the Spanish-born ruling colonial elite

peón a poor wage-earner, usually a country native

petate a mat, traditionally woven of palm leaf

plan political manifesto, usually by a leader or group consolidating or seeking power

plancha outboard motorized launch, sometimes called a *panga*

Porfiriato the 34-year (1876–1910) ruling period of president-dictator Porfirio Díaz

pozole popular stew, of hominy in broth, usually topped by shredded pork, cabbage, and diced onion

presidencia municipal the headquarters, like a U.S. city or county hall, of a Mexican *municipio*, countylike local governmental unit

preventiva state or municipal police, directly responsible for security and keeping the peace

pronunciamiento declaration of rebellion by an insurgent leader

pueblo town or people

puta derogatory term for women

quinta a villa or country house

quinto the royal "one-fifth" tax on treasure and precious metals

retorno cul-de-sac

rurales former federal country police force created to fight *bandidos*

Semana Santa pre-Easter holy week

Tapatío, Tapatía a label, referring to anyone or anything from Guadalajara or Jalisco

taxi especial private taxi, as distinguished from *taxi colectivo*, or shared taxi

telégrafo telegraph office, lately converting to high-tech telecomunicaciones, or telecom, offering telegraph, telephone, money order, and public fax services

tenate soft, pliable basket, woven of dried palm leaf

vaquero cowboy

vecinidad neighborhood

vinchuca "kissing" or "assassin" bug that spreads the dengue fever bacteria

yanqui Yankee

zócalo town plaza or central square

ABBREVIATIONS

Av. *avenida* (avenue)

Blv. *bulevar* (boulevard)

Calz. *calzada* (thoroughfare, main road)

Fco. Francisco (proper name, as in "Fco. Villa")

Fracc. *Fraccionamiento* (subdivision)

Nte. *norte* (north)

Ote. *oriente* (east)

Pte. *poniente* (west)

s/n *sin número* (no street number)

Spanish Phrasebook

Your Mexico adventure will be more fun if you use a little Spanish. Mexican folks, although they may smile at your funny accent, will appreciate your halting efforts to break the ice and transform yourself from a foreigner to a potential friend.

Spanish commonly uses 30 letters – the familiar English 26, plus four straightforward additions: ch, ll, ñ, and rr.

PRONUNCIATION

Once you learn them, Spanish pronunciation rules – in contrast to English – don't change. Spanish vowels generally sound softer than in English. (Note: The capitalized syllables below receive stronger accents.)

Vowels

a like ah, as in "hah": *agua* AH-gooah (water), *pan* PAHN (bread), and *casa* CAH-sah (house)

e like ay, as in "may": *mesa* MAY-sah (table), *tela* TAY-lah (cloth), and *de* DAY (of, from)

i like ee, as in "need": *diez* dee-AYZ (ten), *comida* ko-MEE-dah (meal), and *fin* FEEN (end)

o like oh, as in "go": *peso* PAY-soh (weight), *ocho* OH-choh (eight), and *poco* POH-koh (a bit)

u like oo, as in "cool": *uno* OO-noh (one), *cuarto* KOOAHR-toh (room), and *usted* oos-TAYD (you); when it follows a "q" the **u** is silent, as in *qué* kay (what), or *quiero* kee-AY-roh (I want).

Consonants

b, d, f, k, l, m, n, p, q, s, t, v, w, x, y, z, ch pronounced almost as in English

c like k as in "keep": *cuarto* KOOAR-toh (room), Tepic tay-PEEK (capital of Nayarit state); when it precedes "e" or "i," pronounce **c** like s, as in "sit": *cerveza* sayr-VAY-sah (beer), *encima* ayn-SEE-mah (atop).

g pronounce hard, like g as in "gift" when it precedes "a," "o," "u," or a consonant: *gato* GAH-toh (cat), *hago* AH-goh (I do, make);

otherwise, pronounce **g** soft, like h as in "hat": *giro* HEE-roh (money order), *gente* HAYN-tay (people).

h sometimes occurs, but is silent – not pronounced at all.

j like h, as in "has": *Jueves* HOOAY-vays (Thursday), *mejor* may-HOR (better)

ll like y, as in "yes": *toalla* toh-AH-yah (towel), *ellos* AY-yohs (they, them)

ñ like ny, as in "canyon": *año* AH-nyo (year), *señor* SAY-nyor (Mr., sir)

r is lightly trilled, with tongue at the roof of your mouth like a very light English d, as in "ready": *pero* PAY-doh (but), *tres* TDAYS (three), *cuatro* KOOAH-tdoh (four).

rr like a Spanish r, but with much more emphasis and trill. Let your tongue flap. Practice with *burro* (donkey), *carretera* (highway), and Carrillo (proper name), then really let go with *ferrocarril* (railroad).

Note: The single small but common exception to all of the above is the pronunciation of Spanish **y** when it's being used as the Spanish word for "and," as in "Ron y Kathy." In such a case, pronounce it like the English ee, as in "keep": Ron "ee" Kathy (Ron and Kathy).

Accent

The rule for accent, the relative stress given to syllables within a given word, is straightforward. If a word ends in a vowel, an n, or an s, accent the next-to-last styllable; if not, accent the last syllable.

Pronounce *gracias* GRAH-seeahs (thank you), *orden* OHR-dayn (order), and *carretera* kah-ray-TAY-rah (highway) with stress on the next-to-last syllable.

Otherwise, accent the last syllable: *venir* vay-NEER (to come), *ferrocarril* fay-roh-cah-REEL (railroad), and *edad* ay-DAHD (age).

Exceptions to the accent rule are always marked with an accent sign (á, é, í, ó, or ú), such as *teléfono* tay-LAY-foh-noh (telephone), *jabón* hah-BON (soap), and *rápido* RAH-pee-doh (rapid).

BASIC AND COURTEOUS EXPRESSIONS

Most Spanish-speaking people consider formalities important. Whenever approaching anyone for information or some other reason, do not forget the appropriate salutation – good morning, good evening, etc. Standing alone, the greeting *hola* (hello) can sound brusque.

Hello. *Hola.*
Good morning. *Buenos días.*
Good afternoon. *Buenas tardes.*
Good evening. *Buenas noches.*
How are you? *¿Cómo está usted?*
Very well, thank you. *Muy bien, gracias.*
Okay; good. *Bien.*
Not okay; bad. *Mal* or *feo.*
So-so. *Más o menos.*
And you? *¿Y usted?*
Thank you. *Gracias.*
Thank you very much. *Muchas gracias.*
You're very kind. *Muy amable.*
You're welcome. *De nada.*
Goodbye. *Adios.*
See you later. *Hasta luego.*
please *por favor*
yes *sí*
no *no*
I don't know. *No sé.*
Just a moment, please. *Momentito, por favor.*
Excuse me, please (when you're trying to get attention). *Disculpe* or *Con permiso.*
Excuse me (when you've made a boo-boo). *Lo siento.*
Pleased to meet you. *Mucho gusto.*
My name is . . . *Me llamo . . .*
What is your name? *¿Cómo se llama usted?*
Do you speak English? *¿Habla usted inglés?*
Is English spoken here? (Does anyone here speak English?) *¿Se habla inglés?*
I don't speak Spanish well. *No hablo bien el español.*
I don't understand. *No entiendo.*
How do you say . . . in Spanish? *¿Cómo se dice . . . en español?*
Would you like . . . *¿Quisiera usted . . .*
Let's go to . . . *Vamos a . . .*

TERMS OF ADDRESS

When in doubt, use the formal *cena* (you) as a form of address.

I *yo*
you (formal) *usted*
you (familiar) *tu*
he/him *él*
she/her *ella*
we/us *nosotros*
you (plural) *ustedes*
they/them *ellos* (all males or mixed gender); *ellas* (all females)
Mr., sir *señor*
Mrs., madam *señora*
miss, young lady *señorita*
wife *esposa*
husband *esposo*
friend *amigo* (male); *amiga* (female)
sweetheart *novio* (male); *novia* (female)
son; daughter *hijo; hija*
brother; sister *hermano; hermana*
father; mother *padre; madre*
grandfather; grandmother *abuelo; abuela*

TRANSPORTATION

Where is . . . ? *¿Dónde está . . . ?*
How far is it to . . . ? *¿A cuánto está . . . ?*
from . . . to . . . *de . . . a . . .*
How many blocks? *¿Cuántas cuadras?*
Where (Which) is the way to . . . ? *¿Dónde está el camino a . . . ?*
the bus station *la terminal de autobuses*
the bus stop *la parada de autobuses*
Where is this bus going? *¿Adónde va este autobús?*
the taxi stand *la parada de taxis*
the train station *la estación de ferrocarril*
the boat, ferry *el barco, el transbordador*
the airport *el aeropuerto*
I'd like a ticket to . . . *Quisiera un boleto a . . .*
first (second) class *primera (segunda) clase*
roundtrip *ida y vuelta*
reservation *reservación*
baggage *equipaje*
Stop here, please. *Pare aquí, por favor.*
the entrance *la entrada*
the exit *la salida*

the ticket office *la oficina de boletos*
(very) near; far *(muy) cerca; lejos*
to; toward *a*
by; through *por*
from *de*
the right *la derecha*
the left *la izquierda*
straight ahead *derecho; directo*
in front *en frente*
beside *al lado*
behind *atrás*
the corner *la esquina*
the stoplight *la semáforo*
a turn *una vuelta*
right here *aquí*
somewhere around here *por acá*
right there *allí*
somewhere around there *por allá*
street; boulevard *calle; bulevar*
highway *carretera*
bridge; toll *puente; cuota*
address *dirección*
north; south *norte; sur*
east; west *oriente (este); poniente (oeste)*

ACCOMMODATIONS
hotel *hotel*
Is there a room? *¿Hay cuarto?*
May I (may we) see it? *¿Puedo (podemos) verlo?*
What is the price? (rate) *¿Cuál es el precio? (tipo)*
Is that your best rate? *¿Es su mejor precio? (tipo)*
Is there something cheaper? *¿Hay algo más económico?*
a single room *un cuarto sencillo*
a double room *un cuarto doble*
double bed *cama matrimonial*
king-size bed *cama king-size*
twin beds *camas gemelas*
with private bath *con baño*
hot water *agua caliente*
shower *ducha*
towels *toallas*
soap *jabón*
toilet paper *papel higiénico*
blanket *frazada; manta*

sheets *sábanas*
air-conditioned *aire acondicionado*
fan *abanico; ventilador*
key *llave*
manager *gerente*

FOOD
I'm hungry *Tengo hambre.*
I'm thirsty. *Tengo sed.*
menu *lista; menú*
order *orden*
glass *vaso*
fork *tenedor*
knife *cuchillo*
spoon *cuchara*
napkin *servilleta*
soft drink *refresco*
coffee *café*
tea *té*
drinking water *agua pura; agua potable*
bottled carbonated water *agua mineral*
bottled uncarbonated water *agua sin gas*
beer *cerveza*
wine *vino*
milk *leche*
juice *jugo*
cream *crema*
sugar *azúcar*
cheese *queso*
snack *antojo; botana*
breakfast *desayuno*
lunch *almuerzo*
daily lunch special *comida corrida (or el menú del día, depending on region)*
dinner *comida (often eaten in late afternoon); cena (a late-night snack)*
the check *la cuenta*
eggs *huevos*
bread *pan*
salad *ensalada*
fruit *fruta*
mango *mango*
watermelon *sandía*
papaya *papaya*
banana *plátano*
apple *manzana*
orange *naranja*
lime *limón*

fish *pescado*
shellfish *mariscos*
shrimp *camarones*
meat (without) *(sin) carne*
chicken *pollo*
pork *puerco*
beef; steak *res; bistec*
bacon; ham *tocino; jamón*
fried *frito*
roasted *asada*
barbecue; barbecued *barbacoa; al carbón*

SHOPPING

money *dinero*
money-exchange bureau *casa de cambio*
I would like to exchange travelers
checks. *Quisiera cambiar cheques de
viajero.*
What is the exchange rate? *¿Cuál es el tipo
de cambio?*
How much is the commission? *¿Cuánto
cuesta la comisión?*
Do you accept credit cards? *¿Aceptan
tarjetas de crédito?*
money order *giro*
How much does it cost? *¿Cuánto cuesta?*
What is your final price? *¿Cuál es su último
precio?*
expensive *caro*
cheap *barato; económico*
more *más*
less *menos*
a little *un poco*
too much *demasiado*

HEALTH

Help me please. *Ayúdeme por favor.*
I am ill. *Estoy enfermo.*
Call a doctor. *Llame un doctor.*
Take me to ... *Lléveme a ...*
hospital *hospital; sanatorio*
drugstore *farmacia*
pain *dolor*
fever *fiebre*
headache *dolor de cabeza*
stomachache *dolor de estómago*
burn *quemadura*
cramp *calambre*

nausea *náusea*
vomiting *vomitar*
medicine *medicina*
antibiotic *antibiótico*
pill; tablet *pastilla*
aspirin *aspirina*
ointment; cream *pomada; crema*
bandage *venda*
cotton *algodón*
sanitary napkins use brand name, e.g.,
Kotex
birth-control pills *pastillas anticonceptivas*
contraceptive foam *espuma anticonceptiva*
condoms *preservativos; condones*
toothbrush *cepilla dental*
dental floss *hilo dental*
toothpaste *crema dental*
dentist *dentista*
toothache *dolor de muelas*

POST OFFICE AND COMMUNICATIONS

long-distance telephone *teléfono larga
distancia*
I would like to call ... *Quisiera llamar a ...*
collect *por cobrar*
station to station *a quien contesta*
person to person *persona a persona*
credit card *tarjeta de crédito*
post office *correo*
general delivery *lista de correo*
letter *carta*
stamp *estampilla; timbre*
postcard *tarjeta*
aerogram *aerograma*
air mail *correo aereo*
registered *registrado*
money order *giro*
package; box *paquete; caja*
string; tape *cuerda; cinta*

AT THE BORDER

border *frontera*
customs *aduana*
immigration *migración*
tourist card *tarjeta de turista*
inspection *inspección; revisión*
passport *pasaporte*

profession *profesión*
marital status *estado civil*
single *soltero*
married; divorced *casado; divorciado*
widowed *viudado*
insurance *seguros*
title *título*
driver's license *licencia de manejar*

AT THE GAS STATION

gas station *gasolinera*
gasoline *gasolina*
unleaded *sin plomo*
full, please *lleno, por favor*
tire *llanta*
tire repair shop *vulcanizadora*
air *aire*
water *agua*
oil (change) *aceite (cambio)*
grease *grasa*
My . . . doesn't work. *Mi . . . no sirve.*
battery *batería*
radiator *radiador*
alternator *alternador*
generator *generador*
tow truck *grúa*
repair shop *taller mecánico*
tune-up *afinación*
auto-parts store *refaccionería*

VERBS

Verbs are the key to getting along in Spanish. They employ mostly predictable forms and come in three classes, which end in ar, er, and ir, respectively:

to buy *comprar*
I buy, you (he, she, it) buys *compro, compra*
we buy, you (they) buy *compramos, compran*
to eat *comer*
I eat, you (he, she, it) eats *como, come*
we eat, you (they) eat *comemos, comen*
to climb *subir*
I climb, you (he, she, it) climbs *subo, sube*
we climb, you (they) climb *subimos, suben*
  Got the idea? Here are more (with irregularities indicated).

to do or make *hacer* (regular except for *hago,* I do or make)
to go *ir* (very irregular: *voy, va, vamos, van*)
to go (walk) *andar*
to love *amar*
to work *trabajar*
to want *desear, querer*
to need *necesitar*
to read *leer*
to write *escribir*
to repair *reparar*
to stop *parar*
to get off (the bus) *bajar*
to arrive *llegar*
to stay (remain) *quedar*
to stay (lodge) *hospedar*
to leave *salir* (regular except for *salgo,* I leave)
to look at *mirar*
to look for *buscar*
to give *dar* (regular except for *doy,* I give)
to carry *llevar*
to have *tener* (irregular but important: *tengo, tiene, tenemos, tienen*)
to come *venir* (similarly irregular: *vengo, viene, venimos, vienen*)
Spanish has two forms of "to be." Use *estar* when speaking of location or a temporary state of being: "I am at home." "*Estoy en casa.*" "I'm sick." "*Estoy enfermo.*" Use *ser* for a permanent state of being: "I am a doctor." "*Soy doctora.*"
  Estar is regular except for *estoy,* I am. *Ser* is very irregular:
to be *ser*
I am, you (he, she, it) is *soy, es*
we are, you (they) are *somos, son*

NUMBERS

zero *cero*
one *uno*
two *dos*
three *tres*
four *cuatro*
five *cinco*
six *seis*
seven *siete*
eight *ocho*
nine *nueve*

10 *diez*
11 *once*
12 *doce*
13 *trece*
14 *catorce*
15 *quince*
16 *dieciseis*
17 *diecisiete*
18 *dieciocho*
19 *diecinueve*
20 *veinte*
21 *veinte y uno or veintiuno*
30 *treinta*
40 *cuarenta*
50 *cincuenta*
60 *sesenta*
70 *setenta*
80 *ochenta*
90 *noventa*
100 *ciento*
101 *ciento y uno or cientiuno*
200 *doscientos*
500 *quinientos*
1,000 *mil*
10,000 *diez mil*
100,000 *cien mil*
1,000,000 *millón*
one half *medio*
one third *un tercio*
one fourth *un cuarto*

TIME

What time is it? *¿Qué hora es?*
It's one o'clock. *Es la una.*
It's three in the afternoon. *Son las tres de la tarde.*

It's 4 A.M. *Son las cuatro de la mañana.*
six-thirty *seis y media*
a quarter till eleven *un cuarto para las once*
a quarter past five *las cinco y cuarto*
an hour *una hora*

DAYS AND MONTHS

Monday *lunes*
Tuesday *martes*
Wednesday *miércoles*
Thursday *jueves*
Friday *viernes*
Saturday *sábado*
Sunday *domingo*
today *hoy*
tomorrow *mañana*
yesterday *ayer*
January *enero*
February *febrero*
March *marzo*
April *abril*
May *mayo*
June *junio*
July *julio*
August *agosto*
September *septiembre*
October *octubre*
November *noviembre*
December *diciembre*
a week *una semana*
a month *un mes*
after *después*
before *antes*

Suggested Reading

Some of these books are informative, others are entertaining, and all of them will increase your understanding of Mexico. Virtually all of these will be easier to find at home than in Mexico. Although several of them are classics and out of print, Amazon.com, Barnesandnoble.com, and libraries have used copies. Take some along on your trip. If you find others that are especially noteworthy, let us know. Happy reading.

HISTORY AND ARCHAEOLOGY

Calderón de la Barca, Fanny. *Life in Mexico, with New Material from the Author's Journals.* New York: Doubleday, 1966. Edited by H. T. and M. H. Fisher. An update of the brilliant, humorous, and celebrated original 1913 book by the Scottish wife of the Spanish ambassador to Mexico.

Casasola, Gustavo. *Seis Siglos de Historia Gráfica de Mexico (Six Centuries of Mexican Graphic History).* Mexico City: Editorial Gustavo Casasola, 1978. Six fascinating volumes of Mexican history in pictures, from 1325 to the present.

Collis, Maurice. *Cortés and Montezuma.* New York: New Directions Publishing Corp., 1999. A reprint of a 1954 classic piece of well-researched storytelling. Collis traces Cortés' conquest of Mexico through the defeat of his chief opponent, Aztec emperor Montezuma. He uses contemporary eyewitnesses—notably Bernal Díaz de Castillo—to revivify one of histories greatest dramas.

Cortés, Hernán. *Letters from Mexico.* Translated by Anthony Pagden. New Haven: Yale University Press, 1986. Cortés' five long letters to his king, in which he describes contemporary Mexico in fascinating detail, including, notably, the remarkably sophisticated life of the Aztecs at the time of the Conquest.

Davies, Nigel. *Ancient Kingdoms of Mexico.* London: Penguin Books, 1990. An authoritative history of the foundations of Mexican civilization. Clearly traces the evolution of Mexico's five successive worlds—Olmec, Teotihuacán, Toltec, Aztec, and finally Spanish—that set the stage for present-day Mexico.

Díaz del Castillo, Bernal. *The Discovery and Conquest of Mexico.* Translated by Albert Idell. London: Routledge (of Taylor and Francis Group), 2005. A soldier's still-fresh tale of the Conquest from the Spanish viewpoint.

Garfias, Luis. *The Mexican Revolution.* Mexico City: Panorama Editorial, 1985. A concise Mexican version of the 1910–1917 Mexican revolution, the crucible of present-day Mexico.

Gugliotta, Bobette. *Women of Mexico.* Encino CA: Floricanto Press, 1989. Lively legends, tales, and biographies of remarkable Mexican women, from Zapotec princesses to Independence heroines.

León-Portilla, Miguel. *The Broken Spears: The Aztec Account of the Conquest of Mexico.* New York: Beacon Press, 1962. Provides an interesting contrast to Díaz del Castillo's account.

Meyer, Michael, and William Sherman. *The Course of Mexican History.* New York: Oxford University Press, 1991. An insightful, 700-plus-page college textbook in paperback. A bargain, especially if you can get it used.

Novas, Himlice. *Everything You Need to Know about Latino History.* New York: Plume Books (Penguin Group), 1994. Chicanos, Latin rhythm, La Raza, the Treaty of Guadalupe Hidalgo, and much more, interpreted from an authoritative Latino point of view.

Reed, John. *Insurgent Mexico.* New York: International Publisher's Co., 1994. Republication of 1914 original. Fast-moving, but not unbiased, description of the 1910 Mexican revolution by the journalist famed for his reporting of the subsequent 1917 Russian revolution. Reed, memorialized by the Soviets, was resurrected in the 1981 film biography Reds.

Ridley, Jasper. *Maximilian and Juárez.* New York: Ticknor and Fields, 1999. This authoritative historical biography breathes new life into one of Mexico's great ironic tragedies, a drama that pitted the native Zapotec "Lincoln of Mexico" against the dreamy, idealistic Archduke Maximilian of Austria-Hungary. Despite their common liberal ideas, they were drawn into a bloody no-quarter struggle that set the Old World against the New, ending in Maximilian's execution and the subsequent insanity of his wife, Carlota. The United States emerged as a power to be reckoned with in world affairs.

Ruíz, Ramon Eduardo. *Triumphs and Tragedy: A History of the Mexican People.* New York: W. W. Norton, Inc., 1992. A pithy, anecdote-filled history of Mexico from an authoritative Mexican-American perspective.

Simpson, Lesley Bird. *Many Mexicos.* Berkeley: The University of California Press, 1962. A much-reprinted, fascinating broad-brush version of Mexican history.

Townsend, Richard, et al. *Ancient West Mexico: Art and Archaeology of the Unknown Past.* New York: W.W. Norton, 1998. This magnificent coffee-table volume, with lovely photos and authoritative text, reveals the little-known culture being uncovered at Guachimontones and other sites, notably the "bottle tombs," in the Tequila valley west of Guadalajara. Dozens of fine images illuminate a high culture of sculptural and ceramic art, depicting everything from warriors, ball players, and acrobats to loving couples, animals, and sacred rituals.

UNIQUE GUIDE AND TIP BOOKS

American Automobile Association. *Mexico TravelBook.* Heathrow, FL: 2003. Published by the American Automobile Association (1000 AAA Drive, Heathrow, FL 32746-5063). Short sweet summaries of major Mexican tourist destinations and sights. Also includes information on fiestas, accommodations, restaurants, and a wealth of information relevant to car travel in Mexico. Available in bookstores, or free to AAA members at affiliate offices.

Bayless, Rick. *Rick Bayless's Guide to Mexican Cooking.* New York: Scribner's, 1996. An award-winning author and cook explores the vibrant flavors of a world-class cuisine.

Burton, Tony. *Western Mexico, A Traveller's Treasury.* St. Augustine, FL: Perception Press, 2001. A well-researched and lovingly written and illustrated guide to dozens of fascinating places to visit, both well known and out of the way, in Michoacán, Jalisco, and Nayarit.

Church, Mike and Terry. *Traveler's Guide to Mexican Camping.* Kirkland, WA: Rolling Homes Press (P.O. Box 2099, Kirkland, WA 98083-2099). This is an unusually thorough guide to trailer parks all over Mexico, with much coverage of the Pacific Coast in general and the Guadalajara region in particular. Detailed maps guide you accurately to each trailer park cited and clear descriptions tell you what to expect. The book also provides very helpful information on car travel in Mexico, including details of insurance, border crossing, highway safety, car repairs, and much more.

Franz, Carl, and Lorena Havens. *The People's Guide to Mexico.* Berkeley, CA: Avalon Travel Publishing, 13th edition, 2006. An entertaining and insightful A-to-Z general guide to the joys and pitfalls of independent economy travel in Mexico.

Graham, Scott. *Handle with Care.* Chicago:

The Noble Press, 1991. Should you accept a meal from a family who lives in a grass house? This insightful guide answers this and hundreds of other tough questions for persons who want to travel responsibly in the Third World.

Guilford, Judith. *The Packing Book.* Berkeley: Ten Speed Press, third edition, 2006. The secrets of the carry-on traveler, or how to make everything you carry do double and triple duty. All for the sake of convenience, mobility, economy, and comfort.

Luboff, Ken. *Living Abroad in Mexico.* Berkeley, CA: Avalon Travel Publishing, 2005. A handy package of traveler's tools for living like a local in Mexico. Provides much general background and some specific details on settling (and perhaps making a living) in one of a number of Mexico's prime expatriate living areas, such as Mazatlán, Puerto Vallarta, Lake Chapala, Cuernavaca, and San Miguel de Allende.

Werner, David. *Where There Is No Doctor.* Palo Alto, CA: Hesperian Foundation, 1993(1919 Addison St., Berkeley, CA 94704, tel. 888/729-1796, www.hesperian.org). How to keep well in the tropical backcountry.

SPECIALTY TRAVEL GUIDES

Annand, Douglas R. *The Wheelchair Traveler.* Self-Published, ISBN 9990546738; Amazon. com says they have copies. Step-by-step guide for planning a vacation. Accessible information on air travel, cruises, ground transportation, selecting the right hotel, what questions to ask, solutions to problems that may arise, and accessibility to many wonderful destinations in the United States and Mexico.

Jeffrey, Nan. *Adventuring with Children.* Berkeley, CA: Avalon House Publishing, 1995. This unusually detailed book starts where most travel-with-children books end. It contains, besides a wealth of information and practical strategies for general travel with children, specific chapters on how you can adventure—trek, kayak, river-raft, camp, bicycle, and much more—successfully with the kids in tow.

FICTION

Bowen, David, and Ascencio, Juan A. *Pyramids of Glass.* San Antonio: Corona Publishing Co., 1994. Two dozen–odd stories that lead the reader along a month-long journey through the bedrooms, barracks, cafés, and streets of present-day Mexico.

Boyle, T. C. *The Tortilla Curtain.* New York: Penguin-Putnam 1996; paperback edition, Raincoast Books, 1996. A chance intersection of the lives of two couples, one affluent and liberal Southern Californians, the other poor, homeless, illegal immigrants, forces all to come to grips with the real price of the American Dream.

Cisneros, Sandra. *Caramelo.* New York: Alfred A. Knopf, 2002. A celebrated author weaves a passionate, yet funny, multigenerational tale of a Mexican-American family and of their migrations, which, beginning in Mexico City, propel them north all the way to Chicago and back.

Cohan, Tony. *Mexican Days.* New York: Broadway Books, 2006. A captivating tale of surprise and adventure in a Mexico both old and new.

De la Cruz, Sor Juana Inez. *Poems, Protest, and a Dream.* New York: Penguin, 1997. Masterful translation of collection of love and religious poems by the celebrated pioneer (1651–1695) Mexican nun-feminist.

Doerr, Harriet. *Consider This, Señor.* New York: Harcourt Brace, 1993. Four expatriates tough it out in a Mexican small town, adapting to the excesses—blazing sun, driving rain, vast, untrammeled landscapes—meanwhile interacting with the local folks while the local folks observe them, with a mixture of fascination and tolerance.

Finn, María. *Mexico in Mind*. New York: Vintage Books, 2006. The wisdom and impressions of two centuries of renowned writers, from D. H. Lawrence and John Steinbeck to John Reed and Richard Rodríguez, who were drawn to the timelessness and romance of Mexico.

Fuentes, Carlos. *Where the Air Is Clear*. New York: Farrar, Straus, and Giroux, 1971. The seminal work of Mexico's celebrated novelist.

Fuentes, Carlos. *The Years with Laura Díaz*. New York: Farrar, Straus, and Giroux, 2000. A panorama of Mexico from Independence to the 21st century, through the eyes of one woman, Laura Díaz, and her great-grandson, the author. One reviewer said that she, "as a Mexican woman, would like to celebrate Carlos Fuentes; it is worthy of applause that a man who has seen, observed, analyzed, and criticized the great occurrences of the century now has a woman, Laura Díaz, speak for him." Translated by Alfred MacAdam.

Jennings, Gary. *Aztec*. New York: Forge Books, 1997. Beautifully researched and written monumental tale of lust, compassion, love, and death in pre-Conquest Mexico.

Nickles, Sara, ed. *Escape to Mexico*. San Francisco: Chronicle Books, 2002. A carefully selected anthology of 20-odd stories of Mexico by renowned authors, from Steven Crane and W. Somerset Maugham to Anaïs Nin and David Lida, who all found inspiration, refuge, adventure, and much more, in Mexico.

Peters, Daniel. *The Luck of Huemac*. New York: Random House, 1981. An Aztec noble family's tale of war, famine, sorcery, heroism, treachery, love, and finally disaster and death in the Valley of Mexico.

Rulfo, Juan. *Pedro Paramo*. New York: Grove Press, 1994. Rulfo's acknowledged masterpiece, originally published in 1955, established his renown. The author, thinly disguised as the protagonist, Juan Preciado, fulfills his mother's dying request by returning to his shadowy Jalisco hometown, Comala, in search of his father. Although Preciado discovers that his father, Pedro Páramo (whose surname implies "wasteland"), is long dead, Preciado's search resurrects his father's restless spirit, which recounts its horrific life tale of massacre, rape, and incest.

Traven, B. *The Treasure of the Sierra Madre*. New York: Hill and Wang, 1967. Campesinos, federales, gringos, and indígenas all figure in this modern morality tale set in Mexico's rugged outback. The most famous of the mysterious author's many novels of oppression and justice set in Mexico's jungles.

Villaseñor, Victor. *Rain of Gold*. New York: Delta Books (Bantam, Doubleday, and Dell), 1991. The moving, best-selling epic of the author's family's gritty travails. From humble rural beginnings in the Copper Canyon, they flee revolution and certain death, struggling through parched northern deserts to sprawling border refugee camps. From there they migrate to relative safety and an eventual modicum of happiness in Southern California.

PEOPLE AND CULTURE

Berrin, Kathleen. *The Art of the Huichol Indians*. Harry N. Abrams, New York, 1978. Lovely, large photographs and text by a symposium of experts provide a good interpretive introduction to Huichol art and culture.

Castillo, Ana. *Goddess of the Americas*. New York, Riverhead Books, 1996. Here, a noted author has selected from the works of seven interpreters of Mesoamerican female deities, whose visions range as far and wide as Sex Goddess, the Broken-Hearted, the Subversive, and the Warrior Queen.

Medina, Sylvia López. *Cantora*. New York: Ballantine Books, 1992. Fascinated by the stories of her grandmother, aunt, and mother, the author seeks her own center by discovering a past that she thought she wanted to forget.

Meyerhoff, Barbara. *Peyote Hunt: The Sacred Journey of the Huichol Indians.* Ithaca: Cornell University Press, 1974. A description and interpretation of the Huichol's religious use of mind-bending natural hallucinogens.

Palmer, Colin A. *Slaves of the White God.* Cambridge: Harvard University Press. A scholarly study of why and how Spanish authorities imported African slaves into America and how they were used afterwards. Replete with poignant details, taken from Spanish and Mexican archives, describing how the Africans struggled from bondage to eventual freedom.

Riding, Alan. *Distant Neighbors: A Portrait of the Mexicans.* New York: Random House Vintage Books. Rare insights into Mexico and Mexicans.

Toor, Frances. *A Treasury of Mexican Folkways.* New York: Crown Books, 1947, reprinted by Bonanaza, 1985. An illustrated encyclopedia of vanishing Mexicana—costumes, religion, fiestas, burial practices, customs, legends—compiled during the celebrated author's 35-year residence in Mexico.

Wauchope, Robert, ed. *Handbook of Middle American Indians. Vols. 7 and 8.* Austin: University of Texas Press, 1969. Authoritative surveys of important Indian-speaking groups in northern and central (vol. 8) and southern (vol. 7) Mexico.

FLORA AND FAUNA

Goodson, Gar. *Fishes of the Pacific Coast.* Stanford, California: Stanford University Press, 1988. Over 500 beautifully detailed color drawings highlight this pocket version of all you ever wanted to know about the ocean's fishes (including common Spanish names) from Alaska to Peru.

Howell, Steve N. G. *Bird-Finding Guide to Mexico.* Ithaca, NY: Cornell University Press, 1999. A unique portable guide for folks who really want to see birds in Mexico. Unlike other bird books, the author presents a unique and authoritative site guide, with dozens of clear maps and lists of birds seen at sites all over Mexico. Pacific sites include Mazatlán, San Blas, Puerto Vallarta, El Tuito, Manzanillo, Oaxaca, and many more. Use this book along with Howell and Webb's A Guide to the Birds of Mexico and North America.

Howell, Steve N. G. and Sophie Webb. *A Guide to the Birds of Mexico and Northern America.* Oxford: Oxford University Press, 1995. All the serious birder needs to know about Mexico's rich species treasury. Includes authoritative habitat maps and 70 excellent color plates that detail the male and females of around 1,500 species.

Mason, Jr., Charles T., and Patricia B. Mason. *Handbook of Mexican Roadside Flora.* Tucson: University of Arizona Press, 1987. Authoritative identification guide, with line illustrations, of all the plants you're likely to see in the Guadalajara region.

Morris, Percy A. *A Field Guide to Pacific Coast Shells.* Boston: Houghton Mifflin. The complete beachcomber's Pacific shell guide.

Pesman, M. Walter. *Meet Flora Mexicana.* Published in Arizona, in 1962, by D. S. King, now out of print. Amazon.com has copies, as do some of the larger libraries. Delightful anecdotes and illustrations of hundreds of common Mexican plants.

Peterson, Roger Tory, and Edward L. Chalif. *Field Guide to Mexican Birds.* Boston: Houghton Mifflin, 1999. With hundreds of Peterson's crisp color drawings, this is a must for serious birders and vacationers interested in the life that teems in the Guadalajara region's mountains, forests, lakes, and rivers.

Wright, N. Pelham. *A Guide to Mexican Mammals and Reptiles.* Mexico City: Minutiae

Mexicana, 1989. Pocket-edition lore, history, descriptions, and pictures of commonly seen Mexican animals.

ART, ARCHITECTURE, AND CRAFTS

Baird, Joseph. *The Churches of Mexico.* Berkeley: University of California Press. Mexican colonial architecture and art, illustrated and interpreted.

Cordrey, Donald, and Dorothy Cordrey. *Mexican Indian Costumes.* Austin: University of Texas Press, 1968. A lovingly photographed, written, and illustrated classic on Mexican native people and their dress, emphasizing textiles.

Martínez Penaloza, Porfirio. *Popular Arts of Mexico.* Mexico City: Editorial Panorama, 1981. An excellent, authoritative, pocket-sized exposition of Mexican art.

Morrill, Penny C. and Carol A. Berk. *Mexican Silver.* Atglen, PA: Shiffer Publishing Co.,2007. Lovingly written and photographed exposition of the Mexican silvercraft of Taxco, Guerrero, revitalized through the initiative of Frederick Davis and

William Spratling in the 1920s and 1930s. Color photos of many beautiful, museum-quality pieces supplement the text, which describes the history and work of a score of silversmithing families who developed the Taxco craft under Spratling's leadership. Greatly adds to the traveler's appreciation of the beautiful Taxco silvercrafts. Widely available in many Puerto Vallarta and Guadalajara (Tlaquepaque) shops.

Mullen, Robert James. *Architecture and Its Sculpture in Viceregal Mexico.* Austin: University of Texas Press, 1997. The essential work of Mexican colonial-era cathedrals and churches. In this lovingly written and illustrated life work, Mullen breathes new vitality into New Spain's preciously glorious colonial architectural legacy.

Sayer, Chloë. *Arts and Crafts of Mexico.* San Francisco: Chronicle Books, 1990. All you ever wanted to know about your favorite Mexican crafts, from papier-mâché to pottery and toys and Taxco silver. Beautifully illustrated by traditional etchings and David Lavender's crisp black-and-white and color photographs.

Internet Resources

TRAVEL IN GENERAL
www.travelocity.com
www.expedia.com
Major sites for airline and hotel bookings

www.travelinsure.com
www.worldtravelcenter.com
Good for travel insurance and other services

www.sanbornsinsurance.com
Site of the long-time, very reliable Mexico auto insurance agency, with the only north-of-the-border adjustment procedure. Get your quote online, order their many useful publications, and find out about other insurance you many have forgotten.

SPECIALTY TRAVEL
www.elderhostel.org
Site of Boston-based Elderhostel, Inc., with a broad catalog of ongoing study tours, including some in the Guadalajara region.

www.miusa.org
Site of Mobility International, wonderfully organized and complete, with a flock of services for travelers with disabilities, including many people-to-people connections in Mexico, including Guadalajara.

www.purpleroofs.com
One of the best general gay travel websites is maintained by San Francisco–based travel agency Purple Roofs. It offers, for example, details about gay-friendly Guadalajara hotels, bars, and nightspots, in addition to a wealth of gay-friendly travel-oriented links worldwide.

HOME EXCHANGE
www.homexchange.com
www.homeforexchange.com
Sites for temporarily trading your home with someone else in dozens of places in the world, including Guadalajara and Lake Chapala.

U.S. GOVERNMENT
www.state.gov/travelandbusiness
The U.S. State Department's very good information website. Lots of subheadings and links to a swarm of topics, including Mexican consular offices in the United States, U.S. consular offices in Mexico, travel advisories, and links to other government information, such as importation of food, plants, and animals, U.S. customs, health abroad, airlines, and exchange rates.

MEXICO IN GENERAL
www.visitmexico.com
The official website of the public-private Mexico Tourism Board; a good general site for official information, such as entry requirements. It has lots of summarily informative sub-headings, not unlike an abbreviated guidebook. If you can't find what you want here, call the toll-free information number 800/44-MEXICO (800/446-3942), or email contact@visitmexico.com.

www.mexonline.com
Very extensive, well-organized commercial site with many subheadings and links to Mexico's large and medium destinations, and even some in small destinations. For example, Guadalajara is typical, with manifold links, including for dozens of accommodations, from luxury hotels to modest bed-and-breakfasts. Excellent.

www.mexconnect.com
An extensive Mexico site, with dozens upon dozens of subheadings and links, especially helpful for folks thinking of traveling, working, living, or retiring in Mexico.

www.mexicodesconocido.com.mx
The site of the excellent magazine *Mexico Desconocido* (Undiscovered Mexico) that mostly features unusual and off-the-beaten-track destinations, several in Guadalajara and environs. Accesses a large library of past articles, which

are not unlike a Mexican version of National Geographic Traveler. Click the small "English" button at the top to translate. Excellent, hard-to-find information, in good English translation.

www.planeta.com

Life project of Latin America's dean of ecotourism, Ron Mader, who furnishes a comprehensive clearinghouse of everything ecologically correct, from rescuing turtle eggs in Jalisco to preserving cloud forests in Peru. Contains dozens of subheadings competently linked for maximum speed. For example, check out the Mexico travel directory for ecojourneys, maps, information networks, parks, regional guides, and a mountain more.

www.vrbo.com
www.choice1.com

A pair of very useful sites for picking a vacation rental house, condo, or villa, with information and reservations links to individual owners. Prices vary from moderate to luxurious. Coverage extends to Jalisco, including Lake Chapala, and Puerto Vallarta.

STATE OF JALISCO
www.visita.jalisco.gob.mx

Very good work in progress, with lists of museums, events, hotels, virtual tours, and more. The Guadalajara metropolitan areas are presently best covered, especially for hotels, with many links to hotel websites. Outlying districts are also covered, but with mostly lists and fewer direct links to individual websites. The site may have improved considerably by the time you read this.

GUADALAJARA
www.guadalajaramisdestino.com

Site of the Guadalajara Convention and Visitors Bureau. It contains lists of everything: events, bus service, hotels, and much more. But unfortunately it's all self-contained, with no links to private websites, such as hotels for reservations. It does have an extensive section about the Expo Guadalajara, however.

www.tlaquepaque.gob.mx

Site of Tlaquepaque's municipal government.

www.zapopan.gob.mx

Site of Zapopan's municipal government.

www.guadalajarareporter.com

Site of the English-language Guadalajara newspaper. Very extensive, even more extensive for subscribers. Nonsubscribers, however, have access to the very useful classified section, especially for hotels, bed-and-breakfasts, and house and apartment rentals.

www.rutasjalisco.com

Very useful guide for folks who want to travel around Guadalajara by city bus. Dozens of the most useful lines are accurately mapped out.

LAKE CHAPALA
www.chapala.com

The site of the excellent monthly Chapala-area newspaper, *El Ojo del Agua*. Doesn't contain the entire newspaper—only the (good, however) monthly lead articles per edition, archived back about three years to the beginning of publication. Also the site of parent Coldwell Banker–Chapala Real Estate. Excellent for home rentals and sales. Lots of other information about local goings-on, especially the fine and very active Lake Chapala Society (LCS).

www.ajijicrentals.com

Very complete site that lists dozens of Lake Chapala rentals, from studios to grand villas, from $300 per month upwards.

Index

A

accommodations: general discussion 300-301; business travelers 304; Chapala Riviera 172-176; country inns 199; Downtown 51-54; haciendas 199; Magdalena 228; Mazamitla 196-199; Minerva-Chapultepec 79-84; Plaza del Sol-Chapalita 97-101; San Juan de los Lagos 190-191; Tapalpa 208-209; Tequila 224-225; Tlaquepaque 132-134; Tonalá 150-152; vacation rentals 100-101, 176, 301; Zapopan 115-116
African Mexicans: 243, 262
Agua Caliente: 24, 25, 213
Agustín I (Emperor): 244-245
Ahualulco: 218
airlines: 279-280
air travel: 17, 60-62, 279-281
Ajijic: general discussion 15, 161; accommodations 172-174; food/restaurants 176-178; itinerary tips 22; lakeshore 156, 162; maps 162-163; sightseeing tips 156; town plaza 156, 161
Alacranes Island: 15, 22
alcoholic beverages: 16, 276-278, 298
alebrijes: 271
Alemán, Miguel: 250
Amarillo hot springs and geysers: 219
amusement parks: 306-307
animals: 24, 235-237
apartments: general discussion 301; Chapala Riviera 176; Plaza del Sol-Chapalita 100-101; see also specific place
archaeological sites: general discussion 16; El Iztepete Archaeological Zone 21-22, 31, 69, 95-96, 238; Guachimontones 215-216; itinerary tips 21-22, 23
area codes: 317
armadillos: 235
art galleries: 21
art markets: 96, 97
ATMs: 316; see also specific place
Avenida Independencia: 18, 20, 119, 127-130
Avenida Juárez: 18, 20, 130-131
Ávila Camacho, Manuel: 250
Aztec civilization: 238-240

B

backcountry precautions: 312-313
baggage: 280-281

Ballet Folklórico: 21, 44
Balneario Cañon de las Flores: 24, 215
Balneario El Bosque: 215
Balneario El Paraíso: 24, 224
Balneario El Rincón: 16, 23, 25, 217-218
Balneario Las Tinajitas: 24, 215
Balneario La Toma: 16, 24, 223-224
Balneario Nuevo Paraíso: 113
balnearios: general discussion 16; Bosque de Primavera 214-215; Chimulco 212-213; itinerary tips 23, 24; Río Caliente 213-214; Tequila 223-224; Zapopan 113; see also specific place
banks: general discussion 316; Chapala Riviera 179-180; Downtown 58; Mazamitla 200; Minerva-Chapultepec 88; Plaza del Sol-Chapalita 104; San Juan de los Lagos 192; Tapalpa 211; Tequila 226; Tlaquepaque 138; Tonalá 153; Zapopan 117
bargaining tips: 302-303
Barranca del Río Grande de Santiago: 14, 113, 223-224, 232
Basílica de Nuestra Señora de Zapopan: 18, 69, 110-111
basketry: 266, 268
bathing resorts: see balnearios
bats: 235-236
Battle of Mezcala: 159, 163-164
bed-and-breakfasts: general discussion 300; Plaza del Sol-Chapalita 100-101; see also accommodations; specific place
bicycling: 169
birds/birdwatching: 42-43, 236, 310
birria restaurants: 42, 57
Birrias Nueve Esquinas: 19, 42, 57
blue agave: 220, 234
boating: 170
bookstores: Chapala Riviera 180; Downtown 59-60; Plaza del Sol-Chapalita 96, 104-105
border crossings: 295
Border Industrialization Program: 251
Bosque de Primavera: general discussion 16, 185, 214-215, 233; campgrounds 25; itinerary tips 23, 24
Bosque Los Colomos: 24, 48, 69, 75, 115
botanical gardens: 75
Braniff mansion: 164
brassware: 272
bribes: 285, 287
bullfights: 27, 46, 266

bungie jumping: 206
business hours: 318
business travelers: 304
business visas: 294
bus service: general discussion 17, 281, 283, 289-291; Chapala Riviera 183; Downtown 65-66; Mazamitla 201; Minerva-Chapultepec 90; New Terminal 63-65; Old Terminal 62-63; Plaza del Sol-Chapalita 107; San Juan de los Lagos 193; Tapalpa 211; Tequila 226; Tlaquepaque 139; Tonalá 154; Zapopan 117

C

Calderón, Felipe: 254-256
California exploration: 242
calling cards: 317
cameras: see photographic services/supplies
Camionera Central Nueva: 63-65
Camionera Central Vieja: 62-63
camping/campgrounds: 23, 24-25, 206
candellila: 234
canoeing: 206
Canyon of the Serpent: 75
Capilla de la Cruz Blanca: 145
Capilla de la Purísima: 204
Capilla de Nuestra Señora de Aranzazú: 19, 40, 42
Cárdenas, Lázaro: 249
carriage rides: 19
car travel: general discussion 17, 62, 283-288, 291-293; Chapala Riviera 182-183; driving distances 282, 290; itinerary tips 22-23; Mazamitla 201; permits 295; repairs and maintenance 284-285, 286; safety tips 283-284, 286, 292-293, 313; San Juan de los Lagos 193; Tapalpa 211; Tequila 226; Tonalá 154
Casa de los Artesanos: 125
Casa de los Perros: 39-40
Casa Histórica: 122, 124
Casa Orozco: 18, 74
Catedral Basílica: 16, 185, 189
Catedral de Guadalajara: 14, 18, 19, 27, 32-33
cell phones: 317
Centro Cultural del Refugio: 125
Centro Magno: 71, 74, 78
ceramics: 272-273; see also factory outlets; shopping
Cerro de la Reina: 145
Chagas' disease: 312-313
Chapala: general discussion 15, 161; accommodations 174-175; food/restaurants 178-179; itinerary tips 22; maps 165;

sightseeing tips 162-164, 166; town plaza 162-163
Chapala Pier: 156, 163
Chapala Rail Museum: 164, 166
Chapala Riviera: general discussion 15; accommodations 172-176; entertainment and events 168-169; food/restaurants 176-179; outdoor recreation 169-171; shopping 171-172; sightseeing tips 161-168; tourist information and services 179-182; transportation services 182-183
Chapalita: see Plaza del Sol-Chapalita
Chapalita Circle: 94
charreadas: 27, 46, 47
Chiapas rebellion: 252
Chihuahua pine: 233
children, traveling with: 294, 306-307
Chimulco: 16, 24, 25, 185, 212-213
Chinese pine: 233
chocolatl: 278
church architecture: 38-39
Church of St. Francis Assisi: 162-163
Cihualpilli (Queen): historical background 120, 141, 240; itinerary tips 18, 20; statue 15, 119, 144-145
cinemas: Minerva-Chapultepec 76; Plaza del Sol-Chapalita 96
civil war: 246
climate: 17, 232
clothing shops: 268
clothing tips: 17, 298
cloud forests: 234
coatimundis: 235
Cocas culture: 120, 158
Cola del Caballo: 113
colonial architecture: 14, 18, 19, 36
colonial period: 241-243
community organizations: Chapala Riviera 181; Minerva-Chapultepec 89; Plaza del Sol-Chapalita 105-106
condominiums: 301; see also accommodations; specific place
Constitution of 1917: 258-259
consulates: Chapala Riviera 181; Downtown 58-59; Minerva-Chapultepec 88-89
convents: 39
Copper Canyon: 288
copperware: 272
Cora culture: 262-263
coral snakes: 236-237
corridas de toros: 27, 46, 266
Cortés, Hernan: 31, 239-240
country clubs: 209

country inns: 199
credit cards: 302
criollos: 242-243, 262
Cristero rebellion: 248-249
cruises: 168
Cuervo Distillery: 16, 185, 222
cultural studies programs: 60
currency/currency exchange: 58, 316
customs regulations: 295

D

dance shows: Chapala Riviera 168-169;
   Downtown 44, 46; itinerary tips 18, 20, 21;
   Tlaquepaque 126; Tonalá 147
demographics: 261-263
department stores: general discussion 303;
   Downtown 50; Minerva-Chapultepec 78-79
diarrhea: 311
Díaz Ordaz, Gustavo: 251
Díaz, Porfirio: 246-247
disabled travelers: 305
discos: 46
distilleries: general discussion 16, 185;
   historical background 220; tequila 48, 185,
   222
Doña Marina: 239
Downtown: general discussion 14;
   accommodations 51-54; entertainment and
   events 44-48; food/restaurants 55-57;
   historical background 30-32; itinerary
   tips 18, 19; maps 28-29, 41; outdoor
   recreation 48-49; planning tips 26, 30;
   shopping 49-50; sightseeing tips 27, 32-43;
   tourist information and services 58-60;
   transportation services 60-67
drinking water: 311-312
driving distances: 282, 290
duty-free goods: 296

E

early civilizations: 238-240; see also
   archaeological sites; indigenous population
Echeverría Alvarez, Luis: 251
economy: 251-252, 254, 256-258
educational opportunities: 310; see also
   language schools
Eko-Park Tapalpa: 25, 206
Elderhostel: 305, 310
elections: 254-255
electricity: 318
El Iztepete Archaeological Zone: 21-22, 31, 69,
   95-96, 238
El Parián: 15, 119, 126, 135

El Pocito shrine: 16, 185, 189
El Salto del Nogal: 16, 23, 25, 205-206
El Salto waterfall: 185, 194, 232
El Tabardillo viewpoint: 196
emergency services: general discussion 314;
   air evacuations 312; Chapala Riviera 182;
   Downtown 59; Mazamitla 201; Minerva-
   Chapultepec 90; San Juan de los Lagos 192-
   193; Tapalpa 211; Tequila 226; Tlaquepaque
   139; Tonalá 154; Zapopan 117
entertainment and events: general discussion
   264-266; Chapala Riviera 168-169;
   Downtown 44-48; Magdalena 227; Mazamitla
   194-196; Minerva-Chapultepec 76; Plaza del
   Sol-Chapalita 96; San Juan de los Lagos 189-
   190; Tapalpa 207; Tequila 224; Tlaquepaque
   125-127; Tonalá 147; Zapopan 114-115
entrance arch (Zapopan): 113
environmental issues: 160, 167
escorpión: 237
Estampida sculpture: 74-75
Expo Guadalajara: 69, 94, 304

F

factory outlets: itinerary tips 18, 20-21;
   Minerva-Chapultepec 79; Tlaquepaque 119,
   131-132; Tonalá 15, 119, 149-150
fauna: 24, 235-237
female travelers: 298
fer-de-lance: 237
ferry service: 15
festivals: see entertainment and events
Field Guides tours: 310
Fiesta Cultural de Mayo: 17, 21
Fiesta de la Virgen de Zapopan: 46, 115, 265
Fiesta de Octubre: 17, 46, 265
fiestas: general discussion 264-266; calendar
   267; Chapala Riviera 169; Downtown 46;
   Magdalena 227; Mazamitla 194-196; San
   Juan de los Lagos 190; Tapalpa 207; Tequila
   224; Tonalá 147; Zapopan 114-115; see also
   specific place
film industry: 77
fine art: 21
fire departments: see emergency services
first-aid kits: 313
fishing: 206
flora: 24, 233-235
folkloric dance shows: Downtown 44, 46;
   itinerary tips 18, 20; Tlaquepaque 126
food/restaurants: general discussion 274-278;
   Chapala Riviera 176-179; Downtown 55-57;
   fiestas 169; Magdalena 228-229; Mazamitla

199-200; Mexican food 274-275; Minerva-Chapultepec 84-88; Plaza del Sol-Chapalita 101-104; safety tips 311-312; San Juan de los Lagos 191-192; Tapalpa 209-210; Tequila 225-226; Tlaquepaque 134-137; Tonalá 152-153; Zapopan 116-117
food stalls: *see specific place*
forest-canopy rides: 206
forests: 234-235
fountains: 74
Fox, Vicente: 253-254
Frisa de los Fundadores: 19, 34
fruits: 277
furniture: 269

G

gardens: 75, 94-95, 156, 161-162
gasoline: 284
gay and lesbian travelers: 307
geography: 231-232
getaways: general discussion 16, 184-185; Bosque de Primavera 214-215; Chimulco 212-213; Guachimontones area 215-218; Magdalena 227-230; maps 186; Mazamitla 193-201; planning tips 187; San Juan de los Lagos 187-193; Tapalpa 202-211; Tequila 220-226
geysers: 219; *see also* hot springs
gila monsters: 237
glassware: 269-270; *see also* factory outlets; shopping
Glorietta Minerva: 74
gold jewelry: 14, 49, 270-271
golf courses: Chapala Riviera 170; Lake Chapala 15; Tlaquepaque 127; Tonalá 147; Zapopan 115
government: 258-260
Green Angels: 284
grocery stores: *see* markets
Guachimontones: 16, 21-22, 23, 31, 185, 215-216
Guadalajara Airport: 60
Guadalajara Zoo: 69, 75-76
Guerrero, Vicente: 244
guesthouses: 300; *see also* accommodations; *specific place*
guide books: 329-330
Guzmán, Nuño Beltrán de: 31, 141, 240-241
gyms: Minerva-Chapultepec 78; Plaza del Sol-Chapalita 97; Tlaquepaque 127

H

Hacienda El Carmen: 16, 23, 218-219
haciendas: 199

Hacienda San José: 48, 223
Hacienda Santa Lucia: 113-114
handicrafts: general discussion 14, 15, 266, 268-273, 302-303; Ajijic 162; Chapala Riviera 171-172; courses 182; Downtown 49-50; itinerary tips 18, 19, 20-23; Magdalena 227; Mazamitla 196; Tapalpa 207-208; Tequila 222, 224; Tlaquepaque 121-122, 126; Tonalá 147-149; Zapopan 115; *see also* shopping
health services: *see* medical services
Hidalgo, Miguel: 31, 244
high coniferous forests: 235
highway routes: 287-288, 290
hiking: itinerary tips 23, 24; Lake Chapala 15; Mazamitla 196
historical background: general discussion 238-256; Downtown 30-32; Lake Chapala 158-159; Magdalena 227; Mazamitla 193-194; San Juan de los Lagos 187-188; Tapalpa 202, 204; Tequila 220; Tonalá 141; Zapopan 108, 110
horseback riding: 171, 196, 206
Hospicio Cabañas: general discussion 14, 36, 38; itinerary tips 19, 21; sightseeing tips 27
hospitals: *see* medical services
Hotel Balneario San Juan Cosala: 24, 170, 175
hotels: *see* accommodations; *specific place*
Hotel Villa Montecarlo: 156, 166, 174
hot springs: general discussion 16; Chapala Riviera 161; itinerary tips 23, 24, 212-219; Tequila 223-224; Zapopan 113, 114; *see also* balnearios
Huaxtla: 114
Huichol culture: 112, 262-263, 270

I

ice-skating rinks: 49, 307
illegal drugs: 298
Imolación de Quetzalcoatl: 35
independence struggle: 243-245
indígena groups: 243, 261-263
indigenous population: 30-31, 120, 158, 202, 238-240; *see also* archaeological sites
insects: 312
Instituto Cultural Cabañas: 36, 38, 46, 265
insurance: 281, 283, 292
intercity bus service: 289
Internet access: Chapala Riviera 180; Downtown 59; Mazamitla 200; Minerva-Chapultepec 88; Plaza del Sol-Chapalita 97, 104; San Juan de los Lagos 192; Tequila 226; Tlaquepaque 138; Tonalá 153; Zapopan 117
Internet resources: 334-335

investment services: 317
ironwork: 269
Isla de los Alacranes: 15, 22
Isla de Mezcala: 15, 22, 156, 163-164
itinerary tips: 18-25
Ixcatán: 113

JK

jaguars: 235
Jalisco Philharmonic Orchestra: 21
Japanese Garden: 75
jarabe: 126
Jardín Principal: 204
jewelry: general discussion 270-271; Downtown
    14, 49; Tlaquepaque 129-130
Jocotepec: 169
jogging: Downtown 48; Lake Chapala 169;
    Minerva-Chapultepec 76, 78; Plaza del
    Sol-Chapalita 97; Tonalá 147
José Clemente Orozco Art Museum: 14, 21, 38
Juana Inés de la Cruz, Sister: 94, 105
Juárez, Benito: 246
kayaking: general discussion 15; itinerary tips
    24; Tapalpa 206

L

La Inmaculada: 122
Lake Chapala: general discussion 15, 155, 231-
    232; environmental issues 167; historical
    background 158-159; itinerary tips 22,
    24; maps 157; outdoor recreation 169-171;
    planning tips 158; *see also* Chapala Riviera
Lake of the Birds: 75
lakes: 231-232
language: glossary 319-321; *indígena* groups
    262, 263; useful phrases 322-327
language schools: Chapala Riviera 182;
    Downtown 60; Minerva-Chapultepec 89;
    Plaza del Sol-Chapalita 106
La Parroquia de la Purísima Concepción: 222
La Presa del Nogal: 206
Las Piedrotas: 16, 23, 25, 185, 205
laundry services: Plaza del Sol-Chapalita 104;
    Tonalá 153
lead pigments: 273
leather goods: 269
lechugilla: 234
libraries: Chapala Riviera 180; Plaza del Sol-
    Chapalita 105; Tlaquepaque 138
liquor: *see* alcoholic beverages; tequila
live music: Chapala Riviera 168-169; Downtown
    44-46; itinerary tips 18, 20, 21; Plaza del
    Sol-Chapalita 96

long distance telephone service: 317, 318
López Mateos, Adolfo: 250
López Obrador, Manuel: 254-255
López Portillo, José: 251
Los Arcos: 14, 18, 69, 74
Los Camachos: 24, 113
Los Cazos Park: 185, 194
luggage: 280-281

M

machismo: 299
Madero, Francisco I.: 247
Madrid Hurado, Miguel de la: 251
magazines: 59
Magdalena: 16, 185, 227-230
Magno Centro Joyero: 14, 19, 35, 49
maguey: 234
mail: *see* post offices
Majolica pottery: 272-273
Malinche: 239
maquiladoras: 251
margays: 235
mariachi music: 18, 20, 36, 44-46
Marina, Doña: 239
markets: general discussion 14, 302-303;
    Downtown 49; itinerary tips 19; Mazamitla
    200; Minerva-Chapultepec 78; Plaza del
    Sol-Chapalita 97; San Juan de los Lagos
    191-192; sightseeing tips 27; Tapalpa 210;
    Tequila 225; Tlaquepaque 121-122; Tonalá
    147; Zapopan 111, 115
masks: 271
Maximilian (Emperor): 246
Mazamitla: 16, 24, 193-201
medical services: general discussion 311-314;
    Chapala Riviera 182; Downtown 59;
    Magdalena 230; Mazamitla 201; Minerva-
    Chapultepec 89-90; Plaza del Sol-Chapalita
    106; San Juan de los Lagos 192; Tapalpa 211;
    Tequila 226; Tlaquepaque 139; Tonalá 154;
    Zapopan 117
Mendoza, Antonio de: 241
Mercado Libertad: 14, 19, 27, 35-36, 49
mescal: 234, 276
mesquite grassland: 233-234
mestizos: 243, 261-262
metalwork: 272
Mexican food: 274-275
Mexican Hat Dance: 126
Mexican War of Independence: 159, 163-164
mezcal: 220
Mezcala: 161
Mezcala Island: 15, 22, 156, 163-164

Miguel Hidalgo International Airport: 60
Minerva-Chapultepec: general discussion 14; accommodations 79-84; entertainment and events 76; food/restaurants 84-88; itinerary tips 18; maps 72-73; outdoor recreation 76, 78; planning tips 70; shopping 78-79; sightseeing tips 71, 74-76; tourist information and services 88-90; transportation services 90
Minerva Circle: 74
minibus service: 183
missionaries: 240, 242
Mixtón War: 241
mobile phones: 317
Moctezuma: 239-240
monasteries: 39
money: 58, 316-317
Montezuma pines: 235
Morelos, José María: 244
mosquitoes: 312
mountain biking: 206
movie theaters: Minerva-Chapultepec 76; Plaza del Sol-Chapalita 96
murals: general discussion 14; Downtown 37, 40; itinerary tips 18, 19; Minerva-Chapultepec 74
Museo Casa Taller José Clemente Orozco: 18, 74
Museo de Arqueología: 18, 19, 21, 43
Museo de la Ciudad: 21, 40
Museo de la Virgen: 111
Museo de los Artes: 18, 21, 71
Museo de Paleontología de Guadalajara: 18, 19, 21, 43
Museo Huichol Wirrarica: 18, 21, 69, 111
Museo Nacional de la Cerámica: 20, 145
Museo Regional de Guadalajara: 19, 21, 33
Museo Regional de la Cerámica de Tlaquepaque: 20, 21, 119, 124
Museo Regional Tonallán: 20, 119, 145
Museum of Journalism and Graphic Arts: 39-40
museums: *see specific place*
musical instruments: 272

N
National Museum of Tequila: 222
Negrete, Jorge: 77
Neill James Library and Garden: 22, 156, 161-162, 180
neo-Gothic architecture: 14, 18, 71
New Spain: 240-241
newspapers: Chapala Riviera 180; Downtown 59; Tonalá 153

nightclubs/nightlife: Downtown 46; entertainment and events 76; Plaza del Sol-Chapalita 96
North American Free Trade Agreement (NAFTA): 252
Nueve Esquinas district: 19, 27, 42
nuts: 277

O
oak trees: 233
Obregón, Álvaro: 248
obsidian: 22, 95
ocelots: 235
Old Tlaquepaque: 121-122
opals: 16, 185, 227-228, 229, 271
orchids: 43
Orozco, José Clemente: 19, 37, 74
outdoor markets: 78, 97, 302-303
outdoor recreation: Chapala Riviera 169-171; Downtown 48-49; Minerva-Chapultepec 76, 78; Plaza del Sol-Chapalita 97; Tapalpa 206; Tlaquepaque 127; Tonalá 147; Zapopan 115

P
packing tips: 17, 315
Palacio de Gobierno: 19, 27, 40
Palacio Municipal: 144
Palacio Yarín: 194
paper mills: 205
papier-mâché: 272
parking: 66
Parque Agua Azul: 18, 19, 27, 42-43, 48, 307
Parque Colomos: 307
Parque Cristiana: 164
Parque San Francisco: 27, 40
Parroquia de San Cristóbal: 193-194
Parroquia de Santiago: 145
Parroquia San Pedro: 18, 122
Parroquia San Pedro Apostól: 111
Paseo Teopizintle: 114
passports: 294
pedestrian safety: 313
performing arts: 21, 34, 44-46; *see also* dance shows; live music
permits and licenses: 294-295
peso: 316
pets, traveling with: 294
pewter ware: 272
pharmacies: see medical services
photographic etiquette: 146
photographic services/supplies: Downtown 60; Minerva-Chapultepec 89; Plaza del Sol-Chapalita 104; Tlaquepaque 138; Zapopan 115

piñatas: 272
pine-oak forests: 233
pino triste: 233
planning tips: 17
plants: 24, 233-235
Plaza de Armas: 19, 33, 44
Plaza de las Americas: 111
Plaza de los Hombres Ilustres: 19, 33
Plaza de los Mariachis: 36, 44
Plaza del Sol: 91, 94, 96-97, 101-102
Plaza del Sol-Chapalita: general discussion
    14; accommodations 97-101; entertainment
    and events 96; food/restaurants 101-
    104; maps 92-93; outdoor recreation
    97; planning tips 91; shopping 96-97;
    sightseeing tips 91, 94-96; tourist
    information and services 104-106;
    transportation services 106-107
Plaza Guadalajara: 32
Plaza Liberación: 18, 33, 48
Plaza Nueve Esquinas: 19, 42
Plaza Patria: 115
Plaza San Francisco: 19
Plaza Tapatía: 14, 18, 19, 35
poisonous animals: 236-237
police: *see* emergency services
political reforms: 246, 253
politics: 258-260; *see also* historical
    background
population: 261-263
Posada Alpina: 194
post offices: general discussion 317; Chapala
    Riviera 180; Downtown 59; Magdalena 229;
    Mazamitla 200; Minerva-Chapultepec 88;
    Plaza del Sol-Chapalita 104; Tapalpa 211;
    Tequila 226; Tlaquepaque 138; Tonalá 153;
    Zapopan 117
pottery: 272-273
precipitation: 17, 232
Presa del Nogal: 25
pulque: 220, 276-277
purified water: 311-312
pyramids: 16, 21-22, 30-31; *see also*
    archaeological sites

QR
Quinta Quetzalcoatl: 156, 166, 168, 174-175
rail service: 65, 288
rainfall: 17, 232
Rancho Epenche: 198-199
rattlesnakes: 237
reading suggestions: 328-333
real estate agents: 181, 301, 308

Rectoría de la Universidad de Guadalajara: 14,
    69, 71
religion: 242, 264
religious festivals: 114-115
relocation tips: 307-308
rental cars: general discussion 291-292;
    Downtown 61, 66-67; Minerva-
    Chapultepec 90
reptiles: 236-237
reservoirs: 206
resources: 319-335
Restaurant Casa Bariachi: 19, 87
restaurants: *see* food/restaurants; *specific place*
Restaurant San Miguel: 19, 56
revolution: 247-248
Río Caliente: 23, 24, 213-214
Río Caliente Spa: 214
Río Lerma-Santiago: 232
Río Nogal: 23
rock climbing: 206
rodeos: 27, 46, 47
roller skating: 49, 307
Ruíz Cortínes, Adolfo: 250
Rulfo, Juan: 265
RV travel: general discussion 17, 62; Chapala
    Riviera 182-183; itinerary tips 23, 24-25;
    Minerva-Chapultepec 83-84

S
safety tips: backcountry precautions 312-313;
    car travel 283-284, 286, 292-293, 313;
    female travelers 298; food and water 311-
    312; money 316-317
Salinas de Gortari, Carlos: 252
San Antonio: 15, 161
sangre de drago: 234
San José del Tajo: 25, 84
San Juan Cosala: 15, 161, 175-176
San Juan de los Lagos: 16, 187-193
San Nicolas: 161
Santa Anna, Antonio López de: 245
Santuario del Sagrado Corazón de Jesús: 144
Santuario de Nuestra Señora de la Soledad:
    18, 122
Sauza Museum: 222-223
scenic views: 113
scorpions: 313
seasons: 17, 232
senior travelers: 305-306
Serra, Padre Junípero: 242
shipping agencies: Tlaquepaque 139; Tonalá 153
shopping: general discussion 302-303;
    Chapala Riviera 171-172; Downtown 14, 49-50;

itinerary tips 18, 20-23; Magdalena 227; Mazamitla 196; Minerva-Chapultepec 78-79; Plaza del Sol-Chapalita 96-97; Tapalpa 207-208; Tequila 224; Tlaquepaque 127-132; Tonalá 147-150; Zapopan 115
shopping malls: 303
shuttle services: 61
silver jewelry: 270-271
sisal: 234
skating: 49, 307
snakes: 236-237
social conduct: 298
socially responsible travel: 308-309
Spanish conquest: 31, 141, 158-159, 239-240
spas: 23, 214
sports activities: see outdoor recreation; specific place
stoneware: 273
stonework: 270
strangler figs: 234
student visas: 294
subways: 65, 66
sun protection: 312
supermarkets: see markets
swimming: Downtown 49; itinerary tips 24; Lake Chapala 15, 169-170; Minerva-Chapultepec 78; Plaza del Sol-Chapalita 97; Tlaquepaque 127; Tonalá 147

T

Talavera pottery: 272-273
Tapalpa: 16, 23, 24, 25, 202-211
taxis: 90, 293
Teatro Degollado: general discussion 14, 34, 44; fiestas 265; itinerary tips 19, 21; sightseeing tips 27
Teatro Diana: 19, 21, 44, 265
Tecuexes culture: 120
telephone services: general discussion 317; Chapala Riviera 180; Downtown 59; Magdalena 229-230; Mazamitla 200; Minerva-Chapultepec 88; Plaza del Sol-Chapalita 104; San Juan de los Lagos 192; Tapalpa 211; Tequila 226; Tlaquepaque 138; Tonalá 153
temperatures: 17, 232
Templo de San Francisco de Asis: 18, 19, 40
Templo de Santa María de Gracia: 34
Templo de Santa Monica: 40
Templo Expiatorio: 14, 18, 69, 71
tennis courts: Chapala Riviera 170-171; Downtown 48-49; Lake Chapala 15; Tlaquepaque 127; Tonalá 147

Teotihuacán: 238
tequila (liquor): 48, 185, 221, 276-277
Tequila (town): 16, 24, 220-226
Tequila Express: 27, 48, 223
Teuchtitlán: 218
theft: 283-284, 316-317
Three Sisters of Jalisco: 188
time: 317-318
tipping: 298
Tlaquepaque: general discussion 15; accommodations 132-134; entertainment and events 125-127; food/restaurants 134-137; historical background 120; itinerary tips 18, 20; maps 122-123; outdoor recreation 127; planning tips 121; shopping 127-132; sightseeing tips 121-122, 124-125; tourist information and services 138-139; transportation services 139
Tobolandia: 24, 170
Tonalá: general discussion 15; accommodations 150-152; entertainment and events 147; food/restaurants 152-153; historical background 120, 141; itinerary tips 18, 20; maps 142-143; outdoor recreation 147; planning tips 140, 144; shopping 147-150; sightseeing tips 144-145; tourist information and services 153-154; transportation services 154
tourism board offices: 296-297
tourist information and services: general discussion 316-318; Chapala Riviera 179-182; Downtown 58-60; Magdalena 229; Mazamitla 200-201; Minerva-Chapultepec 88-90; Plaza del Sol-Chapalita 104-106; San Juan de los Lagos 192-193; Tapalpa 210-211; Tequila 226; Tlaquepaque 138-139; Tonalá 153-154; Zapopan 117
tourist permits: 294-295
tours: general discussion 67, 309; Chapala Riviera 181; Copper Canyon 288; factory outlets 20-21; opal mines 228; tequila distilleries 222-223; Tequila Express 27, 48; Tlaquepaque 138; tour guides 66-67, 138, 153, 181, 309
traditional dress: 264, 268
train service: 65, 288
transportation services: general discussion 17, 279-293; Chapala Riviera 182-183; Chimulco 213; Downtown 60-67; driving distances 282; Mazamitla 201; Minerva-Chapultepec 90; Plaza del Sol-Chapalita 106-107; San Juan de los Lagos 193; Tapalpa 211; Tequila 226; Tlaquepaque 139; Tonalá 154; Zapopan 117

travel agents: Mazamitla 200-201; Minerva-Chapultepec 89; Tequila 226; Tonalá 153
travelers checks: 316
traveler's diarrhea: 311
travelers with disabilities: 305
travel guides: 329-330
travel tips: 304-309
trolley service: 71, 90
tropical deciduous forests: 234

UV

University of Guadalajara: 71, 310
vacation rentals: general discussion 301; Chapala Riviera 176; Plaza del Sol-Chapalita 100-101
vegetation: 24, 233-235
Villa, Francisco (Pancho): 247
Virgin of Guadalupe: 122, 190, 243
Virgin of Innocence: 32
Virgin of San Juan de los Lagos: 188, 189
Virgin of Talpa: 188
Virgin of Zapopan: 14, 18, 32, 110-111, 188, 241
visas: 294
Vivero Chapalita: 94-95
volcanoes: 231
voltage: 318

WXYZ

walking: Downtown 48; Lake Chapala 15, 169; Minerva-Chapultepec 76, 78; Plaza del Sol-Chapalita 97; Tonalá 147
warehouse stores: 303
waterfalls: general discussion 16, 232; campgrounds 25; itinerary tips 23; Mazamitla 185, 194; Tapalpa 205-206; Zapopan 113
water hyacinths (lirio): 160
water parks: 24, 170
weather: 17, 232
whitefish (pescado blanco): 160
wilderness reserves: see Bosque de Primavera
wildflowers: 24
wildlife: 24, 235-237
wine: 277-278
women travelers: 298
woolen goods: 273
woven crafts: 266, 268, 273
wrought iron: 269
Zapata, Emiliano: 247
Zapatistas: 252
Zapopan: general discussion 14; accommodations 115-116; entertainment and events 114-115; food/restaurants 116-117; historical background 108, 110; itinerary tips 18; maps 109; outdoor recreation 115; planning tips 108; shopping 115; sightseeing tips 110-114; tourist information and services 117
Zedillo, Ernesto: 252-253
zoos: 69, 75-76, 306-307

Acknowledgments

A host of sympathetic people both at home and in Mexico contributed greatly to this book. I first gratefully thank the multitude of unnamed Guadalajara people—in shops, on the streets, at their front doors, and behind hotel, *turismo,* and bank counters—who tolerantly responded to my queries. At times, their help was vital—such as that unforgettable episode when a dozen-odd *campesinos* pitched in and helped haul my car 100 feet up from a steep, boulder-strewn cornfield where I had suddenly and unexpectedly driven it one night.

To others I am also deeply indebted. In Tlaquepaque, I especially owe a load of thanks to Arturo and Estela Magaña of Quinta Don José for their kind hospitality and time spent treating me to fascinating personal tours of Guadalajara neighborhoods and fine restaurants.

In Guadalajara, I owe much to my friend Ernie Lewis, founder of the excellent newsletter *Adventures in Mexico,* for his many helpful corrections to my first edition text. Also in Tlaquepaque, I owe many thanks to excellent guide Lino Gabriel G. Nuño, ironwork master Roman Gutierrez, and Veronica Flores of Casa de Artesanos. In Tonalá, I thank my super-conscientious and kind guides from Tonalá *turismo,* and Rafael Ángel and his American wife, Diana Romo, of Villas Don Blas. I owe a similar debt to my excellent tour guides from Zapopan tourism.

Farther afield, I am grateful to friendly and knowledgeable workers of Tapalpa tourism, publicity director Franzi at Río Caliente spa, Helena Elena Sauza, the personable director of the Sauza Museum in Tequila, and Javier López Ávila in Magdalena for generously imparting his knowledge and experience of opals to me. This book is much richer because of them.

Thanks also to the others who have encouraged me since then, especially my fellow members of the Society of American Travel Writers and San Francisco Bay Area Travel Writers. Singular among them was the late Rebecca Bruns, whose excellent guidebook, *Hidden Mexico,* has been a major inspiration for my present work.

Back home in Berkeley, thanks for the kind cooperation of the friendly staff at my office-away-from-home, Café Espresso Roma. I am especially grateful for those many dozens of delicious, individually decorated cafe lattes, essential to the successful completion of this book.

Thanks also to my friend and business partner, Halcea Valdes, who generously managed without me while I was away in Mexico.

I owe a debt beyond counting to my late mother, Joan Casebier; my late father and stepmother, Bob and Hilda Whipperman; and my sister, Doris Davis, for their help and patience in making me who I am.

Finally, I owe a mountain of gratitude to my loving life partner, Gundi Ley, who patiently nursed me back to health when I was seriously ill, and tirelessly shared all the field work, both tedious and enjoyable, that made this book possible.

www.moon.com

For helpful advice on planning a trip, visit www.moon.com for the **TRAVEL PLANNER** and get access to useful travel strategies and valuable information about great places to visit. When you travel with Moon, expect an experience that is uncommon and truly unique.

MAP SYMBOLS

▦ Expressway	☾ Highlight	✗ Airfield	⚑ Golf Course				
Primary Road	○ City/Town	✈ Airport	℗ Parking Area				
Secondary Road	◉ State Capital	▲ Mountain	▰ Archaeological Site				
Unpaved Road	⊛ National Capital	✦ Unique Natural Feature	⬧ Church				
Trail	★ Point of Interest		⬚ Gas Station				
Ferry	• Accommodation	⟁ Waterfall	⬭ Glacier				
⊢⊢⊢ Railroad	▾ Restaurant/Bar	⬥ Park	⬚ Mangrove				
Pedestrian Walkway	▪ Other Location	⬛ Trailhead	▨ Reef				
⬚⬚⬚ Stairs	Λ Campground	⬥ Skiing Area	▱ Swamp				

CONVERSION TABLES

°C = (°F − 32) / 1.8
°F = (°C x 1.8) + 32
1 inch = 2.54 centimeters (cm)
1 foot = 0.304 meters (m)
1 yard = 0.914 meters
1 mile = 1.6093 kilometers (km)
1 km = 0.6214 miles
1 fathom = 1.8288 m
1 chain = 20.1168 m
1 furlong = 201.168 m
1 acre = 0.4047 hectares
1 sq km = 100 hectares
1 sq mile = 2.59 square km
1 ounce = 28.35 grams
1 pound = 0.4536 kilograms
1 short ton = 0.90718 metric ton
1 short ton = 2,000 pounds
1 long ton = 1.016 metric tons
1 long ton = 2,240 pounds
1 metric ton = 1,000 kilograms
1 quart = 0.94635 liters
1 US gallon = 3.7854 liters
1 Imperial gallon = 4.5459 liters
1 nautical mile = 1.852 km

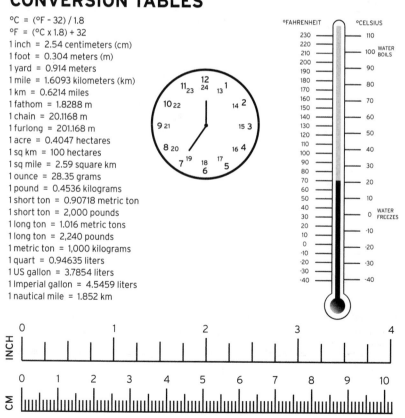

MOON GUADALAJARA
Avalon Travel
a member of the Perseus Books Group
1700 Fourth Street
Berkeley, CA 94710, USA
www.moon.com

Editors: Cinnamon Hearst, Kevin McLain, Michelle Cadden
Series Manager: Kathryn Ettinger
Copy Editor: Kay Elliott
Graphics Coordinator: Nicole Schultz
Production Coordinator: Sean Bellows
Cover Designer: Nicole Schultz
Map Editor: Brice Ticen
Cartographer: Kat Bennett
Indexer: Judy Hunt

ISBN-10: 1-59880-010-8
ISBN-13: 978-1-59880-010-4
ISSN: 1541-3012

Printing History
1st Edition – 2002
3rd Edition – May, 2008
5 4 3 2 1

Some photos and illustrations are used by permission and are the property of the original copyright owners.

Front cover photo: mariachi musician, Guadalajara © James Baigrie/Getty Images
Title page photo: © Bruce Whipperman
Interior photos: pages 4-8 & 14-16 © Bruce Whipperman

Printed in the United States by RR Donnelley

KEEPING CURRENT

If you have a favorite gem you'd like to see included in the next edition, or see anything that needs updating, clarification, or correction, please drop us a line. Send your comments via email to feedback@moon.com, or use the address above.